Look at what you get FREE if you're buying this book new!

New copies of *Foundations of Physical Education, Exercise Science, and Sport* come with the following special resources to help you succeed in class and beyond:

Password for Premium Content on the Online Learning Center for *Foundations of Physical Education, Exercise Science, and Sport*) (www.mhhe.com/wuest15e)

The passcode card bound into the front of your text includes your password to the premium resources found on the Online Learning Center for this text. The Online Learning Center includes tools to help you succeed in your course, such as self-quizzes and links to key resources. The password gives you access to additional tools, as well as articles and current news that can help you as a professional.

If you have purchased a used copy of this book, you can purchase access to the premium content for the Online Learning Center separately; visit the book's Online Learning Center (www.mhhe.com/wuest15e) for more details.

15th Edition

Foundations of Physical Education, Exercise Science, and Sport

Deborah A. Wuest
Ithaca College

Charles A. Bucher
Deceased

Boston Burr Ridge, IL Dubuque, IA Madison, WI New York San Francisco St. Louis
Bangkok Bogotá Caracas Kuala Lumpur Lisbon London Madrid Mexico City
Milan Montreal New Delhi Santiago Seoul Singapore Sydney Taipei Toronto

The McGraw-Hill Companies

FOUNDATIONS OF PHYSICAL EDUCATION, EXERCISE SCIENCE, AND SPORT

Published by McGraw-Hill, a business unit of The McGraw-Hill Companies, Inc., 1221 Avenue of the Americas, New York, NY, 10020.

This book is printed on acid-free paper.

2 3 4 5 6 7 8 9 0 DOC/DOC 0 9 8 7 6

ISBN: 978-0-07-297280-1
MHID: 0-07-297280-7

Editor in Chief: *Emily Barrosse*
Publisher: *Bill Glass*
Senior Sponsoring Editor: *Chris Johnson*
Executive Marketing Manager: *Pamela S. Cooper*
Director of Development: *Kathleen Engelberg*
Developmental Editor: *Carlotta Seely*
Managing Editor: *Jean Dal Porto*
Senior Project Manager: *Jill Moline-Eccher*
Project Manager: *Catherine R. Iammartino*
Art Director: *Jeanne Schreiber*
Lead Designer: *Gino Cieslik*
Photo Research Coordinator: *Natalia Peschiera*
Senior Media Project Manager: *Ron Nelms*
Senior Production Supervisor: *Carol Bielski*
Media Producer: *Lance Gerhart*
Composition: *10/12 Times New Roman by ElectraGraphics, Inc.*
Printing: *Black, 45 # New Era Matte, R. R. Donnelly and Sons, Inc./Crawfordsville, IN.*

Credits: The credits section for this book begins on page 569 and is considered an extension of the copyright page.

Library of Congress Cataloging-in-Publication Data

Wuest, Deborah A.
Foundations of physical education, exercise science, and sport / Deborah A. Wuest, Charles A. Bucher.— 15th ed.
p. cm.
Includes bibliographical references and index.
ISBN 0-07-297280-7 (alk. paper)
1. Physical education and training. 2. Sports. 3. Physical education and training—Vocational guidance. 4. Sports—Vocational guidance. I. Bucher, Charles Augustus, 1912– II. Title.
GV341.W85 2006
796'.07—dc22

2005041576

www.mhhe.com

Brief Contents

Contents

PART IV

Issues, Challenges, and the Future 505

CHAPTER 14

CHAPTER 15

PREFACE

The 15th edition of *Foundations of Physical Education, Exercise Science, and Sport* reflects the continuing growth of these fields. The dynamic nature of the fields is reflected in this textbook designed for introductory and foundation classes. This contemporary text provides an overview of major dimensions of physical education, exercise science, and sport, offering the student both an introduction to the knowledge base as well as information on expanding career opportunities. Career opportunities for qualified individuals have never been greater.

Numerous exciting career opportunities in physical education, exercise science, and sport await qualified professionals. The traditional career of teaching physical education in the school setting has expanded to nonschool settings, such as sports clubs and recreation centers, and to the instruction of people of all ages in physical activity. Coaching opportunities, once predominantly available in schools and colleges, are now available in nonschool settings, such as private clubs, and currently involve working with athletes of all abilities and ages. Today, many young physical education, exercise science, and sport professionals aspire to careers in fitness, cardiac rehabilitation, exercise science, sport management, athletic training, and sport communication.

This text encourages students from the beginning of their career to contribute to the fields of physical education, exercise science, and sport and to be active participants in shaping the nature of these dynamic fields. Students are challenged to fully develop themselves as professionals and make a commitment to excellence. As young leaders, they will work collaboratively with other dedicated professionals to address the issues facing us and confront the challenges that lie ahead.

CHANGES IN THE 15TH EDITION

This edition builds upon the significant revisions made in the 14th revision of the text. At that time, the title of the text was revised to include exercise science and the content related to exercise sciences and sport expanded. This edition brings you updated information on the continued expansion of the fields and growth of the subdisciplines within them. The growing emphasis on a public health role for professionals is discussed. This edition maintains its dual focus on foundational knowledge and career preparation. Students are provided with guidelines to enhance their career preparation and a broad array of career opportunities to explore.

Students are encouraged to pursue excellence and to display the highest levels of professionalism in their endeavors. They are invited to explore the increasingly diverse opportunities for qualified professionals in these fields. Students are called on to take an active leadership role in addressing the problems confronting the fields and in accomplishing our mission of lifespan involvement in physical activity for all people.

Additionally, efforts were made to reorganize the text and to streamline the presentation of information. The need to update and include information about the expanding nature of the field, coupled with the realities of time constraints for covering material in a course and textbook space limitations, has led to the decision to place some of the material on the Web in the Online Learning Center (www.mhhe.com/wuest15e).

In this edition three major changes have been made to the organization of the chapters within the text. In the 14th edition, Chapter 4 was titled Movement: The Keystone; this chapter has been placed on the Web in the Online Learning Center (www.mhhe.edu/wuest15e). The second change relates to Chapter 9, Psychological Foundations, which, in the 14th edition, covered both motor behavior and sport and exercise psychology. In this edition, this chapter is divided into two chapters—Chapter 5, titled Motor Behavior, and Chapter 9, Sport and Exercise Psychology. It is hoped that these changes will provide additional information for those with an interest in the psychological foundations of the fields. The historical foundations chapter is shortened from the 14th edition, and information about the contribution of other cultures to physical education is placed in the Online Learning Center.

In addition to updating relevant studies, this edition contains the latest information on the following important topics:

- Obesity epidemic and U.S. Healthy Lifestyles and Disease Prevention Initiative.
- Update on NASPE's *Moving into the Future* standards for physical education.
- Growing public health role and importance of promotion of physical activity throughout the lifespan.
- Health literacy and its impact on the well-being of people of all ages.
- Recent findings related to physical activity and health, from national surveys, including the National Health Interview Survey, the Behavioral Risk Factor Surveillance System, and the National Health and Nutrition Examination Survey.
- Expanded information on cultural diversity with the fields of physical education, exercise science, and sport.
- No Child Left Behind national education program and its implications for physical education.
- Ergogenic aids, including caffeine, anabolic steroids, and creatine, are discussed both from the standpoint of exercise physiology and from the sociological perspective focusing on the use of performance-enhancing substances.
- Expanded section on goal-setting and self-talk within the chapter on sport and exercise psychology.
- Importance of being a role model, including NASPE's Physical Activity and Fitness Recommendations for Physical Activity Professionals.
- Interstate New Teacher Assessment and Support Consortium (INTASC) competencies for beginning teachers.
- Role conflict and issues it presents for teachers and coaches.
- Technology and enhancement of communication among professionals in the fields.
- Expanded information on sport management and NASPE-NASSM Task Force on Sports Management Competencies.
- Additional career opportunities such as sport tourism and expanded career opportunities such as physical therapy, following graduate study.
- NASPE's characteristics of a quality physical education program.
- Scenario planning and possible futures for nutrition and physical activity.
- Activism and the importance of professionals in ensuring lifelong physical activity opportunities for all people, regardless of race, ethnicity, gender, or socioeconomic status.

This textbook challenges the reader to play a significant role in shaping the future of our dynamic fields.

Organization

The 15 chapters of this book are organized into four parts. Part One provides students with an orientation to physical education, exercise science, and sport. Chapter 1 introduces students to these fields, defines selected terms used throughout the text, discusses various philosophies, introduces sport philosophy, and presents guidelines to help students develop a professional philosophy. In Chapter 2, the objectives of physical education, exercise science, and sport programs are identified and the assessment of objectives is presented. Chapter 3 examines the role of physical education, exercise science, and sport in society and in education as well as the educational reform, fitness, and wellness movements.

In Part Two, the historical and scientific foundations of physical education, exercise science, and sport are presented in five chapters. The historical foundations of physical education, exercise science, and sport are covered in Chapter 4. The development of physical education, exercise science, and sport from early cultures to today is traced. In Chapter 5, an overview of motor behavior is provided, including motor learning and motor development. This is followed by Chapter 6 on biomechanics and Chapter 7 on exercise physiology. In Chapter 8, an overview of sport sociology is presented. This section concludes with Chapter 9, on sport and exercise psychology. These chapters present students with information about the development of the subdisciplines, questions that are typically addressed by researchers within the field, key concepts, and current areas of study.

Part Three, which consists of four chapters, addresses professional considerations, such as career opportunities within the field, preparation for a career in physical education, exercise science, and sport, and professional responsibilities. Chapter 10 focuses on professional development, including professional responsibilities, ethics, leadership, and certification. Chapters 11, 12, and 13 offer in-depth information about specific career opportunities in physical education, exercise science, and sport, including responsibilities associated with each career and specific strategies to enhance one's professional marketability. Chapter 11 describes teaching and coaching careers and how opportunities for these careers have broadened from the school setting and school-aged population to nonschool settings and to include persons of all abilities and ages. In Chapter 12, the many new employment opportunities in fitness and health-related careers are examined. Careers in sport management, sport communication, performance, and other sport-related careers such as officiating are described as well as information on the growing field of sport entrepreneurship in Chapter 13.

Part Four explores issues and challenges confronting professionals today and looks at the future of physical education, exercise science, and sport. Chapter 14 addresses timely issues in physical education, exercise science, and sport. Five issues are examined: the leadership role of the physical education, exercise science, and sport professionals in the physical activity movement; the promotion of values, the role of physical education, exercise science, and sport professionals in youth sports; the growing discipline and the debate over its name; and the gap between research and practice. Four of the challenges facing professionals are making quality daily physical education in the schools a reality, advocacy on behalf of our programs, attaining the health objectives for the year 2010, and promoting lifespan involvement in physical activity for all people. The final chapter, Chapter 15, examines the future of physical education, exercise science, and sport. Societal trends and scenarios are analyzed in light of current developments. To prepare for the future, professionals must be willing to assume the responsibility for the leader-ship of our field and work to improve the man-ner in which we provide services to people of all ages.

Highlights of This Edition

- This edition provides an increased emphasis on health promotion, with a particular focus on the important contribution of physical activity to health and our commitment to promote lifelong physical activity for all people. This edition features updated content, including the latest government reports, information on health literacy, and strategies to promote physical activity.

- The increased focus on the growing field of exercise science and sport is reflected in the expanded content for biomechanics, sport and exercise psychology, sport sociology, motor behavior, exercise physiology, and sport management. The previous edition's Chapter 9 on the psychological foundations has been divided into two chapters—Chapter 5 on Motor Behavior and Chapter 9 on Sport and Exercise Psychology. In revising the textbook, an effort was made to include relevant examples within each chapter for the many different professional careers now associated with physical education, exercise science, and sport.
- For students contemplating a career in these dynamic fields, traditional and new career opportunities are presented. Boxes offer listings of professional organizations and journals. Web site addresses are included to allow easy access to the suggested sites.
- The textbook retains its emphasis on lifespan and cultural perspectives. A box in each chapter highlights questions that researchers might choose to address. These thought-provoking questions can be used for classroom discussion or project ideas.

New or Expanded Topics

Chapter 1: Meaning and Philosophy

- Obesity epidemic and health-related consequences
- Healthy Lifestyles and Disease Prevention Initiative

Chapter 2: Goals and Objectives

- No Child Left Behind and possible effects on school physical education
- Updated NASPE's Moving into the Future standards
- Growing public health role for physical education

Chapter 3: Role in Society and in Education

- Cultural diversity within physical education, exercise science, and sport
- Health literacy
- Updated information on physical activity participation from National Health Interview Survey, Behavioral Risk Factor Surveillance System (BRFSS), and National Health and Nutrition Examination Survey (NHANES)

Chapter 4: Historical Foundations

- Updated recent events and streamlined discussion of previous influences on physical education
- Placed more information regarding the influence of ancient cultures and early modern Europe in the online learning center

Chapter 5: Motor Behavior

- New chapter, with information on motor behavior and motor learning
- Motor development and fundamental motor skills

Chapter 6: Biomechanical Foundations

- Impact of technology on performance

Chapter 7: Exercise Physiology and Fitness

- Health risk factors
- Ergogenic aids, including caffeine, creatine, anabolic steroids, and sports drinks

Chapter 8: Sociological Foundations

- Use of performance-enhancing substances in sport
- Updated information on race and opportunities in sport
- New NCAA graduation rate data

Chapter 9: Sport and Exercise Psychology

- Expanded chapter with additional information about physical activity and mental health
- Goal-setting and self-talk

Chapter 10: Career and Professional Development

- Physical Activity and Fitness Recommendations for Physical Activity Professionals from NASPE

Chapter 11: Teaching and Coaching Careers

- Update salary information
- Interstate New Teacher Assessment and Support Consortium (INTASC) competencies for beginning teachers
- Role conflict

Chapter 12: Fitness- and Health-Related Careers

- Wellness programs
- New section on physical therapy

Chapter 13: Sport Careers

- Expanded information on sports management
- NASPE-NASSM Task Force on Sports Management Competencies
- Sport tourism

Chapter 14: Issues and Challenges

- Youth sports
- Technology and research dissemination

Chapter 15: Future Trends

- Future trends and influence on schooling
- Scenario planning and potential futures for nutrition and physical activity

Successful Features

To facilitate use by instructors and students, the following pedagogical aids have been incorporated into this textbook:

Instructional Objectives. At the beginning of each chapter the instructional objectives and competencies to be achieved by the student are listed. This identifies for the student the points that will be highlighted. Attainment of the objectives indicates the fulfillment of the chapter's intent.

Summaries. Each chapter ends with a brief review of the material covered, assisting the student in understanding and retaining the most salient points.

Self-Assessment Tests. Self-assessment tests and activities are presented at the end of each chapter to enable students to check their comprehension of the chapter material.

References. Each chapter provides up-to-date references to allow students to gain further information about the subjects discussed in the chapter.

Suggested Readings. Additional and easily accessible resources from current literature that relate to the chapter topic have been selected and *annotated.* These readings offer students the opportunity to further broaden their knowledge and understanding of various subjects.

Internet Resources. Each chapter begins with a *Get Connected* feature, which lists Internet sites that provide up-to-date information about relevant topics. The self-assessment exercises include activities that draw on these Internet resources.

Photographs. Carefully chosen photographs, many new, have been used throughout the text to enhance the presentation of material and to illustrate key points.

Writing Style. Foundations of Physical Education, Exercise Science, and Sport has been written in a style that students find readable and that provides them with important insights into the foundations and the roles of physical education and sport in the world today. Students will find substantial information about the career and professional opportunities that exist for knowledgeable, dedicated, and well-prepared professionals committed to the promotion of lifespan involvement in physical activity for all people.

Acknowledgments

My thanks are gratefully extended to the publisher's reviewers for their insightful comments and critical suggestions, which helped greatly in the revision of this book. They include: Thomas Battinelli, Fitchburg State College; Scott E. Frazier, University of Wisconsin-Stevens Point; Susan E. Keith, Angelo State University; and Henry E. White, Johnson C. Smith University. For the previous edition I want to thank these reviewers: Margaret Carlisle Duncan, University of Wisconsin-Milwaukee; Craig A. Harms, Kansas State University; Joyce Graenig, University of Arkansas, Karen McNew Thomas, Texas Woman's University; Sharon L. Van Oteghen, University of Memphis; Jim L. Wasem, Eastern Washington University; and Doris L. Watson, University of Utah.

I would like to extend a special recognition to the outstanding professionals at McGraw-Hill, especially my Developmental Editor, Carlotta Seely. Once again, Carlotta's encouragement, patience, and good humor contributed greatly to the completion of this project. Her sound advice and experience helped shape the revision of this edition. Special thanks are also extended to Jill Moline-Eccher, Senior Project Manager, and Cathy Iammartino, whose great attention to detail helped make this project successful.

I extend most heartfelt thanks to my friends and colleagues, who helped in many ways in the revision of this book. I especially appreciate the help of Sarah Rich for her assistance with photography.

This book is lovingly dedicated to my daughter, Meriber Carola DeVida Wuest, who now, at the age of 13, loves being a student-athlete. This book is also dedicated to my late-night writing companions, my loyal cats, Abby, Jake, and Rosie.

SUPPLEMENTS

Instructor's Resource CD-ROM

This CD includes the Instructor's Manual, Test Bank, and PowerPoint presentation designed to accompany *Foundations of Physical Education, Exercise Science, and Sport.*

Instructor's Manual. The Instructor's Manual for this book includes chapter overviews, chapter objectives, review questions, and suggested class activities.

Computerized Test Bank. The test bank is available on the Instructor's CD-ROM as Word files and with EZ Test **computerized testing software.** EZ Test provides a powerful, easy-to-use test maker to create printed quizzes and exams. EZ Test runs on both Windows and Macintosh systems. For secure online testing, exams created in EZ Test can be exported to WebCT, Blackboard, PageOut, and (beginning fall 2005) EZ Test Online. The EZ Test CD is packaged with a Quick Start Guide; once the program is installed, users have access to the complete User's Manual, including multiple Flash tutorials. Additional help is available at www.mhhe.com/eztest.

PowerPoint Presentation. The chapter-by-chapter PowerPoint for this book is designed to aid the instructor in enhancing student learning.

Online Learning Center

The Online Learning Center to accompany *Foundations of Physical Education, Exercise Science, and Sport* offers a wide variety of resources for both instructors and students:

For the instructor:

- PowerPoint presentation for all chapters
- Professional resources
- Guide to using the Internet
- PageOut

For the student:

- Quizzes: multiple choice and true/false
- Career opportunities
- Chapter-related readings

To access the Online Learning Center for this book, go to: *www.mhhe.com/wuest15e*

PowerWeb

The PowerWeb card packaged with each new copy of this text allows access to a reservoir of course-specific articles and current events. Students can use PowerWeb to take a self-scoring quiz, complete an interactive exercise, click through an interactive glossary, or check the daily news. An expert in each discipline analyzes the day's news to show students how it relates to their field of study.

PART I

Nature and Scope of Physical Education, Exercise Science, and Sport

Part I introduces the reader to the fields of physical education, exercise science, and sport. The first chapter sets the stage for the reader by providing definitions and an introduction to the specialized areas of study within physical education, exercise science, and sport. The influence of various philosophies on programs concludes the first chapter. The second chapter provides the reader with information about the objectives of physical education, exercise science, and sport and their relationship to the objectives of education. The contribution of physical education, exercise science, and sport to society, health, and education and the critical role of professionals in delivering services to people of all ages are described in Chapter 3.

Physical education, exercise science, and sport represent growing and expanding fields. The growth of these fields is reflected in the expanding knowledge base and the development of specialized areas of study. The expansion of physical education, exercise science, and sport has created a diversity of career options for professionals in these fields.

CHAPTER 1

MEANING AND PHILOSOPHY

OBJECTIVES

After reading this chapter the student should be able to—

- Discuss the nature of contemporary physical education, exercise science, and sport and show how it has evolved during the past four decades.
- Define the following specialized areas of study: sport philosophy, sport history, sport sociology, sport and exercise psychology, motor development, motor learning, biomechanics, exercise physiology, sports medicine, sport pedagogy, adapted physical activity, and sport management.
- Clarify the relationship between the discipline and the profession relative to the fields of physical education, exercise science, and sport.
- Explain the relationship of physical education, exercise science, and sport to allied fields of study.
- Discuss key concepts of philosophy and their application to physical education, exercise science, and sport.
- Define sport philosophy and describe its historical development and areas of study.
- Develop a personal philosophy of physical education, exercise science, and sport.

This is one of the most exciting, dynamic times in the history of physical education, exercise science, and sport. Unfolding before us is the vision of lifetime involvement in physical activity for all people. It is a powerful vision, one that is compelling for physical educators, exercise scientists, and sport leaders who choose to embrace it and extraordinary in its potential to affect the well-being and quality of life of people of all ages.

Contemporary physical education, exercise science, and sport have evolved from a common heritage—the traditional program of physical education designed to prepare teachers to serve children and youth in the school setting. Since the 1960s the foundation, scope, and focus of our programs have grown and changed tremendously. As physical education expanded, new fields of study—exercise science and sport—emerged. As the knowledge base comprising these multidimensional fields grew, specialized areas of

GET CONNECTED

Newsletters keep you informed about current developments in physical education, exercise science, and sport. These newsletters are delivered to you via e-mail. They contain current news, professional articles, research reports, information on new products, innovative ideas, and relevant statistics.

Generally, you subscribe to the newsletters using your e-mail address. Before subscribing take a moment to read the information on subscriber privacy. Later, if you want to discontinue your newsletter, you may unsubscribe. These newsletters are free and do not require membership.

ACE Health E-tips Newsletter—sponsored by **American Council on Exercise,** this newsletter offers the latest health and fitness information and tips as well as printable fitness tips.

acefitness.org → click on ACE Fit Facts → then sign up to receive E-Tips

AFPA Newsletter—American Fitness Professionals and Associates newsletter has informative articles on numerous health and fitness topics.

www.afpafitness.com → Select your language and enter the website → click on Newsletter → complete registration information

Character Counts Sports Newsletter—Character Counts promotes ethical coaching and character development through sports. A variety of resources are offered, including a newsletter.

www.charactercounts.org → click on Sportsmanship, then look for link to subscribe to the newsletter

PELinks4U Newsletter—sponsored by **PELINKS4U,** this biweekly newsletter has articles on physical education, including lesson plans and ideas for all levels; coaching and sports; health, fitness, and nutrition; technology; interdisciplinary physical education; and adapted physical education.

www.pelinks4u.org → look for a newsletter box to subscribe

study evolved and exciting new career opportunities began to appear for qualified professionals. Today physical education, exercise science, and sport professionals serve people of all ages in a diversity of settings. Our influence on participants' lives is greater. This greater involvement and changing focus is evident from the descriptions of participants in some of our programs.

> The crowd cheers as the player dribbles down the court toward the basket. With the score tied and only seconds to go on the clock, the player fakes left, drives around the opponent, and lays the ball up on the rim. Score! The buzzer sounds, ending the game. The crowd cheers, acknowledging the great performance of both teams, as the women walk off the court. Sports are not just for boys and men anymore!
>
> Giving one final push, he raises his arms in triumph as he leans toward the finish line of the Boston Marathon—the first wheelchair racer to finish. Working closely with the athletic trainer after his shoulder surgery had brought him back to his pre-injury competitive level, the hard training was really worth it. Few things are more satisfying than winning a hard-fought race.
>
> She practices her somersaults and then works on the balance beam. When the music begins, she joins her group at the mat. As the instructor presents different movement challenges, she responds eagerly, enjoying the chance to be creative and try new things. After the lesson is completed, the toddler runs across the gym to her mother. Although it is expensive, her mother thinks the Kidnastics preschool program is a wonderful contribution to her daughter's development.

Career opportunities in physical education, exercise science and sport, range from teaching in the school setting to instructing in the non-school setting, such as leading aerobics classes in a community or corporate fitness setting.

He hustles out of the locker room, looking forward to his workout. Following warm-ups, he completes his weight-training program. After cooling down, he changes clothes and goes back to his office to finish the project that is due tomorrow. He makes a note on his desk calendar to attend the nutrition seminar tomorrow offered by the fitness center staff. The comprehensive employee fitness program is a great company benefit.

She mounts the medal stand—she has won the silver medal for the 100-meter freestyle swimming event at the state games. Not bad for a 76-year-old grandmother, she thinks to herself as her grandchildren and teammates cheer! This is the healthiest she has felt in years, and she enjoys the new friends she has made in the program.

They work carefully, using the skinfold calipers to take each other's measurements at selected sites on their bodies. After entering the measurements into the computer, the data analysis program produces a profile of their body composition. In another area of the gym, their peers engage in step aerobics, using heart-rate monitors to keep track of their work intensity. In the weight area, students work on their individualized training programs. High school physical education is changing!

The patient stands quietly as the electrodes are attached. The cardiac rehabilitation specialist checks his heart rate on the ECG monitor. He is nervous about starting to exercise so soon after his heart attack. After the specialist reassures him that everything looks fine, he begins his warm-up exercises. The other members of the group, all post–heart attack patients themselves, make him feel welcome with their positive comments and enthusiasm as they exercise beside him. He begins to feel better already.

Getting the family to eat dinner together is difficult. Someone is always rushing off to practice. Tonight it is Mom's turn to hurry off to volleyball practice at the school gymnasium. An active participant in the community sports program, Mom plays soccer in the fall and volleyball in the winter. She looks forward

People of all ages enjoy athletic competition.

to learning to play golf in the spring; the instructors appreciate the enthusiasm of the adults who want to learn new sports to enjoy in their leisure time.

As you can see from reading the descriptions, participants of all ages, genders, and abilities are involved in today's physical education, exercise science, and sport programs.

Welcome to contemporary physical education, exercise science, and sport. Providing an overview of these fields is, quite admittedly, a challenge; for physical education, exercise science, and sport are expanding rapidly and the growth of knowledge within these dynamic fields is unprecedented. This virtual explosion of knowledge has led to the development of new areas of study that are highly specialized and discrete and yet, at the same time, highly interrelated and vitally connected. The expansion of the fields has led to considerable debate among the fields' members, focusing on such issues as the appropriate name for the discipline and how best to define the relationship between scientific research and professional practice. Despite the ongoing debate, the growing consensus is that the central focus of these complex, multifaceted fields is human movement or, more generally, physical activity.

We now know that leading a physically active lifestyle can help prevent disease and positively contribute to health and well-being. If the health of our nation is to improve, physical education, exercise science, and sport professionals must make certain that all people have access to programs, regardless of their age, race, ethnicity, gender, sexual orientation, disability status, income, educational level, or geographic location. This is the challenge that awaits you as future professionals in these dynamic fields.

Physical educators, exercise scientists, and sport leaders need to develop a professional philosophy. Having a specific philosophy will guide your actions, improve your professional practice, and help you explain the value and the contributions of physical education, exercise science, and sport programs to the lives of individuals and to society. Dramatic changes have occurred in the last four decades, and more exciting opportunities and challenges await us in this new millennium.

CONTEMPORARY PHYSICAL EDUCATION, EXERCISE SCIENCE, AND SPORT PROGRAMS

The proliferation of physical education, exercise science, and sport programs during the last four decades has been remarkable. Programs have expanded from the traditional school setting to community, home, worksite, commercial, and medical settings. School-community partnerships bring sport instruction and fitness programs to adults in the community and offer increased opportunities for youth involvement. Community recreation programs offer a great variety of instruction and sport activities for people of all ages and abilities. Personal trainers work with clients in their homes. Adults seeking the convenience of working out at home boosted the sales of home exercise equipment to $3.8 billion a year.[1] Corporations offer employees comprehensive health promotion programs, encompassing fitness classes, cardiac rehabilitation, nutritional counseling, smoking cessation, and occupational safety. Fitness and health clubs enroll millions of members who take advantage of aerobic dance classes, resistance training, and life-enrichment classes such as yoga. Tennis, golf, gymnastics, and karate clubs offer instruction to customers, both young and old. Movement programs span the ages, involving everyone from preschoolers to adults to the aged at senior citizen centers. Hospitals sponsor cardiac rehabilitation programs and increasingly offer fitness programs to community members. Sports medicine clinics treat injured sport and fitness participants. Walkers move briskly through the neighborhood, intent on meeting the daily requirement of including 30 minutes of moderate physical activity in their lives. Joggers, bikers, skaters, and swimmers join the millions who have made daily physical activity an integral part of their lives.

People of all ages are seeking out sport opportunities in many different settings. Youth sports involve more than 25 million children a year. Millions participate in interscholastic and intercollegiate athletics. Sport events such as the New York State Empire State Games, A.A.U. Basketball, Senior Games, the Boston Marathon, and master's swimming competitions involve millions of adults in sport competitions. Community recreational leagues for basketball, softball, soccer, and volleyball provide increased opportunities for participation. Sport events such as the Super Bowl, the Olympics, the World Cup, and the National Collegiate Athletic Association basketball tournament capture the enthusiasm of millions of spectators. Girls and women are participating in sports and physical activities in record numbers.

School physical education programs focus on promotion of lifespan involvement in physical activity. Students learn the skills, knowledge, and attitudes that will enable them to participate in various physical activities throughout their lives. Elementary school physical education programs focus on helping children attain competency in the fundamental motor skills (e.g., throwing and catching) and movement concepts (e.g., balance) that form the foundation for later development of specialized games, sport, fitness, and dance activities. (See Chapter 5.) As children progress through school, skill and fitness development is accompanied by an increased knowledge and understanding of physical activity. High schools offer students the opportunity to choose from several different activities for their physical education program. Some instruction may take place in the community, increasing the range of activities that can be offered to students and encouraging students to use the community facilities during their leisure time. Courses in anatomy, exercise physiology, and athletic training may be included in the curriculum, further developing students' understanding and appreciation of physical activity. Intramural competitions afford students of all skill levels the opportunity to compete against their classmates. Interscholastic athletics offer highly skilled boys and girls the chance to compete against students from other schools.

At the collegiate level, young adults enroll in courses in martial arts or tennis, work out at fitness centers, join aerobic dance classes, and take part in recreational sports programs. Intercollegiate athletic programs for men and women continue to expand, involving more participants and attracting greater interest from the public.

People are engaging in physical activity in record numbers. There is increased public recognition that being active is good for your health. Two national reports, *Physical Activity and Health: A Report of the Surgeon General*[2] and *Healthy People 2010,*[3] present overwhelming evidence that people of all ages can improve their health and quality of life by including moderate amounts of physical activity in their daily lives. Although most people know that physical activity is good for them and participation in physical education, exercise science, and sport programs is at an all-time high, a closer look at the participation data reveals much cause for concern.

Despite the documented health benefits of physical activity, 40% of adults engage in no leisure-time activity.[3] Young children and adolescents are more active than adults are, but their activity levels decrease with age. In 2000, the U.S. government issued the report *Promoting Better Health for Young People through Physical Activity and Sports.*[4] According to the report, "Physical inactivity has contributed to an unprecedented epidemic of childhood obesity that is currently plaguing the United States."[4] Too many children and youth are inactive, unfit, and overweight, placing them at increased risk to develop many chronic diseases.

In the United States, the prevalence of overweight and obesity among children, adolescents, and adults has risen at an alarming rate during the past 20 years. Concerned that health problems associated with overweight and obesity could reverse many of the nation's recent health gains, the U.S. Surgeon General, in 2001, issued *Call to Action to Prevent and Decrease Overweight and Obesity.*[5] The Surgeon General called for individuals and groups across the United States to assist Americans in balancing healthful eating with regular physical activity. Ensuring daily, quality physical education in the schools, incorporating more physical activity into daily life, and increasing opportunities for physical activity at worksites were among the action priorities.

In 2004, with poor diet and physical inactivity identified as the second leading cause of preventable death in the United States, the Department of Health and Human Services again called for America to get active and eat healthier. This initiative, *Healthy Lifestyles and Disease Prevention,* encourages Americans to increase the amount of physical activity in their lives and to make healthier dietary choices.[6] This public health initiative reflects the important role of physical activity in health, not only in terms of quality of life but leading a longer healthier life.

Further examination of health status and physical activity patterns in the United States reveals health disparities and fitness inequities among different population groups. Age, socioeconomic status, race, ethnicity, gender, educational attainment, and geographic location were found to influence physical activity levels. Inactivity is greatest among women, minorities, economically and educationally disadvantaged, people with disabilities, and the aged.[3] These populations have less access to services and face other barriers to the adoption and maintenance of physically active lifestyles. Their limited opportunities for physical activity adversely affect their health, their quality of life, and, ultimately, their lifespan.

Involvement in physical activity should begin at an early age and continue throughout one's life. School physical education programs are the primary avenue for helping children and youth learn the skills, knowledge, and attitudes to lead a healthy, physically active lifestyle. Health policy reports recognize the important contribution physical education can make to health and call for daily, high-quality physical education for all students K–12.[3,7] Unfortunately, the number of children and youth participating in daily physical education programs is declining. Daily participation in physical education by high school students decreased from 42% in 1991 to 25% in 1995 and rose slightly to 32.2% in 2001.[2,8] Many lifelong habits and many diseases have their roots in childhood. That's why it is important to develop positive health habits early in life. Over 52 million students are enrolled in public and private elementary and secondary schools in the United States.[9] Imagine the health benefits if each of these students had access to daily quality physical education pre-K–12. Increasing the number of children and youth that have the opportunity to participate in quality physical education programs on a daily basis is an important priority.

The phenomenal growth of physical education, exercise science, and sport programs—the expansion to new settings and the greater inclusion of people of all ages and abilities—has created a wide array of career opportunities for students interested in these exciting fields. Employment opportunities range from the traditional career of teaching physical education and coaching in the schools to sport instruction and fitness-related careers in community and commercial facilities. Increasingly common are career opportunities in cardiac rehabilitation, athletic training, and worksite health promotion. Careers in sport marketing, sport management, and sport communication are growing in popularity.

The primary challenge facing professionals in these fields is addressing inequities in physical activity opportunities and working to eliminate health disparities. As physical education, exercise science, and sport professionals, we must make a greater commitment to reach out to these populations and

Physical Activity Challenge

Our challenge is to improve participation of populations with low rates of physical activity.

Current participation patterns:

- Women are generally less active than men at all ages.
- African Americans and Hispanics are generally less active than whites.
- People with low incomes are typically not as active as those with high incomes.
- People with less education are generally not as active as those with higher levels of education.
- Adults in the Northeast and South tend to be less active than adults in the North Central and Western States.
- People with disabilities are less physically active than people without disabilities.
- Participation in physical activity declines with age. By age 75, one in three men and one in two women engage in no physical activity.

Source: United States Department of Health and Human Services. *Healthy People 2010: Understanding and Improving Health.* Washington, D.C.: U.S. Government Printing Office, November, 2000.

involve them in our programs. We must address the specific barriers that inhibit the adoption and maintenance of physical activity by different populations groups, utilize new approaches that are sensitive to the needs of increasingly diverse populations, and improve access by developing quality public programs in schools, recreation centers, worksites, and health care settings. All people have the right to good health and the opportunity to be physically active throughout their lifespan.

As you begin your professional career, make a commitment to service. Commit yourself to creating opportunities for all people—regardless of age, income, education, race, ethnicity, gender, sexual orientation, geographic location, or ability—to enjoy and to benefit from lifespan participation in physical activity.

Physical Education, Exercise Science, and Sport Defined

Physical education, exercise science, and sport share a common focus—human movement or, more generally, physical activity. Physical activity is the cornerstone of these dynamic fields.

Historically, physical education programs focused on teaching children and youths in the school setting. The traditional definition of physical education reflects this educational focus. Since the 1960s, a tremendous amount of change has occurred in physical education. The expansion of physical education beyond its traditional realm to nonschool settings and the development of programs to instruct people of all ages in physical activities requires a more inclusive, contemporary definition.

Today, physical education is defined as an educational process that uses physical activity as a means to help individuals acquire skills, fitness, knowledge, and attitudes that contribute to their optimal development and well-being. In this definition, the term *education* refers to the ongoing process of learning that occurs throughout our lifespan. Education, just like physical education, takes place in a variety of settings and is not limited to a specific age group. Home schooling, continuing education through distance learning, worksite health promotion programs, and preschools are just some of the expanded settings for education and physical education programs. Teachers today may be called instructors, leaders, or facilitators. Today's students span the age range, from the very young exploring movement skills in a preschool program to the elderly learning how to play golf through a community recreation program.

Exercise physiologists study the body's short- and long-term adaptations to exercise.

Most physical education programs today are based on a developmental model. This model purports that physical education, through the use of carefully structured physical activity, contributes to the development of the whole person. Physical education includes the acquisition and refinement of motor skills, the development and maintenance of fitness for optimal health and well-being, the attainment of knowledge about physical activities, and the fostering of positive attitudes conducive to lifelong learning and lifespan participation. As Ziegler states, "We have a 'womb to tomb' responsibility for the developmental physical activity for all citizens throughout their lives."[10]

Within the last three decades, there has been an increase in the scholarly study of physical education. Research continues to expand our knowledge with respect to the preparation of physical education teachers, teacher effectiveness, teaching methods, and improvement of student learning. It also provides us with new insights on coaches' and athletes' behaviors.

Exercise science is the scientific analysis of exercise or, more inclusively, physical activity. To study physical activity, exercise scientists draw upon scientific methods and theories from many different disciplines, such as biology, biochemistry, physics, and psychology. The application of science to the study of physical activity led to rapid expansion of the knowledge base of exercise science. As the knowledge base of exercise science grew, so did our understanding of the effects of physical activity on various systems of the body. The significant role that physical activity plays in preventing disease and promoting health became clearer. Exercise's value as a therapeutic modality in the treatment of disease and the rehabilitation of injuries became better known.

Exercise science is a very broad field of study, encompassing the study of many different aspects of physical activity. Through research, scholars gain new insights into how people's movements develop and change across their lifespan and further expand their understanding of how people learn motor skills. Analysis of the performance of motor skills using biomechanics leads to improvement in skill efficiency and effectiveness. Researchers' exploration of the limits and capacities of performers has enabled athletes of all abilities to perform at higher levels of achievement. The psychological effects of physical activity on well-being and strategies to enhance adherence to exercise and rehabilitation programs are some other areas of study in the field of exercise science.

Sports are highly organized, competitive physical activities governed by rules. Rules standardize the competition and conditions so that individuals can compete fairly and achieve specified goals. Sports provide meaningful opportunities to demonstrate one's competence and to challenge one's limits. Competition can occur against an opponent or oneself.

People of all ages and abilities engage in sports for enjoyment, personal satisfaction, and the opportunity to attain victory and/or obtain rewards. The level of competition ranges from recreational sport to elite sport. When sport is highly developed, governing bodies regulate sport and oversee its management. At this level, coaches play a significant role, athletes are highly skilled, specially trained officials ensure the fairness of the competition, records are kept, events are promoted through the media, and spectators assume an important role. *Athletics* refers to highly organized, competitive sports engaged in by skillful participants. Sports occupy a prominent position in our society.

Since the early 1970s, there has been an enormous interest in the scholarly study of sport. These sport studies have focused on the significant role of sport in our society, its tremendous impact on our culture, and its effects on the millions of people who play sport and the millions more who watch and read about them. Scholars study the philosophical, historical, sociological, and psychological dimensions of the sport experience. Examples of areas of investigation include sport ethics, the influence of significant historical events on the sport experience, the inequities in sport opportunities for minorities, and the control of anxiety by athletes during performance. Other researchers have directed their attention to investigating the management of sport and its promotion. The growing popularity of sport and its prominent role in our society makes sport a vital area of study.

The realm of physical education, exercise science, and sport today embraces many different programs, diverse settings, and people of all ages. This recent growth of physical education, exercise science, and sport has been accompanied by an increased interest in its scholarly study. This research has led to the development of specialized areas of knowledge. The subsequent increase in the breadth and depth of knowledge provides a foundation for professional practice. The expansion of physical education, exercise science, and sport has led to a tremendous growth of career opportunities for enthusiastic and committed professionals.

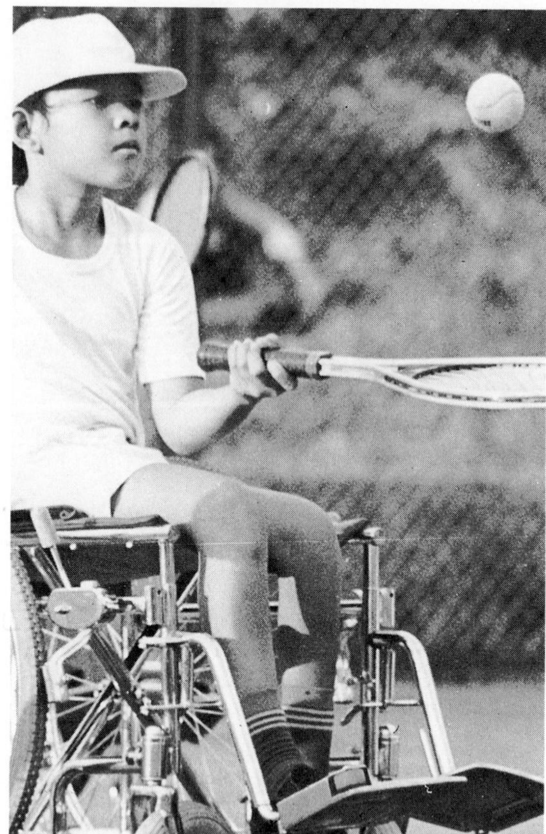

Children with disabilities must have access to sport competition.

Physical Education, Exercise Science, and Sport: The Fields

Corbin[11] defines a field as a "combination of a well-established discipline and one or more professions that deliver a social service" and are "focused on common goals." Disciplinarians engage in research and scholarly endeavors to advance this knowledge base. This knowledge serves as a foundation for the professionals who deliver services to people.[11] Professionals use this knowledge and their skills to design and deliver programs to meet the unique and changing needs of the people they serve. The relationship of the academic discipline to the profession is shown in Figure 1-1. As we continue to grow and become increasingly specialized, we must keep sight of our common focus on physical activity. Both the professional and disciplinary dimensions of these fields enrich our understanding and ability to promote lifespan involvement in regular physical activity for all people.

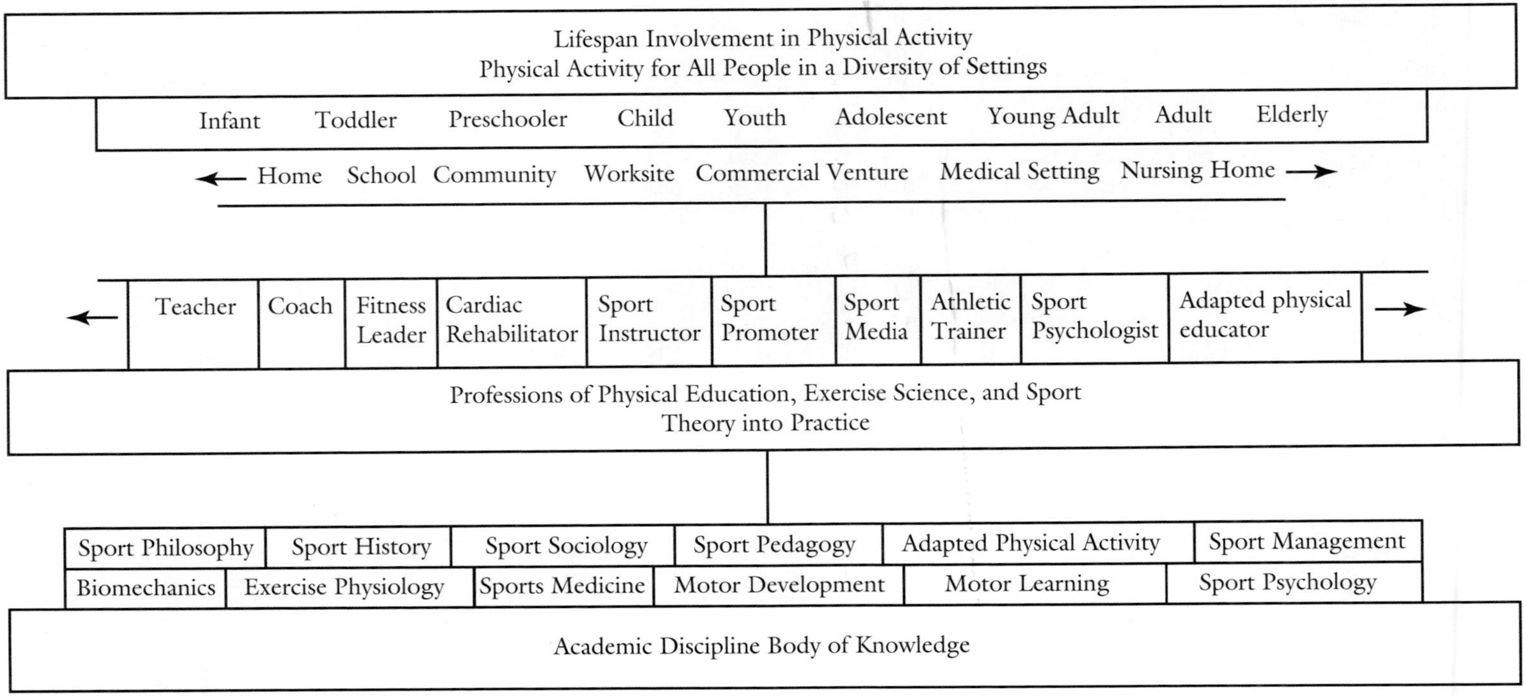

Lifespan Involvement in Physical Activity
Physical Activity for All People in a Diversity of Settings

Infant Toddler Preschooler Child Youth Adolescent Young Adult Adult Elderly

← Home School Community Worksite Commercial Venture Medical Setting Nursing Home →

← Teacher | Coach | Fitness Leader | Cardiac Rehabilitator | Sport Instructor | Sport Promoter | Sport Media | Athletic Trainer | Sport Psychologist | Adapted physical educator →

Professions of Physical Education, Exercise Science, and Sport
Theory into Practice

Sport Philosophy | Sport History | Sport Sociology | Sport Pedagogy | Adapted Physical Activity | Sport Management

Biomechanics | Exercise Physiology | Sports Medicine | Motor Development | Motor Learning | Sport Psychology

Academic Discipline Body of Knowledge

Figure 1-1 The Fields of Physical Education, Exercise Science, and Sport.

The Profession

Physical education, exercise science, and sport can be described with reference to their status as a profession. A *profession* is an occupation requiring specialized training in an intellectual field of study that is dedicated to the betterment of society through service to others. Professionals provide services to others through the application of knowledge and skills to improve people's well-being.

Several characteristics help distinguish a profession from occupations that are not a profession, such as a trade or a craft. These characteristics include:

- An organized and continually expanding body of knowledge that forms the theoretical foundation for practice.
- Educational preparation that includes an extensive course of study focusing on the acquisition of knowledge, development of specialized skills, and attainment of needed competencies.
- Criteria for entry into the profession, which can include participation in an accredited program, a certification process, or licensing procedures.
- Formal associations and opportunities for communication among the membership.
- Established opportunities for continued development and enhancement of professional knowledge and skills.
- A professional code of ethics to govern its membership and provide guidelines for service.
- Recognition by society for its valuable contribution to the welfare of its citizens.
- Dedication to helping others and serving people.

Physical educators, exercise scientists, and sport leaders possess a bachelor's degree and increasingly pursue advanced study via graduate programs in the field. Their professional preparation programs include extensive study in the theoretical aspects of the field, skill development, and often practical experiences that allow them to apply their knowledge and use their skills under the guidance of qualified professionals. Graduates need to fulfill certain requirements to receive their degree. Additional requirements and certifications may be necessary to engage in professional practice.

People of all ages are frequenting fitness centers and health clubs. Many work out on a regular basis. Regular physical activity contributes to good health and overall quality of life.

Many professional organizations offer the opportunity for members to exchange ideas, become aware of new research, and enhance their skills through participation in workshops and clinics. These associations provide a means for communication among their members through conferences, journals, and newsletters. The Internet allows for a rapid exchange of information and communication with professionals worldwide (see Get Connected). Codes of ethics guide professionals as they engage in their work with people.

Today there is increased recognition by society of the valuable contribution professionals in our field make to the lives of others. Our commitment to promoting lifespan physical activity for all members of society benefits the health of the nation. The

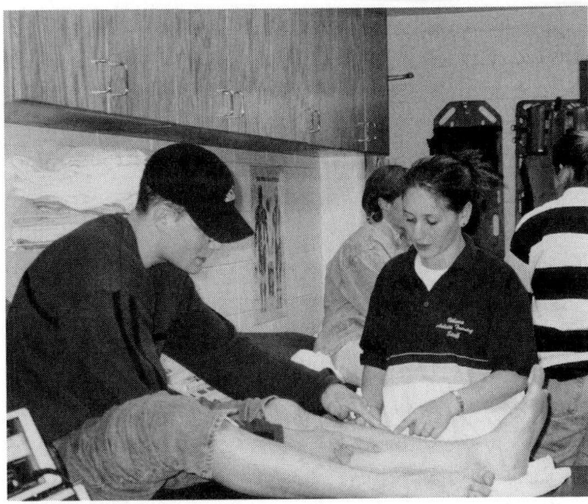

One of an athletic trainer's responsibilities is to evaluate injuries.

expansion of physical education, exercise science, and sport programs to different settings and the involvement of people of all ages in our programs offer professionals increased opportunities to serve others and enhance their well-being.

Traditionally, physical education has been considered part of the teaching profession. Today, our professional emphasis continues to grow as our programs expand to teaching or activity-related careers in nonschool settings, health- and fitness-related careers, and sport-related careers. The emergence of new professional opportunities has created a need for highly qualified professionals who possess a high level of skill, an appreciation and understanding of the needs of an increasingly diverse population, and a sound grasp of the knowledge of physical education, exercise science, and sport.

The Academic Discipline

Since the mid-1960s there has been a phenomenal surge in the scientific study of physical education, which advanced its status as an academic discipline. Henry[12] defines an *academic discipline* as

> an organized body of knowledge collectively embraced in a formal course of learning. The acquisition of such knowledge is assumed to be an adequate and worthy objective as such, without any demonstration or requirement of practical application. The content is theoretical and scholarly as distinguished from technical and professional.

An academic discipline has a focus, a conceptual framework that provides structure for the field, a unique scope in comparison to other fields, and distinct scholarly methods and modes of inquiry leading to the advancement of knowledge and deeper understanding. This body of knowledge is worthy of study for its own sake and does not need to have any immediate application to professional practice. Traditional academic disciplines include biology, psychology, philosophy, history, and mathematics.

The seminal point in the development of the discipline movement occurred in 1964 when Franklin Henry called for the "organization and study of the academic discipline herein called physical education."[12] His clarion call came at a time when forces in society were exerting pressure for educational reform, improved educational standards, and greater academic rigor in the preparation of teachers. Then, physical education teacher preparation programs focused on the application of knowledge and endured criticism for their lack of academic rigor, emphasis on the learning of job-related skills, and their focus on performance courses, such as Basketball Fundamentals.[13]

Henry's call for an academic discipline stimulated greater scholarly activity by academicians at colleges and universities. Developing technologies, theoretical knowledge, and methods of scientific inquiry from other disciplines were directed to the study of physical education and increasingly to exercise and sport. The discipline of psychology, for example, provided the foundation for the development of motor learning and sport psychology. Sociology laid the groundwork for the growth of sport sociology. The proliferation of research and generation of scholarship led to the development of specialized areas of study, commonly called *subdisciplines.*

Subdisciplines of Physical Education, Exercise Science, and Sport

The discipline of physical education, exercise science, and sport consists of 12 subdisciplines. The cross-disciplinary nature of physical education, exercise science, and sport is evident from the names of the subdisciplines. Theories, principles, scientific methods, and modes of inquiry from many other academic disciplines were used by researchers and scholars in the development of these specialized areas of study. Knowledge and research methods from the hard sciences of biology, chemistry, physics, anatomy, physiology, and mathematics strongly influenced the development of the subdisciplines of exercise physiology and sport biomechanics. Psychology, sociology, history, and philosophy, often called the social sciences, formed the foundation for the development of sport and exercise psychology, motor development, motor learning, sport sociology, sport history, and sport philosophy. The rehabilitation sciences, particularly physical therapy, exerted an important influence on the development of sports medicine and adapted physical activity. Educational research significantly affected the development of sport pedagogy. In the subdiscipline of sport management, the influence of management, law, communication, and marketing is evident.

The growth of the subdisciplines broadens the scope of these fields. Equally important, the interdependence between these growing areas offers us valuable knowledge and greater insight as we move toward the accomplishment of our goals. The 12 subdisciplines of physical education, exercise science, and sport are briefly described below.

Exercise physiology is the study of the effects of various physical demands, particularly exercise, on the structure and function of the body. The exercise physiologist is concerned with both short-term (acute) and long-term (chronic) adaptations of the various systems of the body to exercise. The effects of different exercise programs on the muscular and cardiovascular system, the immune system, and the health status of different population groups such as children and the aged are just some areas of study within the field. Clinical exercise testing, design of rehabilitation programs for postcardiac patients, and planning of exercise programs to prevent cardiovascular disease are among the responsibilities of exercise physiologists. (See Chapter 7.)

Sports medicine is concerned with the prevention, treatment, and rehabilitation of sports-related injuries. Athletic trainers' responsibilities are broader than just administering treatment to the injured athlete on the playing field. From the standpoint of prevention, the athletic trainer works with the coach to design conditioning programs for various phases of the season, to correctly fit protec-

Biomechanists analyze the mechanical aspects of athletes' skill performance in order to help them improve.

tive equipment, and to promote the welfare of the athlete, such as counseling the athlete about proper nutrition. With respect to treatment and rehabilitation, the athletic trainer assesses injuries when they occur, administers first aid, works collaboratively with the physician to design a rehabilitation program, provides treatment, and oversees the athlete's rehabilitation. (See Chapter 12.)

Sport biomechanics applies the methods of physics and mechanics to the study of human motion and the motion of sport objects (e.g., baseball or javelin). Biomechanists study the effect of various forces and laws (i.e., Newton's Laws of Motion) on the body and sport objects. The musculoskeletal system and the production of force, leverage, and stability are examined with respect to human movement and sport object motion (e.g., spinning across the circle to throw a discus). Analysis of movements with respect to efficiency and effectiveness is used to help individuals improve their performance. (See Chapter 6.)

Sport philosophy examines sport from many different perspectives. Sport philosophy encompasses the study of the nature of reality, the structure of knowledge in sport, ethical and moral questions, and the aesthetics of movement. Sport philosophers critically examine the meaning of sport for all participants involved and enjoin us to question our beliefs and assumptions about sport. Sport philosophers engage in systematic reflection, use logic as a tool to advance knowledge and arrive at decisions, and seek to understand the relationship between the mind and the body. Sport philosophers debate questions of ethics, morals, and values. (See Chapter 1.)

Sport history is the critical examination of the past, with a focus on events, people, and trends that influenced the development and direction of the field. History is concerned with the who, what, when, where, how, and why of sport.[14] These facts when placed in the social context of the time help us better understand the present and gain insight regarding the future. (See Chapter 4.)

Sport and exercise psychology uses principles and scientific methods from psychology to study human behavior in sport. Sports psychologists help athletes improve their "mental game," that is, develop and effectively apply skills and strategies that will enhance their performance. Achievement motivation, regulation of anxiety, self-confidence, rehabilitation adherence, cohesion, and leadership are among the topics studied by sport psychologists. Recently, sport psychology and exercise psychology have become more closely aligned. Exercise psychology is concerned with exercise addiction, adherence, and other psychological issues affecting the well-being of people who are physically active. (See Chapter 9.)

Motor development studies the factors that influence the development of abilities essential to movement. The motor development specialist uses longitudinal studies (i.e., studies that take place over a span of many years) to analyze the interaction of genetic and environmental factors that affect an individual's ability to perform motor skills throughout their lifespan. The role of early movement experiences, heredity, and maturation on children's development of motor skills is an important focus of study. Professionals use theories of development to design appropriate movement experiences for people of all ages and abilities. (See Chapter 5.)

Motor learning is the study of changes in motor behavior that are primarily the result of practice and experience. The effect of the content, frequency, and timing of feedback on skill learning is a critical area of study. Motor learning is concerned with the stages an individual progresses through in moving from a beginner to a highly skilled performer. The most effective conditions for practicing skills, the use of reinforcement to enhance learning, and how to use information from the environment to modify performance are investigated by motor learning specialists. (See Chapter 5.)

Sport sociology is the study of the role of sport in society, its impact on participants in sport, and the relationship between sport and other societal institutions. Sport sociologists examine the influence of gender, race, and socioeconomic status on participation in sports and, more recently, physical activity. Drug abuse by athletes, aggression and violence, the effect of the media on sport, and player-coach relationships interest sport sociologists. The experience of the millions of children

Sport psychologists help athletes achieve optimal levels of performance.

involved in youth sport has also drawn the attention of sport sociologists. (See Chapter 8.)

Sport pedagogy can be defined broadly to include the study of teaching and learning in school and nonschool settings. Sport pedagogy studies how physical educators and sport leaders provide an effective learning environment, achieve desired learning goals, and assess program outcomes. It seeks to determine the characteristics and skills possessed by effective teachers and coaches and how these influence student/athlete activity and student/athlete learning. The curriculum, its goals, its organization, and how it is implemented are studied. The preparation of teachers is a major focus of this area. (See Chapter 11.)

Adapted physical activity is concerned with the preparation of teachers and sport leaders to provide programs and services for individuals with disabilities. Specialists modify activities and sport to enable people with different abilities to participate. By federal law, adapted physical educators have a role in designing an individualized educational plan for students with disabilities so that they can participate to the fullest extent they are able in school physical education. Advocacy to secure services and leadership to create more opportunities in physical education and sport are important aspects of this field. (See Chapter 11.)

Sport management encompasses the many managerial aspects of sport. These include personnel management, budgeting, facility management, and programming. Other aspects of sport management are law, policy development, fundraising, and media relations. Knowledge from this area can be used by professionals in many different aspects of the sport enterprise, including interscholastic and intercollegiate sports, professional sports, fitness and health clubs, community sport and recreation programs, and sporting goods sales. (See Chapter 13.)

Specialization and Integration

The emergence of subdisciplines led to specialization by both the academicians and practitioners in the field. The creation of new professional societies and scholarly journals provided a forum for professional dialogue, the dissemination of scientific findings, and the sharing of scholarly work. At colleges

Sport sociologists study the behavior of people in sport situations—athletes, coaches, and fans—as well as the impact of sport on the community.

and universities, curricular changes were implemented as new courses were developed and, eventually, new undergraduate majors were added, such as those in sport studies, athletic training, and fitness and cardiac rehabilitation. These new career options attracted an increasing number of students, and the number of graduates of these programs soon exceeded the number of graduates from the traditional teaching program. The graduates of these nonteaching programs often prefer to describe their occupation with reference to their specialized areas of study. Thus, these professionals refer to themselves as athletic trainers, exercise scientists, and sport managers rather than physical educators. The new graduate programs offered at the master's and doctoral levels, such as those in exercise physiology, sport pedagogy, sport management, and sport psychology, reflect the increasingly sophisticated, complex nature of the discipline.

The disciplinary movement will continue to expand our body of knowledge. As specialization increases, it is important not to lose sight of the whole breadth of the field. Even though specialized areas have developed significant knowledge bases, they are not mutually exclusive. There is an overlap in content, ideas, and areas of inquiry, as we are based on a common focus, which has been increasingly defined as physical activity. McNeill defines as the basic focus of our field "our connection and commitment to the health and well-being of all people."[15]

Table 1-1 shows how physical educators, exercise scientists, and sport leaders can use knowledge from each of the subdisciplines to enhance the effectiveness of their programs. In this era of continued growth of the whole field and increased specialization within the field, we should strive to make connections between the subdisciplines. Charles advises that when we eschew boundaries that define the subdisciplines, we can give isolated factors greater meaning by placing them in the perspective of the larger field.[16] Lumpkin suggests that as a field "we should commit to common goals, different roles, and a cross-disciplinary body of knowledge."[17] We must understand the significant contribution of each of these scholarly fields and

Sport pedagogy studies behaviors of teachers and coaches, identifying those that contribute to an effective learning environment. Coach Mike Krzyzewski, Duke University, is recognized for his leadership and coaching excellence. Photo courtesy Duke University Sports Information Department.

the important role each of us play in achieving the goal of lifespan participation in physical activity for people of all ages. It is equally important to remember that as professionals working with people, we are dealing with the whole person—their mind and body in the context of society. We must be sensitive to society's changing needs and capitalize on them as an opportunity for growth. Charles states that "we must recognize and capitalize on indicators of cultural change that point toward a future society that places a premium on health and wellbeing and that values personal fulfillment through physical activity."[16] If we can do this, we can achieve our fullest potential as a significant force in society.

The Name Debate

As the discipline movement grew in the decades following Henry's 1964 call for its development, academicians in higher education engaged in a protracted debate about the proper title for the expanding knowledge base of what had been traditionally known as physical education. What should the discipline be called?

Some scholars expressed concern that the traditional name of *physical education* was too narrow in scope and did not clearly convey the growing academic nature of the field. The title *physical education* also fails to reflect the expanding scholarly interest in sport and exercise science, which have emerged as vital areas of study. Moreover, the name was too closely linked to the traditional profession of teaching in the schools. Teaching, which was once our primary profession, is now one of many professions associated with the discipline. However, other scholars favored the retention of the traditional title *physical education.* Instead of changing the title, these scholars and professionals wanted to focus on changing the image of physical education to more accurately reflect its evolving nature, expanding scope, and changing focus. In short, physical education was experiencing an "identity crisis."

Scholars have engaged in extended discussions to define the field's focus. They sought a new title for the field that would reflect both our disciplinary and professional aspects. As scholars debated, departments of physical education in higher education began changing their names to reflect their expanding mission and changing direction. Starting in the 1960s, some physical education departments in colleges and universities began changing their name to *kinesiology.* Kinesiology is defined as the study of human movement. Proponents of this name believed it reflected the growing scholarly attention to the many facets of human movement. In 1989, after years of debate, the prestigious American Academy of Physical Education voted to change its name to the American Academy of Kinesiology and Physical Education and recommended *kinesiology* as the title of the discipline. Those who opposed this title expressed

TABLE 1-1 Subdisciplines of Physical Education, Exercise Science, and Sport—Application to Fitness Instruction and Program Leadership

Subdiscipline	Types of Questions
Biomechanics	What are the correct techniques for weight training? How can I evaluate a participant's gait?
Exercise Physiology	What is the frequency, duration, and intensity of exercise to yield health benefits? How long will it be before participants will achieve a significant difference in their health status?
Sports Medicine	What exercises will prevent injury? How should exercise be modified for hot, humid weather?
Motor Development	What are the developmental needs of the participants? How can the program be designed to meet these needs?
Motor Learning	What are the best practice conditions for learning a skill? How does the frequency of feedback and praise influence participation?
Sport Philosophy	What is my role as a fitness leader in involving participants in the program? What is the responsibility of the participants in this program?
Sport and Exercise Psychology	What are the best strategies to help program participants adhere to or continue their involvement in the program?
Sport Sociology	What are societal factors that influence the activity choices of the program participants? What are the societal forces that influence their participation?
Sport Pedagogy	What are characteristics of effective teachers? What are guidelines for most effectively presenting instruction?
Adapted Physical Activity	How can the program be modified to meet individual needs? . . . to accommodate individuals with disabilities?
Sport Management	What is the best way to promote the program? How can I bring about a change in policy?

concern about the lack of recognition of the name by the public. Accomplishing our mission is difficult if people do not know what we stand for and recognize the value of what we do.

Exercise science, sometimes in conjunction with *sport science,* became a popular term used by departments in the 1990s. Exercise science defines the broader emphasis of the field and, in terms of name recognition, is easy for the public to understand. Sport, although perceived as too narrow to represent the whole of the field, does capture the growing focus of the field's scholarly endeavors.

Physical education and sport is also a popular title for the field. Ziegler reported that in 1994 it was the most common title used worldwide.[10] By linking physical education with sport, it clearly identifies sport as a vital, but not sole, concern of the field. This designation retains the traditional term *physical education* that is familiar to the public. It includes the term *sport,* which has emerged as a prominent area of scholarly study.

Physical activity sciences is another suggested name for the discipline. Those scholars who favor this name cite its clear and easily recognizable focus—human physical activity. Physical activity sciences reflect the central focus of the discipline—the study of various forms of physical activity from many different perspectives. The name provides a conceptual focus and framework for the many specialized yet interconnected areas of scientific and scholarly study.

Today, there is a growing consensus that physical activity is our central focus. There is still no common agreement as to the title of the field.

Ziegler, in 1997, addressed this continuing dilemma by noting that "the situation has now ballooned into a whirling vortex of more than 150 names in the United States" for departments in higher education. He calls for resolution of the issue, the recognition of developmental physical activity as the focus, and the closer alignment of the "professional and scholarly dimensions of our work."[10] It is time, Ziegler states, "to take bold, positive steps to present a much sharper, more precise image to those who use our services (e.g., students, clients)."[10]

ALLIED FIELDS

Health, recreation, and dance are frequently referred to as allied fields of physical education, exercise science, and sport. These fields share many purposes with physical education, exercise science, and sport, namely the development of the total individual and concern for quality of life. However, the content of the subject matter of the allied fields and the methods used to accomplish their goals may vary from the subject matter and methods of physical education, exercise science, and sport. The title of the largest professional organization, the American Alliance for Health, Physical Education, Recreation and Dance (AAHPERD), reflects the close and important relationship between these fields. AAHPERD's membership consists of professionals in physical education, sport, athletics, exercise science, health, safety, recreation and leisure, and dance.

Health

Health education concerns itself with the total well-being of the individual, encompassing physical, mental, social, emotional, and spiritual health. Three areas within health education are health instruction, the provision of health services, and environmental health.

Teaching the basics of healthful living is the focus of health instruction. Health instruction is targeted at individuals of all ages, ranging from preschoolers to the elderly, and is delivered through a diversity of agencies—including educational institutions at all levels, public health services, and private programs. Health instruction can encompass many areas, including disease prevention, mental health, nutrition, physical fitness,

Corporate fitness programs are becoming increasingly popular. Tenneco employees participate in step aerobics classes offered as part of their health and fitness programs.

Physical activity contributes to health and fitness throughout life. Bicycling is an excellent activity for people of all ages.

stress management, and dealing with abuse of drugs and alcohol.

Delivery of health services is the second area of health education. These services are concerned with developing and maintaining a satisfactory level of health for all people. Health services are provided at educational institutions at all grade levels and are more frequently becoming an integral part of employee health services offered by corporations. Services may include routine eye examinations, cholesterol and blood pressure monitoring, and cancer screening.

Environmental health is the third area included within health education. Its primary concern is the development of healthful and safe environments. Standards have been developed to ensure that individuals within an environment are not needlessly exposed to hazards such as toxic chemicals or infectious materials.

Americans are becoming increasingly conscious of the instrumental role physical activity plays in one's quality of life. Data supporting the health benefits of participation in appropriate physical activity on a regular basis continue to mount. Accrued benefits of regular physical activity include the prevention of coronary heart disease, hypertension, noninsulin-dependent diabetes, mellitus, osteoporosis, obesity, and mental health problems.[2,3] Other benefits may include the reduction of the incidence of stroke and the maintenance of the functional independence of the elderly.[2,3] Additionally, it has been found that, on average, individuals who are physically active outlive individuals who are physically inactive.[2,3] The strong role regular and appropriate physical activity plays in the health and well-being of individuals further confirms the allied nature of health and physical education, exercise science, and sport.

Recreation

Another area allied with physical education, exercise science, and sport is recreation. Recreation is generally thought of as self-chosen activities that provide a means of revitalizing and refreshing one's body and spirit. The spectrum of activities ranges from active to passive and from group to individual in nature. Recreation is important for individuals of all ages. Through recreation, individuals can learn to use their leisure time constructively in ways that are personally fulfilling.

Like physical education, exercise science, and sport, recreation is experiencing a period of rapid growth and expansion. The number and types of available activities have increased, the settings in which programs are offered have become more diverse, and the number and range of populations served have expanded. Concern for the environment has also led to calls for resource management by national and local authorities to preserve the environment while providing for the careful expansion of outdoor recreational facilities.

Recreational opportunities abound. Schools, communities, and businesses offer a wide range of activities to meet the fitness and leisure needs of individuals. Worksite fitness programs, industrial sport leagues, commercial fitness programs, competitive recreational leagues, instructional clinics, and open facilities for drop-in recreation are increasing in number. During nonschool hours, school facilities are the site for various recreational offerings for people of all ages. Many individuals and families pursue recreational activities independently as well.

Therapeutic recreation focuses on providing a broad range of services for individuals of all ages who have disabilities. Through a diversity of interventions, the individual's quality of life is enhanced, the development of leisure skills is encouraged, and the integration of the individual into community recreational opportunities and life is emphasized.

Recreation, like physical education, exercise science, and sport, can contribute to the quality of an individual's life. It provides opportunities for individuals to engage in freely chosen activities during their leisure time.

Dance

The third allied area is dance. Dance is a popular activity of people of all ages and is both a physical activity and a performing art that gives participants an opportunity for aesthetic expression through movement.

People dance for a variety of reasons. Dance is used to communicate ideas and feelings and is considered a creative art form. As with all of the arts, dance should be an integral part of the educational experience. As a form of recreation, dance provides opportunities for enjoyment, self-expression, and relaxation. Dance also can be used as a form of therapy, providing opportunities for individuals to express their thoughts and feelings. It provides a means to cope with the various stresses placed on individuals. Dance is increasingly used as a means to develop fitness.

There are many forms of dance that are enjoyed by individuals—including ballet, ballroom, folk, clog, modern, square, and tap. Cultural heritage is reflected in and passed on through dance activities.

Within the past two decades, aerobic dance, and its many variations, has grown in popularity. Aerobic dance provides participants with an opportunity to develop fitness and experience the fun and enjoyment of working out to music.

Health, recreation, and dance are allied fields to physical education, exercise science, and sport. The overall focus of these fields of endeavor is the development of the total individual and the enhancement of each person's quality of life. Attainment of these aims involves health promotion, pursuit of worthy leisure-time activities, and creative expression through dance. These experiences, coupled with the movement activities that compose the realm of physical education, exercise science, and sport, offer the potential to enhance the lives of people of all ages. Fulfillment of this potential will depend on the quality of leadership provided by professionals in health, recreation and leisure, dance, physical education, exercise science, and sport.

TERMINOLOGY

Within the last 50 years, great strides have been made in our understanding of health and physical activity. Our definition of health and other terms such as *physical activity* and *physical fitness* have changed considerably. In 2000, the President's

Components of Fitness

HEALTH-RELATED FITNESS COMPONENTS

- Body composition
- Cardiorespiratory endurance
- Flexibility
- Muscular endurance
- Muscular strength

PERFORMANCE-RELATED FITNESS COMPONENTS

- Agility
- Balance
- Coordination
- Power
- Reaction time
- Speed

Council on Physical Fitness and Sport (PCPFS) developed a compendium of common terms that reflected the latest thinking in the field and published them in *Research Digest.*[18] The definitions of terms in this section are based upon the PCPFS definitions as well as current documents, such as the Surgeon General's report entitled *Physical Activity and Health,*[2] *Healthy People 2000,*[7] and *Healthy People 2010.*[3]

Health is a state of positive well-being associated with freedom from disease or illness. Traditionally, health was defined as the absence of disease and infirmity. Thus, by definition, if an individual was not sick, he or she was well. Today, health is viewed as an optimal state of well-being—wellness—and possessing a high quality of life.

Wellness is a state of optimal well-being. It is a state of positive biological and psychological well-being that encompasses a sense of well-being and quality of life. Today, the primary causes of death and disease in our society are related to lifestyle choices. Achieving wellness requires that the individual make lifestyle choices that will reduce disease risk factors and promote health. These choices include following sound nutritional practices, being physically active on a regular basis, taking time for rest and relaxation, managing stress effectively, adhering to sound safety practices, and eliminating controllable risk factors, such as smoking or excessive alcohol consumption.

Holistic health is closely aligned with wellness. The basic tenet of holistic health is that an individual's health is affected by most aspects of an individual's life. Physical, mental, emotional, social, spiritual, environmental, and genetic factors all interact to influence an individual's state of health.

Quality of life is an overall sense of well-being. It holds different meanings for each individual, but to many people it means a life that is healthy, satisfying, meaningful, and enjoyable. Quality of life can be viewed from both a health-related and non-health-related perspective. Health-related quality of life refers to individuals' perceived physical and mental health.[19] Medical and health professionals use health-related quality of life as a means to assess the effects of illness and disability on individuals' sense of well-being and satisfaction with daily living. Non-health-related quality of life is a general concept that relates to individuals' physical, psychological, and spiritual well-being.[19] It reflects individuals' perceptions of factors that contribute to the goodness and meaning of life, as well as their happiness.[19]

Physical activity is bodily movement produced by the contraction of the skeletal muscles that substantially increases energy expenditure above the baseline level. Physical activity has many different forms. Exercise, sport, leisure activities, dance, activities of daily living, and occupational tasks are forms of physical activity.

Exercise is a specific form of physical activity that is performed with the intention of developing physical fitness. Exercise is planned, structured, and repetitive. The duration, intensity, and frequency of exercise can be measured.

Physical fitness is the capacity of people to perform physical activities. It is a set of attributes that people have or achieve that allow them to carry out daily tasks without undue fatigue and enable them to have the energy to participate in a variety of physical activities. It is a state of well-being associated with low risk of premature health problems. Physical fitness can be described in relationship to health and performance.

Health-related physical fitness is comprised of those fitness components that have a relationship to good health and well-being. Health-related fitness components are body composition, cardiorespiratory endurance, flexibility, and muscular strength and endurance. Health-related fitness is important to all persons throughout their lifespan.

Performance-related physical fitness consists of those components of physical fitness that are associated with enhanced performance in sports and motor skills. The performance-related fitness components are agility, balance, coordination, power, reaction time, and speed.

• • •

PHILOSOPHY

For some people the term *philosophy* conjures up visions of an individual sitting in the ivory towers of a university pondering seemingly unanswerable questions. Or it may call up the image of an individual sitting atop a rock next to the bank of a stream, looking at the water rippling by and contemplating the meaning of life. Perhaps you think of philosophy as too abstract in nature to have practical value. Maybe it would help you to appreciate the worth of philosophy if it was defined simply as a set of beliefs that guides one's actions and gives direction to one's life.

What Is Philosophy?

Philosophy, derived from the Greek word *philosophia,* means the love of wisdom.[20] Philosophers pursue the truth through the systematic investigation of reality, knowledge, meanings, and values. Philosophy can also be defined as a set of beliefs relating to a particular field, for example, a philosophy of sport, fitness, or physical education. Philosophy is a system of values by which one lives and works. Your system of beliefs and values guides your conduct in both your personal and professional life. Philosophy helps individuals address the problems that confront them through the use of critical thinking, logical analysis, and reflective appraisal.

Questions that reflect the concerns of philosophers include the following:

- What is the role of human beings on this earth?
- What are the origin and nature of the universe?
- What constitutes good and evil, right and wrong?
- What constitutes truth?
- Is there a God?
- Do human beings have souls, that is, some essence that exists yet cannot be seen?
- What is the function of education in society?
- What relationship exists between mind and matter?

Philosophy is conventionally divided into four domains or branches of study, providing a framework for examination of philosophical concerns. Each branch contributes to our understanding and offers us greater insight in our search for wisdom.

Branches of Philosophy

Philosophy's branches of study are generally divided into four domains: metaphysics, epistemology, axiology, and logic. *Metaphysics* seeks to address the ultimate nature of reality, that is, what is real and exists. Speculative in its approach, metaphysics may be used to understand the relationship between mind and body or the essential meaning of sport. *Epistemology* is the branch of philosophy concerned with examining the nature of knowledge. It uses critical, analytical methods to examine the structure of knowledge, its origin, and limits. This approach can help us in defining the nature of the discipline (i.e., body of knowledge) of physical education, exercise science, and sport. *Logic* focuses on the examination of ideas in an orderly and systematic way. Logic uses a critical approach to study how ideas relate to each other, and applies sound and reasoned judgment to decision making. Logic can help members of our

Branches of Philosophy

Branch	Focus	General Questions	Physical Education, Exercise Science, and Sport Questions
Metaphysics	Nature of reality	What is the meaning of existence? What is real?	What experiences in a physical education program will better enable the individual to meet the challenges of the real world?
Epistemology	Nature of knowledge and methods of obtaining knowledge	What is true?	What is the validity of the knowledge pertaining to physical activity and its influence on the development of the individual?
Logic	Systematic and orderly reasoning	What is the method of reasoning that will lead to the truth?	What process should a researcher use to determine the value of physical education to program participants?
Axiology	Aims and values of society	How do we determine what has value, and on what criteria is this judgment based?	What is the value of physical education programs to the individual?
Ethics	Issues of conduct, right and wrong	What is the highest standard of behavior each person should strive to attain?	How can sport be utilized to develop ethics?
Aesthetics	Nature of beauty and art	What is beauty?	Why are skilled performers' movements beautiful to view?

fields design sound research approaches or organize facts to document the contribution of physical activity to well-being. *Axiology* examines the nature of values. Two extensions of axiology are ethics and aesthetics. *Ethics* is concerned with issues of right and wrong, responsibility, and standards of conduct. Speculative in nature, ethics examines moral values. Moral reasoning helps people determine what is the right thing to do in a given situation or circumstance. The development of character, nature of fair play, and issues of justice are just a few of the ethical concerns of physical education, exercise science, and sport. *Aesthetics* is the study of the nature of beauty and art. The beauty of skilled movement and artistic expression through dance enable us to see movement as an art form.

These branches represent different aspects of philosophy. In developing a comprehensive philosophy for a discipline, such as physical education, exercise science, and sport, each of these areas is addressed. (See the Branches of Philosophy box.) It gives a definition of each branch of philosophy, a typical question posed, and an example of a question that might be asked concerning physical education, exercise science, and sport.

Why Have a Philosophy?

In today's changing society, a sound philosophy of life and physical education, exercise science, and sport is necessary for the professional to be effective. Professionals must ask themselves the following important questions:

- What has value in today's society?
- What is relevant to the needs of people today?
- What are some inequities that must be addressed?

Physical educators, exercise scientists, and sport leaders also may find a philosophy helpful in addressing more specific questions confronting them. For example:

- Should youth sport programs mandate equal playing time for all participants?
- Should intercollegiate athletes be required to maintain a certain grade-point average to participate?
- Should athletic trainers be required to report illegal drug use by an athlete?
- Should the coach, athletic trainer, or athlete make the final determination whether an injured athlete can play?
- Should employees be required to participate in a corporate fitness program?
- Should certification be required of all health/fitness club employees?
- Should individuals who have tested HIV positive be allowed to participate in physical education classes and on athletic teams?
- Should the media scrutinize the private lives of professional athletes?
- Should fitness instructors be role models and "practice what they preach"?

A well-developed professional philosophy gives physical education, exercise science, and sport professionals guidance in resolving these questions as well as a multitude of questions and issues that confront them.

A professional philosophy serves several functions. Philosophy assists in the development and clarification of beliefs and values, which serve as a foundation for one's behavior. Philosophy aids in decision making. When confronted with ethical decisions, professionals use philosophy to reflect on how they ought to act, what is right and wrong in a given situation, and what is just and unjust. Philosophy guides physical educators, exercise scientists, and sport leaders in determining the goals, objectives, and methods of instruction used in their programs. A sound and reasoned philosophy helps professionals evaluate their programs to determine if they are meeting participants' needs and are being conducted in an ethical manner.

General Philosophies

The five philosophies most often examined in relationship to education are idealism, realism, pragmatism, naturalism, and existentialism. These philosophies have influenced the goals, objectives, educational content, methodology, and values associated with education as well as the roles and responsibilities of teachers and students in the education process. Because of physical education's historic association with education, its programs have been influenced by these philosophies. These philosophies can also be applied to contemporary physical education, exercise science, and sport. An overview of these philosophies is provided and examples show how they can influence the nature and conduct of physical education, exercise science, and sport programs.

Idealism

As a philosophy, idealism emphasizes the mind as central to understanding. Idealism encompasses such general concepts as: The mind is the focus of the person's being. All reality comes from the mind. In the scheme of the universe, people are more important than nature because nature is interpreted by the mind. Values and ideals exist independently of individuals and are universal and absolute; they never change. An individual exercises free will in choosing between right and wrong. Reasoning and intuition help individuals arrive at the truth.

When the general principles of idealism are applied to physical education, exercise science, and sport, they result in such concepts as: Physical education, exercise science, and sport involve more than the "physical." Even though the mind and body are to be developed as one, in reality ide-

Central Beliefs Underlying Traditional Philosophies

Idealism	The mind interprets events and creates reality; truth and values are absolute and universally shared.
Realism	The physical world is the real world and it is governed by nature; science reveals the truth.
Pragmatism	Reality is determined by an individual's life experiences; the individual learns the truth through experiences.
Naturalism	Reality and life are governed by the laws of nature; the individual is more important than society.
Existentialism	Reality is based on human existence; individual experiences determine what is true.

alism emphasizes the development of the mind and thought processes. Physical fitness and activities are valued for their contribution to the development of one's personality. Ideals are emphasized in the physical education, exercise science, and sport program. The physical education, exercise science, and sport professional is a role model for the program's participants, particularly in terms of character and values. Self-development is emphasized.

Realism

The physical world is the central focus of the philosophy of realism. Realism deals with such concepts as: The physical world of nature is the real world. All physical events that occur in the universe are the result of the laws of nature; nature is in control. The truth can best be determined through the scientific method. People's senses and experiences also help them to understand nature. The mind and the body have a close, harmonious relationship.

When these general principles are applied to the area of physical education, exercise science, and sport, they result in such concepts as: Education is for life. Physical education, exercise science, and sport should focus on the development of the total person. Physical education, exercise science, and sport programs are valuable because of their contribution to health. A healthy person can lead a fuller life and be more productive. Programs are based on scientific knowledge and an orderly progression. Drills are used extensively, and learning is evaluated objectively.

Pragmatism

According to the philosophy of pragmatism, experiences—not ideals or realities—are the means to achieving the truth. Pragmatism deals with such concepts as: Truth is based on one's experiences. Because individuals experience different circumstances and situations, reality changes in pragmatism. Success is the only criterion of the value and truth of a theory. Truth is situational; whatever works in a given situation is correct at that time. Values are relative and are derived from one's experiences. Social responsibility is important; individuals are an integral part of a larger society.

When the general principles of pragmatism are applied to the area of physical education, exercise science, and sport, they result in such concepts as: The program content should be based on the needs and interests of the students. The program should be varied to provide a diversity of experiences for learning. Learning is accomplished through the problem-solving method. Social outcomes from participation in the program are important. The physical education, exercise science, and sport professional serves as a guide.

Naturalism

A belief that life is governed by the laws of nature is central to the philosophy of naturalism. Naturalism includes such general concepts as: Any reality

Philosophy influences athletes' attitudes toward winning and helps them interpret the meaning of success.

that exists is found only within the physical realm of nature. Nature itself is the source of value. The individual is more important than society, but society is necessary to prevent chaos.

When the principles of naturalism are applied to the area of physical education, exercise science, and sport, they result in such concepts as: Physical activity is important for the development of the total person; it provides a medium for the development of physical, mental, social, emotional, and moral skills. Instruction is paced according to the individual's needs. Participants are self-directed. Individualized learning through self-activity leads to the attainment of individual goals. Highly competitive performance between individuals is discouraged; competition against oneself is encouraged, however. Play is an important part of the educational process. Noncompetitive activities and outdoor pursuits provide beneficial opportunities for individual growth.

Existentialism

Reality is determined by individual experiences, according to the existentialist philosophy. Existentialism deals with such concepts as: Human existence is the only true reality. Individuals must accept responsibility for themselves and the choices they make. An individual's experiences and choices are unique, affecting their perception of reality. Individuals must determine their own systems of values and follow them, but they also must accept the consequences of their actions. Individuals are more important than society; however, they must acknowledge their societal responsibility.

When the general principles of existentialism are applied to the area of physical education, exercise science, and sport, they result in such concepts as: Each participant is free to choose from a variety of activities within the program. Individual activities provide opportunities for participants to develop self-awareness and self-responsibility. The physical education, exercise science, and sport professional serves as a counselor, promoting reflective thinking while allowing participants to make choices and deal responsibly with the consequences of those choices.

The principles of idealism, realism, pragmatism, naturalism, and existentialism influence educational programs, including physical education. Although the discussion of these philosophies focused primarily on the schools and physical education, their influence can be seen in contemporary physical education, exercise science, and sport programs.

Most schools today follow a modern educational philosophy that is based on much of what was advocated by John Dewey, leader of the progressive education movement.

Modern Educational Philosophy

Today's educational philosophy reflects several influences. Dewey's ideas were influential in shaping American education. Humanism, a philosophy that grew popular in the 1960s and 1970s, also altered the focus of American education.

Dewey's ideas of *progressive education* reflect a pragmatic orientation. Progressives believed that education was the avenue to improve the social conditions of society. This child-centered approach to learning emphasized children taking an active role in their learning, as opposed to being passive recipients of knowledge conveyed to them by the teacher.[13] Dewey's approach of "learning by doing" significantly changed the nature of American education. Furthermore, Dewey believed in the unity of

Some sports, such as the martial arts, emphasize the development of the mind and spirit as well as the body.

the mind and the body. Educational activities were viewed as contributing to the development of the total person, not just the mind. The tenets of progressive education lent support to the inclusion of physical education in the school curriculum. Physical activity developed the physical as well as contributing to the intellectual and social goals of education. This philosophy of education through the physical was to become one of the most important influences on twentieth-century physical education.[13]

A *humanistic philosophy* emphasizes the development of the full potential of each individual. Personal growth, self-actualization, and the development of values are central tenets of this philosophy. Treating students as individuals, valuing the dignity of each person, enhancing self-esteem, fostering personal and social development, and promoting self-responsibility were hallmarks of this approach. Within the realm of physical education, exercise science, and sport, humanism encourages a greater emphasis on meeting individual needs and recognizes that one type of program is not suited to all individuals. The feelings, needs, goals, capabilities, and limitations of individuals should carefully be considered in conducting programs. Although the popularity of this approach to education has decreased, the influence of humanism on professional practice can be readily discerned, both within and outside of the educational setting. For example, in corporate fitness programs, programs are designed to meet the needs of individual clients, assumption of responsibility for one's own health and fitness is stressed, and a holistic approach to health is emphasized.

The Mind-Body Relationship

What is the relationship between the mind and the body? Are they separate, independent entities? Or, are the mind and body as one, a unified, interdependent, dynamic organism? Philosophers have long debated these questions. Their answers hold great significance for physical education, exercise science, and sport.

The belief that the mind and the body are separate entities is termed *dualism*. Dualism views the mind and the body as independent, with either the mind or the body being superior. Usually, dualists emphasize the superiority of the mind over the body, relegating the body to an inferior role. The reduction or elimination of school physical education programs in order to increase the time for more "academic" pursuits reflects the emphasis on the mind at the expense of the development of the body. There are other times in physical education, exercise science, and sports programs when the emphasis is placed on development of the body. When the development of the body is emphasized under this philosophical approach, this is referred to as *education of the physical.* Because the mind and the body are separate entities, educating or developing the body has no effect on the mind.

In contrast to the dualist approach, *monism* views the mind and the body as a fused, unified entity. Because the mind and the body are viewed as a unified whole, neither one can be subservient to the other. Physical activity is as important as intellectual activity. From this philosophic perspective, physical education is as important as the rest of the courses in the educational curriculum. When physical education, exercise science, and sport adopt this philosophical approach, physical activity is seen as the medium for the development of the total person. This *education through the physical approach* is the most dominant force in contemporary physical education.

The monist, holistic approach is central to our mission of promoting lifespan participation in physical activity. Achievement of lifespan participation requires that physical educators, exercise scientists, and sport leaders embrace the developmental approach to physical activity: that is, design physical activity programs to promote fitness and motor skills and to instill in participants an appreciation for the contribution of physical activity to one's total well-being.

Eclectic Approach to Philosophy

One common approach to philosophy is the eclectic approach. The major philosophies that have influenced education and physical education and sport practices have been reviewed in previous sections. Many people find it difficult to believe in all the tenets associated with a particular philosophy. Thus, in an effort to develop a philosophy that they can believe in, they have combined a variety of concepts and tenets from different philosophical schools into a set of compatible beliefs. The combining of the beliefs from various philosophical schools is called *eclecticism.* While this combination of beliefs resembles no single philosophical school, these beliefs, when woven thoughtfully together, provide a sound philosophy for the individual.

Sport Philosophy

Sport philosophy emerged as a specialized area of study in the mid-1960s and 1970s. The definition, scope, historical development, and areas of study are discussed in this section.

Definition and Scope

Sport philosophy is the systematic and reflective study of the truth, meanings, and actions of sport. Sport philosophers use logic and reasoning to gain a broader understanding of how sport contributes to our lives and to analyze the principles that guide our professional practices and actions. Sport philosophers study the values connected with sport, examine the relationship between the mind and body, and debate ethical dilemmas. They call upon us as physical education, exercise science, and sport professionals to critically reflect upon our beliefs and assumptions about sport and challenge us to use our insight and knowledge for the well-being of others.

Historical Development

Sport philosophy traces its roots to physical education. Kretchmar[21] describes the evolution of sport philosophy as a progression through three periods: the eclectic philosophy of education approach (1875–1950); the comparative systems approach (1950–1965); and the disciplinary approach (1965 to present).

Historically, the period between the late 1800s and the 1950s was marked by educational reform. Progressive education advocates directed their efforts at reforming an educational system that stressed rote memorization, focused on the 3 Rs—reading, writing, and arithmetic, and emphasized order and conformity, rather than meeting the individual needs of children. As schools changed in response to pressures for reform, more active, individualized learning experiences were provided for the students and support for the inclusion of other subjects in the educational curriculum emerged. At this time, physical education's contribution to the physical development and health of children had been generally recognized. Yet there was little recognition of the potential of physical education and sport to contribute to the psychosocial development of children and enrich their lives. Physical educators such as Thomas Wood, Charles Hetherington, Jesse Feiring Williams, Rosalind Cassidy, Charles McCloy, and J. B. Nash helped reshape physical education. The New Physical Education, as it came to be called, emphasized games, sports, play, and dance rather than rote exercises. These leaders articulated the contributions physical education and welfare of children. These leaders held varying beliefs about the emphasis that should be given to the different objectives of physical education. Some leaders advocated "education of the physical," an approach that focused on physical education's contribution to health and the biological systems of the body. Other leaders favored the "education through the physical" approach, which viewed physical education as a medium through which children developed not only physically but psychosocially as well.

Although these physical education educators differed in their approaches to physical education, they did agree on the importance of including physical education in the educational curriculum. Their scholarly efforts were directed at analyzing how physical education contributed to the attainment of educational objectives and the promotion of social values. Much of their efforts focused on justifying the inclusion of physical education as an integral part of the educational curriculum of children and youth.

From 1950 to 1965, the systems approach was the dominant philosophical approach used by scholars in the field. The major tenets of the traditional educational philosophies of idealism, realism, pragmatism, naturalism, and existentialism were compared (e.g., naturalism versus realism) and applied to the goals, objectives, values, and conduct of educational programs. These comparisons were then extrapolated to physical education and implications for practical concerns, such as program content and teaching methodology, were discussed. Physical education philosophers of this time focused their efforts largely on physical education and its effects on students. They gave limited attention to the critical analysis of sport and human movement outside of the educational setting.

In the mid-1960s and during the 1970s, as the physical education disciplinary movement grew and sport assumed an increasingly prominent role in our society, sport philosophy emerged as a specialized area of study. The sport philosophers of this era focused their efforts on critically analyzing the many complex dimensions of the sport experience and directed less attention to the study of physical education. They addressed such questions as the nature of sport, values achieved through participation, and the meaning of competition. Ethical issues, such as cheating, intentional fouling, use of performance-enhancing drugs, and promoting equity, also captured scholars' attention. As sport philosophy expanded, sport was defined more broadly, and more attention was given to the study of other forms of physical activity engaged in by people of all ages and abilities.

With the growth of sport philosophy, a forum for the ongoing exchange of ideas and for dissemination of scholarly work was needed. The founding of the Philosophic Society for the Study of Sport (PSSS), now called the International Association for the Philosophy of Sport (IAPS), in 1972 helped meet this need. In 1974 the society published the *Journal of the Philosophy of Sport.* The society has played a leadership role in forging an identity for sport philosophy and promoting the philosophic study of sport, physical education, and physical activity. The Sport Philosophy Academy of the National Association of Sport and Physical Education of the American Alliance for Health, Physical Education, Recreation, and Dance provides another opportunity for the exchange of ideas. Sport philosophy research and scholarly articles are also published in *Quest* and, infrequently, in the *Research Quarterly for Exercise and Sport.* The annual meetings of the IAPS and AAHPERD offer opportunities for scholars to share their work with colleagues.

Areas of Study

As sport philosophy became more organized and more sophisticated, sport philosophers undertook the investigation of a wider array of topics. Their work may now focus on the value of sport or the relationship of the mind and the body. They also encourage the use of logic and analytical skills to address ethical issues and making the use of insight and knowledge to promote positive change. Some of the questions sport philosophers may investigate include:

- What is the meaning of competition for athletes with disabilities?
- What are the ethical implications of genetic engineering and its potential use in elite sport?
- What role does sportsmanship play in influencing the values derived from competition?
- How does culture influence the meaning derived from participating in sport?
- Why do some athletes risk permanent disability by continuing to participate in sport when injured?
- Why do adults persist in emphasizing winning in sports when children want to emphasize the fun elements associated with play?
- Does participation in sport develop character?
- Does a coach have the right to control the athlete's lifestyle choices (e.g., curfew, code of conduct)?
- What is the relationship between play, work, and sport?
- How does athletic ability influence the meaning for the participant? Are the values derived from participation in sport different for athletes of different abilities?
- How can the sport experience be made more just and equitable?

Sport philosophy helps us understand the meaning of sport to the participants. This knowledge can help professionals make decisions and develop guidelines that will lead to a more positive experience for those involved. Sport philosophy offers us a systematic, reasoned approach to examine our beliefs, to explore the connections and relationships between our personal values, to critically reflect on societal values, and to align our actions according to the goals and aims to be achieved. As previously discussed, one of the challenges facing physical education, exercise science, and sport in the twenty-first century is eliminating disparities in physical activity. Sport philosophy offers us guidance in addressing inequities in physical activity opportunities experienced by underserved populations. Sport philosophy invites us to think critically about what we do, what we ought to do, and how we can change to provide more inclusive, equitable opportunities in sport for all people.

Your Philosophy of Physical Education, Exercise Science, and Sport

A philosophy of physical education, exercise science, and sport is essential for all physical educators, exercise scientists, and sport leaders. Traditionally, philosophy as it applies to physical education and sport programs in schools and colleges has been emphasized; however, the implications are clear for programs outside the schools. A philosophy of physical education, exercise science, and sport also must be applicable to these diverse programs. For example, the importance of physical activity is now stressed for all segments of the population, including industrial employees, the elderly, youths, and the public in general. Physical education, exercise science, and sport professionals who serve as leaders, administrators, and instructors for these groups should also be concerned with developing a sound philosophy of physical education, exercise science, and sport. Most of the concepts of a philosophy for programs

Lifespan and Cultural Perspectives: Sport Philosophy

- What is the meaning of competition for an athlete with a disability?
- How has the emphasis on winning influenced the meaning of youth sport for the participants?
- How do cultural differences influence the meaning of competition?
- Regarding genetic engineering and sport, what are the ethics of fair play?
- Does competition and the values derived from it enhance the quality of life of the masters sport athlete?
- Is sport as a transmitter of social values instilling the "right" values in youth?

in schools and colleges are applicable to programs that exist outside the educational realm. A professional philosophy for both school and nonschool programs should be humanistic in its approach, commit to meeting the unique needs of participants, have a sound scientific basis, and understand the role of physical activity in enhancing the quality of life for people.

What is your philosophy of physical education, exercise science, and sport? Development of a philosophy is a difficult task but one that is necessary as you proceed toward your goal of becoming a physical educator, exercise scientist and sport leader. Perhaps the place to start is with your personal philosophy.

What is your philosophy of life? What are the values by which you lead your life? Maybe your philosophy of life is succinctly captured by one of these often heard adages:

- "Do unto others as you would have them do unto you."
- "The end justifies the means."
- "Look out for number one."
- "Honesty is the best policy."
- "Things work out for the best."
- "Keep your nose to the grindstone, your shoulder to the wheel."
- "Be the best you can be."

These adages are only a few examples of the beliefs that guide some individuals' lives. If your philosophy of life is not represented by the above statements, can you capture its essence in a single, noteworthy expression? How is your philosophy represented by the manner in which you lead your life? Are your actions congruent with your beliefs?

Many readers of this textbook have participated in athletics at some level, be it youth, interscholastic, or intercollegiate. Critically reflect back on this experience. What was your coach's philosophy? How did that philosophy translate into the conduct of practices and games? Is your coach's philosophy reflected in one of the statements below?

- "Winning is everything."
- "Play hard, play fair."
- "No pain, no gain."
- "Win at all costs."

How did your coach's philosophy contribute to your experience and the value you derived from participation?

As you continue your education and pursue a career in your chosen area, it is important that you have a philosophy to guide your actions and efforts. During your undergraduate professional preparation, you will be encouraged in your classes to develop your own philosophy, to think logically and analytically about your beliefs. The following guidelines are presented to help you in your endeavors to determine, define, and articulate your philosophy of physical education and sport.

1. **Review your past experiences in physical education, exercise science, and sport.** Examine them critically. What were some of your most outstanding experiences in this field? What were some of your most disheartening ones? Why? Is there a physical educator that you particularly admire, one that served as a role model for you and even prompted your entry into this field? If so, what was his or her philosophy?
2. **Read about the different philosophies.** What theories are compatible with your beliefs? What theories are at odds with them? How do these theories translate into practice? What are the characteristics of programs conducted from this philosophical perspective?
3. **Review the philosophies of the leaders in physical education, exercise science, and sport.** Determine the philosophies of leaders in the field. Then determine which of their beliefs are compatible with yours and which are not compatible.
4. **Take advantage of opportunities you have during your professional preparation to talk to various professors about their philosophies.** What beliefs are evident in their teaching? Critically examine your experiences during your professional preparation. Ask why things are as they are. Speculate on how things could be changed. Talk with practitioners in the career you are seeking to enter and determine the beliefs that guide their actions.
5. **Review the codes of conduct and ethical standards of various professional organizations.** Many physical education, exercise science, and sport professional organizations have standards of conduct that serve as guidelines for their members. What are the standards of conduct expected of professionals entering your prospective field? What are the expectations for service to the profession and to others?
6. **Express your philosophy.** Undoubtedly during your preparations you will be asked to write and discuss your philosophy several times. Take advantage of these opportunities for expression to clarify your thinking and more closely examine your beliefs. You may wish to save your papers so that you can look back and see how your philosophy has evolved during your education.

Developing a personal philosophy is a difficult task and some would say a never-ending process. Your philosophy will likely change and mature during your experiences in the field. Try to be open to the various experiences in your life, reflect upon them, learn from them, and view your life as an ongoing process of change and growth.

Focus on Career: Sport Philosophy

PROFESSIONAL ORGANIZATIONS	• International Association for the Philosophy of Sport (www.dmu.ac.uk/dept/schools/pesl/affiliat/iaps.htm) • AAHPERD/NASPE/Sport Philosophy Academy (www.aahperd.org→NASPE→Academies)
PROFESSIONAL JOURNALS	• *Journal of the Philosophy of Sport* • *Quest*

SUMMARY

Contemporary physical education, exercise science, and sport are rapidly changing, dynamic fields. Physical education is defined as an educational process that uses physical activity as a means to help individuals acquire skills, fitness, knowledge, and attitudes that contribute to their optimal development and well-being. Education is the ongoing process of learning that occurs throughout our lifespan. Education, just like contemporary physical education, takes place in a multiplicity of settings and reaches out to involve individuals of all ages. Exercise science is the scientific analysis of exercise or, more inclusively, physical activity. Sport is a highly organized, competitive physical activity governed by rules where the outcome is largely determined by skill and strategy. Rules standardize the competition and conditions so that individuals can compete fairly.

The fields of physical education, exercise science, and sport include both disciplinary and professional dimensions. The discipline is the body of knowledge of the field. Scholars and researchers engage in activities designed to provide greater scientific understanding and insight. The professional dimension of the field focuses on providing services to people of all ages in many different settings. Professionals use the body of knowledge and specialized skills to meet the unique needs of people and help them improve their health and quality of life. The growth of knowledge in physical education led to specialized areas of study, such as sport and exercise psychology, sport sociology, sport pedagogy, sport philosophy, sport biomechanics, exercise physiology, motor development, motor learning, adapted physical activity, sport history, and sport management. Each practitioner should be knowledgeable about these specialized areas of study as well as appreciate their interrelatedness and their contribution to the discipline as a whole.

Philosophy is critical to our endeavors. The major branches of philosophy include metaphysics, epistemology, axiology, ethics, aesthetics, and logic. Philosophies such as idealism, realism, pragmatism, naturalism, and existentialism have influenced the nature and practice of education and physical education and sport programs. As the twentieth century has progressed, the philosophy of education through the physical has significantly influenced physical education, exercise science, and sport programs.

Sport philosophy emerged as a specialized area of study in the mid-1960s and during the 1970s. As this area grew, emphasis shifted from philosophical issues associated with physical education in the schools to the study of sport. Sport philosophers use logic and critical reasoning to study the meaning of sport and the mind-body relationship.

Each professional should develop his or her own philosophy. One's philosophy influences the objectives or outcomes sought from one's programs and the methods by which these objectives are attained. The objectives of physical education, exercise science, and sport are discussed in the next chapter.

SELF-ASSESSMENT TESTS

These tests are designed to help you determine if you have mastered the materials and competencies presented in this chapter.

1. Without consulting your text, describe the 12 subdisciplines of physical education, exercise science, and sport. Discuss how these areas are interrelated. Use examples to illustrate why it is important to be knowledgable about the various specialized areas within the discipline.
2. Compare the characteristics of physical education, exercise science, and sport programs, in either the school or nonschool setting, guided by each of the following philosophies: idealism, realism, pragmatism, naturalism, and existentialism.
3. Attempt to write your philosophy of physical education, exercise science, and sport. Try to follow the suggestions for the development of a philosophy. Reflect on your experiences, review various

philosophies, and take time to talk with some of your professors about their philosophy.

4. The Get Connected box on page 3 lists newsletters for physical education, exercise science, and sport. Subscribe to one of these newsletters. Discuss the benefits the Internet offers to professionals in the field. For the semester, keep copies of your newsletters and summarize what you have learned at the end of the semester.

REFERENCES

1. Sporting Goods Manufacturers Association: Sales of U.S. Recreational Products Push $70 Billion, Press Release, June 29, 2004.
2. US Department of Health and Human Services: Physical activity and health. A report of the Surgeon General, Atlanta, Ga., 1996, US Department of Health and Human Services, Centers for Disease Control and Prevention, National Center for Chronic Disease Prevention and Health Promotion.
3. US Department of Health and Human Services: Healthy people 2010: understanding and improving health, Washington, D.C., 2000, US Government Printing Office.
4. US Department of Health and Human Services: Promoting better health for young people through physical activity and sports: A report to the president from the Secretary of Health and Human Services and the Secretary of Education, Washington, D.C., 2000, US Government Printing Office.
5. US Department of Health and Human Services. The Surgeon General's call to action to prevent and decrease overweight and obesity. Washington, D.C., 2001.
6. US Department of Health and Human Services. Citing "Dangerous Increase" in Deaths, HHS launches new strategies against overweight epidemic. March 9, 2004. Available online at http://www.smallstep.gov/sm_steps/news_updates.html.
7. US Department of Health and Human Services: Healthy people 2000: national health promotion and disease prevention objectives, Washington, D.C., 1990, US Government Printing Office.
8. Centers for Disease Control and Prevention 2001 CDC Youth Risk Behavior Surveillance Survey. Washington, D.C., 2001. Available online at http://www.cdc.gov.
9. National Center for Education Statistics: Projections of education statistics to 2011, Available online at http://nces.ed.gov (Publication number NCES 2001083, 2001.
10. Ziegler EF: From one image to a sharper one! Physical Educator 54(2):72–77, 1997.
11. Corbin C: The field of physical education—common goals, not common roles, JOPERD 64(1):79, 84–87, 1993.
12. Henry F: Physical education: an academic discipline, Journal of Health, Physical Education, and Recreation 37(7):32–33, 1964.
13. Siedentop D: Introduction to physical education, fitness, and sport, ed 3, Mountain View, Calif., 1998, Mayfield.
14. Freeman WH: Physical education and sport in a changing society, ed 5, Boston, MA, 1997, Allyn & Bacon.
15. McNeill AW: Reflections on scholarship reconsidered, Quest 48:140–151, 1996.
16. Charles JM: Scholarship reconceptualized: the connectedness of kinesiology, Quest 48:152–164, 1996.
17. Lumpkin A: Introduction to physical education, exercise science, and sport studies, ed 5, Dubuque, Ia., 2002, McGraw-Hill.
18. President's Council on Physical Fitness and Sport: Definitions: health, fitness, and physical activity, Research Digest, March 2000.
19. Centers for Disease Control and Prevention: Health-related quality of life. Available online www.cdc.gov/nccdphp/reqol/, 2001.

20. Mechikoff RA and Estes SG: A history and philosophy of sport and physical education, ed 3, Dubuque, Ia., 2002, McGraw-Hill.

21. Kretchmar RS: Philosophy of sport. In Massengale JD & Swanson RA, The history of exercise and sport science (pp. 181–201), Champaign, Ill, 1997, Human Kinetics.

SUGGESTED READINGS

Charles JM: Scholarship reconceptualized: the connectedness of kinesiology, Quest 48:152–164, 1996.

The connectedness between the subdisciplines, the connection of kinesiology to society, and professional challenges are discussed.

Charles JM: Zen in the art of kinesiology, Quest, 53:151–164, 2001.

Discusses how both Western aesthetics and Eastern approaches can be integrated to study the art of movement, such as the beauty of the body in motion, the artistry of performance, and the personal meaning of movement.

Dixon N: Canadian figure skaters, French judges, and realism in sport, Journal of the Philosophy of Sport 30:103–117, 2003.

Studies the controversial incidences associated with figure skating in the 2002 Olympics and links these actions to various theories of judgment in sport.

Fraleigh WP: Intentional rules violations—one more time, Journal of the Philosophy of Sport 30:166–177, 2003.

Examines various philosophical positions and issues associated with the commission of intentional fouls in sport, including a discussion on cheating.

Fry JP: Sports and "the fragility of goodness," Journal of the Philosophy of Sport 31:34–47, 2004.

A thoughtful examination of passionate sport participants' engagement in sport and its relationship to the good life.

Hall SJ: Resources and resourcefulness, Quest 55: 258–266, 2003.

Hall perceives the academic fields related to health and exercise have a strong future if its members can capitalize on the national awareness of the health benefits of physical activity, further highlight our research, and continue to increase the diversity and visibility of our fields of study.

Kretchmar RS: Movement subcultures: sites for meaning, JOPERD 71(5):19–25, 2000.

Learning is enhanced when educational experiences are perceived as important and personally meaningful. Several approaches for promoting meaning are explored, meaning is analyzed from a philosophic perspective, and strategies that teachers can use to help students find deeper meaning in movement are presented.

Lumpkin A, Stoll SK, and Beller, JM: Sports ethics: applications for fair play, ed 2, New York, 2001, McGraw-Hill.

Moral reasoning provides the foundation for a discussion of ethics in relation to violence, ergogenic aids, commercial sport, and equity issues in sports.

Massengale JD and Swanson RA, editors: The history of exercise and sport science, Champaign, Ill., 1997, Human Kinetics.

The authors trace the historical development of the subdisciplines of sport pedagogy, adapted physical activity, sport sociology, sport history, philosophy of sport, motor behavior, sport and exercise psychology, biomechanics, and exercise physiology. Future directions for the fields are explored.

Mechikoff RA and Estes SG: A history and philosophy of sport and physical education, ed 4, New York, 2006, McGraw-Hll.

The authors trace the development of physical education and sport, including the Olympics, from ancient civilizations to modern times.

Sessions WL: Sportsmanship as Honor, Journal of the Philosophy of Sport 31:47–59, 2004.

Discusses how part of the anxiety experienced by competitors may rise from concern regarding their opponents' character and whether or not they will be treated honorably.

US Department of Health and Human Services: Physical activity and health. A report of the Surgeon General, Atlanta, Ga., 1996, US Department of Health and Human Services, Centers for Disease Control and Prevention, National Center for Chronic Disease Prevention and Health Promotion.

This noteworthy document reviews the historical background, responses to exercise and physical activity, relationship of physical activity to health, patterns and trends, and recommendations.

Ziegler, EF: From one image to a sharper one! Physical Educator 54(2):72–77, 1997.

Ziegler calls for bold steps in resolving the dilemma of the name for the field and the competencies required by its members.

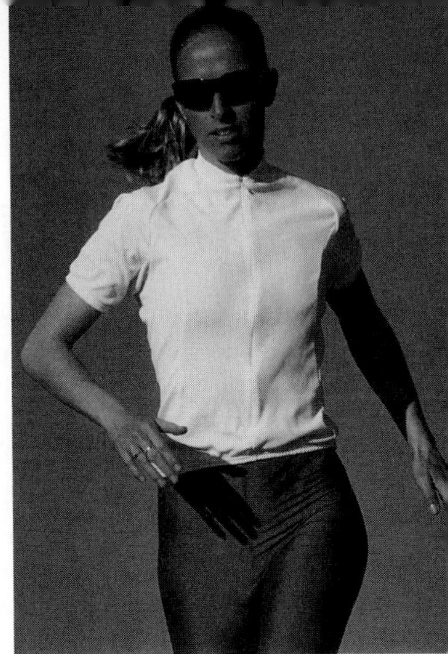

CHAPTER 2

GOALS AND OBJECTIVES

OBJECTIVES

After reading this chapter the student should be able to—

- Describe the goals of education in our society.
- Discuss the goals and objectives of physical education, exercise science, and sport.
- Identify the characteristics of a physically educated person.
- Explain what is meant by the cognitive, affective, and psychomotor domains of behavior and how education contributes to development within these domains.
- Articulate the contributions of physical education, exercise science, and sport to education.
- Describe the purposes and the importance of assessment in physical education, exercise science, and sport.

American education faces the challenge of preparing children and youth—with a wide range of abilities, a multitude of needs, and from increasingly diverse backgrounds—to live as responsible, active citizens and productive members of society both in today's and tomorrow's world. What skills, knowledge, behaviors, and attitudes are necessary for students in the twenty-first century? *Goals 2000* sets forth the nation's education goals for the beginning of the twenty-first century. The No Child Left Behind (NCLB) education law, passed in 2002, is designed to make sure that all children achieve, regardless of their economic status, race, ethnicity, or disability. As a part of the educational curriculum, physical education can contribute to the attainment of educational goals in many meaningful ways.

High-quality physical education programs contribute to the development of students' motor skills and promote health-enhancing fitness. Students acquire knowledge about a wide variety of physical activities, learn to interact respectfully with others, and gain an appreciation for the opportunities that physical activity provides for challenge, enjoyment, and well-being. Furthermore, through interdisciplinary teaching, physical education can reinforce and expand upon learning in other subject areas. Today more than 52 million children and youth are enrolled in our nation's elementary and secondary

GET CONNECTED

National Association of Sport and Physical Education (NASPE). NASPE, part of AAHPERD, offers information about national standards for physical education, national standards for athletic coaches, codes of conduct for sport and physical educators, information about the exercise science, sport studies, and physical education academies, and access to several professional resources.

www.aahperd.org→click on the link for NASPE

National Center for Educational Statistics site includes access to current education statistics and publications on the status of American education, including *The Condition of Education* annual report.

nces.ed.gov

Cooper Institute site gives information about the **Fitnessgram** and **Activitygram** assessments, fitness resources, and research.

www.cooperinst.org

schools. School-based physical education programs offer the greatest opportunity to reach children from diverse populations and help them gain the skills, knowledge, and habits for lifetime participation in regular physical activity.

Just as *Goals 2000* established specific outcomes for education, the National Association for Sport and Physical Education (NASPE) developed national standards for physical education and benchmarks for their achievement. These standards help answer the question, What are the skills, behaviors, knowledge, and values of a physically educated person? Like NCLB, NASPE emphasizes the importance of accountability for student learning and making sure all students become "physically educated."

Goals and objectives help us focus our efforts on the most important outcomes, direct our resources so that they are used most effectively, guide our selection of instructional methodologies, and enable us to assess whether the desired outcomes have been achieved. Goals and objectives are important for physical education, exercise science, and sport programs.

Historically, physical education goals and objectives are stated for school-based programs. Contemporary physical education, exercise science, and sport programs have expanded beyond the traditional school setting and operate in a variety of settings. Millions of participants of all ages engage in physical education, exercise science, and sport programs. As professionals, we must define the goals and objectives of our programs based on the context in which we work, whether in a corporate fitness center, cardiac rehabilitation program, or a community sports program. Clearly defined goals and objectives are essential if the potential of physical education, exercise science, and sport to foster optimal human development, to enhance health, and to enrich the quality of life is to be fulfilled.

If your career aspirations lie outside of the educational arena, remember that learning is a process that takes place in many different settings. As physical educators, exercise scientists, and sport leaders, many of you will be involved in teaching—instructing participants in your program to move efficiently and effectively, engaging them in carefully designed fitness activities to help them achieve and maintain a healthy level of fitness, providing them with knowledge to enable them to achieve a high state of wellness, and/or designing experiences that enhance their psychosocial development. Goals and objectives are important for nonschool-based physical education, exercise science, and sport programs.

Each individual's level of development should be considered in planning activities.

As a physical education, exercise science, and sport professional, you should keep in mind that the nation's schools are a major societal institution and exert a major influence on all members of society. Thus, it is important for you to understand the goals and objectives of education and the contribution of our programs to their attainment. Education and school-based physical education programs form the foundation for future learning. Today's students are tomorrow's adults, many of whom will be participants in our programs. What were their physical education experiences? School physical education programs influence adults' participation patterns and their physical activity habits.

This chapter discusses the role of education in society, the goals of education, and the goals of physical education, exercise science, and sport. The contribution of physical education, exercise science, and sport programs to learning in the cognitive, affective, and psychomotor domains is discussed. In order to determine whether our program participants have achieved the stated goals and objectives, assessment is necessary. We can use several different approaches to determine whether our participants have achieved the desired outcomes.

ROLE OF EDUCATION IN SOCIETY

As a major institution of our society, education significantly influences the life of our nation. Today, at the beginning of the twenty-first century, we are entering an era in which technological advances, scientific progress, exponential knowledge growth, and greater diversity within our population will transform our society in many dramatic ways. It is within this context that America's educational institutions face the challenge of preparing today's students to live and to work in tomorrow's world.

Educational institutions are responsible for preparing our children and youth for future education, employment, and citizenship. The economic prosperity of the United States, our leadership position in the world community, and our freedom depend on it. Our commitment to high-quality education for all children, regardless of race, ethnicity, socioeconomic class, intellectual and physical ability, and gender will significantly influence the future of our country.

Intellectual development is one of the central missions of education. Acquisition of the basic skills of literacy and communication, such as reading, writing, speaking, and listening, and development of competency in core subjects, such as mathematics and science, are important goals of education. The nurturing of problem-solving skills, development of critical thinking abilities, and the creation of the foundation for lifelong learning are important in preparing our children and youth for the future.

In our democracy, preparing students for citizenship is one of the most important responsibilities of America's educational institutions. Students need to learn about our government, their rights and freedoms, and their civic responsibilities. They need to know how to be effective participants in our democracy, and understand how to advocate for justice, work for reform, and act as agents of societal change. In our increasingly diverse society, it is essential that students learn to appreciate how diversity enriches our personal lives and our society and to be respectful of differences. Community involvement, public service, and working for the common good are other aspects of citizenship.

Educational institutions are charged with the responsibility of preparing students for the world of work. Well-qualified and productive workers contribute to the nation's prosperity and its leadership in the world community. Students who lack career skills may find themselves economically disadvantaged, and this will negatively affect them in many aspects of their life (e.g., health). As technology advances and impacts on more and more jobs in our rapidly changing world, students will need to learn different skills and change careers as new jobs are developed and others become obsolete.

The overall personal development of each student is one of the primary purposes of education. Physical development has long been considered the unique contribution of physical education programs in the school. Physical education programs teach motor and sport skills and promote fitness. In recent years, schools have taken a greater, more comprehensive role in promoting the health of students. Character development, promotion of moral and ethical values, and preparation for a meaningful self-directed existence are often cited as aspects of personal development. Development of expressiveness, encouragement of personal interests, and learning how to develop and sustain meaningful and satisfying personal relationships are part of the personal development goal of education.

As we move farther into the twenty-first century, dramatic changes in education will occur. We will see the continued incorporation of new technologies, accompanied by a greater emphasis on distance and lifelong learning. Education will expand to different settings and be directed at a greater number of older adults. As education changes, our goals will be refined and new goals added in response to changing societal needs.

Goals and *Objectives* Defined

Before a discussion of the goals and objectives of education and physical education, exercise science, and sport, defining these terms may be helpful. *Goals* are statements of purposes, intents, and aims that reflect desired accomplishments. Goals are expressed as general statements and are very broad in their direction. They state long-term outcomes to be achieved by participants in the program. A goal of contemporary education is to help all students acquire the necessary knowledge and competencies to engage in lifelong learning. A goal of contemporary physical education, exercise science, and sport is to help people acquire the necessary knowledge, skills, and appreciations to participate in physical activity throughout their lifespan.

Objectives are derived from goals. Objectives describe learning, specifically what individuals should know, do, or feel as a result of instruction. Objectives are more specific than goals. They are short-term statements of specific outcomes that build cumulatively to reach a goal. Objectives can be stated in many different ways and vary in their degree of specificity. They can be stated with reference to general behavior or with reference to specific outcomes. For example, one goal of *Healthy People 2010* is to increase life expectancy.[1] A general objective that will contribute to this goal is to increase the number of people who engage in exercise to achieve cardiorespiratory fitness. A more specific objective related to physical activity is to increase from 15% to 30% the proportion of adults who engage regularly, preferably daily, in moderate physical activity for at least 30 minutes per day.

Well-constructed objectives can take on many different forms and can be stated in many different ways. Most importantly, whatever the format, objectives should describe the behavior the individual will demonstrate when the desired outcome is achieved. When objectives are stated in terms that are measurable, they provide a means to assess the individual's progress toward the achievement of the goal. (See the Examples of Physical Education, Exercise Science, and Sport Objectives box.)

Objectives may be developed for different areas of learning, that is, intellectual development, physical development, or social-emotional development. Objectives guide the development of assessment procedures and instructional experiences. They help professionals focus their efforts on the subject content that is most important for participants to learn.

Quality programs have a clearly defined mission and well-articulated goals. Objectives relate to the goals and are relevant to society's and participants' needs, experiences, and interests. Instruction is designed to help participants achieve the desired objectives and, ultimately, attain stated goals. Ongoing assessment yields meaningful information about participants' progress toward achievement of the goal.

Examples of Physical Education, Exercise Science, and Sport Objectives

Regardless of the setting in which they are conducted, all physical education, exercise science, and sport programs should have objectives that are clearly defined and relevant to the needs and interests of the participants. Can you identify the program associated with these objectives? Are these objectives for students in a secondary school physical education program, employees in a corporate fitness program, clients enrolled in a commercial fitness club, or adults involved in a community fitness and recreation program?

PHYSICAL FITNESS DEVELOPMENT OBJECTIVE

- The participant will complete a 20-minute aerobic dance routine designed to improve cardiovascular fitness.

MOTOR SKILL DEVELOPMENT OBJECTIVE

- The participant will demonstrate the proper technique in executing the tennis forehand.

COGNITIVE DEVELOPMENT OBJECTIVE

- The participant will be able to explain the scoring system used in golf.

AFFECTIVE DEVELOPMENT OBJECTIVE

- The participant will demonstrate an appreciation for the contribution of exercise to his or her life by participating in an unsupervised program of vigorous physical activity three times a week.

Goals of Education: Historical Development

The needs of society and those of the individual influence the goals of education. Justification for inclusion of subjects in the curriculum of the school is based on their potential to contribute to the attainment of educational goals and to the total development of the individual.

Over the years, many national commissions and noted authorities have set forth many purposes and goals for education. In 1918, a committee of the National Education Association stated the "Seven Cardinal Principles of Education": health, command of fundamental processes, vocation, citizenship, worthy home membership, worthy use of leisure time, and ethical character.[2] In 1938, the Educational Policies Commission consolidated the Seven Cardinal Principles into four comprehensive aims: self-realization, human relationship, economic efficiency, and civic responsibility.[3] In 1944, these aims were expanded into the 10 "imperative needs of youth"[4]; among them were good health and physical fitness and good use of leisure time. Over twenty years later, in 1966, a commission of the American Association of School Administrators identified nine imperatives of education, which included making the best use of leisure time.[5] In 1978, the "Seven New Cardinal Principles of Education" were advanced in an effort to make the original principles more relevant to the changing world. These principles were enhancement of personal competence and development, skilled decision making, promotion of civic interest and participation, global concern for humankind, fostering family cohesiveness, development of moral responsibility and ethical action, and respect for nature and the environment.[6]

In 1994 President Clinton signed into law the *Goals 2000: Educate America Act.* This act identified eight goals for American education for the year 2000. These goals have since become the benchmarks against which we continue to measure America's progress in educating its children and youth at the beginning of the twenty-first century. These goals provide clear direction and focus for our educational efforts. (See the Educational Goals for the Year 2000 box.)

Educational Goals for the Year 2000

- All children will start school ready to learn.
- High school graduation rates will be at least 90%.
- Students will leave grades 4, 8, and 12 having demonstrated competency in challenging subject matter, including English, mathematics, science, history, and geography; students will be prepared for responsible citizenship, future learning, and productive employment.
- U.S. students will be first in the world in math and science.
- All adults will be skilled and possess the knowledge and skills necessary to compete in the global economy and uphold the rights and responsibilities of citizenship.
- Every school will be free of drugs and violence and offer a safe, disciplined environment conducive to learning.
- Teachers will have access to programs for continued development of their professional skills.
- Schools will promote partnerships that will increase parental involvement in promoting the social, emotional, and academic growth of their children.

From: United States Department of Education: *The Goals 2000: educate America act—launching a new era in education,* Washington, D.C., 1994, US Government Printing Office.

Contemporary Goals of Education

Goals 2000 encompasses eight areas: (1) ensuring readiness to learn, (2) improvement of graduation rates, (3) attainment of competency in five core subjects, (4) achievement of international prominence in math and science, (5) promotion of literacy in adults, (6) establishment of a positive, safe learning environment, (7) provision of greater opportunities for professional development for teachers, and (8) creation of partnerships by schools to promote parental involvement in education.[7]

Readiness to learn focuses on the importance of all children starting school with the necessary basic skills and knowledge to serve as the foundation for a lifetime of learning. Achievement of this goal requires that greater attention be directed to the needs of preschool children. In particular, we must address the inequalities that adversely affect students' readiness to learn. Many young children who are socially and economically disadvantaged lack access to opportunities that promote readiness, such as quality preschool programs or adequate nutrition. Other children have disabilities

Goals 2000 strives for U.S. students to be first in the world in math and science.

that affect their ability to learn. National education authorities have identified several objectives central to achieving this goal. These include providing access to quality preschool programs for children who are disadvantaged and disabled, focusing on the role of the parent as the child's first teacher, and ensuring that children arrive at school healthy. Learning readiness must be nurtured throughout the children's school years.

Improvement of graduation rates from the current 71% to the targeted level of 90% requires a multifaceted approach.[8] It involves preventing dropouts from occurring in the first place and reaching out to those who have withdrawn to enroll them in a degree or degree equivalency program. Additional efforts must be targeted at preventing dropouts among children of color, who are overrepresented in the dropout rate.

A diversity of social and environmental factors contribute to the student's potential for dropout. Low self-esteem and perceptions that school does not provide an avenue for personal success are part of the problem. Lack of a strong family structure places children at risk for dropping out. To improve the graduation rate, schools need to offer opportunities for success in meaningful areas, nurture the self-concept of learners, develop a strong network of support that addresses students' needs, and foster within its students the motivation to work toward relevant goals.

Competency in core subjects emphasizes attainment of proficiencies in five core subjects: English, mathematics, science, history, and geography. Learning must include acquisition of competencies for lifelong learning and for employment in a competitive global economy. Although not identified as core subjects, this goal calls for all students to have access to health education and physical education to ensure that they are healthy and fit. This goal also promotes the development of good citizenship, values, and appreciation for cultural diversity.

World leadership in math and science achievement aims to have U.S. students be first in the world in mathematics and science. For the United States to be the best in this area requires strengthening the mathematics and science components of the educational curriculum, especially courses offered in the early school years. Courses must become more challenging, and more stringent standards need to be established to assess students' performance in these areas. Achievement of these higher standards will enable students as adults to live, work, and compete effectively in a global economy.

Adult literacy advocates that all adults should be literate. An educated workforce contributes to enhanced economic success. Yet, many adults today do not have basic literacy skills. More than 42 million Americans, 22% of the population, cannot read; 50 million, 27% of the population, read at or below the fifth-grade reading level.[9] A disproportionate number of these adults are minorities. Opportunities for lifelong learning should be developed so that all adults have the opportunity to get a degree or its equivalent. Furthermore, provision must be made to ensure that adults can receive additional education and training throughout their lifetime, so that they may continue to meet the changing job needs of the twenty-first century.

Adults must also have opportunities to acquire the skills necessary for responsible citizenship. These include the ability to evaluate information and engage in decision making and problem solving. They must have the opportunities to exercise their rights as citizens of the nation.

A safe and positive learning environment that is conducive to achievement is necessary for all students. Today, reports of violence in schools abound. The incidence of drug use by students and the selling of drugs within the school itself have raised considerable alarm. Other social issues that affect students' lives and their ability to learn include the disintegration of the family unit and resulting lack of support for children, and health-related issues such as AIDS and teen pregnancy. If our educational goals are to be achieved, schools must be involved as part of a comprehensive approach to address these societal problems.

The professional development of teachers is crucial to the achievement of our education goals. Teachers must have access to programs that allow them to acquire the skills and knowledge to instruct effectively and prepare students for the next century. Greater opportunities for training allow teachers to learn about new technologies, acquire competencies in new instructional techniques to teach learners of all abilities, develop new curricula to achieve the national standards, and gain skill in using assessment techniques to monitor students' progress.

The goal of *parental involvement* charges schools to promote partnerships with parents. Parents are actively encouraged to become involved in the education of their children. Besides eliciting parental support, schools are encouraged to forge partnerships within their local communities to accomplish educational goals.

Goals 2000 reflects an emphasis on attainment of competencies that will allow students to participate effectively as adults in our workforce and that will enable the United States to be competitive in the global economy. The goals stress providing students and adults with the skills and knowledge necessary for lifelong learning. Preparing individuals for responsible citizenship and preparing them to function as contributing members of society are valued outcomes of the educational process.

In 1997, President Clinton's *Call to Action for American Education in the 21st Century* set forth 10 goals. These include:

- The development of rigorous national standards with periodic testing to make sure children are achieving.
- Making sure there is a talented and dedicated teacher in every classroom.
- Expansion of preschool programs and greater efforts to involve parents in their children's education.
- Increased use of technology to enable students to achieve at higher levels.
- Ensuring our schools are safe, disciplined, and drug free and instill American values.
- Increased educational accountability.
- Opening the doors of college to those who qualify, making the 13th and 14th years of education as universal as high school.[10]

Further efforts must be focused on addressing inequities in the schools, such as programs to reduce the dropout rate and improve the achievement of disadvantaged youth. Students from racial and ethnic minority backgrounds and low-income families are at greater risk for poor school outcomes. In 1998, the *Hispanic Dropout Project* revealed the Hispanic dropout rate to be 30%.[11] This was 2.5 times the rate for blacks and 3.5 times the rate for white students.[11] Of even greater concern, Hispanics make up 56% of all U.S. immigrants; however, they make up nearly 90% of all immigrant dropouts.[13] If this continues, many adults in United States' soon-to-be largest minority group will be underprepared for employment and engaging in civic life.[11]

The *Condition of Education 2000* reveals that the achievement gap between the economically advantaged and disadvantaged, and between whites and minority students persists.[12] In 2001 President

George W. Bush proposed a new educational initiative, *No Child Left Behind* (NCLB), to narrow the achievement gap.[13] He stated, "We have a genuine national crisis. More and more, we are divided into two nations. One that reads, and one that doesn't. One that dreams, and one that does not."[15] His initiative presents a blueprint to further strengthen our elementary and secondary schools.

NCLB calls for greater accountability for student learning. The use of standards and frequent assessments are part of the accountability movement. The focus is student attainment of proficiency in reading, mathematics, and science. NCLB requires that federal school funding be directed to programs that use instructional techniques that are based on sound research and that have been proven to work.[14] Teacher quality is a critical component of this educational reform effort. Greater emphasis is placed on the recruitment, preparation, and ongoing training of teachers.[14] Safe schools, free from drugs and violence, are essential if student learning is to improve. Parents are given a greater role in the education of their children and provided with an array of choices designed to help their children achieve, including the option of moving from schools that consistently demonstrate low levels of achievement.[14]

As we begin the twenty-first century, professionals must take an active role in eliminating inequities and work hard to ensure equal educational opportunities for all students.

High-quality physical education, exercise science, and sport programs, such as master's swim teams, benefit participants physically, mentally, emotionally, and socially.

Physical Education and the Goals of Education

Physical education programs in the school can contribute to the goals of education in many significant ways. First, physical education makes a unique contribution to the development of the total person. It is the only area of the school curriculum that promotes the development of motor skills and fitness. No other curricular area contributes to development in the psychomotor domain.

Second, a quality physical education program enhances the health and well-being of its students. Healthy students can learn more effectively, have more energy to expend on educational tasks, and possess a greater vigor and vitality not only for learning but for daily living. Since one primary goal of education is to prepare students to be productive members of society, attention must be given to the health and welfare of the individual. Adults who are healthy can work more efficiently and effectively. Participation in regular physical activity enhances one's overall health. A quality physical education program helps students acquire the skills, knowledge, and attitudes that will result in a lifetime of participation in physical activity, thus contributing to good health in adulthood and increased productivity.

Third, physical education can contribute to learning readiness. The first *Goal 2000* states that all children should enter school ready to learn. Movement experiences are critical to learning readiness. Movement is the means by which infants explore their environment, develop their senses, and lay the foundation for future learning in all domains. As infants move from crawling to walking, they enlarge their world and become engaged in the exciting process of discovery. Their language skills expand as they learn to describe what they encounter in their environment, and their cognitive skills grow as they investigate their world. Through movement and play, young children become independent as they explore, gain confidence as they accomplish new feats, and acquire social skills as they interact with others. Additionally, movement stimulates growth and development and enhances the child's health.

Fourth, physical education can be an important part of an integrated educational curriculum. Traditionally, schools have organized subject matter into discrete areas—mathematics, science, health, English, physical education, and so on. It was assumed that students, on their own, could integrate what they had learned into a meaningful whole and see the interrelatedness among various areas.

Today we see a greater emphasis on multidisciplinary learning, with the integration of subject content across the curriculum. Integration provides opportunities for students to see new relationships, to transfer what they have learned from one setting to the next, and to reinforce learning in various ways. Physical education offers some exciting possibilities as part of a multidisciplinary approach to learning. The content from physical education can be transferred across the curriculum, and content from other curriculum areas can be integrated into physical education. For example, physical education can provide a laboratory for students to use the information they learned in physics about the laws of motion, forces, levers, and mechanics.[15] Through various movement experiences, they can see how concepts from physics apply to their lives and affect their daily living, including their movements. Learning experiences focusing on fitness provide opportunities for students to study biochemical changes associated with exercise, reinforce what they have learned about anatomy and physiology, use their mathematical skills to calculate energy expenditure and evaluate fitness results, and support what they have learned in health class about the importance of good nutrition. A multidisciplinary approach to learning helps students understand how the various subjects are interrelated in the real world.

NCLB did not identify physical education specifically as a subject in which children should become proficient. However, NCLB does have implications for physical education. The law requires that schools close the gap in achievement among students and stresses the importance of accountability for student learning. As physical educators, we, too, must be committed to closing the achievement gap between those students who are fit and unfit, those who are skilled and unskilled, and those who are active and those leading a sedentary lifestyle. No child should be left behind, whether in reading or physical education.

Standards and assessment of learning are important in physical education, too, not just in math or reading. Standards should be meaningful and reflect our significant content. Establishment of clear goals and objectives and assessment of individual achievement using methods aligned to instructional content contribute to accountability. During teacher preparation, physical educators need to develop a strong disciplinary foundation and effective instructional techniques as well as proficiency in a variety of assessment approaches.

Quality teachers are the cornerstone of a quality program, one in which there is accountability for student learning. Attention must be directed at the recruitment of qualified individuals into the field, strong professional preparation both in disciplinary content and pedagogy, and ongoing professional development.

A safe school learning environment is another important tenet of NCLB. Physical educators can contribute to the safe school learning environment by emphasizing instructional approaches that include personal responsibility, respect for others, and information about the harmful effects of drug use.

Quality physical education programs contribute to students' physical, intellectual, and social-emotional development. However, whether the potential of physical education to contribute to educational outcomes is fulfilled depends heavily on teachers' commitments to conducting quality programs, and the support they receive for their work from within the school system and from their community.

GOALS OF PHYSICAL EDUCATION, EXERCISE SCIENCE, AND SPORT

Physical education, exercise science, and sport have as their primary goal the improvement of the well-being and quality of life of individuals who participate in our programs. We can accomplish this by socializing individuals into the role of participants who will make a long-term commitment to participation in enjoyable and meaningful physical activity and sport experiences. Our main purpose is to provide people with the skills, knowledge, and attitudes to participate in regular physical activity throughout their lifespan.

Increasingly, a significant public health role for physical education has been embraced by many professionals in the field. Corbin states, "Physical Education has much to offer society and it is my belief that it can be an effective agent of change—especially in promoting the health of our nation."[16] Corbin adds, "Our principal goal should be healthy lifestyle promotion with an emphasis on active living for a lifetime. Physical educators can help every child find some form of activity that can be performed and enjoyed throughout life."[16]

Since virtually all children attend schools, effective school programs can have a significant impact on the nation's health and are, perhaps, our greatest chance to change society for the better. But teaching skills and developing fitness are not enough. Students need to learn to value and enjoy physical activity. Additionally, students need both the knowledge and the self-management skills that lead to lifetime adherence. Students need to know how to self-assess their fitness level and modify their activity accordingly; they need to know how to set goals and plan programs so they can adapt their activities to their changing needs as they move into adulthood. If we can agree that this is our common goal and we focus on the delivery of quality programs to people of all ages, physical education can be a significant force in our society.

As education programs continue to expand beyond the traditional school setting, contemporary physical education, exercise science, and sport programs, in both public and private settings, can contribute to the attainment of educational goals. In order for this to occur, physical education, exercise science, and sport leaders must be cognizant of the goals of education and carefully design their programs to contribute to these desired outcomes.

Historical Development

Physical education, exercise science, and sport programs today trace their goals and objectives to those of school-based physical education programs. Throughout the years, many leaders in the field have articulated the goals and objectives of physical education. When we trace the historical development of the goals and objectives of physical education, we see a shift from emphasizing education *of* the physical to a focus on education *through* the physical; that is, the focus has shifted from exercising the body to enhancing the development of the whole person. In the twentieth century, the developmental model, education through the physical, emerged as the dominant focus.[17]

The developmental model began to take shape in the late nineteenth and early twentieth century. A leading physical educator of that time, Thomas Wood, in 1883, stressed that physical education should contribute to the complete education of the individual. In the 1880s, Dudley A. Sargent, the Director of Physical Education of the Hemenway Gymnasium at Harvard University, cited hygienic, educative, recreative, and remedial objectives to be achieved by participants in his program. In 1910, Clark Hetherington, the acknowledged "father of modern physical education," viewed physical education's contribution to the educational process as encompassing organic education, psychomotor education, intellectual education, and character education. These objectives of the "new" physical education greatly influenced the nature and conduct of programs in the nation's schools. Most of the objectives set forth by leaders of physical education and sport today can be encompassed within the four areas originally defined by Hetherington.

Over a half century later, in 1964, Charles Bucher,[18] identified four developmental objectives for physical education. These objectives were physical (organic) development, motor and movement development, mental development, and social development. Achievement of the outcomes associated with each of these objectives contributes to the development of "well-rounded individuals who will become worthy members of society."

The American Alliance for Health, Physical Education, Recreation and Dance (AAHPERD), one of our largest professional organizations, and its forerunners have taken a leadership role in delineating the goals, purposes, and objectives for physical education. In 1934, the American Physical Education Association's (APEA) Committee on Objectives listed physical fitness, mental health and efficiency, social-moral character, emotional expression and control, and appreciation as desired objectives. In 1950, the American Association for Health, Physical Education and Recreation (AAHPER) stated these objectives for physical education: (1) to develop and to maintain maximum physical efficiency, (2) to develop useful skills, (3) to conduct oneself in socially useful ways, and (4) to enjoy wholesome recreation.

In 1965, AAHPER in a document entitled *This Is Physical Education* stated five major objectives:

1. To help children move in a skillful and effective manner in all the selected activities in which they engage in the physical education program, and also in those situations that they will experience during their lifetime.
2. To develop an understanding and appreciation of movement in children and youth so that their lives will become more meaningful, purposive, and productive.
3. To develop an understanding and appreciation of certain scientific principles concerned with movement that relate to such factors as time, space, force, and mass-energy relationships.
4. To develop through the medium of games and sports better interpersonal relationships.
5. To develop the various organic systems of the body so that they will respond in a healthful way to the increased demands placed on them.[19]

These objectives stressed the role of physical education in preparing students for lifetime involvement in physical activity. Besides the development of fitness and movement skills, intellectual, social, and emotional development were emphasized.

The 1971 Physical Education Public Information (PEPI) project of AAHPER sought to inform the public, educators, policy makers, and funding agencies about the goals and values of physical education. PEPI defined a "physically educated" person as possessing knowledge and skill concerning his or her body and how it functions.[20] Further emphasized was the significant contribution physical education can make to the education and lives of students, both as youths and adults. Among the values highlighted are the following:

- Physical education is health insurance.
- Physical education contributes to academic achievement.
- Physical education provides skills and experiences that can last a lifetime.
- Physical education helps in developing a positive self-image and the ability to compete and cooperate with others.

As you review the goals and objectives of physical education in Table 2-1, some commonalities can be seen, although the wording of the objectives varies. The prominent emphasis is on the development of the whole person, not just the body. The goals and objectives of physical education are encompassed within four primary areas: fitness development, skill development, knowledge, and social-emotional development. The contribution of physical education to preparation for life as a contributing member of society is also a highly regarded outcome.

Educational athletics—that is, sports associated with educational institutions—have justified their inclusion within the school by stressing their contribution to the total development of the individual. The commonly cited developmental objectives for sports programs are similar to the objectives of physical education.

Although the leaders have disagreed on the number of objectives and their wording, the objectives of physical education can be encompassed

TABLE 2-1 Goals and Objectives of Physical Education: The Last One Hundred Years

Late 1800s	1910	1934	1950	1964	1965	1971	1990
Sargent	**Hetherington**	**APEA***	**AAHPER****	**Bucher**	**AAHPER****	**AAHPER****	**AAHPERD*****
Hygienic Educative Recreative Remedial	Organic education Psychomotor education Intellectual education Character education	Physical fitness Mental health and efficiency Social-moral character Emotional expression and control Appreciation	Develop and maintain maximum physical efficiency Develop useful skills Conduct oneself in socially useful ways Enjoy wholesome recreation	Physical development Motor and movement development Mental development Social development	Skillful and effective movement Development of organic systems of the body Understanding and appreciation of movement Understanding and appreciation of scientific principles related to movement Development of interpersonal relationships	Health insurance Contributes to academic achievement Skills and experiences to last a lifetime Positive self-image Ability to compete and cooperate with others	Skills to perform a variety of physical activities Physical fitness Regular participation in physical activity Knows benefits and implications of involvement in physical activity Values physical activity and its contribution to a physically active lifestyle

* American Physical Education Association.

** American Association for Health, Physical Education and Recreation.

*** American Alliance for Health, Physical Education, Recreation and Dance.

within four main groups: physical fitness development, motor skill development, cognitive development, and affective development. These objectives have strongly influenced our contemporary physical education, exercise science, and sport programs.

Contemporary Goals and Objectives

Contemporary physical education, exercise science, and sport programs are growing in popularity. These programs are diverse in content, varied in setting, and serve people of all ages. What are the goals and objectives of these contemporary programs? What outcomes should participants in these programs achieve? These questions can be addressed by reflecting on and drawing parallels from the goals and objectives established for school-based physical education programs. In 1986 the National Association for Sport and Physical Education, an association of AAHPERD, appointed an Outcomes Committee to answer the question, "What should students know and be able to do?" The Outcomes Project defined a physically educated person as one who

- Has learned the skills necessary to perform a variety of physical activities.
- Is physically fit.
- Does participate regularly in physical activity.
- Knows the implications of and the benefits from involvement in physical activities.
- Values physical activity and its contribution to a healthful lifestyle.[21]

In 1990, this definition was expanded to 20 specific outcomes. (See the Characteristics of a Physically Educated Person box.)

In 1995 NASPE published *Moving into the Future: National Content Standards for Physical Education: A Guide to Content and Assessment.*[22] This document identified content standards for physical education (see the Content Standards in Physical Education box). It also identified assessment guidelines and offered teachers sample benchmarks to assist them in assessing student learning (see Sample Content Standards and Benchmarks for Achievement for a Fourth-Grade Child box). NASPE's effort reflects one of the primary goals of the national education reform movement—the clarification of important goals and the establishment of content standards for each area of the school curriculum. The development of national content standards for physical education parallels the development of national standards for each of the other areas of the school curriculum.

In 2004, NASPE published the revised standards for physical education in the second edition of the document *Moving into the Future.*[23] These revised standards (see the 2004 National Standards for Physical Education box) reflect what students should know and be able to achieve through participation in a quality physical education program.

Though developed in reference to school physical education, these significant goals and objectives are relevant to physical activity and sport programs in nonschool settings serving people of all ages. As Zeigler[24] stated:

> The profession has a responsibility to function and serve through the entire lives of people, not just when they are children and young people in schools and colleges. This means we should serve both boys and girls and men and women of all ages who are "special," "normal," and "accelerated."
>
> This can be carried out throughout the lifespan by both public and private agencies, as well as by families and individuals in their own ways. To assume lifetime responsibility would permit us to enlarge the scope—the breadth and the depth—of our profession's outlook.

NASPE's initiatives offer physical educators, exercise scientists, and sport leaders in both school and nonschool settings a common conceptual framework to guide their endeavors. This framework clearly identifies goals and outcomes associated with quality programs. Professionals in all settings can incorporate the assessment benchmarks, points of emphasis, criteria, and suggested assessment techniques into their programs. The assessment guidelines provide both a means to evalutate their participants' achievements and, at the same time, enrich learning by incorporating assessment strategies into the instructional process.

Characteristics of the Physically Educated Person

A physically educated person:

HAS learned skills necessary to perform a variety of physical activities.

- Moves using concepts of body awareness, space awareness, effort, and relationships
- Demonstrates competence in a variety of manipulative, locomotor, and nonlocomotor skills
- Demonstrates competence in combinations of manipulative, locomotor, and nonlocomotor skills performed individually and with others
- Demonstrates competence in many different forms of physical activity
- Demonstrates proficiency in a few forms of physical activity
- Has learned how to learn new skills

IS physically fit.

- Assesses, achieves, and maintains physical fitness
- Designs safe personal fitness programs in accordance with principles of training and conditioning

DOES participate regularly in physical activity.

- Participates in health-enhancing physical activity at least three times a week
- Selects and regularly participates in lifetime physical activities

KNOWS the implications of and the benefits from involvement in physical activities.

- Identifies the benefits, costs, and obligations associated with regular participation in physical activity
- Recognizes the risk and safety factors associated with regular participation in physical activity
- Applies concepts and principles to the development of motor skills
- Understands that wellness involves more than being physically fit
- Knows the rules, strategies, and appropriate behaviors for selected physical activities
- Recognizes that participation in physical activity can lead to multicultural and international understanding
- Understands that physical activity provides the opportunity for enjoyment, self-expression, and communication

VALUES physical activity and its contributions to a healthful lifestyle.

- Appreciates the relationships with others that result from participation in physical activity
- Respects the role that regular physical activity plays in the pursuit of lifelong health and well-being
- Cherishes the feelings that result from regular participation in physical activity

Reprinted by permission of National Association for Sport and Physical Education, Physical Education Outcomes Committee: *Definition of the physically educated person; outcomes of quality physical education programs,* Reston, Va., 1990, AAHPERD.

The past one hundred years have seen the emergence of a consensus about the primary objectives of physical education and, more recently, the characteristics of a physically educated person. Both in the traditional school and nonschool settings, quality physical education, exercise science, and sport programs can contribute to the development of the whole person. The four primary objectives of physical education and, by extension, exercise science, and sport—physical fitness, motor skill development, cognitive development, and social-emotional development—and the goals and outcomes characteristic of a physically educated person relate to the three domains of learning. The three learning domains—cognitive, affective, and psychomotor—help us understand the needs of participants and the skills and abilities to be acquired. In education as well as within the fields of

Content Standards in Physical Education

A physically educated person:

- Demonstrates competency in many movement forms and proficiency in a few movement forms.
- Applies movement concepts and principles to the learning and development of motor skills.
- Exhibits a physically active lifestyle.
- Achieves and maintains a health-enhancing level of physical fitness.
- Demonstrates responsible personal and social behavior in physical activity settings.
- Demonstrates understanding and respect for differences among people in physical activity settings.
- Understands that physical activity provides opportunities for enjoyment, challenge, self-expression, and social interaction.

National Association for Sport and Physical Education, *Moving into the future: national standards for physical education,* 1995. Reprinted with permission from the National Association for Sport and Physical Education (NASPE), 1900 Association Drive, Reston, VA 20191-1599.

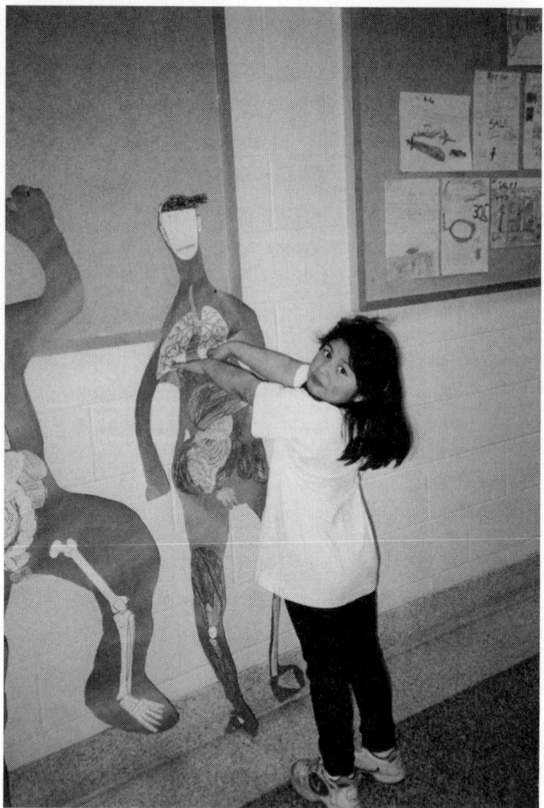

Physical education can help children understand the human body. This 8-year-old is pointing to the lungs, which she says "help you live and get air to run hard."

physical education, exercise science, and sport, achievement of goals and objectives have traditionally been described with reference to learning in the three domains, as will be discussed in the next section.

LEARNING IN THE THREE DOMAINS

Objectives for learning can be classified into three domains or areas of behavior: cognitive (thinking), affective (feeling), and psychomotor (doing). The cognitive domain is concerned with the acquisition of knowledge and its application. The affective domain includes the promotion of values, the fostering of social skills, and enhancement of emotional development. The psychomotor domain involves the development of motor skills and physical fitness.

It is critical that professionals consider all three domains when planning learning experiences to meet individuals' needs. Separation of behaviors into domains simplifies the formulation of objectives. It enables us to more readily take into account individuals' levels of development in each domain as we design and conduct activities. However, these domains are interrelated and, as professionals, we must keep this at the forefront of our minds as we work with people in our programs.

Physical education, exercise science, and sport can contribute to learning in each of the three domains. In the school setting, physical education, like other subjects in the educational curriculum, supports cognitive and affective development.

Sample Content Standards and Benchmarks for Achievement for a Fourth-Grade Child

CONTENT STANDARD

Achieves and maintains a health-enhancing level of physical fitness.

By the fourth grade, students will begin to match different types of physical activity with underlying physical fitness components and should participate in moderate to vigorous physical activities in a variety of settings. Students should begin to be able to interpret the results and understand the significance of information provided by formal measures of physical fitness. Fitness testing may be introduced at this level. Meeting the criterion health standards prescribed by Fitnessgram is available.

The emphasis for the fourth-grade student will be to:

- Identify several activities related to each component of physical fitness.
- Associate results of fitness testing to personal health status and ability to perform various activities.
- Meet the health-related fitness standards as defined by the Fitnessgram.

Sample Benchmarks

1. Engages in appropriate activity that results in the development of muscular strength.
2. Maintains continuous aerobic activity for a specified time and/or activity.
3. Supports, lifts, and controls body weight in a variety of activities.
4. Regularly participates in physical activity for the purpose of improving physical fitness.

Assessment Examples

1. Student project.
   Have the students collect pictures of people participating in physical activities and identify those activities that contribute to each component of health-related fitness.

   Criteria for Assessment
   a. Provides a minimum of two examples for each fitness component.
   b. Associates activity with the appropriate component of fitness.

2. Student project.
   Students are asked to select an exercise intended to achieve a personal fitness-related goal. Practice the exercise regularly over the course of several weeks (specify the exact length of time). Have the student record the results of each exercise session and graph the progress.

   Criteria for Assessment
   a. Correctly identifies a personal goal that needs work.
   b. Records progress toward goal on a regular basis.
   c. Shows consistent improvement over time.
   d. Meets own goal at the end of the month.

National Association for Sport and Physical Education, *Moving into the future: national standards for physical education,* 1995. Reprinted with permission from the National Association for Sport and Physical Education (NASPE), 1900 Association Drive, Reston, VA 20191-1599.

However, it places the greatest emphasis on the psychomotor domain. The extent to which physical education, exercise science, and sport contribute to cognitive and affective development depends heavily on the degree to which this development is emphasized within the specific program.

Physical education's unique contribution to the educational curriculum is in the psychomotor domain. Development in this domain encompasses the objectives of motor skill development and physical fitness. While the psychomotor domain is our primary focus, there are many ways that we can accomplish our goals in this area while enhancing development in the other two domains.

Education is a process of learning that can take place in many different settings. In programs

2004 National Standards for Physical Education

Physical activity is critical to the development and maintenance of good health. The goal of physical education is to develop physically educated individuals who have the knowledge, skills, and confidence to enjoy a lifetime of healthful physical activity.

A physically educated person:

Standard 1: Demonstrates competency in motor skills and movement patterns needed to perform a variety of physical activities.

Standard 2: Demonstrates an understanding of movement concepts, principles, strategies, and tactics as they apply to the learning and performance of physical activities.

Standard 3: Participates regularly in physical activity.

Standard 4: Achieves and maintains a health-enhancing level of physical fitness.

Standard 5: Exhibits responsible personal and social behavior that respects self and others in physical activity settings.

Standard 6: Values physical activity for health, enjoyment, challenge, self-expression, and/or social interaction.

National Association for Sport and Physical Education, *Moving into the future: national standards for physical education* (2nd edition), 2004. Reprinted with permission from the National Association for Sport and Physical Education (NASPE), 1900 Association Drive, Reston, VA 20191-1599.

conducted outside the school setting, physical education, exercise science, and sport contribute to the cognitive, affective, and psychomotor development of program participants. These programs involve people of all ages, in a diversity of settings, and with many different goals. As we continue to expand our programs, we must actively seek to extend the opportunity for participation to all people, regardless of sex, race, ethnic and cultural background, and socioeconomic status.

Taxonomies

Taxonomies serve as a guide for professionals in planning for learning outcomes and achievement of the desired goals. A taxonomy organizes educational objectives in a hierarchy, using developmental theories as a basis for formulating objectives. Objectives are ordered progressively from low to high. Behaviors at one level serve as the foundation and prerequisite for behaviors at a higher level. Stated more simply, lower-order objectives serve as stepping stones to the attainment of higher levels of achievement.

Taxonomies have been developed for each domain. Although these taxonomies are often described with reference to education and the school setting, they offer guidelines for professionals in all fields who work with people to enhance learning and promote human development. Quality physical education, exercise science, and sport programs contribute to development in each domain.

Cognitive Domain

The cognitive domain is concerned with the acquisition of knowledge and the development of intellectual skills. Bloom and his colleagues developed a taxonomy of educational objectives for this domain in the 1950s.[25] These objectives reflect an increase in complexity at each level of development. Learning facts is the initial objective, and from this grows understanding and application of concepts, critical analysis, synthesis, and evaluation. (The Cognitive Domain box presents the objectives for this domain.)

Development of knowledge and understanding is an important objective for physical education, exercise science, and sport programs in all settings. Our programs are concerned with educating individuals about the many dimensions of human movement, including the knowledge within our discipline.

Physical education, exercise science, and sport contribute to knowledge of the human body, exercise, disease, and health. In the school setting, physical education is the sole area of the curriculum that teaches students about human movement

The Cognitive Domain

Category	Description
1. Knowledge	Memory; ability to recall; bringing to mind appropriate information; represents lowest level of learning outcomes in cognitive domain
2. Comprehension	To grasp the meaning of material; understanding without perceiving implications; interpret; translate; estimate; predict; one step beyond memory; represents lowest level of understanding
3. Application	Ability to use learned information in new situations; can apply rules, methods, and concepts; higher level of understanding
4. Analysis	To break down material into its component parts; organization and relationships between parts made clear; identifying; selecting; inferring; higher intellectual level
5. Synthesis	To put parts together to form a new whole; produce new patterns, routines, or structures; creative behaviors stressed
6. Evaluation	Judge value of ideas, concepts, based on definitive criteria or standards; highest learning outcome because it contains elements of all other categories and judgments based on specific criteria

and explores its many dimensions. Through the physical education program, individuals can gain a greater understanding of the various organ systems of the body (e.g., cardiorespiratory system), how they function, and how they can best be maintained. The relationship between exercise and physical activity, disease, and health is an important one for students to comprehend. Students who apply this knowledge to their own lives can enhance their health and reduce their chances for disease, enabling them to lead happier and more productive lives. In other settings, such as wellness clinics in hospitals or worksite health promotion programs, professionals who help adults learn how incorporating physical activity into their daily lives can help them lead longer, healthier lives.

The learning of physical activities involves various cognitive processes. Learners must understand the techniques of the skill being taught and then be able to translate this information into an appropriate, coordinated movement. Related principles and concepts of movement should also be taught so that individuals can move more effectively. For example, children should know that a throw is more effective when one steps in the direction of the throw and follows through toward the intended target. Moreover, successful performance in many sport activities requires modifying movements to meet the demands of a changing situation (e.g., applying backspin to the tennis ball to catch one's opponent off-guard). This requires individuals to learn from their experiences (e.g., which modifications of a skill lead to success). Cognitively, individuals must analyze their performance, synthesize the information, and apply it to the new situation.

Professionals in all settings need to place more emphasis on the scientific principles and concepts underlying the performance of various activities. Physical activities are not performed in a vacuum. As such, instructors should continually provide appropriate knowledge and information for participants and encourage them to question what they are doing. "Why should I exercise regularly? How will this exercise contribute to the rehabilitation of my knee? Why is warming up before exercising important? How can I get more distance for my golf drive? What can I do to throw the ball farther? Why is it important to play by the rules?" Participants should be provided with more opportunities to think, to apply problem-solving skills to physical activity situations, and to experience situations that allow for creativity and individual expression.

Knowing how to monitor your heart rate, calculate your training zone, and modify your fitness program to meet your individual needs are cognitive outcomes that can be achieved in programs.

Children at Agassiz Middle School, in Fargo, North Dakota, learn about the Fitness Education Pyramid.

Teachers can also use fitness activities to stimulate cognitive development. Students can self-analyze their fitness levels, identify areas of improvement, apply their knowledge to design an individualized exercise program, and evaluate their progress regularly, adjusting their program as needed. These cognitive skills of analysis, identification, application, and evaluation contribute to the educational goal of preparing students to be lifelong learners. These activities also give students skills to modify their fitness programs during their adult lives as their needs change, a critical feature of lifespan involvement.

Technology is increasingly being used to enhance the teaching of concepts of physical activity. For example, a physical education teacher at the Agassiz Middle School, Fargo, North Dakota, uses heart-rate monitors to help students understand important concepts related to physical activity.[26] Students learn about the Fitness Education Pyramid, which graphically depicts the different types of health benefits associated with varying levels of activity intensity. The heart-rate monitors give students vivid feedback about the effects of activity on their hearts and enable them to monitor their efforts as they participate. This feedback enhances the students' understanding of important fitness concepts.

Our programs can contribute to our understanding of sport, a major institution in our society and in many other cultures throughout the world. Sport affects a country's economy, politics, government, and educational system. Sport dominates the newspapers, magazines, radio, and television. Millions of people of all ages are involved as participants in sport, and millions more enjoy sport as spectators. Because sport is a part of our culture and others throughout the world, it should be understood from a sociological and psychological perspective. Of course, a body of sport knowledge also exists concerning such things as rules, strategy, safety measures, terminology, and etiquette.

Physical education, exercise science, and sport professionals can help people become wise consumers of goods and services that influence their health and fitness. The health and fitness industry is a multibillion-dollar industry. Unfortunately, it is an area in which goods and services of doubtful value find a ready market. Advertisements in popular magazines promise a quick weight loss or a rapid shape up. Infomercials promoting exercise equipment and nutritional supplements capture the attention of thousands of people. Professionals can help participants in their programs learn how to evaluate such pronouncements critically and be wise consumers in the burgeoning marketplace.

Within the school setting, physical education can contribute to cognitive development in many significant ways. Like other curricular areas, it can promote the development of critical thinking skills, and it can provide exciting opportunities for multidisciplinary study. Uniquely, physical education is the one area of the curriculum in which students can obtain knowledge about human movement, fitness, and sport to serve as a foundation for a lifetime of participation.

Affective Domain

Many factors influence individuals' learning, including their feelings about themselves, the learning experience, and the subject. Recognizing this, Krathwohl and his associates developed the taxonomy for the affective domain.[27] This taxonomy reflects the development of values, appreciations, attitudes, and character. As individuals progress through the levels within this domain, they move from a concern about themselves to a value structure that embraces concern for others. At the highest level, their internalized values directly influence their choices and actions. Affective development also encompasses the social and emotional development. (The objectives are shown in The Affective Domain box.)

Quality physical education, exercise science, and sport programs conducted by qualified leaders can enrich development in the affective domain. These desirable outcomes should not be left to chance, but actively sought through carefully planned approaches designed to promote growth in this area.

All people have certain basic social needs. These include a feeling of belonging, recognition, self-respect, and love. Fulfillment of these needs contributes to social development. Physical education, exercise science, and sport programs can help participants meet some of these social needs. For example, elderly participants who join an exercise program typically benefit not only physically but socially, deriving pleasure from meeting with their group regularly and forming new friendships. Such interactions help to diminish the feelings of isolation experienced by many elderly who live alone.

Valuing physical activity for enjoyment and challenge is an example of an affective outcome.

Social development is further encouraged by opportunities to interact with program participants. For example, in school physical education programs, students have more opportunities to interact with one another and work together than in any other area of the educational curriculum. Interscholastic sport programs have long extolled their value in promoting learning that teaches athletes

The Affective Domain

Category	Description
1. Receiving	Sensitivity to the existence of certain events, stimuli; awareness; willingness to receive or attend to phenomena
2. Responding	Actively attending to stimuli; reacts to situation beyond mere perception; overt response
3. Valuing	Stimuli or phenomena assigned worth; learner places a value on events; characteristics of a belief or an attitude; appreciation
4. Organizing	Internalizes values and organizes them into a system; determines interrelationship among values; arranges values in hierarchical form; compares, relates, synthesizes values
5. Characterizing by a value or complex	Acts in accordance with internalized values; behavior consistent with accepted values and becomes a part of personality; highest level of affective domain

how to work together as part of a team, compete fairly, accept responsibility, and respect the rights of others.

Promotion of a positive self-concept and enhancement of feelings of self-worth and self-respect are desired outcomes associated with this domain. One way that physical education, exercise science, and sport activities can contribute to these outcomes is to provide opportunities for individuals to develop competence in physical skills and to challenge themselves to attain new levels of achievement and realistic goals. Experiences should be structured to allow for meaningful success for all involved. Individuals who perceive themselves as competent and have confidence in themselves as movers are more likely to seek involvement in physical activities.

Helping young people develop a healthy self-esteem is important. Drug and alcohol abuse and a myriad of other social problems have been linked to low self-esteem. Programs that empower participants through opportunities for leadership, promotion of competence, and development of improved self-image through establishing and maintaining a high level of fitness enhance the self-esteem of participants.

The development of positive attitudes and appreciation for the contributions that engaging in regular physical activity makes to lifelong health and well-being are outcomes that physical education, exercise science, and sport professionals are increasingly emphasizing. Knowledge of the benefits of physical activity and the development of the skills to participate in various activities are not, in and of themselves, sufficient to promote lifespan involvement. If we are to achieve our goal of promoting regular physical activity, we must instill in participants the motivation to lead a healthy, active lifestyle. Our programs should help participants appreciate the contribution that physical activity can make to their health, performance, and rewarding use of leisure time.

Professionals should be concerned with helping individuals clarify and think through their value judgments. We must move beyond the lower-order objective of creating an interest in physical activity. Helping participants achieve the higher-order objective of internalizing values should be our focus. At this level, values directly influence what individuals choose to do and how they behave. Thus, we must help individuals develop values that will lead to a physically active lifestyle. Additionally, we must give attention to developing their decision-making and self-management skills, which will help them in translating their values into action.

Decision-making skills and self-management skills are particularly important for achieving wellness. Many lifestyle choices that individuals make have the potential to influence their health. Decisions that individuals make about eating, exercising, managing stress, and using leisure time can have a positive or negative impact on their health. Helping individuals clarify their values and make decisions congruent with their beliefs can enhance their quality of life.

Professionals can promote social responsibility, an important component of good citizenship. Hellison[28] developed a model to promote responsibility that has been successfully used with at-risk students in both school- and community-based programs. This model emphasizes personal growth through self-control, involvement, goal setting, and assisting others. Success, personal awareness, problem solving, and self-reflection are also incorporated within this model. This approach and other thoughtfully designed instructional experiences can do much to promote the development of socially acceptable values.

Professionals must also give careful thought to the influence of their own behaviors, values, and actions on their program participants. How important is it for professionals to practice what they preach? Professionals who aspire to promote affective development must carefully weigh this question. As leaders, they serve as models for participants. Consideration for the needs and feelings of others, respect for each individual, and enthusiasm for physical activity are some behaviors physical educators, exercise science, and sport professionals should exhibit if they want to promote the same behaviors within their participants.

Physical education, exercise science, and sport also provide a venue to develop ethics and morals. In physical education classes and sport experiences, students and athletes have the opportunity to respond to codes of conduct, to decide what is right or wrong, and to make choices that have moral implications. Professionals can promote further development in this area by having students and athletes reflect on their decisions and behavior. Students can also be asked to assume officiating responsibilities in games or to make their own calls (e.g., calling one's own fouls in a game or calling the ball in or out in a tennis match). Discussion of students' and athletes' behaviors following these situations can help participants further clarify their values.

Our programs have long been extolled as a means through which character development can occur. However, character development can be either positive or negative in nature. As Docheff points out, "The outcome of character development is determined by a number of factors—that is, the character of those that support and drive the endeavor, including coaches, teachers, administrators, parents. . . ."[29] Professionals can exert a great influence on character development. However, as professionals, "we must take personal responsibility for the development of good character in others by the demonstration of good character in ourselves." Gough suggests that the most significant character-building challenge is "often more a matter of doing the good, than a matter of knowing the good, more a matter of having the strength of character to do that right thing than a matter of analyzing and resolving complicated moral dilemmas. . . ."[30] Helping individuals develop the habit of "doing good" is critical to our character-building endeavors.

Physical education, exercise science, and sport programs can contribute to an appreciation of beauty. The ancient Greeks stressed the "body beautiful" and did their exercises and athletic contests in the nude to display the fine contours of their bodies. Physical activity is one key to a beautiful body. Also, a beauty of movement is developed through physical activity. When people move, whether it is to perform an everyday task or a sport skill, their movements can have a degree of elegance and beauty. For example, when a person picks up an object from the floor, it can be done with a great deal of skill and grace, or it can be done awkwardly. Included in the performance of such acts as catching a football, making a basketball goal, executing a high jump, completing a two-and-one-half somersault dive, or performing a complex dance can be rhythm, grace, poise, and ease of movement that are beauty in action.

Physical education, exercise science, and sport fosters development in the affective domain. The enhancement of self-esteem, promotion of social responsibility, clarification of values, development of attitudes, and appreciation of beauty are just some contributions that physical education, exercise science, and sport can make to the development of the whole person.

Acquisition of motor skills is one focus of the psychomotor domain.

Psychomotor Domain

Developed by Harrow, the taxonomy of objectives in the psychomotor domain shows a progression of development that provides the foundation for programs of physical activities.[31] The lower-order objectives focus on the acquisition of basic movements and perceptual abilities. The higher-order objectives emphasize the development of fitness and highly skilled movements, as well as increased creativity in the use of these movements. (The Psychomotor Domain box lists the objectives of this domain.)

Development of fitness is also included within this domain. Corbin presents a taxonomy that moves in progression from exercising to achieving fitness and then to establishing personal exercise habits.[32] The higher-order objectives focus on learning how to evaluate one's own fitness level and resolve fitness problems.

The psychomotor domain is the main focus of our fields. Psychomotor development of the individual is our primary contribution to the educational curriculum. Although physical education can contribute in many meaningful ways to development in the other domains, psychomotor development in the schools is the unique responsibility of the physical educator. Psychomotor development is concerned with two of the primary objectives of physical education: motor skill development and physical fitness development.

Motor Skill Development

The development of motor skills is sometimes referred to as the development of neuromuscular or psychomotor skills because effective movement depends on the harmonious working together of the muscular and nervous systems. The acquisition and refinement of motor skills essential for everyday activities such as posture and lifting and for movement in a variety of physical activities, such as dance, sports, aquatics, or outdoor pursuits, are important outcomes of motor skill development. The development of motor skills focuses on helping individuals learn how to move effectively to accomplish specific goals efficiently, that is, with as little expenditure of energy as possible.

The Psychomotor Domain

Category	Description
1. Reflex movements	Actions elicited without conscious volition in response to some stimuli; flexing, extending, stretching, postural adjustments; provides base for movement behavior
2. Basic fundamental movements	Inherent movement patterns based on combinations of reflex movements; patterns provide starting point for improvement of perceptual and physical abilities; basis for complex skilled movement
3. Perceptual abilities	Interpretation of stimuli from various modalities so adjustments can be made; includes auditory, visual, tactile, kinesthetic, coordinated perceptual abilities
4. Physical abilities	Characteristics that, when developed to a high degree, provide learner with a sound, efficiently functioning body; organic vigor essential to development of highly skilled movement; endurance, strength, agility, flexibility
5. Skilled movements	Degree of efficiency in performing a complex movement task; consists of a vertical and horizontal continuum, based on inherent movement patterns
6. Nondiscursive communication	Movement expressions that are part of a movement repertoire; movement interpretations that include any efficiently performed skilled movement; movement patterns designed to communicate a message to the viewer; ranges from facial expressions through sophisticated choreographies

Motor skill development is a sequential process that occurs throughout one's lifespan. Infants possess reflexive, involuntary movements that are replaced with voluntary movements as they mature. Fundamental movements, such as running and throwing, begin to develop in early childhood around the time the child can walk independently. These fundamental motor skills progress through various stages, leading to the mature form of the skill. As children progress through these stages, they exhibit a greater degree of proficiency in their movements, enhanced control and precision of response, and improved coordination.

Fundamental movements form the basis for the development of specialized motor and sport skills in the later childhood years. Fundamental movements such as running, kicking, trapping, and dodging now can be applied to a sport such as soccer. Movements such as running, striking, and sliding can be incorporated into a game of tennis. In these situations, increased demands are placed on the individual with respect to form, speed, accuracy, and complexity of skill performance. If we are to achieve our goal of lifespan participation in physical activity, careful attention must be paid to the development of each individual's motor skills. As our programs expand to meet the needs of people of all ages, from preschoolers to the elderly, we must be prepared to promote the acquisition and refinement of motor skills in diverse populations.

The development of individuals' motor skills to their fullest potential requires that individuals have the opportunity to be involved in structured movement experiences that are appropriate to their development level. These experiences should provide meaningful instruction, offer sufficient opportunity for skill practice, and encourage effort and continued practice outside the structured setting. Physical educators who work with young children play a critical role in achieving our goal of promoting lifelong participation. It is important that children acquire competency in the basic, fundamental motor skills so that they can adapt these skills to the more stringent demands of sports and other physical activities such as dance and recreational pursuits. Individuals who lack the prerequisite skills will have trouble meeting these demands. Learning experiences that provide for success while developing skill proficiency increase the probability that students will incorporate physical activity into their lifestyle.

Physical education is the only area within the school that helps students in developing their motor skills. Through a progressive curriculum, students move from competency in the basic movements to the performance of skilled movements, including sport skills. They are provided with opportunities to learn how to modify these movements to meet changing situational demands and unique personal needs. They also have the opportunity to explore movement as a medium for communication, as a vehicle for creativity, and as a means to understand other cultures. Though many current physical education curriculums are emphasizing fitness promotion, the development of motor skills should not be neglected. This is essential for lifespan participation. The likelihood of individuals engaging in physical activity regularly increases if they have the skills to participate successfully in activities that are enjoyable and personally satisfying.

School physical education programs should offer a balanced variety of activities that allow young people to develop competency in lifetime activities that are personally meaningful and enjoyable. A balance should exist in any physical education program among team, dual, and individual (lifetime) sports. Team sports such as basketball and soccer provide an opportunity for students to develop skills and to enjoy working and competing together as a team. However, in many school physical education programs, team sports dominate the curriculum at the expense of various individual and dual sports, such as tennis, swimming, badminton, and golf. In such cases, the students are deprived of the opportunity to develop skills in activities that they can participate in throughout their adult lives. Only through a balanced program of team, dual, and individual sports is it possible to develop well-rounded individuals.

In adulthood, an individual's participation in sports and recreational activities is influenced by a number of factors. Past exposure, interests, abilities, enjoyment, motivation, opportunity, time, and financial considerations are just a few factors that influence the nature and level of adults' participation. If one primary purpose of physical education, exercise science, and sport is to promote a physically active lifestyle that will contribute to the optimal development and health of the individual, we must provide individuals of all ages with the necessary motor skills to do so. The skills individuals acquire will help determine how they spend their leisure time as well as what path they will choose to develop fitness. For example, a person who excels in swimming may spend much of his or her leisure time engaged in related activities, or choose to follow a fitness program based on swimming. If an individual excels in tennis, he or she may frequent the courts.

Physical education, exercise science, and sport professionals working outside the school setting with adults face special challenges in teaching motor skills. Adults may want to learn a new sport, yet lack proficiency in the prerequisite fundamental movement skills. They may, for example, exhibit poorly developed running or throwing skills. Professionals working with these adults must use instructional strategies to help them master the fundamental movements while incorporating instruction about the sport skills into the lesson to challenge the adults.

Physical education also contributes to the educational goal of promoting worthy use of leisure time. Sports, aquatics, and dance give individuals enjoyable activities for use during their free time. They offer a pleasurable means to relax after work and are popular recreational pursuits on the weekends. Development of motor skills for participation in sport and recreational activities is important for people of all ages, including those individuals with disabilities. Physical education, exercise science, and sport professionals in all settings must be prepared to teach individuals with a diversity of needs and to modify activities and instructional strategies to be appropriate to the abilities of the individuals with whom they are working. Challenging activities that lead to skill development and meaningful participation are essential to providing a positive learning experience for all individuals, including those with special needs.

Physical Fitness Development

The evidence supporting the contribution of physical activity and health-related fitness to the well-being and quality of life is overwhelming. Development and maintenance of physical fitness has long been heralded as one of the most important outcomes of school physical education programs. Fitness promotion is the focus of many nonschool physical education, exercise science, and sport programs as well.

Educational institutions are charged with preparing individuals to be productive members of society. An individual's health status directly affects his or her ability to lead a productive life. Thus, promotion of fitness as well as the skills and knowledge to maintain it throughout one's lifetime are important contributions of physical education to educational goals.

A progressive, systematic approach to the development of physical fitness should be used. First and foremost, the program should consider the needs of the individual. Based on these needs, the program should be designed to accomplish the desired outcomes. Careful attention should be given to helping individuals identify and develop proficiency in activities that are enjoyable and meaningful to them while contributing to the attainment of fitness. This will encourage individuals to make these activities an integral part of their lifestyle.

Improving fitness is an important goal of many worksite health promotion programs, such as the one offered at the Taking Care Center, in Hartford, Connecticut.

If we are to accomplish our objectives related to physical fitness, a multifaceted approach is needed. Obviously, we must teach exercises and activities that promote fitness. However, this is not enough. Through our programs, individuals must acquire the knowledge to design and modify their fitness program to meet their changing needs. Moreover, our programs must instill within each individual the desire to make fitness a lifelong pursuit, the enjoyment of physical activity, and the appreciation of the value of leading a healthy, active lifestyle.

Contemporary physical education, exercise science, and sport support the development of physical fitness and physically active lifestyles for people of all ages. Unfortunately, the majority of our nation's people are not involved in physical activity on a regular basis and thus do not realize the concomitant health benefits. Minorities, people who are economically disadvantaged, women, older adults, and persons with disabilities are disproportionately inactive. As professionals, we must increase our efforts to reach out and involve people from these populations in our programs.

Quality school-based physical education programs can contribute significantly to the education of the individual and to the goals of education. They enhance learning and development in all three domains: cognitive, affective, and psychomotor. For physical education, exercise science, and sport professionals working in settings outside the school, an understanding of the behavioral domains, taxonomies, and objectives helps them to more effectively structure their programs to achieve desired outcomes. Physical education, exercise science, and sport professionals in all settings must also assess the progress of their participants in achieving the desired outcomes. Assessment should be an integral part of all physical education, exercise science, and sport programs.

ASSESSMENT OF LEARNING

How do professionals determine whether the participants in their physical education, exercise science, and sport programs have achieved the stated objectives? How do we diagnose the needs of the individuals engaged in our programs? What is the best way to monitor participants' rates of progress? How do participants know when they have accomplished their goals? How can we motivate people to persist in their endeavors? What changes can we make in our programs to be more effective? How can we show the worth of our programs in this era of accountability? How can we, as professionals, enhance our own abilities to meet the needs of participants in our programs? Assessment enables us to answer these and many other important questions.

Assessment is a critical component of quality physical education, exercise science, and sport programs. Assessment should be a dynamic, ongoing process integrated into programs and viewed as an essential, crucial element of any program, be it conducted in a school or nonschool setting. The development of quality physical education, exercise science, and sport programs requires establishing clear goals, assessing participants' needs, setting specific objectives, planning learning experiences, providing effective instruction, and evaluating the outcomes.

Assessment can yield important information about participants' progress, program quality, instructional practices, and the effectiveness of professionals. Evaluation promotes accountability. Participants are accountable for their performance, and physical education, exercise science, and sport leaders are accountable for participants' achievements. Today, more than ever, demonstrating the worth and value of our programs is critical. Assessment is central to this purpose because it provides meaningful information about learning and achievement related to goals, objectives, and outcomes in the affective, cognitive, and psychomotor domains. Assessment links the content standards to the instructional process and to the participants' achievements. Figure 2-1 shows a sample physical education report. Assessment is a continual endeavor, one that is essential to the learning process.

Assessment Defined

Assessment is a process used to gather information about the participant's achievement and to make decisions and judgments based on that evidence for many purposes. Measurement and evaluation are closely related processes. *Measurement* is the process of gathering information or collecting data. *Evaluation* is the process of interpreting the information or data. Assessment is more encompassing in its scope than evaluation, including data collection, interpretation, and decision making.

NASPE identifies "the primary goal of assessment as the enhancement of learning, rather than documentation of learning."[22] Assessment has a broader purpose than the assignment of a grade or using a checklist to denote progress. As a critical component of any program, assessment helps professionals make decisions and conduct programs that are in the best interests of the participants.

Assessment encompasses a variety of measurement, evaluation, and assessment techniques that have as their primary purpose the gathering and interpretation of information. This information is used to make decisions that will enhance the outcomes achieved and the experiences of participants in physical education, exercise science, and sport programs.

Purposes of Assessment

There are many purposes for assessment. As an integral component of quality physical education, exercise science, and sport programs, assessment, when used correctly, can contribute in many ways to the achievement of learning and enhancement of development in the cognitive, affective, and psychomotor domains. The main purposes of assessment include diagnosis, placement, monitoring of progress, determination of achievement, motivation, program improvement, and teacher effectiveness.

Essential for Good Health—A Physically Active Lifestyle

Child's Name ____________________ Class __________

I CAN Physical Education Report
5th 6-week period 1998–99
Grade 4

We are learning how to learn. Your child has rated his/her ability level in the space next to each skill. ***If my rating is different from your child's rating, you will see my rating in GREEN.*** *Please ask your child "What do these letters you wrote mean?" Hopefully you will get a thoughtful answer such as "I put L for learning because I can do that some of the time, but not all of the time." If my rating is different, you may also want to ask why s/he thinks they are different. There may be a good reason. Encourage your child to think about what s/he needs to work on and celebrate new skills. Thanks, Dolly Lambdin, Physical Education Teacher*

B = Beginning – I can do it once in a while.
L = Learning – I can do it most of the time – but I have to really think about it.
M = Mastered – I can always do it – It is easy for me.
P = Problems – I have problems with this.

In physical education we learn to move our bodies and objects with skill and confidence.

Basketball

__ I can dribble with one hand at a time without looking at the ball.
__ I can dribble (without stopping and dribbling again) when someone is guarding me.

__ I can do three kinds of basketball passes.
They are ________________, ________________, and ________________.
__ I can pivot when not dribbling the ball.

__ When I shoot, I start with the ball in front of my forehead.
__ When I shoot, I remember to follow through with a wave.

__ I know when to guard my partner.
__ I know how to guard my partner.

We encourage and support each other and make class a good place to learn.

__ I listen during instructions.
__ I follow the directions.
__ I do **quality work.**
__ I move safely.
__ I work well with any partner.
__ I help make fair teams.
__ I like to play basketball.

Thanks for reading this 5th report card. Have your child return this slip for a "playdough" treat.
Child's Name ________________ **Parent's Signature** ________________
Walk, jog, bike, EXERCISE with your children!!! Enjoy a healthy lifestyle.

Figure 2-1 Sample physical education report card that includes both self-assessment and teacher assessment.

Computerized fitness equipment is becoming increasingly common. This technology makes it easier for people to monitor their workout and self-assess their fitness status.

Diagnosis is one of the most important uses of assessment. Diagnostic procedures can be used to identify individuals' strengths and weaknesses, levels of abilities, and developmental status in the various domains. When working with children with disabilities, the adapted physical activity specialist may use the Denver Developmental Screening Test to identify motor, language, and personal-social skills of the children. A sport psychologist working with an intercollegiate athletic team to improve its performance uses several paper-and-pencil tests to find out athletes' satisfaction, perception of team climate, attentional styles, and leadership roles. Additional knowledge gleaned from interviews of the athletes and coaches and from personal observation of the team during practice and games helps the sport psychologist identify factors limiting the team's achievement.

Prescription uses diagnostic information to design programs to meet identified needs. A cardiac rehabilitation specialist uses the results of an exercise stress test to prescribe an exercise program for the postcardiac patient. A personal trainer reviews the various assessments of a client's fitness levels, nutritional status, and lifestyle habits and then designs an individualized wellness program for the client. Working with the athlete's physician, an athletic trainer plans a program of exercise to restore the full range of motion to the athlete who is recovering from a rotator cuff injury.

Classification or placement of individuals into groups based on their abilities is another purpose of assessment. For children with disabilities, assessment influences their educational placement and the type of services they receive. Sport activity instructors commonly assign people to ability groups for instruction, believing that same ability grouping facilitates learning.

Determination of achievement is one of the primary purposes of assessment. Physical education, exercise science, and sport programs involve purposeful activity directed toward the attainment of certain goals. Have the program participants achieved the stated objectives? Does the senior citizen know how to modify his walking program as he increases in fitness? Are the children in a youth sport program mastering the basic skills of soccer? Do the physical fitness test results reveal that the student has achieved a satisfactory level of health-related fitness? Does the running log of a participant in the community fitness program reveal a commitment to exercising on a regular basis? Without assessment, how would we know whether our participants have achieved the desired objectives? Assessment can provide an indicator of achievement at the end of a program. When assessment is done at both the beginning and the end of the program, improvement can be seen. Incorporation of various assessment techniques throughout the program allows for the tracking of participants' progress.

Assessment can enhance the motivation of participants, encouraging them to improve further. Learning experiences that provide for frequent self-testing and incremental successes allow sixth-grade students to see that their volleyball skills are improving and that hard work yields results. An athlete is motivated to continue to rehabilitate her knee when she sees that the weight that she can lift with her injured leg increases each week. An employee in a corporate fitness program is motivated to continue to exercise each day at 6 A.M. when he sees a decrease in his time to complete a mile and perceives himself as having more energy to meet the demands of the day. Assessment is also motivating to professionals when they see that the time and effort they have invested in their programs have benefitted the program's participants.

Assessment affects participants in varied ways. Assessment influences participants' perceptions of themselves as learners and, more specifically, their perceptions of their competence as movers. It can enhance their confidence in their abilities and create positive attitudes toward participation. Participants can use assessment to focus their learning on relevant tasks, to guide their expenditure of time, to consolidate their learning, and to develop learning strategies for the future.

Another purpose of assessment is program evaluation. Assessment can provide evidence of the effectiveness of the program. Corporate fitness directors can document the progress and concomitant health gains made by employees enrolled in the program. This lets the employer know whether the program is beneficial to the employees and whether the investment in the program has yielded cost savings. This more global approach can also be used to improve the program. From this perspective, items such as program content, progression of instructional experiences, administration and organization, facilities and equipment, and time allocation are addressed as part of the overall program assessment. This enables professionals to make improvements in their programs to heighten their effectiveness.

Physical educators, exercise scientists, and sport leaders who care deeply about their professional endeavors reflect upon all the information gathered via the assessment process to improve their own effectiveness. They might ask themselves, "Are there any changes that I can make in my presentation? Is the order of the instructional tasks the best sequence to enhance participants' developments? Do I need to give participants more guidance? These and other questions can help professionals enhance their effectiveness and thus influence the outcomes of the participants in their programs.

There are many different avenues that professionals can use to assess the outcomes achieved by participants in their programs. The ability of assessment procedures to enhance learning by connecting assessment to instruction and to enrich the experience of program participants makes it critical that assessment is included as an integral part of physical education, exercise science, and sport programs.

The Role of Technology in Assessment

Technology is increasingly influencing the assessment processes. Computers help in maintaining records of test results or keeping a log of participants' involvement in the program.

One example of computerized record keeping is the Cooper's Institute for Aerobics Fitnessgram.[33] The Fitnessgram is used in many schools throughout the nation to provide students and their parents with information about the student's fitness profile. The program measures the health-related components of fitness—cardiorespiratory endurance, muscle strength and endurance, flexibility, and body composition. The Fitnessgram can be seen in Figure 2-2. The Fitnessgram provides a computerized report on the fitness status of each student. The profile is constructed from the individual's performance on the test items. When necessary, exercise recommendations are made, based on the test performance of the individual. The Fitnessgram also makes it easy for teachers, parents, and students to compare their performance on the current test to performances on previous tests. This makes it easy to note where improvements have been made and identifies fitness areas that require attention. The Fitnessgram helps teachers keep track of their students' fitness level and determine whether the stated program objectives are being achieved.

A new feature of Fitnessgram is the Activitygram, which is shown in Figure 2-3.[33] The Activitygram provides an assessment of the student's physical activity both on school and nonschool days. This assessment was included in the Fitnessgram to help reinforce to students the importance of being physically active on a daily basis.[33] In order to maintain fitness, students must develop lifetime habits of regular physical activity. The Activitygram helps students become more aware of their physical activity patterns.

Computerized assessment and recordkeeping systems are becoming increasingly popular. One system is the HealthFirst TriFit system. The HealthFirst TriFit system enables physical education, exercise science, and sport professionals to perform a complete fitness assessment and design personalized exercise and nutrition programs for their students or clients.[34] Assessment of cardiovascular function, body composition, flexibility, muscular strength, and a variety of biometric measures can be performed. The testing instruments, such as the bicycle ergometer used to assess cardiovascular endurance or the skinfold calipers used to help determine body composition, are directly interfaced with the computer. Additional information from other assessments can be entered into the computer by the professional. The HealthFirst software analyzes the results of the tests performed and creates a profile of the student's or client's health fitness status. Personalized fitness programs can then be created using the HealthFirst software. Progress reports can also be generated, allowing the tracking of fitness activities and assessments over a period of time. Additionally, there is an online learning center that students and clients can access to perform health risk appraisals or find out additional information on a multitude of topics pertaining to fitness and wellness.

Corporate fitness centers also use microcomputers in their fitness programs. A computerized check-in system records employee participation. After exercising, employees use the computer to record the type of exercise they performed, the duration of the exercise period, and their weight. A record of each employee's progress toward his or her goals is easily maintained. This information is helpful to program managers in charting facility usage, calculating the benefits of the programs, and documenting program effectiveness.

Heart-rate monitors are valuable tools for teaching children and adults about fitness in both school and nonschool settings. These monitors, worn on the wrist, track heart rate and provide positive reinforcement to the wearers as they work to achieve their goals. They provide physical education teachers, exercise scientists, and sport leaders with valuable information that they can use to modify their teaching methods. A printout of the exercise session provides a permanent record of participants' work.

The impact of computer technology has been felt throughout the fields of physical education, exercise science, and sport. Exercise physiologists use computers to regulate equipment during highly complex tests of cardiovascular function and to analyze the voluminous amounts of data generated. Athletic trainers assess the extent of an injury, carry out a course of treatment, and monitor the rehabilitation process. Computerized equipment, such as the Cybex, offers both the injured athlete and the athletic trainer continuous feedback on their weight-training efforts during rehabilitation. Biomechanists use special computer programs to analyze motions and force

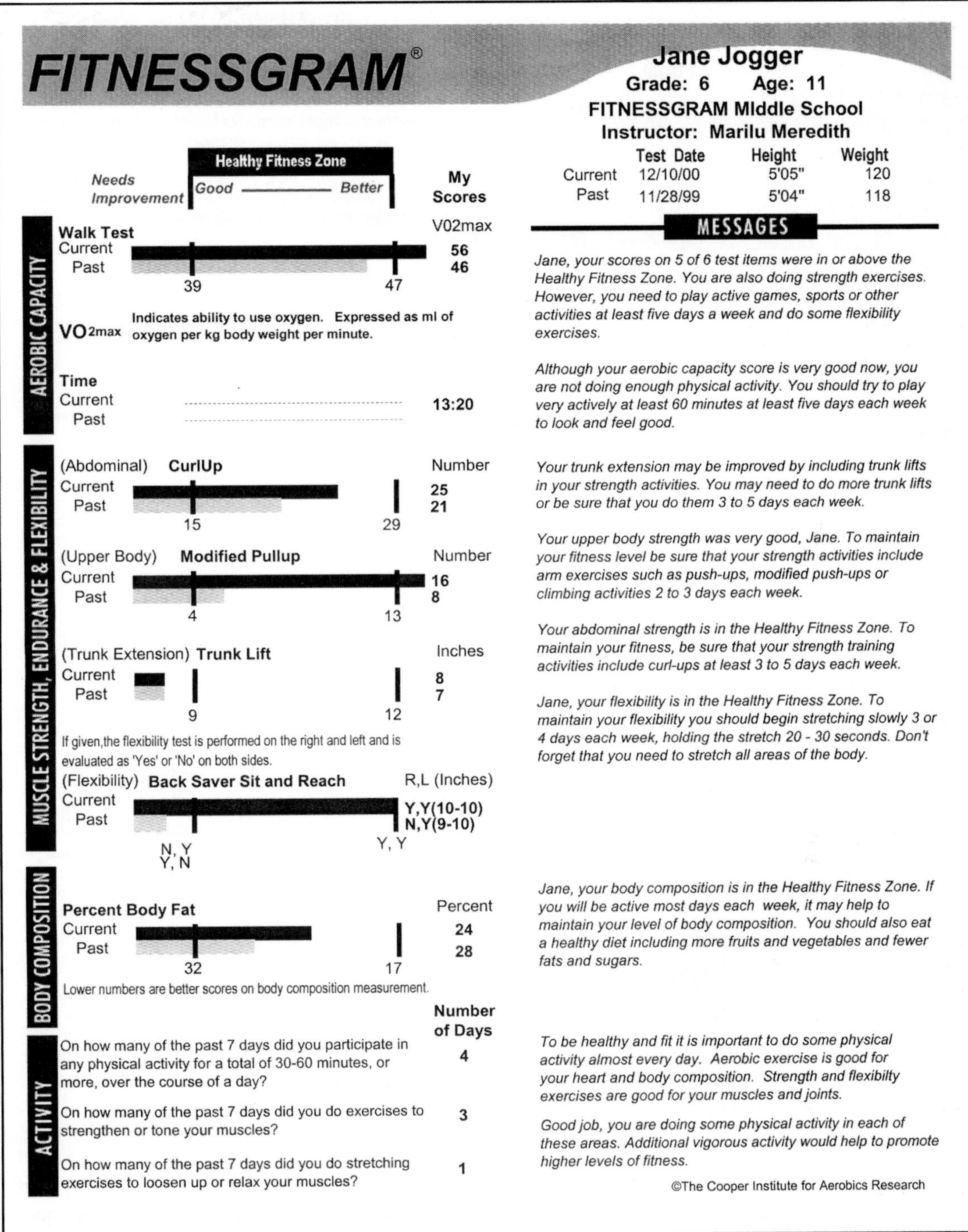

FITNESSGRAM®

Jane Jogger
Grade: 6 Age: 11
FITNESSGRAM MIddle School
Instructor: Marilu Meredith

	Test Date	Height	Weight
Current	12/10/00	5'05"	120
Past	11/28/99	5'04"	118

Healthy Fitness Zone: Needs Improvement | Good —— Better | My Scores

AEROBIC CAPACITY

Walk Test — V02max
Current 56
Past 46
(Healthy Fitness Zone: 39 – 47)

VO2max — Indicates ability to use oxygen. Expressed as ml of oxygen per kg body weight per minute.

Time
Current 13:20
Past

MUSCLE STRENGTH, ENDURANCE & FLEXIBILITY

(Abdominal) **CurlUp** — Number
Current 25
Past 21
(15 – 29)

(Upper Body) **Modified Pullup** — Number
Current 16
Past 8
(4 – 13)

(Trunk Extension) **Trunk Lift** — Inches
Current 8
Past 7
(9 – 12)

If given, the flexibility test is performed on the right and left and is evaluated as 'Yes' or 'No' on both sides.

(Flexibility) **Back Saver Sit and Reach** — R,L (Inches)
Current Y,Y(10-10)
Past N,Y(9-10)
(N, Y / Y, N – Y, Y)

BODY COMPOSITION

Percent Body Fat — Percent
Current 24
Past 28
(32 – 17)

Lower numbers are better scores on body composition measurement.

ACTIVITY — Number of Days

On how many of the past 7 days did you participate in any physical activity for a total of 30-60 minutes, or more, over the course of a day? 4

On how many of the past 7 days did you do exercises to strengthen or tone your muscles? 3

On how many of the past 7 days did you do stretching exercises to loosen up or relax your muscles? 1

MESSAGES

Jane, your scores on 5 of 6 test items were in or above the Healthy Fitness Zone. You are also doing strength exercises. However, you need to play active games, sports or other activities at least five days a week and do some flexibility exercises.

Although your aerobic capacity score is very good now, you are not doing enough physical activity. You should try to play very actively at least 60 minutes at least five days each week to look and feel good.

Your trunk extension may be improved by including trunk lifts in your strength activities. You may need to do more trunk lifts or be sure that you do them 3 to 5 days each week.

Your upper body strength was very good, Jane. To maintain your fitness level be sure that your strength activities include arm exercises such as push-ups, modified push-ups or climbing activities 2 to 3 days each week.

Your abdominal strength is in the Healthy Fitness Zone. To maintain your fitness, be sure that your strength training activities include curl-ups at least 3 to 5 days each week.

Jane, your flexibility is in the Healthy Fitness Zone. To maintain your flexibility you should begin stretching slowly 3 or 4 days each week, holding the stretch 20 - 30 seconds. Don't forget that you need to stretch all areas of the body.

Jane, your body composition is in the Healthy Fitness Zone. If you will be active most days each week, it may help to maintain your level of body composition. You should also eat a healthy diet including more fruits and vegetables and fewer fats and sugars.

To be healthy and fit it is important to do some physical activity almost every day. Aerobic exercise is good for your heart and body composition. Strength and flexibilty exercises are good for your muscles and joints.

Good job, you are doing some physical activity in each of these areas. Additional vigorous activity would help to promote higher levels of fitness.

Figure 2-2 The Fitnessgram can be used by teachers to generate a computerized report of the physical fitness status of students.

ACTIVITYGRAM

JOE JOGGER
ACTIVITYGRAM - 09/20/00
FITNESSGRAM Middle School

MINUTES OF ACTIVITY

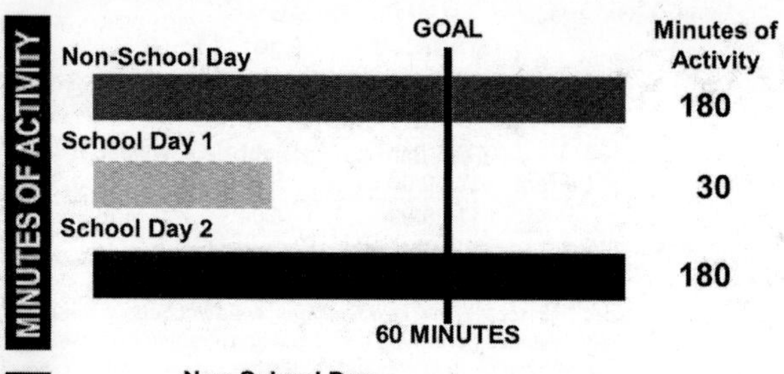

MESSAGES

The chart shows the number of minutes that you reported doing moderate (medium) or vigorous (hard) activity on each day. Congratulations, your log indicates that you are doing at least 60 minutes of activity on some days. This will help to promote good fitness and wellness. For fun and variety, try some new activities that you have never done before.

TIME PROFILE

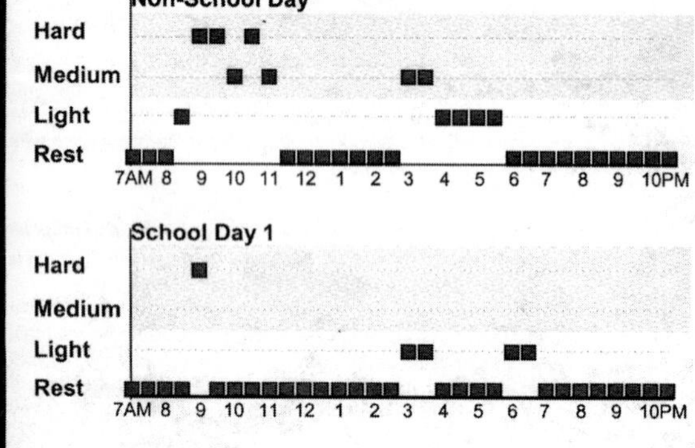

School Day 2
Hard
Medium
Light
Rest
7AM 8 9 10 11 12 1 2 3 4 5 6 7 8 9 10PM

The goal in ACTIVITYGRAM is to find ways to include activity in levels medium and hard each day (shaded areas are medium to hard).

The time profile shows the activity level you reported for each 30 minute period of the day. Your results show that you were somewhat active during school but quite active on the weekends. To increase your activity level, try to be more active on school days.

ACTIVITY PROFILE

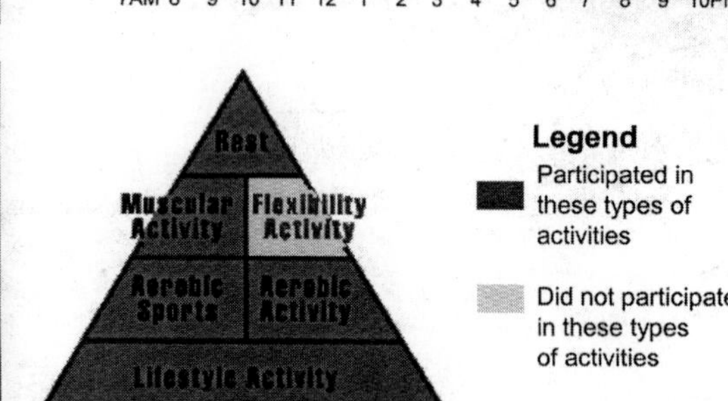

Legend

Participated in these types of activities

Did not participate in these types of activities

The activity pyramid reveals the different types of activity that you reported doing over a few days. Your results indicate that you participated in regular lifestyle activity as well as some activity from the other levels. This is great! The variety in your program should help you stay active. Your results indicate that you spend an average of 4 hours per day watching TV or working on the computer. While some time on these activities is okay, you should try to limit the total time to less than 2 hours.

ACTIVITYGRAM provides information about your normal levels of physical activity. The report shows what types of activity you do and how often you do them. It includes information that you reported for two or three days during one week.

ACTIVITYGRAM is a module within FITNESSGRAM 6.0 software. FITNESSGRAM materials are distributed by the American Fitness Alliance, a division of Human Kinetics. www.americanfitness.net

Figure 2-3 The Activitygram can be used to assess students' activity levels during both school and nonschool days.

Focus on Career: Education

PROFESSIONAL ORGANIZATIONS
- American Alliance for Health, Physical Education, Recreation and Dance (www.aahperd.org)
- National Education Association (www.nea.org)
- Association for Supervision and Curriculum Development (www.ascd.org)

PROFESSIONAL JOURNALS
- *JOPERD*
- *Strategies*
- *Educational Leadership*
- *Journal of Curriculum and Supervision*

production. Sport sociologists and sport psychologists use computers to conduct sophisticated data analysis. Fitness professionals rely on computers for record keeping. Club members punch in their personal code on a computer console next to each piece of exercise equipment. As a digital display shows weight lifted and repetitions performed, the computer keeps track as well, providing the member and the professional with a continuous record of the member's progress.

There are many interactive Web sites on the Internet that allow individuals to complete a health risk appraisal and have ready access to information they can use to modify their lifestyles. Interactive logs enable individuals to keep track of their physical activity and dietary intake, making it easy for them to track and continually monitor their fitness program from any location worldwide.

Physical education, exercise science, and sport professionals use handheld computers or Personal Digital Assistants (PDAs) to enter fitness data, analyze assessment results, and monitor attendance and participation. Handheld devices expedite the assessment process by allowing professionals to quickly enter data and then later upload the information they have collected to their desktop computer for further analysis and inclusion in their database.

As we move forward in the twenty-first century, technology will play an important role in helping physical education, exercise science, and sport professionals assess a multitude of outcome measures and to monitor the progress of participants in their programs.

SUMMARY

American education faces the challenge of preparing individuals with a wide range of abilities and from diverse backgrounds to function effectively in today's and tomorrow's world. Physical education as an integral part of the school curriculum can play a significant role in this endeavor.

Because education is a major societal institution and school physical education programs serve millions of children and youth, an understanding of education's goals and objectives is important for all physical education, exercise science, and sport professionals. Goals are broad statements of aims that reflect desired accomplishments. Objectives are more specific statements of outcomes that build progressively to the achievement of goals. *Goals 2000* identifies American educational goals for the next century. These include readiness to learn, improvement of graduation rates, increased competency in core subjects, international prominence in math and science, improvement of adult literacy, creation of a safe learning environment, professional development for teachers, and school-parent partnerships. Physical education programs in the school can help achieve these goals by enhancing school readiness, contributing to the health and vitality of students, facilitating an integrated approach to learning, and promoting lifelong learning. NCLB stresses accountability for learning.

The goals of physical education have historically been defined for school-aged populations. Today, our programs embrace a wide range of ages and settings. Contemporary physical education, exercise science, and sport emphasize the development of the whole person through participation in quality physical education, exercise science, and sport programs. The objectives of physical education, exercise science, and sport encompass four areas: fitness development, skill development, knowledge, and social-emotional development.

The past decade has seen professional efforts devoted to identifying the qualities of a physically educated person. According to NASPE, a physically educated person has learned skills to perform a variety of physical activities, is physically fit, participates regularly in physical activities, knows the benefits of involvement in physical activity, and values the contribution of physical activity to a healthy lifestyle. NASPE developed content standards for physical education and guidelines for assessment. These standards and guidelines offer professionals in all settings a valuable framework to guide their efforts.

Human behavior is often described with reference to three domains: cognitive, affective, and psychomotor domains. Taxonomies organize the objectives associated with each domain into hierarchies. These taxonomies guide professionals in designing programs to meet the needs of their participants. Physical education, exercise science, and sport programs contribute in many ways to learning in these three domains.

Assessment of learning is critical in physical education, exercise science, and sport. Assessment is a continual process that serves many purposes. These include diagnosis, prescription, classification, determination of achievement, documentation of progress, enhancement of motivation, program improvement, and professional development. There are many types of assessment methods for professionals to utilize.

Technology is increasingly influencing the assessment process. Computers have been used for record keeping, regulation of testing equipment, and data analysis. Professionals in all settings have found technology to be of great value in their endeavors.

The next chapter will discuss the role of physical education, exercise science, and sport in our society, as well as the educational reform movement and its impact on our programs.

SELF-ASSESSMENT TESTS

These tests are designed to help you determine whether you have mastered the material and competencies presented in this chapter.

1. Carefully review *Goals 2000.* How did *Goals 2000* influence your high school curriculum? What impact did it have on your physical education program? What was the contribution of your physical education program to *Goals 2000*?

   Using the information provided in Get Connected, access one of the education sites to find out the latest information on *Goals 2000.* Is the United States making progress toward the attainment of the goals?
2. Review carefully the characteristics of a physically educated person and the outcome statements. Then compare your knowledge, skills, and attitudes to the desired outcomes. Are you physically educated?
3. Reflect on your experiences in youth, interscholastic, and intercollegiate sport. How did these experiences contribute to your development in the cognitive, affective, and psychomotor domains? What changes could have been made in the conduct of the programs to further enhance development?
4. Select a future career. For each domain of learning, develop two goals and two specific objectives for participants in your program.

REFERENCES

1. US Department of Health and Human Services: Healthy people 2010: understanding and improving health, Washington, D.C., 2000, US Government Printing Office.

2. Commission on reorganization of secondary education: Cardinal principles of secondary education, Washington, D.C., 1918, US Government Printing Office.
3. Educational policies commission: The purposes of education in an American democracy, Washington, D.C., 1938, National Education Association.
4. Educational policies commission: Education for all American youth, Washington, D.C., 1944, National Education Association.
5. Association of School Administrators: Imperatives in education, Washington, D.C., 1966, Association of School Administrators.
6. Gross RE: Seven new cardinal principles, Phi Delta Kappan 60:291–293, 1978.
7. US Department of Education: The goals 2000—launching a new era in education, Washington, D.C., 1994, US Government Printing Office.
8. Children's Defense Fund: Children 1990: a report card, briefing book, and action primer, Washington, D.C., 1990, Children's Defense Fund.
9. National Center for Educational Statistics: Adult literacy in America, Washington, D.C., 1999, US Department of Education.
10. US Department of Education: US mayors support President Clinton's call for action for American education, Washington, D.C., Community Update, 49:5, 1997.
11. US Department of Education: Hispanic dropout project, Washington, D.C., 1998, US Department of Education.
12. US Department of Education: The condition of education 2000, Washington, D.C., 2001, US Department of Education.
13. US Department of Education: No child left behind, Washington, D.C., 2001, US Department of Education.
14. United States Department of Education. No child left behind overview. 2004. Available online at www.nclb.gov.
15. Sadler WC, Tentinger LG, and Wiedow GA: American 2000: implications for physical education, Physical Educator 50:77–86, 1993.
16. Corbin CB: Physical education as an agent of change. Quest 54, 182–195, 2002.
17. Siedentop D: Introduction to physical education, fitness, and sport, ed 3, Mountain View, Calif., 1998, Mayfield.
18. Bucher CA: Foundations of physical education, ed 4, St. Louis, 1964, Mosby.
19. American Association for Health, Physical Education, and Recreation: This is physical education, Washington, D.C., 1965, American Association for Health, Physical Education, and Recreation.
20. Biles F: PEPI—The physical education public information project, Journal of Health, Physical Education, and Recreation 41(7):53–55, 1971.
21. National Association for Sport and Physical Education: Definition of a physically educated person: outcomes of quality physical education programs, Reston, Va., 1990, AAHPERD.
22. National Association for Sport and Physical Education: Moving into the future: national standards for physical education: a guide to content and assessment, St. Louis, 1995, Mosby.
23. National Association for Sport and Physical Education, Moving into the future: National standards for physical education (2nd ed.), Reston, Va., 2004, AAHPERD.
24. Ziegler E: The professional's relationship to fitness for people of all ages, Journal of Physical Education, Recreation and Dance 56(1):15, 1985.
25. Bloom BS, editor: Taxonomy of educational objectives: the classification of education goals, handbook I: cognitive domain, New York, 1956, David McKay.
26. Strand B, Mauch L, and Terbizan D: The fitness education pyramid—Integrating the concepts with the technology, JOPERD 68(6):19–27, 1997.
27. Krathwohl DR, Bloom BS, and Masia BB: Taxonomy of educational objectives, handbook II: the affective domain, New York, 1964, David McKay.
28. Hellison D: Teaching personal and social responsibility in physical education. In S Silverman and C Ennis, editors, Student learning in physical education: applying research to enhance instruction, Champaign, Ill., 1996, Human Kinetics.
29. Docheff D: Character in sport and physical education—summation, JOPERD 69(2):24, 1998.
30. Gough RW: Character development—A practical strategy for emphasizing character development in sport and physical education, JOPERD 69(2):18–20, 23, 1998.

31. Harrow A: A taxonomy of the psychomotor domain, New York, 1964, David McKay.
32. Corbin CB: Becoming physically educated in the elementary school, Philadelphia, 1976, Lea & Febiger.
33. The Cooper Institute for Aerobics Research, The Fitnessgram, Dallas, Tex., 1999, The Cooper Institute for Aerobics Research.
34. HealthFirst USA, TriFit, Albuquerque, N. Mex., 2001, HealthFirst USA.

Suggested Readings

AAHPERD: Research Quarterly for Exercise and Sport. June 2000. Entire Issue.

This issue is devoted to assessment of physical activity and issues related to assessment. The status, limitations, and future directions for assessment among different population groups such as women, children, and older adults are discussed.

Anderson DR: The humanity of movement or "it's not just a gym class," Quest, 54:87–96, 2002.

Concern is raised that the emphasis on the disciplinary aspect of the fields and the emphasis on the scientific outlook have led to minimizing the humanistic features of movement.

Block BA: Literacy through movement: an organizational approach, JOPERD 72(1):39–48, 2001.

How literacy can be developed through physical education is the focus of this article. This article contains extensive charts and illustrations of how movement experiences can be designed to help promote literacy.

Corbin CB: Physical education as an agent of change. Quest 54:182–195, 2002.

Physical education must have clear objectives if it is to be an effective agent of change in our society. Because virtually all children attend school, physical education can play a significant role in enhancing the health of the nation and reversing disease trends.

Fortes, S: Climbing the walls to write in physical education. JOPERD 74(8):12–14, 2003.

Illustrates how technology and physical education activities, such as a climbing wall, can be used to create meaningful educational experiences for students that encompass the three learning domains.

Gabbei R and Hamrick D: Using physical activity homework to meet national standards, JOPERD 72(4):21–26, 33, 2001.

Physical activity homework can be used to help students achieve the NASPE content standard of exhibiting a physically active lifestyle outside of the school setting.

Gallo, AM: Assessing the affective domain. JOPERD 74(4):44–49, 2003.

Physical educators often make claims that they promote learning in the affective domain. This article offers suggestions on how to assess affective outcomes, evaluate the teaching process, and create a positive learning environment.

McBride RE and Carrillo D: Incorporating critical thinking into a secondary school wellness unit, JOPERD 71(9):20–25, 2000.

Physical education can contribute in many ways to the goals of education. This article illustrates how physical education can be used to develop critical thinking skills.

Docheff D, editor: Character in sport and physical education, JOPERD 68(9), 1997.

A five-part feature on character development, this includes information on the history of character education, physical education's impact on character development, sports' effect on character, measurement, and practical strategies for character development in physical education and sport.

National Association for Sport and Physical Education: Moving into the future national standards for physical education, Reston, Va., 2004.

National content standards and student expectations provide practitioners with a framework for their work.

Nilges L and Usnick V: The role of spatial ability in physical education and mathematics, JOPERD 71(6):29–33, 2000.

Six spatial abilities and their relationship to learning in mathematics and physical education are discussed. This article shows one of the ways that physical education can be used to contribute to educational goals.

Tannehill D, editor: Assessment Series K–12 Physical Education, National Association for Sport and Physical Education, Reston, Va., 1999.

This series provides a multitude of assessment ideas to improve student learning. Included are assessment of motor skills in elementary physical education, student responsibility and teamwork, elementary heart health, and games. Additional books in the series focus on creating rubrics for physical education, standards-based assessment of student learning, and portfolio assessment for K–12 physical education.

CHAPTER 3

ROLE IN SOCIETY AND IN EDUCATION

OBJECTIVES

After reading this chapter the student should be able to—

- Understand the changing demographics of the United States and their implications for physical education, exercise science, and sport.
- Interpret to colleagues and to the public the role of physical education, exercise science, and sport in the promotion of health and the attainment of wellness.
- Discuss the physical activity of people of all ages and the implications for physical education, exercise science, and sport.
- Discuss the current educational reform movement and its implications for school physical education programs.

Societal trends influence the role of physical education, exercise science, and sport in our society. One significant trend is the changing demographics of our population. Our society is more culturally diverse than at any other time in its history. This diversity will become even greater as we move farther into the twenty-first century. As professionals committed to enriching the lives of all people, we must, as DeSensi states, increase our "consciousness and appreciation of differences associated with heritage, characteristics, and values of people."[1]

Two other societal trends that hold implications for physical education, exercise science, and sport are the wellness movement and the fitness and physical activity movement. The wellness movement emphasizes the individual's responsibility to make informed choices that will lead to an optimal state of health. Disease prevention and health promotion are the cornerstones of this movement. Participation in physical activity by people of all ages should be encouraged. There is substantial evidence to support the value of leading a physically active lifestyle across the lifespan.

GET CONNECTED

Centers for Disease Control and Prevention presents information on a variety of health status indicators, including news, health information, and statistics. This site offers access to *Morbidity and Mortality Weekly Report.*

www.cdc.gov

Healthy People 2010 site offers information about the nation's health goals, leading health indicators, and specific objectives for the different areas, including physical activity.

www.health.gov/healthypeople/default.htm

Physical Activity and Health: A Report of the Surgeon General contains a wealth of information about physical activity and health, including information about the physical activity status and participation of different population groups.

www.cdc.gov/nccdphp/sgr/sgr.htm

United States Department of Education site provides current news and information about educational initiatives.

www.ed.gov

United States Department of Health and Human Services Office of Minority Health highlights minority health initiatives and provides links to minority health resources, including *Closing the Gap,* a newsletter on reducing disparities in health.

http://omhrc.gov

Another significant trend is the educational reform movement. During the past three decades, calls to redesign, revitalize, and strengthen the educational system have increased. The nature of the educational reforms implemented could have far-reaching consequences for the conduct of physical education and sport programs in our schools. Participation in daily physical education decreased during the 1990s. Furthermore, physical activity among children declines during adolescence. School-based programs offer us a great opportunity to address inequities in participation in physical activity and to encourage continued involvement in physical activity throughout the lifespan.

CHANGING DEMOGRAPHICS

As the twenty-first century begins, the United States is in the midst of demographic changes that will profoundly influence our future as a nation and will greatly affect the nature and conduct of physical education, exercise science, and sport programs.[2–6*] Racial and ethnic diversity grew dramatically in the United States during the last three decades of the twentieth century and will increase even more in the decades to come. Our growing diversity requires that we, as physical educators, exercise scientists, and sport leaders, be able to work effectively in cross-cultural situations. Changes within and among different population groups, such as children and the aged, determine the demand for education, health care, facilities, and other services that meet the needs of different segments of the population. This, in turn, will influence job opportunities, funding for services, and the nature and conduct of programs designed to serve these populations.

In the United States, we are living longer and healthier lives. Public health initiatives, advances in

* Data compiled from United States Department of Commerce, US Census Bureau, Census 2000 (www.census.gov); Centers for Disease Control and Prevention, National Center for Health Statistics (www.cdc.gov/nchs); National Center for Education Statistics (nces.ed.gov/); Federal Interagency Forum on Child and Family Statistics (www.childstats.gov); United States Department of Health and Human Services (www.cdc.gov).

medical science, and improvements in standards of living have contributed to dramatic improvements in the longevity of the population. At the beginning of the twentieth century, the average life expectancy in the United States was 47.3 years. In 2001, life expectancy for the U.S. population rose to an all-time high of 77.2 years. U.S. Health and Human Services Secretary Tommy G. Thompson said, "Americans on the average are living longer than ever before, and much of this is due to the progress we've made in fighting diseases that account for a majority of deaths in the country. But we can do even more by eating right, exercising regularly and taking other simple steps to promote good health and prevent serious illness and disease."[5]

During the twentieth century, life expectancy disparities narrowed, but continued to exist among population groups. In 2001, whites continued to live considerably longer than blacks. The gender gap in life expectancy narrowed but still persists, with women outliving men by over 5 years.

Improvements in health have contributed to the growth of the older population during the last century. In 1900, about 4% of the population was 65 years and older. In 2000, an estimated 35 million people or about 13% of the population was 65 years and older. The number of older Americans is projected to grow rapidly in the first half of the twenty-first century. In 2011, the "baby boom" generation, born between 1946 and 1964, will begin to turn 65. By 2030, it is projected that one in five people or 20% of the population will be 65 years of age or older. The most rapidly growing segment of the older population is the age 85 and older group. In 2000, about 2% of the population was age 85 and older. By 2050, it is projected that nearly 5% of the U.S. population will be age 85 and older.

The number of children in the United States influences the demand for schools and teachers, health care services and professionals, and other facilities and services that serve children and their families. In 2000, there were 70.4 million children or 26% of the population under the age of 18. This was a decline from the peak of 36% at the end of the "baby boom" in the twentieth century. The percentage of children in our population is projected to remain relatively stable and is estimated to comprise 24% of the population in 2020. School enrollment is projected to continue to increase slightly through 2010.

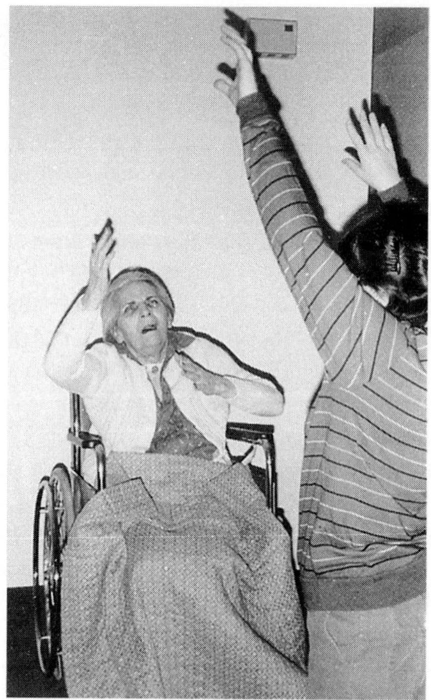

Participation in appropriate exercise can help elderly people increase their flexibility.

America is remarkable in its diversity, home to a wonderful mixture of cultures, races, and ethnicities. To facilitate the collection and analysis of information about our population, in the 1970s the federal government created broad racial and ethnic categories. According to federal classifications, blacks (African Americans), American Indians and Alaskan Natives, Asian Americans and Pacific Islanders, and white Americans (Caucasians) are races. Ethnicity is categorized as non-Hispanic or Hispanic. Hispanic or Latino can include people of any race. (See the Race and Ethnicity in the United States—Census 2000 box.) These broad categories are misleading, for they mask substantial differences among these groups. For example,

Race and Ethnicity in the United States: Census 2000

U.S. Census Race and Ethnicity Category Definitions

White	People having origins in any of the original peoples of Europe, the Middle East, or North Africa
Black or **African American**	People having origins in any of the Black racial groups of Africa.
American Indian and **Alaska Native**	People having origins in any of the original peoples of North and South America (including Central America), and who maintain tribal affiliation or community attachment
Asian	People having origins in any of the original peoples of the Far East, Southeast Asia, or the Indian subcontinent
Native Hawaiian and **Other Pacific Islander**	People having origins in any of the original peoples of Hawaii, Guam, Samoa, or other Pacific Islands
Some other race	People who were unable to identify with the five categories
Hispanic or **Latino**	Persons of Cuban, Mexican, Puerto Rican, South or Central American, or other Spanish culture or origin regardless of race
Non-Hispanic	Persons who are not of Hispanic origin regardless of race

Population by Race and Hispanic Origin

Race and Hispanic Origin	Percent
RACE	
Total population	**100.00**
One Race	97.6
White	75.2
Black or African American	12.3
American Indian and Alaskan Native	.9
Asian	3.6
Native Hawaiian and Other Pacific Islander	.1
Some other race	5.5
Two Races	2.4
HISPANIC or LATINO	
Total population	**100.00**
Hispanic or Latino	12.5
Not Hispanic or Latino	87.5

From United States Census Bureau, *Overview of Race and Hispanic Origin Census 2000 Brief,* US Census Bureau, Washington D.C., March 2001.

within the classification Asian Americans and Pacific Islanders are more than 40 ethnic groups with over 100 different spoken languages. Looking beyond these broad classifications for race and ethnicity helps us see how truly diverse our nation is.

As a nation, our cultural diversity continues to grow. The surge in immigration increased our diversity tremendously. The 2000 Census data revealed that 12.5% of the population was Hispanic, which can be people of any race, and 87.5% of the population was non-Hispanic. With respect to race, 75.2% of the population was white, 12.3% of the population was African American, .9% American Indian or Alaskan Native, 3.6% Asian, and .1% Native Hawaiian and other Pacific Islanders. About 2% of the population identified themselves as multiracial. By the year 2010, projections indicate that ethnic and racial minority groups will account for 32% of the population compared to 20% of the population in 1980. The Hispanic population is the fastest growing of any other racial and ethnic group, and it is estimated that 25% of the population will be Hispanic by the year 2050.

Changes in the racial and ethnic diversity of the United States are reflected in all age groups. For example, the elderly are becoming more racially and ethnically diverse. In 1994, only 1 person in 10 was a minority but this should climb to 2 in every 10 persons by 2050. The proportion of elderly who are Hispanic is expected to rise from 4% to 16% over the same period.

More dramatic changes are expected in the school-age population. In 1999, 38% of public school students were minorities, an increase from 22% in 1972. Black and Hispanic students accounted for 16.5% and 16.2%, respectively, of public school enrollment. In 2050 it is projected that Hispanic children will comprise 31% of all children, compared to 43% and 16% for whites and African Americans, respectively.

The changes in the racial and ethnic composition of student enrollments have altered the diversity of language and culture in the nation's schools. In 1999, 2.6 million school-age children spoke a language other than English at home and had difficulty in speaking English; this is double the number in 1979. There are several school systems in the United States where more than 100 languages are spoken by the students. The variety in culture and language enriches the learning environment while at the same time creating great challenges for the schools.

Socioeconomic status exerts a significant influence on many aspects of an individual's life including health status, educational attainment, and future employment. Poverty is associated with poor health outcomes for all ages, including higher rates of mortality. Unfortunately, many adults and children live in poverty today, and poverty rates vary by age, sex, race, ethnicity, family composition, and employment. Poverty level differs by the size of the household. The 2003 poverty threshold was an annual income below $9,573 for a single person or below $18,979 for a family of four.[7] In 2003, 12.5% of the population or 35.9 million people lived below the poverty level. The poverty rate for white non-Hispanics was 8.0%, for blacks 24.1%, for Hispanics 21.8%, and Asians and Pacific Islanders 12.5%.[7]

During the twentieth century remarkable changes in our nation's demographics occurred. Projections for the twenty-first century show a future in which our society will become increasingly diverse, with this diversity being reflected in all age groups. Our longevity will continue to increase, and our elderly population will reach an all-time high. The population of children will remain relatively stable. Poverty rates decreased in the twentieth century, but today still too many of our society live in poor socioeconomic conditions and suffer adverse consequences with respect to health and their quality of life as a result.

What Are the Implications of These Changing Demographics for Physical Education, Exercise Science, and Sport?

The many demographic changes that are occurring in the twenty-first century present physical educators, exercise scientists, and sport leaders with great challenges and with extraordinary opportunities. As we reflect on these demographic and societal changes, we must ask ourselves what we can do to provide opportunities for participation in physical activity for all people. How can we involve a greater number of older persons in our programs? How can we design programs that are sensitive to the values and needs of different racial and ethnic populations? How can we provide access to our programs for individuals living in poverty? How do we reach underserved populations and, most importantly, what is our commitment to do so? Attainment of our goal of lifespan participation in physical activity for all people requires that we do much more than we are currently doing to reach people of all ages, socioeconomic backgrounds, and different population groups.

Our nation's increasing cultural diversity makes it imperative that physical education, exercise science, and sport professionals reflect carefully on their view of cultural diversity and their commitment to providing opportunities for lifelong involvement in physical activity for all people. De Sensi defines cultural diversity as the "differences associated with gender, race, national origin, ethnicity, social class, religion, age, and ability/disability, but it can also be extended to include differences in personality, sexual orientation, veteran status, physical appearance, marital status, and parental status."[1] De Sensi's broad definition embraces many different groups. As you reflect on this definition, do you feel prepared to work with culturally diverse populations, whether in a school, community, work site, health care, or private setting? Are you culturally competent?

Culture plays a complex, significant role in the health and well-being of people of all ages. Culture influences an individual's health, beliefs, behaviors, activities, access to care, adherence to programs, and treatment outcomes. Communication between the professional and the client/patient/student is influenced by cultural norms, including norms related to language used and usage, eye contact, personal space, expression of symptoms and concerns, openness or extent of disclosure, and degree of formality in the interaction. Because health is significantly influenced by cultural beliefs, cultural issues should be a major consideration in the design and implementation of health promotion and prevention services, including physical activity programs.

The U.S. Department of Health and Human Service Office of Minority Health defines cultural and linguistic competence as "a set of congruent behaviors, attitudes and policies that come together in a system, agency or among professionals that enables effective work in cross-cultural situations. 'Culture' refers to integrated patterns of human behavior that include the language, thoughts, communications, actions, customs, beliefs, values, and institutions of racial, ethnic, religious or social groups. 'Competence' implies having the capacity to function effectively as an individual and an organization within the context of the cultural beliefs, behaviors and needs presented by consumers and their communities."[8]

How do you achieve cultural competency? The U.S. Department of Health and Human Services Bureau of Primary Health Care publication *Cultural Competency: A Journey*[9] states that achieving cultural competency is a journey, an ongoing developmental process of personal reflection and growth. The journey begins with an awareness of and reflection on your own cultural heritage, your values, beliefs, biases, and prejudices and how they may affect your perceptions and interactions with people of other cultures. Cultural competency requires thoughtful examination of your own cultural heritage and the privileges and disadvantages associated with your culture. It necessitates understanding how power, privilege, oppression, discrimination, stereotypes, and prejudice influence opportunities for different cultural groups. Gaining knowledge of other cultural beliefs, values, and behaviors of other cultures, recognizing that people of different cultures have different ways of communicating and behaving, and learning another language are part of the journey toward cultural competency.

However, there is more to cultural competency than just being knowledgeable about different cultures or being able to speak a second language. The United States Administration on Aging guidebook *Achieving Cultural Competence* states,

> To achieve cultural competency, professionals must first have a sense of compassion and respect for people who are culturally different. Then, practitioners can learn behaviors that are congruent with cultural competence. Just learning the behavior is not enough. Underlying the behavior must be an attitudinal set of behavior skills and moral responsibility. It is not about the things one does. It is about fundamental attitudes. When a person has an inherent caring, appreciation, and respect for others, they can display warmth, empathy, and genuineness. This then enables them to have culturally congruent behaviors and attitudes. When these three elements intersect, practitioners can exemplify cultural competence in a manner that recognizes, values, and affirms cultural differences among their clients.[10]

The increased recognition of the important role that culture plays in health and the overwhelming disparities in the health status of minorities when compared to whites led the U.S. Department of Health and Human Services Office of Minority Health (OMH) to develop national standards for culturally competent care. These standards for culturally and linguistically appropriate services (CLAS) serve as guidelines to improve services to underserved populations. They help ensure that persons entering the health care system, regardless of their race or ethnicity, receive equal, fair, and quality care that is compatible with their cultural health beliefs, practices, and preferred language.

During the twenty-first century, physical education, exercise science, and sport professionals will assume a greater role in health promotion and disease prevention as the role of physical activity in improving health, preventing disease, and extending the length and enhancing the quality of life becomes even more widely accepted. The health disparities among different population groups, as reflected in life expectancy, are significant. The United States Bureau of Primary Health Care views cultural competence as an essential component of their program "100% Access, 0 Disparities," which seeks to eliminate health disparities among underserved populations by increasing access to quality treatment and health promotion programs.[11] As physical education, exercise science, and sport professionals, cultural competence is likewise critical to our efforts to promote lifespan involvement in physical activity for all people.

When professionals practice in a culturally competent way, they design and implement programs that appropriately serve people of diverse cultures in a manner that affirms participants' worth and dignity. Programs incorporate the values, traditions, and customs of the cultural group. Members of the cultural group are involved in meaningful ways in the creation and conduct of the health promotion/disease prevention program. Professionals respect individual rights, use effective communication skills that convey respect and sensitivity, and appreciate how diversity enriches our

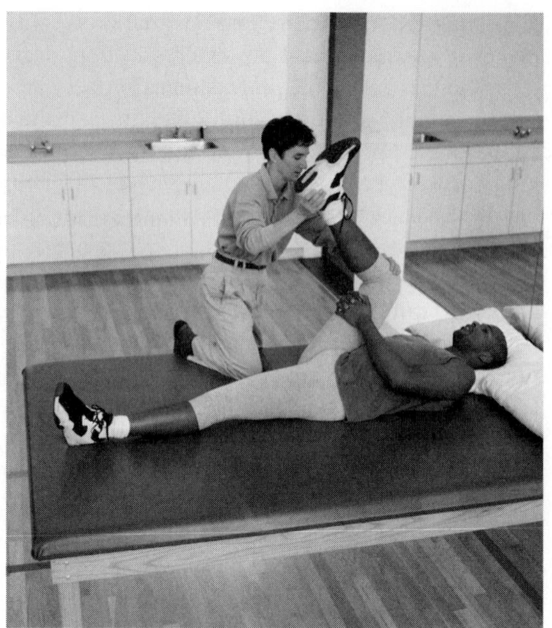

Cultural competency is important for athletic trainers because it can enhance treatment outcomes.

lives. When the culture of a specific population group or community is incorporated into programs, professionals are more likely to be effective in their efforts.

Racial and linguistic minorities are underrepresented in education, health promotion and health care occupations, as well as in physical education, exercise science, and sport occupations. The majority of educators and health professionals are from the white Anglo culture, the dominant culture in our society. Are you sensitive to the fact that cultures different from the dominant culture may suffer oppression, discrimination, and lack of access to many of the opportunities enjoyed by the dominant culture? Are you willing to work toward social justice and elimination of inequalities?

As a professional in the field, you need to recognize how culture influences an individual's behavior and worldview. At times, you may work with individuals from a different culture than your own. For example, minorities are underrepresented in athletic training, an allied health profession. According to the National Collegiate Athletic Association (NCAA), only 5% of the Division I head athletic trainers are African Americans. Yet, at the Division I level, 23% of athletes are African Americans.[12] It is likely that athletic trainers will be working with athletes from different cultures than their own. Ford writes, "Patients' cultures influence their perception of care, compliance, communication, and the injury or illness assessment and management process."[13] When cultural competence is an important part of clinical practice, a patient's culture is considered in the assessment, delivery of treatment, and development of effective management plans. Ford emphasizes that optimal outcomes are achieved when athletic trainers respond with sensitivity to cultural issues.[13]

Within the school setting, there is a lot of diversity among students. However, there is significantly less diversity among faculty and staff. Currently, in the elementary and secondary schools, 35% of the students are children of color. Yet the majority of teachers are White Americans.[14] Only 13% of teachers are minorities.[14] Given the diversity inherent in the school setting, it is important that physical educators have the opportunity to develop the skills to work successfully with students from different social, ethnic, and cultural backgrounds as well as students with different abilities. According to Burden, Hodge, O'Bryant, and Harrison, physical education professional preparation programs have a "responsibility to implement diversity training such that novice teachers are trained and socialized with culturally relevant content knowledge, pedagogy and management skills and multiple experiences teaching culturally, linguistically, and ethnically diverse learners."[15] Such training is critical if we are to achieve our goals of eliminating disparities in physical activity levels, improve the health of participants in our programs, and socialize our learners into being physically active throughout their lifespan.[15]

Cultural competency is essential to the achievement of lifespan involvement in physical activity for all people. The significant and complex role that culture plays in the health and well-being of people of all ages makes it important that physical education, exercise science, and sport professionals develop cultural competency. Understanding culture helps professionals appreciate cultural differences and utilize their knowledge of the strengths and beliefs of different groups to achieve positive health outcomes and avoid stereotypes and biases that limit services and further contribute to health disparities among different groups. When professionals practice in culturally competent ways, they recognize, value, and appreciate cultural differences.

WELLNESS MOVEMENT

The twentieth century saw a gradual, epidemiologic transition from infectious to chronic disease as the leading causes of death. In 1900, the leading causes of death were influenza, pneumonia, tuberculosis, and gastrointestinal problems (e.g., diarrhea). Life expectancy was 47.3 years. Half a century later, in 1950, there was a phenomenal rise in life expectancy to 68 years. The development of antibiotics, the availability of vaccines, and improvements in housing, sanitation, food and water supplies, and diet were instrumental in achieving this dramatic gain. In 2000, the leading causes of death were chronic diseases, specifically heart disease, cancer, and stroke.[16]

As this shift from infectious to chronic diseases occurred, evidence accumulated regarding the role behavioral risk factors play in disease and early mortality. Health risk factors can be categorized as those factors that are modifiable and those that are not. Nonmodifiable risk factors are age, sex, and heredity. Modifiable risk factors include smoking, physical inactivity, diet, obesity, and alcohol use. Modifiable risk factors play a significant role in the occurrence of chronic diseases.

In the United States, the Centers for Disease Control and Prevention reports that "chronic diseases—such as cardiovascular disease (primarily heart disease and stroke), cancer, and diabetes—are among the most prevalent, costly, and preventable of all health problems."[17] Chronic diseases account for about 70% of all deaths and approximately 75% of health care costs each year.[17] More than 1.7

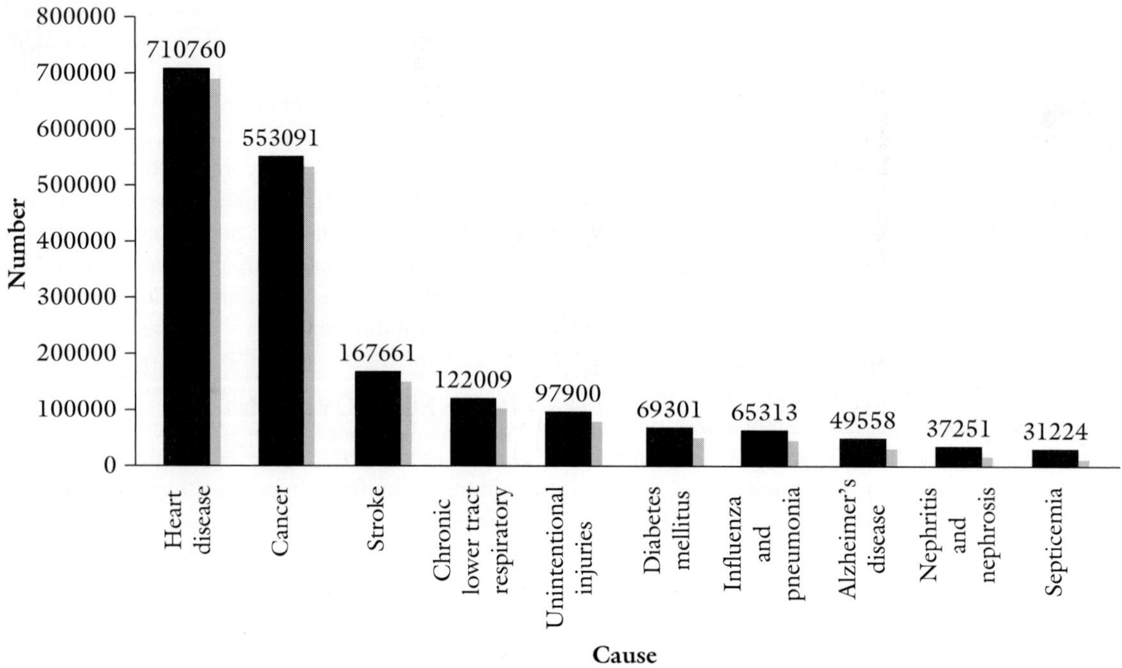

Figure 3-1 Leading causes of death in U.S. in 2000.
Data from American Cancer Society, Statistics for 2004.

million people or 7 out of 10 Americans die each year from a chronic disease.[17] Moreover, millions of individuals suffer due to disability associated with chronic disease and pain, decreasing their quality of life. Additionally, 1 in every 10 Americans experiences major limitations in activity due to chronic disabling conditions.[17]

Two of the most prevalent chronic diseases are cardiovascular disease and cancer, the number one and number two causes of death in the United States. Cardiovascular disease, which includes coronary and congestive heart disease, stroke, and hypertensive disease, is the number one killer of males and females in the United States. Nearly 930,000 people died from cardiovascular disease in 2001.[17] Physical inactivity, poor nutrition, obesity, and tobacco use contribute to cardiovascular disease. Sedentary persons have twice as much risk of cardiovascular disease as those who are active. Smokers have twice as much risk of cardiovascular disease as nonsmokers. Although the risk for inactivity and smoking are similar, the prevalence of inactivity in the nation is greater than the incidence of smoking. Cancer is the number two cause of death in the United States. According to the American Cancer Society, approximately one-third of the over 500,000 cancer deaths are related to poor nutrition, physical inactivity, overweight, obesity, and other lifestyle factors (see Figure 3-1).[18] Addressing these modifiable risk factors will lead to improvement in the health of the nation.

The top three modifiable causes of death in the United States are tobacco use, poor diet and physical inactivity, and alcohol consumption (see Figure 3-2).[19] Tobacco use is the leading cause of death, and physical inactivity and poor diet the second most prevalent cause. The Centers for Disease Control and Prevention (CDC) reported that deaths due to poor diet and physical inactivity rose by 33 percent over the last decade.[19] Together, inactivity and unhealthy eating are responsible for at least 400,000 preventable deaths each year; to-

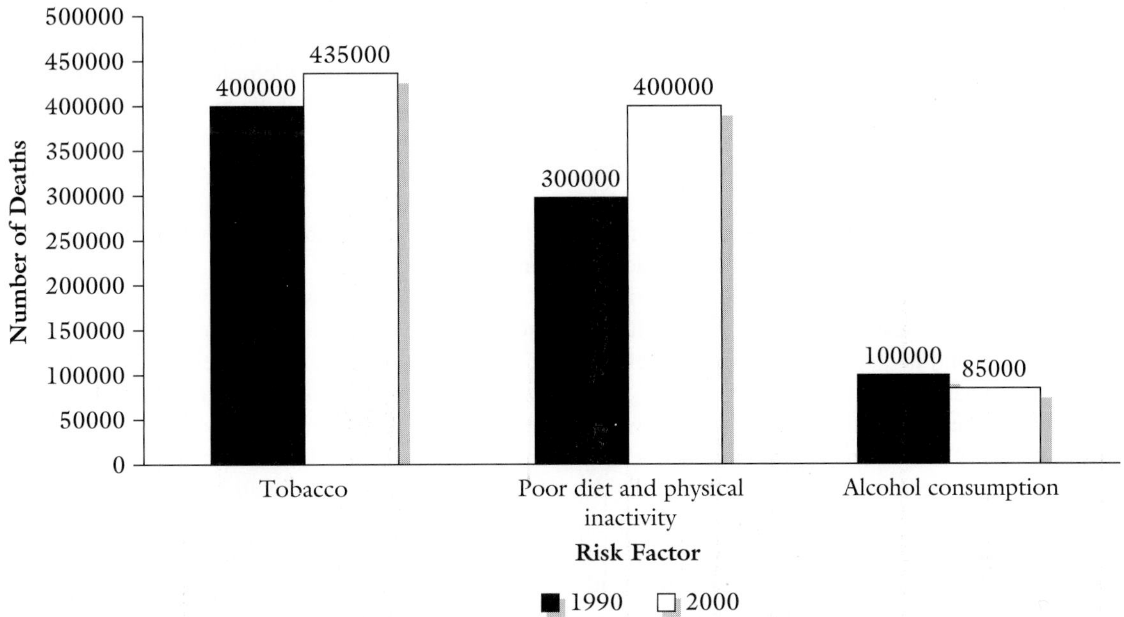

Figure 3-2 Top three modifiable risk factors and associated deaths in the U.S. for 1990 and 2000.
Data from United States Department of Health and Human Services, Study shows poor diet, inactivity close to becoming leading preventable cause of death, March 9, 2004.

bacco is a factor in 435,000 deaths each year.[20] Director of the CDC Dr. Julie Gerberding stated, "The fact that more than a third of deaths in America each year are related to smoking, poor eating habits and physical inactivity is both tragic and unacceptable, because these are largely preventable behaviors."[19] Poor eating habits and physical inactivity play a major role in obesity.

Obesity poses severe health risks to people of all ages. Obesity is closely linked to coronary heart disease, stroke, type 2 diabetes, and certain types of cancer, such as colon cancer. Obesity increases mortality from all causes. Unfortunately, the prevalence of overweight and obesity continues to rise. In 1976, 47% of adults were considered overweight or obese.[21] This rose to 56% in 1994 and to a high of 64% in 2000.[21] The problem of obesity and overweight is not limited to adults. The percentage of children who are overweight has tripled since 1980.[21] About 15% of children and adolescents age 6 to 19 years are overweight. From the perspective of public health, this is of great concern.[21] CDC Director Dr. Julie Gerberding notes that many children who are overweight grow up to be overweight or obese adults, placing them at greater risk for health problems such as heart disease or diabetes.[19] It is estimated that half of the youngsters who are overweight as children will carry the burden and risks of overweight into adulthood.[18] Seventy percent of overweight adolescents will remain overweight as adults.[18]

Physical inactivity is a risk factor for many chronic diseases, such as cardiovascular disease and cancer. It is also a contributing factor in obesity and overweight. In 2001, at least half of adults did not engage in the recommended amount of physical activity (minimum of 30 minutes of moderate-intensity activity on most days of the week).[22] Physical activity is greater among children and adolescents. More than 60% of high schoolers engaged in vigorous physical activity, and more than 25% in moderate physical activity on a regular basis.[23] However, offsetting this active involvement is the increasing amount of time adolescents devote to sedentary pursuits such as television watching and using computers. Nearly 40% of students reported watching television three or more hours a day.[23] Inactive youths are more likely to grow up to be sedentary as adults. Regular physical activity contributes to good health and reduces the morbidity and mortality from many chronic diseases. However, despite the known benefits, too many adults and youth are sedentary and not active enough to achieve health benefits. The high incidence of physical inactivity as well as obesity in both children and adults must be addressed if the health of the nation is to improve.

During the twentieth century, our view of health changed. Traditionally the public viewed good health as freedom from disease. If an individual was not ill, he or she was considered healthy. This perspective changed during the twentieth century. While it is generally agreed that not being ill is one part of being healthy, health can also be defined in terms of being well. According to the World Health Organization (WHO), health is a "state of complete physical, mental, and social well-being and not merely the absence of disease and infirmity."[24] Health, then, is not solely concerned with one's physical state; it extends beyond concern with the body to include emotional and social well-being.

In the later part of the twentieth century, the holistic approach to health grew in popularity. The holistic approach is an even broader approach to health than presented in the WHO definition. Besides encompassing the physical, mental, and social dimensions of health, holistic health also incorporates the intellectual and spiritual dimensions of well-being. Holistic health focuses on the whole person. Individuals who are healthy, according to the holistic definition of health, are said to have achieved a high level of wellness.

Wellness is a state of optimal health and well-being. It is living life to the fullest and maximizing one's potential as a whole person. Wellness incorporates five different components: physical wellness, emotional wellness, social wellness, intellectual wellness, and spiritual wellness. Physical wellness encompasses physical fitness and proper nutrition. Emotional wellness focuses on emotional stability and managing stress effectively. Social wellness emphasizes the development of interpersonal skills and healthy, fulfilling relationships. Intellectual wellness is characterized by sound decision-making skills, intellectual growth, and values. Spiritual wellness takes on different meanings according to the beliefs of the individual.

Wellness emphasizes individuals taking personal responsibility for their health and leading a lifestyle that enhances their well-being. However, while focusing on individual responsibility, it is important to recognize that a multitude of forces—environmental, genetic, societal, and personal—interact to affect one's well-being. Living conditions, heredity, and societal conditions such as poverty and discrimination also exert a significant influence on one's health and well-being.

Americans today are taking a more active role in protecting and enhancing their health. There is a growing realization that our health and our quality of life are significantly influenced by the manner in which we live our lives. Many lifestyle choices we make, whether to smoke tobacco or to exercise on a regular basis, influence our potential for health, function, and well-being both on a daily basis and across our lifespan. This realization is accompanied by a greater understanding of the important role of personal responsibility—that is, informed and responsible behavior—in achieving good health, both on a personal and national level.

During the 1980s and 1990s, societal interest in promoting health and preventing disease increased. The accumulation of evidence supporting the fact that changes in behavior could reduce individuals' risks of disease, increase their span of healthy life, and improve their quality of life stimulated the growth of health promotion and disease prevention initiatives. These health initiatives set forth ambitious plans for improving the nation's health by the end of the twentieth century. The first document, *Healthy People: The Surgeon General's Report on Health Promotion and Disease Prevention,*[25] was released in 1979 and established national goals for improving health. It focused on

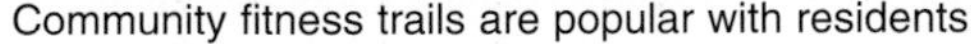
Community fitness trails are popular with residents.

reducing premature deaths and preserving independence for older adults. In 1980, *Promoting Health/Preventing Disease: Objectives for the Nation*[26] established 226 public health objectives to be achieved by 1990 that would lead to the accomplishment of the nation's health goals. In 1990, the Department of Health and Human Services released *Healthy People 2000: National Health Promotion and Disease Prevention Objectives,*[27] which identified health improvement goals and objectives to be achieved by the year 2000.

Healthy People 2000 sought to significantly improve the nation's health through a comprehensive emphasis on disease prevention and health promotion initiatives. *Healthy People 2000* had three broad health goals: to increase the span of healthy life, to reduce disparities in health among population groups, and to achieve access to preventive services for all Americans.

During the past two decades, health promotion and disease prevention initiatives resulted in dramatic progress in improving some aspects of the nation's health. Infant mortality rates significantly declined, childhood vaccinations rose to an all-time high, and death rates for coronary heart disease and stroke decreased.[28] However much more needs to be done. Heart disease remains the nation's number one killer, the incidence of diabetes continues to rise, HIV/AIDS continues to be a serious health problem, and all too often mental health disorders go undiagnosed and untreated.[28] Smoking among adolescents has increased during the past decade.[28] Obesity in adults has increased 50%, and at least half of the adults fail to engage in the recommended amount of physical activity to realize health benefits;[21] both obesity and inactivity contribute significantly to heart disease and other chronic health conditions. Medical and health professionals are greatly concerned about the increase in obesity among children and youth and their sedentary lifestyle.

The latest report, *Healthy People 2010,*[28] seeks to improve the health of the nation through a comprehensive emphasis on health promotion and disease prevention. *Healthy People 2010* recognizes that "individual health is closely linked to community health—the health of the community and the environment in which individuals live, work, and play. Likewise, community health is profoundly affected by the collective beliefs, attitudes, and behaviors of everyone who lives in the community."[28] The underlying premise of *Healthy People 2010* is

Healthy People 2010 Focus Areas and Goals

Focus Area	Goal
1. Access to Quality Health Services	Improve access to comprehensive, high-quality health care services.
2. Arthritis, Osteoporosis, and Chronic Back Conditions	Prevent illness and disability related to arthritis and other rheumatic conditions, osteoporosis, and chronic back conditions.
3. Cancer	Reduce the number of new cancer cases as well as the illness, disability, and death caused by cancer.
4. Chronic Kidney Disease	Reduce the new cases of chronic kidney disease and its complications, disability, death, and economic costs.
5. Diabetes	Through prevention programs, reduce the disease and economic burden of diabetes, and improve the quality of life for all persons who have or are at risk for diabetes.
6. Disabilities and Secondary Conditions	Promote the health of people with disabilities, prevent secondary conditions, and eliminate disparities between people with and without disabilities in the U.S. population.
7. Educational and Community-Based Programs	Increase the quality, availability, and effectiveness of educational and community-based programs designed to prevent disease and improve health and quality of life.
8. Environmental Health	Promote health for all through a healthy environment.
9. Family Planning	Improve pregnancy planning and spacing and prevent unintended pregnancy.
10. Food Safety	Reduce foodborne illnesses.
11. Health Communication	Use communication strategically to improve health.
12. Heart Disease and Stroke	Improve cardiovascular health and quality of life through the prevention, detection, and treatment of risk factors; early identification and treatment of heart attacks and strokes; and prevention of recurrent cardiovascular events.
13. HIV	Prevent human immunodeficiency virus (HIV) infection and its related illness and death.
14. Immunization and Infectious Diseases	Prevent disease, disability, and death from infectious diseases, including vaccine-preventable diseases.

that the health of the individual is virtually inseparable from the health of the community and that the health of every community determines the overall health of the nation.[28] From this premise comes the vision for *Healthy People 2010*—"Healthy People in Healthy Communities."

Healthy People 2010 is a blueprint for improving the health of individuals and the health status of the nation during the first decade of the twenty-first century. *Healthy People 2010* has two overarching goals to be achieved within the next 10 years:

- Increase quality and years of healthy life
- Eliminate health disparities

These goals reflect our nation's changing demographics—the facts that our population is growing older and is becoming increasingly diverse. The goals provide a general focus and direc-

Healthy People 2010 Focus Areas and Goals (*continued*)

Focus Area	Goal
15. Injury and Violence Prevention	Reduce injuries, disabilities, and deaths due to unintentional injuries and violence.
16. Maternal, Infant, and Child Health	Improve the health and well-being of women, infants, children, and families.
17. Medical Product Safety	Ensure the safe and effective use of medical products.
18. Mental Health and Mental Disorders	Improve mental health and ensure access to appropriate, quality mental health services.
19. Nutrition and Overweight	Promote health and reduce chronic disease associated with diet and weight.
20. Occupational Safety	Promote the health and safety of people at work through prevention and early intervention.
21. Oral Health	Prevent and control oral and craniofacial diseases, conditions, and injuries and improve access to related services.
22. Physical Activity and Fitness	Improve health, fitness, and quality of life through daily physical activity.
23. Public Health Infrastructure	Ensure that federal, tribal, state, and local health agencies have the infrastructure to provide essential public health services effectively.
24. Respiratory Diseases	Promote respiratory health through better prevention, detection, treatment, and education efforts.
25. Sexually Transmitted Diseases (STDs)	Promote responsible sexual behaviors, strengthen community capacity, and increase access to quality services to prevent sexually transmitted diseases and their complications.
26. Substance Abuse	Reduce substance abuse to protect the health, safety, and quality of life for all, especially children.
27. Tobacco Use	Reduce illness, disability, and death related to tobacco use and exposure to secondhand smoke.
28. Vision and Hearing	Improve the visual and hearing health of the nation through prevention, early detection, treatment, and rehabilitation.

From US Department of Health and Human Services. *Healthy People 2010.* 2nd ed. With Understanding and Improving Health and Objectives for Improving Health. 2 vols. Washington, D.C.: US Government Printing Office, November 2000.

tion for our disease prevention and health promotion efforts. To accomplish these goals, 467 specific objectives in 28 focus areas were established (see the *Healthy People 2010* Focus Areas and Goals box.) Ten leading health indicators were identified in order to track the nation's progress toward achievement of the two *Healthy People 2010* goals.

The first goal of *Healthy People 2010* is to help individuals of all ages live longer and improve their quality of life. Life expectancy increased dramatically in the twentieth century. Every age group experienced an increase in life expectancy. Individuals who are 65 years old today can expect to live an average of 18 more years to the age of 83, and those persons who are 75 years old can expect to live an average of 11 more years to the age of 86 years. By 2050, life expectancy is projected to increase to 79.7 years for males and 84.3 years for females. However, as previously discussed in this chapter, there are significant disparities in life expectancy between different population groups in the United States, and these disparities must be eliminated.

As strides are made toward increasing life expectancy, efforts must also be directed toward increasing the quality of life. Quality of life is a subjective measure and reflects one's overall sense of happiness and satisfaction. According to *Healthy People 2010,* health-related quality of life "reflects a personal sense of physical and mental health and the ability to react to factors in the physical and social environment."[28] The subjective nature of health-related quality of life makes it difficult to measure. One means of assessment is to measure the years of healthy life, that is, years of life spent in optimal health without acute or chronic limitations. From 1990 to 1996, years of healthy life increased from 64.0 years to 64.2 years. During the same time period life expectancy increased a full year. Progress in improving the healthy years of life is not as rapid as progress in improving life expectancy.

Although remarkable gains in life expectancy and years of healthy life have been made in the past two decades, there is substantial need for improvement. *Healthy People 2010* seeks to increase life expectancy and enhance the quality of life by helping all individuals gain knowledge, develop and sustain motivation, and participate in health promotion and disease prevention programs. *Healthy People 2010* encourages local communities and states to develop initiatives that promote healthy behaviors, create healthy environments, and increase access by all people to high-quality health care.

The second goal of *Healthy People 2010* is to eliminate health disparities among different demographic groups in the United States. Health disparities are differences that occur by gender, race and ethnicity, education and income, disability, geographic location, or sexual orientation. Health disparities are reflected in the overall health of the nation, with one of the most telling disparities being the difference in life expectancy for various demographic groups.

There are significant gender differences in health between men and women. Men have a higher death rate for each of the 10 leading causes (e.g., cardiovascular disease, cancer) of death; their overall life expectancy is 6 years less than that of women. Some of these differences are obviously gender specific, such as deaths due to cervical and prostate cancers.

Significant health disparities exist among racial and ethnic groups. *Healthy People 2010* identified several disparities among different population groups:

- African Americans have an infant mortality rate that is more than twice the rate for whites.
- The death rate from heart disease for African Americans is more than 40% higher than for whites.
- African Americans' death rates for all cancers are 30% higher than for whites.
- Compared to whites, the death rate for African Americans from HIV/AIDS is seven times higher.
- African Americans' rates of homicide are six times higher than that of whites.
- Hispanics have higher rates of high blood pressure and obesity than non-Hispanic whites.
- Hispanics are almost twice as likely to die from diabetes as non-Hispanic whites.
- American Indians and Alaskan Natives have an infant mortality rate that is nearly double that for whites.
- American Indians' and Alaskan Natives' rate of diabetes is more than double the rate for whites.
- American Indians and Alaskan Natives have disproportionately higher death rates from unintentional injuries and suicide.

Elimination of disparities among races and ethnicities is critical to our nation's well-being. To improve the health of the nation, we must improve the health of all our people.

Differences in income and education are associated with disparities in life expectancy and disease, including heart disease, diabetes, obesity, and low birth weight. Population groups with the worst health status have the highest poverty rates and the least education. Those with higher incomes and higher education typically are healthier. For example, among white men aged 65, those with the highest incomes were expected to live 3 years longer than those in the lowest income groups.[28] Activity limitation caused by chronic disease occurred three times more frequently in people in the lowest income group compared to people in the highest income group. Higher incomes allow people increased access to quality medical care and opportunities to engage in health-promoting behaviors. The greater the level of education achieved, the better the health status. For example, among adults aged 25 to 64 years, the overall death rate for those adults with less than 12 years of education is more than twice the death rate for those with 13 or more years of education.[28]

Disparities in health are also associated with disabilities, geographic location, and sexual orientation. People with disabilities have fewer days of vitality, lower rates of physical activity, and higher rates of obesity compared to persons without disabilities.[28] Geographic location influences health. Rural populations experience higher rates of heart disease, cancer, diabetes, and injury-related deaths than people living in urban areas.[28] Rural populations are also less likely to exercise regularly.[28] A diverse community with a variety of health concerns, the homosexual population faces major health issues. For gay men, major health issues are HIV/AIDS, substance abuse, depression, and suicide. For example, gay male adolescents are more than twice as likely to commit suicide than their heterosexual peers.[28] It appears that lesbians have higher rates of stress compared to heterosexual women.[28]

The exact cause of health disparities among specific population groups is hard to identify. These disparities are believed to be the result of the complex interaction of a variety of social, behavioral, cultural, environmental, gender, economic, physiological, and genetic factors. What is clear, however, is that the overall health of our nation depends upon the elimination of health disparities among population groups. A multitude of factors must be understood and addressed in order to design, implement, and evaluate health promotion and disease prevention interventions to improve health and the quality of life.

Achieving the *Healthy People 2010* overarching goals of increasing quality and years of healthy life and eliminating health disparities represents a range of health challenges that must be addressed by individuals, communities, states, and the nation. Achievement of health equity requires a multidisciplinary approach. According to *Healthy People 2010,* the "greatest opportunities for reducing health disparities are in empowering individuals to make informed health care decisions and in promoting community-wide safety, education, and access to health care."[28] The guiding principle of *Healthy People 2010* is that every person—regardless of age, gender, race or ethnicity, income, education, geographic location, disability, and sexual orientation—deserve equal access to comprehensive, culturally competent health care.[28]

These goals established the health agenda for the United States. To accomplish these goals and monitor progress, 467 specific objectives were developed and organized into 28 focus areas, each representing an important public health area and each containing a goal, the achievement of which will contribute to the overall health of the nation. Achieving the vision of "Healthy People in Healthy Communities" requires individuals and families making healthy lifestyle choices for themselves. Communities and businesses are encouraged to support health-promotion initiatives in the school, work site, and community setting.

Leading health indicators were established to help individuals, institutions, and communities plan actions to improve health and to provide a way to measure progress throughout the decade. Each of the 10 leading health indicators have been paired with *Healthy People 2010* objectives to facilitate the tracking of progress. (See the Leading Health Indicators box.)

Healthy People 2010 selected physical activity as both a leading health indicator and as a focus area, thus affirming the significant benefits and critical contribution of physical activity to good health. During the 1990s, there was a shift in focus

Leading Health Indicators

Indicator		Objective
1. Physical Activity	**22.2**	Increase the proportion of adults who engage regularly, preferably daily, in moderate physical activity for at least 30 minutes per day.
	22-7	Increase the proportion of adolescents who engage in vigorous physical activity that promotes cardiorespiratory fitness 3 or more days per week for 20 or more minutes per occasion.
2. Overweight and Obesity	**19.2**	Reduce the proportion of adults who are obese.
	19.3c	Reduce the proportion of children and adolescents who are overweight or obese.
3. Tobacco Use	**27-1a**	Reduce cigarette smoking by adults.
	27-2b	Reduce cigarette smoking by adolescents.
4. Substance Abuse	**26-10a**	Increase the proportion of adolescents not using alcohol or any illicit drugs during the past 30 days.
	26-10c	Reduce the proportion of adults using any illicit drug during the past 30 days.
	26-11c	Reduce the proportion of adults engaging in binge drinking of alcoholic beverages during the past month.
5. Responsible Sexual Behavior	**13-6a**	Increase the proportion of sexually active persons who use condoms.
	25-11	Increase the proportion of adolescents who abstain from sexual intercourse or use condoms if currently sexually active.
6. Mental Health	**18-9b**	Increase the proportion of adults with recognized depression who receive treatment.
7. Injury and Violence	**15-15a**	Reduce deaths caused by motor vehicle crashes.
	15-32	Reduce homicides.
8. Environmental Quality	**8-1a**	Reduce the proportion of persons exposed to air that does not meet the U.S. Environmental Protection Agency's health-based standards for ozone.
	27-10	Reduce the proportion of nonsmokers exposed to environmental tobacco smoke.
9. Immunization	**14-24a**	Increase the proportion of young children who receive all vaccines that have been recommended for universal administration for at least 5 years.
	14-29a,b	Increase the proportion of noninstitutionalized adults who are vaccinated annually against influenza and ever vaccinated against pneumococcal disease.
10. Access to Health Care	**1-1**	Increase the proportion of persons with health insurance.
	1-4a	Increase the proportion of persons who have a specific source of ongoing care.
	16-6a	Increase the proportion of pregnant women who begin prenatal care in the first trimester or pregnancy.

From US Department of Health and Human Services. *Healthy People 2010.* 2nd ed. With Understanding and Improving Health and Objectives for Improving Health. 2 vols. Washington, D.C.: US Government Printing Office, November 2000.

from intensive vigorous exercise to a broader range of health-enhancing physical activities. A growing consensus among epidemiologists, exercise scientists, fitness experts, and health professionals led to the recommendation for moderate physical activity for 30 minutes or more on most, if not all, days of the week. Additional health benefits could be gained through increasing the intensity and/or amount of physical activity. Promoting active lifestyles is important to the health of the nation. Virtually all individuals benefit from regular physical activity.

If you want to lead a longer, healthier life, engage in physical activity on a regular basis. Physically active people outlive sedentary people. Regular physical activity helps maintain the functional independence of older adults and enhances the quality of life for people of all ages. Regular physical activity helps prevent disease and assists in the management of many diseases, including coronary heart disease, hypertension, diabetes, and some types of cancer. Health benefits appear to be proportional to the amount of physical activity. For people who are inactive, even small increases in physical activity can be beneficial to their health. Moderate physical activity offers people many different options to incorporate physical activity into their lives, according to personal preference and life circumstances. It is hoped that those who dislike vigorous physical exercise or find it difficult to adhere to a program may find it easier to incorporate moderate physical activity into their lives on a regular basis. Vigorous physical activity is recommended for the improvement of cardiorespiratory endurance.

In the physical activity focus area are 15 objectives. (See the Healthy People 2010 Objectives for Physical Activity and Fitness box.) The objectives focus on increasing physical activity and reducing disparities in physical activity among different population groups. Despite the documented health benefits of physical activity, too many adults and children lead sedentary lives.

The *Healthy People 2010* physical activity objectives center on increasing the proportion of adults who accrue health benefits from participation in physical activity. Therefore, *Healthy People 2010* strives to reduce the proportion of adults who are sedentary and increase the proportion of adults who engage in moderate and vigorous physical activity on a regular basis. Additionally, there is increasing evidence that supports the importance of muscular strength, muscular endurance, and flexibility to good health; therefore, *Healthy People 2010* seeks to increase the proportion of adults who engage in physical activities that enhance these health-fitness components. The efforts to increase physical activity are not limited to adults; improvement of physical activity patterns of adolescents is a priority.

Improving the proportion of adolescents who engage in moderate and vigorous physical activity will help adolescents develop healthy habits as they enter adulthood. Decreasing television watching and other forms of sedentary behavior will help increase physical activity. School physical education plays an important role in accomplishing the objectives for physical activity. *Healthy People 2010* calls for increasing the number of schools requiring daily physical education for their students and increasing physical activity during physical education class time.

Healthy People 2010 recognizes that the places in which people live, work, and play—our communities—can have a significant impact on our ability to participate in physical activity. Access to facilities and safe places to walk, for example, can increase participation in physical activity by all age groups. The physical activity objectives call for increasing the number of the nation's schools that provide access to their physical activities and spaces outside of the normal school hours. Encouraging people of all ages to increase the number of trips they make by walking or bicycling will lead to more people including physical activity into their daily lives. Further increasing the proportion of work sites that offer employee health promotion programs will increase opportunities for a large number of adults to participate in a multitude of physical activities.

Healthy People 2010 Objectives for Physical Activity and Fitness

Number	Objective	Baseline Percent	Target Percent
22-1	Reduce the proportion of adults who engage in no leisure-time physical activity.	40	20
22-2	Increase the proportion of adults who engage regularly, preferably daily, in moderately physical activity for at least 30 minutes per day.	15	30
22-3	Increase the proportion of adults who engage in vigorous physical activity that promotes the development and maintenance of cardiorespiratory fitness 3 or more days per week for 20 or more minutes per occasion.	23	30
22-4	Increase the proportion of adults who perform physical activities that enhance and maintain muscular strength and endurance.	18	30
22-5	Increase the proportion of adults who perform physical activities that enhance and maintain flexibility.	30	43
22-6	Increase the proportion of adolescents who engage in vigorous physical activity for at least 30 minutes on 5 or more of the previous 7 days.	27	35
22-7	Increase the proportion of adolescents who engage in vigorous physical activity that promotes cardiorespiratory fitness 3 or more days per week for 20 or more minutes per occasion.	65	85
22-8	Increase the proportion of the nation's public and private schools that require daily physical education for all students.		
	a. Middle and junior high schools	17	25
	b. Senior high schools	2	5
22-9	Increase the proportion of adolescents who participate in daily school physical education.	29	50
22-10	Increase the proportion of adolescents who spend at least 50% of school physical education class time being physically active.	38	50
22-11	Increase the proportion of adolescents who view television 2 or fewer hours on a school day.	57	75
22-12	Increase the proportion of the nation's public and private schools that provide access to their physical activity spaces and facilities for all persons outside of normal school hours (that is, before and after the school day, on weekends, and during summer and other vacations).	Develop-mental. No data available	
22-13	Increase the proportion of work sites offering employer-sponsored physical activity and fitness programs.	46	75
22-14	Increase the proportion of trips made by walking—trips 1 mile or less.		
	a. Adults aged 18 years and older	17	25
	b. Children and adolescents aged 5 to 15 years	31	50
22-15	Increase the proportion of trips made by bicycling.		
	a. Adults aged 18 years and older—5 miles or less	.6	2.0
	b. Children and adolescents aged 5 to 15 years—2 miles or less	2.4	5.0

From US Department of Health and Human Services. *Healthy People 2010: Understanding and Improving Health.* 2nd ed. Washington, D.C.: US Government Printing Office, November 2000.

Jumping rope is one way to develop fitness.

Unfortunately, disparities in physical activity exist among population groups, contributing to disparities in health status among different populations. Women are more inactive than men and African Americans and Hispanics are more inactive than whites. Inactivity is higher among older adults than younger adults. The less affluent are more inactive than the more affluent. Participation in physical activity decreases as children get older. People with lower levels of education and income tend to be less active in their leisure time than people with higher levels of education and greater income. Health promotion and disease prevention programs need to utilize multidimensional approaches to address these inequities and to promote the adoption and maintenance of physical activity by different population groups.

Health promotion and disease prevention efforts have the potential to significantly constrain the enormous and rapidly escalating cost of health care in the United States. In 1999, health care expenditures totaled $1.2 trillion and consumed over 13% of the U.S. gross national product (GNP), more than any other industrialized nation.[29] In 2002, just 4 years later, costs had risen to $1.6 trillion dollars, or 14.9% of the GNP.[30] Costs continue to rise at an astronomical rate and are projected to reach $3.4 trillion dollars or 18.4% of the GNP in 2013.[30]

Poor health is costly as are the choices individuals make regarding their lifestyles. Secretary of Health and Human Services Tommy G. Thompson stated, "The choices we make about diet, activity and tobacco affect not only our own lives, but also affect the economic health of our families, our businesses and even our nation as a whole."[31] Taking into account both direct and indirect costs of diseases and lifestyle choices helps you to see the economic consequences of poor health. For example, in 2004, the estimated cost of cardiovascular disease was $368.4 billion.[32] In 2003, the overall costs for cancer was $189.5 billion.[32] In 2000, the total cost of obesity in the United States was estimated to be $117 billion; the costs of inactivity was estimated to be $76 billion.[23,34] Addressing these conditions can significantly reduce health care costs and make dramatic improvements in the health of the nation, reducing premature death and disability and enhancing the quality of life.

Spiraling health care costs are a major concern of U.S. businesses. Illness and premature employee death cost American industry billions of dollars a year. Poor health and fitness contribute to decreased productivity and increased absenteeism. Premiums for medical insurance continue to rise. The growing health care costs and the realization of the benefits to be gained through health promotion and fitness programs has led many corporations to establish programs for their employees. Corporations have found that such programs make economic sense. On the average, the net benefit is $5.64 for every dollar invested.[33] An increasing number of corporations are offering health promotion programs to their employees. Corporations

Obesity and Physical Activity—Quick Facts

PREVALENCE

- Obesity in the U.S. has reached epidemic proportions. Approximately 64% of adults are overweight, and 30% are obese. During the last decade, obesity rates among adults have risen by more than 60%.
- Approximately 15% of children and adolescents, ages 6–19 years of age, are considered to be overweight. Since 1980, overweight has doubled among children and tripled among adolescents.
- Over 50% of adults do not get enough physical activity to provide health benefits. Over 25% of adults participate in no physical activity during their leisure time.
- Approximately a third of high school students did not meet the physical activity recommendations for moderate or vigorous physical activity. Only 32% participate in daily high school physical education classes.

OBESITY, INACTIVITY, AND HEALTH

- Obesity is associated with increases in death from all causes.
- Physical inactivity and poor diet contribute to 400,000 preventable deaths a year; only tobacco contributes to more deaths per year—435,000.
- Physical inactivity and unhealthy eating contribute to obesity, cancer, cardiovascular disease, diabetes, osteoporosis, and arthritis.
- Overweight or obese individuals experience social stigmatization and discrimination in academic and employment situations.

ECONOMIC CONSEQUENCES

- In 2000, health care costs associated with obesity were $117 billion.
- In 2000, health care costs associated with inactivity were $76 billion.
- If only 10% of adults started a regular walking program, an estimated $5.6 billion in heart disease costs could be saved.

PHYSICAL ACTIVITY AND HEALTH BENEFITS

- Adults of all ages can realize benefits from regular, moderate physical activity, such as 30 minutes of brisk walking 5 or more times a week. Greater amounts of activity will yield additional health benefits.
- Children and adolescents can realize benefits from participation in at least 60 minutes of moderate physical activity on most days of the week.

Data compiled from the Centers for Disease Control and Prevention, National Center for Health Statistics, and the President's Council on Physical Fitness and Sports.

have found that medical costs and absenteeism drop and productivity increases after the introduction of a health promotion program.

In 2001, U.S. Surgeon General David Satcher, concerned about the rising incidence of overweight and obesity and associated health consequences, issued a "call to action." Satcher said, "Communities can help when it comes to health promotion and disease prevention. When there are no safe places for children to play, or for adults to walk, jog, or ride a bike, that's a community responsibility. When school lunchrooms or workplace cafeterias don't offer healthy and appealing food choices, that is a community responsibility. When new or expectant parents are not educated about the benefits of breast-feeding, that's a community responsibility. And when we don't require daily physical education in our schools, that is also

Community-based Strategies to Prevent and Decrease Overweight and Obesity

- Ensure daily quality physical education for all school grades.
- Ensure that more food options that are low in fat and calories, as well as fruits, vegetables, whole grains, and low-fat or nonfat dairy products, are available on school campuses and at school events.
- Make community facilities available for physical activity for all people, including on the weekends.
- Create more opportunities for physical activity at work sites.
- Reduce time spent watching television and engaging in other sedentary behaviors.
- Educate all expectant parents about the benefits of breast-feeding, which has been found to reduce the likelihood of children becoming overweight as they grow older.
- Change the perception of obesity so that health, not personal appearance, becomes the chief concern.
- Increase research on the behavioral and biological causes of overweight and obesity. Direct research toward prevention and treatment, and toward ethnic/racial health disparities.
- Educate health care providers and health profession students on prevention and treatment of overweight across the lifespan.

From "The Surgeon General's Call to Action to Prevent and Decrease Overweight and Obesity" (www.cdc.gov).

a community responsibility."[35] This report, entitled "The Surgeon General's Call to Action to Prevent and Decrease Overweight and Obesity," outlines community strategies that can be used to help address these problems. The report calls for daily quality physical education, creating more opportunities for physical activity in the community and workplace, reducing sedentary behaviors, and providing healthier food options (see the Community-Based Strategies box).

In 2002, President George W. Bush set forth his Healthier U.S. Initiative, which called for government, business, church and civic groups, and community agencies to work together to help Americans lead longer and healthier lives.[36] The four key objectives for a healthier United States are daily physical activity; good nutrition and sound dietary habits; greater use of preventive screenings; and responsible choices with respect to alcohol, tobacco, drugs, and safety. In 2004, the Healthy Lifestyles and Disease Prevention Initiative was launched, which encourages Americans to take small, manageable steps to bring about changes in their behaviors to ensure good health. These small steps, like including 10 minutes of walking into a daily routine, would ultimately lead to lifestyle changes that would yield significant health benefits. Moreover, if 10% of adults began a regular walking program, $5.6 billion a year in heart disease costs could be saved.[35]

A focused effort is needed if the *Healthy People 2010* objectives are to be met. *Healthy People 2010* progress reports for the areas of physical activity and nutrition and overweight, released in 2004, show little progress in achieving the objectives associated with these areas. Little change has been seen in the 1997 baseline levels for various physical activity objectives.[36] With respect to nutrition and overweight, compared to the 1988–1994 and 1996 baseline data, the prevalence of overweight and obesity has increased.[36] As you will see in the next section on physical activity and fitness, too many people of all ages are inactive, fail to achieve the recommended amount of regular physical activity, make unhealthy food choices, and are overweight or obese.

The wellness movement encourages people to make lifestyle decisions that will enhance their health and well-being. An increased emphasis on health promotion and disease prevention has led to some improvements in the health of our nation. People are aware that the manner in which they live and their personal choices significantly impact on their health and quality of life. Additionally, there is a greater understanding of how the environment, society, and economic status influence people's health and quality of life. Elimination of disparities in health and, ultimately in lifespan, is one of the nation's top health priorities.

What Are the Implications of the Wellness Movement for Physical Education, Exercise Science, and Sport?

What role should physical education, exercise science, and sport take in promoting health and achieving national public health goals? The public health focus on health promotion and disease prevention presents a tremendous opportunity for physical education, exercise science, and sport professionals to increase their contributions to the health and welfare of all people. As you review the *Healthy People 2010* goals and the specific objectives for physical activity, ask yourself the following questions:

- How can physical education, exercise science, and sport contribute to the realization of these objectives and the goal of optimal health and well-being for all segments of the population?
- What are the implications of these objectives for the structure and content of physical education, exercise science, and sport programs in all settings and for a diversity of populations?
- What are the implications for the manner in which we deliver services? How can we expand our services to reach underserved populations?
- What are the implications for job opportunities in the field?

The potential of physical education, exercise science, and sport to contribute to the national health objectives for physical activity and fitness is tremendous. Physical education, exercise science, and sport programs in both school and nonschool settings provide an avenue for people of all ages to be active and to learn the skills, knowledge, and values conducive to leading a physically active lifestyle.

School physical education programs have a critical role to play in achieving the national health goals. If the health of the nation is to be improved, effective use must be made of school health and physical education programs. The schools provide an efficient means to reach over 50 million students a year. The school offers us the best vehicle to address disparities in opportunities associated with socioeconomics status. As professionals, we must be strong, passionate spokespersons on behalf of physical education and sport. The decline in the number of children participating in daily physical education must be reversed. Quality programs are critical to this effort. The inclusion of physical education as an integral component of a comprehensive school health program is another approach to increase physical education programs. During these impressionable years, much can be done by schools and parents working together to lay the groundwork for healthy living as an adult.

School physical education programs should provide the foundation for participation in physical activities throughout one's lifespan. Physical education programs for young children should focus on attainment of proficiency in fundamental skills and movement concepts. In the upper-elementary grades and middle-school years, students should be exposed to a variety of activities in the areas of sports, dance, aquatics, and outdoor pursuits. This exposure allows students to identify activities that are enjoyable and satisfying to them.

In high school, students should have the opportunity to develop competency in several activities that are personally meaningful. Fitness promotion is important. Teachers must provide a sequence of experiences that will give students a knowledge base of physical education and sport so that they can learn how to direct their own exercise programs, modify physical activities to suit their changing needs, and wisely select activities to participate in during their leisure time. Physical educators must also remember it is important to offer experiences that are challenging, meaningful, and personally satisfying to participants and are con-

Physical education is an educational basic.

ducive to developing motivation for continued participation throughout life. The entire physical education program should be seen as developmental in nature, offering a series of planned learning experiences that focus on development of fitness, motor skills, knowledge, and values that will lead to lifespan participation.

The school setting also offers a means to reach adults. Over 5 million adults are employed by the schools, both in instructional and noninstructional positions. More schools are offering worksite health promotion programs, similar to those found in corporations, to their employees. These programs often encompass fitness promotion, skill development, and health education.

The use of the school as a community center has not reached its full potential. Although more schools are opening their doors to the community during evening hours, on the weekend, and during the summer, many schools remain unused and others underutilized. The use of the school as a community center would enable us to reach adults and offer a diversity of programs to meet their needs. Moreover, adult school-based programs offer a means to bring physical activity and sport experiences to adults who lack the financial resources to join a fitness club or do not have a program at their work site. They provide an avenue to reach all people within the community. Programs can be designed to focus on the needs of people of all ages, ranging from young adults to the elderly, at a minimal cost. Other programs can be started that foster family participation, emphasizing children and parents' participating in activities together.

The growing number of older Americans makes it important to have physical activity programs to meet their many needs. Their needs are quite diverse. Millions of older Americans participate in sports. Other older Americans can benefit from physical activity programs that help them maintain the necessary health and vitality to live independently for as long as possible. In this manner, physical education, exercise science, and sport can increase the number of years of healthy life as well as make life more satisfying.

Worksite health promotion programs have grown tremendously. Many worksite programs have increased their scope of offerings from just a fitness program to include an array of different activities. Programs vary but may include fitness programs, recreation activities, and health promotion programs such as cancer and hypertension screening, nutritional counseling, and smoking cessation. Another change is that businesses have moved from viewing these programs as the perks of upper management to making these programs available to employees at all levels. This growth of programs has led to an increase in career opportunities in this sector.

Commercial fitness clubs and community agency programs, such as those at the YMCA, are growing. Additionally, they have expanded the populations served. Although these programs were initially targeted toward adults, they are now reaching out to the elderly and preschool children. These programs provide instruction in skills, encourage the development of fitness, offer education, and strive to promote regular participation.

Physical educators, exercise scientists, and sport leaders can also contribute to the attainment of public health goals by contributing, directly or indirectly, to the achievement of objectives in the other *Healthy People 2010* priority areas. For example, physical education class provides a ready means to discuss how the use of tobacco, excessive alcohol consumption, and drug abuse are deterrents to fitness, thereby contributing to the objectives in three priority areas. Physical educators can reinforce nutritional concepts and provide opportunities for students to explore the impact of nutrition on performance. Teaching stress reduction techniques, such as progressive relaxation, or sharing with students how physical activity can help alleviate stress, or how fitness can serve as a stress buffer, can contribute to attaining the objectives for mental health.

In addition to contributing to the priority areas associated with health promotion, physical education, exercise science, and sport professionals can also promote health protection and preventive services. For example, by teaching swimming and water safety skills to all students, schools can help reduce the number of drownings, an objective related to the priority area of unintentional injuries. Physical activity can reduce risk for heart disease and stroke, another priority area.

As the United States becomes more diverse, the challenge of addressing disparities in health status and access to opportunities will become greater. Greater efforts must be made to reach racial and ethnic minorities, people with disabilities, and people with low incomes. As Siedentop states, professionals should understand inequities that may limit access to opportunities to participate in activity based on "irrelevant attributes such as race, gender, age, handicapping condition, or socioeconomic status. Individuals should value fair access to participation so much that they are willing to work at local, regional, and national levels to make that activity more available to more people."[37]

Enjoyable physical activity is a good approach to developing health-fitness components.

If we are to improve the health of the nation, a greater emphasis needs to be placed on school-community partnerships. Both the resources of the school and the community need to be used if the objectives for the year 2010 are to be achieved. If physical education, exercise science, and sport professionals are to take on a public health role, they must be willing to work as part of a comprehensive team dedicated to the improvement of the nation's health status. Physical education, exercise science, and sport professionals must realize that physical activity is only a part of the means to achieving optimal health. Nutritionists, health educators, medical personnel, and others have a critical role to play in the wellness movement. It is important that all professionals work cooperatively to achieve the

Task Force on Physical Activity Effective Interventions

- Information Approaches
  - Community-wide campaigns
  - Point-of-decision prompts
- Behavioral and Social Approaches
  - School-based physical education
  - Social support interventions in community settings
  - Individually adapted health behavior change
- Environmental and Policy Approaches
  - Access to places for physical activity

realization of the nation's health goals and the attainment of optimal well-being for each individual.

What are the best ways to increase physical activity within a community and achieve the physical activity objectives of *Healthy People 2010*? In 2001, the Task Force on Physical Activity[38] released its report, which identified interventions that were effective in increasing physical activity. Knowledge of which interventions are most effective can help policy makers and physical activity and health professionals use their community resources most effectively to reach *Healthy People 2010* physical activity objectives. To be included in the report, studies had to demonstrate improvements in physical activity behavior outcomes (e.g., increased time spent walking) or increases in selected fitness measures (e.g., increased aerobic capacity).

After a systematic review of 94 studies, the task force recommended six interventions to increase physical activity (see accompanying box): two information approaches (community-wide campaigns and point-of-decision prompts), three behavioral and social approaches (school-based physical education, social support interventions in community settings, and individually adapted health behavior change) and one environmental and policy approach (creation and/or enhanced access to places for physical activity in conjunction with informational outreach activities).

Simple interventions can be effective in increasing physical activity. The task force found that point-of-decision prompts to encourage people to use nearby stairs for health benefits or weight loss were successful. These prompts increased the number of people taking the stairs rather than elevators or escalators. These prompts can be incorporated into many different settings within the community: schools, transportation centers, workplaces, and shopping malls.

Community-wide, high-intensity, sustained promotional campaigns that promote physical fitness using a variety of media (newspapers, television, radio, flyers) were effective in increasing physical activity. Community-wide campaigns that incorporated many different components to encourage physical activity, including a promotional component, were also recommended as effective. Multicomponent programs, which include support, self-help groups, physical activity counseling, risk factor screening, education, community events, and the creation of walking trails, were strongly recommended. The task force noted that it was impossible to separate out the incremental benefits of each component.

Health-behavior change programs that were tailored to fit the needs of the individual were strongly recommended. These individually designed programs consider the person's readiness to change or specific interests. These programs were designed to help individuals incorporate more physical activity into their daily routines by teaching them behavioral skills such as goal-setting and self-monitoring, building social support, behavioral reinforcement through self-reward and positive self-talk, structured problem-solving, and relapse prevention.

School-based physical education programs were strongly recommended by the task force as an intervention approach. Physical education programs that were effective modified their policies to increase the amount of time spent in physical education class or increase the time the students were active during class. Other interventions improved students' moderate and vigorous physical activity during scheduled classes by changing the activities played (e.g., switching from softball to soccer) or modifying the rules (e.g., using a smaller number of players and mini-games) to create more opportunities to be active. In some of the interventions, health education was incorporated into the program. These interventions were effective in increasing the amount of physical activity and aerobic capacity. It was noted that in the majority of cases comparison groups received "standard" health and physical education curricula.

Another strongly recommended intervention was the use of social support interventions. These interventions help persons change their level of physical activity by building and strengthening social networks and developing relationships that supported persons' efforts to change. Using social support at the workplace, setting up a buddy system, or establishing walking groups that offer friendship and support are effective in increasing physical activity and aerobic capacity.

Increasing access to places for physical activity received a strong recommendation as an intervention. Creating new facilities or building walking trails provides additional opportunities for physical activity participation. Removing barriers limiting access to places for physical activity is an effective intervention strategy; this could include reducing fees for participation or setting aside time for facility use for members of the community. Worksite health promotion programs were found to be an effective intervention because they provide an accessible, convenient, low-cost place for people to engage in a variety of physical activities.

The task force found insufficient evidence, that is, areas of uncertainty in studies or indication of the need for continuing research, for several physical activity interventions. These include single component multimedia campaigns, classroom-based health education focusing on information provision and behavioral skills, classroom-based health education focusing on reducing television and video game playing, college-age physical education and health education, and social support interventions in family settings.

The findings of the task force allow physical education, exercise science, and sport professionals to consider these evidence-based recommendations and the needs and goals of the local community when selecting an intervention to promote increased physical activity. Sedentary lifestyles contribute to premature mortality and increase the risk for heart disease, stroke, diabetes, and other diseases and conditions. Achievement of *Healthy People 2010* requires effective interventions in communities in which people live, work, and play.

PHYSICAL ACTIVITY AND FITNESS MOVEMENT

Enthusiasm for exercise and fitness is at an unprecedented level in the United States today, with millions of people spending countless hours and billions of dollars on exercise and sport. The fitness movement, which began as a trend in 1970s, has over three decades later grown to be an enduring feature of our society. Men and women of all ages are participating in fitness and sport activities to an extent not witnessed before in this country. It appears that being physically active is for many children and adults an ingrained part of American life.

However, when data about participation are closely examined, the widespread extent of the physical activity and fitness in American society is not supported. Available data show that many children and adults are leading sedentary lives.

In 1996, *Physical Activity and Health: The Surgeon General's Report*[39] was released. This landmark document convincingly set forth the contribution physical activity can make to the health and lives of all people. The contribution of physical activity to health is shown in The Benefits of Regular Physical Activity box.

Several key messages are presented in this document:

- People of all ages can benefit from physical activity.
- People can improve their health by engaging in a moderate amount of physical activity on a regular basis.

The Benefits of Regular Physical Activity

Regular physical activity improves health in the following ways:

- Reduces the risk of dying prematurely.
- Reduces the risk of dying from heart disease.
- Reduces the risk of developing diabetes.
- Reduces the risk of developing high blood pressure.
- Helps reduce blood pressure in people who already have high blood pressure.
- Reduces the risk of developing colon cancer.
- Reduces feelings of depression and anxiety.
- Helps control weight.
- Helps build and maintain healthy bones, muscles, and joints.
- Helps older adults become stronger and better able to move about without falling.
- Promotes psychological well-being.

US Department of Health and Human Services: *Physical activity and health: a report of the Surgeon General*, Atlanta, Ga., US Department of Health and Human Services, Centers for Disease Control and Prevention, National Center for Chronic Disease Prevention and Health Promotion, 1996.

- Greater health benefits can be achieved by increasing the amount of physical activity, through changing the duration, frequency, or intensity of effort.

Moderate physical activity is defined as physical activity that results in an energy expenditure of 150 calories a day or 1,000 calories per week. Walking for 30 minutes, swimming laps for 20 minutes, or wheeling oneself in a wheelchair for 30–40 minutes will satisfy the requirement for moderate physical activity. Physical activity can be accumulated throughout the day by doing intermittent activities such as walking 3 times a day for 10 minutes.

The recommendation to include moderate physical activity as part of one's daily schedule represents an effort to broaden the scope of physical activity recommendations. Traditionally, an exercise period of 20 minutes at an intensity of 60% to 85% maximum heart rate performed 3 or more times per week was the recommended standard for promoting health fitness and preventing disease. In 1995, the American College of Sports Medicine and the Centers for Disease Control and Prevention, in an effort to encourage greater involvement in physical activity, emphasized participation in moderate physical activity on most days of the week. It is hoped that with additional opportunities to engage in beneficial physical activity, more people will participate. While participation in some cases is not of sufficient intensity to develop cardiovascular fitness, being physically active does yield health benefits.

The Surgeon General's report stresses that physical inactivity is a national problem. Inactivity contributes to the burden of unnecessary illness and premature death. It is estimated that poor diet and lack of activity together account for more than 400,000 deaths per year. Lifestyle factors, such as lack of physical activity, diet, and tobacco use, account for more than half of premature deaths and disabilities.[39]

The emphasis on moderate physical activity and the focus on integration of physical activity into one's lifestyle offer additional opportunities for sedentary individuals to improve their health through participation in physical activities that are enjoyable, personally meaningful, and fit more easily into their daily schedules. Healthy lifestyle patterns, including regular physical activity, should be developed when people are young. These lifestyle patterns can then be carried into adulthood, reducing the risk of disease. People who regularly participate in moderate amounts of physical activity can live longer, healthier lives.

Before reading a description of the fitness and physical activity status of children, youth, and adults, you may find it helpful to understand how the data are collected. Several different national surveys track physical activity, nutrition, and health status of people in many different age groups. Each survey strives to obtain a representative sample that includes different population groups—race,

Situps are often used as part of a health fitness assessment.

ethnicity, age, gender, etc. The Behavioral Risk Factor Surveillance System (BRFSS) uses telephone surveys to collect data from over 200,000 people in all the states, the District of Columbia, Puerto Rico, Guam, and the U.S. Virgin Islands.[40] The National Health Interview Survey (NHIS) uses personal interviews to collect data on progress toward *Healthy People 2010* objectives. About 40,000 households and 100,000 respondents take part in this survey.[40] The Youth Risk Behavior Survey (YRBS) is a school-based survey of students in grades 9–12. About 15,000 students take part in this survey.[40]

The National Health and Nutrition Examination Survey (NHANES) uses a combination of personal interview and direct physical examination to collect data on children and adults on many aspects of health.[40] For example, unlike other surveys that rely on self-reported measures of height and weight, NHANES personnel obtained this information through direct measurement of height and weight following standardized measurement techniques.

Because of the different approaches to data collection, estimates vary. Typically on self-reported measures, respondents tend to report data that provide a more positive profile of themselves. For example, researchers have found that individuals tend to underreport their weight, which leads to lower measures of the prevalence of overweight and obesity than when the weight is actually measured by the researcher.[40]

To determine whether an individual was at a healthy weight, Body Mass Index (BMI) was used. BMI is calculated by dividing weight in kilograms by height in meters squared ($BMI = weight/height^2$). Children and youth were considered to be at risk for overweight if their BMI equaled or was greater than the 85th percentile and less than the 95th percentile on the gender- and age-specific CDC Growth Charts for the United States.[41] Overweight was defined as having a BMI greater than the 95th percentile.[41] For adults, overweight is defined as a BMI of 25 or more, obese is a BMI of 30 or more, and extreme obesity is a

BMI of 40 or more.[41] A BMI of 30 indicates a person is about 30 pounds overweight; a 6' person who is 221 pounds or a 5'6" person who is 186 pounds has a BMI of 30.[42] It should be noted that while the BMI provides a quick and inexpensive method to determine whether an individual is at a healthy weight, it does have its limitations. Very muscular individuals may have a high BMI, yet not be at risk for poor health.[42]

Estimating physical activity levels and healthy body weight for children, adolescents, and adults is a challenging task. Despite the variability in survey estimates for physical activity and overweight/obesity and the limitations of the BMI, it is clear that both the children and adults of the country need to be more active and to eat healthier.

Since physical activity patterns are formed in childhood, children must be encouraged to spend less time watching TV and more time being active. Computer time should be limited as well.

Fitness and Physical Activity of Children and Youth

Are our nation's children and youth fit? Are they participating in sufficient physical activity to gain health benefits and reduce their risk for disease? The answers to these questions hold important implications for the achievement of our public health goals and for the health and future well-being of children and youth.

It is difficult to arrive at a clear picture of the fitness status and physical activity patterns of the nation's children and youth. The historical shift from performance-related to health-related fitness, the growing emphasis on the accrual of moderate to vigorous physical activity, and the variability in procedures involved in testing and sampling of subjects contribute to the difficulty. There has been no large-scale fitness testing of children and youth since the 1980s. However, there is sufficient information to help us understand that we, as physical education, exercise science, and sport professionals, need to do much more to help children and youth lead a more active lifestyle.

The 1996 Surgeon General's report on *Physical Activity and Health*[39] reached the following conclusions about the physical activity patterns of our nation's adolescents and young adults:

1. Only about one-half of young people ages 12–21 regularly participate in vigorous physical activity. One-fourth engage in no vigorous physical activity.
2. Approximately one-fourth of young people engage in light to moderate physical activity, that is, walking or biking, nearly every day.
3. About 14% of young people are inactive, reporting no vigorous or no light to moderate activity. The prevalence of inactivity is higher among females than males and among African American females than Caucasian females.
4. Males are more likely than females to engage in strengthening activities, light to moderate activities (biking and walking), and vigorous physical activity.
5. Participation in physical activity declines markedly as age or grade in school increases.
6. About 80% of 9th grade students are enrolled in physical education. This figure declines strikingly during the next years in high

People who participate in physical education programs often learn sports that they will enjoy for a lifetime. These students at Concord High School, in Connecticut, are receiving instruction in golf.

school. By 12th grade, only about 40% of the students are enrolled in physical education.

7. From 1991 to 1995, the number of students enrolled in daily physical education decreased from 42% to 25%.
8. Within physical education class, the number of students who reported being active for at least 20 minutes a class period declined from 81% to 70% during the first half of the 1990s.
9. Among students who attended daily physical education, only 19% report being active for 20 minutes or more.

Lack of participation among youth is a serious problem. During this important period between childhood and adulthood, adult habits begin to emerge. If we are to become a healthier nation, the decline in physical activity during this critical time period must be addressed. Moreover, special efforts must be made to reach out to population groups that have low physical activity participation rates, such as minorities and females.

During the 1990s, several assessments were made of children's and youths' fitness status and physical activity patterns. The Centers for Disease Control and Prevention developed the Youth Risk Behavior Surveillance System (YRBSS) to monitor health-risk behaviors of youth and young adults. National surveys are conducted periodically. Among the health-risk behaviors monitored are physical inactivity and unhealthy dietary behaviors.

In 2003, over 15,000 students in grades 9–12 completed the YRBSS questionnaires.[43] The findings relative to physical activity offer us insight into the youths' physical activity patterns and their school physical education experiences. The students completed questions on participation in physical activity during the 7 days preceding the survey. The YRBSS revealed:

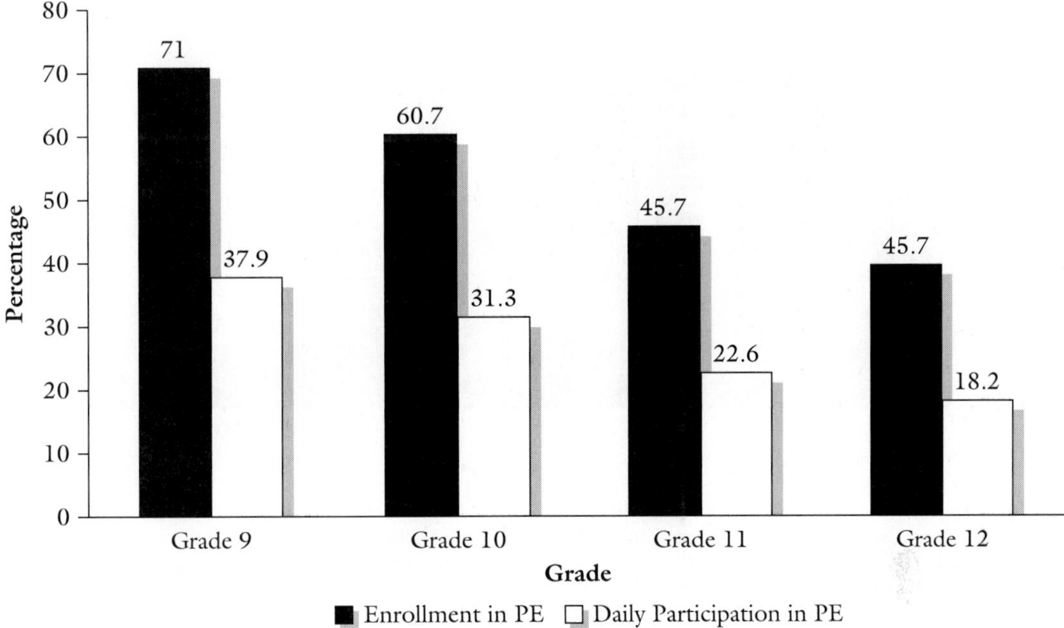

Figure 3-3 The 2003 YRBSS revealed that as school grade levels increased, enrollment and participation in physical education decreased.
Data from 2003 YRBSS.

- Approximately two-thirds (62.6%) of the students reported they engaged in vigorous physical activity that made them sweat or breathe hard for 20 minutes or more on 3 or more of the 7 days preceding the survey.
- Approximately one-quarter (24.7%) of the students participated in activities that did not make them sweat or breathe hard for 30 minutes or more on 5 or more of the 7 days preceding the survey (i.e., moderate physical activity).
- About one-half (51.9%) of students had done strengthening exercises (e.g., push-ups, sit-ups, and weightlifting) on 3 or more days of the 7 days preceding the survey.

The YRBSS reported that male students were typically more active than female students; males participated in more vigorous, moderate, and strengthening physical activities than did female students. Similar differences were found among different racial/ethnic groups. Generally, white students participated more in vigorous physical activities, moderate physical activities, and strengthening exercises than black or Hispanic students did. Participation in physical activity tended to decrease as students' grade levels increased. Television watching was surveyed since sedentary behaviors reduce the time youths have available to be active. Nationwide, 38.2% of students reported that they watched television 3 or more hours during a school day.

The YRBSS gathered information on enrollment, daily participation, and activity time in physical education. Nationwide, 55.7% of students were enrolled in a physical education class. As shown in Figure 3–3, as students' grades in school increased, enrollment in physical education decreased. Only 28.4% of students participated in daily physical education; this is a marked decrease from 41.6% in 1991. The percentage of students who attended physical education decreased as the students' grade levels increased (Figure 3-4).

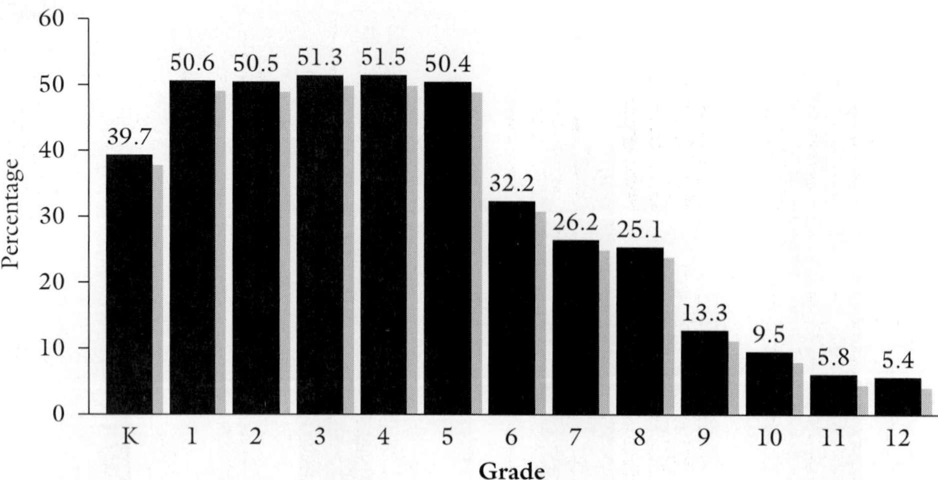

Figure 3-4 The School Health Policies and Programs Study 2000 shows that physical education requirements in schools decrease dramatically from grades 5 through 12.

Centers for Disease Control and Prevention, National Center for Chronic Disease and Health Promotion, Adolescent and School Health, School Health Policies and Programs Study 2000, 2000.

Participation on sports teams contributes to youths' physical activity. During the 12 months preceding the survey, 57.6% of students had played on a sports team. Male students (64.0%) participated on teams significantly more than female students (51.0%). Across all racial/ethnic groups, males were significantly more involved on sports teams than females.

Obesity presents a serious health risk for youth and adversely affects body composition, one of the health-fitness components. According to the YRBSS,[43] nationwide, 15.4% of the students were at risk for becoming overweight. The prevalence was similiar for both male and female students. Risk for overweight was higher among black and Hispanic students than white students, 18.3% versus 17.3% versus 14.1%. More than 1 in 10 students, 13.5%, were overweight. Compared to female students, male students were significantly more likely to be overweight than female students were, 17.4% versus 9.4%, respectively. The prevalence of overweight was higher among black students than white students.

The National Health and Nutrition Examination Survey (NHANES) is a survey conducted by the National Center for Health Statistics (NCHS), Centers for Disease Control and Prevention. The NHANES is designed to obtain information about the health and diet of children, youths, and adults and is conducted periodically.

In 2000, NHANES estimated that 15% of children ages 6–11 years and 15% of adolescents ages 12–19 years were overweight.[41] Comparison of the data from NHANES II (1976–1980) and NHANES III (1988–1994) revealed that the prevalence of overweight among children and adolescents is rising. The prevalence of overweight among children increased from an estimated 7% to 15%. For adolescents, the prevalence of overweight increased from 5% to 15%. The prevalence of overweight among adolescents is of great concern because of their increased risk to become overweight adults. As overweight adults, they have a greater risk for many diseases, including heart disease, diabetes, and other obesity-related health conditions.

The findings from the *Healthy People 2010,* the Surgeon General's Report on *Physical Activity and Health,* the YRBSS, and the NHANES indicate that too many of our nation's children and youth are inactive and overweight. Too many of our youth reduce their physical activity during their adolescent years. Quality physical education, exercise science, and sport programs are needed that focus on helping all young people get active and stay active. Special efforts must be made to address disparities in activity among population groups. These activity disparities tend to persist, contributing to disparities in health seen in adulthood. Because females tend to be less active than males, special efforts must be made to encourage them to stay involved in physical activities.

Racial/ethnic disparities in activity also need to be addressed by offering programs led by culturally competent physical educators, exercise scientists, and sport leaders; increased efforts must be made to sustain and increase racial/ethnic minority youth participation in physical activities. The decline in enrollment in physical education programs and decrease in daily physical education further reduce opportunities for involvement in physical activity by all youth.

Physical education, exercise science, and sport professionals should collaborate with policy makers, teachers, parents, and community members to develop and maintain quality physical activity programs in the school and in the community. The emphasis should be on enjoyable participation in physical activity. A diverse range of noncompetitive and competitive activities appropriate for different ages and abilities should be offered, both in school and community settings. Children and youth need opportunities to learn skills, knowledge, and attitudes to lead a physically activity lifestyle. Special efforts must be made to encourage and sustain participation by underserved populations. Quality programs, however, are not enough; programs need to be accessible. Affordable programs remove socioeconomic barriers to participation, and when programs are offered where children and youth live, they invite participation on a regular basis. Lifespan involvement in physical activity begins with promoting a healthy, active lifestyle in children and youth.

Fitness is important for all people. This woman, who is visually impaired, trains with a personal trainer at a local fitness center.

Fitness and Physical Activity of Adults

Information about the fitness and physical activity patterns of adults as well as information related to healthy weight and body composition is available from large-scale surveys. Sales of exercise equipment and health club membership offer additional insight regarding adult participation in physical activity and fitness.

The *Healthy People 2010* objectives for physical activity and fitness for adults revealed additional information about the activity patterns of Americans. *Healthy People 2010*[28] reported the following findings regarding participation in physical activity by adults aged 18 years and older:

- 40% of adults engaged in no leisure time activity.
- Only 15% of adults engaged in moderate physical activity for at least 30 minutes 5 or more days per week, which was sufficient to yield health benefits.
- 23% of adults engaged in vigorous physical activity 3 or more days per week for 20 minutes or more each time, which leads to improvements in cardiorespiratory fitness.
- 18% of adults engaged in physical activities to improve and maintain muscular strength and endurance.
- 30% of adults performed stretching exercises.

Time constraints, inadequate access to convenient facilities, unsafe environments, lack of motivation, and lack of knowledge are frequently cited as reasons for the lack of physical activity. Furthermore, while many people start a physical activity program, too few sustain participation over time.

Differences in physical activity were found among population groups. These findings are important to consider if we are to achieve the *Healthy People 2010* goal of eliminating disparities in health. *Healthy People 2010* identified the following disparities among population groups:

- Males were more active than females; more males than females engaged in moderate and vigorous physical activities, and performed muscular strength and endurance exercises. In every age group, females had higher levels of inactivity.
- Greater levels of physical activity were found for whites and for non-Hispanics than for other racial and ethnic groups. Nearly 40% of non-Hispanics were inactive compared to over 50% of Hispanics. American Indian and Alaskan Natives, Asians or Pacific Islanders, and blacks have higher levels of inactivity than whites.
- Non-Hispanics and whites were the most active compared to other population groups; these groups had higher levels of engagement in moderate and vigorous physical activity and exercises to improve and maintain muscular strength and endurance.
- Inactivity progressively increased as age increased. Thirty-one percent of adults aged 18–24 participated in no leisure time behavior compared to 65% of adults aged 75 years and older. Participation in vigorous and moderate physical activities decreased as age increased, as did participation in exercises designed to enhance and maintain muscular strength, muscular endurance, and flexibility.
- Inactivity decreased and participation in physical activities increased as level of education attainment increased. For example, nearly 75% of adults aged 25 and older with less than a 9th grade education were inactive compared to about 25% of adults who were college graduates. Inactivity was higher among the less affluent than the more affluent.
- Persons with disabilities were more inactive than persons without disabilities. Compared to persons with disabilities, a greater percentage of persons without disabilities engaged in moderate and vigorous physical activities and muscular strengthening and endurance activities.

The 1999–2001 National Health Interview Survey (NHIS)[44] indicated that 38.6% of adults were inactive during their leisure time. More than half of the adults, 61.4%, engaged in at least some physical activity during their leisure time. Overall, 31.3% of adults engaged in regular physical activity—either at the light-moderate level at least 5 times a week for a minimum of 30 minutes each time and/or vigorous physical activity at least 3 times a week for a minimum of 20 minutes each time. Almost one-fourth of the adults (23.1%) engaged in strengthening activities.

According to the NHIS, men were more likely than women to engage in regular physical activity, participate in strengthening activities, and be active during their leisure time (Figure 3-5). Engagement

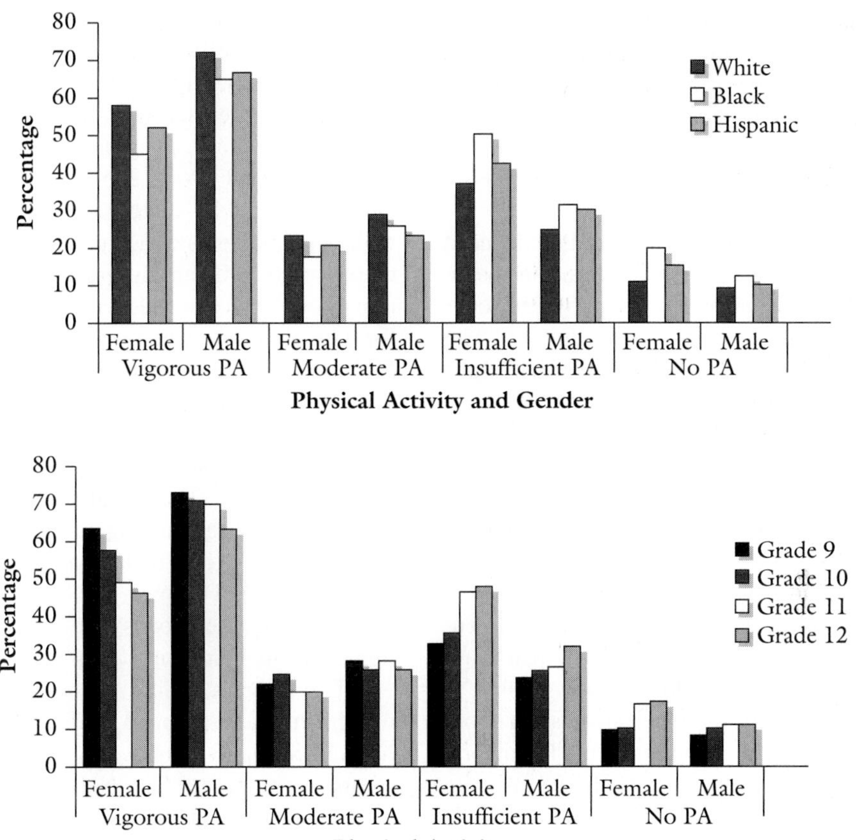

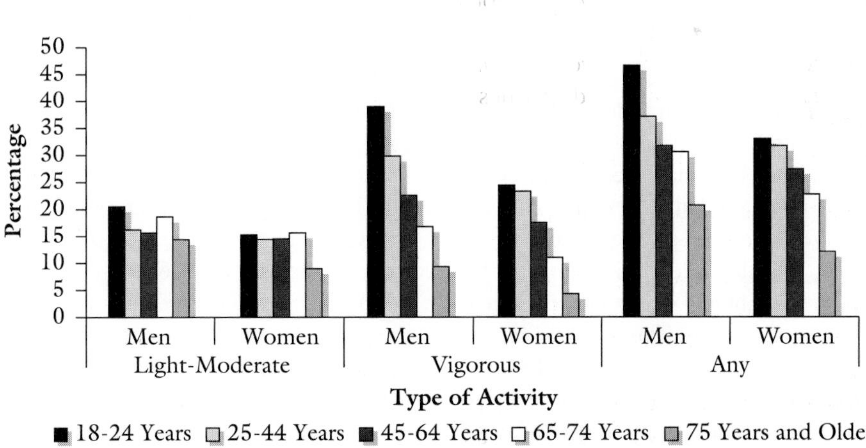

Figure 3-5 Youth and adult participation in physical activity reveals differences by age, gender, race, and ethnicity. **A,** Students' level of physical activity (PA) by race, ethnicity, and gender. **B,** Participation in physical activity by grade level and gender. **C,** Adult participation in regular leisure time physical activity by gender and age group.

Data from 2003 YRBSS and 2000 National Health Interview Survey.

in leisure-time physical activities decreased with age, with younger adults (19–24 years) more likely than older adults (greater than 75 years) to participate. Younger adults engaged in regular physical activities more often than older adults (39.7% of adults aged 18–24 compared to 15.6% of adults 75 years of age and older).

Engagement in physical activity is influenced by race, ethnicity, level of education, and socioeconomic status. Engagement in regular physical activity was more prevalent among white adults (32.7%) than among Asian adults (27.8%) and black adults (23.9%). Non-Hispanic white adults (65.7%) were more likely to engage in regular physical activity than non-Hispanic black adults (24%) and Hispanic adults (22.4%). Adults with higher levels of education were more likely to participate in regular physical activity than those adults who had lower levels of educational attainment. Adults whose income was above the poverty line were more likely to engage in some regular physical activity than those adults whose income fell below the poverty line.

Two other surveys provide information about the physical activity of adults. The Behavioral Risk Factor Surveillance System (BRFSS)[45] data for 2000–2001 revealed that only 45.4% of adults engaged in physical activities consistent with the recommendation of a minimum of 30 minutes of moderate-intensity activity on most days of the week. Over 50% of adults were not active enough to meet the recommendations for health. Additionally, 26% of adults reported no leisure-time physical activity. Another survey, the National Health Interview Data for 2003,[46] revealed that 32.9% of adults engaged in regular leisure-time physical activity.

Maintaining a healthy weight is important for good health. Overweight and obesity pose a health risk to individuals of all ages. The National Health and Nutrition Examination Survey (NHANES) measures the height and weight of survey participants using standardized techniques. NHANES reported that, in 2002, only 33% of adults were at a healthy weight.[41] The prevalence of overweight or obesity among adults was 65.1% percent. More specifically, 30.4% of adults were obese and 4.9% were extremely obese.

Across most age, racial/ethnic groups, the prevalence of overweight exceeded 50%. With respect to obesity, there was no significant difference in the prevalence of obesity among men across racial/ethnic categories for all age groups. Obesity ranged from 22.9% for non-Hispanic white men aged 20–39 to 32.2% for non-Hispanic white men 60 years of age and older. For women, there were significant differences among population groups. The prevalence ranged from 24.9% for non-Hispanic white women ages 20–39 to 50.6% for non-Hispanic black women ages 40–59. Women had a significantly higher prevalence of obesity than men. With respect of extreme obesity, differences were seen among age, race, and ethnicity for women. The prevalence of extreme obesity was highest among non-Hispanic black women (13.5%) and highest among those 40–59 years (15.1%). For men, little differences were found among the groups; the prevalence of extreme obesity among men was 3.3%.

Two surveys, using self-reported height and weight measures, found different results than NHANES. The BBRFSS estimated that 20.9% of adults were obese.[47] The NHIS estimated 25.5% of adults were obese. NHANES reported the prevalence of adult obesity to be 30.4%.[46] The differences in the prevalence may be due to individuals underestimating their weight when they responded to the survey.

Although different surveys report different estimates for overweight and obesity, it is easy to see that too many people are at risk for poor health due to their weight. Additionally, the prevalence of overweight and obesity has increased dramatically in the last two decades. Comparison of the NHANES data with previous results revealed that the prevalence of overweight, obesity, and extreme obesity is increasing. Adjusted NHANES data from 1976 to 1980 showed 46% of adults were overweight; that figure increased to 64.5% in 2002.[41] Similarly, obesity increased from 14.4% in the earlier survey to 30.5% in the most recent survey.[42] The prevalence of extreme obesity increased from 2.9% in 1988–1994 to 4.7% in 2002.[42] Obesity and overweight have reached epidemic proportions and pose a serious public health challenge. *Healthy People 2010*'s objective for nutrition and overweight is to increase the prevalence of adults at a healthy weight from the current 33% to 60%. Another objective is to decrease the prevalence of obesity among adults to 15%. If these objectives are to be achieved, greater efforts must be directed at achieving these outcomes, especially toward groups in which there are significant disparities.

Surveys of adult physical activity patterns during the 1990s and the early 2000s consistently report high levels of inactivity and low levels of regular moderate physical activity. Additionally, disparities among population groups were consistently found. Women, racial and ethnic minorities, less affluent, aged, and adults with lower levels of education had greater levels of inactivity. Physical education, exercise science, and sport professionals need to develop and implement strategies that encourage greater participation in physical activity, especially in those populations that have a high level of inactivity. Physical activity also plays an important role in maintaining a healthy weight. Since sedentary behavior is a risk factor for a variety of degenerative and chronic health conditions, attainment of our national health goals necessitates that a greater proportion of the population get involved in physical activity and stay active throughout their life-span.

Although many adults lead a sedentary lifestyle, many other adults are active. The picture of fitness in our society is quite perplexing and often contradictory—health club membership is booming, fitness participation remains steady, and overweight and obesity has reached epidemic proportions.[48]

American Sports Data (ASD) tracks physical activity for the sporting goods and fitness and health club industries, including The Sporting Goods Manufacturers Association (SGMA) and the International Health, Racquet and Sports Club Association (IHRSA). The ASD 2000 survey reveals another dimension of adult participation and helps us see a broader picture of adult physical activity patterns. The 2000 survey studied trends in fitness behavior from 1987–1999.[48] Among the findings reported are the following:

- The number of adults who exercised frequently (i.e., performed specific fitness activities at least 100 times a year) remained steady throughout the 1990s, about 20% of the population.
- Frequent home exercisers grew from 11.3 million participants in 1987 to a high of 18.5 million in 1997 and declined to 17.4 million in 1999. During the same time period, engagement in outdoor fitness activities increased from 25.0 million participants in 1987 to 26.5 million participants in 1999.
- The use of cardio equipment to exercise remains popular. Cardio equipment use rose from 9.0 million in 1987 to a high of 17.3 million in 1999. Strength training is flourishing, growing from 10.8 million users in 1987 to 19.2 million users in 1999.
- During the 1990s, membership at health clubs increased nearly 50%, and the number of people who worked out frequently at clubs, more than 100 days a year, rose by 84%. However, annual health club turnover rates remain between 30% and 40%.
- The overweight population can be quite active and boast a surprisingly high percentage of sports/fitness participants. Whereas 59% of the population perceives itself to be a little or considerably overweight, the overweight percentage for very active people reached 51%.

Additionally, it was noted that the reason for exercising shifted over the decade. The emphasis on cosmetic fitness—that is, exercising to look good—is decreasing and the emphasis on function fitness, that is, being healthy and strong enough to live fully, is increasing. Functional fitness focuses on having enough energy to get more out of life, whether it is participating in sports, engaging in physical activities, or having more energy for work and activities of daily living.[48]

Participation in fitness activities is highest among older adults. ASD reported in 2000 that 26% of persons over the age of 55 engaged in fitness activities on at least 100 occasions compared to 23% for those persons aged 35–54 and 20% for persons 18–34 years of age.[49] Why is participation higher in this age group? According to ASD, many of the active older adults were involved in the fitness booms of the 1970s and 1980s and now have moved into the older age bracket.[49] Additionally, the increased frequency of exercise being mandated by a medical health professional is another contributing factor.[49] Lastly, as people age and confront their mortality, preventive health concerns inspire one to engage in life-prolonging activity.[49]

Health clubs experienced tremendous growth since 1987. The 2003 IHRSA data[50] revealed that:

- In 2003, health club membership was 39.4 million compared to 17.3 million in 1987 and 32.8 million in 2000.
- In 1987, 39% of health club members were aged 35 and older compared to 59% in 2000.

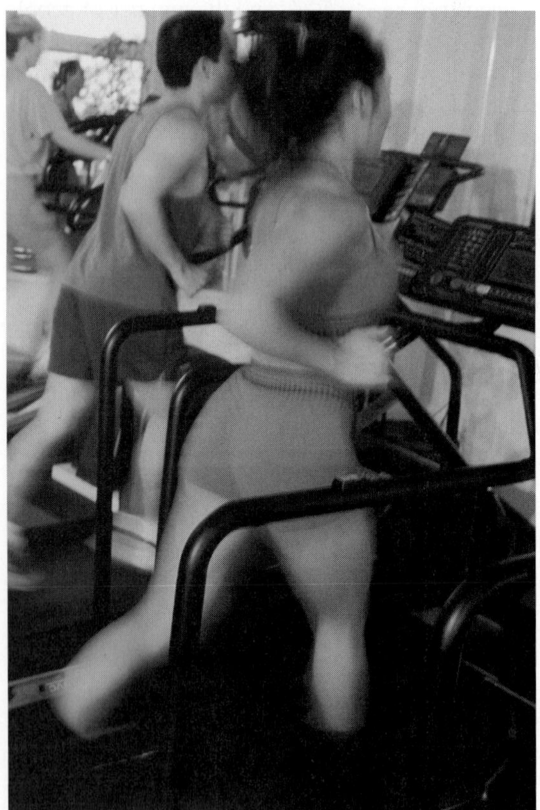

Health club membership continues to rise. Treadmills remain a popular means of working out.

- The greatest increase in health club membership occurred in members aged 55 and older. Since 1987, the membership increased 393%, from 1.5 million to nearly 7 million. In 2003, this age group accounted for 17.4% of all health club members.
- Membership by "baby boomers" (ages 37–54) accounts for 37.6% of all health club memberships.
- Women represent slightly more health club members than men (53% versus 47%).
- Forty-six percent of the members have a household income greater than $75,000, whereas only 11% have a household income of less than $25,000.

Health club membership in both profit and nonprofit (e.g., YMCA) clubs increased steadily in the 1990s. Clubs offer members their choice of a wide range of activities, opportunities for group exercise, and the chance to work out under the supervision of a fitness professional. ASD reports a dramatic surge in the number of people who engage the services of a personal trainer; there was a 30% increase from 1999 to 2002, and over 5 million people employ a personal trainer.[51]

Surveys and expenditures for sport and exercise equipment can also help us understand the extent of participation in physical activity programs by adults. In 2000, the SGMA[51] reported that:

- Between 1990 and 2000, free weight training by both sexes increased 67%. Women comprise 46% of the users of free weights and are more likely to use hand weights while men prefer barbells or dumbbells.
- Women outnumber men in fitness walking, treadmill exercise, stationary bicycling, stair-climbing machine exercise, aerobic rider exercise, cross-country ski machine exercise, elliptical motion trainers, aerobic dance exercise, abdominal machines, yoga/tai chi, fitness swimming, aquatic exercise, cardio kickboxing, and stretching.
- Americans spent approximately $5.6 billion on home exercise equipment in 2000 compared to $1.9 billion in 1990. Treadmills still lead the

way in sales but free weights and home gyms sales have grown steadily.

- Of the 36.2 million fitness walkers, 10.3 million say it is their favorite activity.
- The majority of the 15 most popular sports for adults 55 years of age and older are related to fitness. The fitness activities engaged in on 100 or more days per year are fitness walking, treadmill exercise, stretching, hand weights, weight/resistance machines, stationary cycling, calisthenics, and free weights—dumbbells.
- Consumer spending for athletic footwear rose 3.6% in 2000 to $8.98 billion after two years of declining spending. The running/jogging shoe topped all categories with sales of $2.61 billion in sales, followed by basketball shoes and cross-training shoes with $1.49 billion and $1.34 billion in sales, respectively.

The SGMA report indicates that many Americans are active on a regular basis. However, buying home exercise equipment does not guarantee use on a regular basis. Additionally, many people buy athletic footwear for fashion reasons, rather than for the purpose of working out or engaging in physical activity. ASD research found that most Americans, over 80% of the population, realize that physical activity is good for their health even though only 20% of the population gets enough exercise.[48] Health club membership and consumer spending on sports and fitness equipment show that American attitudes have changed. But there is a wide gap between positive attitudes and actual fitness behavior.[48]

Daily, moderate physical activity is important for all members of the family.

Physical activity is beneficial for the health and well-being of people of all ages, including the older population. Even among the frail and very old adults, mobility and function can be maintained and improved through engagement in regular physical activity. *Healthy People 2010* reported that over 50% of adults aged 65 to 74 years were sedentary and that increased to 65% in the over 75 age group.[28] As this segment of the population grows during the twenty-first century, it is critical that more of our efforts be directed toward helping older Americans stay active throughout their life-span.

Adults of all ages need to increase their participation in moderate and vigorous physical activity. Although the percentage of adults that are active enough to receive health benefits and the percentage of adults that are leading sedentary lives vary from report to report, it is clear that too many adults are inactive. Inactivity coupled with the rising increase in obesity places too many adults at increased risk for chronic diseases. Most adults know that physical activity is good for them; however, the gap between "knowing" about physical activity and "doing" physical activity is quite large. Physical education, exercise science, and sport professionals have an important role to play in closing the gap between knowledge and action and helping all persons adopt and maintain a program of moderate physical activity throughout their lifespan.

What Are the Implications of the Fitness Movement for Physical Education and Sport?

Although many Americans of all ages are not exercising vigorously with sufficient frequency, intensity, and duration to maintain an adequate level of health-related fitness, many people are making a commitment to incorporating moderate physical activity into their lifestyle. Furthermore, the increased documentation of the positive relationship between adequate levels of health-related fitness and wellness offers strong support for physical education, exercise science, and sport programs. It also emphasizes the need for fitness and physical activity programs to reach all ages of our society, regardless of sex, race, educational level, occupation, economic status, and community setting. As professionals, we must capitalize on the interest in fitness and its contribution to health to promote and secure funding for our programs.

Physical education, exercise science, and sport professionals must also become leaders in the fitness movement and exert a significant influence on its direction. Corbin[52] pointed out that medical doctors, self-appointed experts, and movie stars are at the vanguard of the fitness movement. Many of these people lack the qualifications, training, and expertise to direct this movement. Additionally, the proliferation of products and programs related to exercise and fitness has raised some concern about their validity. Physical education, exercise science, and sport professionals have the necessary knowledge and skill and must take over the leadership responsibilities within the movement. As Corbin states, in assuming the burden of leadership, we must practice what we preach. Professionals should be role models and should reflect a commitment to a healthy lifestyle, with physical activity as an integral component of that lifestyle. Failure to practice what we preach damages our credibility.

Findings relative to the physical activity levels of the nation's youth show an urgent need for the physical activity movement to reach the children and youth of our nation. Schools should emphasize lifelong fitness, and this education should begin early in life. School-based programs must teach students the skills for lifetime participation and foster an appreciation for the value of fitness and physical activity in maintaining an optimal state of well-being. Fitness education should also be extended to parents. Parents' roles in shaping their children's physical activity habits should be recognized, and professionals should involve them in creating positive physical activity patterns. Because much of children's and youths' physical activity takes place outside of the school setting, school and community physical activity programs should be closely coordinated so that the maximum benefits are derived from participation. The Centers for Disease Control and Prevention (CDC) has developed guidelines for school and community programs to promote physical activity among the nation's youth.[53] These guidelines make it clear that promoting lifelong physical activity requires a coordinated effort between the home, school, and community. (See the CDC Recommendations for Promoting Lifelong Physical Activity box.) Moreover, it emphasizes the inclusion of physical education as part of a comprehensive school-wide approach to promote well-being.

Many adults, when questioned about reasons for lack of participation in physical activity, cite lack of time. With the new recommendations on physical activity, more options are provided to incorporate physical activity into daily life. Furthermore, as the number of worksite programs continues to grow, greater opportunities for involvement will be available. Convenience is a factor that influences whether or not people will work out. On-site opportunities with flexible hours will make it more convenient for adults to incorporate physical activity into their daily routine. Some corporations are also rewarding individuals who work out by reducing their out-of-pocket costs for insurance. The growth in sales of home exercise equipment is also a positive sign that people are meeting their need to exercise by placing equipment in their homes. Some adults have hired personal trainers to guide their home exercise programs.

There must be increased efforts to reach out to underserved populations. This is true for both children and adults. The family is an important role model for physical activity involvement. However, an increasing number of children in single-parent families, many of whom are at risk for poor school outcomes, may not have the parental support for involvement. Collingwood states that physical fitness programs for at-risk youths require strong leadership, role modeling, and a focused, structured effort to achieve the desired outcomes.[54] Besides fitness promotion, structured physical fitness

CDC Recommendations for Promoting Lifelong Physical Activity

1. **Policy.** Establish policies that promote enjoyable, lifelong physical activity.
   - Schools should require daily physical education and comprehensive health education (including lessons on physical activity in grades K–12).
   - Schools and community organizations should provide adequate funding, equipment, and supervision for programs that meet the needs of and interests of all students.
2. **Environment.** Provide physical and social environments that encourage and enable young people to engage in safe and enjoyable physical activity.
   - Provide access to safe spaces and facilities and implement measures to prevent activity-related injuries and illnesses.
   - Discourage the use or withholding of physical activity as punishment.
   - Provide health and promotion programs for school faculty and staff.
3. **Physical Education Curricula and Instruction.** Implement sequential physical education curricula and instruction in grades K–12 that
   - Emphasize enjoyable participation in lifetime physical activities such as walking and dancing, not just competitive sports.
   - Help students develop the knowledge, attitudes, and skills they need to adopt and maintain a physically active lifestyle.
   - Follow the National Standards for Physical Education.
   - Keep students active most of the class time.
4. **Health Education Curricula and Instruction.** Implement health education curricula and instruction that
   - Feature active learning strategies that follow National Health Education Standards.
   - Help students develop the knowledge, attitudes, and skills they need to adopt and maintain a healthy lifestyle.
5. **Extracurricular Activities.** Provide extracurricular physical activity programs that offer diverse, developmentally appropriate activities, both noncompetitive and competitive, for all students.
6. **Family Involvement.** Encourage parents and guardians to support their children's participation in physical activity, be physically active role models, and include physical activity in family events.
7. **Training.** Provide training to enable teachers, coaches, recreation and health care staff, and other school and community personnel to promote enjoyable, lifelong physical activity for young people.
8. **Health Services.** Assess the physical activity patterns of young people, refer them to appropriate physical activity programs, and advocate for physical activity instruction and programs for young people.
9. **Community Programs.** Provide a range of developmentally appropriate community sports and recreation programs that are attractive to all young people.
10. **Evaluation.** Regularly evaluate physical activity instruction, programs, and facilities.

Centers for Disease Control and Prevention: *Guidelines for school and community programs to promote lifelong physical activity among young people, Morbidity and Mortality Weekly Report,* March 7, 1997, 46(RR-6); 1–36.

programs can affect many risk factors associated with the problems of at-risk youth. Properly designed and led by committed leaders, programs can increase well-being, enhance self-esteem, and teach important life skills such as goal-setting, planning, and values development.[54]

Socioeconomic status is a significant influence on participation in physical activity. Individuals who come from affluent backgrounds have greater involvement than those from less affluent circumstances. They have more disposable income they can use to support their involvement in fitness and sports. Children, youths, and adults from lower economic strata have fewer resources available. Their limited resources—money, energy, and time—must be spent on securing the necessities of life: food, shelter, clothing, safety, and medical care. There is little left for the less crucial activities of life such as exercise and sports. Even access to physical activity programs that are affordable may be difficult for those living in low-income neighborhoods. The relatively poor health of people in lower socioeconomic groups may also limit their participation. Harris notes that these obstacles to physical activity are "outward manifestations of the relative lack of power that accompanies low socioeconomic status."[55] Compared to those who are wealthier, those who are poor have less control over their lives, encounter greater stress, receive less social support from others, and must deal with the realization that they are deprived. "In general, they encounter serious barriers to an immediate access to a high quality of life, to chances of attaining such a life in the future . . . and have little power to bring about changes that might improve the situation."[55] As professionals, we must understand these inequities, the powerful feelings they evoke, and the type of strategies that can be effectively employed to change this situation.

During the 1990s, there was enormous growth in private sector industries related to sport and fitness, such as gymnastics clubs and fitness clubs. These industries provided greater opportunities for participation for those able to afford the fees. Historically, the most widely available opportunities for participation have been in the public sector in schools, community recreation programs such as youth soccer, and public facilities such as parks and swimming pools. As the shift toward private opportunities continues, efforts must be directed at expanding public sector opportunities and making them available to people of all socioeconomic classes. Offering low-cost programs and reduced fees for those unable to pay will allow individuals from low-income groups to participate. However, reducing fees may not be sufficient. For example, one city pool lowered its fees for children but found it did little to increase the number of participants from lower-income families. When the city offered free bus transportation to the pool, participation increased in record numbers. Not only must opportunities be provided, but steps must be taken to ensure that people can access these opportunities. Even in the public sector, fees may limit participation.

Culturally competent physical education, exercise science, and sport professionals are needed to design and implement programs that are sensitive to the needs and values of different population groups, such as racial and ethnic minorities, females, and the aged. Health promotion and prevention programs are most effective when they incorporate the cultural beliefs and practices of the targeted population. Not only must we make a special effort to encourage underserved populations to be more active, but also we must recognize and address the barriers that serve to limit participation in physical activity. Barriers such as cultural beliefs, financial constraints, physical limitations, or unsafe neighborhoods influence participation in physical activity. Prejudice and discrimination needlessly limit opportunities. Addressing disparities in participation and inequities in opportunities requires that physical education, exercise science, and sport professionals make a commitment to challenging the status quo and working to increase opportunities for underserved populations. Equity-oriented physical educators, exercise scientists, and sport leaders are needed if we are going to achieve our goal of lifespan involvement in physical activity for all people.

A large segment of our population is over 50 and that segment is growing rapidly. Because of the remarkable increases in longevity and the growing awareness that some of the risks associated with disease and disability can be reduced, healthy promotion is emerging as a significant theme in geriatrics. Physical activity is a critical component of a healthy lifestyle. In 2001, the Robert Wood Johnson Foundation released its report, *National Blueprint: Increasing Physical Activity among Adults Aged 50 and Older.*[56] The *Blueprint* called for a coordinated effort by medical and health professionals, including physical activity professionals, to take a more prominent role in promoting physical activity in older adults. To increase physical activity among older adults, the diversity within this population must be recognized and planned for when designing and implementing programs. Physical activity programs must address the needs of a broad range of people from various cultural and ethnic backgrounds, socioeconomic and educational status, and of all races and genders. Within these populations are the frail elderly, older adults with chronic health conditions and disabilities and active, healthy senior citizens. The "one size fits all" program will not work. Physical activity programs must be tailored to fit the needs of specific populations.

Regular moderate physical activity can yield important health benefits for people of all ages.

Physical education, exercise science, and sport professionals can contribute in many different ways to the promotion of physical activity in older adults. Exercise physiologists can take a leadership role in determining the amount of physical activity necessary for health benefits for different population groups. The impact of physical activity on disease, disability, and quality of life needs to be tracked over a period of time. Exercise physiologists have the qualifications to play a leading role in this effort. Other research is needed to ascertain the factors that motivate individuals to participate in physical activity programs or self-directed activities and to incorporate these factors into programs to sustain ongoing involvement by the program's participants. Physical education, exercise science, and sport professionals have the expertise to undertake these and other endeavors.

Physical educators, exercise scientists, and sports leaders are needed to conduct high-quality programs for older adults in may different settings, such as community settings, retirement communities, work sites, schools, assisted living facilities, senior citizen centers, health and sport clubs, hospital wellness programs, and other settings easily accessible to the older populations. A greater effort must be made to assist individuals in selecting physical activity options that match their interests, lifestyles, and functional abilities as well as identifying avenues for them to pursue them. Educating medical and other health care professionals about the value of physical activity and disseminating information about "best practices" programs that can be replicated in other settings is a role that physical education, exercise science, and sport professionals can capably undertake. The *Blueprint* encourages more physical education, exercise science, and sport professionals to become trained in working with older adults as this segment of our population continues to grow. More qualified professionals are needed to conduct programs to meet the needs of this diverse population.

A concerted effort by professionals must be made to reach all segments of the adult population and to give them the necessary skills, knowledge, and attitudes to develop and maintain adequate levels of health-related fitness. We must sustain participation by that small segment of society, the individuals who exercise vigorously enough to maintain an adequate level of health-related fitness. We must encourage the people who engage in moderate physical activity to upgrade the intensity of their efforts to achieve the full benefits of appropriate vigorous exercise. Finally, we must reach out to those individuals who exercise irregularly, if at all, and help them to begin to incorporate physical activity into their lives. Accomplishment of these goals requires committed, qualified professionals and a diversity of programs conducted in a variety of settings and targeted to all segments of the population.

EDUCATIONAL REFORM

The 1970s and 1980s were marked by calls for the reform of America's schools. These calls were prompted by several factors, including the public's desire for accountability, the poor reading and writing performance of students, the reduction of academic standards for high school graduation, the relaxation of requirements for college entrance, and the loss of professional status by teachers. The growing social disorder and problems within the school environment, such as student drug abuse, contributed to the public's dissatisfaction. Concern was also raised by the significant differences in performance between whites and minority students and between the affluent and the poor.

The 1983 report, *A Nation at Risk,* issued by the National Commission on Excellence in Education captured the public's attention with its bold declaration that "the educational foundations of our society are presently being eroded by a rising tide of mediocrity that threatens our very future as a Nation and a people."[57] America's preeminent position in commerce, industry, science, and technological innovation was being challenged and overtaken by countries throughout the world. Our educational system was faulted for failing to develop in the country's youth the skills necessary to compete within the world marketplace. The report stressed that individuals who do not possess the necessary skills, literacy, and training will be disadvantaged economically and disenfranchised from a chance to participate fully in our society.

A Nation at Risk, The Paideia Proposal: An Educational Manifesto,[58] *High School: A Report on Secondary Education in America,*[59] and other reports of this time called for reform of the educational system. In general, these reports called for strengthening the educational system and improvement of student learning. It was recommended that a greater emphasis be placed on the basics, such as mathematics, reading, writing, and science. Elimination of the "frills" in the curriculum would provide more time for students to master the basics and increase their level of achievement.

Improvement of teaching was another area cited by the reports: opportunities for meaningful continuing education, more stringent entrance requirements into teacher preparation programs, and changes in the content and format of teacher preparation. Competency testing was suggested as a means to ensure that teachers had mastered the content they were teaching and had the ability to effectively use basic pedagogical skills.

A third area of improvement focused on the organizations of schools and their funding. To provide more time for instruction, lengthening of the school day and year was recommended. Creation of school and community/industry partnerships to improve learning opportunities was another strategy to improve student learning and to assist school systems that were economically disadvantaged.

Increased emphasis on core subjects, such as mathematics, reduces the time available for daily physical education.

Many educators view the publication of *A Nation at Risk*[57] as the start of the national education standards movement. Standards serve to clarify expectations and provide a means to assess achievement. At an educational summit in 1989, President Bush and the nation's governors identified five school subjects—English, mathematics, science, history, and geography—for which challenging national achievement standards would be established.[60]

During the 1990s, pressures for educational reform continued. In 1994, *The Goals 2000: Education America Act* established goals for the year 2000.[61] These national education goals served as the benchmark against which America's progress in education was measured. As previously discussed in Chapter 2, these goals emphasized a more challenging curriculum and higher academic standards. Foreign languages, the arts, economics, and civics and government were added to the previously defined competency areas in which students must demonstrate high levels of achievement. Another goal declared that U.S. students would be first in the world in mathematics and science achievement. Other goals called for improving the readiness of children entering school, creating a better learning environment, enhancing the professional development of teachers, promoting greater parental and community involvement in the schools, and giving more emphasis to lifelong learning. If educational reform is to succeed, greater attention must be directed to the societal problems that influence the education process and outcomes.

The 1990s saw an increased emphasis on accountability for performance by the schools and standards-based education. Standards for what students "should know and should be able to do" for most school subjects, including mathematics, science, and physical education, were established. The establishment of standards increased pressure on school administrators and teachers to improve academic performance. This pressure to demonstrate increased student achievement, particularly in the areas of science and mathematics, has led to efforts to increase the time available for learning. Some schools lengthened the school day and/or the school year; other schools reduced the time allotted to other school subjects, such as physical education.

In 2001, President George W. Bush set forth his *No Child Left Behind*[62] initiative, designed to strengthen the educational experience of all children, regardless of race, ethnicity, gender, or socioeconomic background. This initiative called for the establishment of standards, frequent assessment of student programs, and greater accountability of schools for student learning.

The *Condition of Education* is published annually by the U.S. government to provide information progress and trends in education in such areas as student achievement, dropout rates, and degree attainment. The *Condition of Education 2004*[63] revealed that progress had been made in the areas of mathematics and science. For example, between 1982 and 2000, the percentage of high school graduates who had completed advanced courses in mathematics rose from 26 to 65 percent, and in science it increased from 35 percent to 63 percent of graduates. It also revealed that it is more likely that high school students in high-poverty and high-minority public schools were taught English, science, and mathematics by out-of-the field teacher than their peers in low-poverty and low-minority schools, contributing to significant differences in achievement.

Despite the improvements that have occurred, disturbing disparities in achievement still exist among different population groups. For example, reading and mathematics scores have improved during the decade, but the gap in performance between white and black students persists, although it has narrowed. Poverty adversely affects educational achievement. For instance, nearly 70% of inner-city fourth graders are unable to read at a basic level on national reading tests. The gender gap in educational attainment still exists, but it has narrowed. Females read and write better than males, although they perform worse than males in science and mathematics. Females are more likely to go to college immediately after high school than males are.

Disparities in education are a great concern. High levels of educational attainment are associated with good health (*Healthy People 2010* noted that the highest levels of sedentary behavior were associated with the lowest levels of educational attainment).[28] Income is also associated with health; People who are affluent have better health status than people who are less affluent. Education is often a predictor of income. For example, in 2000, the average annual income for men with a bachelor's degree was $56,334, and for women it was $40,415.[64] In contrast, men who had not completed high school earned $25,095 a year and women earned $17,919 a year.[64]

Another area where the relationship between educational attainment and health is reflected in individuals' *health literacy.* Health literacy is the "degree to which individuals have the capacity to obtain, process and understand basic health information and services needed to make appropriate health decisions."[28] An estimated 90 million adults have lower-than-average reading skills.[65] People with a low level of literacy are more likely to experience difficulty in accessing, understanding, and applying information, including information related to health.[65] Additionally, individuals with limited literacy skills may not be knowledgeable about health-related facts, such as the acceptable range for blood pressure, the recommended amount of daily physical activity, or the type and number of fruits and vegetables that should be consumed each day.[65]

The consequence of poor health literacy is poorer health status; researchers suggest that the reason is that individuals are less likely to understand how to prevent disease and to benefit from advances in health care.[28] Health literacy is a critical aspect of both primary and preventive health care. Improving health literacy can save lives, reduce medical costs, and affect the health and well-being of millions of Americans. Providing individuals with easy-to-read information, presenting information in a way that is compatible with the culture and in the language of the individual, and using a variety of communication channels are some ways to improve health literacy and, ultimately, health outcomes.[65]

Getting a quality education is one of the best ways to improve one's life, particularly for those who are socially or economically disadvantaged. Many minorities are at an educational disadvantage for several reasons, including a lower level of parental education, greater likelihood of living with a single parent, fewer community resources, attending a disadvantaged school that is less conducive to learning, and a greater likelihood of living in poverty. Additionally, the surge in immigration has resulted in an increase in students for whom English is their second language. Learning to read and write in English, while at the same time mastering learning in the other content areas of the school, poses a great challenge. Minorities have made great gains in education since the advent of *A Nation at Risk,* but compared to their white, non-Hispanic peers, too many minorities are disadvantaged with respect to educational access, achievement, and level of educational attainment.

Changes in the racial and ethnic composition of our country have altered the diversity of language and culture in our schools. Children and youth from many different cultural backgrounds, a variety of family situations, and a wide range of economic circumstances present a challenge to an educational system charged with providing equal opportunities for all students. This challenge must be met and each child should be educated to his or her fullest potential. Failure to help each child achieve "threatens our very future as a nation and a people."[57]

What Are the Implications of the Educational Reform Movement for Physical Education?

Physical education is an integral component of the educational curriculum. However, many advocates of educational reform do not share this point of view. Some proponents of educational reform regard physical education as a "frill" or a nonessential subject. Several leading educational reports failed to mention physical education; other reports relegated physical education to the status of a personal service or ancillary course. In essence, physical education is viewed by some as a subject that cannot be justified for inclusion in the educational curriculum.

The focus of educational reform on standards-based achievement in the "basic" subjects has led many schools to alter their curriculums to increase the time available for core academic subjects and reduce the time spent on "nonessential" subjects. One consequence of this is that content that is not tested, or perceived as "nonessential," becomes lower in priority, such as physical education, art, and music.[66] Despite the potential of physical education to contribute educational goals, schools are eliminating or reducing the time available for physical education. The time "wasted" on physical education could be used to improve academic performance. Some proponents of educational reform, however, support the inclusion of physical education within the school curriculum. The Carnegie Commission report, *High School,* stated: "Clearly no knowledge is more critical than knowledge about health. Without it no other life goal can be successfully achieved."[59] The commission recommended a course in lifetime fitness for all students.

The National Association for Sport and Physical Education (NASPE) believes that physical education should be an integral part of the school curriculum at all levels of instruction. NASPE's Council on Physical Education for Children position paper, entitled *Physical Education is Critical to a Complete Education,*[67] notes that physical education can affect both academic learning and the physical activity patterns of students. "The healthy, physically active student is more likely to be academically motivated, alert, and successful. . . . Throughout the school years, quality physical education can promote social, cooperative, and problem-solving competencies. Quality physical education programs in our nation's schools are essential in developing motor skills, physical fitness, and understanding of concepts that foster lifelong healthy lifestyles."[67]

Healthy children have more energy available for learning. Additionally, research has shown that children engaged in daily physical education "show superior motor fitness, academic performance, and attitude toward school compared to their peers who did not participate in physical education."[66] After a review of the literature on physical education and academic performance, Shepard offers this perspective:

> Daily programs of physical education should not be introduced with the expectation that they will lead to major gains in academic performance. However, available data suggest that the rate of academic learning per unit of class time is enhanced in physically active students, so that lack of curricular time is not a valid reason for denying children a daily program of quality physical education.[68]

Furthermore, the importance of developing and sustaining positive health habits early in the child's development cannot be overlooked. Physical education is important for the overall education of the students. There is strong support from many different groups for requiring daily, quality physical education for all grade levels. The U.S. Senate and the House of Representatives passed a resolution in 1987 encouraging state and local governments and local educational institutions to

Congressional Physical Education Resolutions

To encourage state and local governments and local educational agencies to provide quality daily physical education programs for all children from kindergarten through grade 12.

Whereas physical education is essential to the physical development of the growing child;

Whereas physical education helps improve the overall health of children by increasing cardiovascular endurance, muscular strength and power, flexibility, weight regulation, improved bone development, improved posture, skillful moving, increased mental alertness, active lifestyle habits, and constructive use of leisure time;

Whereas physical education helps improve the mental alertness, academic performance, readiness to learn, and enthusiasm for learning of children;

Whereas physical education helps improve self-esteem, interpersonal relationships, responsible behavior, and independence of children;

Whereas children who participate in quality daily physical education programs tend to be more healthy and physically fit;

Whereas physically fit adults have significantly reduced risk factors for heart attacks and strokes;

Whereas the Surgeon General, in *Objectives for the Nation,* recommends increasing the number of school-mandated physical education programs that focus on health-related physical fitness;

Whereas the Secretary of Education, in *First Lessons—A Report on Elementary Education in America,* recognized that elementary schools have a special mandate to provide elementary school children with knowledge, habits, and attitudes that will equip the children for a fit and healthy life; and

Whereas a quality daily physical education program for all children from kindergarten through grade 12 is an essential part of a comprehensive education: now, therefore, be it

Resolved by the Senate (the House of Representatives concurring), that Congress encourages state and local government and local educational agencies to provide quality daily physical educational programs for all children from kindergarten through grade 12.

provide quality, daily physical education programs for all students in kindergarten through 12th grade. The resolution notes the many contributions physical education makes to educational objectives (see the Congressional Physical Education Resolutions box.) The resolution recognized that elementary schools have a special mandate to teach students knowledge, skills, and habits and develop the attitudes that will enable them to lead a fit and healthy life.

National health reports clearly support the inclusion of daily, quality physical education programs in the school curriculum. Daily, quality physical education programs for all school children can contribute to the attainment of our national health goals. Never before have we seen such national support for physical education in the schools.

Healthy People 2010 recognizes the contribution physical education can make and calls for increasing the number of schools that require daily physical education for all students. Additionally, the 1996 *Surgeon General's Report on Physical Activity and Health,* the 1997 *Centers for Disease Control and Prevention Guidelines for Schools and Community Programs to Promote Lifelong Physical Activity Among Young People*[53] both recommended requiring daily physical education for all students from kindergarten through 12th grade. In 2000, the *Report to the President: Promoting Better Health for Young People through Physical Activity and Sports*[69] identified the substantial health benefits gained from regular participation in physical activity. Quality, daily physical education was recommended as one strategy that would benefit the health of children and youth and enable them to incorporate more physical activity into their daily lives. School physical education programs can reach over 50 million students at an important time in their lives. Developing positive health habits at an early age is crucial in sustaining a healthy lifestyle as an adult. Importantly, school physical education programs provide one of the greatest means of reaching disadvantaged populations. The schools have a critical role to play in promoting the health of the nation.

Since 1987, the National Association for Sport and Physical Education (NASPE) has periodically conducted the *Shape of the Nation Report* to summarize the status of physical education in the American educational system. In interpreting the results, NASPE recommends keeping in mind that there is no federal law requiring that physical education be provided to students, and that states may set some minimum requirements for time and content and then defer more specific decisions for physical education to local school districts. This approach accounts for considerable variability in the delivery of physical education and some other subject areas, such as art or music.

The 2001 *Shape of the Nation Report*[66] revealed that most states do not require daily physical education for all students in kindergarten through 12th grade. Illinois is the only state that mandates daily physical education for all students K–12; however, a waiver program allowing exemption from daily physical education has been implemented. Forty-eight states have a state mandate for physical education. However, in many states the legislated mandate requires only that physical education be provided, with local school districts in charge of the content and the format.

Adolescence is a critical time for forming health habits, including regular participation in physical activity. National surveys of physical activity among children and youth showed that physical activity decreased markedly during the adolescent years. The Centers for Disease Prevention and Health Promotion School Health Policies and Programs Study 2000 (SHPPS 2000)[70] revealed that as students progress from kindergarten to 12th grade, their opportunity to participate in physical education decreases. About 50% of schools require physical education in grades 1 through 5; by grades 11 and 12 only about 5% of the schools require physical education.[70] Only 29.1% of students in grades 9 through 12 participated in daily physical education; this is a decrease from 41.6% in 1991.[71] NASPE found that the majority of high school students take physical education for only one year between the 9th and 12th grades.[66]

Another distressing trend is the policy of exempting students from the required physical education courses. SHPPS 2000 reported that 16.7% of elementary schools, 25.3% of middle schools, and 40% of senior high schools exempt students.[70] Among the reasons for the exemption are high physical competency test scores and participation in community sports and community service activities. At the middle and high school levels, students were also exempted for participation in school sports, engaging in vocational training, and enrollment in other school courses. The *Shape of the Nation*[66] reported that 27 states allow substitutions for high school physical education. Reasons for substitution include medical reasons, religious reasons, participation in school sports, ROTC, marching band, and other special activities.[66]

The *Shape of the Nation* revealed that time requirements for physical education vary widely. At the elementary school level, state mandated times range from 30 to 150 minutes per week; NASPE recommends 150 minutes per week. At the middle school level, NASPE recommends 225 minutes per week; state requirements range from 80 minutes per week to 225 minutes per week. High school time requirements are highly variable, ranging from no time specified to 225 minutes a week, which is the time recommended by NASPE.

NASPE recommends that elementary school students should have a minimum of 60 minutes a day of moderate and vigorous physical activity every day, while middle and high school students should accumulate a minimum of 30 minutes every day. NASPE suggests that to achieve that amount of physical activity schools must make physical education instruction "the cornerstone of a systematic physical activity promotion in school that also includes recess, after-school clubs and intramurals as well as competitive athletics. The cocurricular activities must be designed to attract all students especially those not interested in traditional athletic programs."[67]

One outcome of the standards-based education movement is the development of standards for physical education. As discussed in Chapter 2, in 1995 NASPE published *Moving Into the Future: National Standards for Physical Education.*[71] Both content—"what students should know and be able to do in physical education" and performance—"how good is good enough" standards were identified for students in grades K through 12. *The Shape of the Nation*[67] reports that most states have established, or are in the process of establishing, standards for physical education. The incorporation of the content standards into physical education lets students know what they have accomplished and helps parents, school policy makers, and community members to more clearly understand the contribution of physical education both to the education of students and to their health and well-being.

Promoting Better Health for Young People Through Physical Activity and Sports[69] calls upon us, as a nation, to do more to promote lifelong participation in physical activity. Quality, daily physical education enhances the health and well-being of young people. Through physical education, children and youth acquire the skills, knowledge, and attitudes for lifetime participation, contributing to good health throughout the lifespan. Daily physical education is one part of a comprehensive approach to helping young people be active and stay active. Resources must be directed at creating a wide range of accessible, safe, and affordable opportunities to be active within the school and the community. Special efforts must be made to ensure that programs reach out to involve those with the greatest needs, including girls and racial/ethnic minorities. Programs must be responsive to the needs of different population groups, and resources invested in "creative, culturally sensitive, linguistically appropriate programs to give all young Americans the opportunities and motivation they need to become more active."

Strategies were developed to create additional opportunities for participation in physical activities for all children and youth. According to the report, "to obtain the opportunities and motivation that will enable them to increase their levels of physical activity and fitness, young people can benefit from:

- Families who model and support participation in enjoyable physical activity.
- School programs, including quality, daily physical education; health education; recess; and extracurricular activities that help students develop the knowledge, attitudes, skills, behaviors, and confidence to adopt and maintain physically active lifestyles, while providing opportunities for enjoyable physical activity.
- After-school care programs that provide regular opportunities for active, physical play.
- Youth sports and recreation programs that offer a range of developmentally appropriate activities that are attractive to all young people.
- A community structured environment that makes it easy and safe for young people to

Learning tennis skills is one way in which people with disabilities can participate in recreational activities.

walk, ride bicycles, and use close-to-home physical activity facilities.
- Media campaigns that increase motivation of young people to be physically active."[69]

Full implementation of the recommended strategies requires the commitment of resources, hard work, and collaboration between governments at all levels, nongovernmental organizations, and the private sector. The implementation of these strategies will create increased opportunities for children to participate in enjoyable physical activity during their childhood and through adolescence, encouraging the continuation of physical activity into adulthood.

What can be done to increase quality, daily physical education for all students in our schools? Physical education, exercise science, and sport professionals must take a leadership role in advocating for physical education. As advocates, be able to articulate the benefits of quality physical education and be knowledgeable about the role of physical activity in advancing the nation's health goals. Conduct quality programs, incorporate the physical education content standards, and assess student learning on a regular basis. Professionals must forge collaborative relationships with policy makers, community and school leaders, parents, and youths to increase physical education in the schools and expand opportunities for involvement in physical activity within the community. Conducting quality programs, advocating for increased opportunities for physical activity, including daily physical education, and becoming actively involved in working for change are just some ways that physical education, exercise science, and sport can contribute to increasing physical activity opportunities for all people.

It seems ironic that at a time when we know more than ever before about the significant relationship between physical activity and health, we are under greater pressure than ever before to defend our programs. Never before in our history have we had greater recognition of the contribution of physical activity to health and the importance of being physically active throughout life. Physical education, exercise science, and sport professionals must capitalize on this support to make quality, daily physical education a reality for all students.

Focus on Career: Health and Aging

PROFESSIONAL ORGANIZATIONS

- American Association for Active Lifestyles and Fitness/AAAHPERD (www.aahperd.org → AAALF)
- American Association for Health Education/AAHPERD (www.aahperd.org → AAHE)
- American Public Health Association (APHA) (http://apha.org)
- The Geronotological Society of America (www.geron.org)

PROFESSIONAL JOURNALS

- *American Journal of Health Education*
- *American Journal of Public Health*
- *The Gerontologist*
- *Journals of Gerontology*
    - Series A: *Biological Sciences and Medical Sciences*
    - Series B: *Psychological Sciences and Social Sciences*

SUMMARY

The role of physical education, exercise science, and sport in our society is influenced by societal trends. One significant trend is the changing demographics of our population. Our society is more culturally diverse than at any point in its history, and the diversity will increase as we move farther into the twenty-first century. We are living longer. Our society is becoming older; the number of people 65 years of age and older will increase from about 13% of the population in 1997 to 18.5% in 2025. The number of people with disabilities continues to grow. The structure of the family is changing. Too many Americans lives in poverty; poverty is associated with poor health and school outcomes. As physical educators, exercise scientists, and sport leaders, we must be committed to providing opportunities for lifelong involvement in physical activity for all people. Cultural competency is important in working with people from diverse population groups to adopt and maintain a physically active lifestyle. Cultural competency includes an appreciation of differences, valuing the uniqueness of individuals, and commitment to addressing inequities in opportunities.

The wellness movement and physical activity and fitness movement also hold several implications for physical education and sport. The wellness movement emphasized health promotion and disease prevention through lifestyle modification and individual responsibility for one's own health. Physical activity and fitness are integral parts of a healthy lifestyle. The evidence supporting the contribution of physical activity to health continues to mount. *Healthy People 2010* and *Physical Activity and Health: A Report of the Surgeon General* document the significant role physical activity plays in promoting well-being. Within the past few decades there has been a tremendous surge of interest in physical activity and fitness. However, when participation patterns are examined, too many children and adults lead a sedentary lifestyle. Professionals need to increase their efforts to involve people in physical activity. The wellness and physical activity and fitness movements offer strong support for the development of nonschool physical education, exercise science, and sport programs to reach people of all ages.

The educational reform movement received its impetus from a series of reports decrying the status of education in America's schools and identifying specific areas for reform. The reports call for a greater emphasis on the core subjects and standards. Lifelong learning is stressed. These reports disagree on the status of physical education as an educational basic. Thus, it is up to physical educators to make a strong case for physical education as a basic before physical education is eliminated from the educational curriculum. The emphasis on lifelong learning supports the need for physical education, exercise science, and sport programs for individuals of all ages.

SELF-ASSESSMENT TESTS

These tests are designed to help you determine if you have mastered the material and competencies presented in this chapter.

1. You have been invited to speak to a community group on the role of physical activity in the promotion of health and attainment of wellness. Prepare a short speech reflecting the contribution of physical education, exercise science, and sport to a healthy lifestyle. Use the information provided in the Get Connected box to locate current information about the value of physical activity.
2. For each of the *Healthy People 2010* objectives for physical activity and fitness, provide specific examples of how school and nonschool physical education, exercise science, and sport programs can help in their attainment.
3. As can be seen from the information on changing demographics, our society is becoming more diverse. What specific steps can physical education, exercise science, and sport take to reach underserved populations? Are you culturally competent to work with our nation's increasingly diverse populations?
4. The school board of your hometown is considering a proposal to decrease the time allocated to physical education in the school curriculum. Specifically, the board is considering a proposal to eliminate daily

physical education for K–12. Students would then take physical education 3 days a week until 10th grade, at which time it would become an elective. Under the new policy, students who participate in interscholastic athletics and marching band would be excused from physical education during the season. As a professional, what arguments would you make against this resolution? What arguments would you offer in support of this resolution? What would be your position as a parent of a child in this school?

REFERENCES

1. De Sensi JT: Understanding multiculturalism and valuing diversity: a theoretical perspective, Quest 47:34–43, 1995.
2. National Center for Health Statistics: Health United States 2001, Hyattsville, Md., 2001 (www.cdc.gov/nchs).
3. US Department of Commerce, US Census Bureau, Census 2000, Washington, D.C., 2001 (www.census.gov).
4. US Department of Education, A back to school report on the baby boom echo: Growing pains, US Department of Education, Washington, D.C., 2000 (www.ed.gov).
5. US Department of Health and Human Services: Life expectancy hits new high in 2000: mortality declines for several leading causes of death, October 10, 2001 (www.cdc.gov).
6. Federal Interagency Forum on Child and Family Statistics: America's children: key indicators of well-being, 2001. Washington, D.C., 2001, Federal Interagency Forum on Child and Family Statistics (childstats.gov).
7. Armas GC: National poverty rate rises for 2nd year in a row, September 27, 2003 (www.montana forum.com/rednews/2003/09/27/build/economy/poverty2.php?nnn=6).
8. US Department of Health and Human Services Office of Minority Health: Revised CLAS Standards from the Office of Minority Health, Closing the Gap, February/March 2001 (www.omhrc.gov).
9. Bureau of Primary Health Care, Health Resources and Services Administration, US Department of Health and Human Services: Cultural competence: a journey, Washington, D.C., 1998, Bureau of Primary Health Care (bphc.hrsa.gov/cultural competency/ Default.htm).
10. US Department of Heath and Human Services Administration on Aging: Achieving cultural competence: a guidebook for providers of services to older Americans and their families, Washington, D.C., 2001, Department of Health and Human Services (www.aoa.gov).
11. US Department of Health and Human Services Bureau of Primary Health: Moving toward 100% access and 0 disparities, Washington, D.C., 1998, Department of Health and Human Services (bphc.hrsa.gov/campaign).
12. National College Athletic Association, 2001–2002 Race Demographics of NCAA Member Institutions' Athletic Personnel, 2003 (www.ncaa.org).
13. Ford MG: Working toward cultural competence in athletic training, Athletic Therapy Today, 8, 60–66, 2003.
14. National Education Association, NEA and teacher recruitment: An overview, 2004 (www.nea.org).
15. Burden JW, Jr., Hodge SR, O'Bryant CP, and Harrison L, Jr.: From colorblindness to intercultural sensitivity: infusing diversity training in PETE programs, Quest 56, 173–189, 2004.
16. Centers for Disease Control and Prevention, Fact Sheet—Actual Causes of Death in the United States, 2000 (www.cdc.gov/nccdphp/factsheets/death_causes2000_access.htm).
17. Centers for Disease Control and Prevention, Chronic Disease Overview, 2004 (www.cdc.gov/nccdphp/overview.htm).
18. American Cancer Society, Statistics for 2004 (www.cancer.org/docroot/STT/stt_0.asp).
19. United States Department of Health and Human Services, Study shows poor diet, inactivity close to becoming leading preventable cause of death, March 9, 2004 (www.smallsstep.gov/sm_steps/news_updates.html).
20. Mokdad AH, Marks JS, Stroup DF, Gerberding JL: Actual Causes of Death in the United States, 2000, JAMA 291,1238–1245, 2004.

21. Active Living Leadership, Physical activity facts and figures, 2004 (www.activelivingleadership.org).
22. Centers for Disease Control and Prevention, National Center for Health Statistics, Adult Inactivity.
23. President's Council on Physical Fitness and Sport, Fact Sheet—Physical Activity and Health, 2004 (www.fitness.gov).
24. World Health Organization: Constitution of the World Health Organization, Chronicle of the World Health Organization, 1:29–43, 1947.
25. US Department of Health, Education, and Welfare: Healthy people: The Surgeon General's report on health promotion and disease prevention, Washington, D.C., 1979, US Government Printing Office.
26. US Public Health Service, US Department of Health and Human Services: Promoting health/preventing disease: objectives for the nation, Washington, D.C., 1980, US Government Printing Office.
27. US Public Health Service, US Department of Health and Human Services: Healthy people 2000: national health promotion and disease prevention objectives, Washington, D.C., 1996, US Government Printing Office.
28. US Department of Health and Human Services: Healthy people 2010: understanding and improving health, ed 2, Washington, D.C., 2000, US Government Printing Office (www.healthypeople.gov/healthypeople).
29. US Department of Health and Human Services, Health Care Financing Administration, National health care expenditures, 1999 (www.hcfa.gov/stats).
30. Centers for Medicare and Medicaid Services: Highlights—National Health Expenditures, 2002, 2004 (www.cms.gov).
31. US Department of Health and Human Services: HHS issues report on the impact of poor health on businesses, September 16, 2003 (www.hhs.gov/news/presss/20030916.html).
32. National Center for Chronic Disease Prevention and Health Promotion: Preventing obesity and chronic diseases through good nutrition and physical activity, August 2003 (www.cdc.gov/nccdphp/pe_factsheets/pe_pa.htm).
33. Serxner S, Anderson DR, and Gold D: Building program participation: Strategies for recruitment and retention in worksite health promotion programs, The Art of Health Promotion, March/April 2004, 1–5.
34. US Department of Health and Human Services: Overweight and obesity threaten U.S. health gains, December 13, 2001 (www.surgeongeneral.gov/news/pressreleases/pr_obesity.htm).
35. US Department of Health and Human Services: Prevention: A blueprint for action, 2002 (aspe.hhs.gov/health/blueprint/overview.shtml).
36. US Department of Health and Human Services: Healthy People 2010 Progress Reports, 2004 (www.healthypeople.gov).
37. Siedentop D: Valuing the physically active life: contemporary and future directions, Quest 48: 266–274, 1996.
38. Centers for Disease Control and Prevention: Increasing physical activity: a report on recommendations of the task force on community preventive services, MMWR, 50(No. RR-18), 2001.
39. US Department of Health and Human Services: Physical activity and health: a report of the Surgeon General, Atlanta, GA, 1996, US Department of Health and Human Services, Centers for Disease Control and Prevention, National Center for Chronic Disease.
40. Centers for Disease Control and Prevention: An explanation of U.S. physical activity surveys, May 9, 2003. (www.cdc.gov/nccdphp/dnpa/physical/physical_surveys.htm).
41. Hedley AA, Ogden CL, Johnson CL, Carroll MD, Curtin LR, and Flegal KM: Prevalence of overweight and obesity among US children, adolescents, and adults, 1999–2000, JAMA, 291, 2847–2850, 2004.
42. National Institutes for Health, National Heart, Lung, and Blood Institute: Clinical guidelines on the identification, evaluation, and treatment of overweight and obesity in adults, Washington, D.C., 1998, National Institutes of Health.
43. Centers for Disease Control and Prevention: Youth Risk Behavior Surveillance—United States, 2003 (www.cdc.gov/yrbss).
44. Schhoeborn CA, Adams PF, Barnes PM, Vickerie JL, and Schiller JS: Health behaviors of adults: United States, 1999–2001. National Center for Health Statistics. Vital Health Stat(10)(219), 2004.
45. Centers for Disease Control and Prevention: Prevalence of physical activity, including lifestyle

activities among adults—United States, 2000–2001, MMWE, 52(32):764–769, 2003.

46. Centers for Disease Control and Prevention: National Health Interview Survey, 2003 (www.cdc.gov/nchs).
47. Centers for Disease Control and Prevention, National Center for Health Statistics, BRFSS, 2004 (www.cdc.gov/nchs).
48. American Sports Data, Inc.: Booming health clubs, slipping fitness participation, and healthier diets all coexist in the overweight society, Press release August 28, 2000 (www.americansportsdata.com).
49. American Sports Data, Inc.: Grandparents fitter than grandchildren? Press release July 23, 2001 (www.americansportsdata.com).
50. International Health, Racquet and Sportsclub Association, Industry Statistics, 2004 (www.ihrsa.org).
51. Sport Goods Manufacturing Association, Industry Statistics, 2004 (www.sgma.com).
52. Corbin CB: Is the fitness bandwagon passing us by? Journal of Physical Education, Recreation and Dance 55(9):17, 1984.
53. Centers for Disease Control and Prevention: Guidelines for school and community programs to promote physical activity among young people, 1997, United States. Public Health Service, US Department of Health and Human Services, Washington, D.C. (www.cdc.gov).
54. Collingwood TR: Providing physical fitness programs to at-risk youth, Quest 49:67–88, 1997.
55. Harris JC: Enhancing quality of life in low-income neighborhoods: Developing equity oriented individuals, Quest 48:366–377, 1996.
56. Robert Wood Johnson Foundation: National blueprint: Increasing physical activity among adults aged 50 and older, 2001, Robert Wood Johnson Foundation, Princeton, N.J. (www.rwjf.org).
57. Gardner D: A nation at risk: the imperative for educational reform, Washington, D.C., 1983, US Government Printing Office.
58. Adler M: The Paideia proposal: an educational manifesto, New York, 1982, Macmillian.
59. Boyer E: High school: a report on secondary education in America, New York, 1983, Harper & Row.
60. US Department of Education: The Charlottesville Summit, National Education Goals 2000 (www.ed.gov).
61. US Department of Education: The goals 2000: educate America act—launching a new era in education, Washington, D.C., 1994, US Government Printing Office.
62. US Department of Education: No child left behind, 2001 (nces.ed.gov).
63. US Department of Education: Condition of Education, 2004 (www.ed.gov).
64. US Department of Education: National Center for Educational Statistics, 2004 (www.nces.gov).
65. U.S. Agency for Health Care Research and Quality. New evidence report illustrates links between health literacy and health care use and outcomes. Press Release, April 8, 2004 (www.ahrq.gov).
66. National Association for Physical Education and Sport: Shape of the nation report, 2001, Reston, Va., 2001, American Alliance for Health, Physical Education, Recreation and Dance.
67. National Association for Physical Education and Sport, Council of Physical Education for Children: Physical education is critical to a complete education, Reston, Va., 2001, American Alliance for Health, Physical Education, Recreation and Dance.
68. Shepard RI: Curricular physical activity and academic performance, Pediatric Exercise Science 9:117–126, 1997.
69. Centers for Disease Control and Prevention Healthy Youth: Promoting better health for young people through physical activity and sports: a report to the president from the Secretary of Health and Human Services and the Secretary of Education, 2000, Healthy Youth Center for Disease Control and Prevention, Silver Springs, Md. (www.cdc.gov/nccdphp/dash/presphysactrpt).
70. Centers for Disease Control and Prevention, National Center for Chronic Disease Prevention and Health Promotion, Division of Adolescent and School Health: School health policies and programs study 2000 (www.cdc.gov/nccdphp/dash/shpps/factsheets/fs00_pe.htm).
71. National Association for Sport and Physical Education: Moving into the future: national standards for physical education, New York, 1995, WCB/McGraw-Hill.

SUGGESTED READINGS

Burden JW, Jr., Hodge SR, O'Bryant CP, and Harrison L, Jr.: From colorblindness to intercultural sensitivity: infusing diversity training in PETE programs, Quest 56, 173–189, 2004.

Diversity training across teacher preparation programs and curricular is important to enhance culture sensitivity of preservice teachers and help them work more effectively with children from all backgrounds.

Centers for Disease Control and Prevention: Increasing physical activity: a report on recommendations of the Task Force on Community Preventive Services, Morbidity and Mortality Weekly Report, 50 (No. RR-18), October 26, 2001.

Reviews physical activity interventions for different settings and identifies approaches that are recommended on the basis of increasing physical activity and improving aerobic capacity.

Centers for Disease Control and Prevention Healthy Youth: Promoting better health for young people through physical activity and sports: a report to the president from the Secretary of Health and Human Services and the Secretary of Education, 2000, Healthy Youth Center for Disease Control and Prevention, Silver Springs, Md. (Free PDF download at www.cdc.gov/nccdphp/dash/presphysactrpt).

Outlines 10 strategies to promote health and encourage lifelong participation in enjoyable physical activities; appendices include many significant physical activity documents.

Fabiano P, and Swinford PL: Serving racial and ethnic populations with health promotion, American Journal of Health Promotino, 18, 5:8–13.

Health promotion models should address the specific needs of racial and ethnic populations. Models should take into consideration the environmental circumstances of the population served if optimal results are to be achieved.

Ford MG: Working toward cultural competence in athletic training, Athletic Therapy Today, 8:60–66, 2003.

The importance of athletic trainers, as allied health professionals, being able to administer care in a cultural competent manner in order to achieve optimal results.

Harrison L and Worthy T: "Just like all the rest": developing awareness of stereotypical thinking in physical education, JOPERD, 72(9):20–24, 2001.

Discusses stereotyping, the self-fulfilling prophecy, self-stereotyping, and suggestions for reducing stereotyping in physical education classes.

Kulinnna PH: Teaching students to achieve and maintain a health-enhancing level of physical fitness, JOPERD, 72(8):30–33, 2001.

Students need cognitive, affective, psychomotor, and behavioral skills if they are to develop physically active lifestyles as well as encouragement to participate in physical activity both within and outside of school; includes strategies for developing fitness at the elementary and secondary levels.

Langford GA and Carter, L: Academic excellence must include physical education, Physical Educator, 60:28–34, 2003.

Physical education should be an integral part of the school curriculum and should be sequenced in progressive fashion to promote lifelong physical activity.

The Robert Wood Johnson Foundation: National blueprint: increasing physical activity among adults 50 and older, 2001, Princeton, N.J., The Robert Wood Johnson Foundation.

Guide to help organizations and professionals design and implement strategies to help people age 50 and over increase their physical activity (free download at www.rwjf.org).

US Department of Health and Human Services Health Resources and Health Services Administration: Cultural competence works, US Department of Health and Human Services, 2001, Health Resources and Health Services Administration, Merrifield, Va., (free PDF download at www.hrsa.gov/cmc).

Offers ideas for health care professionals to become more culturally competent in the delivery of services; since many physical education, exercise science, and sport professionals work in healthy promotion much of the information may be helpful in working with diverse populations.

II

Foundations of Physical Education, Exercise Science, and Sport

In Part I the terms *physical education, exercise science,* and *sport* were defined and their philosophy and objectives discussed. Part II builds on that knowledge by discussing the foundations of physical education, exercise science, and sport. Trained physical education, exercise science, and sport professionals should understand the foundations of their field. Part II begins with a discussion of the historical foundations of physical education, exercise science, and sport in Chapter 4. Chapter 5 provides an overview of motor behavior. Chapters 6, 7, 8, and 9 present the biomechanical, physiological, sociological, and psychological bases from which physical education, exercise science, and sport derive their principles and concepts. These areas of study are the major sciences or subdisciplines of physical education, exercise science, and sport—namely, exercise physiology, motor behavior, sport and exercise psychology, sport sociology, and biomechanics. The principles and concepts discussed in these chapters introduce the professional to the knowledge needed to plan and conduct meaningful programs in physical education, exercise science, and sport.

C H A P T E R 4

Historical Foundations

Objectives

After reading this chapter the student should be able to—

- Identify events that served as catalysts for physical education, exercise science, and sport's growth.
- Identify some of the outstanding leaders in physical education, exercise science, and sport over the course of history and the contributions each made to the field.
- Discuss recent developments in physical education, exercise science, and sport.
- Draw implications from the discussion of history of principles that will guide the professional future of physical education, exercise science, and sport.

Contemporary physical education, exercise science, and sport in the United States are built on a rich heritage. Our programs today have been influenced by the philosophies, practices, and sports from other cultures, but particularly the programs of Ancient Greece, Rome, Great Britain, Sweden, and Germany. Events in the United States, such as colonialism, the expanding frontier, the Great Depression, the growth of public school education, urbanization, and technology, have affected the growth and direction of our fields. Within the United States, dynamic, visionary leaders advanced the scope and status of physical education, exercise science, and sport. This chapter provides a brief overview of the history of physical education, exercise science, and sport from ancient times to recent developments. Space limitations preclude a more detailed approach. Additional information is provided at the Online Learning Center. Generally, the terms *physical education* and *sport* are used in reference to early historical developments, with physical education typically used to refer to school-based programs and sport used to refer to organized, competitive contests. It is only in the latter decades of the twentieth century that the term *exercise science* emerged.

History enlightens us—it enables us to understand how contemporary physical education, exercise science, and sport has been shaped by the lead-

GET CONNECTED

Amateur Athletic Foundation of Los Angeles offers access to the history of the Olympics and sports, including a wonderful catalog of art and artifacts, research articles on children and the media, gender and sport; *Journal of Olympic History,* and *Journal of Sport History.*

www.aafla.com

Hickok's Sport History site offers information about the history of specific sports and biographies of athletes from many different sports and times.

www.hickoksports.com/history.shtml

North American Society for Sport History provides access to NASSH news, related sites, and *Journal of Sport History.*

www.nassh.org/index1.html

ers and events of the past. History guides us—it suggests future possibilities and courses of action that might be most effective in the years to come. History is a scholarly field of study, focusing on the study of change over time. Historians engage in descriptive and interpretive research.

Descriptive research objectively describes, in as much detail as possible, what has happened in the past. According to Mechikoff and Estes, "descriptive history explores the who, what, when, and where of the past, and it tries to do so without transposing ideas, values, and judgments from the present onto the events of the past. Interpretive history seeks to explain the how and why of events that happened in the past. . . . Unlike descriptive history, the interpretive perspective introduces the historian's subjective bias into the interpretation, and history is no longer 'just the facts'."[1] The interpretive perspective seeks to explain the significance of historical events within the historical and social context of the time. Mechikoff and Estes state that the interpretative approach "allows much of the fullness and richness of the history to come forth, and it makes the narrative much more open to discussion and understanding. In contrast, descriptive histories are not better or worse than interpretive histories; they are merely different types of accountings of what occurred in the past."[1] History expands our understanding of society as well as physical education, exercise science, and sport.

SPORT HISTORY

Sport history emerged as a subdiscipline within the realm of physical education, exercise science, and sport in the late 1960s and early 1970s. The definition, scope, historical development, and areas of study are discussed in this section.

Definition and Scope

Struna describes sport history as a "field of scholarly inquiry with multiple and often intersecting foci, including exercise, the body, play, games, athletics, sports, physical recreations, health, and leisure."[2] The term *sport* in this discussion is used broadly to incorporate the multiple foci of the field, as suggested by Struna. Sport historians examine the historical development of sport. They describe and analyze the actions and behaviors of leaders, examine and interpret significant events, study the evolution of organizations, and explore the emergence of trends. It is difficult to appreciate the evolution of sport without understanding the practices, philosophies, and beliefs that were popular at that time. Sport historians are interested

Women's basketball at Smith College, Northampton, Massachusetts, 1904.

in how the past has shaped sport as we experience it today.

Historical Development

There has long been an interest in the history of sport. Early works on the history of sport typically were descriptive in nature, describing the development of a specific sport (e.g., baseball), chronicling the contributions of a leader to physical education (e.g., Dudley Sargent), or documenting certain events (e.g., development of the forerunner to the American Alliance for Health, Physical Education, Recreation, and Dance). However, as interest in the history of sport grew, more interpretive analytical studies were undertaken. These interpretive studies, which incorporated information about the historical and social context of the time, greatly enriched our understanding of sport. Through analytical studies of sport, we gain insight into the following:

- How games and sports came to be included in the school physical education curriculum
- How Victorian-era conceptions of morality influenced sports participation by females
- The impact of segregation on sports opportunities for blacks
- How the "new physical education" developed and how the philosophy of "education through the physical" evolved
- An appreciation of the contributions of past physical education leaders to the field
- An understanding of the conditions under which the exercise and sports sciences emerged.

Sport history is a dynamic field. Struna reports that prior to the 1960s, much of the research on sport history was produced by scholars in the departments of history.[2] Physical educators who conducted historical studies were more narrow in their approach, focusing on activities and individuals who had a role in shaping physical education. By the 1980s, Struna found that this trend had reversed. Many of the leading sport historians were faculty in the departments of exercise and sport science.[2] Additionally, scholars from other fields besides history and physical education, such as the humanities and anthropology, began to investigate sport. The scholars used different perspectives for their work, thus enhancing our understanding of the many different dimensions of sport.

As sport history grew as a fertile area of research, sport historians undertook a wider range of questions. Throughout the 1970s, historians focused primarily on describing and explaining organized, competitive sports, its evolution and its programs. However, as the field grew, a wider range of questions were addressed, using more analytical approaches. As Struna points out, historians came to understand that "modern" sport—organized, competitive physical contests—needs to be interpreted in light of the context in which it was created. Historians need to understand that sport is constructed by a particular group of people during a particular time. This understanding has elicited a wider range of questions—not only about the history of the sport, but about the context in which it developed. Struna notes that questions arise about . . . "practices and conceptions of exercise and health, about multiple contexts in which games and exercise and physical training existed, and about the sources of variance in experiences over time."[2] This recognition that sport needs to be studied in the context of the time and society in which it was created has helped historians "to understand our past experiences on their own terms, rather than on ours, and to employ multiple frames to make sense of the many dimensions of past experiences."[2]

With the growth of interest in the history of sport, in 1973, the North American Society for Sport History (NASSH) held its first meeting. NASSH provides a central forum for sport history scholars from all disciplines to exchange ideas and share their work. NASSH's *Journal of Sport History* is recognized as one of the preeminent publications in the field and provides a means for scholars to disseminate their research.[2] Other journals that provide avenues for sport history research are the *Canadian Journal of History of Sport and Physical Education, International Journal of Sport History, Sport History Review,* and *Journal of Olympic History.*

Areas of Study

As sport history grew as a specialized area of study, sport historians sought to investigate a wider array of topics within the realm of sport, including physical education, dance, play, conceptions of the body, sport, and exercise. Sport historians also came to recognize that many groups—such as racial and ethnic minorities and females—have been overlooked in historical research on sport. Some of the questions sport historians may investigate include:

- How did urbanization influence the development of sports in America?
- How did the sport activities of Native Americans influence the recreational pursuits of the early colonists?
- How was the growth of intercollegiate sports for women influenced by the beliefs and actions of women physical education leaders in the 1920s and 1930s?
- What role did the expanding American frontier play in the development of sports in the United States?
- What factors influenced the inclusion of physical education in the curriculum of the schools?
- What factors influenced the development of muscular Christianity and how did that philosophy influence the rise of sport?
- How did youth sport develop and what is its impact on youth culture?
- How did segregation influence the participation of blacks in sports?
- What factors contributed to the establishment of the National Collegiate Athletic Association?
- How have Greek ideals influenced the development of sportsmanship?
- What are the events that led to the development of the fitness movement in the 1970s?

As Mechikoff and Estes point out, history often provides us with an illuminating perspective.[1] It helps us understand why we think and act the way we do and gives us some idea about what may happen in the future.[1] Sport history helps physical education, exercise science, and sport professionals gain a greater understanding of the events, forces, and leaders that shaped the field today, and offers us guidance for our behaviors and actions in the future.

ANCIENT GREECE AND ROME

One profound influence on the development of physical education and sport was the civilization of Ancient Greece (prehistoric times—338 B.C.). The city-states of ancient Greece, particularly Athens, placed a high value on physical activity, viewing sports, exercise, and fitness as integral to education and life. The Greek ideal stressed the unity of the mind, body, and spirit. Reflecting this principle, Greek education encompassed both intellectual and physical development. The expression "a sound mind in a sound body" exemplifies this belief. "Gymnasiums" served as centers for intellectual discussions as well as sport instruction and physical training. Males received instruction in physical actvities, such as wrestling, running, and jumping. Development of the body was valued, and the Greeks engaged in training to develop their physiques. The guiding principle of Athenian society, arête, a pursuit of excellence, encouraged individuals to push themselves to achieve to the highest extent possible.

This Greek vase, called an *amphora,* was found in eastern Greece and dates to about 550 to 525 B.C.

In honor of the gods, Greeks held festivals, where sporting events gave Greek men the opportunity to demonstrate the beauty of their physique as well as their athletic abilities. The most renowned of these festivals was the Olympic Games, held in honor of Zeus, the chief god. Beginning around 776 B.C., the Olympic Games were held every 4 years and featured music, feasting, and athletic contests spanning at least 5 days. The Olympic Games were so important that the frequently warring city-states declared a truce so that contestants from all city-states could safely travel to the games and participate in the games.

During the Ancient Rome period (500 B.C.–27 B.C.), physical activity was also regarded with importance, although its role was different than that in Greece. Being fit and having athletic prowess were important to Rome's military success. Males received training in many physical activities, such as archery, wrestling, riding, and fencing. Strength development was important so that the men could be successful in defending the state and waging war as Rome sought to expand its empire. After Rome conquered Greece, Greek gymnastics were introduced to the population, but were not popular. Romans preferred professional sports, often blood sports such as gladiatorial contests, men's fighting wild animals, and men's fighting each other until the death of one. Spectators enjoyed these and other events, such as chariot races. Feasting and drinking bouts in conjunction with little physical activity led to the decline of the fitness of the Roman population. Ultimately, the Roman Empire came to an end, with the poor physical condition of its citizens one of the contributing factors in its decline.

The programs of Ancient Greece and Rome influenced physical education programs in the United States. The Greek ideal of the unity of the mind and body is reflected in many contemporary physical education programs. The development of the body and the pursuit of excellence stand as the motive for many who welcome the challenge of competition at their own level and who value achievement over winning.

EARLY MODERN EUROPEAN PROGRAMS

During the late 1700s and 1800s, early modern Europe experienced the rising tide of nationalism. Against this backdrop, physical education programs in Germany, Sweden, and Great Britain developed and expanded. During the 1800s, proponents of these programs introduced them to the United States.

Germany

During the early modern European period, physical education in Germany focused on the development of strong citizens through programs in the schools and community associations. Physical education leaders of the time, such as *Johann Bernhard Basedow* (1723–1790), *Johann Christoph Friedrich Guts Muths* (1759–1839), and *Adolph Spiess* (1810–1858), were instrumental in promoting school gymnastics. Their programs focused on exercises and instruction in activities such as gymnastics, games, marching, running, and wrestling. Gymnastic apparatus included wooden horses and rope ladders. These leaders believed that physical education deserved a place in the school curriculum.

Friedrich Ludwig Jahn (1778–1852) is credited with the development of the *Turnverein* movement, an association of gymnasts. During Jahn's

Drawing of a *turnplatz,* a German exercise ground that included equipment for jumping, vaulting, balancing, climbing, and running.

Associations of gymnasts called *Turnverein societies* were still popular in the 1920s. At left, a society member practices his skills on an apparatus in the turnplatz. At right, members of the Durlach Turnverein are shown.

lifetime, Napoleon overran Germany. Jahn deeply loved his country and wanted to help free it from Napoleonic control. He believed that he could help accomplish this by molding German youth into strong, hardy citizens who would be capable of throwing over foreign control.

Jahn, a teacher at Plamann's Boys' School, instructed the students regularly in various outdoor activities. He set up an exercise ground outside of the city where he erected various apparatuses. Equipment for jumping, vaulting, balancing, climbing as well as a place to run gave the boys opportunities to develop their skills and strength. The program grew in popularity; soon hundreds of boys were regularly visiting the exercise ground or *turnplatz* and more apparatuses were added.

Jahn's system of gymnastics was recognized throughout Germany, and in many cities, Turnvereins were formed. German immigrants to the United States formed Turnvereins where they settled. Proponents of the German system of gymnastics also helped promote this system in the United States during the 1800s.

Sweden

During this time period, physical education in Sweden gained recognition for its scientific approach. *Per Henrik Ling* (1776–1839) used the sciences of anatomy and physiology to examine the effect of physical activity on the body. He sought to determine the mechanism by which physical activity helped the body function in an optimum capacity. Ling examined the effect of exercise on the heart, musculature, and various organ systems of the body. Ling believed that through the scientific approach, instructors of physical education would be better able to understand the needs of the body and select and apply physical activity intelligently.

Ling's program of gymnastics incorporated Swedish apparatus, such as stall bars, and exercises designed to correct posture and improve health. Ling believed that physical education was necessary for strong and weak persons. It was important to prescribe exercise on the basis of individual differences. Both the mind and the body must be developed to function harmoniously together. Ling believed that teachers of physical education must have foundational knowledge of the effects of exercise on the body. Ling established the Royal Central Institute of Gymnastics at Stockholm to train physical educators. Teachers of physical education received their preparation in one of three categories—educational gymnastics, military gymnastics, or medical gymnastics.

Ling's scientific approach to teaching physical education and his development of programs based on the specific needs of the individual were among the most important of his contributions. His gymnastics programs and his approach to training teachers were promoted in the United States by his followers.

Great Britain

Great Britain during the early 1800s took a different approach to physical education. While other European countries stressed organized programs of gymnastics, Great Britain emphasized programs of organized games and sports. Sports have a long, rich heritage in Great Britain. Swimming, rowing, archery, riding, hockey, quoits, tennis, golf, football (soccer), and cricket were played prior to the 1800s.

One of the leaders of physical education in Great Britain was *Archibald Maclaren* (1820–1884). Maclaren had a background in both sports and in medicine. He believed that it was important to treat physical training as a science. He wrote several books on training, including *Training in Theory and Practice* and *A System of Physical Education.* In his work, he stresses that the objectives of physical education should take into consideration that the promotion of health is more important than the development of strength. Maclaren recognized that physical action is an antidote for tension, weariness, nervousness, and hard work. He noted that the recreative exercise found in games and sport is not enough in itself for growing boys and girls and that physical exercise is essential to optimum growth and development. According to Maclaren, physical training and mental training are inseparable. The mind and body represent a "oneness" in human beings and sustain and support each other. Maclaren stated that exercises should be adapted to an individual's level of fitness and that exercises should be progressive in nature. Additionally, Maclaren believed that physical education should be an essential part of any school's curriculum.

During the early and mid-1800s, the philosophy of *muscular Christianity* developed and grew in popularity. Following the Reformation in the sixteenth century, Protestant sects, including the Puritans, enacted rigid prohibitions against participation in many physical activities and sports. Participation was viewed as sinful. Muscular Christianity argued that sports activities provided a means to teach and reinforce moral values and virtues, thus serving as a means to build character.

Proponents of muscular Christianity suggested that physical weakness reflected moral and spiritual weakness; thus, engaging in physical activities and sport to develop the body reflected one's commitment to develop desirable Christian qualities. Other advocates of muscular Christianity believed that the body was the soul's temple and, as Christians, individuals were obligated to care for their physical being. Muscular Christianity—engaging in sport to build moral character—helped reconcile sport and religion. The philosophy of muscular Christianity greatly influenced English educational institutions, which came to promote the inclusion of sport in schools as a means to develop fair play, honor, and self-discipline among students and to prepare students for life.

The contributions of Germany, Sweden, and Great Britain to physical education and sport influenced the development of programs in the United States. As individuals trained in these programs or systems of gymnastics came to the United States, they took an active role in promoting their approach to physical education. Their leadership influenced the development of programs in the United States during the 1800s.

PHYSICAL EDUCATION AND SPORT IN THE UNITED STATES

The growth of physical education and sport in the United States was influenced by European ideals, systems of gymnastics (exercises), and philosophies. In more recent years, there has been a greater incorporation of activities and beliefs from ancient Asian cultures, such as yoga, the martial arts, and the beliefs about the relationship between the mind, body, and spirit.

Colonial Period (1607 to 1783)

Colonists coming from Europe to settle the New World found Native Americans leading a very active existence. Native Americans hunted, fished, canoed, ran from place to place, and engaged in a multitude of physical activities as they sought food, built shelters, and communicated with other tribes. Young men had to successfully complete a series of challenging physical tests in order to become warriors. Various forms of physical activity were included within their rituals (i.e., burial services, fertility-based ceremonies, and medicinal rites), which were performed in an effort to influence the religious forces they believed directed their lives.[3] Sport, dance, and dramatic enactments were incorporated into Native American festive celebrations and engaged in as forms of relaxation. Ray reports that numerous tribes engaged in sport as a substitute for intervillage or intertribal warfare.[4] Prior to major competitions, there was a period of preparation of the mind, body, and spirit. According to Ray, games and sport played important roles in the lives of Native Americans; they promoted group identity, served as an outlet for creativity, and offered opportunities for individual recognition.[4]

Tribal differences in culture and lifestyle influenced the physical activity of Native Americans, although there were many similarities in the games and sports of tribes across North America. Men, women, and children participated in various sports and games, with some activities being relegated to certain age groups and gender, while others were enjoyed by both males and females or adults and children.[4] Physical prowess, cunning, skillfulness, skill, speed, and endurance were valued. Baggataway (lacrosse) was popular, and rituals often surrounded the game. The game was also used as a means to settle disputes. Rules and playing equipment varied by tribe. Shinny, a game similar to field hockey, in which a stick was used to propel a ball into a goal, was played by both males and females. Footraces often extended over many miles and allowed members of the tribe to demonstrate their speed and endurance. Swimming, canoeing, archery, various types of ball games, and games of chance were other popular activities among Native Americans.

When the first colonists from Europe arrived in North America, they were confronted with harsh conditions and focused their efforts primarily on survival. When they were not working, they engaged in recreational activities. The colonists' recreational activities varied according to their heritage, their religious beliefs, and the area of the country in which they settled. In the New England area, religious beliefs led to prohibitions against many physical activities. The Puritans saw pleasurable physical activities, such as dance and many games, as leading to sin and eternal damnation. Hard work, stern discipline, austerity, and frugality were thought to be secrets to eternal life and blessedness.

People in other sections of the nation, however, brought the knowledge and desire for various types of sport with them from their native countries. The Dutch in New York liked to engage in sports such as skating, coasting, hunting, and fishing. However, the outstanding favorite was bowling. In Virginia, many kinds of sports were popular, such as running, boxing, wrestling, horse racing, cockfights, fox hunts, and later, cricket and football.

Education during this time period was limited. Children attended academies that focused their efforts on helping students attain some degree of proficiency in the basic subjects of reading, writing, and arithmetic. Although advanced educational institutions existed, few students continued their education beyond the elementary level. Physical education was not part of the school curriculum. Recreational games and sports provided a diversion from hard work and allowed opportunities for socializing.

National Period (1784 to 1861)

During the National Period, interest in education grew, and more schools were established for both females and males. The growth of female seminaries (private schools) increased educational opportunities for women. During the 1800s, free public education began to slowly become available for girls and boys, although opportunities for secondary school education and college education were limited. In the 1820s and 1830s, physical education began to be incorporated into school curriculums.

During the 1820s, German gymnastics were introduced to the United States by German immigrants. In 1825, *Charles Beck* (1798 to 1866), a Turner, introduced Jahn's gymnastic program of exercise and apparatus to his students at the Round Hill School in Northampton, Massachusetts. Beck built an outdoor gymnasium and started the first school gymnastics program. In 1826, *Charles Follen* (1796 to 1840) organized exercise classes, based on the German system, for students at Harvard University.

Catharine Beecher (1800 to 1878) was the director of the Hartford Female Seminary for Women in Connecticut, an institution of higher education for young women. In 1828, she developed and implemented a program of physical education within the educational curriculum of the school. The program consisted of calisthenics performed to music. These exercises included Swedish gymnastics and were designed to improve the health and vitality of her students and to prepare them more fully for their future role as homemakers and mothers. She was among the first to advocate for the inclusion of daily physical activities into the public schools.

In the 1840s, many Germans immigrated to the United States, fleeing from the unstable political situation in Germany. The Germans brought with them their customs, and within a short period of time, Turnvereins, or German gymnastic societies, began to be established. In 1851, in Philadelphia, the first national Turnfest was held. Turners from New York, Boston, Cincinnati, Brooklyn, Utica, and Newark engaged in this competition. As Germans moved westward to settle, they established Turnverein societies in their communities.

During the early to mid-1800s, more schools and colleges opened their doors to both males and females. Gymnasiums and swimming pools were constructed, increasing opportunities for participation. Intercollegiate athletics began during this period of time. In 1852, the first intercollegiate competition occurred. A crew race between Harvard and Yale was held, with Harvard winning the race. Intercollegiate athletics would begin to assume an increasingly prominent role on college campuses.

Sports participation grew as settlers became more established and religious prohibitions relaxed. Horseracing and foot races were popular. Baseball, which had evolved from the English sport of rounders, was "invented" in 1839. Rowing was a popular, and competitive, pastime. One of the favorite activities, however, was gambling on sport events.

Civil War Period until 1900

Many outstanding leaders with new ideas influenced the development of physical education and sport during the Civil War period and the late 1800s. Physical education was increasingly included in the schools, and sports grew in popularity.

In 1860, *Dioclesian Lewis* (1823 to 1886) developed the Lewis system of "light" gymnastics and introduced his system to men, women, and children living in Boston. Lewis's program of gymnastics was directed at improving the health and well-being of his participants. Exercises to improve the cardiovascular system were performed to music. Posture and flexibility exercises and light apparatus, such as wands, Indian clubs, and beanbags, were incorporated into his program. Schools adopted his program of gymnastics, and Lewis recognized the need to train teachers to instruct children using his system. In 1861, Lewis established the Normal Institute for Physical Education in Boston to prepare teachers. Courses in anatomy and physiology, hygiene, and gymnastics comprised the 10-week professional preparation program. This was the first teacher-training program in the United States.

Edward Hitchcock (1828 to 1911) and *Dudley Sargent* (1849 to 1924), both of whom were physicians, were central figures in the development of college physical education programs. In 1861, Hitchcock was named the director of health and hygiene at Amherst College. In this position, Hitchcock was responsible for the physical development and health of the students. Physical education classes consisted of developmental exercises performed using horizontal bars, rings, ropes, ladders, Indian clubs, vaulting horses, and weights. Marching and calisthenics were included within the curriculum, as were some sports skills. To monitor the progress of his students, Hitchcock used anthropomorphic or bodily measurements (e.g., height, weight, chest girth, etc.), taking measurements before and then after the completion of training. Hitchcock is recognized for his pioneering work using the scientific approach in physical education.

In 1879, Sargent was appointed director of the new Hemenway Gymnasium at Harvard University. Students who elected to take physical

Wand drills were an important part of physical education program activities in the 1890s.

Staff and students of the first physical education class at the Chautauqua School in New York in 1886.

education received a medical examination and underwent a battery of anthropomorphic tests as the basis for an individually prescribed conditioning program. Sargent developed specially designed exercise equipment, which the students used in conjunction with carefully selected German and Swedish gymnastic exercises, to work out. Students were also encouraged to participate in sports, such as baseball, fencing, and rowing. In 1881, Sargent founded the Sanatory Gymnasium, a school to prepare physical education teachers to utilize his scientific and comprehensive approach to physical education. Later this school became the Sargent School for Physical Education, and today it is the Sargent College of Boston University.

Delphine Hanna (1854 to 1941) attended Sargent's school and received training in his approach to physical education. In 1885, Hanna accepted a teaching position at Oberlin College. Active in conducting physical education classes, Hanna used anthropomorphic research as part of her work. Hanna's training program for prospective teachers eventually evolved into one of the first professional preparation programs for physical education. Among her students were future physical education leaders Thomas Wood and Luther Gulick.

Dr. George Fitz (1860 to 1934), a research physiologist at the Harvard Lawrence Scientific School, called for physical education programs to be based on scientific principles. Research was needed to determine the body's physiological responses to exercise so that the actual benefits of exercise could be determined. In 1892, Fitz established a laboratory to conduct research on physical activity at Harvard University.

During the 1880s, the complete Swedish system of gymnastics was introduced in the United States and became popular in the eastern section of the country. *Hartvig Nissen* (1855 to 1924) pioneered this effort. In 1883, he began teaching Swedish gymnastics at the Swedish Health Institute in Washington, D.C. and later continued his teaching in Boston. *Baron Nils Posse* (1862 to 1895), graduate of the Royal Central Institute of Gymnastics, came to Boston in 1885 and began teaching Swedish gymnastics. Bostonian philanthropist *Mary Hemenway,* became an advocate of the Swedish system and wanted to have school children reap the benefits of this program. To train teachers in Swedish gymnastics, Hemenway underwrote the establishment of the Boston Normal School of Gymnastics in 1889. *Amy Morris Homans* (1848 to 1933) assumed a leadership position in this school,

This graphic for Dr. Rich's Institute for Physical Education shows students engaging in a variety of physical education activities.

and Posse served as an instructor. Homans played an influential role in getting the Boston public schools to adopt the Swedish system of physical education in 1890, a system that was later adopted by schools throughout the state of Massachusetts. The Swedish system soon eclipsed the German system in popularity in the East, but the German system remained more prevalent in the Midwest.

The late 1880s were marked by considerable debate among physical educators regarding which system of gymnastics should serve as the curriculum in American schools. This controversy is often referred to as the "Battle of the Systems." Advocates for each system—the German, Swedish, and various systems developed by Americans (e.g., Hitchcock, Sargent)—articulated the merits of their system and advanced reasons why that particular system should be the national curriculum of the schools. In 1889, a pivotal point occurred in the development of the American system of physical education—the Boston Conference on Physical Training. Organized and led by Mary Hemenway, with the assistance of Amy Morris Homans, the Boston Conference brought together prominent leaders in physical education to discuss and evaluate the various systems. The conference was significant because it stimulated discussion about the purpose of American physical education and which program would best serve the needs of the American people. No consensus was reached about which system should be the national curriculum. Nils Posse suggested that what was needed was an American system designed for the American people.

The growth of physical education was encouraged by the efforts of the Turners. The Turnvereins took an active role in promoting physical education, advocating for its inclusion in the schools. In order to prepare teachers for their system, the Turners, in 1866, established the North American Gymnastic Union in New York City. The curriculum of this one-year program included physical education, anatomy, gymnastics instruction, and teaching methodology. This school eventually relocated to the Midwest, and expanded to a two-year training program in 1885. In 1907, the school moved to Indianapolis, and eventually became associated with Indiana University.

Another stimulus to the growth of physical education during this time was the Young Men's Christian Association (YMCA). Founded in London in 1844, the first YMCA opened in the United States in 1851. Because of the interest in gymnastics and other health-promoting activities, the YMCAs added physical education after the Civil War. To ensure qualified teachers for its programs, in 1885, the YMCA International Training School was founded in Springfield, Massachusetts; this school later became Springfield College. *Luther Gulick, M.D.* (1865 to 1918), played an instrumental role in the YMCA Training School for over 15 years, serving first as an instructor and then as the superintendent. Gulick designed the YMCA logo, an equilateral triangle stressing the unity of the body, mind, and spirit and reflecting the importance of developing the whole person—physically, mentally, and spiritually. Gulick later became the Director of Physical Training for the New York City Public Schools.

At the close of the century, there was greater recognition of the value of physical education to the educational progress. Organized physical education programs began to appear as part of the curriculum in elementary and secondary schools in the 1850s. California was the first state to require schools to offer physical education in 1866, followed by Ohio in 1892. In 1881, the acceptance of physical education grew when the National Education Association recognized physical education as a curricular area.

A significant step in the development of physical education was the founding, in 1885, of the Association for the Advancement of Physical Education (AAPE). *William Anderson, M.D.,* a teacher at Adelphi Academy in Brooklyn, was interested in learning more about how other physical education professionals were teaching and structuring their programs. He organized a meeting at Adelphi Academy and invited professionals in the field. There was considerable support for the development of an organization to facilitate ongoing professional exchange; thus, AAPE was founded. Dr. Edward Hitchcock served as the first president. When the group met again in 1886, they changed their name to the American Association for the Advancement of Physical Education (AAAPE). This organization was the forerunner of today's American Alliance for Health, Physical Education, Recreation, and Dance (AAHPERD). It should be noted that many professionals initially involved in AAPE were physicians and held M.D. degrees. They supported physical education because of the beneficial health effects it provided.

During the mid- to late 1800s, considerable progress occurred in the growth of organized sports. Tennis was introduced in 1874, and in 1880, the United States Lawn Tennis Association was organized. Golf was played in the United States in the late 1880s, and in 1894, the United States Golfing Association was formed. Bowling had been popular since the time of the early Dutch settlers in New York, but it was not until 1895 that the American Bowling Congress was organized. Basketball, one of the few sports originating in the United States, was invented by James Naismith in 1891. Some other sports that became popular during this period were wrestling, boxing, volleyball, skating, skiing, lacrosse, handball, archery, track, soccer, squash, football, and swimming. In 1879, the National Association of Amateur Athletics of America was developed, from which the American Athletic Union (AAU) was later formed.

The AAU has played an instrumental role in the participation of the United States in the Olympic Games. In 1896, the Olympic Games were revived in Athens, Greece. Baron Pierre de Coubertin worked for several years to reestablish the games. A pedagogist, he was attracted to the idea of using sport as a means to develop pride and honor among the youth of France. His efforts to use athletic competition to develop character were not well received.

During a visit to the United States, he met with Princeton history professor William Sloane, who shared with him information about the ancient Olympic Games. An idealist, Coubertin saw that the Olympics could embody the ideals to which he ascribed: amateurism, fair play, good competition, promotion of good will, and fostering of understanding among athletes of the world.

Upon returning to France in 1892, he proposed the reestablishing of the Olympic Games to the governing athletic organization. His proposal was not endorsed. Coubertin persisted and continued to work toward his goal. At an international meeting of amateur athletic associations in Paris in 1894, Coubertin was successful in establishing the modern Olympics and nurtured its growth as the first president of the newly created International Olympic Committee.

The first modern Olympics were held in Athens in 1896. A small delegation of American athletes, organized by Professor Sloane, participated in the Athens Olympics. Participation was limited to males and to 28 events in four sports: track and field, gymnastics, target shooting, and fencing. From the first modern Olympiad in 1896, the Olympics grew in scope and popularity to become the event that it is today.

Intercollegiate athletics grew during this time period. With the first intercollegiate meet in the form of a crew race between Harvard and Yale in 1852, intercollegiate sports began to play a prominent role on college campuses. Williams and Amherst played the first intercollegiate baseball game in 1859, and Rutgers and Princeton, the first football game in 1869. Other intercollegiate contests soon followed in tennis, swimming, basketball, squash, and soccer. Although mostly males participated in athletics, opportunities were available for women. For example, in 1896, the first intercollegiate women's basketball game was held, with teams from the University of California and Stanford University competing.

Initially, intercollegiate athletics were organized and directed primarily by the students. Athletics were viewed by school administrators and faculty as extracurricular activities because they were not perceived as central to the educational mission of the university. However, as athletics grew in popularity and prominence, problems and abuses became more frequent. Faculty raised concern about student-athletes' academic performance, eligibility, commercialization, payment of athletes, and overemphasis on athletics at the expense of academics.

To address these and related concerns and to control its future growth, faculty and administrators became involved in the governance of athletics. Faculty athletic committees were formed on campus. Harvard University was the first to establish a committee in 1892. The next step in assumption of faculty control was the development of university associations to govern athletics. In 1895, the Intercollegiate Conference of Faculty Representatives was formed. Comprising faculty representatives from seven Midwestern institutions, it established eligibility requirements for students pertaining to enrollment and academic performance, imposed limits on athletic financial aid, and developed guidelines for the employment and retention of coaches. This conference, which later became the Big Ten, was the forerunner of other conferences established throughout the country to govern intercollegiate athletics and to define its role in university life.

Opportunities for women to participate in sport were limited by the social constraints of the time. Women's sports consisted of those in which they could participate and continue to be ladylike; Victorian sensibilities and contemporary standards of morality led to women's participating in activities in which they could be fully dressed and not break out in a sweat. Individual sport activities, such as archery, were acceptable. As physical education programs grew in the schools, more women became interested in participating in a wider range of physical activities. Women's team sports, such as basketball, became popular around the turn of the century; however, some schools and members of the public discouraged women's participation. Around 1870, the high-wheeler bike, with a huge front wheel about 5 feet tall and a small rear wheel, became popular. However, the bike was rather unstable, and riders were prone to frequent accidents. Around 1886, the safety bicycle, the

Ina Getings, a student at the University of Nebraska, pole vaulting in 1905.

forerunner of today's bicycle, was invented, and both males and females began to ride in great numbers. The popularity of the bicycle led to changes in women's attire; women began dressing in ways that allowed for more freedom of movement and enabled greater participation in a wide variety of physical activities. It is also important to realize that during this time women had not yet gained the right to vote.

Opportunities for blacks to participate in sports were also limited by societal constraints. After slaves were freed following the Civil War, they engaged in a variety of sports, with baseball, boxing, and horseracing being the most popular. A rising tide of racism in the late 1800s led to the passage of "Jim Crow" laws that led to the segregation of blacks and whites in many areas of life, including schools, playgrounds, and sports. The banning of competition between blacks and whites led to the formation of separate sport leagues and college athletic conferences. This segregation continued through the 1900s, and integration in many sports did not occur until after World War II. Major league baseball remained segregated until 1946.

Early Twentieth Century

The early twentieth century marked a significant period of growth and development for both physical education and sport. From the 1900s to the 1940s, remarkable changes occurred in the philosophy, nature, and conduct of physical education programs. Physical education changed its focus from the narrow emphasis on systems of gymnastics, exercise regimes, and calisthenics to a broader focus that encompassed games, sports, aquatics, dance, and outdoor activities. The "new physical education" developed, which emphasized a program of activities and the contribution of physical education to the total education of the individual. Physical education leaders debated whether physical education should emphasize education *of* the physical or education *through* the physical. Physical education teacher training programs grew in

Students participate in playday at the John Muir School in 1924.

number, and graduate degrees in physical education began to be awarded with greater frequency.

Sport became increasingly organized during this time and grew tremendously in popularity. Extensive programs were established in schools and universities, and recreation programs flourished. Intercollegiate athletics were brought under more rigid academic control. Intramurals became more popular as the emphasis on sports for all gained momentum.

During the first decade of the twentieth century, Luther Gulick continued to promote play as important to the development of children. In 1903, he founded the Public School Athletic League in New York City which initially focused on providing opportunities for boys to participate in sports. Gulick played an instrumental role in the formation of the Playground Association of America in 1906, which sought to promote the development of urban and rural playgrounds, and served as its first president. Recreational opportunities for children and adults began to expand. By 1930, the Playground Association had evolved into the National Recreation Association.

Physical education began to change in scope. At the forefront of this change was *Thomas Dennison Wood, M.D.* (1864 to 1951), who advocated the development of a new program of physical education that would enhance the development of the whole individual through participation in play, games, sports, and outdoor activities. Wood studied with Hanna at Oberlin College, served as the first director of the physical education department at Stanford University, and taught at Teachers College of Columbia University from 1901 to 1932. In an 1893 speech at the International Conference on Education, Wood presented his vision for a new physical education, one with an "aim as broad as education itself. . . . The great thought in physical education is not the education of physical nature, but the relationship of physical training to completed education, and then the effort to make the physical contribute its full share to the life of the individual, in environment, training, and culture."[5]

Wood's program was a departure from the physical education programs of the day, which emphasized gymnastics, health, and the development of the body. Wood called for a broader program of activities and a greater responsiveness to the needs of the individual. His program was first introduced under the title "Natural Gymnastics," but later became known as the "new physical education."

Robert Tait McKenzie, M.D. (1867 to 1938), physician, physical educator, and noted artist-sculptor, was on the faculty of McGill University (Canada) and the University of Pennsylvania. McKenzie worked to help develop physical education programs for individuals with disabilities. McKenzie is recognized for his authorship of many books, among them *Exercise in Education and Medicine,* published in 1910. A renowned sculptor, McKenzie's works focused on the portrayal of athletes in many different sporting events.

World War I (1916 to 1919)

World War I started in 1914, and the United States' entry, in 1918, had a critical impact on the nation and education. The Selective Service Act of 1917 called to service all men between the ages of 18 and 25 years.

Social forces were also at work during this period. The emancipation of women was furthered by passage of the Nineteenth Amendment. Women also began to show interest in sport and physical education, as well as in other fields formerly considered to be "off limits."

During World War I many physical educators provided leadership for physical conditioning programs for the armed forces and also for the people on the home front. Dudley Sargent, Luther Gulick, and R. Tait McKenzie contributed their services to the armed forces. The Commission on Training Camp Activities of the War Department was created, and Raymond Fosdick was named the head of this program. Joseph E. Raycroft of Princeton University and Walter Camp, the creator of "All-Americans," were named to head the athletic divisions of the Army and the Navy, respectively. Women physical educators were also active in conditioning programs in communities and industries at home.

When the war ended, the public had an opportunity to study the medical examiner's report for the men who had been called to military duty. One-third of the men were found physically unfit for armed service, and many more were physically inept. Also, a survey by the National Council on Ed-

Women playing field hockey at Smith College, in Northampton, Massachusetts, in 1904.

ucation in 1918 showed that children in the elementary and secondary schools of the nation were woefully subpar physically. The result was the passing of much legislation in the various states to upgrade physical education programs in the schools.

Golden Twenties (1920 to 1929)

Many advances in physical education occurred during this time that had a profound influence on physical education for decades to come. The "new physical education" began to take shape during this period, influenced by the leading progressive education theorists of the time, including John Dewey. *Clark Hetherington* (1870 to 1942) taught at New York University from 1923 to 1928 and at Stanford University from 1929 to 1938. Hetherington's philosophy of physical education was influenced by Wood's beliefs and his "natural gymnastics" approach. In 1910, Hetherington articulated the four objectives of physical education as organic development (fitness), psychomotor development (skill), character development (social), and intellectual development (mental). Hetherington, like Wood, believed that physical education had a broader purpose than the development of the physical aspects of the individual, which was the popular approach of the times. Hetherington is often credited with inventing the phrase "new physical education" to describe the changing emphasis of the field that was initially described by Wood. In 1922, Hetherington wrote *School Programs in Physical Education,* setting forth his beliefs about the content and conduct of physical education.

Rosalind Cassidy (1895 to 1980), like Wood and Hetherington, was an advocate of "education through the physical"—the position that held that carefully designed programs of physical education could contribute to the development of the whole person. Cassidy's career as a teacher spanned over 40 years; she began teaching at Mills College in 1918 and then was hired by the University of California at Los Angeles in 1947, where she worked until 1962. In 1927, Cassidy co-authored with Wood *The New Physical Education; a Program of Naturalized Activities for Education Toward Citizenship,* which described how physical education could contribute to the education of children through a well-planned program of physical education activities. A prolific writer, Cassidy's works helped promote the "education through the physical" approach. Her writings included textbooks on humanizing physical education, secondary methods for adolescent girls, and human movement.

Early physical education attire for American women.

Jesse F. Williams, M.D. (1886 to 1966) also advocated "education through the physical" and helped shape the direction of the field with his efforts to promote this philosophy. Williams taught at Teachers College of Columbia University for over 25 years, ending his tenure there in 1941. In 1927, Williams published the *Principles of Physical Education,* which set forth his beliefs that social responsibility and moral values can be developed through physical education. Williams' beliefs were based on the unity of mind and body. Physical education should be included within the school curriculum because of its ability to contribute to the development of the whole child. Games and sports were recognized as a means through which desired educational outcomes could be achieved. Williams argued for the inclusion of athletics in school. According to Williams, athletics could perform a vital role in creating socially responsible citizens, a goal of both physical education and schools.

There was considerable debate among professionals regarding the philosophical direction of the field that continued for many decades. The "education through the physical" position emphasized a broad approach to physical education, with advocates claiming that students' participation in carefully selected physical activities would enhance not only their health and fitness, but contribute to the building of character and intellectual development. The "education of the physical" proponents stressed a more narrow approach to physical education. Advocates of this approach pointed out the unique contribution of physical education to the physical development of the individual, and believed that programs should be structured to promote fitness, skills, and health outcomes.

In 1926, *Jay B. Nash* (1886 to 1965) began what would prove to be an illustrious career at New York University. Nash strongly believed in the value of recreation and thought that through experiences such as camping, individuals would gain both an appreciation of nature and an understanding of the principles of democracy. The physical education curriculum should be designed to prepare students to use their leisure time in a worthy manner. Physical education should teach students recreational skills that they can use for enjoyable participation throughout their lifetime.

The 1920s and 1930s marked a time when an increasing emphasis was placed on defining the scientific basis of physical education. Measurement was used as a means of grouping students, assessing achievement, prescribing exercises, and motivating performance. Some leaders argued that it was important to be able to demonstrate outcomes and identify which programs of exercise yielded beneficial results. The growth of doctoral programs in physical education also stimulated an interest in research. In 1924, Teachers College of Columbia University and New York University offered the first doctoral degrees in physical education, and other programs began to develop around the country as well. In 1930, the American Physical Education Association published the *Research Quarterly,* now called the *Research Quarterly for Exercise and Sport.*

Many problems arose in regard to college athletics. As a result, the Carnegie Foundation provided a grant, in 1923, for a study of intercollegiate athletics in certain institutions in the South by a Committee of the Association of Colleges and Secondary Schools. Later, a study of athletic practices in American colleges and universities was conducted. The report of this study was published in 1929 under the title *American College Athletics.* The report denounced athletics as being professional rather than amateur in nature and as a means of public entertainment and commercialization. Problems such as recruiting and subsidizing athletes also were exposed.

During this period the intramural athletic programs increased in colleges and universities. Women's programs experienced an increase in the number of staff, hours required for student participation, activities offered, and physical education buildings in use.

Depression Years (1930 to 1939)

The 1929 stock market crash ushered in the Great Depression, which affected education. Unemployment and poverty reigned. Health and physical

Tennis at the turn of the century at Smith College, in Northampton, Massachusetts.

education had a difficult time surviving in many communities.

During the period of economic depression in the United States, many gains achieved by physical education in the schools of the nation were lost. Budgets were cut back, and programs in many cases were either dropped or downgraded. Between 1932 and 1934, an estimated 40% of the physical education programs were dropped completely. Legislative moves were made in several states such as Illinois and California to do away with the physical education requirement.

Another development during the depression years was that physical educators became more involved in recreation programs in the agencies and projects concerned with unemployed persons. These later programs were being subsidized with special government assistance. The national association, recognizing the increased interest in recreation, voted to change its title to include the word *recreation*—the American Association for Health, Physical Education, and Recreation.

One of the leaders of this time was *Charles McCloy* (1886 to 1959). McCloy served as a YMCA instructor and director in China for more than 10 years and taught physical education at several colleges in the United States. In 1932, McCloy received his doctoral degree in biology from Columbia University. As a professor at the University of Iowa, McCloy was active in research, including anthropometry. In 1940, McCloy wrote *Philosophical Bases for Physical Education.* McCloy advocated "education of the physical," espousing the belief that school physical education's unique contribution to the education of the individual is organic and psychomotor development. According

American physical education leaders William G. Anderson and Amy Morris Homans.

to McCloy, school physical education programs should focus their efforts on promoting fitness and teaching sports skills. Furthermore, McCloy recognized the importance of physical educators being able to document results and measure progress using scientific data. During and after World War II, McCloy served as a fitness consultant to the United States Armed Forces.

Interscholastic athletic programs continued to grow and in some situations dominated physical education programs and created many educational problems. The collegiate athletic program received a temporary setback from the Carnegie Report but then started to grow again. The National Association of Intercollegiate Basketball was established in 1940 for the purpose of providing an association for the smaller colleges. It later changed its name to National Association of Intercollegiate Athletics in 1952. In 1937, representatives of the Junior Colleges of California met for the purpose of forming the National Junior College Athletic Association.

Intramural athletics continued to grow in colleges and universities. Women's athletic associations also increased in number. The principles that guided such programs were established largely during the early years by the National Section of Women's Athletics.

Mid-Twentieth Century (1940 to 1970)

Physical education made progress in the middle of the twentieth century. World War II had a great impact on physical education and sport programs. The country was jolted from depression by World War II. Physical education received an impetus as physical training programs were established under Gene Tunney in the Navy, Hank Greenburg in the Air Force, and sports leaders in other branches of the armed forces. Schools and colleges were urged to help develop physical fitness in the youth of the nation. A return to more formalized conditioning programs resulted.

The need for a national program of physical fitness was evident as a result of Selective Service examinations and other indications that young people were not in sound physical condition. Several steps were taken in this direction. President Franklin Roosevelt appointed John B. Kelly of Philadelphia as National Director of Physical Training. In 1942, a Division of Physical Fitness was established in the Office of Defense, Health, and Welfare Services. In 1943, John B. Kelly was appointed chairman of a Committee of Physical Fitness within the Office of the Administrator, Federal Security Agency.

The war years had their impact on programs of physical education in the nation's schools and colleges. In many instances, elementary school physical education classes met daily, and secondary and college classes also increased in number. The program of activities took on a more formal nature with the purpose of physically conditioning the children and youth of the United States for the national emergency that existed. Girls and women, as well as boys and men, were involved in these programs.

The Physical Fitness Movement

In December, 1953, an article was published in the *Journal of Health, Physical Education, and Recreation* entitled "Muscular Fitness and Health." The article reported the results of the Kraus-Weber Minimal Muscular Fitness tests given to European and American children. Nearly 60% of the American children had failed, compared with only 9% of the European children. The fitness test primarily measured flexibility and abdominal strength. Nevertheless, the deplorable condition of the American youth was cause for concern.

James B. Kelly of Philadelphia and Senator James Duff of Pennsylvania alerted the President of the United States to the information discussed in this article. In July, 1955, President Eisenhower gathered a group of prominent sports figures in Washington, D.C., to discuss the fitness problem. Later he called a Youth Fitness Conference at the Naval Academy in Annapolis. At the conclusion of the conference President Eisenhower issued an executive order establishing a President's Council on Youth Fitness and appointed Dr. Shane MacCarthy as executive director. After this, a President's Citizens Advisory Committee on Fitness of American Youth was appointed.

As a result of President Eisenhower's decrees there was a greater interest in fitness in the United States. Several states established their own committees on physical fitness. The YMCA, AAU, and other organizations put forth special efforts to promote fitness. Several business concerns became involved. *Sports Illustrated* magazine devoted regular features to fitness. The National Research Council of the AAHPERD authorized physical fitness testing of American children. The College Physical Education Association for Men published a special report entitled "Fit for College." Operation Fitness USA was inaugurated by the AAHPERD to promote fitness, leadership, public relations, and research. The project established motivational devices such as certificates of recognition, achievement awards, and emblems for students at various levels of achievement.

When John F. Kennedy became President of the United States, he appointed Charles "Bud" Wilkinson to head his council on youth fitness. The name was changed to the President's Council on Physical Fitness. The council introduced its "Blue Book" with suggestions for school-centered programs. Later, the council's name was again changed to its current name, the President's Council on Physical Fitness and Sports.

Professional Preparation and Development

The war and postwar teacher shortage represented a critical problem for the nation. During the war, 200,000 teachers left jobs, and 100,000 emergency certificates were issued. Many of those who left did not return, and inadequately trained replacements were hired. The critical shortage forced administrators to reduce their standards in selecting teachers.

Professional preparation programs increased in number during this period, with over 600 colleges and universities offering programs. Some of the larger institutions developed separate professional programs for health, physical education, and recreation professionals, whereas many smaller institutions were concerned with only physical education.

Early leaders in physical education were physicians, not physical educators. As professional preparation programs in physical education developed, physical educators assumed many of the leadership roles. Some physicians retained their interest in physical education and sport. In 1954, a group of 11 physicians founded the Federation of Sports Medicine; the name of the organization was changed to the American College of Sports Medicine (ACSM) in 1955. Today, ACSM has over 17,000 members in over 70 countries. Members are committed to improving the well-being of people through medicine and exercise. Members include physicians, physical educators, exercise physiologists, and biomechanists.

As sports programs expanded and participation increased, there was a need for qualified individuals to treat the injured athletes and to design programs to prevent injuries. Physical educators, coaches, and other individuals began working as athletic trainers. In 1950, the National Athletic Trainers' Association (NATA) was founded by a group of 200 athletic trainers at a meeting in Kansas City. Today, NATA membership includes more than 27,000 allied health professionals and spans the globe.

Sports

Four significant developments occurred in athletics during the mid-twentieth century. Renewed interest was shown in girls' and women's sport, intramurals, lifetime sports, and sport programs for boys and girls below high school age.

Girls' and Women's Sports In 1962, the Division for Girls' and Women's Sports (DGWS) and the Division of Men's Athletics of the AAHPERD held their first joint conference so that the views of both men and women in the profession could be expressed. Two years later the first National Institute on Girls' Sports was held to promote sports for girls and women. In 1965, a study conference met to discuss and develop guidelines needed in the areas of competition for girls and women. Other steps taken to promote girls' and women's sports included the development of a liaison with Olympic Games officials as a part of the Olympic development movement, the publication of guidelines for girls and women in competitive sports by the DGWS, and the exploration of the social changes in society that had implications for sport programs for women. All these steps represented movement toward providing greater opportunities for girls and women to engage in competitive sports at both the high school and college levels.

Intramurals As sport became increasingly popular at various educational levels, interest was renewed in providing sport competition for all students, not just for the skilled elite. A meeting that helped to spur this movement was held in 1956, when the National Conference on Intramural Sports for College Men and Women met in Washington, D.C. Its purpose was to consider intramural programs for college men and women, to formulate principles, to recommend administrative procedures relating to current and future programs, and to provide greater opportunity for more young men and women to participate in healthful recreational activities. The intramural movement continued to grow, with leadership being provided by the National Intramural Association.

Lifetime Sports An increased emphasis was placed on including sports into the physical education curriculum that could be played during a person's entire lifetime. Giving leadership to this movement was the establishment of the Lifetime Sports Foundation in 1965. Its purpose was to promote fitness and lifetime sports and to give assistance to groups engaged in these areas. This same year the AAHPERD approved the Lifetime Sports

Lifespan and Cultural Perspectives: Sport History

- How did the ancient Greek beliefs about the body influence the development of physical education?
- What role did sport play in the lives of the early Native Americans?
- How did Victorian conceptions of femininity influence women's participation in sports in the United States?
- What events have led to a greater emphasis on physical activity for older adults?
- How did segregation influence opportunities for blacks in sport?
- How did beliefs about the development of children influence the physical education curriculum in the 1800s?

Education Project, an adjunct of the Lifetime Sports Foundation. School and college physical education programs reflected the influence of such projects, with greater emphasis being given to teaching activities such as bowling, tennis, golf, and badminton.

Sport Programs Below the High School Level

Considerable controversy was generated during this period concerning sports for children below the high school level. In 1953, a National Conference on Program Planning in Games and Sports for Boys and Girls of Elementary School Age was held in Washington, D.C. It was the first time that organizations representing medicine, education, recreation, and other organizations serving the child had ever met with leaders of organizations who promote highly organized competitive activities for children. Two recommendations to come out of this conference were (1) that programs of games and sport should be based on the developmental level of children and that no contact sports should be allowed for children under 12 years of age and (2) that competition is inherent in the growth and development of the child and will be harmful or beneficial depending on a variety of factors.

International Developments

International meetings of leaders of health, physical education, and recreation from various parts of the world were initiated in the mid-twentieth century. In 1958, at the annual meeting of the World Confederation of Organizations of the Teaching Profession (WCOTP), a committee was appointed to make plans for a World Federation of National and International Associations of Health Education, Physical Education, and Recreation. The purpose was to provide a way in which to unite representatives from all associations of these fields in a worldwide organization. The following year the WCOTP established the International Council of Health, Physical Education, and Recreation (ICHPER).

Programs for Individuals with Disabilities

In the mid-twentieth century physical educators realized that their field of specialization could make a contribution to students with special needs, including individuals who are developmentally disabled, physically disabled, and/or culturally disadvantaged. One event that accented this movement was a grant from the Joseph P. Kennedy, Jr., Foundation in 1965, which enabled AAHPERD to establish the Project on Recreation and Fitness for the Mentally Retarded for the purposes of research, program development, and leadership training. Since its inception in 1968, the Special Olympics has provided competitive sport opportunities for individuals with mental retardation.

Adapted physical education programs received increasing attention, with special programs being included in professional preparation institutions to provide leadership for this area. Furthermore, governmental grants of funds enabled greater emphasis to be placed on this particular area of the physical education program.

Research

The need for research in physical education assumed greater importance in the eyes of physical educators than it had heretofore. The Research Council of the AAHPERD was established in 1952 as a section under the General Division. Its functions and purposes included promoting research along strategic lines, developing long-range plans, preparing and disseminating materials to aid research workers in the field, and synthesizing research materials in areas related to the professional fields.

Research became increasingly specialized. Studies were conducted in areas such as exercise physiology, motor learning, sociology of sport, and pedagogy.

SIGNIFICANT RECENT DEVELOPMENTS (1970 TO PRESENT)

Physical education, exercise science, and sport currently is in one of its most exciting eras. So many changes have occurred since 1970 that capturing them all in such a limited space is difficult. They include the disciplinary movement, the quest for identity, the emergence of the subdisciplines, new directions in professional preparation, and increased career opportunities in these dynamic fields. The national emphasis on disease prevention and health promotion and increasing evidence of the positive relationship between physical activity and health have stimulated participation by people of all ages and created new opportunities within the realm of physical education, exercise science, and sport. Sport participation at all levels and within all segments of the population has exploded. Legislation has increased opportunities for girls and women in sports and for people with disabilities. The Olympics have experienced a period of growth, withstood the politicization of the Games, and emerged as a commercial venture of huge proportions. Technology has contributed in many ways to the continued growth of physical education, exercise science, and sport. Many of these recent developments are included within other chapters.

The Discipline

The disciplinary movement is generally acknowledged to have begun with Franklin Henry's 1964 clarion call for the study of the academic discipline of physical education.[6] It was, however, during the 1970s, and continuing to this date, that the body of knowledge composing the discipline of physical

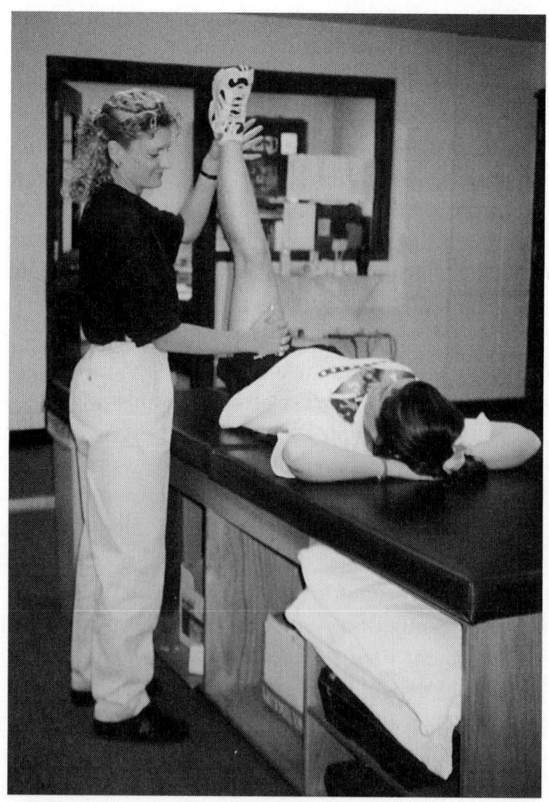

New professional preparation programs train students for nontraditional careers, such as athletic training.

education, exercise science, and sport grew most rapidly. Expanded and rigorous research efforts by dedicated academicians, coupled with improvements in technology, have contributed to the explosion of knowledge. Specialized areas of study or subdisciplines such as exercise physiology, motor learning, and sport psychology have emerged (see Chapter 1). Professionals have engaged in protracted discussions about what should be the primary focus of our field. In the late 1990s, there was a growing consensus that physical activity is the central focus of our field.

The disciplinary movement that has been evolving since the 1970s led to considerable debate about the best name for our field of endeavor. The traditional name of *physical education* was perceived by some as too narrow and as failing to convey the expanding scholarly interest in sport. In 1989, the prestigious American Academy of Physical Education voted to change its name to the American Academy of Kinesiology and Physical Education and recommended *kinesiology* as the title of the discipline. Other popular names were *physical education and sport, exercise science,* and *exercise and sport science.* In 1994, Ziegler reported that *physical education and sport* was the most widely used title for the field worldwide.[7] As the disciplinary movement continued to grow in the 1970s and 1980s, departments of physical education in colleges and universities changed their name in an effort to convey more accurately the nature of their work. In 1997, in the United States, there were more than 150 different names for departments in higher education.[8]

The growth of the discipline influenced professional preparation programs at colleges and universities. New courses were developed to embrace the knowledge within the subdisciplines. At the undergraduate level, these courses were initially incorporated into teacher preparation programs. Graduate programs were further developed to offer study within those areas of specialization. Beginning in the late 1970s, an increasing number of undergraduate programs offered their students the opportunity to specialize. To this end, undergraduate programs in specialized areas such as exercise science, sport studies, or sport management were developed. The broadening of professional preparation programs within physical education, exercise science, and sport to encompass specialized areas of study has allowed students to prepare for a diversity of career opportunities within these expanding fields.

In the late 1960s and early 1970s, the proliferation of research and the desire to share findings with colleagues helped stimulate the formation of specialized scholarly organizations. For example, the North American Society for the Psychology of Sport and Physical Activity was founded in 1967, and the Philosophic Society for the Study of Sport was begun in 1972. Interest in research grew markedly, and in 1980 the *Research Quarterly* was renamed the *Research Quarterly for Exercise and Sport.* Today there exist many professional organizations and journals focusing on specialized fields of study within physical education, exercise science, and sport, providing a plethora of outlets for the dissemination of research findings through presentations at conferences and through professional journals.

The scope of physical education, exercise science, and sport widened considerably in the 1970s, and it appears that it will continue to do so during the twenty-first century. Physical education, exercise science, and sport programs have expanded from serving school- and college-age populations to serving people of all ages—from preschoolers to the elderly. Expansion of programs from the traditional school setting to nonschool settings such as community centers and corporate fitness centers has occurred at an increasing rate. There has also been a growing shift to private sector physical education, exercise science, and sport programs. These programs, part of the health-enhancement and leisure-services industry, have created a diversity of career opportunities for well-prepared individuals. Certification programs for professionals began to increase in number. The American College of Sports Medicine (ACSM), the National Athletic Trainers Association (NATA), National

Strength and Conditioning Association (NSCA), and Aerobics and Fitness Association of America (AFAA) offer certification programs for professionals. (Professional preparation programs and career opportunities are discussed in Part III.)

One milestone in this period was the celebration, in 1985, by the American Alliance for Health, Physical Education, Recreation, and Dance (AAHPERD) of the one-hundredth anniversary of its founding as the American Association for the Advancement of Physical Education.

Disease Prevention and Health Promotion

One of the most significant changes in society during these past decades is the increased emphasis on disease prevention and health promotion. As disease prevention and health promotion initiatives grew, greater attention was directed at helping individuals improve their health by incorporating health-enhancing behaviors into their lifestyle. At this time there was an emerging consensus of epidemiologists, experts in exercise science, and health professionals, as well as a growing body of evidence, that supported the contribution of physical activity to health and well-being. Four national health reports—*Healthy People* (1979),[9] *Objectives for the Nation* (1980),[10] *Healthy People 2000* (1990),[11] and *Healthy People 2010*[12]—clearly identified the contribution that physical activity could make to well-being. These reports established specific objectives to be accomplished by physical education, exercise science, and sport, the attainment of which would lead to the improvement of the health of the nation. Among these objectives were promoting a greater national participation in physical activity, increasing the number of schools offering daily physical education, expanding community recreation programs, and establishing worksite health promotion programs.

In 1996, the landmark report *Physical Activity and Health: A Report of the Surgeon General*[13] affirmed the contribution of physical activity to the attainment and maintenance of health. This report on physical activity and health emphasized that all Americans can substantially improve their health and quality of life by including moderate amounts of physical activity in their daily lives. It is a national call to action to improve the health of the nation and offers a tremendous challenge to all members of our field.

School Physical Education

Public health initiatives since 1970 have emphasized the critical role that school physical education programs can play in helping children acquire the skills, knowledge, and habits to be active throughout their lives. The emphasis on lifetime sports has continued, with activities such as orienteering, cross-country skiing, and golf being part of the school curriculum. Movement education, with its emphasis on exploring skillful movement, understanding and application of knowledge of human movement, and the joy and significance of movements has been an important influence on elementary-school physical education programs. The child-centered developmental approach has influenced content, teaching methods, and assessment techniques.

Many different curriculum frameworks have emerged since the 1970s. Some have emphasized fitness, including both fitness development and understanding of the underlying fitness concepts. Other models, such as adventure or sports education, bring a different focus to school physical education. Adventure education models capitalize on the interest in outdoor pursuits, such as backpacking, high-ropes course, or challenge initiatives in which members of a group have to work together to solve a task, such as getting everyone over a 12-foot-high wall. The sport education model involves all students, not just the elite athletes, in the sport experience. This model recognizes that within the playful competition of sport, educational values can be achieved by all students. In contrast to the traditional physical education program, students are divided into teams that practice together throughout the sport season (traditional unit) and participate in formal competition that ends in a culminating event. Students assume the role of the coach, referee, and administrator.[14]

These decades have been marked by efforts to promote physical education and advocacy on behalf of daily quality physical education in the schools. In 1971, the *Physical Education Public Information Project* (PEPI) was begun to inform the public, educators, and policy makers about the value of physical education. PEPI emphasized that "physical education is health insurance."[15] In 1986, the National Association of Physical Education and Sport (NASPE), an association of AAHPERD, defined the characteristics of a "physically educated person" (see Chapter 2).[16] In 1992, NASPE developed national content standards for physical education. This was followed by the development of assessment guidelines. In 1995, the NASPE published *Moving into the Future: National Standards for Physical Education: A Guide to Content and Assessment.*[17] This document offered physical educators for the first time a national framework to guide their efforts.

In 1987, Congress passed a resolution urging individual states to mandate high-quality, daily physical education programs for all school-aged children. Organizations supporting the resolution included the National Education Association, American Heart Association, American Medical Association, and the American Alliance for Health, Physical Education, Recreation, and Dance.

Periodic surveys such as AAHPERD's the *Shape of the Nation* and the Youth Risk Behavior Surveillance System (YRBSS) have been conducted to monitor the status of school physical education. The first *Shape of the Nation* survey in 1987 revealed that only one state, Illinois, required daily physical education for all its students, K–12.[18] This is still the case in 2004. Examination of the results of the YRBSS revealed that the prevalence of high school students' attending daily physical education declined significantly from 41.6% in 1991 to 25.4% in 1995. There was only a slight improvement from 1995 to 2003; participation rose from 25.4% to 28.4%.[19]

The national health reports, such as *Healthy People 2010,* called for increasing daily quality physical education for all students. School physical education is regarded as a key setting in which to increase the physical activity of children and youth as well as lay the foundation for a lifetime of physical activity. Yet, despite the recognition that physical education can make a significant contribution to students' health, physical educators are facing tremendous pressures to justify their program. Increasing pressures for academic reform have led to efforts to make more time in the curriculum for educational basics and reduction in the time for "frills" such as art, music, and physical education (see Chapters 2 and 3). Furthermore, physical educators have reported tremendous pressure to justify their programs due to fiscal constraints.

As the twenty-first century progresses, greater efforts must be directed at promoting physical education as an educational basic, an integral part of the school curriculum for children and youth in all grades.

Physical Fitness and Participation in Physical Activity

The fitness movement began as a trend in the 1970s and has continued to expand. Many people of all ages lead an active lifestyle, engaging in such activities as jogging, biking, walking, and weight training to an extent never before seen. For example, the Sporting Goods Manufacturers Association (SGMA) reported that in 2000 there were an estimated 36 million fitness walkers.[20] Sales of home exercise equipment top billions of dollars and continue to grow. In 2003, sales of home gyms reached $305 million.[20]

However, while it appears America is an active nation, studies report that too many adults engage in no physical activity during their leisure time (see Chapter 3). Too many children and youth were found to be inactive. Inactive people of all ages need to incorporate more physical activity into their lives on a daily basis. Recent studies have also raised alarm regarding the growing percentage of children, youth, and adults who are overweight and obese. While more individuals of all ages are participating in physical activities to an extent never before seen, much more needs to be done to encourage people to be active and to eat healthy.

Sales of sports equipment have increased dramatically in the last decade, creating many new career opportunities in sports retailing.

Historically, starting in 1970s, there was a gradual shift from an emphasis on performance-related fitness to health-related fitness. During the 1970s and 1980s, as the emphasis on disease prevention and health promotion grew, the contribution of fitness to health gained increased recognition. Physical inactivity was linked to disease. To improve health, it was recommended that people engage in fitness activities on a regular basis. In terms of cardiovascular fitness, this required engaging in vigorous physical activity 3 to 5 times a week, at 60% to 90% of the age-adjusted maximum heart rate, for at least 20 minutes a session.

At this time, there also was a shift in fitness development and testing in the schools. The emphasis shifted from performance-related fitness to health-related fitness. In 1980, AAHPERD inaugurated the Health-Related Physical Fitness Test.[21] This test was designed to measure the physical fitness components associated with health. The components measured were cardiovascular endurance, body composition, lower back and hamstring flexibility, and abdominal muscle strength and endurance.

As evidence of the health benefits of being fit and incorporating regular physical activity into one's lifestyle mounted, concerns were raised regarding the fitness and physical activity patterns of the nation's youth. In 1985, the National Children and Youth Fitness Study (NCYFS I), the first nationwide assessment of youth fitness in nearly a decade, revealed that only one-third of youths aged 10 to 17 participated in appropriate physical activity necessary for the maintenance of cardiorespiratory endurance.[22] In 1987, the National Children and Youth Fitness Study (NCYFS II) results for children ages 5 to 9 revealed a low level of cardiorespiratory endurance within this population.[23] For both children and youth, the percentage of body fat was greater than in their counterparts of the 1960s. NCYFS I and II raised concern that the current school physical education programs may be inadequate to promote lifetime fitness and that changes in the conduct of the programs were necessary.

To address these concerns and to educate students about the multiple dimensions of fitness, in 1988, AAHPERD introduced a new fitness test and educational program entitled Physical Best.[24] Physical Best emphasizes not only the physical dimension of fitness but the cognitive and affective dimensions as well. The fitness test assesses five components of fitness—cardiovascular endurance, body composition, flexibility, and upper body and abdominal strength and endurance—with the use of the distance run, skinfold measurements, sit-and-reach, pull-ups, and sit-ups, respectively. The educational component was designed to help teachers assist students to attain desirable fitness habits through individualized goal setting, motivation techniques, and encouragement of participation in physical activities outside the school setting.

In 1994, AAHPERD and the Cooper Institute for Aerobic Research (CIAR) announced an agreement to collaborate on youth fitness testing and education. AAHPERD agreed to adopt the CIAR's Prudential Fitnessgram system for testing and assessment of youth fitness. CIAR agreed to use AAHPERD's Physical Best educational materials that promote healthy lifestyles for all children and youth.

As researchers continued to investigate the relationship between fitness, physical activity, and health, they found that health-related benefits could be obtained at more moderate levels of activity intensity than previously realized. In 1995, guidelines for physical activity reflecting this finding were issued by the Centers for Disease Control and Prevention (CDC) and the American College of Sports Medicine (ACSM). The CDC and ACSM recommended that all adults should accumulate 30 minutes or more of moderate-intensity activity on most, preferably all, days of the week.[13] The National Institute of Health (NIH) Consensus Development Conference on Physical Activity and Cardiovascular Health recommended that all population groups, including children and youth, accumulate at least 30 minutes a day of moderate-intensity physical activity.[13] The new recommendations by the CDC, ACSM, and NIH also emphasized that greater benefits would accrue by engaging in moderate-intensity activities for a great period of time or participating in more vigorous physical activity.[13]

The fitness movement and the recognition of the importance of leading a healthy, active lifestyle were significant features of the past three decades. The shift from performance to health-related fitness reflects recognition by professionals in the fields of the important role of physical activity in promoting the health and well-being of people of all ages.

The Growth of Sports

Participation in sports has experienced phenomenal growth at all levels since the 1970s. Participation by children and youth involved in organized sport activities outside the school setting, under the guidance of public or private agencies, has grown tremendously. It is estimated that children and youth sports involve more than 25 million children, 3 million adult volunteer coaches, and 500,000 paid coaches, working primarily in private sports clubs with elite performers. Among the most popular programs are soccer, baseball, softball, and swimming. Children and youth are also enrolling in record numbers in commercial sport organizations, such as gymnastics and tennis clubs.

Participation in interscholastic sports has grown from 3,960,932 boys and girls in 1971 to 6,903,552 in 2003–2004.[25] More than 50% of students had played on a sports team in a given year. There is an increased trend toward specialization at an early age in a specific sport. A youth may play on the school soccer team in the fall, participate in recreational league indoor soccer in the winter, play spring soccer, and then attend soccer camp in the summer. Some school districts, facing budgetary difficulties, have instituted "pay-to-play" plans in which athletes are charged fees to participate. Considerable concern has been raised that these fees will limit participation and disproportionately affect students from lower socioeconomic groups. The National Federation of State High School Associations opposes this practice, stating that sports have educational value and therefore students should have access to them as part of their educational experience.

At the collegiate level, participation in sports has increased as well. The National Collegiate Athletic Association (NCAA) reported that during the 1989–1990 academic year, 266,268 collegians participated in intercollegiate athletics; in 2002–2003, 377,641 collegians participated.[26] Thousands more collegiate athletes participate at the over 300 schools that are members of the National Association of Intercollegiate Athletes (NAIA)[28] and at the over 460 community colleges that are governed by the National Junior College Athletic Association (NJCAA).[27] Moreover, during this time, sport has emerged as big business in NCAA Division I schools. Media revenues for televising football and basketball games and tournaments have reached millions of dollars. For example, the major NCAA Division I-A football schools shared more than $100 million in revenue for the bowl games.

Participation in recreational leagues by adults has increased enormously as well. "Over-55" basketball leagues and softball leagues have been added as part of the popular adult leagues in many communities. Many different kinds of sporting interests are accommodated in these recreational programs. Adult soccer and volleyball leagues have increased in popularity. Road races attract thousands of participants. Amateur competitions draw millions of competitors of all ages. Master's programs in swimming and track and field, the National Senior Games, and the National Olympic Festival; and state games, such as the New York Empire State Games, engage people of all ages in various levels of competition in a multitude of sports.

Professional sports have also increased during this time. Since the 1970s, expansion has resulted in the addition of many professional hockey, football, and baseball teams. Salaries of professionals have increased dramatically; multimillion dollar contracts have become increasingly common.

The past decade has seen the growth of professional basketball opportunities for women. The Women's National Basketball Association (WNBA), backed by the National Basketball Association, began its inaugural season in 1997. The Women's United Soccer Association (WUSA), the women's professional soccer league, played its first season in 2001. Unfortunately, due to financial issues, the league suspended its operations in 2003, but there is an effort to revive the league and continue play in the future. The number of women participating in professional sports, such as the Ladies Professional Golf Association (LPGA), has grown tremendously. Male and female athletes in both tennis and golf now compete for prizes worth millions of dollars.

Girls and Women in Sports

Participation by girls and women in sports began to grow rapidly in the 1970s and continues. The changing attitudes toward women in society was one factor that promoted the growth of participation. Participation was also greatly enhanced by the passage of Title IX of the Educational Amendments Act of 1972. In essence, Title IX states, "No person in the United States shall on the basis of sex be excluded from participation in, be denied the benefits of, or be subjected to discrimination under any education program or activity receiving Federal financial assistance." This legislation has had wide-ranging effects on physical education and athletic programs in the United States.

One major reason Title IX came into existence was to ensure that girls and women receive the same rights as boys and men. Testimony before congressional committees prior to the enactment of this legislation showed that girls and women were being discriminated against in many educational programs, including physical education and athletics. Although Title IX applies to all types of educational programs, probably the most dramatically affected have been sport and physical education programs. Girls' and women's athletic programs, in particular, have grown rapidly.

Participation in sports by girls and women has risen dramatically since the enactment of Title IX. According to the National Federation of State High School Associations, during 1971, the year before Title IX legislation, 3,366,000 boys and 294,000 girls competed in interscholastic sports in the United States. In 2003–2004, the Federation reported that 4,038,253 boys and 2,865,299 girls took part in interscholastic sports.[25] This is an all-time high for participation by girls. Participation by women at the intercollegiate level also showed substantial increases. For example, according to the NCAA, 32,000 women competed in intercollegiate sports in 1972, whereas in 2002–2003, the NCAA reported that 160,650 women competed. (These figures include only NCAA-sponsored championship sports; thus the number of participants is greater than reported here.)

Title IX mandated certain provisions for physical education and athletic programs. With respect to physical education, no discrimination could occur in program offerings, quality of teachers, and availability and quality of facilities and equipment. Physical education classes must be organized on a coeducational basis. However, classes may be separated by sex for contact sports such as wrestling, basketball, and football. Also, within classes, students may be grouped by ability or another basis, except sex, although such groupings may result in single-sex or predominately single-sex groupings.

Title IX also caused changes in the conduct of athletic programs. Separate teams for men and women or a coeducational team must be provided in schools and colleges. For example, if only one team is organized in a particular school for a sport such as swimming, then students of both sexes must be permitted to try out for this team. Both sexes in educational institutions must be provided with equal opportunities for the following: equipment and supplies, use of facilities for practice and games, medical and training services, coaching and academic tutoring, travel allowances, housing and dining facilities, compensation of coaches, financial assistance, and publicity. Equal aggregate expenditures are not required; however, equal opportunities for men and women are mandated.

There have also been changes since 1972 in the governance of women's intercollegiate sports. The Association of Intercollegiate Athletics for Women (AIAW), founded in 1972, initially was the governing body for women's intercollegiate sports. The AIAW established policies and procedures governing competition and conducted national championships for women's intercollegiate sports. In 1980–1981, 960 institutions were members and 99,000 women participated in AIAW events; the AIAW conducted 39 national championships encompassing 17 sports. The NCAA used its vast financial resources to entice teams to leave the AIAW; over a period of time, this led to the demise of the AIAW. In 1982, the NCAA and the NAIA assumed the governance of intercollegiate sports for women at all NCAA and NAIA institutions.

Throughout its history, many challenges to Title IX have been heard by the courts. In 1984, the United States Supreme Court in a 6 to 3 decision ruled in the *Grove City College v. Bell* case that Title IX should be regarded as program specific. In essence, this narrow interpretation of Title IX held that only programs directly receiving federal aid were required to comply with Title IX, not the institution as a whole. Before this ruling, Title IX was interpreted broadly; that is, institutions receiving any federal funds were required to comply with Title IX in all institution activities. Since athletic programs typically receive little, if any, direct federal funding, the threat of losing funding for noncompliance and nonsupport of women's athletics is without substance. While some institutions remained deeply committed to women's athletics, the fear existed that some institutions, without the threat of noncompliance, would allow women's athletics to stagnate or even to become victims of budgetary cutbacks.

In 1988, the Civil Rights Restoration Act superseded the 1984 United States Supreme Court ruling. Once again, Title IX was interpreted broadly and its applicability to athletics was reinstated. In 1991, the Office of Civil Rights announced that investigation of Title IX athletic complaints would be one of the office's priorities.

Title IX has led to dramatic changes in the conduct of physical education and athletic programs and to significant increases in participation by girls and women within these programs. However, the impact of Title IX has been limited by several factors, including gender biases, limited budgets, inadequate facilities, lack of qualified leadership (i.e., coaches), and resistance to change. Although equal opportunity is mandated by law and great strides have occurred within the last decades, much still needs to be accomplished within both physical education and athletic programs to achieve equity.

Programs for Individuals with Disabilities

In recent years, many judicial decisions and legislative acts have supported the rights of individuals with disabilities to have the same opportunities as other individuals. These mandates have resulted in significant changes in the conduct of physical education programs and athletic programs for individuals with disabilities. The rights of persons

Competitors in wheelchair archery take aim at the 2004 Paralympic Games in Athens.

with disabilities in programs for which schools and other sponsoring organizations receive federal funds were guaranteed by Section 504 of the Rehabilitation Act of 1973 (P.L. 93-112). This law provided for access to all school programs, including physical education and athletics.

The most widely known and important law related to education for people with disabilities is P.L. 94-142, or the Education of All Handicapped Children Act of 1975. This law provided for a free and appropriate education for children 3 to 21 years of age. Section 121a.307 of the regulations stated that physical education services were to be made available to every child with a disability. All educational services are to be provided for students with disabilities in the least restrictive environment. In essence, this means that a child with a disability is placed in a special class or mainstreamed into a regular class or moved between the two environments as dictated by his or her abilities and capabilities. Furthermore, the school assumes the responsibility of providing the necessary adjunct services to ensure that students with disabilities perform to their optimum capacity, whether they are integrated into a regular program or left in a special class. Each child with disabilities must have an individualized educational plan or IEP.

In 1986, the Education for All Handicapped Children Amendments of 1986 (P.L. 99-457) was passed, and implementation began in 1990. This law mandated that educational services to individuals with special needs from 0 to 2 years of age be provided and that services for 3- to 5-year-olds be expanded. Special educational services, including

Wheelchair basketball at the 2004 Paralympic Games in Athens.

A man, who is an amputee, gets ready to race at the cycling competition at the 2004 Paralympic Games in Athens.

physical education, are required. Preschool physical education programs had to be expanded to accommodate the diverse needs of these individuals and to fulfill the mandate of the law.

In 1990, P.L. 101-476, the Individuals with Disabilities Education Act (IDEA) was passed. Among its mandates was a requirement that all references to "handicapped children" be changed to "children with disabilities." It mandated that transitional services be provided to students as early as 14 and no later than 16 years of age. Transitional services are a coordinated set of activities designed to help students with disabilities make the transition from the school to post-school life in the community. It emphasizes creating linkages between the school and private and public services within the community. For example, if fitness development was part of the IEP, then linkages need to be created between the school and local fitness programs. IDEA also provides more opportunities for children with disabilities to receive assistive technologies to improve their abilities. For example, students can get racing wheelchairs or other specialized equipment that would enhance their ability to participate. Children with disabilities must have the opportunity to participate in extracurricular activities and services, such as athletics, intramurals, and the art club.

IDEA stated that physical education and sport must be available to every child who is receiving a free and appropriate education. Each student with a disability must be afforded the opportunity to participate in a regular physical education program with children who do not have a disability unless the child is enrolled full-time in a separate facility or needs a specially designed physical education program. The philosophy, known as inclusion, is based on the rights of children with disabilities, regardless of severity, to attend their home schools and participate in the regular educational setting rather than be isolated from their peers in special programs. An alternative approach is the use of the least restrictive environment. The least restrictive environment places a child in the educational setting that is most appropriate for his or her abilities and developmental level. The environment can range from full inclusion in the regular setting to special programs in a self-contained setting. Regardless of the approach, it is important that children with disabilities have individualized programs that are appropriate for their developmental levels and that optimize their potential.

Federal legislation directed toward improving conditions of persons with disabilities and meeting their educational needs has caused many changes. Schools are now required to provide physical education, intramurals, recreational programs, and athletic programs for students with disabilities. Adapted physical education programs have expanded. Teachers have had to learn different strategies to enhance the learning opportunities for students with disabilities participating in regular physical education classes. Facilities have to be altered and modified to meet the needs of the disabled. It is hoped that the commitment to improve the educational opportunities and to meet the educational needs of individuals with disabilities will continue in the years ahead. A greater emphasis also must be placed on meeting the activity needs of individuals with disabilities by developing expanded opportunities for participation in the community setting.

In 1990, a landmark law, the Americans with Disabilities Act (ADA) (P.L. 101-336) was passed. This law seeks to end discrimination against individuals of all ages with disabilities and to remove barriers to their integration into the economic and social mainstream of American life. Five areas are addressed by the law: employment, public accommodations, public services, transportation, and telecommunications. The effects of this law are far-reaching. For example, the ADA mandates that all facilities, including recreational and sport facilities, must provide equal access and equal services to individuals with disabilities. This law opens playgrounds, swimming pools, gymnasiums, and health spas, for example, to individuals with disabilities, increasing their opportunities to participate in fitness and sport activities. In 1998, professional golfer Casey Martin sued the Professional Golfers Association under the ADA for the right to ride a motorized cart in competition. Martin has Klippel-Trebauney-Weber syndrome, a painful ailment that affects the circulation in his lower right leg and limits his ability to walk the golf course. It was ruled that the PGA Tour must accommodate Martin. This ruling was appealed, but in 2001, the United States Supreme Court upheld this decision.

Since the 1970s, the number of individuals with disabilities participating in competitive sports has increased. The Amateur Sports Act of 1978 (P.L. 95-606) charged the United States Olympic Committee to encourage provisions for sporting opportunities for the disabled, specifically to expand participation by individuals with disabilities in programs of athletic competition for able-bodied individuals. This charge served as the impetus for the formation of the Committee on Sports for the Disabled in 1983. The committee is to promote participation in sport by individuals with disabilities and to support amateur sports programs for athletes with disabilities. Participation in national and international competitions and games by athletes with specific disabilities continues to rise. Competitions include the Paralympics, the Special Olympics, World Games for the Deaf, and the World Wheelchair Games, to name a few. Competition at the state and local level, such as Connecticut's Nutmeg Games for the Disabled, continues to grow. It is likely that this trend will continue as all segments of our society find participation in sport to be a meaningful and satisfying experience.

Olympics

In 1996, the Centennial Olympic Games were held in Atlanta, Georgia. In the 100 years since their rebirth in 1896, the Olympics have evolved into an event of global magnitude. In the 1896 Olympics held in Athens, 311 athletes from 11 nations competed. In Atlanta, 10,750 athletes from 197 nations competed.

The modern Olympic Games, organized originally with the idealistic goal of fostering understanding among the people of the world, have become an instrument for political goals. Ideological differences have exerted a profound influence on the conduct of the Games. The 1972 Munich Olympics were marked by terrorism. Eight armed Arab guerrillas entered the Olympic Village complex occupied by the Israelis; a day later eleven Israelis, five terrorists, and one German policeman were dead. Millions of people around the world mourned the slain athletes. After a memorial ceremony, the Munich Olympics continued.

Social and political issues led to boycotts at the 1976 Olympics in Montreal over the issue of representation of China and the issue of apartheid. The United States led a boycott of the 1980 Olympics in Moscow in protest of the Soviet Union's invasion of Afghanistan. The Soviet Union, in turn, led a boycott of the 1984 Olympics in Los Angeles, claiming that the United States failed to adhere to the Olympic ideals. The 1988 Olympics in Seoul, Korea, saw the Americans and Soviets competing in the XXIVth Olympiad. The International Olympic Committee took a strong position against drug "doping." Canadian sprinter Ben Johnson tested positive for steroid use after winning the 100 meters, and American Carl Lewis was then awarded the gold medal.

Several monumental events in the early 1990s had a significant impact on the world and the Olympics. The collapse of the Berlin Wall that had separated East Germany from West Germany and the collapse of the Soviet Union contributed to the end of the Cold War and a decrease in East-West tensions. In 1992, the Germans competed in Barcelona as a unified team, and athletes from the former Soviet Union competed as part of the Commonwealth of Independent States. South Africa competed for the first time in decades, and the Baltic States participated as independent countries for the first time since World War II. As more countries began to be more open about paying their athletes for their performances, the issue of amateurism became a moot point. Professional athletes began to participate in the Games in increased numbers. Public attention was focused on the United States basketball "Dream Team," largely comprised of professionals such as Michael Jordan, David Robinson, and Larry Bird. Growing commercialism and concern about the use of drugs continued.

In the 1996 Centennial Olympic Games in Atlanta, a record number of athletes, nearly 11,000, from a record number of nations, 197, made the Games a memorable event. The athletes participated in 271 events. The event was broadcasted to an estimated 3.5 billion people. NBC paid the International Olympic Committee $456 million dollars for the broadcast rights; compare this to the $394,000 paid by CBS to telecast the 1960 Games in Rome. Rights to the 2000 Olympic Games in Sydney and the 2002 Winter Games in Salt Lake City, Utah, were purchased by NBC for $1.27 billion. Commercialization extended further than broadcast rights. To be an official corporate sponsor of the Games costs each of the selected companies $40 million.

The 2000 Summer Olympic Games, held in Sydney, Australia, drew a record number of nations: 199. Twenty-eight sports were included, and 10,651 athletes (6,582 men and 4,069 women) competed in over 300 events. In 2001, Jacques Rogge was elected the 8th president of the International Olympic Committee, succeeding Juan Antonio Samaranch, who had served as president of the IOC for 21 years, from 1980–2001. During his tenure, many landmark events occurred and the Games experienced unprecedented growth and prosperity.

In 2001, in a controversial decision, the IOC selected Beijing, China, as host of the 2008 Olympic Games. The Summer Olympic Games have only been held in Asia twice, Tokyo in 1964 and Seoul in 1988. China, the most populous nation on earth, is home to 1.3 billion people. Human rights advocates questioned awarding the Games to a country that has a long history of human rights violations. Other individuals asked whether the Olympics would have a transforming effect on China, opening up its society, promoting social change, and modernizing the nation. Would it offer Olympic sponsors an economic advantage, giving them access to one-fifth of the world's people? Does awarding the Games to China follow the Olympic ideals of separating politics from sports? Does it fulfill the Olympic mission of universality?

In 2004, the Summer Olympics returned to its birthplace and to the place where the Games were revived—Athens, Greece. A record number of athletes, 11,099, participated. Participation by women also reached an all-time high. Representatives of 202 countries took part in the Games. Some of the events, particularly those in track, are intrinsically tied to the origins of the Olympic Games. For the first time in modern history, an Olympic sporting event—the shotput—was held in the Ancient Olympia Stadium. One new event added for this Olympics was women's wrestling. Like previous Olympics, corporations paid billions of dollars for sponsorship rights for this event. For U.S. broadcast rights, NBC paid $793 million. It is estimated that the Olympics were watched by over 4 billion viewers worldwide.

The Winter Games also flourished during this time and mirrored the changes seen in the Summer Games. In the early 1990s, the International Olympic Committee voted to stagger the Winter and Summer Games in a 2-year rotation instead of a 4-year rotation. This started with the 1994 Winter Games in Lillihammer, Norway. It was believed that, given the high degree of public interest in the Olympics, the public would embrace this change. There would also be an economic benefit to the International Olympic Committee if the games were held every 2 years rather than every 4.

Focus on Career: Sport History

PROFESSIONAL ORGANIZATIONS

- North American Society for Sport History www.nassh.org/index1.html
- International Society for the History of Physical Education and Sport www.umist.ac.uk/UMIST_Sport//ishpes.html
- History of Sport and Physical Education Academy www.aahperd.org → NASPE → Academies

PROFESSIONAL JOURNALS

- *Journal of Sport History*
- *Sport History Review*
- *The International Journal of the History of Sport*
- *Journal of Olympic History*
- *Canadian Journal of History of Sport and Physical Education*

Participation by women has increased during these past decades. Women's softball in 1996, and women's ice hockey in 1998, are just two of the new sports added to the Games. In 1998, following the Winter Games in Nagano, Japan, the International Olympic Committee stated that no new events would be added to the competition unless a comparable event could be added for women.

"Nontraditional" sports have been added to the Olympic Games. Beach volleyball, mogul skiing, and snowboarding are just a few of the new sports included in the Olympics.

The Paralympics is an international Olympic competition for persons with disabilities. The disability categories are amputee, cerebral palsy, intellectual disability, les autres, vision-impaired, and wheelchair. In the early 1990s, the International Olympic Committee mandated that the Paralympics would be the responsibility of the same country that hosted the Olympic Games. The same venues would be used, and the Paralympics would take place immediately following the closing of the Olympic Games. The 2004 Paralympics in Athens involved over 4,000 athletes and 2000 team officials representing 130 countries. The athletes participated in 18 sports.

In recent years the Olympics have been used as a means to further political ideologies. The line between amateurism and professionalism has disappeared. Commercialization has reached new heights and continues to grow. The Olympics have become an embedded component of our global culture.

SUMMARY

History provides the foundation for the fields of physical education, exercise science, and sport. Many of our programs and activities today have been shaped by our heritage. Studying history also provides one with an appreciation for other cultures and the role of physical activity in these societies.

An adage states that "history tends to repeat itself." Recurring themes are apparent throughout the history of physical education, exercise science, and sport. For example, wars frequently served as the impetus for societies to intensify their physical education program or to justify its existence. Physical fitness was promoted among the populace to prepare for these war efforts.

However, studying history allows us to understand more fully many of the changes that have occurred in our field. The impact of different philosophies on the content and structure of physical education, exercise science, and sport programs and changes in the nature and the importance of objectives can be discerned throughout the years. It is important to be aware of the events that served as catalysts and deterrents to our growth of physical education, exercise science, and sport.

The recent history of physical education, exercise science, and sport reveals many changes. Since the 1970s, the growth of the discipline, the emphasis on disease prevention and health promotion, changes in school physical education, the fitness movement and emphasis on physical activity, and the phenomenal growth of sports have contributed greatly to our fields. By understanding the history of physical education, exercise science, and sport, a professional can better understand the nature of the field, appreciate the significant developments of today, and project trends for the future.

SELF-ASSESSMENT TESTS

These tests are designed to help you determine if you have mastered the materials and competencies presented in this chapter.

1. Describe events that served as catalysts for the growth of physical education, exercise science, and sport, and events that served as deterrents to the growth of physical education, exercise science, and sport throughout history.
2. Using the information provided in the Get Connected box, explore the history of the Olympic Games or other sports.
3. Project future developments for physical education, exercise science, and sport based on historical events, including events from both early and recent times.

REFERENCES

1. Mechikoff RA and Estes SG: A history and philosophy of physical education and sport: from ancient civilizations to the modern world (2nd ed.), New York, 2002, WCB/McGraw-Hill.
2. Struna NL: Sport history. In JD Massengale and RA Swanson, eds., The history of exercise and sport science, Champaign, Ill., 1997, Human Kinetics.
3. Salter M: Play in ritual. An ethnohistorical overview of Native North America, Stadion, 3(2):230–243, 1977.
4. Ray HL: Let's have a friendly game of war, Quest, 14 June, 28–41, 1970.
5. Davenport J: Thomas Denison Wood: Physical educator and father of health education, JOPERD 55(8):63–64, 68, 1984.
6. Henry F: Physical education: an academic discipline, Journal of Health, Physical Education, and Recreation 37(7):32–33, 1964.
7. Ziegler EF: Physical education and kinesiology in North America: professional and scholarly foundations, Champaign, Ill., 1994, Stipes.
8. Ziegler EF: From one image to a sharper one! Physical Educator 54(2):72–77, 1997.
9. US Department of Health, Education, and Welfare: Healthy people: the Surgeon General's report on health promotion and disease prevention, Washington, D.C., 1979, US Government Printing Office.
10. US Public Health Service, US Department of Health and Human Services: Promoting health/preventing disease: objectives for the nation, Washington, D.C., 1980, US Government Printing Office.
11. US Public Health Service, US Department of Health and Human Services: Healthy people 2000: national health promotion and disease prevention objectives, Washington, D.C., 1990, US Government Printing Office.
12. US Department of Health and Human Services: Healthy people 2010: understanding and improving health (2nd ed.). Washington, D.C., 2000, US Government Printing Office (www.healthypeople.gov/healthypeople).

13. US Department of Health and Human Services: Physical activity and health: a report of the Surgeon General, Atlanta, Ga., 1996, US Department of Health and Human Services, Centers for Disease Control and Prevention, National Center for Chronic Disease Prevention and Health Promotion, and The President's Council on Physical Fitness and Sports.
14. Siedentop D, Mann C, and Taggart A: Physical education: teaching and curriculum strategies for grades 5–12, Palo Alto, Calif., 1986, Mayfield.
15. Biles F: The physical education public information project, JOHPER 41(7):53–55, 1971.
16. National Association for Sport and Physical Education: Definition of a physically educated person: outcomes of quality physical education programs, Reston, Va., 1990, AAHPERD.
17. National Association for Sport and Physical Education: Moving into the future: national standards for physical education: a guide to content and assessment, St. Louis, Mo., 1995, Mosby.
18. National Association for Sport and Physical Education: Shape of the nation 1993, Reston, Va., 1993, American Alliance for Health, Physical Education, Recreation, and Dance.
19. Centers for Disease Control and Prevention: youth risk behavior surveillance system, Atlanta, Ga. (www.cdc.gov/nccdphp/dash/yrbs/).
20. Sporting Goods Manufacturers Association: Tracking the fitness movement—2001. (www.sgma.com)
21. American Alliance for Health, Physical Education, Recreation, and Dance: Health-related fitness test, Reston, Va., 1980, AAHPERD.
22. Ross JG and Gilbert CG: The national children and youth fitness study: a summary of the findings, JOPERD 56(1):45–50, 1985.
23. Ross JG and Pate RR: The national children and youth fitness study II, JOPERD 58(9):51–56, 1987.
24. American Alliance for Health, Physical Education, Recreation, and Dance: Physical best, Reston, Va., 1988, AAHPERD.
25. National Federation of State High School Associations: Participation sets record for sixth straight year, 2004. (www.nfhs.org)
26. National Collegiate Athletic Association: Participation statistics, 2002–2003. (www.ncaa.org)
27. National Junior College Athletic Association: 2001. (www.njcaa.org)
28. National Association of Intercollegiate Athletes: 2001. (www.naia.org)

SUGGESTED READINGS

Amateur Athletic Foundation of Los Angeles (AAFLA). (www.aafla.com/index.html)

Access the AAAFLA site and navigate to the searchable archives to read back issues of the Journal of Sport History and Journal of Olympic History as well as the biography of Pierre de Coubertin. Access the Sports Art & Artifacts and download Preserving Sports Heritage: Arts and Artifacts collection focusing on the heritage of sports. AAF Research Reports contains articles on children and sports media, gender stereotyping in televised sport, and portrayal of race and ethnicity in media coverage of sport.

Cazers G and Miller GA: The German contribution to American physical education: a historical perspective, JOPERD 71(6):44–48, 2000.

This interesting article examines the German influence on the evolution of physical education in the United States.

Davenport J, editor: The normal schools: exploring our heritage, JOPERD 65(3):25–56, 1994.

A series of eight articles that describe the normal schools of the 1800s, which provided professional education for individuals seeking to enter the field.

Dyreson M: American ideas about race and Olympic races from the 1890s to the 1950s: Shattering myths or reinforcing scientific racism, Journal of Sports History, 28(2):173–215.

Examines the role of athletic performance at the Olympics by minorities and discusses whether or not it perpetuates racism.

Guttmann, A: Sport, politics and the engaged historian, Journal of Contemporary History: 38:363–374.

Discusses the topics of historical studies by sports historians studying the relationship between politics and sports. Topics include roles of sports under fascist regimes and communist societies, relationships between sports and ethnicity, race, and gender.

Hutzler Y: Attitudes toward the participation of individuals with disabilities in physical activity: A review, Quest 55:347–374, 2003.

An extensive review of articles published during the past two decades on attitudes toward the participation of individuals with disabilities in various forms of physical activity, including sport.

Magdalinski T: Sports history and the East German national identity; Peace Review, 11(4):539–546, 1999.

Role of sports in the German Democratic Republic, with a focus on sports' impact on the national culture and socialization of its citizens.

Massengale JD and Swanson RA, editors: The history of exercise and sport science, Champaign, Ill., 1997, Human Kinetics.

This books presents in depth the historical development of the exercise and sport sciences, including sport pedagogy, adapted physical activity, sport sociology, sport history, philosophy of sport, motor behavior, sport and exercise psychology, biomechanics, and exercise physiology.

Mechikoff R and Estes S: A history and philosophy of sport and physical education, ed 2, Dubuque, Iowa, 1998, McGraw-Hill.

Provides an overview of significant philosophies and traces the development of sport and physical education from the time of the ancient Greeks to the present day, including the history of the modern Olympics.

Motley ML and LaVine ME: Century marathon: a race for equality in girls' and women's sports, JOPERD 72(6):56–60, 2001.

Traces the progress in athletic opportunities for females during the twentieth century.

Wrynn A: Contesting the canon: Understanding the history of the evolving discipline of kinesiology, Quest 55:244–257, 2003.

Reminds readers that memory plays an important role in history, and that our history should be carefully reexamined for consistency.

CHAPTER 5

Motor Behavior

OBJECTIVES

After reading this chapter the student should be able to—

- Define motor behavior, motor development, motor control, and motor learning and understand the influence of readiness, motor development, motivation, reinforcement, and individual differences in the learning of motor skills.
- Understand the information-processing model of motor learning and the stages of learning and be able to draw implications for instruction in physical education, exercise science, and sport.
- Apply to the teaching of physical education, exercise science, and sport basic concepts of motor learning such as feedback, design of practice, and transfer.
- Describe the fundamental movements and the phases of motor development.

Motor behavior is a broad umbrella term used to encompass the areas of motor control, motor learning, and motor development. Motor control and motor learning trace their roots to experimental psychology, whereas motor development traces its roots to developmental psychology.

During the last 30 years, motor behavior has grown tremendously and has become increasingly specialized. This chapter provides a short introduction to motor behavior. In this chapter, the terms "teacher" and "learner" are used in their broadest sense to encompass physical education, exercise science, and sport professionals who provide instruction to people of all ages in a diversity of settings.

MOTOR BEHAVIOR

One of the primary concerns of physical education, exercise science, and sport professionals is the learning and refinement of motor skills. Learning is defined as a relatively permanent change in behavior or performance as a result of practice or experience. Motor behavior is concerned with the learning or acquisition of skills across the lifespan and encompasses three areas:

GET CONNECTED

Inner Body Online uses graphics and animations to help you learn about various anatomical systems of the body.
www.innerbody.com

Motor Development Academy site, one of the National Association of Sport and Physical Education academies, offers links to information pertaining to motor development, including minimum competencies in undergraduate motor development.
www.aahperd.org > NASPE > Academies > Motor Development

Saskatchewan, Canada, Evergreen Curriculum—Physical Education provides information about the development of motor skills at the elementary, middle, and secondary levels.
www.sasked.gov.sk.ca/docs/physed.html

Lifespan and Cultural Perspectives: Motor Behavior

- How does aging affect the control of movements?
- How does early sensory stimulation affect the development of motor skills?
- How does socioeconomic status affect the development of motor skills?
- How does a deficit in auditory or visual processing affect the learning of specific motor skills?
- At what age can children safely engage in resistance training?

motor learning, motor control, and motor development. Thomas and Thomas identify three goals of motor behavior: first, "to understand how motor skills are learned"; second, "to understand how motor skills are controlled"; and third, "to understand how learning and control of motor skills changes across the life span."[1] All of these areas, although highly specialized, are interrelated. Although researchers in these areas focus on slightly different questions, a more highly integrated approach to research is seen today.

As motor behavior expanded as a field of study, scholars sought avenues to disseminate their research and opportunities to exchange ideas. In 1969, the *Journal of Motor Behavior* was founded by Richard Schmidt, and it continues to serve as one of the major outlets for researchers in the field. Additionally, the *Research Quarterly for Exercise and Sport* also publishes research on motor behavior. Motor learning, motor development, and sport psychology emerged as subdisciplines of physical education at relatively similar times and for awhile their interests were aligned. In 1967, researchers in these fields founded the North American Society for the Psychology of Sport and Physical Activity (NASPSPA). Today, NASPSPA continues to provide a forum for motor behavior and sport and exercise psychologists, although both groups have their own interests and focus within the organization. Researchers also present papers at the American Alliance for Health, Physical Education, Recreation, and Dance convention. NASPE's Motor Development Academy, which was founded in 1979, also provides a forum for discussion and exchange of ideas through its program at the AAHPERD national convention and its newsletter.

MOTOR LEARNING AND MOTOR CONTROL

Motor learning and motor control are interrelated. The definition and scope of these specialized areas of study, historical development, and areas of interest are briefly described in this section.

Definition and Scope

Motor learning is the study of the acquisition of motor skills as a result of practice and experience. Learning is inferred from changes in performance. For example, an instructor determines whether an individual has learned a tennis serve by observing and assessing the individual's performance. As the individual receives instruction and practices, his/her performance of the tennis serve should improve: that is, become more consistent, effective, and efficient. You would then infer from the individual's performance that learning had occurred. Motor skills range in scope from simple skills, such as learning to walk, to highly complex skills, such as those of an elite gymnast performing intricate tumbling passes as part of a floor exercise routine. Motor learning focuses on studying the cognitive aspects of motor skill acquisition. According to Thomas and Thomas, the goals of motor learning are "understanding the influence of feedback, practice, and individual differences, especially how they relate to the retention and transfer of motor skill."[1]

Intimately related to the area of motor learning is motor control. Motor control is the study of the neurophysiological and behavioral processes affecting the control of skilled movements. Thomas and Thomas summarize the goals of motor control as understanding "how the muscles and joints are coordinated during movement, how a sequence of movements is controlled, and how to use environmental information to plan and adjust movements."[1] Researchers in motor control are in-

With practice, motor performance becomes more efficient, effective, and consistent.

terested in the processes underlying the learning and performance of motor skills, such as how the nervous system works with the muscular system to produce and coordinate movement and how cognitive processes are involved in the learning and execution of motor skills.

Historical Development

The history of motor learning and motor control can be divided into three eras: the Early Period (1880–1940), the Middle Period (1940–1970), and the Present Period (1970–today).[2]

During the early period, although researchers investigated the acquisition of motor skills, their research focused on trying to understand how the mind worked rather than seeking to understand how skilled movements were produced.[2] One significant development was Thorndike's research on learning (1927), which became known as the Law of Effect. Thorndike found that when responses to a situation were rewarded, they were strengthened, used more frequently, and hence became learned behaviors. Thorndike's work influenced subsequent work on the impact of feedback on motor skill acquisition.[2] Adams reports that it was during this early period that the basis for research in five major areas of motor learning was laid: knowledge of results, distribution of practice, transfer of training, retention, and individual differences. Motor control research also began during this time, with some of the early work focusing on the qualities of muscle. The discovery that the brain produces electrical activity stimulated interest in the relationship between brain electrical activity and movement, which helped further researchers' understanding of how the nervous system controls muscles and movement.

The start of the middle period was marked by a surge of interest in motor learning. World War II had stimulated an interest in pilot selection and training. Motor learning research focused more on application, investigating such areas as transfer of training (e.g., What factors would enable a pilot to easily and successfully switch from flying one type of aircraft to another aircraft that was of a different size, with controls positioned differently?).

In the late 1940s, Craik advanced his ideas about the similarities between the human brain and the computer, which gave new insight into how the brain processes and uses information to determine the motor response.

In the 1960s, Franklin Henry published his landmark paper on the "memory drum theory," which discussed the role of cognitive activity in motor learning.[2] Often considered the "father of motor behavior," Henry and his contemporaries, Fitz Hubbard, Jack Adams, Arthur Slater-Hammel, and John Lawther, helped set the stage for the emergence of the subdiscipline in the 1970s.[2] In 1968, Robert N. Singer published *Motor Learning and Human Performance,* the first book in the subdiscipline.

The 1970s marked the emergence of motor learning and motor control within physical education programs. As the subdiscipline emerged and evolved, motor behavior scholars began to move from the application of theories from psychology to explain motor skills to the development and use of their own theories and models to explain motor skill acquisition. Adams' (1971) closed loop theory explained how feedback, following the performance of slow and discrete movements, is used to update the cognitive representation of the movement and improve subsequent performances of the motor skill.[3] In 1975, Schmidt's schema theory proposed the idea of a generalized motor program; that is, movement patterns such as kicking or throwing could be generalized to a variety of sports and settings. More recently, the dynamical systems theory, developed by Scott Kelso and other researchers, suggests that the neuromuscular system plays a prominent role in the selection of movements. According to Thomas and Thomas, the "information-processing view of motor behavior (motor programs or schema) based on the role of cognition and a central processing mechanism, has dominated the research literature in motor behavior for over 30 years. However, the dynamical systems view (movements organized by environmental constraints) has provided an alternative explanation and challenged information processing as the dominant theory in recent years."[1]

Areas of Study

Since the 1970s, many topics have captured the interests of researchers. Researchers have investigated the effectiveness of various types of practice, the impact of different types of feedback on motor performance, the use of cognitive strategies to improve performance, reaction time, and transfer of learning—how skills learned in one setting can enhance or hinder learning in another setting. Some researchers have focused their efforts on understanding motor problems in special populations—such as postural and coordination control in the aging.

Motor control also grew as a specialized area of study during this modern period. Motor control researchers have tried to determine how movements are coordinated, how the sequence of our behaviors is controlled, and how information obtained from the environment is used to plan and modify movements.

Researchers in motor learning and motor control may address questions such as these:

- How do the type and frequency of feedback impact skill acquisition?
- How does the structure of practice influence the retention of skills?
- What can be done to facilitate the transfer of previous learning to the learning of new skills?
- How does skill performance change as beginners move from novice to advanced levels of performance?
- How can an individual's perception of cues in the environment be enhanced to improve performance?
- How does the aging process affect motor control? How do specific diseases, such as Parkinson's disease, affect an individual's ability to perform motor skills?
- When teaching a skill such as pitching or the tennis serve, should you first emphasize speed or accuracy?
- How do differences in individuals' learning styles influence their ability to learn motor skills?

As we begin the twenty-first century, advances in technology and a greater emphasis on cross-disciplinary research will further our understanding of how motor skills are learned and controlled.

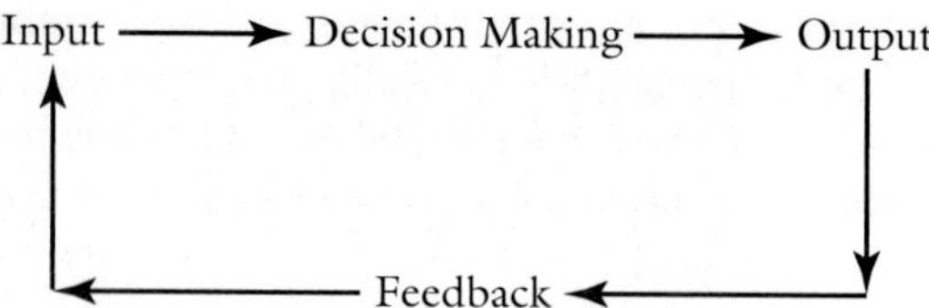

Figure 5-1 Information-processing model.

Information-Processing Model

Many theories have been advanced to explain the process by which motor skills are learned and controlled. One popular model to describe motor skill acquisition and performance is the information-processing model. In its simplest form, the information-processing model comprises four components or processes: input, decision making, output, and feedback. This model is illustrated in Figure 5-1.

Input is the process of obtaining information from the environment. This information is obtained through the senses. Visual, auditory, kinesthetic, and other sensory information is transmitted through the nervous system to the brain where the process of *decision making* occurs. During this procedure the input is processed; that is, it is sifted, evaluated, and interpreted. Relevant environmental cues are identified. Using this current information and relevant past experiences stored in memory, the individual selects an appropriate

Fencing is a sport that requires rapid processing of information as well as split-second decision making skills.

response. A decision is reached about what movement to make. The response is organized; a "motor program" that will control the response is retrieved from memory. The muscles are directed to contract in proper order, with the proper amount of force and with the correct timing to produce the desired movement. The response and its execution are the *output. Feedback* is information about the performance of the movement and its quality, appropriateness, and/or outcome. This information can be used to provide *input* for making ongoing adjustments in performance or to modify the next skill attempt. The knowledge gained from feedback can be used to improve the decision-making process as well as the succeeding output. As an individual becomes more adept at performing the skill, often he or she also becomes more skilled at using the feedback to improve performance.

How the information-processing model works can be illustrated by this simple example. Suppose you are in a soccer game and are in possession of the ball within shooting range of the goal. Should you retain the ball and continue to dribble while maneuvering for a more favorable position? Should you pass to a teammate? Or should you shoot for the goal?

To make this choice, you must first obtain information about your position on the field, the positions of your teammates and the opposing players, and the distance between you and the goalie. This information serves as input. Next, as part of the decision-making process you must analyze and interpret this information with reference to your past experience in the game of soccer and specifically in situations similar to the present one. Within a fraction of a second, based on this analysis and evaluation, you must choose the response to make. The decision is influenced by your own and your teammates' past successes in similar situations, the probable actions of the opposing team given their past reactions in similar situations, appropriateness of the various strategies available, and perhaps directions or guidelines from the teacher or coach concerning the desirable course of action in such situations. You may also consider your own ability as well as your level of confidence in your ability to execute the selected option, be it dribble, pass, or shoot.

After these considerations and deliberations you select an option. Next, you execute the selected movement—you dribble, pass, or shoot. Finally, both during and after execution of the response, you receive feedback about your performance. The feedback may focus on whether you executed the movement as intended and/or whether the outcome was successful (e.g., you scored a goal).

Teachers should be familiar with the manner in which individuals learn skills as well as the factors that influence their performance. This understanding will help them design practices that facilitate an individual's opportunity to learn through appropriate structuring of the learning environment. The teacher must give learners appropriate input through the careful selection of teaching methods, materials, and procedures. The teacher must help the learner understand the goal of the movement and then distinguish between relevant and irrelevant information or cues with respect to that goal, drawing the learner's attention to cues essential for the decision-making process and teaching the learner to disregard the irrelevant ones.

The teacher next must help the learner to become a wise decision maker. This can be accomplished by helping the learner evaluate his or her past experiences, by explaining the "why" underlying skills and strategies, by instructing the learner on how to use the available feedback, and by making sure that the learner is attending to the right cues and interpreting the information correctly. The teacher can facilitate the learner's development of the desired skill using proper progressions and by giving the learner appropriate and sufficient practice opportunities.

Finally, the teacher can help the learner by providing feedback about the learner's performance and communicating this information to the learner in an understandable manner. Additionally, the teacher must draw the learner's attention to the feedback available during the execution of the skill as well as the information regarding the outcome of the performance. This information can provide the basis for adjustments in the learner's movements.

As you can see from the information-processing model, the senses play a critical role in motor learning and performance. Vision is one of the most important senses for gathering information or input from the environment to use for decision making. An area of study that is gaining increasing emphasis is sports vision training. *Sports vision training* combines vision science, motor learning, biomechanics, sport psychology, and neuroanatomy to help individuals improve their performance.[4]

Research focusing on the process and mechanism by which motor skills are controlled and learned is entering an exciting era at the beginning of the twenty-first century. The dynamical systems theory is receiving considerable attention from researchers at the present. Advances in technology, increasingly sophisticated research methodology, and interdisciplinary approaches hold great promise for enhancing our understanding of motor skill acquisition and control.

An understanding of the manner in which individuals learn skills can help the teacher make the learning process more effective and more enjoyable—that is, less frustrating for the learner. The professional must also be aware that skill learning occurs in stages.

Stages of Learning

As an individual learns motor skills and makes the transition from unskilled to skilled performer, he or she progresses through several stages. Fitts and Posner[5] identified three stages of learning: the cognitive stage, the associative stage, and the autonomous stage. The teacher must be cognizant of the characteristics of the learner at each stage to plan for instruction. Different instructional strategies and techniques are required at each stage to make practice more effective. (See Table 5-1.)

Cognitive Stage

The first stage of learning is the cognitive stage. During this stage the learner is endeavoring to understand the nature and/or goal of the activity to be learned. During this stage the learner might be concerned with such questions as "How do I stand?" "How do I hold the tennis racquet?" "How do you score in this game?" "What is the sequence of actions in this swimming stroke?" The learner

TABLE 5-1 Characteristics Associated with Stages of Learning

Cognitive	Associative	Autonomous
Learner's focus		
Cognitive understanding of the goal of the skill	Concentration on temporal aspects or timing of movements	Concentration on use of the skill in performance situations, use of strategies
Concentrate on spatial aspects or sequence of skill components		
Performance characteristics		
Lacks smoothness, inefficient, variable, large number of gross errors	Smoother, less variability, more efficient, reduction of extraneous movements, fewer and reduced range of errors	Smooth, efficient, highly refined and well organized spatially and temporally, adaptable to environmental demands
Teacher's focus		
Provide overview of nature of skill and goal; feedback on intent of skill; information and demonstration of skill, cognitive understanding	Direct learner's attention to critical cues and feedback available, provide numerous practice opportunities, accommodate individual differences	Focus on refinement of response, consistency for closed skills and flexibility for open skills, use of skill in performance situations, feedback for refinement of movements

also needs to pay close attention to the information provided by the instructor; this includes verbal directions as well as visual information, perhaps from demonstration of a skill or a videotape of a performer executing this skill. After analyzing this information, the learner formulates a plan of action based on his or her understanding of the task and the specific directions provided by the instructor. Formulating a plan of action is referred to as establishing a motor plan or an executive plan. A high level of concentration on the task is required as the learner tries to put together the various parts of the skill in the correct sequence.

As the learner makes initial attempts at performing the skill, the performance is characterized by a large number of errors, usually gross in nature, and a great deal of variability. Although the learner may have an idea about what he or she is doing incorrectly, the learner may not know how to correct it. To improve skill performance, the learner needs specific feedback from the instructor, communicated in understandable terms. For example, someone just learning the tennis forehand must concentrate on moving to the correct position on the court, the grip of the racquet, the stance, turning the body, keeping an eye on the ball, making contact with the ball with the head of the racquet so that it goes over the net, shifting the body's weight, following through, and returning to ready position. The beginner at times will hit the ball over the net; with the next attempt the learner might hit the ball into the net or out of the court or miss the ball entirely. The learner's actions, although performed in the correct sequence, may lack the smooth, polished look and the consistency of a highly skilled performer.

Associative Stage

The second stage is the associative stage. At this point the basics of the skill have been learned and the learner concentrates on refining the skill. During this stage the learner works on mastering the timing needed for the skill; the learner's performance looks smoother. Fewer errors are committed, and the same type of error tends to recur. The learner is also aware of some of the more obvious errors he or she is making in executing the task and can use this information to adjust subsequent performance. The tennis player learning the forehand may notice more success in getting the ball over the net and inside the boundaries of the court, although he or she cannot place the ball with any assurance. The player may notice a frequent failure to follow through after contacting the ball, but he or she is not aware that the angle of the racquet face needs adjustment. The instructor can provide the learner with additional instruction focusing on specific actions and point out relevant cues.

Autonomous Stage

The third stage is the autonomous stage. This stage of learning is reached after much practice. The learner can perform the skill consistently with few errors. The skill is well coordinated and may appear to be performed effortlessly. During this stage the skill has become almost automatic. The learner does not have to pay attention to every aspect of the skill; he or she can perform the skill without consciously thinking about it at all. The tennis player no longer has to concentrate on the fundamentals of the skill; instead, his or her focus can be directed to placing the ball in the court, varying the speed of the shot, placing spin on the ball, or game tactics. The learner also becomes more skilled at detecting errors and making adjustments, in a sense becoming his or her own teacher.

Individuals do not proceed through these stages at the same rate. It may also be difficult at times to identify what stage an individual is in. To plan practices to promote effective learning, however, the professional must be cognizant of the characteristics and the needs of the learner in the various stages. The professional also needs to be aware of the forces that influence learning.

Highly skilled performers exemplify the autonomous stage of learning.

Forces Influencing Learning

Learning implies a change in a person—a change in the method of both practicing and performing a skill or a change in an attitude toward a particular thing. Learning implies a progressive change of behavior in an individual, although some changes are rapid, such as when one gains insight into a problem. It implies a change that occurs as a result of experience or practice. It results in the modification of behavior as a consequence of training or environment. It involves such aspects as obtaining knowledge, improving skill in an activity, solving a problem, and making an adjustment to a new situation. It implies that a person has acquired knowledge or skill through instruction or personal study. Learning continues throughout life.

To create an effective learning situation, teachers must be cognizant of the forces influencing learning. Four of these forces—readiness, motiva-

Learning experiences should be appropriate for the participant's abilities.

tion, reinforcement, and individual differences—will be discussed.

Readiness

Successful acquisition of new information or skills depends on the individual's level of readiness. *Readiness* can be defined in terms of physiological and psychological factors influencing an individual's ability and willingness to learn. Physiological readiness in children is development of the necessary strength, flexibility, and endurance, as well as development of the various organ systems, to such a degree that children can control their bodies in physical activities. Psychological readiness refers to the learner's state of mind. One's feeling or attitude toward learning a particular skill—in other words, the desire and willingness to learn—will affect one's acquisition of that particular skill. To create an effective learning environment, the teacher must keep in mind the individual's physiological and psychological readiness.

Teachers planning learning activities must be cognizant of the individual's cognitive, affective, and physical characteristics as well as the individual's past experiences. This knowledge will help the teacher plan an atmosphere conducive to learning. The teacher should structure the learning experience so that the individual experiences success rather than the frustration that may come from trying to learn a task that is too difficult or beyond the individual's ability at that time. The teacher may need to modify the task to make it either easier or more challenging. For example, many Little League baseball teams have started letting the younger children hit the ball off a batting tee rather than hit a pitched ball. This adjustment was made because it was realized that the younger children were having difficulty tracking and successfully hitting a moving object. By allowing children to hit the ball while it was stationary—sitting atop a batting tee—the children were able to practice the skill of striking an object, or batting, and experience success in their endeavors. Certainly hitting the ball from the tee was more satisfying to the children than swinging at the pitched ball and missing. Adjusting the learning task to the individual's ability requires consideration of the individual's physiological readiness. Planning learning experiences that promote success enhances the individual's psychological readiness to learn.

Motivation

Motivation is a basic factor in learning. The term *motivation* refers to a condition within an individual that initiates activity directed toward a goal. The study of motivation focuses on the causes of behavior, specifically those factors that influence the initiation, maintenance, and intensity of behavior.

Needs and drives form the basic framework for motivation. When individuals sense an unfulfilled need, they are moved to do something about it. This desire prompts people to seek a solution to the recognized need through an appropriate line of action. This line of action may require practice, effort, mastery of knowledge, or other behavior to be successful. For example, an individual who is hungry becomes motivated to seek food, whereas at the cognitive level, the individual who wants to pass a certification desires to acquire the necessary knowledge.

Motivation refers to an individual's general arousal to action. It might be thought of as the desire or drive a person must have to achieve a goal to satisfy a particular need. The term *need* refers to an internalized deficiency of the organism. The need might be physiological or psychological. The term *drive* refers to the concept of the stimulus for action. Motivation, for example, might be associated with the drive to exercise to satisfy the need to keep the body healthy. The motivating factor might be internal, resulting from the individual's own desire to be fit, or it might be the result of some outside force, such as peer pressure to be thin.

Although motives are internal in nature, they may be affected by external influences. However, it is common to describe an individual's motives as being either internal or external. Motives such as the desire to develop one's body, to have fun, or to test one's limits are examples of internal motives for learning. The desire to win awards, to appease parental pressures for participation, or to win money are examples of external motives for participation. An employee may decide to participate in an employee fitness program because of the desire to enhance his or her health status (internal motivation); on the other hand, the employee may participate because he or she was pressured to do so by the boss (external motivation). Internal motivation is more conducive to positive learning and performance and sustained participation than external motivation. The worth of the activity should be the inducement for learning and participation rather than rewards, punishments, or grades. In physical education, exercise science, and sport programs, motives such as the desire to develop one's body, the desire to learn basic movement skills and eventually develop more advanced skills for specialized games, or the desire to do one's best are all valid and should be encouraged.

The professional should be aware of the motives for the individual's participation in physical education, exercise science, and sport programs. Individuals' motives for learning and participation may differ considerably, so consideration of individual differences is important. For example, as previously mentioned, some participants in an employee fitness program may be internally motivated to join, while others, whose presence was suggested by their employer, may be externally motivated and perhaps even reluctant to participate in the activities. During the course of the program, however, the externally motivated participants may develop an internal motivation. The change could result because the professional made the program challenging, meaningful, and satisfying to the employee. As a consequence, the once reluctant employee may become an enthusiastic participant in the program.

The actions of the teacher can often have a positive effect on the individual's motivation. In a physical education and sport program not all individuals will be motivated to the same extent to learn new skills; in fact, some individuals may not be motivated to learn at all. The teacher can enhance an individual's motivation for learning through goal setting, that is, establishing challenging, albeit attainable, goals for the individual. Motivation can also be enhanced by structuring the learning environment for success and by making the learning experience positive and enjoyable. An individual's level of motivation may also be enhanced through reinforcement.

Reinforcement

Physical education, exercise science, and sport professionals should be alert to the need to reinforce the learning of skills and other behaviors of those under their supervision when the desired performance takes place. *Reinforcement* is using events, actions, and behaviors to increase the likelihood of a certain response (e.g., a skill or a behavior) recurring. Reinforcement may be positive or negative. Reinforcement is considered positive when it is given following the desired response, and it is deemed negative when it is withheld following a desired response. Providing encouragement, praise, commendation, or a pat on the back following successful execution of a skill is an example of positive reinforcement. Such an acknowledgment of an individual's success not only will serve to reinforce correct skill performance but will also likely motivate the individual to continue in his or her efforts to master the skill. If a teacher belittles an individual's unsuccessful effort to perform a skill and discontinues this behavior when the individual successfully executes the skill, the teacher is using negative reinforcement.

Two types of reinforcers are tangible and intangible. Tangible reinforcers are material items such as a medal or money. Intangible reinforcers include verbal praise, a pat on the back, or a nod of approval.

Research suggests that reinforcement is more effective when given immediately after a response than when it is delayed. Random reinforcement tends to be more effective than continual reinforcement. For reinforcement to be effective it must be meaningful to, important to, or desired by the recipient.

Reinforcement, motivation, readiness, and development are important forces in learning. Another important consideration in planning for learning is individual differences.

Individual Differences

In any learning situation, be it with children or adults, the teacher must provide for individual differences among the learners. The importance of considering individual differences in readiness, motivation, and reinforcement has already been discussed. The teacher also should consider other differences when planning for learning.

Differences in social and economic backgrounds should be considered—some individuals come from middle-class families while others are

Physical educators must accommodate individual differences among learners. These elementary school students are working with objects of different shapes as part of a perceptual-motor program.

economically disadvantaged. These factors can greatly influence the prior experiences these individuals bring to the learning situation. Differences in physical abilities among individuals in the learning situation may be pronounced. Differences in intelligence and preferred learning styles hold implications for the manner in which the skills are to be taught. Personality differences must also be considered. Some individuals are outgoing, whereas others are shy and withdrawn. Some individuals are eager to try new skills while others are reluctant or intimidated by the prospect of learning something new.

Designing learning experiences to accommodate individual differences requires careful planning and commitment on the part of the teachers. It is not an easy task to design learning experiences for a diversity of abilities, but it is not impossible. Physical education, exercise science, and sport professionals should strive to help each person to be the best he or she can be.

Motor Learning Concepts

In planning for motor learning, the professional must consider a learner's level of readiness, development, individual characteristics, motivation, and need for reinforcement. At this point it will be helpful to consider additional concepts, factors, and conditions that promote the learning of motor skills and improve performance.

1. *Practice sessions should be structured to promote optimal conditions for learning.* The manner in which practice sessions are organized can have a critical impact on the amount of learning that occurs. Practices should be organized so that distracting elements are eliminated from the setting. The instructor should ensure that the proper mental set has been established in the mind of the learner, the proper facilities and equipment are available, the learner has the proper background to understand and appreciate the material being presented, and conditions are such that a challenging learning situation exists.

Much research has been done on the organization of practice with reference to the relationship between practice periods and rest periods. (In the literature this is referred to as massed versus distributed practice.) Schmidt,[6] after reviewing the research, stated that "we should recognize that a single, optimal distribution of practice and rest periods does not exist." The design of practice should consider the nature of the task to be learned, the characteristics of the learner, the energy costs of the tasks, and safety. Magill[7] stressed that practice sessions should be structured to maximize the number of opportunities the learner has to try the task. Siedentop[8] emphasizes the need to maximize the amount of time the learner is practicing a task (time-on-task) and the need for the task to be appropriate for the level of the learner.

2. *Learners must understand the task to be learned.* Helping the learner acquire a cognitive understanding of the nature of the task to be learned is one of the first steps in the learning process. As previously discussed in the stages of learning, the learner must establish an executive or motor plan for action; this involves understanding the nature of the task, analyzing the task demands, and devising techniques to achieve the task goal. This conception of the task or image serves as a guide for the learner's initial attempts.

Typically, learners have been helped to establish an image of the task or skill through verbal instructions provided by the teacher. However, the teacher may overuse instructions when faced with the task of describing a complex movement. Too many instructions may overwhelm learners, and in an effort to cope with the avalanche of information about what to do and when to do it, they may disregard much of the information. Instructions should focus on key elements of the task.

Succinct, accurate instructions in conjunction with other techniques such as demonstrations may be more useful than instructions alone in helping the learner understand the task. Demonstrations of the skill allow the learner to form an image of the task. The teacher can use instructions to call the learner's attention to the critical components of the skill. During the learner's initial performances of the task, the learner can model the performance exhibited. Children frequently learn skills on their own by imitating or modeling the performance of others. Teachers may also use films or videotapes of skilled performers to provide a model for performance.

3. *The nature of the skill or task to be learned should be considered when designing practice.* Skills can be classified in a variety of ways. To facilitate learning, practices should be appropriate to the type of skill to be learned.

Skills are generally classified on a continuum. One common classification is *open* versus *closed* skills. This classification is based on whether the environment is changing or not changing during the performance of a skill. An open skill is performed in an environment that is changing or variable during the performance of the skill. A closed skill is performed in a stable, unchanging environment. Shooting a goal during a soccer game, hitting a tennis forehand during a match, batting a pitched ball, and dribbling down the basketball court to execute a layup are examples of open skills. Driving a golf ball off the tee, executing a forward 2½ somersault dive from the 3-meter springboard, performing an uneven bars or parallel bars routine in gymnastics, and shooting a foul shot in basketball are examples of closed skills.

The teacher's design of practice should reflect the nature of the skill and the conditions under which the skill will eventually be performed. In practicing closed skills, where the environment remains relatively stable during the performance of the skill, the teacher should emphasize achieving consistency of movement. In performing open skills, the changing environment requires that the performer make alterations in performance to adjust to the changing conditions (e.g., movements of opponents and teammates, speed and direction of the ball, etc.). Thus, practice should be variable, with the student exposed to a variety of situations similar to those he or she will actually encounter when performing the skill.

During the initial stages of teaching an open skill, the teacher may structure the environment to be stable (closed) to make learning easier for the beginner. For instance, in learning to bat a pitched ball, the teacher may start the performer out hitting a ball off a batting tee; then the teacher may use a pitching machine set to pitch a ball at a certain speed and height. Finally the performer is given the opportunity to hit balls thrown by a pitcher and must then learn how to adjust his or her swing to the varying speeds and heights of the ball. Thus, while open skills may be practiced under closed conditions initially, once the performer is ready, open conditions should prevail. In teaching open skills, the teacher must help the performer identify relevant cues in the environment that signify the need to change his or her response. Unlike closed skills in which attainment of response consistency is emphasized, achieving response flexibility and diversity is stressed in open skills. Providing the performer with variable practice conditions is important in learning open skills.

Other motor skill classifications are fine versus gross, discrete versus continuous, and self-paced versus externally paced motor skills. Further information on these skills may be found in the suggested readings at the end of this chapter.

4. *The nature of the task and the background of the learner should be considered in deciding whether to teach the skill by the whole or the part method.* The instructor must decide whether to teach a skill as a whole or to break it down into its component parts. For example, do you teach a skill such as the front crawl stroke as a whole, or do you break the stroke down and teach it by parts—arm action, leg action, and breathing? What about teaching the jump shot in basketball? Or the tennis serve? If the learner is highly skilled and has had previous experience in the sport, is the whole or the part method better?

This area has been much researched, but the findings are somewhat confusing. At the risk of generalizing, the instructor should teach a highly complex task as parts. Parts should consist of individual, discrete skills. Tasks in which the skill components are highly interrelated, such as the jump shot in basketball, should be taught as a whole. Highly skilled learners with previous experience in the sport will probably be able to learn effectively if the whole method is used. Low-skilled learners or individuals with short attention spans such as young children may find it easier to learn if taught by the part method. It appears that all learners would benefit from seeing a demonstration of the whole skill; this may enhance the organization of the information provided to the learner and the learner's understanding of the goal of the skill.

If the teacher were to teach the high jump by the part method, the learners would be taught the approach (run to the bar); then they would be taught the jump; next, they would be taught the landing. After all components had been taught, the learners would practice the total skill.

Another option is to use the progressive part method, which consists of initially teaching the first two parts of the skill, combining these two parts into a whole, teaching a third part, then connecting this to the first two parts, and so on. For example, the first two sequences in a dance routine would be taught and practiced, then the third sequence taught; then the third sequence would be added to the first two sequences, and all three sequences practiced together. This process of progressively adding parts of a skill is continued until the entire skill is learned.

In summary, the structure of the task, both its complexity and organization, and the characteristics of the learner must be considered in selecting methods of instruction.

Teachers must decide whether to emphasize speed or accuracy when teaching a skill that requires both elements.

5. *Whether speed or accuracy should be emphasized in learning a skill depends on the requirements of the skill.* Teachers are often required to make a judgment as to whether speed or accuracy should be emphasized in the initial stages of learning a skill. For example, a highly skilled tennis player endeavors to serve the ball with as much velocity as possible into the service court. When teaching the tennis serve, should the teacher emphasize speed, accuracy, or both speed and accuracy? When teaching pitching, should the teacher emphasize throwing the ball as fast as possible, getting the ball into the strike zone all the time, or pitching the ball into the strike zone as fast and as often as possible? This dilemma—whether to emphasize speed or accuracy—is often referred to as a speed-accuracy trade-off. In essence, to perform the skill as accurately as possible means that the performer will have to sacrifice some speed and perform the skill more slowly. Attainment of maximum speed or velocity in performing a skill is at the expense of accuracy. When both speed and accuracy are desired, both qualities will decrease.

Different sport skills have different speed and accuracy requirements. Pitching a ball or performing a tennis serve requires a high degree of both speed and accuracy. In throwing the javelin, speed is more important than accuracy, whereas in the tennis drop shot, accuracy in terms of court placement is more important than speed. The teacher must understand the requirements of the task and design practices accordingly.

The research seems to suggest that skills should be practiced as they are to be performed. This advice is relatively straightforward when the skill emphasizes either speed or accuracy. For example, based on the research findings, speed should be emphasized in teaching the javelin throw, and accuracy emphasized in the tennis drop shot. However, what about skills that place a premium on being both fast and accurate, such as pitching a ball or executing a tennis serve? One approach is to have the learner execute the skill as fast as possible and work on accuracy and control after speed has been attained. Another approach is to have the learner focus on being as accurate as possible by reducing the speed of the movements; then, once accuracy is attained, increasing the speed of the movements would be stressed. Emphasizing both speed and accuracy is another approach. The research suggests that when both speed and accuracy are of paramount concern, both variables should receive equal and simultaneous emphasis. The rationale is that mastery is sacrificed when an individual practices a motor skill at slower speed than is needed in the game situation, because the person must readjust to the faster situation. The teacher should understand the speed and accuracy demands of a skill and structure practices so that the learner can practice the skill as it is to be ultimately performed.

6. *Transfer of learning can facilitate the learning of motor skills.* The influence of a previously learned skill on the learning or performance of a new skill is called transfer of learning. The influence exerted may be positive or negative. When a previous experience or skill aids in the learning of a new skill, positive transfer occurs. For example, the student who knows how to play tennis readily learns how to play badminton because both skills require similar strokes and the use of the racquet. Most researchers agree that positive transfer most likely occurs when two tasks have similar part-whole relationships. Again, to use the example of racquet games, since many racquet games such as platform tennis, squash, tennis, racquet ball, and badminton have similar part-whole relationships, it is believed that some transfer takes place. Transfer, however, is not automatic. The more meaningful and purposeful the experience, the greater is the likelihood of transfer. Transfer of training occurs to a greater degree in the following situations: with more intelligent participants, in situations that are similar, where an attitude exists and an effort is made by the learner to effect transfer, when the principles or procedures that are foundational to the initial task are understood, and in situations where one teaches for transfer.

Teachers must also be aware of negative transfer. Negative transfer occurs when a previously learned skill interferes with the learning of a new skill. For example, an individual being introduced to the game of golf for the first time experiences difficulty in swinging the club because of his or her previous experience in another skill such as softball or baseball. In such cases the expression often heard is "You're swinging the golf club like a baseball bat."

Physical educators and coaches have become interested in transferring skills learned in practice sessions to actual game situations. To this end, they strive to make their drills as much like a game as possible, or they make an effort in the practice environment to familiarize their team with situations it may encounter in the game. For example, during practice sessions before a basketball game, coaches may have their substitutes imitate the actions of the opponents so that the varsity team is familiar with the opponents' style of play on the night of the game.

Transfer may either facilitate or hinder the acquisition of a skill. Physical educators need to be aware of the principles of transfer so they can use positive transfer to promote skill learning and enhance performance and can readily counteract the effects of negative transfer.

7. *Feedback is essential for learning.* One of the most critical factors affecting learning is feedback. Feedback is information about an individual's performance. Feedback can serve several functions. It provides the learner with information about his or her performance. Using this information, the learner can make adjustments in the response prior to the next attempt. Second, feedback can serve to reinforce the learner's efforts, strengthening the correct response. Finally, feedback may also serve to motivate the learner by providing information about his or her progress.

Feedback may be classified in many ways. Feedback for error correction may focus on the outcome of the movement or the movement itself. Knowledge of results (KR) provides information about the effects of the movement on the environment, information that tells the learner whether or not the goal of the movement was achieved. Knowledge of performance (KP) provides information about the movement itself. The learner's awareness and feelings about how correctly the movement was executed in relation to the intended movement is knowledge of performance. For example, in shooting a foul shot in basketball, the player can readily see if the goal of the movement—putting the ball in the basket—was attained. This is knowledge of results. However, the player may know even before the ball goes in the basket that the shot will be good because the movement "felt right." This is knowledge of performance. Knowledge of performance depends on the learner being sensitive to the "feelings" associated with correct and incorrect performance; in other words the learner becomes aware of what feels right and what feels wrong. Changes in performance occur as the learner compares information about the outcome (KR) with the desired outcome and information about performance (KP) with his or her intended movement. The learner then adjusts his or her performance accordingly until the correct response is achieved.

Feedback may also be classified according to its source or according to when it is presented to the learner. Feedback may be described as intrinsic when the source of the information is the outcome of the task or skill itself.[9] Scoring an ace with a tennis serve, having the shot go slightly wide of the goal in soccer, and scoring on a foul shot in basketball are examples of intrinsic feedback. Information from external sources such as an instructor, friend, or videotape is classified as extrinsic or augmented feedback.[9] When the learner receives information during the performance of the skill, this feedback is referred to as concurrent. Feedback given after the performance is completed is called terminal feedback. Often feedback is a combination of information from various sources. For example, comments from the teacher during the learner's performance provide the learner with extrinsic concurrent feedback. A soccer player seeing the kicked ball go in the goal receives intrinsic terminal feedback.

How can professionals use feedback effectively? Docheff[10] states that the most effective use of feedback includes both general and specific information. One simple method to guide physical education, exercise science, and sport professionals in giving feedback is the use of a "feedback sandwich." The feedback sandwich combines all three functions of feedback: reinforcement, information, and motivation. For example, "Good job, Bob. With your elbow in line, you will always have good alignment when shooting the basketball. Keep up the good work." Physical education, exercise science, and sport professionals should plan for specific feedback. Feedback should be positive and relate to teaching cues. The feedback sandwich offers professionals a guide to increase the meaningfulness and effectiveness of their feedback.

The importance of feedback in the learning of skills is well recognized. Feedback is especially critical during the initial stages of learning a skill. It appears that knowledge of results is more helpful to the individual performing open skills and that knowledge of performance is more valuable to the individual executing a closed skill. With highly skilled performers, whether they are performing a closed or an open skill, knowledge of performance is more helpful. Feedback should be communicated to the learner in a meaningful manner. The teacher should help the learner become aware of the feedback available and teach the learner how to use this information to improve his or her performance.

8. *Learners may experience plateaus in performance.* The extent to which an individual has learned a skill may be inferred from his or her performance. When learning a new skill, an individual may initially demonstrate a sharp improvement in performance. This may be followed by a plateau, or a period in which little or no progress is made. Finally, additional practice results in further improvements in performance.

The plateau may occur for a variety of reasons, such as loss of interest and lack of motivation, failure to grasp a clear concept of the goal to be attained, lack of attention to the proper cues or attention to irrelevant cues, preparation for a transition from fundamental skills to more complex skills in the learning process, or poor learning conditions. Teachers should be cognizant of the plateaus and the conditions under which learners make little or no apparent progress in the activity. They should be especially careful not to introduce certain concepts or skills too rapidly, without allowing sufficient time for their mastery. They should also watch for certain physical deterrents to progress, such as fatigue or lack of strength. Some individuals cannot go beyond a given point because of physiological limits in respect to speed, endurance, or other physical characteristics. Often, however, it is not physiological limits but rather psychological limits that must be overcome. By implementing techniques to enhance the learner's interest and enthusiasm, these limits can be overcome.

9. *Self-analysis should be developed.* During the early periods of instruction when the basic techniques of the skill are being learned, learners need frequent instruction and help from the teacher. However, as the skill is mastered, the learner should rely less on the teacher's help and more on internal resources. A good teacher will help the learner to be his or her own teacher. This involves providing the learner with opportunities for self-criticism and analysis. The learner should be taught how to detect errors and how to correct them. By helping the student become aware of his or her performance and techniques by which it can be improved, the teacher is promoting lifelong learning.

10. *The leadership provided determines to a great degree how much learning will take place.* The teacher should make sure that the learner has a clear idea of the objective to be accomplished. Practices should be designed to maximize the learner's opportunities to perform the skill and minimize unproductive activities such as waiting. The teacher should be continually alert to detect correct and incorrect responses and encourage correct performance. The learner's motivation can be enhanced by providing him or her with opportunities to experience success and by presenting meaningful activities. The teacher should present material appropriate to the learner's level of understanding and be cognizant of individual differences. The teacher should use his or her leadership to promote participants' learning. The Guidelines for Physical Activity Instruction box summarizes motor learning concepts that will improve performance.

• • •

MOTOR DEVELOPMENT

Motor development is also encompassed within the broad area of motor behavior. The definition and scope of motor development, its background and emergence as a subdiscipline of physical education, and areas of study are briefly described in this section.

Definition and Scope

Motor development is the study of the origins of and changes in movement behavior throughout the lifespan. Motor development encompasses the study of biological (heredity) and environmental influences on motor behavior from infancy to old age.[11] It involves understanding how motor behavior is influenced by the integration of psychological, sociological, cognitive, biological, and mechanical factors.[12]

According to Gallahue and Ozmun, the study of motor development uses both a process and a product approach."As a process, motor development involves the underlying biological, environmental, and task demands influencing both motor performance and movement abilities of individuals from infancy through older adulthood. As a product, motor development may be regarded as descriptive or normative and is typically viewed in stages (infancy, childhood, adolescence, and adulthood) that reflect the particular interest of the researcher."[12]

Historical Development

Motor development traces its roots to developmental psychology. Gallahue and Ozmun[12] describe the history of motor development as moving through three periods of growth, based on the

Guidelines for Physical Activity Instruction

1. Use the information-processing model of learning to assist in the planning of learning experiences.
2. Match the type of instruction to the individual's stage of learning.
3. Consider the individual's level of readiness when teaching new skills and information.
4. Plan instructional experiences that take into account the individual's level of development in all three domains—cognitive, affective, and psychomotor.
5. Use the powerful influence of motivation to facilitate learning.
6. Provide positive reinforcement to strengthen desirable responses.
7. Take individual differences into account when teaching by selecting approaches that accommodate a diversity of abilities and needs.
8. Structure practice sessions to promote optimal conditions for learning.
9. Help individuals gain an understanding of the task to be learned and its requirements.
10. Consider the nature of the skill or task when designing practice sessions.
11. Evaluate the task demands and assess the learner's background in deciding whether to use the whole or part method to teach a skill.
12. Study the requirements of the skill to determine whether speed or accuracy should be emphasized in teaching.
13. Facilitate learning by using positive transfer.
14. Incorporate appropriate meaningful feedback to help individuals correct their performance, motivate them, and reinforce their efforts.
15. Be prepared to deal with plateaus in performance.
16. Assist individuals to develop self-analysis skills.
17. Provide strong leadership that contributes to the attainment of the desired objectives.

explanations used to describe the developmental process: the "maturational period" (1928–1946), the "normative/descriptive period" (1946 through the 1970s), and the "process-oriented period" (1980s to the present).

The maturational period marked the beginning of the growth of motor development as an area of study within physical education. During this time, researchers were interested in studying the underlying biological processes governing maturation. Early researchers such as Arnold Gesell (1928), Myrtle McGraw (1935), Mary Shirley (1931), and Nancy Bayley (1935) studied the sequences of motor development in young children, beginning in infancy. Their work led to a better understanding about the sequence of normal development, moving from the acquisition of early rudimentary movements to the attainment of mature movement patterns. The researchers found that although the rate at which children acquired motor skills varied, the sequence in which the children learned was relatively the same. Wild's 1938 study of throwing behavior in school-aged children was the first research to focus on the development of fundamental movements in children rather than infants. Wild classified children's overhand throwing patterns into stages; her work later served as a model for classifying developmental movement patterns in children and influenced work in the field for years to come.

The normative/descriptive period focused on describing the motor performance of children, rather than the motor development of infants. Much of the work was undertaken by physical educators; Anna Espenschade, Ruth Glassow, and G. Lawrence Rarick were leading contributors of this era. These leaders were interested in children's acquisition of skills and how growth and maturation affect performance. Their research efforts and leadership in the establishment of doctoral programs in motor development during the 1950s and 1960s contributed to the emergence of motor development as a field of study within physical education.

Another area of research during this time was perceptual-motor development. When performing motor skills, sensory information, especially visual information, often guides performance. As Gallahue and Ozmun describe, incoming sensory information is integrated with past information in memory to guide the movement response.[12] Sensory feedback from the movement itself is also an important aspect of perceptual-motor development.[12]

Motor development, along with motor learning and motor control, emerged as subdisciplines within the growing academic discipline of physical education during the late 1960s and early 1970s. As research expanded, the work of the previous period was extended and new areas of research developed. Researchers during the 1960s through the 1980s, such as Rarick and Robert Malina, concentrated their efforts on understanding the influence of growth and maturation on motor performance. Ralph Wickstrom's work on fundamental movement abilities helped us more fully understand these critical motor skills. Lolas Halverson, Mary Ann Roberton, Vern Seefeldt, and John Haubenstricker focused their efforts on understanding the development of fundamental motor skills: that is, the levels or stages that children passed through as they acquired skills.

In the 1970s, researchers became increasingly interested in exploring the processes underlying the development of motor skills across the lifespan. Kevin Connolly's edited book *Mechanisms of Motor Skill Development* set the foundation for further research into the cognitive processes associated with motor skill development.[2] Jerry Thomas was one of the leaders in researching how cognitive factors influence children's motor skill acquisition. David Gallahue and Kathleen Hayward contributed much to our understanding of lifespan motor development. Other researchers such as Esther Thelen, Scott Kelso, and Jane Clark developed theoretical frameworks to study motor development based on dynamical systems theory. The emphasis on understanding the processes involved in motor development plays an important role in research today.

Areas of Study

Many broad areas of study fall within motor development, including the influence of age on the acquisition of skills and the development of theories to serve as a framework for our understanding of how movements are developed and controlled. Specialists in motor development may investigate questions such as these:

- What are the heredity and environmental factors most significantly associated with obesity?
- At what age can children safely engage in resistance training?
- How does socioeconomic status affect the development of motor skills?
- What are the developmental stages individuals go through as they acquire fundamental motor skills? What factors affect the rate of development?
- How does early sensory stimulation affect the development of motor skills?
- What are the changes in motor skill development experienced across the lifespan?

Since physical education, exercise science, and sport professionals are concerned with helping individuals of all ages acquire and improve their motor skills, motor development, both from its theoretical and applied perspectives, is important to professionals in our fields.

Phases of Motor Development

The study of motor development today emphasizes consideration of a multitude of factors that influence all aspects of development across the lifespan. Development is a highly interrelated process. According to Gallahue, the study of motor development must "encompass both the biological and environmental aspects of cognitive and affective behavior that impact on motor development, and it must look across various age periods of development. If it is to be of any real value to the practitioner, the study of motor development must not only focus on the skilled performer . . . but must instead analyze and document what individuals of all ages can do . . ."[12]

Gallahue developed an hourglass model (see Figure 5-2) to illustrate how development is a continuous process, beginning at conception and

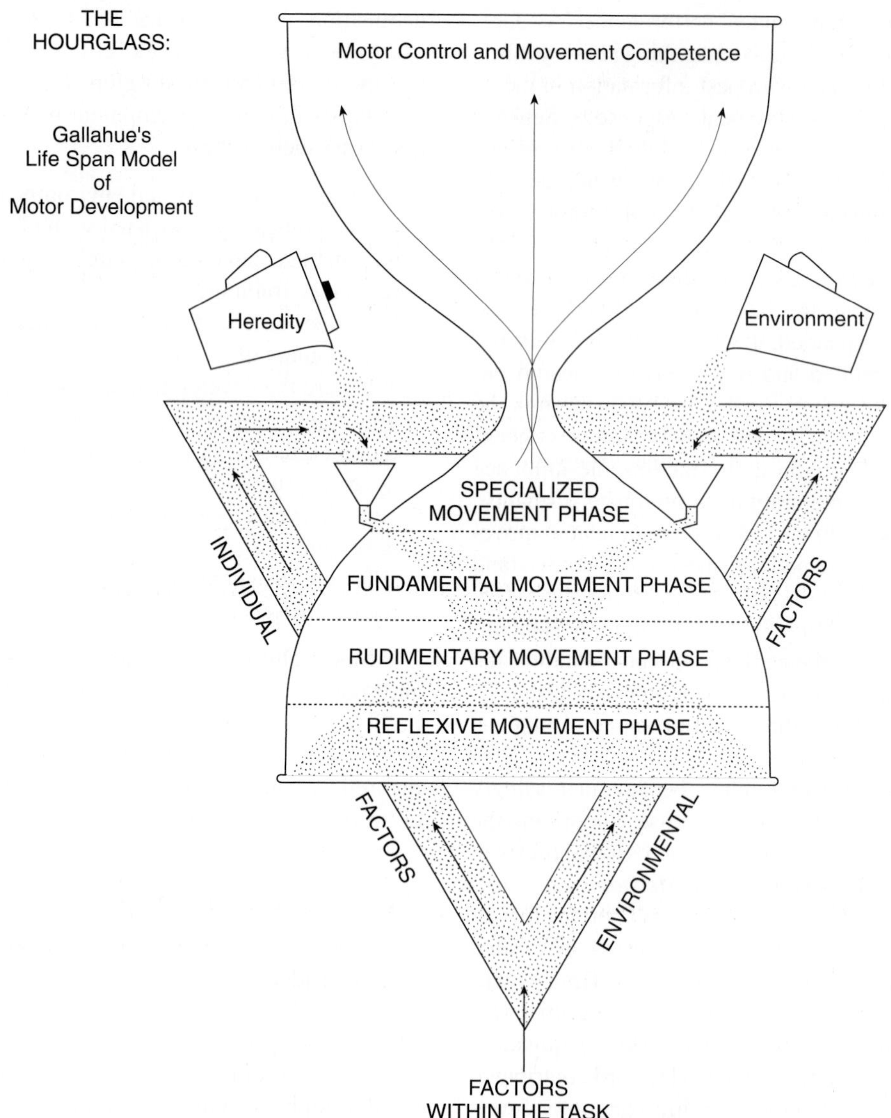

Figure 5-2 Gallahue's Model of Life Span Motor Development. Filling the hourglass with "sand" (i.e., the stuff of life).
From Gallahue DL and Ozmun JC: Understanding motor development: infants, children, adolescent, adults, ed 5, New York, 2002, McGraw-Hill, p. 53.

continuing throughout the lifespan, ceasing at death. In our hourglass is the "stuff of life: 'sand.'" Gallahue[11] views sand entering our hourglass from two containers, which symbolize the heredity and environmental contributions to the process of development. The heredity container has a lid, reflecting that at conception our genetic makeup is determined, thus the amount of sand in that container is fixed. The second container, the environment, has no lid; thus, more sand can be added to it from the environment and additional sand poured into our hourglass.

During the early reflexive (in utero to about 1 year of age) and rudimentary movement (birth to about 2 years of age) phases of motor development, the sand pours into the hourglass primarily from the hereditary container. During the first two years of life, the sequential progression of motor development is quite rigid and invariable. For example, with the rudimentary movements, children learn to sit before they stand and stand before they walk. However, there is considerable variability in the rates at which children acquire these rudimentary skills. This variability in motor skill acquisition occurs throughout life. Motor skill acquisition is enhanced when individuals—infants, children, adolescents, and adults—receive additional opportunities for practice, encouragement, and instruction in an environment conducive to learning. When these opportunities are absent, acquisition of motor skills is inhibited. The rate of acquisition is also influenced by the nature and the requirements of the task.

During the fundamental movement phase (2–7 years of age), children begin to develop the fundamental movement skills, such as running, jumping, throwing, catching, and kicking. Gallahue divides the acquisition of these fundamental movement skills into three separate, but somewhat overlapping, stages: initial, elementary, and mature (these will be briefly described next).[11] Encouragement, instruction, and plentiful opportunities for practice are crucial for children to move through these stages.

Acquisition of specialized movement skills, from about 7 to 10 years of age and older, is influenced by the attainment of mature, fundamental skills. Specialized motor skills are developed, refined, and combined; these skills are used for activities of daily living, recreational activities, and sports. These skills have improved form, greater accuracy, and better control than the fundamental motor skills.

After showing how our movements are developed, Gallahue then portrays the hourglass as turning over at some point in our lives and sand begins to pour out, typically in our late teens and early 20s[11] (see Figure 5-3). The time for the "turnover" is quite variable and influenced more by social and cultural factors than by physical factors. Sand falls through two filters—the hereditary filter and the lifestyles filter. Filters can be dense, allowing sand to go through slowly or very porous, in which case sand will pass through rapidly.

The hereditary filter represents our inherited predispositions, whether they are toward longevity or coronary heart disease. Sand also passes through the lifestyle filter, which is environmentally based and over which we have some degree of control. Physical fitness, nutritional status, physical activity, stress resistance, and spiritual well-being influence the density and, hence, the rate at which sand falls through this filter. Although we cannot stop the sand from flowing through the hourglass—that is, the aging process, we can control the rate at which it falls by as much as 40%. Gallahue describes the wonderful opportunities that we as professionals in these fields have to help people add more sand to their hourglass and to develop "lifestyle filters" that will slow the rate at which sand falls through the hourglass.[11] He points out that even when the hourglass is overturned and sand is flowing through to the bottom, we can still take advantage of many opportunities for continued development and activity, thereby adding more sand to our hourglass and increasing our longevity.[11]

Selected Fundamental Motor Skills

Fundamental motor skills encompass a broad range of skills that form the foundation for successful participation in games, sports, dance, and fitness activities. These skills can be categorized into locomotor, nonlocomotor, and manipulative skills. Locomotor skills are those in which the body moves through space and include running, jumping, and sliding. Nonlocomotor skills, or axial movements, are typically done from a relatively stationary position, using a stable base of support. Generally performed in place, nonlocomotor skills include bending, stretching, and

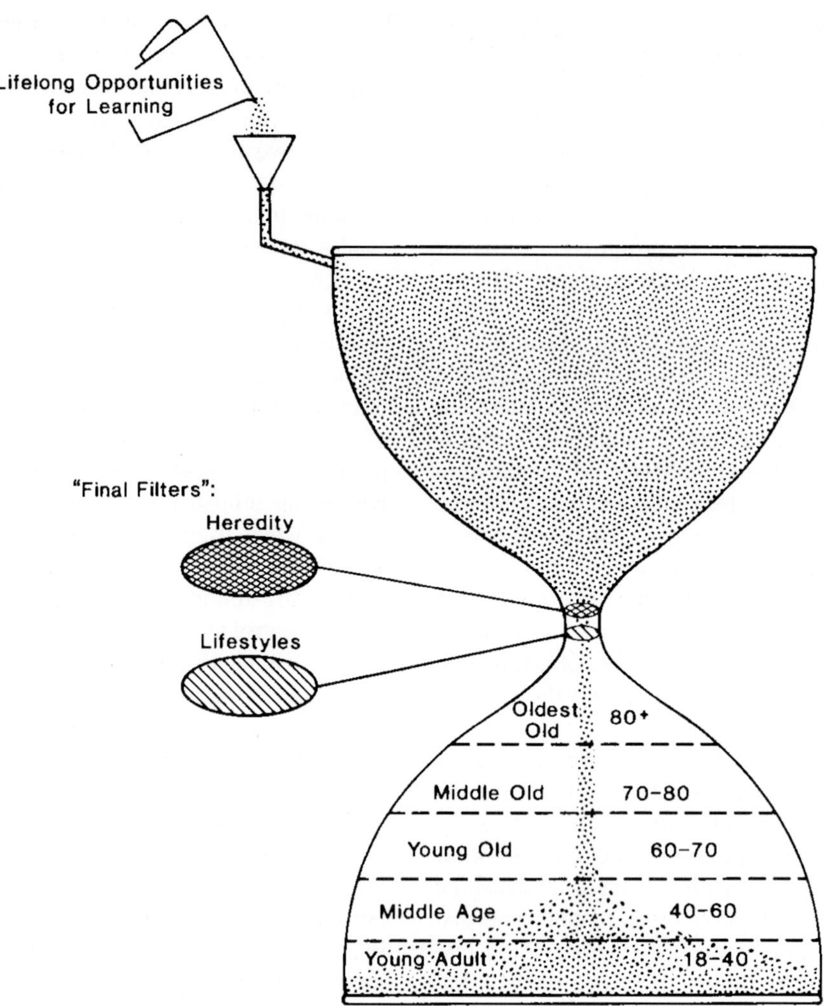

Figure 5-3 Emptying the overturned hourglass of life.
From Gallahue DL and Ozmun JC: Understanding motor development: infants, children, adolescent, adults, ed 5, New York, 2002, McGraw-Hill, p. 55.

pushing. Manipulative skills are skills used in handling objects; throwing, catching, striking, and kicking are examples of manipulative skills.

Fundamental motor skills are combined to create the specialized movement necessary in many activities. For example, the softball throw requires a combination of sliding (locomotor skill) and throwing (manipulative skills) and twisting (nonlocomotor skill). Other specialized sport skills require more complex combinations of movements.

The next section contains a brief analysis of selected locomotor, nonlocomotor, and manipulative motor skills. As children learn the skills, they should also acquire knowledge of the critical elements important to skill performance. This knowledge increases children's understanding of the technique and forms the foundation for future learning.

Fundamental Motor Skills

Locomotor Skills	Nonlocomotor Skills	Manipulative Skills
Walk	Bend and stretch	Throw
Run	Twist and turn	Catch
Jump and land	Push and pull	Strike an object
Hop	Swing and sway	Dribble
Leap		Kick
Slide		Volley
Gallop		
Skip		
Dodge		

Locomotor Movements

The following locomotor skills are discussed: walking, running, jumping (for distance and height), hopping, leaping, skipping, sliding, and galloping. These are the skills most commonly used by elementary schoolchildren. Opportunities for students to explore and use these skills by themselves and in combination with nonlocomotor movements creates a sufficient foundation for more complex movement skills.

Walking Walking involves the transfer of weight from one foot to the other while moving. The weight of the body is transferred in a forward direction from the heel to the ball of the foot and then to the toes. The feet should move parallel to each other, with the toes pointing straight ahead. One foot is in contact with the ground at all times; this is the support foot. The body is erect, with the head up. The arm action is coordinated with leg action; the opposite arm and leg move in the same direction. These movements should be rhythmical and natural.

Running Running is similar to walking in several ways. However, some critical differences exist. In running, the speed of the movement is faster. The length of the stride is longer, the flexion and extension of the legs are greater, and there is a momentary period of flight when the body is not supported at all. The body leans slightly forward to place the center of gravity above the front foot in the stride. The arms swing forward and back, opposing the legs, and contribute power to the movement.

Jumping Jumping varies according to the goal of the task. Jumping for distance and jumping for height are common skills. The standing long jump, for example, is done by bending the knees and lowering the upper body into a crouched position. As the body rocks back on the feet, the arms are brought down and beyond the hips. At takeoff, the forward and upward swing of the arms is coordinated with the powerful extension of both the feet and legs. The body is propelled forward as if reaching for an object in front of the body. The knees bend in midair so that the feet do not touch the ground prematurely. The landing is on the feet, with the knees bending to absorb the impact, and the body falling forward.

Hopping Hopping involves forcefully pushing off the ground from one foot, a brief suspension in the air, and landing on the same foot. The push-off from the ground is made from the toes and the ball of the foot (supporting foot), with the knee of the opposite foot bent and the foot off the ground (nonsupporting foot). The arms are thrust upward to aid in body lift. The landing is on the toes, ball, and heel of the foot in that order. The knee is bent slightly to help absorb the shock of the landing. To aid in balance, the arms and nonsupporting foot are used. Hopping should be practiced with both feet.

Leaping Similar to the run, a leap is a long step forward to cover distance or to go over an obstacle. It is an exaggerated running step, with the stride longer and the body projected higher in the air. In the leap, the toes of the takeoff foot leave the floor last, and the landing is on the ball of the opposite foot. The arms should be extended

Hopping is one of the fundamental skills. Games, such as hopscotch, provide enjoyable opportunities to develop this motor skill.

upward and forward to give added lift to the body during the leap. Often the legs are extended in the air. Before the execution of the leap, usually a short run is taken to gain momentum for the leap itself.

Skipping A skip is a combination of a step and a hop, with feet alternating after each step-hop. A long step is taken on one foot, followed by a hop on the same foot, and then a step with the opposite foot, again followed by a hop. Balance is aided by swinging the arms in opposition to the legs.

Sliding A slide is a sideways movement in which the weight of the body is shifted in the direction of the slide. In a slide to the right, the right foot steps sideways (leading foot); then the left foot (trailing foot) is quickly drawn close to the right foot. Weight is shifted from the lead foot to the trailing foot. The same foot continues to lead in sliding movements. The body maintains an upright posture and the arms are used for balance. The legs should not be crossed. The slide should be practiced in both directions.

Galloping Galloping is similar to sliding, but the movement is performed in a forward direction. One foot leads in the forward direction (leading foot). After a step by the leading foot, the rear or trailing foot is brought quickly forward and close to the lead foot. The stepping leg is always the lead leg. Opportunities to lead with the right foot and with the left foot should be included in practicing the gallop.

Nonlocomotor Movements

Nonlocomotor movements are generally performed using a stable base of support. The nonlocomotor movement skills discussed are bending, stretching, twisting, turning, pushing, pulling, and swinging. Generally, they are performed in place and can be done from a variety of body positions (e.g., standing or sitting). They can also be combined with locomotor movements.

Bending and Stretching Bending is a movement occurring at the joints of the body in which body parts are brought closer together. For example, by bending the body at the hips to touch the toes, a person is decreasing the angle between the upper and lower body at the hip joint. This is called flexion. Bending movements may be in several directions: for example, forward, backward, sideways, or in a circular motion. The range of bending movements is determined by the type of joint at which the movement occurs. Ball-and-socket joints permit the greatest movement. Hip joints and shoulder joints are examples of ball-and-socket joints. Hinge joints permit only backward and forward movements. The knee joint is a hinge joint.

A stretch is an extension or hyperextension at the joints of the body. Stretching is the opposite of bending. Most movements require complete extension only where the body parts adjacent to the joints are at a straight angle (180°). However, in movements such as the wrist cock before a throw, hyperextension is needed to give added impetus to the throw.

Bending and stretching are necessary to maintain flexibility—the full range of movement about a joint. Bending and stretching are common to most of the activities of daily life (e.g., dressing and bathing), and they are very important to physical education activities. Teachers should provide daily activities in which these skills can be practiced and refined.

Twisting and Turning Twisting is a rotation of the body or a body part around its axis while maintaining a fixed base of support. Twisting movements can take place at the neck, shoulders, spine, hips, ankles, and wrist. The body can be in different positions: for example, standing or lying down. As in bending and stretching movements, the range of a twisting movement is determined by the type of joint.

Turning generally refers to a rotation of the body around in space. When the body is turned, the base of support is shifted from one position to another. Jumping up and landing facing the opposite direction and pivoting are examples of turns. A twisting action is typically used to initiate a turn. Turns should be practiced in both directions, left and right or clockwise and counterclockwise.

Pushing and Pulling Pushing is a forceful action directed toward increasing the distance between the body and an object. A push can be used to move an object away from the body or the body away from an object. Pushing an opponent away in a wrestling match or a box across the floor are two examples of pushing. Proper body position enhances the effectiveness of a push. A forward stride position enlarges the body's base of support, and bending the knees lowers the center of gravity and increases the body's stability. Proper body alignment helps prevent back injuries.

Pulling is a forceful action designed to decrease the distance between the body and an object. A pull brings the body and the object closer together. As in pushing, widening the base of support and lowering the center of gravity increase effectiveness. In a tug-of-war, participants widen their base of support and dig their heels in as they try to pull their opponents across the dividing line. Partner resistance exercises and rowing use both pushing and pulling. Steady, controlled movements are recommended for both pulling and pushing.

Swinging A swing is a circular or pendular movement of a body part or of the entire body around a stationary center point. The center point may be a joint, such as the shoulder in swinging the arm, or an outside axis, such as the swing on a high bar. When the force necessary to hold a body stationary is released, the force of gravity will cause that body part to swing. In most body movements, the force of muscular contractions is necessary to maintain body swing. Swinging movements should be continuous, rhythmical, and free flowing.

Manipulative Skills

Manipulative skills involve the propulsion and control of objects. The body is used to apply force to an object and to absorb force when receiving or controlling an object. The manipulative skills of throwing, catching, kicking, and striking are briefly described.

Throwing Throwing an object may involve the use of the underhand, sidearm, or overhand pattern. Since the overhand throwing pattern is most frequently employed by children and adults, this movement will be described.

When throwing, the ball is held in the fingers of the throwing hand. As the throwing action is initiated, the ball is brought back and the body rotates so the opposite side is toward the target. Weight is transferred back to the foot on the same side as the throwing hand. The arm is bent at the elbow, and the elbow leads slightly as the arm is brought forward for the throw. As the arm accelerates, a step forward onto the opposite foot is taken and the hips rotate forward. The arm quickly extends, the wrist snaps, and the ball is released. The arm follows in the direction of the throw, coming down and across the body.

Catching Catching involves the use of hands to stop and gain control of an object. As the object approaches, the individual makes a judgment about where it can be intercepted and moves to a location directly in line with the object, placing the hands in a position for effective reception. The eyes follow the flight of the object, and both hands reach out toward it. The object is grasped by the hands and pulled in by the arms and hands toward the body to absorb the object's force.

Kicking Kicking is imparting force to an object by the foot and the leg. The kicking of a stationary object is the foundation for the kicking of a moving object and for punting.

In kicking, the supporting foot is placed alongside the object. The kicking leg, knee bent, moving freely from the hip, swings through an arc toward the object. As the foot contacts the object, the knee is extended and the body leans back for balance. The kicking leg follows through, continuing its movement toward the direction of the flight of the object. The arms, relaxed, move in opposition to the legs. The eyes focus on the object throughout the kick.

Striking Striking involves using a body part (e.g., hand) or an implement (e.g., paddle, racquet, bat) to apply force to a stationary or moving object. The length, size, and weight of the implement as well as characteristics of the object being struck influence the nature of the movement pattern. Kicking, described earlier, is also considered a striking task.

For the striking action typically seen in batting, the body is positioned perpendicular to the line of flight of the oncoming ball. The feet are placed in a forward-backward stride position, approximately shoulder-width apart. The trunk is rotated back, the weight is shifted to the rear foot, and a backswing is taken. The flight of the ball is followed by the eyes until just before making contact. Body weight is shifted onto the forward foot in the direction of the intended flight of the ball. With the hips leading, the hips and trunk are rotated in the same direction as the weight shift. Arms move forward into contact, and the follow-through action occurs in the direction of the line of flight.

Fundamental motor skills are the foundation for the development of specialized game, sport, dance, and fitness activities. These skills are the building blocks for the future. Acquisition of skills for lifetime participation begins with the mastery of these fundamental motor skills. All children, the skilled and the unskilled, need sufficient opportunities and a variety of experiences to master these important movement basics. (See the online learning center for more information on the development of motor skills.)

Development of Fundamental Motor Skills

Motor development specialists also investigate the sequential and overlapping stages children proceed through as they acquire skills. To illustrate the changes that occur as skills are developed, a brief overview of the stages associated with the acquisition of fundamental motor skills is presented. In acquiring fundamental motor skills,

TABLE 5-2 Developmental Sequence for Overhand Throwing

I. Throwing
   A. Initial stage
      1. Action is mainly from elbow
      2. Elbow of throwing arm remains in front of body; action resembles a push
      3. Fingers spread at release
      4. Follow-through is forward and downward
      5. Trunk remains perpendicular to target
      6. Little rotary action during throw
      7. Body weight shifts slightly rearward to maintain balance
      8. Feet remain stationary
      9. There is often purposeless shifting of feet during preparation for throw
   B. Elementary stage
      1. In preparation, arm is swung upward, sideward, and backward to a position of elbow flexion
      2. Ball is held behind head
      3. Arm is swung forward, high over shoulder
      4. Trunk rotates toward throwing side during preparatory action
      5. Shoulders rotate toward throwing side
      6. Trunk flexes forward with forward motion of arm
      7. Definite forward shift of body weight
      8. Steps forward with leg on same side as throwing arm
   C. Mature stage
      1. Arm is swung backward in preparation
      2. Opposite elbow is raised for balance as a preparatory action in the throwing arm
      3. Throwing elbow moves forward horizontally as it extends
      4. Forearm rotates and thumb points downward
      5. Trunk markedly rotates to throwing side during preparatory action
      6. Throwing shoulder drops slightly
      7. Definite rotation through hips, legs, spine, and shoulders during throw
      8. Weight during preparatory movement is on rear foot
      9. As weight is shifted, there is a step with opposite foot

II. Developmental Difficulties
   A. Forward movement of foot on same side as throwing arm
   B. Inhibited backswing
   C. Failure to rotate hips as throwing arm is brought forward
   D. Failure to step out on leg opposite the throwing arm
   E. Poor rhythmical coordination of arm movement with body movement
   F. Inability to release ball at desired trajectory
   G. Loss of balance while throwing
   H. Upward rotation of arm

From Gallahue DL and Ozmun JC: Understanding motor development: infants, children, adolescents, adults, ed 5, New York, 2002, McGraw-Hill, p. 222.

children pass through three stages: initial, elementary, and mature. Table 5-2 and Figure 5-4 show the three stages of the development of the overhand throwing pattern.

The initial stage reflects the child's early attempts at performing the skill. Poor spatial and temporal integration of the movements comprising the skill characterize this stage. The movements

INITIAL

ELEMENTARY

MATURE

Figure 5-4 Stages of the overhand throwing pattern

From Gallahue DL and Ozmun JC: Understanding motor development: infants, children, adolescent, adults, ed 5, New York, 2002, McGraw-Hill, p. 223.

exhibit improper sequencing of parts of the skill, little body rotation, often exaggerated use of the body, poor rhythm, and difficulties in coordination. This stage is generally seen in 2-year-olds.

The elementary stage reflects greater control and rhythmical coordination of the movements. The temporal and spatial elements of the movement are better synchronized, and the movement is better coordinated. The movements are still restricted or exaggerated, and mechanical principles are not consistently applied to the performance. Typical 3- or 4-year-olds are at this stage. Gallahue and Ozmun[12] note that many individuals fail to move beyond the elementary stage in some of their movements. If you've watched adults using the overhand throw, you may observe an adult throwing with an elementary stage pattern, for example, stepping forward with the foot on the same side as the throwing arm rather than stepping forward with the opposite foot.

The mature stage is marked by increased efficiency, enhanced coordination, and improved control of movements. Increases in size and strength contribute to greater force production. According to Gallahue and Ozmun, most children should be at the mature stage by 5 or 6 years of age.[12] However, some skills may develop later, particularly manipulative skills that require tracking and intercepting moving objects, such as catching or striking. The greater visual-motor requirements of these tasks contribute to their later development. Greater range of motion, increased accuracy, and better adaptation to environmental conditions characterize this stage. Development of the mature form of the skills is enhanced when plentiful opportunities for practice are provided, along with instruction and encouragement—opportunities that would be available through a developmentally appropriate, quality elementary physical education program. Failure to acquire the mature form of the skill adversely impacts the development of more specialized skills in the later years.

Physical education, exercise science, and sport professionals working with adults in the areas of sport instruction, recreation activities, or fitness may find some adults in their program exhibit elementary or poorly developed mature forms of fundamental motor skills. Professionals must be prepared to help these adults improve and refine their motor skills, so that they have a better foundation for the development and application of more specialized skills.

More information on the fundamental movement patterns and processes is found in the Online Learning Center. Space precludes the discussion of further information about motor development. However, with the growing emphasis on early childhood education and the increase in the aging population in the United States, it is likely that greater attention will be directed toward understanding motor development within these age groups.

This chapter was designed to provide the reader with a brief overview of some of the concepts and concerns in the realm of motor behavior. An understanding of how individuals learn motor skills will help physical education, exercise science, and sport professionals design experiences to promote effective learning. Promoting effective learning is a concern of professionals working in both school and nonschool settings. In the school setting, for example, elementary school physical educators are concerned with helping children master fundamental motor skills, high school teachers focus their efforts on assisting students to acquire skills in a variety of lifetime sports, and coaches spend countless hours helping their athletes refine the skills necessary for high-level performance. In the nonschool setting, athletic trainers may help injured athletes regain efficient motor patterns, while exercise leaders in a corporate or community program may help adults attain proficiency in such lifetime sports as golf or tennis. Thus, understanding how learning occurs and can be facilitated is important foundational knowledge for professionals to possess. The manner in which individuals control their movements (motor control) and the impact of development (motor development) on learning are also important considerations in designing learning experiences.

Focus on Career: Motor Behavior and Movement

PROFESSIONAL ORGANIZATIONS

- National Association for Sport and Physical Education (NASPE) Council on Physical Education for Children (www.aahperd.org→NASPE→Physical Education Councils)
- National Association for Sport and Physical Education (NASPE) Middle and Secondary School Physical Education Council (www.aahperd.org→NASPE→Physical Education Councils)
- NASPE Motor Development Academy (www.aahperd.org→NASPE→Academies)
- North American Society for the Psychology of Sport and Physical Activity (NASPSPA)

PROFESSIONAL JOURNALS

- *JOPERD*
- *Strategies*
- *Teaching Elementary Physical Education*
- *Journal of Motor Behavior*
- *Journal of Teaching in Physical Education*
- *Research Quarterly for Exercise and Sport*

SUMMARY

Motor behavior—specifically motor control, motor learning, and motor development traces its roots to psychology. These fields emerged in the mid-1960s and 1970s from the parent discipline of psychology and developed identities as subdisciplines in the growing academic discipline of physical education, now referred to as physical education, exercise science, and sport.

Motor behavior is a broad term, encompassing motor control, motor learning, and motor development. Motor control is the study of the neural mechanisms and processes by which movements are learned and controlled. Motor learning is the acquisition of motor skills as a consequence of practice and experience. Motor development is the study of the origins and changes in movement behavior throughout the lifespan.

Many theories and models have been advanced to describe learning. One popular theory is the information-processing model. According to this model, learning and performance of skills can be described as a series of information-processing tasks consisting of input, decision making, output, and feedback. Individuals pass through three stages when learning a motor skill: cognitive, associative, and autonomic. Learning is influenced by readiness, motivation, reinforcement, and individual differences. To facilitate motor learning, physical education, exercise science, and sport professionals should incorporate concepts from motor learning into the design of their practices.

Fundamental motor skills form the foundation for learning more complex skills. In developing these fundamental skills, individuals move through three stages: initial, elementary, and mature. Professionals should understand how motor skills develop so they can design learning experiences to facilitate their acquisition.

SELF-ASSESSMENT TESTS

These tests are designed to help you determine if you have mastered the material and competencies presented in this chapter.

1. You are a teacher in the school setting, a sport instructor in a community setting working with senior citizens, or a fitness leader in a corporate

fitness program working with adults. How would you incorporate each of the following concepts into your program: readiness, reinforcement, motivation, and individual differences?
2. Select a skill you are familiar with from your previous experiences. Describe how you would teach this skill to a beginner. In your description, describe what the individual would experience at each of the three stages of learning and how you would use the information-processing model of learning to enhance the individual's skill acquisition.
3. Review the list of motor learning concepts that promote the learning of motor skills and improve performance. Select five of those concepts and illustrate how you would apply them to the teaching of a fundamental skill or sports skill.

REFERENCES

1. Thomas JR and Thomas KT: Motor behavior. In SJ Hoffman and JC Harris, editors: Introduction to kinesiology: studying physical activity, Champaign, Ill., 2005, Human Kinetics.
2. Thomas JR: Motor behavior. In JD Massengale and RA Swanson, editors: The history of exercise and sport science, Champaign, Ill., 1997, Human Kinetics.
3. Adams, JA: Historical review and appraisal of research on the learning, retention, and transfer of human motor skills, Psychological Bulletin, 101: 41–74, 1987.
4. Knudson D and Kluka DA: The impact of vision and vision training on sport performance, JOPERD 68(4):17–24, 1997.
5. Fitts PM and Posner MJ: Human performance, Belmont, Calif., 1967, Brooks/Cole.
6. Schmidt RA: Motor control and learning, ed 3, Champaign, Ill., 1999, Human Kinetics.
7. Magill RA: Motor learning and control: concepts and applications, ed 7, New York, 2004, McGraw-Hill.
8. Siedentop D: Developing teaching skills in physical education, ed 4, Mountain View, Calif., 2000, Mayfield [McGraw-Hill].
9. Rink JE: Teaching physical education for learning, ed 4, New York, 2002, McGraw-Hill.
10. Docheff DM: The feedback sandwich, JOPERD 61(9):17–18, 1990.
11. Gallahue DL: Understanding motor development: infants, children, adolescents, Indianapolis, 1989, Benchmark.
12. Gallahue DL and Ozmun JC: Understanding motor development: infants, children, and adolescents, ed 5, New York, 2002, McGraw-Hill.

SUGGESTED READINGS

Goodway JD, Crowe H, and Ward P: Effects of motor skill instruction on fundamental motor skill development. Adapted Physical Activity Quarterly 20: 298–315, 2003.

The impact of instruction in fundamental motor skills, specifically locomotor and object control, on the skill development of preschoolers who are at risk of developmental delay is described.

Okely AD, Booth ML, and Chey T: Relationships between body composition and fundamental movement skills among children and adolescents. Research Quarterly for Exercise and Sport, 75: 238–248, 2004.

This study examined the relationship between overweight and motor skill performance. For locomotor skills, nonoverweight boys and girls possessed more advanced motor skills than their overweight peers. There was no significant difference found, however, for object-control skills. The study suggests that intervention approaches to help children and youth prevent unhealthy weight gain include strategies to enhance motor skill proficiency.

Rink J: It's okay to be a beginner, JOPERD 75(6), 31–35, 2004.

The article offers insight into what motor learning concepts would be helpful to students in physical education classes to know and how these concepts would be beneficial to them as adults leading a physically active lifestyle.

Steinberg GM: Using the five-step strategy to teach motor skills to older adults, JOPERD 71(5):40–44, 46, 2000.

The sequential process of readying, imaging, focusing, executing, and evaluating are applied to the teaching of motor skills to older adults.

Valenti NC and Rudsill ME: An inclusive mastery climate intervention and the motor skill development of children with and without disabilities. Adapted Physical Activity Quarterly 21:330–348, 2004.

A learning climate that promotes mastery of motor skills benefits children with or without disabilities. A 12-week intervention program was successful in significantly improving motor skills of those students in the mastery approach.

Williams K: What's motor development got to do with physical education? JOPERD 75(6):35–40, 2004.

This article examines relevant motor development and motor learning concepts and how knowledge of these areas can be helpful for both physical education students and their parents.

CHAPTER 6

BIOMECHANICAL FOUNDATIONS

OBJECTIVES

After reading this chapter the student should be able to—

- Define the term *biomechanics* and indicate its relationship to kinesiology.
- Identify the value of biomechanics for physical education, exercise science, and sport professionals.
- Understand some of the terminology associated with the subdiscipline of biomechanics.
- Explain the meaning of mechanical principles and concepts that relate to stability, motion, leverage, and force. Illustrate the application of these principles to physical skills and sport techniques.
- Describe some of the techniques used to analyze motion.

Understanding the factors that govern human movement is essential for physical education, exercise science, and sport professionals. Physical educators, exercise scientists, and sport leaders are concerned with helping individuals learn how to move efficiently and effectively. In elementary physical education classes, the teacher is concerned with helping students learn fundamental motor skills such as throwing and running, which provide a foundation for learning more advanced sport skills. In competitive athletics, where the difference between winning and losing may be one hundredth of a second or a fraction of a centimeter, a coach may use scientific methods such as high-speed photography and computer simulation to fine-tune an athlete's form. The weekend golfer, seeking to break par, requests the assistance of the golf pro to eliminate a troublesome slice from his or her swing. The golf pro may then videotape the golfer's performance to determine the source of error and to illustrate to the golfer the needed changes. The athletic trainer rehabilitating an athlete recovering from shoulder surgery uses knowledge of the range of motion of this joint to help develop an effective rehabilitation program. The adapted physical educator analyzes the gait of a child with cerebral palsy in order to prescribe physical activities to improve it. The exercise

GET CONNECTED

Biomechanics Magazine Online offers access to a diversity of topics, including athletic training, braces, chiropractic, diabetic shoes, gait analysis, orthotics, and prosthetics.

www.biomech.com

Exploratory Activities in the Health Sciences is designed for children, but includes many activities that use principles from biomechanics, such as application of biomechanical principles to skateboarding, baseball, and hockey.

www.exploratorium.edu/sports/index.html

International Society of Biomechanics in Sport gives access to abstracts of articles on sport engineering, neuromuscular biomechanics in sport, modeling and simulation in sport biomechanics, sports injuries, prevention and rehabilitation; newsletter and current news; links to societies and resources.

www.uni-stuttgart.de/External/isbs

Sport and Science—Winter Olympics is sponsored by Montana State University–Bozeman and offers excellent online modules, including physics and biomechanics, sports and nutrition, sport physiology and sport psychology.

http://btc.montana.edu/olympics/physbio/default.htm

instructor closely monitors a client working on a Nautilus machine to ensure the exercise is being performed properly through the range of motion. These examples show how physical education, exercise science, and sport professionals use the scientific knowledge of human motion from the realms of kinesiology and biomechanics to help individuals move efficiently and effectively.

KINESIOLOGY AND BIOMECHANICS

The study of human movement is the focus of kinesiology and biomechanics. *Kinesiology* is the scientific study of human movement. The term *kinesiology* is derived from the Greek *kinesi,* meaning "motion." Defined more broadly, kinesiology is used by some professionals as an umbrella term to encompass the subdisciplines that emerged from physical education in the 1970s. In this chapter, the term *kinesiology* will be used in a more narrow, traditional sense to refer to the anatomical and physiological study of human movement. To understand human movement fully, one needs an understanding of body movement, or kinesiology.

Kinesiology focuses on the anatomical and musculoskeletal analysis of human movement. It involves the study of the skeletal framework, the structure of muscles and their functions, the action of the joints, and the neuromuscular basis of movement. Kinesiology helps us appreciate the intricacies and wonder of human motion. Luttgens and Hamilton[1] write,

> One who gives it any thought whatever cannot help being impressed not only by the beauty of human motion but also by its apparently infinite possibilities, its meaningfulness, its orderliness, its adaptability to the surrounding environment. Nothing is haphazard; nothing is left to chance. Every study that participates in the movement of the body does so according to physical and physiological principles.

Kinesiology helps us see human motion through new eyes and gain a greater appreciation for human movement.

Students of physical education, exercise science, and sport study kinesiology in order to learn how to improve performance by analyzing the movements of the body and applying the principles of movement to their work. Luttgens and

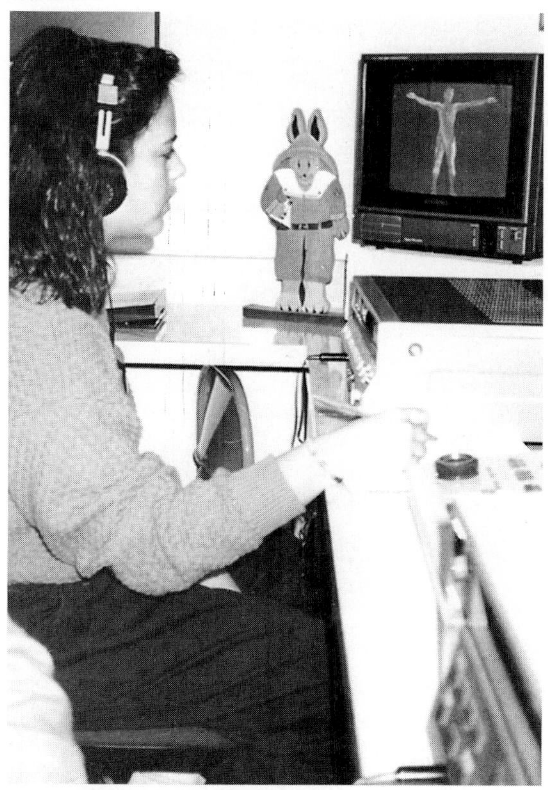

Kinesiology is concerned with the anatomical basis of movement. This student is using a self-paced instructional module to review anatomy.

Hamilton[1] identify three important purposes for the study of kinesiology by students in the fields of physical education, exercise science, and sport. Physical education, exercise science, and sport professionals can use their knowledge of kinesiology to help the people with whom they work perform with optimum safety, effectiveness, and efficiency. Safety is of paramount concern for all professionals. We design and conduct movement experiences for participants in our programs so that participants avoid doing harm to their body. Professionals and participants work together to set goals for effective performance. Typically, the effectiveness of a performance is judged by success or failure in meeting those goals. Our programs should be designed to enable our participants to achieve their goals. Professionals and participants strive to achieve their stated goals as efficiently as possible—that is, with the least expenditure of effort. Thus, according to Luttgens and Hamilton, safety, effectiveness, and efficiency are the underlying aims of using kinesiology in physical education, exercise science, and sport.[1]

Kinesiology helps prepare physical education, exercise science, and sport professionals to teach fundamental motor skills and specialized sport skills to people of all ages, as a means of optimizing performance. Kinesiology offers professionals a background from which to evaluate exercises and activities and how they affect the body.

Definition and Scope

Biomechanics, as a subdiscipline of physical education, exercise science, and sport, focuses on the application of the scientific principles of mechanical physics to understand movements and actions of human bodies and sport implements (e.g., a tennis racquet). The term *biomechanics* can be better understood by examining the derivation of the word. *Bio* is from Greek and refers to life or living things and *mechanics* refers to the field of Newtonian physics and the forces that act on bodies in motion. Biomechanists study how various forces affect human motion and how movements can be improved in terms of efficiency and effectiveness.

Kinesiology and biomechanics are integrally related. An understanding of how the body moves, including the function and actions of the joints, muscles, and bony structure, is essential to the understanding of biomechanics. In order to effectively study the influences of forces on motion—biomechanics—one must be knowledgeable about the actions of the joints and the muscles that cause these forces; this is the realm of kinesiology. Both kinesiology and biomechanics are fundamental to understanding human movement and to helping individuals attain their fullest potential.

The principles of biomechanics can be applied in many fields of study outside of physical

Biomechanists study the movements of athletes to improve performance as well as to reduce the occurrence of injury.

education, exercise science, and sport. These include biology, physiology, engineering, aerospace engineering, physical and occupational therapy, and medicine.

Historical Development

Biomechanics traces its roots back to the 1890s, but emerged from physical education as a specialized area of study in the mid-1960s and 1970s. During the early history of biomechanics in the United States, the term *kinesiology* was used to refer to the science of applying mechanics to the study of movement and, until recently, the terms were used interchangeably. Wilkerson chronicles the growth of biomechanics through three stages: the early foundations (referred to as the Kinesiology Era), the organization of the subdiscipline or the Biomechanics Era, and the Development of Biomechanics.[2]

The Kinesiology Era spanned the late 1800s and the first six decades of the twentieth century, and represented the infancy of biomechanics. During this time frame, the term *kinesiology* was used to refer to the application of mechanics to the study of movement. Atwater credits Nils Posse as the first to use the term *kinesiology.* Posse wrote "The Special Kinesiology of Educational Gymnastics," published in 1894.[3]

Scholars of the early to the mid-twentieth century contributed to the growth of kinesiology/biomechanics through their teaching, research, and writing. Arthur Steindler, Charles McCloy, Ruth Glassow, Thomas Cureton, M. Gladys Scott, Katharine Wells, Marion Broer, and John M. Cooper were some of the early kinesiologists who led the way in developing and promoting the application of mechanical principles to the study of human movement. In 1935, Steindler, a physician and professor at the University of Iowa, where he taught kinesiology classes, became the first person to use the term *biomechanics* in the physical education literature. These early kinesiologists laid the foundations of biomechanics.

Wilkerson described the 1960s as the beginning of a new era in the development and growth of biomechanics—the emergence from physical education of biomechanics as a subdiscipline within the evolving exercise and sport sciences.[2] During this time the term *biomechanics* started to slowly replace the term *kinesiology* and was used more frequently to describe the scientific application of mechanics to the study of human movement. There was a greater emphasis on the study of both the anatomical and mechanical aspects of human movement. Advances in technology, instrumentation, and methodology contributed to the proliferation of research during this time.

Courses in kinesiology/biomechanics increased at both the undergraduate and graduate levels. At the graduate level, biomechanics began to emerge as an area of specialization. In 1977, the first national symposium on teaching kinesiology/biomechanics was held, during which there was considerable discussion about the differences between the terms *kinesiology* and *biomechanics.* Additionally, this meeting served as the impetus for the development of guidelines for teaching undergraduate kinesiology/biomechanics; *Guidelines and Standards for UndergraduateBiomechanics/Kinesiology* was first published in 1980, and revised in 1992.[4] According to the guidelines, biomechanics/kinesiology at the undergraduate level should provide students with "(1) an understanding of how the human body and external forces create human movement, (2) the knowledge necessary to undertake a systematic approach to the analysis of motor skills activities and exercise programs, and (3) the experience of applying that knowledge to the execution and evaluation of both the performer and the performance in a clinical or educational milieu."[4] These guidelines influenced the learning experiences of countless physical educators, exercise scientists, and sport leaders as well as other future professionals concerned with the study of human movement.

The development of the biomechanics era was marked, according to Wilkerson, by the formation of scholarly societies, the organization of academic workshops and seminars, and the creation of scholarly journals; these provided a forum for the exchange of ideas, dissemination of research findings, and opportunity for communication within the field.[2] In 1963, the formation of a kinesiology interest group within the American Association for Health, Physical Education, Recreation, and Dance (AAHPERD) began which, in 1965, officially became the Kinesiology Section of AAHPERD. In 1974, the Kinesiology Section became the Kinesiology Academy, and in 1993, it changed its name to the Biomechanics Academy.

Several scholarly societies were formed by those interested in biomechanics and, more specifically, the biomechanics of sports. In 1973, the *International Society of Biomechanics* was founded, and in 1976, the *American Society of Biomechanics* was formed. These societies were very broad in their focus, including professionals from physical education, medicine, ergonomics, biology, and engineering. The growing interest in biomechanics in sports and the desire to help bridge the gap between biomechanics research and the teaching and coaching of sports led to the establishment, in 1982, of the International Society for Biomechanics in Sports (ISBS).

During this time, several journals were created to serve as an outlet for research and an exchange of ideas. In 1968, the first issue of the *Journal of Biomechanics* was published. The *International Journal of Sport Biomechanics* first appeared in 1985 and was later renamed the *Journal of Applied Biomechanics.* Most recently, in 2002, ISBS published its new journal, *Sports Biomechanics.*

The growth of biomechanics has been remarkable. As biomechanics emerged and flourished, specialized areas of interest have developed within the subdiscipline. Biomechanists may specialize in a particular sport, such as swimming, or focus their research on a specific topic, such as footwear. Other biomechanists choose to direct their attention to more clinical concerns, such as rehabilitation. Other areas of interest in the broad and ever-expanding field include gait and posture analysis and computer simulation.

Cyclists have benefited greatly from improvements in equipment design and research designed to help them streamline and refine their body position to improve performance.

Biomechanics enables physical education, exercise science, and sport professionals to analyze human movement scientifically, increasing their ability to help individuals more safely, efficiently, and effectively achieve their movement goals. There is a growing trend within the fields of exercise and sport sciences to refer to biomechanics as *sport biomechanics.* Additionally, as we move toward the future, there is a greater interest in using biomechanics to work not only with elite athletes, but with persons of all abilities and to strengthen and improve their performance of a diversity of movement tasks.

Reasons for Studying Biomechanics

Biomechanics is recognized as a subdiscipline of physical education, exercise science, and sport. As a result of reading this chapter, prospective professionals will have a better understanding of the parameters of this field of study and will recognize the value it has for them in future careers. In some cases, perhaps, it will motivate further study and specialization in this field of endeavor.

Many professionals can profit from the study of biomechanics. To be effective as practitioners, physical educators, exercise science, and sport professionals should have an understanding of the principles of biomechanics. Knowledge of biomechanics will provide the professional with a better understanding of the human body and the various internal and external forces that affect human movement, as well as the forces that act on object motion. This in turn will enable professionals to be better instructors, coaches, and leaders of the many physical activities and skills within physical education, exercise science, and sport.

Coaches who want to be expert in their field need a sound foundation in the area of biomechanics. Biomechanics offers important scientific knowledge that can improve performance, and the best coaches are taking advantage of this knowledge. Coaches of athletes today who are involved in many areas of high school, college, and Olympic sport find competition very intense. Therefore, coaches of athletes who wish to excel must use all this knowledge and the best techniques available. Biomechanics can be used to improve sport techniques and equipment, thus enhancing athletes' performance while assuring their safety.

Biomechanics is often at the forefront of changes in technique and technology. In the late 1960s and early 1970s, our understanding of swimming changed and new techniques emerged as elite coaches and biomechanists worked together. Coach James Counsilman, author of *The Science of Swimming,* worked with biomechanists to study the forces involved in propulsion in swimming.[5] In 1971, Brown and Counsilman filmed swimmers wearing lights on their hands as they swam in a darkened pool. This allowed the pattern of the swimmers' hands and feet to be identified and their actions carefully studied. It was found that the traditional technique of the arm pull, based on drag forces for propulsion, was not as efficient as an arm pull technique that created lift forces.[6] Counsilman's continued work in this area, along with that of other coaches and researchers, soon revolutionized the sport of swimming.

Innovations by athletes have also advanced biomechanics research. Athletes have created new techniques that have led to higher levels of performance, for example, in high jumping and tennis.

Lifespan and Cultural Perspectives: Biomechanics

- How can shoes be better designed to reduce the chances of persons with diabetes experiencing ulcerations on their feet?
- Which type of exercise would be most effective in reducing falls in individuals over the age of 70?
- What is the optimum design of a snowboard?
- How does an individual's posture when using exercise equipment (stepper, weights, etc.) influence gains achieved from exercise?
- How do the performance patterns of elite divers differ from the 3-meter board to the 10-meter platform?
- How can a sport biomechanist use computer-enhanced images to improve the performance of an age-group swimmer?
- How does an individual's gait change when using a brace for a torn anterior cruciate ligament (ACL)? Which type of brace is most effective?

Until the late 1960s, high jumpers approached the bar from an angle, thrust an arm and a leg up and over, then executed a kick, and the body "rolled" over the bar. In 1968, high-jumper Dick Fosbury, utilizing his unorthodox flop style of jumping, won the Gold Medal at the Olympic Games in Mexico. The "Fosbury Flop" style of jumping used a curved approach to the bar with the jumper going over backward in a twisting lay-back of the body. Within 10 years, the traditional, long-used roll style of jumping was replaced by the flop style and records soared to new heights. As a young tennis player, Chris Evert used a two-handed backhand drive to return the ball over the net. Now it is common to see players use this stroke, which gives greater control and speed than the traditional one-handed backhand stroke.

Some other professionals within the field of physical education, physical science, and sport who use the principles of biomechanics to improve an individual's movements and skill performance are adapted physical educators, athletic trainers, and exercise leaders. Knowledge of kinesiology and biomechanics helps these professionals design and conduct programs to enhance individual movement skills.

There are many specialized areas of study within biomechanics. Developmental biomechanics focuses on studying movement patterns and how they change across the lifespan, from infancy to old age and with people with disabilities. Especially with the aged, an understanding of the biomechanical principles involved in activities of daily living, such as walking, climbing stairs, lifting, and carrying, is important in designing activities to enable individuals to remain independent and able to care for their needs.

The biomechanics of exercise is another specialized area of study. Exercise should be based on both physiological and biomechanical principles. An understanding of the biomechanics of exercise can help maximize the benefits of exercise and reduce the chances of injury. Physical educators, exercise scientists, and sport leaders can use biomechanical principles of exercise to make sure individuals are performing the exercise correctly and achieving maximum benefits.

Rehabilitation biomechanics is applied to the study of the movement patterns of people who are injured or who have a disability. This helps professionals understand how the injury or disability has altered the normal movement pattern of individuals. This information is then used to design programs to help individuals move optimally within their constraints and to restore normal function when possible.

Physical education, exercise and sport professionals, when helping individuals perform exercises, should make sure that each movement is performed correctly and conforms to accepted biomechanical principles. This is important for safety reasons as well as to help ensure the individual achieves desired benefits. Work is performed as the individual moves the weight through the range of motion of this exercise.

Equipment design is a growing area of biomechanics. Changes in equipment can lead to dramatic increases in performance. The speedskating event at the 1998 Nagano Olympics served as a showcase for new technology: the clap skate. The Dutch-invented clap skate, with its hinged blade, redefined record times. With conventional skates, the skater uses the quadriceps, not the calf muscles, and pushes through the back side of the skate. The clap skates use a hinge-and-spring mechanism to attach the front of the skate boot to the blade. The heel is not attached to the blade; thus when the foot is raised above the ice, the blade snaps back to the heel, making the characteristic clapping noise. The clap skate allows the skater to use his/her calf muscles, making the push more powerful. The blade also remains on the ice for a longer time, allowing for a longer stride and greater speed.

Biomechanists are also involved in the testing of new fabrics, evaluating them in terms of their potential to contribute to performance. New fabrics, developed after years of testing, help competitors in several different sports decrease their times by reducing water or air resistance. In the 2000 Olympic Games in Sydney, swimmers wore new bodysuits created out of a special material that offered less resistance through the water than human skin. Modeled on a shark's skin, Speedo's "Fastskin" material helped competitors shave seconds off their times, critical in a sport where the difference between winning and finishing second can be as little as a hundredth of a second.[7] In the 2002 Utah Winter Olympic Games, similar "speed suits" were worn by speedskaters. Nike's "Swift Skin" and Descente "Vortex" suits, along with the accompanying hoods, gloves, and skate covers, allowed speedskaters to cover their body from head to foot in a material designed to decrease air resistance.[7] Extensive testing went into the development of these fabrics, designed to decrease friction and, subsequently, improve performance.

Biomechanists working in the area of equipment design have also contributed to great changes in sport techniques, higher levels of performance, reduction of injury, and increased safety. The design of running shoes has changed radically since the early 1970s. More cushioning, greater attention given to injury prevention, establishment of greater variety of sizes, and designs to fit specific purposes (e.g., running, cross training, basketball, court shoes, etc.) are reflected in athletic shoes today. Athletic shoes are designed today to accommodate users' special needs, such as pronation, and to enhance comfort and performance. Greater attention has also been given to the needs of women. The sporting goods industry, since the mid-1980s, is building equipment, such as skis or running shoes, specifically for women as opposed to simply manufacturing a scaled-down version of the men's models. An understanding of the way the body works, knowledge of the demands of the sport, and the ability to apply biomechanical principles are important in equipment design.

The application of biomechanical principles is not limited to the realm of physical education, exercise science, and sport. Biomechanists working in industry use this information to ensure safe working conditions and efficient performance from the workers. In medicine, knowledge from biomechanics can be used by orthopedists to evaluate how pathological conditions affect movement or to assess the suitability of prosthetic devices for patients. As the field of biomechanics continues to expand, its contribution to our understanding of human movement will become even more significant.

Major Areas of Study

Biomechanics is concerned with two major areas of study. The first area is biological in nature as implied in the term *biomechanics.* Motion or movement involves biological aspects of the human body, including the skeletal and muscular systems. For example, movement occurs as a result of such things as force applied to bones, contraction of muscles, and bones acting as levers. Bones, muscles, and nerves work together in producing motion. It is not possible to understand motor skill development without first knowing about biological aspects underlying human movement such as joint action, anatomical structures, and muscular forces.

The second major area of study in biomechanics relates to mechanics. This area of study is important because it utilizes the laws and principles of Newtonian physics and applies them to human motion and movement. Biomechanics is also concerned with object motion. The study of mechanics includes *statics,* or the study of factors relating to nonmoving systems or those characterized by steady motion (e.g., the center of gravity in positions of balance). It also includes *dynamics,* or the study of mechanical factors that relate to systems in motion. In turn, dynamics can involve a *kinematic* or *kinetic* approach. Kinematics is concerned with the study of time and space factors in motion such as velocity and acceleration, whereas kinetics is involved with forces such as gravity and muscles that act on a system.

Research in biomechanics is concerned with studying movement and factors that influence performance. The kinds of questions that may be studied are listed below:

- How do running motions change as children develop?
- How do forces summate to produce maximum power in the tennis serve?
- What are the movement patterns of world-class hurdlers?
- How can athletic shoes be designed to reduce injuries on artificial turf?
- What is the wrist action of elite wheelchair marathon athletes?
- What is the optimal design of the javelin?
- What are the critical performance elements of throwing? Of various fundamental motor skills? Of various sport skills? What are the common errors associated with the performance of these skills, and how can they best be remediated? How do the mechanics of these fundamental motor skills change with age?
- Which techniques are best for increasing the range of motion after reconstructive surgery of the shoulder?
- What is the best body position for swimming the butterfly stroke?
- Is a specific brand of rowing ergometer safe to use? Can individuals of all fitness levels effectively use this piece of fitness equipment? Are the benefits claimed by the manufacturer for its use accurate?

These are only a few of the questions that can be addressed through biomechanical research techniques. In answering these questions, researchers measure such factors as joint angles and muscle activity, force production, and linear and angular acceleration. The next section presents selected biomechanical terms.

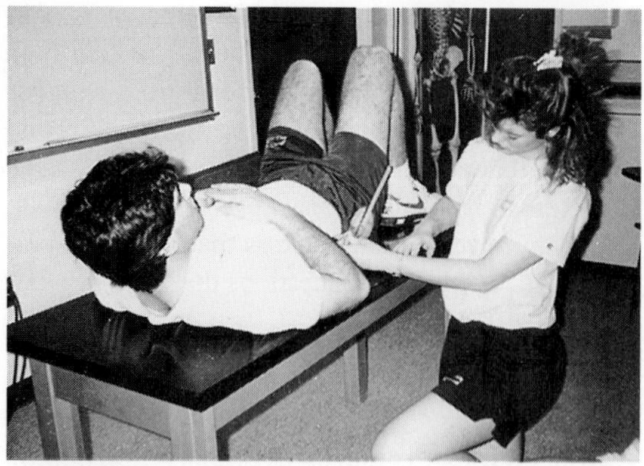

Students use goniometry to measure joint angles.

SELECTED BIOMECHANICAL TERMS RELATED TO HUMAN MOTION

The field of biomechanics has a specialized scientific vocabulary that describes the relationship between force and motion. As previously defined, kinematics is concerned with understanding the spatial and temporal characteristics of human movement: that is, the direction of the motion and the time involved in executing the motion. Important terms related to kinematics include *velocity, acceleration, angular velocity, angular acceleration,* and *linear* and *angular motions.* Kinetics is concerned with the forces that cause, modify, or inhibit motion. Terms related to kinetics are *mass, force, pressure, gravity, friction, work, power, energy,* and *torque.* (See Table 6-1.)

Velocity refers to the speed and direction of a body and involves the change of position of a body per unit of time. Because bodies in motion are continually changing position, the degree to which the body's position changes within a definite time span is measured to determine its velocity. For example, the velocity of a baseball from the time it leaves the pitcher's hand to the time it arrives in the catcher's glove can be measured in this manner.

Acceleration refers to the change in velocity involving speed or direction of a moving body. An individual playing basketball, for example, can add positive acceleration when dribbling toward the basket on a fast break, or the player can change pace and slow down (decelerate) to permit another player to screen for him or her.

Angular velocity is the angle that is rotated in a given unit of time. *Angular acceleration* refers to the change of angular velocity for a unit of time. For example, when a bowling ball is rolled down a lane, its angular velocity can be computed mathematically in terms of revolutions per second. The angular acceleration, on the other hand, occurs after the bowling ball is released and the ball actually starts rolling, instead of sliding, which occurs immediately on release.

The relationship between *linear* and *angular motions* of body parts should be understood. Northrip, Logan, and McKinney[8] cite the following examples: (1) a throwing motion involves angular velocity of the wrist joint, which helps to determine throwing speed; (2) kicking a football involves the angular velocity of the kicker's ankle joint, which helps to determine kicking performance. The final linear velocity that results in both cases is achieved as the sum of many angular motions at the body joints. Because most body movements are rotational movements at the body's joints, to achieve the best results in skill performance, it is necessary to integrate linear and angular motions.

Mass is the amount of matter possessed by an object. Mass is a measure of the object's inertia: that is, the resistance of the object to efforts made to move it and, once the object has begun to move, resistance to changing its motion. The mass of an object influences the amount of force needed to produce acceleration. The greater the mass, the larger the force needed. For example, in track and field a larger force would be needed to produce an acceleration of a 16-pound shot than a 12-pound shot.

Force is any action that changes or tends to change the motion of an object. Forces have both a magnitude (i.e., size) and a direction. Forces on the body can occur internally, such as when a muscle contracts and exerts forces on the bone to which it is attached. External forces such as gravity also can act on the body.

Pressure refers to the ratio of force to the area over which the force is applied. For example,

TABLE 6-1 Selected Biomechanical Terms

Kinematics—study of space and time factors in motion such as velocity and acceleration
Kinetics—study of forces that act on a system, such as gravity and muscles
Velocity—change in the speed and/or direction of a body per unit of time
Acceleration—change in velocity
Angular velocity—angle that is rotated in a given unit of time
Angular acceleration—change in angular velocity for a given unit of time
Mass—amount of matter possessed by an object
Force—any action that changes or tends to change the motion of an object. Forces are described in terms of magnitude and direction
Pressure—ratio of force to the area over which the force is applied
Gravity—force that accelerates all objects vertically toward the center of the earth
Center of gravity—point at which all of an object's mass is balanced at a specific moment
Friction—force that occurs when surfaces come in contact with each other
Work—force that is applied to a body through a distance and in the direction of the force
Power—amount of work accomplished in a one unit of time
Energy—capacity of a body to perform work
Torque—twisting, turning, or rotary force applied to the production of angular acceleration

16-ounce boxing gloves will distribute a given force over a larger surface area than 12-ounce boxing gloves, thus reducing pressure. In this case, distributing the pressure will ensure less chance of injury from blows when the 16-ounce gloves are used.

Gravity is a natural force that pulls all objects toward the center of the earth. An important feature of gravitational pull is that it always occurs through the center of weight or mass of an object. In the human body, the center of weight is known as the *center of gravity.* The center of gravity is the point at which all of the body's mass seems to be located and the point about which an object would balance. The center of gravity is constantly changing during movement. It can be either within or outside the body, depending on the shape of the body. It always shifts in the direction of movement or the additional weight. When human beings stand erect with their hands at their sides, the center of gravity is located at the level of the hips. Athletes can use their knowledge about the center of gravity to better their skills. For example, the basketball player during a jump ball swings both arms forward and upward to assist in gaining height. Once in the air, the player allows one arm to drop to his or her side and strives to get maximum reach with the other arm. By dropping one arm to the side, the player can reach farther beyond the center of gravity than with two arms overhead.

Friction is a force that occurs when surfaces come in contact and results when the surfaces move past each other. The roughness of the surface and the amount of force pressing the surfaces together influence the amount of friction. The rougher the surface and the greater the force, the greater the magnitude of friction. Friction plays an important role in traction. Traction is important to athletes. The ability of athletes to make quick turns, change direction rapidly, stop, and propel themselves forward without losing footing depends on having the right amount of traction.[8] Shoe manufacturers design shoes to provide athletes with the right amount of traction for the specific sport, playing surface, and weather conditions.[8] Reduction of friction is important in sports such as skating and skiing, where the ability to glide over ice and snow is critical to performance.[8]

Work refers to the force that is applied to a body through a distance and in the direction of the force. An individual who bench presses 240 pounds

Understanding of the principles of biomechanics can assist gymnasts in improving their performance.

through 2 feet is doing work. The direction of the motion is the same as the direction of the force, and therefore the total amount of work is figured by multiplying 240 pounds by 2 feet, which equals 480 foot-pounds of work for each repetition.

Power is the amount of work accomplished in one unit of time. For example, a person performs a certain task, such as running, and exerts a certain amount of horsepower to perform the task in a given amount of time. In order to exert twice as much horsepower, the runner would have to perform the same task and accomplish the same amount of work (i.e., run the same distance) in half the amount of time.

Energy relates to the capacity of a body to perform work. Two types of energy used in biomechanics are (1) kinetic energy, the energy a body has because it is moving (such as a skier whose weight and velocity determine kinetic energy); and (2) potential energy, the energy that accrues as a result of the position that a body occupies relative to the earth's surface. The weight of the body and its height above the surface are used to determine potential energy. For example, a diver at the peak of a dive has the capacity to do work because of his or her position relative to the earth's surface. When he or she falls toward the water, the weight of the body does work equal to its magnitude times the distance the body moves in the direction of force.

Torque represents a twisting, turning, or rotary force related to the production of angular acceleration and is contrasted with the force necessary to produce linear acceleration. Torque can also be produced as a result of the rotation of a body or body part. For example, supination and pronation of the radioulnar joint can produce torque. The production of torque is essential in gymnastics because of the many movements required in routines that use apparatus such as the high bar, parallel bars, uneven parallel bars, and rings.

MECHANICAL PRINCIPLES AND CONCEPTS RELATED TO MOVEMENT

Movements are governed by mechanical principles. Biomechanists use these principles in the analysis of movement. To illustrate, some mechanical principles, selected principles and concepts relating to stability, motion, leverage, and force are presented in this section.

Stability

Stability is an important factor in all movement skills. It is related to equilibrium and balance. When all the forces acting on the body are counterbalanced by equal and opposite forces so that the sum of the forces equals zero, equilibrium is maintained. A state of equilibrium occurs when the body's center of gravity is over its base of support and the line of gravity (a line drawn from the center of the gravity to the center of the earth) falls within the base. The base of support of the body is the area outlined when all the points in contact with the ground are connected. The greater the body surface in contact with the ground, the larger the base of support. Thus, a sitting position has a larger base of support than a standing position. A stance that places four points of the body in contact with the ground, rather than just two points as in standing, typically increases the base of support.

Stability is the body's ability to return to a position of equilibrium after it has been displaced. The greater the body's stability, the more difficult it is to affect its equilibrium.

Static equilibrium occurs when the center of gravity is in a stable position (e.g., when one is sitting or performing a handstand in gymnastics). Dynamic equilibrium is a state in which the center of gravity is in motion (e.g., when one is running or performing a cartwheel in gymnastics). In sport and movement terminology, stability is often referred to as balance. The body's ability to maintain stability or balance is governed by three primary principles.

Principle

The lower the center of gravity is to the base of support, the greater the stability. When performing activities that require stability, individuals should lower their center of gravity. In running, for example, individuals can stop more efficiently and quickly if they bend their knees, thereby lowering the center of gravity, and place their feet in a forward stride position. Other examples include a wrestler taking a semicrouched position and the football lineman assuming a three-point stance.

Principle

The nearer the center of gravity is to center of the base of support, the more stable the body. When the center of gravity extends beyond the boundaries of the base of support, balance is lost. Keeping the body's weight centered over the base of support helps promote stability. However, in activities where the objective is to move quickly in one direction, shifting the weight in the direction of the movement can aid performance. For example, in starting a sprint race, the runners will lean forward to get out of the starting blocks quickly.

Tai Chi has been found to improve balance in the elderly. The wide base of support offers the instructor stability as she leads the class through the movement.

Some activities such as walking on a balance beam require a small base of support. It is very easy to lose one's balance in these types of activities. When balance is lost while performing on the balance beam, the arm or leg on the opposite side from which the person is leaning is raised to shift the center of gravity back toward the base of support.

Principle

Stability can be increased by widening the base of support. Widening the base of support helps achieve greater stability. When standing, for example, spreading the feet in the direction of movement adds stability. For activities in which a stance is required, using both hands and feet will create the widest base.

To increase stability in situations when receiving or applying force, the direction of the force must be considered. When receiving either a fast-moving object or a heavy force, widen the base of support in the direction from which the force is coming. When applying a force, widen the base in the direction from which the force is to be applied.

Motion

Motion implies movement, which consists of destroying or upsetting the equilibrium of the body. A force is required to start a body in motion, to slow it down, to stop it, to change the direction of its motion, or to make it move faster. Everything that moves is governed by the laws of motion formulated by Sir Isaac Newton. These laws describe how things move and make it possible to predict the motion of an object.

Newton's First Law

The law of inertia states that a body at rest will remain at rest and a body in motion will remain in motion at the same speed and in the same direction unless acted on by some outside force.

For a movement to occur, a force must act on a body sufficiently to overcome that object's inertia. If the applied force is less than the resistance offered by the object, motion will not occur.

Concepts

1. Once an object is in motion it will take less force to maintain its speed and direction (i.e., momentum). For example, it takes an individual more effort to start pedaling a bicycle to get it under way than it does to maintain speed once the bicycle is moving.
2. The heavier the object and the faster it is moving, the more force that is required to overcome its moving inertia or to absorb its momentum. In football an opponent will have to exert more force to stop a massive, fast-moving lineman than he would to stop the lighter-weight and slower-moving quarterback.

Newton's Second Law

The law of acceleration states that a change in velocity (acceleration) of an object is directly proportional to the force producing it and inversely proportional to its mass.

If two unequal forces are applied to objects of equal mass, the object that has the greater force applied will move faster. Conversely, if two equal forces are applied to objects of different masses, the lighter mass will travel at the faster speed.

For example, in shot putting the athlete who is stronger and thus able to expend more force will toss the 12-pound shot farther than an athlete who possesses less strength. Also, an athlete will find more force is needed to propel a 16-pound shot than a 12-pound shot.

Concepts

1. The heavier the object, the more force needed to speed it up (positive acceleration) or slow it down (negative acceleration).
2. An increase in speed is proportional to the amount of force that is applied; the greater the amount of force that is imparted to an object, the greater the speed with which that object will travel.
3. Momentum is a measure of both speed and mass. If the same amount of force is exerted for the same length of time on two bodies of different mass, greater acceleration will be produced in the lighter or less massive object. If the two objectives are propelled at the same speed, the heavier object will have greater momentum once inertia is overcome and will exert a greater force than the lighter object on something that it contacts.

Newton's Third Law

The law of action and reaction states that for every action there is an equal and opposite reaction.

Bouncing on a trampoline and springing from a diving board are examples of the law of action and reaction. The more force one exerts on the downward bounce, the higher the bounce or spring into the air. The thrust against the water in swimming is another example of an equal and opposite reaction—the water pushes the swimmer forward with a force equal to the force exerted by the swimmer on the backward thrust of the strokes.

Concept

1. Whenever one object moves, another object moves too and in the opposite direction. When you push something, it pushes back; when you pull on something, it pulls back.

Linear and Rotary Motion

Motion is linear or rotary. The human body usually employs a combination of both. The rotary action of the legs to propel the body in a linear direction is an example.

Linear Motion

Linear motion refers to movement in a straight line and from one point to another. In running, for example, the body should be kept on a straight line from start to finish. Also the feet and arm movements should be back and forth in straight lines rather than from side to side across the body.

Rotary Motion

Rotary motion consists of movement of a body about a center of rotation, called the *axis*. In most human movements rotary motion is converted into linear motion. Rotary motion is increased when the radius of rotation is shortened. Conversely, rotary motion is decreased when the radius of the moving body is increased. Examples include tucking the head when performing tumbling stunts to increase the rotation of the body and holding the arms out when executing a turn on the toes on ice to slow the body.

Leverage

Efficient body movement is made possible through a system of levers. A lever is a mechanical device used to produce a turning motion about a fixed point, called an *axis*. A lever consists of a fulcrum (the center or axis of rotation), a force arm (the distance from the fulcrum to the point of application of force), and a weight or resistance arm (the distance from the fulcrum to the weight on which the force is acting). The bones of the body act as levers, the joints act as the fulcrums, and the force to move the bone or lever about the joint or fulcrum is produced by the contraction of the muscles.

Three types of levers are determined by the relationship of the fulcrum (axis), the weight, and the point of application of force. In a *first-class lever* the fulcrum is located between the weight and point of application of force. In a *second-class lever* the weight is between the fulcrum and the force. In a *third-class lever* the force is between the fulcrum and the weight. (See Figure 6-1.)

Levers enable one to gain a mechanical advantage by producing either strength or speed. First-class levers may produce both strength and speed, unless the fulcrum is in the middle of the force and weight, which produces a balanced condition. Second-class levers produce force, and third-class levers favor speed. The movements of the body are produced mostly through third-class levers. In third-class levers, the point of application of the force (produced by the muscles) is located between the fulcrum (the joint) and the resistance (the object to be moved).

The length of the force arm is the key to producing either force or speed. If great force is desired, the force arm should be as long as possible. If great speed is desired, the force arm should be shortened. The internal levers of the body cannot be controlled in regard to the length of the force arm. However, when using implements such as bats and racquets, long force arms would be created by holding the implement near the end, thereby producing greater force. If a person was interested in greater speed to swing a bat, he or she would "choke up" on the bat to reduce the force arm. When using an implement to produce greater force or speed, the size and the length of the implement must match the strength of the person who is handling the implement.

Concepts

1. Levers are used to gain a mechanical advantage by either producing speed or force.
2. Greater speed is produced by lengthening the resistance arm, and greater force is produced by lengthening the force arm.

Force

Force is the effect that one body has on another. It is invisible, but it is always present when motion occurs. It should be pointed out, however, that there can be force without motion. An example of

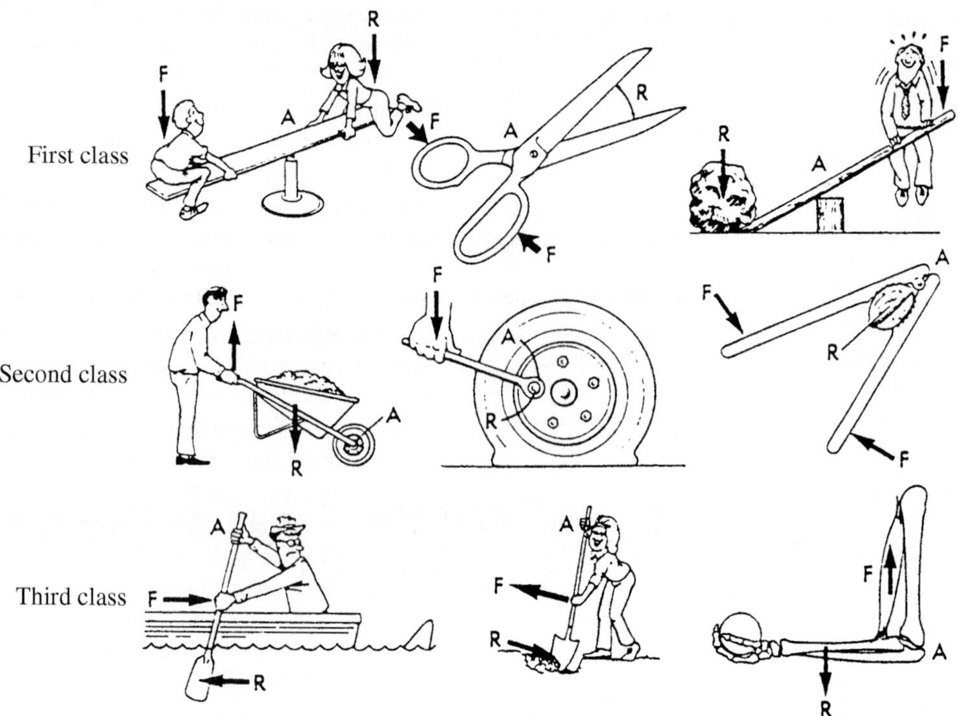

Figure 6-1 First-, second-, and third-class levers (A = axis, F = force, R = resistance).

a force in which no motion is evident is the push against a wall by a person. The wall does not move, although great force might be exerted. Another example occurs when two arm wrestlers are pushing against each other with equal force and their arms remain relatively motionless.

Professionals should be aware of the principles relating to the production, application, and absorption of force when they teach movement activities.

Production of Force

Body force is produced by the actions of muscles. The stronger the muscles, the more force the body is capable of producing. However, the force of the muscle group or groups must be applied in the same direction and in proper sequence to realize the greatest force. In the high jump, for example, the body should be lowered on the last step before the jump. This lowering of the body will enable the jumper to contract the muscles of the thigh, which are the strongest of the body. The upward movement of the arms will give added force to the jump when coordinated with the upward push of the legs. It should be remembered that the principles of stability and the laws of motion must be observed in the performance of the high jump if the greatest height is to be attained.

Force also must be generated to propel objects. The same principles apply as mentioned above. In the swing of a softball bat the application of force is possible because of the production of force by different muscle groups in a coordinated manner. For maximum force the body should be rotated at the hips, shoulders, arms, and hands in a sequential order. The summation of these forces will produce the greatest momentum. A follow-through is necessary both to avoid jerky movements and to reduce the possibility of injury to the muscles or tendons.

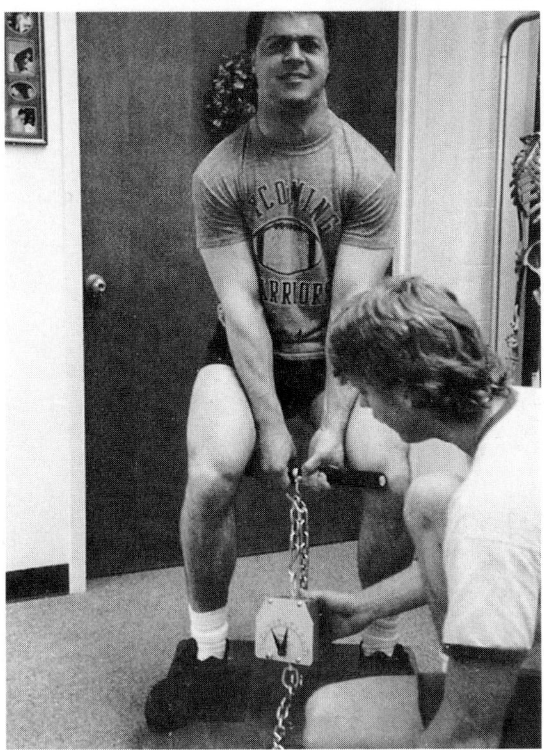
A dynamometer is used to measure strength.

Application of Force

The force of an object is most effective when it is applied in the direction that the object is to travel. Many activities in sport involve the projection of the body or another type of object into the air. To project an object or the body forward most efficiently, the force should be applied through the center of the weight of the object and in a forward direction. To move the body upward, the body must be straight and all the force must be directed upward through the center of the body. The example of the high jump will illustrate this principle. Force from the legs must be applied through the center of the body if the greatest force is to be applied to the jump. Some of the force will be dissipated if the jumper leans to one side when pushing off from the ground.

When someone throws an object, the following three main factors are of concern: (1) the speed of the throw, (2) the distance of the throw, and (3) the direction that the object will travel.

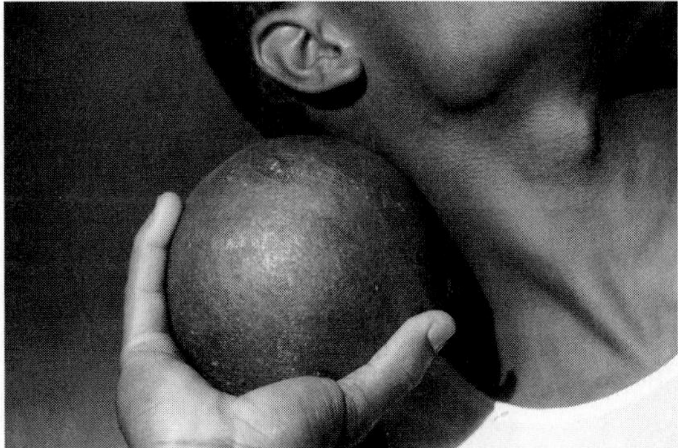
Force production is a critical component in many sports, such as the shot put.

The *speed* of the throw depends on the speed of the hand at the moment of release of the object. The speed of the arm can be increased by lengthening it to its fullest, rotating the body, shifting the weight properly, and taking a step in the direction of the throw. These movements must be done in a continuous motion to maintain momentum. If an implement such as a bat or paddle is used, it becomes an extension of the arm. Therefore the same principle applies. The implement should be held as close to the handle end as possible to create a long movement arm. This will enable the person to apply more force.

The *distance* of the throw will be affected by the pull of gravity and air resistance. The distance that an object will travel, therefore, will depend on the angle of release in addition to the force imparted to the throw. The pull of gravity and air resistance will affect thrown objects less if they are released at an angle of approximately 45°. This represents a compromise between releasing an object at a large angle and having it remain in the air but not go very far because of wind resistance and releasing the object at a smaller angle where the pull of gravity will keep it from traveling very far.

The *direction* or accuracy of the throw depends on the point of release of the object. The release must be a point in the arc of the arm at which the object is tangent to the target. To better achieve the desired angle of release, the throwing arm should be moved in a flatter arc at the time of release. In making the overhand throw in softball, for example, the hand should travel in the straightest line possible toward the target, both on the backswing and the follow-through.

In addition to gravity and air resistance, the flight of thrown and batted objects is also affected by the spin of the object. The object will travel in the direction of the spin.

Absorption of force is important in catching objects. The catcher's mitt, which distributes the force over a greater area, and "giving" with the catch help absorb the force of the pitched ball.

Absorption of Force

Many instances occur when persons must receive or absorb force. Examples include absorbing the force of a thrown object, as in catching a football or softball; landing after a jump; and heading a soccer ball. The impact of the force should be gradually reduced, and it should be spread over as large an area as possible. Therefore, when someone catches a ball, the arms should be extended to meet the ball. On contact, the hand and arms should "give" with the catch. When landing from a jump, the person should bend the hips, knees, and ankles to gradually reduce the kinetic energy of the jump, thereby reducing the momentum. The feet must also be spread slightly to create a large area of impact (base).

Concepts

1. The more muscles that are used, the greater the force that is produced (provided, of course, that they are the same sized muscles).
2. The more elasticity or stretch a muscle is capable of, the more force it can supply. Each working muscle should be stretched fully to produce the greatest force.
3. When objects are moved, the weight of the objects should be pushed or pulled through the center and in the direction that they are to be moved.
4. When heavy objects are moved or thrown, the force of the muscles should be used in a sequential manner. For example, the order in throwing should be trunk rotation, shoulder, upper arm, lower arm, hand, and fingers.
5. When body parts (arms and legs) or implements such as bats and paddles are used, they should be extended completely when making contact with an object to be propelled. This creates a long movement arm, thereby creating the greatest force; the implements should be gripped at the end.
6. When receiving or absorbing the force of a thrown object (as in catching a ball), a fall, or a kick, the largest possible area should be used to absorb the force. For example, the student should use two hands to catch a hard-thrown ball; more area will be available to absorb the force of the ball.
7. The absorption of force should be spread out as long as possible by recoiling or "giving" at the joints involved in the movement.

To analyze an individual's motor performance, physical education, exercise science, and sport professionals need to be cognizant of the principles governing movement. Selected principles pertaining to stability, motion, leverage, and force were discussed in this section. Professionals are also concerned about such concepts as friction, aerodynamics, hydrodynamics, and ball spin and rebound in the evaluation of performance. An understanding of both biomechanics and kinesiology provides the professional with a foundation for understanding and analyzing human movement.

BIOMECHANICAL ANALYSIS

Various instruments and techniques are used by biomechanists to study and analyze motion. During the past 15 years improvements in instrumentation coupled with advances in computers and microchip technology have greatly assisted biomechanists in their endeavors. Additionally, the development of better and more creative methods of using these instruments has greatly enhanced the understanding of human movement and the ability to improve performance.[9] These tools include computers, anthropometry, timing devices, cinematography, videography, electrogoniometry, electromyography, dynamography, and telemetry. Sometimes researchers use wind tunnels. These tools, as well as visual observation, can be used to perform quantitative and qualitative analysis of human movement.

Instruments

Computers have become increasingly important in biomechanical research. Biomechanical analysis requires dealing with prodigious amounts of data. The use of the computer in dealing with such data has become a necessity. Additionally, much of the instrumentation used in biomechanical research is linked to a computer. Much of the analysis of information can be performed on-line so that the results can be available almost instantly.

Computers can also be used to simulate movements. *Simulation* requires the use of mathematical formulas to develop models of a specific movement. Then, this computer model can be used to assist biomechanists in determining the effects of certain modifications in the movement or certain variables on performance. For example, simulation can address such questions as What is the effect of altering the takeoff position of a dive on the subsequent performance? Or How does air resistance affect a skier's performance? This approach helps researchers determine how a performance can be improved. Comparisons of the optimal or ideal performance and an individual's actual performance are enhanced through the use of computer technology. The computer is used to generate graphic representations of the ideal performance and the actual performance. The drawing of the actual performance is compiled from analysis of the films of the performer. These graphic representations of the ideal performance and an individual's actual performance can then be compared. This helps to detect errors and identify strategies to improve performance. Computers offer biomechanists tremendous assistance in understanding human movements.

Cinematography is one of the basic tools employed in biomechanical research. Sophisticated cameras are used to film an individual's performance. These high-speed cameras capture details of movements that may escape the unaided eye of the professional observing the performer's movements. As a result of cinematography, it is possible to film movement and capture such things as the speed, angle, range, and sequence of moving segments. Cinematography provides a permanent record that can be studied after the movement action takes place. Slow-motion and stop-action techniques aid in the study of the performance. From the film, graphic representations of the movement can be developed, either through hand drawing or through computer analysis. Completion of mathematical calculations based on information provided from the films is an essential part of movement analysis. This process is greatly speeded and simplified through the use of computers.

Stroboscopy is a photographic technique that also is used for the study of movement. This technique allows filming to take place against a darkened background, with light being flashed onto the subject being filmed. The total movement is recorded on a single frame of film as a sequence of images. For example, with this technique it is possible to take a picture of the total forehand stroke in tennis, which shows the path of the various body segments in the total execution of the stroke. This facilitates the analysis of the individual's movements. With this technique, one person's execution of a movement skill (e.g., the forehand tennis stroke or the wrist action used) can be compared with that of another person or the ideal performance.

Videography is the use of video systems to record an individual's performance. Video systems consist of a video camera, recorder, and a playback unit. Unlike cinematography, video systems are relatively inexpensive, easy to use, and readily available to practitioners. The ability to directly play back what has been recorded allows for immediate viewing by the analyst and prompt feedback to the performer. Videography systems can be interfaced with computers to provide movement analysis. This is one of the most inexpensive high-technology systems for the analysis of movement. Advances in technology have led to better quality cameras as well as sophisticated playback capabilities that yield greater clarity of still and stop-action images.

Anthropometry is concerned with the measurement of the human body. The length, width, diameter, circumference (girth), and surface area of the body and its segments are measured. Correct identification of anatomical landmarks is crucial to obtaining accurate measurements. Information about the structure of the human body is used to calculate the forces acting on the joints of the body and the forces produced by movement. Information about the structure of an individual's body is important in developing computer models of performance.

Timing devices or chronoscopes are used to record speeds of body movements. Some types of timing devices are stop watches, digital timers, counters, switch mats, photoelectric cells, and real-time computer clocks. The chronoscope is started at a preselected point in time, typically the initiation of a movement, and then stopped at a preselected time, such as the completion of a movement. The speed of movement is then calculated. Radar guns can also be used to provide instantaneous information about speed.

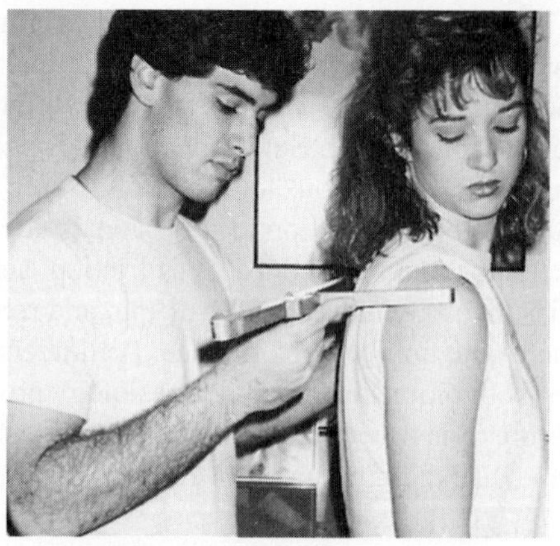

Anthropometry is the measurement of the human body. Various devices are used to provide information about the body and its segments.

Electrogoniometry is a technique that can be used to provide information about the angles of the joint as part of a total motion pattern. Another term for an electrogoniometer is an elgon. A goniometer (see Chapter 7 for information about the use of goniometers to measure flexibility) is used in conjunction with an electrical device called a *potentiometer* to measure the degrees of movement at a joint. This information can be transferred directly to a computer, recording paper, or oscilloscope. For example, this instrument would permit the study of the knee-joint action when a particular skill, such as walking or running, is executed. It can also measure range of motion, angular velocity, and acceleration. Electrogoniometry may be particularly useful when combined with electromyography.

Electromyography (EMG) is used to measure the electrical activity produced by a muscle or

Light-emitting diodes facilitate the tracking and analysis of movements.

muscle group. When properly processed, this measurement serves as an approximate indicator of the amount of force being developed by a muscle. This provides a means to observe the involvement of a particular muscle or muscle group in a movement. Surface electrodes are placed over the muscle or muscle group or fine wire electrodes are inserted into the muscle to be observed. Electrical impulses from muscle activity are then processed, recorded, and displayed on an oscilloscope, recording paper, or computer. EMG can be used to record the muscle activity associated with a particular performance; when EMG is done during various periods of time, a record of progress can be made. Certain rhythms of muscle activity are associated with a performance. An athlete who is not performing well or is in a slump may display a different EMG rhythm than normal. This information can be used to assist the athlete to correct errors and regain the desired form. EMG is often used in conjunction with electrogoniometry. Researchers may also make recordings of brain wave activity using the electroencephalograph (EEG) concurrently with EMG activity; this provides the researcher with information on how the brain influences motor activity (this is studied within the realm of motor control).

Dynamography is a technique used to measure the forces produced during a movement. To measure strength, particularly static strength, spring devices and cable tensiometers are used. Strain gauges are devices that are also used to measure strength. They have been incorporated into equipment such as athletic footwear insoles, bicycle pedals, and uneven parallel bars to measure the force produced by the performers using this equipment. Another device that is used to measure force is the force platform. Force platforms can be built into the floor to measure forces such as those associated with a foot striking the floor during walking. They can also be designed to measure force production by athletes during sprint starts, pole vaulting, and gymnastics.

Telemetry involves the wireless recording of various aspects of movement. Telemetry systems consist of specialized electrodes that are attached to the individual and a transmitter that sends the information to the receiver that records it. Telemetry systems can be used to transmit information about heart rate or joint angles (electrogoniometry) during a performance. A distinct advantage of this technique is that it permits movement data to be recorded without encumbering the performer with wires and other equipment that can hinder performance.

Wind tunnels are used in many ways to improve athletes' performance. Nike used a wind tunnel to measure air resistance during the development of their "Swift Skin."[7] Wind tunnels are used to determine whether equipment design can be improved: for example, whether the shape of a new helmet for cycling or a change in the composite of a bike wheel actually reduces air resistance. Reducing air resistance helps athletes achieve better times in their sports.

Skiers and sledders (such as bobsledders or lugers) used the wind tunnel to refine their movements for optimum efficiency and speed.[7] These athletes experiment with various body positions inside the wind tunnel. Researchers, including biomechanists, analyze the videotapes of the athlete to provide information about the aerodynamics of each position. Sometimes special force-measuring devices are used to provide additional information to assist in the identification of the optimum body position. Working together, researchers, coaches, and athletes use this information to assist athletes in making form adjustments that will lead to optimum performance.

Advances in computers and instrumentation as well as the manner in which they are used have contributed much to the understanding of human movement. For example, the intersection of biomechanics and biofeedback has stimulated the development of new devices to improve sport. Biofeedback is the provision of information about a physiological parameter, such as muscle tension, to an individual. The individual then uses this information to modify his or her response. The Swing Trainer and the Cycle Trainer developed by Innovative Sports Training can be used in rehabilitation or as an aid to improve performance. The Swing Trainer provides complete real-time, 3-D golf swing analysis and biofeedback training (Figure 6-2). Using sensors that easily attach to the body, the swing trainer captures the full range of the golf swing and provides precise information on all aspects of the golf swing. Audio and visual biofeedback ensures optimal body positioning. When the individual is out of position, a tone alerts the individual, and a video displays the proper position. The Cycle Trainer works in a similar fashion. The Cycle Trainer measures critical orthopedic angles, body positions, pulse, and power output during cycling.

The Swing Trainer, developed by Innovative Sports Training, provides real-time, 3-D golf swing analysis.

Analysis

Quantitative and qualitative methods can be used to analyze human movement. *Quantitative analysis* uses many of the techniques described previously to provide specific numerical information about the movement being studied. Specific information, for example, about the joint angles during movement, the force generated, and the speed of movement is provided. Quantitative analysis is used predominantly in research efforts and is increasingly incorporated as part of the overall training program of elite athletes to help them optimize their performance (e.g., biomechanists work with elite athletes at the U.S. Olympic Training Center at Colorado Springs, Colorado).

Qualitative analysis also provides important information about the movement being studied. Qualitative analysis relies most commonly on visual evaluation of the movement. The movement can be described in such terms as successful or unsuccessful or performed with difficulty or with ease. An individual's performance also can be compared with another individual's performance or against a standardized model. Videography, which can be used for quantitative analysis, can also be used effectively for qualitative analysis. Instead of using the videotape to calculate various kinematic and kinetic measures, the videotape of an individual's movement can be studied to identify performance errors and to determine effective corrections.

Qualitative analysis is most commonly used by practitioners. It offers practitioners who may

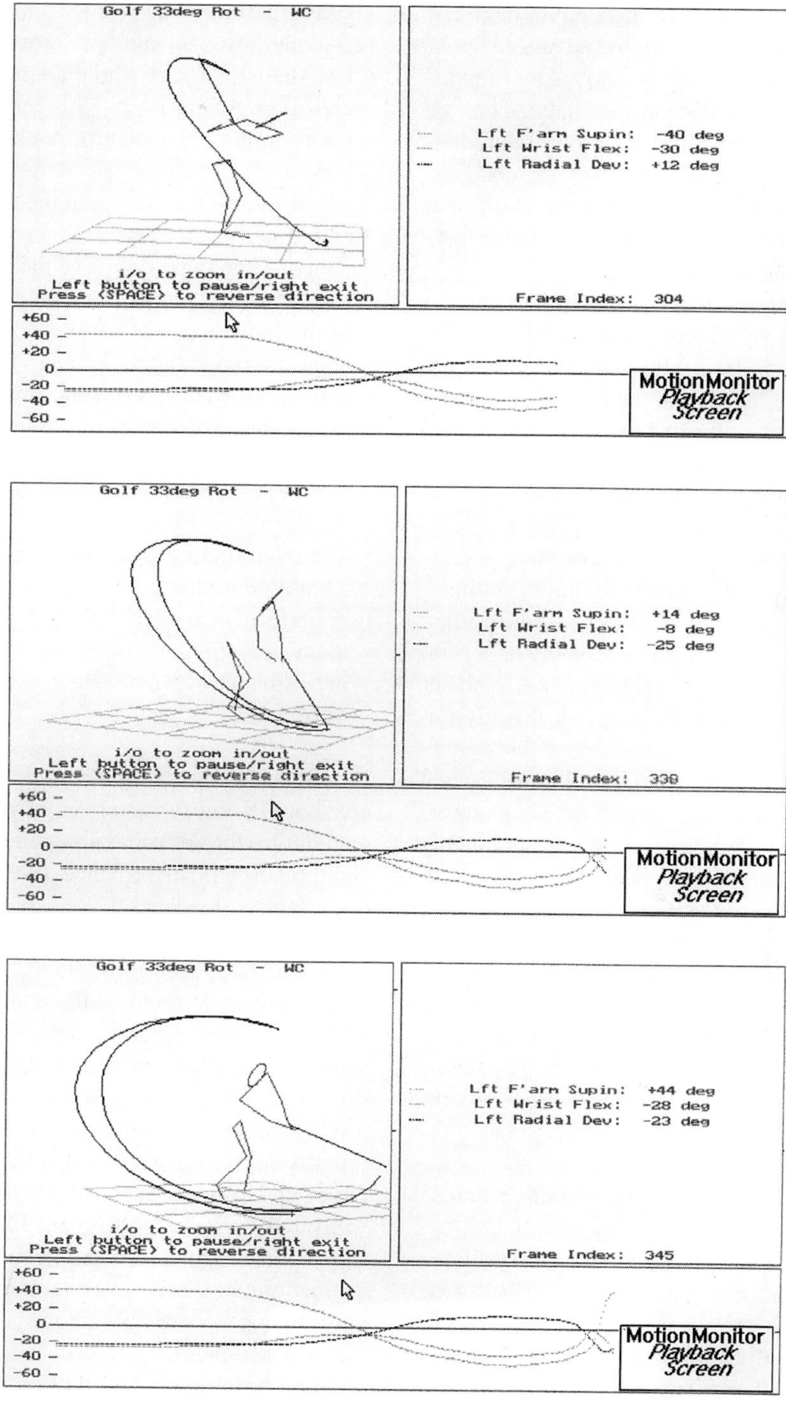

Figure 6-2 Printout of the Swing Trainer playback screen, showing three forearm and wrist angles for monitoring.

not have access to sophisticated equipment nor have the background to employ advanced techniques a method to effectively analyze an individual's movements. Biomechanical analysis can be used by athletic trainers in designing a rehabilitation program, by physical educators for conducting an evaluation of fundamental motor skills, and by exercise leaders in ensuring that clients perform each exercise correctly.

Teachers and coaches can use biomechanical analysis to improve students' and athletes' performance of sport skills. Additionally, teachers and coaches are often faced with the task of evaluating several performers of diverse skill levels in a short period of time. The use of videotape and slow-motion/stop-action playback can be useful to the practitioner in assessing an individual's performance. Videotape equipment has become increasingly available in school and community settings.

If videotape equipment is not available, then the professional must rely directly on his or her observations of the individual's performance. Whether the professional is using videotape or directly observing the individual's performance, the professional should keep in mind relevant biomechanical principles, have a mental image of the ideal performance of the skill being observed, and thoroughly understand the nature of the skill being performed. As an observer, the professional should be objective and proceed in a systematic fashion.

Adrian and Cooper[10] and Brown[11] offer several suggestions to physical education, exercise science, and sport professionals using visual evaluation techniques to assess skill performance. These suggestions, which can be incorporated into the practitioner's observation plan, are listed below:

- Observe the skill from a correct vantage point. Being in the correct position is essential to observe the critical components of the skill. When possible, view the skill from at least two perspectives.
- Observe the individual perform the skill several times before offering suggestions for improvement. This will permit the identification of consistent performance problems that may not be evident during a single performance attempt.
- Use the whole-part-whole method for the observation. After observing the total movement, focus on the movement of the body parts (e.g., legs, trunk). Observe the sequencing and timing of these parts. Observe the range of motion and look for unnecessary or extraneous movements. Then, again observe the whole body and focus on the coordination and sequencing of the movements of various body parts with respect to each other.
- If the performer is using an implement such as a racquet, or imparting force to another object such as throwing a discus or kicking a ball, it is also important to focus on the action of the implement.
- The overall effectiveness of the movement should be evaluated.
- A performance checklist can be used to guide the observation and to ensure that critical performance elements are viewed and not overlooked.

Once the observation is completed, practitioners should identify the errors in performance and give the performer accurate and relevant feedback about his or her performance. (See Chapter 5 for a discussion of feedback.)

Knudson suggests that professionals use a comprehensive approach when performing qualitative analysis of motor skills in order to intervene to improve performance.[12] Rather than focusing solely on error detection and provision of corrections, or limiting themselves to biomechanical factors, professionals should take a more holistic and interdisciplinary approach, using many of the exercise and sport sciences as they design an intervention to improve performance. Knudson's four-step approach includes preparation, observation, evaluation/diagnosis, and intervention.[11] Accuracy and consistency are important in conducting qualitative assessment.

During preparation, physical education, exercise science, and sport professionals must gather

At the US Olympic Training Center in Colorado Springs, biomechanists work with elite athletes to refine their skills and optimize their performance.

information about the movement to be analyzed and about the performer. What are the critical features of the movement? What are the abilities of the performer? Knudson encourages professionals to strive to increase their knowledge of human movement by being a "student" of movement, studying movements and factors that influence the performance.[12]

Analysis of the kinematics of movement must be combined with observational experiences to accurately perceive critical features of movement. It is important to correctly select the critical features of the movement that are necessary for optimal performance. These critical features determine whether a movement is safe, efficient, and effective. Knowledge of biomechanics helps professionals determine which are the critical features of a skill.

Professionals benefit from a systematic approach to observation. The traditional approach emphasizes observing critical features based on the temporal phases of a skill—preparation, action, follow-through.[11] Other professionals prefer a more holistic approach, watching several trials of a skill in order to form an overall impression of performance and then focusing on critical features.[11]

Accurate diagnosis requires determining the underlying strengths and weaknesses of the performance. Here the movement is analyzed relative to the predefined critical features.

In the intervention phase, the professional focuses the performer's attention on one critical feature of the movement, rather than overwhelming the performer with multiple corrections. Knudson suggests that the professional identify the intervention that would create the most improvement in performance and one that is the least difficult for the performer to implement.[11] Interventions are more likely to be successful when the diagnosis is accurate.

Consistency is another important aspect of qualitative analysis. According to Knudson, multiple observations of the performer improve the consistency and reliability of the analysis.[11] Consistency is further enhanced when the critical features have been precisely and clearly defined. Lastly, a simple approach to classifying critical features can improve consistency.

Physical education, exercise science, and sport professionals use qualitative analysis in many different ways to help participants in their programs move safely, efficiently, and effectively. Developing skills in qualitative analysis requires an understanding of biomechanical principles and the ability to accurately and consistently observe, assess, and prescribe strategies to improve the performer's movement, whether the movement is a sport skill, a specific exercise, or a task of daily living.

The Future

Technology will continue to drive the advancement of knowledge. Adrian and Cooper state, "With today's sophisticated technology, we have been able to learn more about human movement in the past ten years than in any previous decade."[9] To answer the questions of the next decade, Adrian and Cooper assert that "we must use basic concepts about what is known to pose the questions of the future and create more effective, safe, and rewarding human movement."[10]

Adrian and Cooper state that mathematical modeling of the anatomical characteristics of individuals coupled with computer simulation techniques enables biomechanists to make predictions of performance as well as to develop new and advanced performance techniques.[10] Expertise in mathematics, anatomy, physiology, physics, and computers is necessary to take advantage of these approaches. Data collected via the tools of cinematography, videography, dynamography, electrogoniometry, electromyography, and accelerometry form the foundation for modeling and are entered into the computer where the data are analyzed using various software packages. Simulations allow movements to be varied with respect to speed, timing, range of motion, and environment. Through simulations these changes in movement variables can be explored and determinations can be made about the optimization of performance and its safety. Computer-assisted drawing and design programs can expedite the design of equipment.

Advances in the analysis of human movement continue to be made at a rapid pace. The increased availability of technology at a decreased cost will make sophisticated analyses readily available to teachers, coaches, athletic trainers, athletes, fitness participants, and practitioners. The use of multidisciplinary teams, composed of sport scientists from the various subdisciplines, will facilitate the integration of data from multiple sources, enhancing our comprehension and enabling physical education and sport professionals to work more effectively with students, athletes, and individuals of all ages seeking to move more efficiently and effectively. The integration of biomechanics with motor development can increase our understanding of movement across the lifespan and enable us to more readily design solutions to remediate problems and safely advance the motor performance of people of all ages and abilities.

Expert profiling and simulations advance the frontier of knowledge and lead to improvements in performance. The United States Olympic Committee Sports Science and Technology Committee has funded several projects, including simulations of bobsled runs and modeling and simulation of paddles and oar blades for rowing and canoeing.

Worldwide databases make data available to interested researchers throughout the world. These databases allow for diagnosis of movement problems, profiling, and collaborative research ventures.

The World Wide Web offers a wealth of information to individuals interested in biomechanics. For example, one site—*Biomechanics World Wide* (see Get Connected box)—offers links to profiles of different biomechanists, laboratories worldwide, and even a place to trade or sell equipment. Specialized areas of study are represented, including gait and locomotion, sport and exercise biomechanics, muscle, motor control, computer simulations, ergonomics, orthopedics, prosthetics, and biomedical engineering. Also included on the site is information on biomechanics societies, career opportunities, and professional journals. This site and other related sites offer access to current information and a venue to share ideas and stimulate collaborative endeavors.

Focus on Career: Biomechanics

PROFESSIONAL ORGANIZATIONS	• International Society of Biomechanics www.isbweb.org • International Society for Biomechanics in Sport www.umist.ac.uk/UMIST_Sport//ishpes.html • Biomechanics Academy www.aahperd.org → NASPE → Academics • American Society of Biomechanics http://asb-biomech.org • International Sports Engineering Association www.sports-engineering.co.uk
PROFESSIONAL JOURNALS	• *Journal of Applied Biomechanics* • *Journal of Biomechanics* • *Research Quarterly for Exercise and Sport* • *Sports Biomechanics* • *Sports Engineering*

As we move into the twenty-first century, another exciting trend is the shift in the population that biomechanists study and with whom they work.[2] Wilkerson suggests that in the future we will see a great emphasis on research on women and the elderly, two populations that were not studied in the past.[2] Additionally, there wil be a shift toward studying people with a wider range of abilities and in a greater array of settings; our research will expand from a focus on the elite athlete to a broader focus on people participating not only in sports, but carrying out their tasks of daily living.

SUMMARY

Understanding the factors that govern human movement is essential for physical education, exercise science, and sport professionals. Physical education, exercise science, and sport professionals are concerned with helping individuals optimize their movements. To accomplish this task, they need to thoroughly understand the mechanical principles that regulate movement. The analysis of human movement and sport object movement using the principles of physics and mechanics is called biomechanics. In recent years the study of biomechanics has grown tremendously in the United States and is commonly recognized as a subdiscipline of physical education, exercise science, and sport.

Biomechanics is concerned with two major areas of study. The first area focuses on the anatomical aspects of movements while the second area concerns itself with the mechanical aspects of movement. Needless to say, these areas are closely related. Biomechanists have a specialized scientific vocabulary to describe their area of study. The terms *power, acceleration, velocity, mass, pressure, friction, work, energy, angular velocity* and *acceleration, torque,* and *gravity* are defined in this chapter. Selected biomechanical principles and concepts pertaining to stability, motion, leverage, and force are explained and illustrated.

Within the last 15 years, improvements in instrumentation and its application have been numerous, which has greatly expanded the knowledge base. Although the practitioner may not have access to much of the specialized equipment used by the biomechanist researcher, the practitioner can use available equipment such as videotape equipment or direct observation to analyze performance. Understanding the principles of biomechanics is essential in improving individuals' performance.

SELF-ASSESSMENT TESTS

These tests are designed to help you determine if you have mastered the materials and competencies presented in this chapter.

1. Write a short essay of 250 words on the worth of biomechanical knowledge to the practitioner in physical education, exercise science, and sport. Write the essay from the perspective of a practitioner in a career that you are considering for the future: that is, teacher, coach, athletic trainer, exercise physiologist, or sports broadcaster.
2. Explain and illustrate the meaning of each of the following terms: power, acceleration, velocity, mass, pressure, friction, work, energy, torque, and center of gravity.
3. Using a sport with which you are familiar, illustrate principles and concepts relating to stability, motion, leverage, and force.
4. Using the information provided in the Get Connected box, access *Biomechanics Magazine.* Select an article of interest and write a short summary of the article and its application to your future career.
5. Using the information provided in the Get Connected box, access *Exploratory Activities in Health Sciences.* Find one activity that is of interest to you and write a short description of that activity to present to the class.
6. Using the information provided in the Get Connected box, access *Sport and Science—Winter Olympics.* Read the section on Physics and Biomechanics. What other sports use these principles? Write a short report on a sport you have selected showing how biomechanics influence sport performance.

REFERENCES

1. Hamilton N and Luttgens K: Kinesiology, ed 10, New York, 2002, McGraw-Hill.
2. Wilkerson JD: Biomechanics. In JD Massengale and RA Swanson, editors: The history of exercise and sport science. Champaign, Ill., 1997, Human Kinetics.
3. Atwater AE: Kinesiology/biomechanics: perspectives and trends, Research Quarterly for Exercise and Sport 51:193–218, 1980.
4. Biomechanics Academy. National Association for Sport and Physical Education, AAHPERD: Guidelines and standards for undergraduate biomechanics/kinesiology, Reston, Va., 1992, AAHPERD.
5. Counsilman JE: The science of swimming, Englewood Cliffs, N.J., 1968, Prentice Hall.
6. Brown RM and Counsilman JE: The role of lift in propelling swimmers. In J Cooper, editor: Biomechanics, Chicago, 1971, The Athletic Institute.
7. Boyle A: The high-tech race for the Olympic gold. Available online at www.msnbc.com/news/693675 (retrieved 11/09/04).
8. Aerodynamics, fluid dynamics, and friction. Available on line at www.athleteproject.com/sportsbiomechafd.htm (retrieved 11/9/04).
9. Northrip JW, Logan GA, and McKinney W: Introduction to biomechanical analysis of sport, ed 2, Dubuque, Iowa, 1979, William C. Brown.
10. Adrian MJ and Cooper JM: The biomechanics of human movement, Dubuque, Iowa, 1987, Benchmark Press.
11. Brown EW: Visual evaluation techniques for skill analysis, Journal of Physical Education, Recreation, and Dance 53(1):21–26, 1982.
12. Knudson D: What can professionals qualitatively analyze? JOPERD 71(2):19–23, 2000.

SUGGESTED READINGS

Abendroth-Smith J and Kras J: More B-BOAT: the Volleyball Spike, JOPERD, 70(3):56–59, 1999.

Written for practitioners, practical strategies for biomechanical analysis of the volleyball spike are presented.

Adrian M and Cooper J: Biomechanics of human movement, ed 2, Dubuque, Iowa, 1997, Brown & Benchmark.

Basic biomechanical principles are explained, tools for movement analysis presented, and application of principles to development across the lifespan, exercise, sport, rehabilitation, occupational settings, and the arts described.

Bladin C, McCrory P, and Pogorzelski A: Snowboarding injuries: current trends and future directions, Sports Medicine, 34:133–139, 2004.

Analyzes snowboarding injuries and offers injury-prevention strategies to enhance snowboarders' safety. Suggests that the next decade will see further advances in understanding of the biomechanical factors involved in snowboarding injuries.

Carr G: Mechanics of sports: a practitioner's guide, Champaign, Ill., 1997, Human Kinetics.

A practical approach to the analysis of mechanical concepts underlying sport performance is presented. This text provides the reader with information to guide the observation, analysis, and correction of sport techniques.

Greenwald RM, Penna LH, and Crisco JJ: Differences in batted ball speed with wood and aluminum baseball bats: A batting cage study, Journal of Applied Biomechanics, 17:241–252, 2001.

This article illustrates how biomechanics can be used to investigate various questions in sports, including the differences in ball speed associated with different bats.

Hall SJ: Basic biomechanics, ed 4, McGraw-Hill, 2001, New York.

Offers an introduction to biomechanics, including both quantitative and qualitative examples of different biomechanical principles.

Hamilton N and Luttgens K: Kinesiology: scientific basis of human motion, McGraw-Hill, 2002, New York.

Introduces basics of anatomy, physiology, and applications of kinesiology, including biomechanical concepts.

Reeve J, editor: Qualitative analysis: putting it all together, Feature, JOPERD 71(1), 2000.

A series of 5 articles on the use of qualitative analysis appearing in 2 issues of JOPERD. These are listed below:

- Reeve J: Introduction, JOPERD 71(1):16–17, 2000.
- Pinheiro VED: Qualitative analysis for the elementary grades, JOPERD 71(1):18–21, 25, 2000.
- Morrison CS: Why don't you analyze the way I analyze?, JOPERD 71(1):22–25, 2000.
- Wilkinson S: Transfer of qualitative skill analysis ability to similar sport-specific skills, JOPERD 71(2):16–18, 23, 2000.
- Knudson D: What can professionals qualitatively analyze? JOPERD 71(2):19–23, 2000.

Salo A and Bezodis I: Which starting style is faster in sprint running—standing or crouch start? Sport Biomechanics, 3:43–55, 2004.

The study examined the differences between two starting methods in spring running to ascertain whether one of the methods provided better acceleration and was faster.

Scientific American—September 2000 Issue—The Elite Athletes.

Articles include information on biomechanics and the development of the running shoe, drug use in sports, and the impact of technology on sport. (www.sciam.com)

Strohmeyer HS: Biomechanical concepts for the physical educator, JOPERD, 75(7): 17–22, 2004.

Provides information about concepts and principles of biomechanics presented in an easy-to-understand format. Topics include tension, gravity, equilibrium, force absorption, and friction; and examples show how physical educators can integrate these concepts into their teaching.

Tsang WWN and Hui-Chan CWY: Effect of 4- and 8-wk intensive Tai Chi training on balance control in the elderly, Medicine and Science in Sport and Exercise, 36:648–657, 2004.

An intensive program of Tai Chi, even as short as 4 weeks in duration, was found to improve balance in older adults.

CHAPTER 7

EXERCISE PHYSIOLOGY AND FITNESS

OBJECTIVES

After reading this chapter the student should be able to—

- Define exercise physiology and understand the importance of exercise physiology to the practitioner.
- Understand concepts of health- and performance-related fitness.
- Understand and appreciate the role of physical activity in health.
- Explain the principles and guidelines for designing fitness programs.
- Use the FITT formula to design a fitness program.
- Describe other factors related to fitness and performance.

Exercise physiology is the study of the body's responses and its adaptation to the stress of exercise. Exercise physiologists are concerned with investigating both the immediate (acute) and the long-term (chronic) effects of exercise on all aspects of body functioning. These effects include the responses of the muscular system, the action of the nervous system during physical activity, the adjustments of the respiratory system, and the dynamics of the cardiovascular system. Improving the body's response to exercise also is an important area of study. The effects of exercise are examined at different levels, ranging from the subcellular level to the systemic level. Describing and explaining the myriad of functional changes caused by exercise sessions of variable frequency, duration, and intensity is one major area of study for exercise physiologists.

The field of exercise physiology offers professionals a strong foundation of knowledge about the effects of exercise on the body. Professionals, whether teachers in a school or nonschool setting, coaches, fitness leaders employed in a commercial club, or exercise physiologists working in a corporate fitness setting or a hospital, must understand the body's responses to exercise. Knowledge of the principles governing different types of training programs and the guidelines to be followed in constructing an exercise prescription enables professionals to design programs to meet each individual's physical activity needs and goals.

GET CONNECTED

American College of Sports Medicine offers access to position papers and their free newsletter *Fit Society Page;* also information about certification and upcoming conferences.

www.acsm.org/newsletters.htm

The Athlete Project serves as a resource for those interested in sport and exercise sciences. Comprehensive information is provided on several topics, including exercise physiology, sport biomechanics, ergonomics, and coaching.

www.athleteproject.com

President's Council on Physical Fitness and Sport offers the latest research via their Research Digests, access to all publications via their Reading Room, and resources for physical education, exercise science, and sport professionals.

www.fitness.gov

Gatorade Sports Science Institute gives you the opportunity to see sports science in action as well as access to "hot" topics papers and Ask the Expert.

www.gssiweb.com

Exercise physiology has become increasingly sophisticated. New research procedures and measurement techniques coupled with advances in equipment, computer technology, and other related disciplines such as biochemistry have contributed to rapid expansion of the knowledge base. While fitness and the elite performer long have been a key concern of the exercise physiologist, interest in recent years has encompassed virtually all aspects of human performance and people of all skill abilities and of all ages, from the very young to the elderly, including individuals with disabilities.

EXERCISE PHYSIOLOGY: AN OVERVIEW

Exercise physiology is one of the most rapidly growing areas of specialization within the fields of physical education, exercise science, and sport. The definition, historical development, and areas of study and scope are discussed in this section.

Definition

Exercise physiology is the study of the effects of exercise on the body. Specifically, exercise physiology is concerned with the body's responses and adaptations to exercise, ranging from the system level to the subcellular level. These modifications can be short term—that is, lasting only for the duration of the activity—or long term—present as long as the activity is continued on a regular basis. Knowledge of exercise physiology is essential for professionals in physical education, exercise science, and sport.

As a subdiscipline, exercise physiology is one of the largest and most popular areas of study within the realm of physical education, exercise science, and sport. It has one of the richest traditions; interest in the effects of exercise on the body can be traced to ancient times. Today the depth and breadth of knowledge in exercise physiology is growing rapidly because of the proliferation of research, which is facilitated by increasingly sophisticated technology and by the widespread interest of professionals in this field.

Historical Development

Exercise physiology emerged as a specialized area of study in the mid-1960s and 1970s. Exercise physiology traces its roots to the mid- to late 1800s and early 1900s. Then, as now, the discipline of physiology influences the ongoing work in exercise physiology.

According to Buskirk, Edward Hitchcock, Dudley Sargent, Thomas D. Wood, Robert Tait McKenzie, and George Fitz were instrumental in laying the early foundations of exercise physiology and promoting the scientific basis of physical education.[1] While at Amherst College in the 1860s, Edward Hitchcock used anthropometric techniques to measure changes in his students' development after they participated in his physical training program. At Harvard University, in 1879, Dudley Sargent used anthropometry in his physical education classes to investigate the effects of exercise on the body. In the 1890s, Thomas D. Wood helped promote the scientific basis of physical education. During his tenure at Stanford University, Wood developed a four-year degree program leading to an undergraduate degree in physical training and hygiene. Students took courses in anatomy and physiology and physiology of exercise as part of their degree program.

Physiologist Dr. George Fitz established the first formal exercise physiology laboratory at Harvard University in 1892. At a time in physical education's history when the merits of the various systems were being debated, Fitz advocated using a scientific approach to evaluate each system, so that the actual benefits of each system could be determined. Fitz conducted research in his lab, taught exercise physiology in the Department of Anatomy, Physiology, and Physical Training as part of its four-year Bachelor of Science degree program, authored numerous research studies, and published *Principles of Physiology and Hygiene* in 1908. Noted physician, physical educator, and sculptor R. Tait McKenzie advocated investigating the effects of exercise on various systems of the body and helped promote the idea of preventive medicine.[1] In 1910, he published *Exercise in Education and Medicine.*

During the early 1900s, James McCurdy played an instrumental role in developing physiologic research at Springfield College.[1] In 1924, McCurdy published the first edition of his textbook *Physiology of Exercise.* Peter Karpovich continued McCurdy's work at Springfield College, expanding the exercise physiology laboratory and opening up new avenues of study.[1] In 1923, Arthur Steinhaus established an exercise physiology laboratory at Williams College in Chicago, where he and his students conducted research on a diversity of topics related to physiology, exercise, and muscular activity.[1] One of his most widely recognized papers is his work entitled "Chronic Effects of Exercise," written in 1933.

One of the seminal events in the growth of exercise physiology was the founding of the Harvard Fatigue Laboratory in 1927. Lawrence J. Henderson and G. E. Mayo established the lab, and David Bruce Dill served as its director until the lab's closing in 1946. The lab attracted many notable researchers who conducted groundbreaking research on exercise and environmental physiology. During the lab's existence its researchers published over 50 papers on the effects of exercise and environmental conditions on humans.[1] Many of these researchers established research laboratories throughout the country, for which the Fatigue Lab served as a model.

Following World War II, more colleges and universities began to establish programs. For example, in 1948, Thomas K. Cureton established the Physical Fitness Research Laboratory at the University of Illinois, which focused on investigating the physiological foundations of fitness.[2] Fitness tests of the nation's youths and results from the physicals of men called for military service increased society's interest in fitness.

In the mid-1960s and the early 1970s, the growth of exercise physiology as a specialized area of study was stimulated by university and physical education leaders' calls for more stringent teacher training and a greater emphasis on scholarship and academic rigor in graduate programs in physical education. Graduate programs in physical education were strengthened, and curriculums modified so that more specialized training could occur in a myriad of areas, including exercise physiology. Ultimately, undergraduate areas of specialization evolved, and undergraduate majors were developed within this expanding area of study. Among the majors that developed were exercise science, adult fitness, and cardiac rehabilitation. Eventually, separate departments were established, with the mission of preparing students to be exercise scientists, including exercise physiologists.

During the 1970s, the American Physiological Society (APS) accorded greater recognition to the rapidly expanding field of exercise physiology. Exercise physiology was officially included as part of one of the APS's speciality sections. Additionally, the APS changed the title of its journal to include exercise physiology. Thus, the *Journal of Applied Physiology* was renamed the *Journal of Applied Physiology: Respiratory, Environmental and Exercise Physiology;* in the mid-1980s, the title was changed back to the *Journal of Applied Physiology.* As Tipton explains, "The collective significance of these events was that exercise physiology had finally achieved official recognition as a legitimate specialty area in physiology by the American Physiological Society. This fact not only provided academic credence to the exercise physiologist, but it also enhanced the acceptance of exercise physiology as a major discipline within the profession of exercise science."[2]

The 1980s and 1990s marked an era where there was greater understanding of the significant relationship between physical activity and health. In 1996, the first Surgeon General's Report on *Physical Activity and Health*[3] was released. National health reports, such as *Healthy People 2010,*[4] secured greater public recognition of the role of physical activity and well-being.

As research in the realm of exercise physiology continued to grow, more scholarly journals and professional organizations were established to serve as outlets for the dissemination of scientific work. Some of the early researchers' works were published in the *American Journal of Physiology,* which issued its first volume in 1898. In 1948, the American Physiological Society established the *Journal of Applied Physiology,* which published research on the responses by humans to a variety of stressors, including exercise.[2] The *Research Quarterly,* which began publication in 1930, and, subsequently, became the *Research Quarterly for Exercise and Sport,* served as an outlet for researchers' work. Researchers also presented papers and conducted workshops at meetings of AAHPERD.

In 1954, physicians, physiologists, and physical educators came together to establish the American College of Sports Medicine (ACSM). In 1969, *Medicine and Science in Sports* began its publication, and in 1980, this periodical was renamed *Medicine and Science in Sports and Exercise.* In 1974, ACSM published its first edition of *Guidelines for Graded Exercise Testing and Prescription* and in 1975, conducted the first certification exams in exercise leadership and cardiac rehabilitation. In 1997, ACSM published its first issue of *Health and Fitness Journal.* More recently, ACSM developed a clinical exercise physiology registry and in 2000 offered its first certification exam for *Clinical Exercise Physiologists.*

As exercise physiology grew, other journals were founded and offered additional outlets for scholars to share their research; these include *Physician and Sports Medicine, Exercise and Sport Science Reviews, American Journal of Sports Medicine,* and *International Journal of Sports Medicine.*

Scope and Status

Exercise physiology encompasses a broad range of topics. Examples of some areas of study are listed below:

- Effects of various exercise programs on the systems of the body, including circulatory, respiratory, nervous, skeletal, muscle, and endocrine systems.
- Relationship of energy metabolism to performance.
- Effectiveness of various training programs in promoting gains in specific components of fitness (e.g., effects of Nautilus training on strength).
- Effects of various environmental factors such as temperature, humidity, altitude, pollutants, and different environments (e.g., space or

undersea) on physiological responses to exercise and performance.

- Effects of individual differences such as age, sex, initial level of fitness, or disability on fitness development and performance.
- Identification of factors that limit performance.
- Effectiveness of various rehabilitation programs on the recovery of injured athletes, on diseased individuals, and on individuals with disabilities.
- Effects of ergogenic aids such as drugs or music on performance.
- Health and therapeutic benefits to be accrued from engaging in appropriate levels of physical activity.
- Effects of nutrition on performance.

Exercise physiologists can work in many different settings. They can be involved in conducting research in a laboratory setting, teaching exercise science courses at a college or university, or engaged in a variety of clinical activities, such as guiding an elite athlete through a graded exercise test on a treadmill, directing a cardiac rehabilitation program at a hospital, or administering a worksite health promotion program.

Historically, performance and fitness are the two areas of research that have dominated exercise physiology. Much attention has been directed by researchers to the area of cardiovascular exercise physiology, which examines how oxygen is used by the cardiovascular system during exercise. Researchers have also focused a great deal of effort on the study of exercise metabolism, investigating the metabolic responses to exercise and training conducted under a variety of conditions.

In recent years, cardiac rehabilitation and exercise biochemistry are two areas that have become increasingly popular as major fields of study. *Cardiac rehabilitation* focuses on the assessment of cardiovascular functioning and on the determination of the effectiveness of various exercise programs in preventing cardiovascular disease and rehabilitating individuals suffering from the disease. *Exercise biochemistry* involves examination of the effects of exercise at the cellular level, specifically within the muscle cell. Two emerging areas of study within exercise physiology are exercise epidemiology and pediatric exercise science. *Exercise epidemiology* focuses on studying the relationship between physical activity and mortality. The increasing public health role for professionals in physical education, exercise science, and sport requires that we have a greater understanding of the relationship between physical activity, morbidity, and mortality. *Pediatric exercise* science encompasses the scientific study of the response of the body to exercise during childhood, including the effects of growth and maturation and differences in response between children and adults.

The application of knowledge from the realm of exercise physiology appears to focus predominantly on studying the effects of physical activity and exercise on the body. Two primary areas of application can be discerned: first, the enhancement of fitness, promotion of health, and prevention of disease; and second, the improvement and refinement of motor performance, especially in sport. The principles of exercise physiology can be used to improve and maintain both health-related fitness and motor skill-related fitness. As in the other subdisciplines of physical education, exercise science, and sport, there is a growing emphasis on research and application across the lifespan, from the very young to the aged.

Knowledge of and skills associated with exercise physiology are used in many different ways by professionals in physical education, exercise science, and sport. Physical education teachers help children set and attain fitness goals, both in physical education class and through participation in physical activity outside the school. Coaches typically use training guidelines to help their athletes achieve the high levels of fitness essential for performance in specific sports. Cardiac rehabilitation specialists work in hospitals, clinics, work sites, or community settings, enhancing the fitness of post-heart attack patients, performing fitness evaluations, and leading preventive programs. Fitness professionals in private clubs, community programs, and corporate settings design, conduct, and evaluate fitness programs for people of all ages. Strength-training specialists work with professional and intercollegiate athletes and in rehabilitation. Athletic trainers develop preventive programs and rehabilitation programs for injured athletes.

The current tremendous interest in health, fitness, and physical activity by the public and the expansion of the knowledge base of this field also have enhanced professional opportunities. An increasing number of young people are undertaking undergraduate and graduate study in exercise physiology and preparing to pursue careers in adult fitness, cardiac rehabilitation, and strength development. (Career opportunities in these areas are discussed in Chapter 12.)

Exercise physiology is an exceptionally broad area of study, with a long, rich history. Exercise physiology incorporates knowledge from many scientific disciplines, such as biology, chemistry, physiology, and anatomy. Additionally, given the depth and breadth of the discipline, it is difficult within the limitations of this chapter to provide a worthy introduction to the area. Therefore, it was decided to focus on one area of exercise physiology—fitness—and approach it from an applied perspective. It is hoped that this approach would allow students enrolled in this introductory course to gain insight into the field of exercise physiology and be able to relate the information they are learning to their own experiences with exercise, fitness, and performance. As students continue their undergraduate preparation, they will have the opportunity to study exercise physiology more extensively.

Physical Fitness

Physical fitness is one area of study within exercise physiology. *Physical fitness* is the ability of the body's systems to function efficiently and effectively. Individuals who are physically fit have the ability to "carry out daily tasks with vigor and alertness, without undue fatigue, and with ample energy to enjoy leisure-time pursuits and to meet unforeseen emergencies."[5]

Contemporary professionals commonly view physical fitness as a quality comprising 11 different components, each with specific requirements for its development and maintenance. Fitness components typically are classified into two categories: those pertaining to health and those pertaining to motor-skill performance.[5] The Definitions of Physical Fitness Components box identifies and defines the health and skill-performance components.

Health fitness is important for all individuals throughout their lifespan. The achievement and maintenance of those qualities necessary for an individual to function efficiently and to enhance his or her health through the prevention and remediation of disease are the central focus of health fitness. An increasing body of research supports the contribution of regular, appropriate physical activity to health and quality of life.

Performance-related or *skill-related physical fitness* emphasizes the development of those qualities that enhance the performance of physical activities such as sport. Whereas health fitness is concerned with living better, performance-related fitness is concerned with performing sport-related skills better and more efficiently. Moreover, performance-related fitness is specific to the sport or activity in which the individual engages. Different degrees of performance-related fitness components are needed, depending on the specific motor activity. For example, the degree of power, agility, and speed needed by a football player is different from that required by a tennis player, though both individuals need these qualities to perform at an optimal level.

Fitness, be it health-related or performance-related, must be viewed in relation to an individual's characteristics (e.g., age, health status, occupation, preferences), needs, goals, and the tasks that must be performed. All individuals possess certain levels of each of the health- and performance-related fitness components. The extent to which each quality is developed depends on the individual. A weekend tennis player needs a different level of physical fitness than a competitive wheelchair marathoner; a 70-year-old grandparent requires a different level of fitness than the 10-year-old grandchild. Professionals charged with the responsibility of designing and conducting fitness programs should ask the program participants, "Fitness for what?" Does the participant desire physical fitness that will contribute to general

Definitions of Physical Fitness Components

Fitness Component	Definition
Health-Related Fitness Components	
Body composition	Amount of body fat relative to fat-free content expressed as a percentage
Cardiorespiratory endurance	Maximum functional capacity of the cardiorespiratory system to sustain work or physical activity involving large muscle groups over an extended period
Flexibility	Range of movement possible at a joint or joints
Muscular endurance	Ability of a muscle or muscle group to repeat muscular contractions against a force or to sustain a contraction over time
Muscular strength	Maximum amount of force that can be exerted by a muscle or muscle group against a resistance during a single contraction
Skill-Related Fitness Components	
Agility	Ability to change direction rapidly with control
Balance	Ability to maintain equilibrium while stationary or moving
Coordination	Ability to execute movements smoothly and efficiently
Power	Ability to produce force at a fast speed; a combination of strength and speed usually applied during a short period
Reaction time	Time elapsed between the administration of a stimulus and the body's response to the stimulus
Speed	Ability to move the body quickly

health or to outstanding performance in a particular sport? All people should seek to achieve and maintain an optimal level of physical fitness with respect to their individual needs.

Proper development and maintenance of physical fitness require the application of knowledge from the realm of exercise physiology. Because exercise physiology is concerned with both the body's immediate and long-term responses to exercise, the development and conduct of fitness programs to meet an individual's specific fitness needs should be guided by knowledge from this field. Elite athletes preparing for competition, healthy adults wanting to work out on a regular basis, patients recovering from heart disease, youth sport athletes training for competition, injured participants rehabilitating from injury, elderly citizens aspiring to live independent lives, and individuals with disabilities who are striving to meet the challenges of life can all benefit from participation in a well-designed physical fitness program based on the principles of exercise physiology.

Physical Activity, Physical Fitness, and Health

Research on the effects of physical activity and fitness on the health status of the individual is a major area of research in exercise physiology today. A major threat to the health and well-being of Americans is chronic diseases, many of which can be categorized as hypokinetic diseases. *Hypoki-*

netic diseases are caused by insufficient physical activity, often in conjunction with inappropriate dietary practices. Coronary heart disease, hypertension, osteoporosis, noninsulin-dependent diabetes, chronic back pain, and obesity are examples of hypokinetic diseases.

Health Risk Factors

Researchers have identified risk factors that contribute to chronic disease, such as heart disease and cancer—the major causes of death in the United States today. The causes of these diseases are a complex interaction of biological, environmental, and behavioral factors. Inherited and biological factors, such as gender, race, age, and inherited susceptibility to disease, can not be changed. However, other risk factors associated with the environment and behavior may be amenable to change, reducing the individual's risk for disease. These controllable risk factors can be organized into environmental and behavioral factors.

Environmental risk factors, including physical factors, such as air quality, and socioeconomic factors, such as poverty, are associated with poor health outcomes. While they can be changed, people may face obstacles in doing so. It is difficult to move above the poverty line, especially in troubled economic times. However, there are other factors that people can address. People can take an active role in their community to bring about change. They can speak out for clean air and support community-based health initiatives, such as low-cost serum cholesterol screenings. They can reduce their interactions with environments that are unhealthy, such as avoiding places where they would be exposed to second-hand smoke.

Behavioral factors, such as smoking, inactivity, and poor nutrition, reflect individual behavior choices. These factors can be changed by individuals taking personal responsibility for their health and reducing the presence of chronic disease factors in their lifestyle. Taking responsibility for eating healthy, incorporating physical activity into one's lifestyle, and using alcohol in moderation are steps individuals can take to reduce their risk factors and enhance their overall level of health.

Physical inactivity has been identified as a risk factor for several diseases. Individuals who lead a sedentary—that is, physically inactive life—have increased risk of morbidity and mortality from a number of chronic diseases.[3,4,6] One striking example is the relationship between physical activity and coronary heart disease, the leading cause of death in the United States. Individuals who are inactive have almost twice the risk of coronary heart disease as those who are active.[3,4] The degree of risk is similar to those better known risk factors of cigarette smoking, hypertension, and obesity.

Dose-Response Debate

There has been an ongoing debate about the amount of physical activity necessary to achieve health benefits. This *dose-response debate* has centered on questions such as these: "What kind of activity should be performed? For how long, at what intensity, and how often should physical activity be performed to realize health benefits?" Appropriate, sustained vigorous exercise promotes health fitness and leads to the achievement of desirable health outcomes, reduction in risk for disease, and increased longevity.[3,4] The 1996 document *Physical Activity and Health: A Report of the Surgeon General* showcased the growing body of scientific evidence that regularly engaging in moderate physical activity, below the threshold to promote physical fitness, can also lead to substantial health gains. Individuals who engage in moderate-intensity exercise (e.g., walking, taking the stairs) for at least 30 minutes a day for most, or preferably all days of the week, can improve their health and decrease their risk for disease.[3,4] Additional health benefits can be derived from increasing the time engaged in moderate-intensity physical activity or by participating in more vigorous physical activity associated with health fitness. Even very sedentary individuals who begin an appropriate physical activity program in middle age can achieve health benefits. It is never too late to be active!

In 2000, an international symposium convened to address issues pertaining to the dose-response relationship between physical activity and health. Participants in this symposium engaged in a comprehensive review of the evidence on 24 critical topics related to physical activity and health. The evidence was summarized in a Consensus Statement, which addressed the contribution of physical activity to health, the dose-response relationship between physical activity and health, and research recommendations.

The Consensus Statement reported that "there is an inverse and generally linear relationship for rates of all-cause mortality, total CVD (Cardiovascular Disease), and coronary heart disease incidence and mortality and for the incidence of type 2 diabetes."[6] As physical activity increased, disease risk decreased. According to Lee and Skerrett, minimal adherence to the current physical activity guidelines, which call for the accumulation of at least 30 minutes of moderate-intensity physical activity (e.g., brisk walking) on most days of the week—yielding an energy expenditure of at least 1,000 kcal • wk^{-1}—is "associated with a significant 20–30% reduction in all-cause mortality."[7]

Although being physically active on a regular basis was found to be associated with other health outcomes, such as reduction in obesity or enhancement of quality of life, it was difficult to determine the dose-response relationship. However, "it may be sufficient to discover a level of physical activity or fitness that results in a beneficial effect."[6] Greater health benefits accrued as physical activity increased. However, when attempting to establish an optimal dose of physical activity for health, "consideration must be given not only to the dose that induces the greatest health benefit but also to the potential risk" of injury or harm.[6]

Health Benefits

The relationship between physical activity, physical fitness, and health gives professionals in physical education, exercise science, and sport the opportunity to make a significant contribution to the health of the nation. Professionals can help people of all ages in a diversity of settings incorporate physical activity into their lives and improve their health. Furthermore, professionals can help people achieve greater health benefits by encouraging them to increase their activity to a sufficient level to develop health fitness.

Aerobic classes are a popular fitness offering at employee fitness centers, community programs, and fitness clubs.

Enhanced cardiovascular function is one health benefit of physical activity. This helps reduce the risk of heart disease. Benefits accrued include a more efficient level of cardiovascular function, stronger heart muscles, lower heart rate, reduced blood pressure, increased oxygen-carrying capacity of the blood, and improved coronary and peripheral circulation. Resistance to atherosclerosis is improved as desirable serum cholesterol levels are maintained; low-density lipids are reduced and protective high-density lipids are increased. Thus, the risk of a heart attack is lessened, and the chances of surviving a heart attack are increased. Physical activity can also help reduce other risk factors associated with cardiovascular disease such as obesity and hypertension.

Physical activity can help maintain a desirable body composition. Excessive body fat is hazardous to one's health and it can shorten one's life. Elevated serum cholesterol levels, diabetes, hypertension, gallbladder disease, cardiovascular disease, osteoarthritis of the weight-bearing joints, and some types of cancer are all associated with being overweight. Additionally, many adults and children who are obese experience psychological stress and self-concept problems. Being physically active on a regular basis helps maintain a healthy body composition by using excess calories and by preventing the addition of undesirable weight, thus reducing susceptibility to disease. Because overweight children often become overweight adults, and because the tendency to be overweight increases with age, it is important that proper activity habits as well as balanced nutritional practices are acquired early in life. Physical activity also can contribute to improved physical appearance and self-image.

Muscular strength, muscular endurance, and flexibility also are important to good health. Millions of Americans suffer from problems with low-back pain. Many of these problems can be attributed to muscular weakness and imbalance, which in turn can be attributed to inactivity or participation in inappropriate activities. Millions of elderly and disabled individuals may have trouble performing tasks of daily living because of insufficient development of these fitness components. Regular and appropriate physical activity can help these individuals achieve functional independence. Reduced risk of muscle and joint injury is also a positive outcome of regular and appropriate activity.

The value of physical activity is not limited only to the body; it also contributes to sound mental health. It may help alleviate mental illness and reduce susceptibility to depression and anxiety. Being active can help individuals withstand and manage stress more effectively. Many people find exercising provides a release from tensions. Exercise makes a person feel better. Those who exercise often comment about this directly: "I feel more alive," "I have more energy," "I'm not as tired in the evening," "I can do a lot more with my life."

Regular participation in physical activity can contribute to the development of a positive self-concept and greater self-esteem. It enhances self-confidence, emotional stability, assertiveness, independence, and self-control.

Socialization is another benefit of participation in exercise and physical activities. Sports, recreational activities, and exercise groups offer opportunities to fulfill the desire to belong to a group as well as the desire for recognition. These are important psychosocial needs.

Besides enhancing health, health fitness can contribute to increased work efficiency. Individuals who are fit have more energy, which contributes to greater productivity and efficiency of both physical and mental tasks. More energy is available for recreational activities and leisure-time pursuits. Fit individuals can also better withstand fatigue. Physical exercise can improve one's sleeping patterns.

Health fitness can improve overall general motor performance. Physical activities associated with daily living as well as sport skills can be performed more efficiently by individuals who are fit. Additionally, fit individuals recover more quickly from vigorous exercise and work than do unfit individuals. Physical activity enhances one's appearance and posture through the development of proper muscle tone, greater flexibility, and an enhanced sense of well-being.

Regular exercise can help mitigate the debilitating effects of old age. To be most effective in mitigating the effects of aging, the integration of regular physical activity into one's lifestyle should begin early in life. Individuals who remain active and physically fit throughout their life will retain a more desirable level of cardiovascular health, muscular strength, muscular endurance, and body composition.

Individuals who exercise regularly are likely to engage in other positive forms of health-promoting behavior. Because they do not want to negate the benefits accrued from exercise, they may also strive to eat properly, get sufficient rest and relaxation, and manage the stress in their lives. Personal health and well-being become an important personal priority.

Regular and appropriate physical activity has many benefits. However, to realize these benefits, a person must be active all year. To function properly and at a high level, the human organism needs exercise as an essential ingredient on a regular basis, just as it demands nutritious food every day. Being active throughout one's life is essential for continued good health.

FITNESS DEVELOPMENT

In order to plan a fitness program, physical education, exercise science, and sport professionals must have a knowledge of how energy is produced for physical activity. Understanding the energy demands helps in structuring the fitness program to achieve desired results. Principles of fitness training offer guidance for program planning. In developing fitness programs, the frequency, intensity, time, and type of physical activity must be specified.

Energy Production for Physical Activity

Energy is necessary for the performance of physical activity, whether it is physical activity associated with the activities of daily living, moderate-intensity activity to improve health, exercise to improve fitness, participation in sports for recreation, or involvement in highly competitive athletics. Muscles must produce energy to move. Metabolism is the sum of all chemical reactions in the body, including energy production and energy utilization.

Energy for muscular contraction is produced from the breakdown of food we eat; food serves as a fuel source for the body. Protein, carbohydrates, and fat nutrients from food are broken down via a series of processes to three main molecules—amino acids, glucose, and fatty acids. These molecules, in turn, are delivered via the bloodstream to the cells. In the cells, through a series of chemical reactions, *adenosine triphosphate,* or *ATP,* is created. ATP is used as energy to perform muscular activity.

There are two major ways that energy, specifically ATP, is generated for activity: the anaerobic system and the aerobic system. *Anaerobic* means without oxygen; *aerobic* means with oxygen. The type of task performed, specifically the duration of the activity and its intensity (or the rate at which energy is expended), determines which energy system will contribute the majority of the energy required.

The anaerobic system provides energy for tasks that demand a high rate of energy expenditure for a short period—for example, the 100-yard dash, 50-yard freestyle swim sprint, or shot put—or in events where power—that is, quick, explosive movements—is necessary, such as in gymnastics or football.[8] This system produces energy quickly to meet immediate demands. It uses ATP and other necessary molecules for the chemical reactions that are stored in the muscle cells. When these small stores of ATP are used up, the body then uses stored glycogen as an energy source. Glycogen is broken down to glucose, which is then metabolized within the muscle cells to generate ATP for muscle contraction. Because body fuels can be metabolized to produce small amounts of ATP for energy without the use of oxygen, this is referred to as anaerobic metabolism. However, the amount of work that can be performed anaerobically is limited. The anaerobic system can support high-intensity exercise for only about 1 minute. One product of anaerobic energy production is lactic acid, which accumulates in the muscles and contributes to fatigue.

When exercise continues for a prolonged time, the aerobic system provides the energy for physical activity. Physical activities requiring a lower rate of energy expenditure over a longer time, such as jogging 5 miles, cross-country skiing 10 kilometers, or engaging in a basketball game, use aerobic metabolism to supply the energy.[8] For performing aerobic activities, a constant supply of oxygen is required by the muscles performing the work. Oxygen is used as part of a more complex process to generate ATP from carbohydrates and fats. The aerobic system is tremendously efficient at extracting ATP from the food nutrient molecules and without producing fatiguing by-products such as lactic acid.

In many activities, these systems function simultaneously. For example, many physical activities that would be considered aerobic in nature, such as basketball, soccer, racquet ball, or long-distance races, include an anaerobic component. These activities require periodic bursts of vigorous activity. Sprinting up the court for a long pass, accelerating past an opponent to an open space, and sprinting toward the finish line are examples of when a burst of speed or power is needed.

TABLE 7-1 Energy Systems Used

Energy System	Length of Time	Type of Activity
Anaerobic	6–60 seconds	Any type of sprint (running, swimming cycling) Short-duration, explosive activities
Combined systems	1–3 minutes	Medium-distance activities (400 and 800 meters) Intermittent sports activities
Aerobic	More than 3 minutes	Long-distance events Long-duration intermittent sport activities

Source: From Prentice W: Fitness and wellness for life, ed 6, New York, 1999, McGraw-Hill.

The relative contribution of each of these energy systems will depend on the intensity of the exercise and its duration. (See Table 7-1.) For intense efforts lasting approximately 1 minute or less, the anaerobic system supplies the required energy. As the activity becomes less intense and the duration longer, the aerobic system predominates.

The anaerobic and aerobic systems of the body can be improved through training. Anaerobic training typically involves alternating high-intensity activity with rest periods of varying lengths; the number of repetitions in this cycle depends on the goal of the training. Anaerobic training increases the ability to do anaerobic work, tolerance for lactic acid, and muscle size. In contrast, aerobic training generally involves exercising at a lower intensity for a longer amount of time. Aerobic training improves the capacity of the body to transport and use oxygen, to generate ATP aerobically, and to utilize carbohydrates and stored fats for energy production. Aerobic training improves the function of the cardiovascular system. Understanding the different energy systems is important in developing, implementing, and evaluating training programs to improve fitness.

Principles of Fitness Training

Knowledge from the field of exercise physiology offers guidelines for professionals to use when planning and conducting programs to improve fitness. These principles should be followed whether the exercise program is being designed by an elementary school physical educator to improve students' health fitness, by a coach to improve athletes' performance, by an exercise leader to enhance adults' fitness, or by an exercise specialist as part of a patient's cardiac rehabilitation program. Several physiological and behavioral factors must be taken into account if the sought-after benefits—improvement and maintenance of fitness—are to be realized.

1. **Principle of overload.** Overload is essential if fitness gains are to be realized. Simply stated, for improvements in fitness to occur, one must perform more than one's normal amount of exercise. For example, if improvement in muscular strength is wanted, the muscles must be exercised with more intensity than normal. Once the desired level of fitness has been reached, individuals must continue to train at a level that will maintain the desired level.
2. **Principle of specificity.** The kinds of physiological changes that occur because of training are related to the type of training employed. Training programs should be designed with specific goals in mind. Therefore, it is imperative that professionals understand the demands of the sport or requirements for physical activity so that a specific training program can be designed. For example, to realize the maximum gains in cardiorespiratory endurance, activities and programs should be designed specifically to achieve this aim.

3. **The individual's initial level of fitness must be considered.** An individual embarking on an exercise program should obtain approval from a physician. Following approval, the individual's present level of fitness should be assessed by qualified professionals. The individual's current fitness status should be taken into consideration in designing the exercise program. Those who have a relatively low level of fitness or lead a sedentary lifestyle should start their exercise program at a lower level of intensity than individuals who have a relatively high level of fitness.
4. **Progression should be followed in planning a program.** The use of progression is critical if a fitness program is to be effective. Progression depends on the individual. With the initial level of fitness as a starting point, exercises being performed should increase as an individual becomes adjusted to the exercise program. This can be done by increasing the frequency, duration, or intensity of the exercise. Progression should be steady and progress carefully monitored so that the individual is challenged by the exercise program but not overwhelmed.
5. **Individual differences must be taken into account.** The individual's needs and objectives must be taken into account when planning an exercise program. Factors that may influence the individual's performance warrant attention as well. The nature of the individual's work, diet, and lifestyle should be considered when designing an exercise program. The amount of stress an individual is currently experiencing also may significantly affect his or her performance.
6. **The elements of a training program should include a warm-up, the workout, and a cool-down.** Warm-up and cool-down activities are important. Warm-up activities of at least 5 to 10 minutes in duration should precede the vigorous part of the exercise session. Warm-up activities can help prevent injury and prepare the body for the strenuous activities that are part of the exercise program. Following the workout, a cool-down period of 5 to 10 minutes is recommended to allow the body to begin returning to its normal state. Individuals with low levels of fitness or individuals who are middle-aged and older should take more time to warm up and cool down. Stretching exercises and low-level aerobic activity are suggested for warm-up and cool-down.
7. **Safety is paramount.** Safety of the individual should be a primary concern. Before starting an exercise program, individuals should have a thorough medical screening. This is particularly critical when special conditions exist, such as beginning an exercise program after a long period of inactivity or for rehabilitation after an illness (e.g., heart attack). Individuals engaged in physical activities involving body contact or other hazards should be strongly cautioned to use essential protective equipment, especially for the head, neck, eyes, and teeth (e.g., individuals playing racquetball should be required to use eye guards). Individuals should be warned of proper precautions to take when exercising in special weather conditions such as intense heat, high humidity, or extreme cold. Finally, individuals should learn how to monitor carefully their responses to exercise and to report any unusual occurrences (e.g., excessive breathlessness) to the professional conducting the program or to a physician.
8. **Behavioral factors should be considered in developing and implementing a fitness program.** Consideration must be given to motivating individuals to adhere to their fitness programs and to incorporate their program into their daily living. Essentially, how can physical education, exercise science, and sport professionals facilitate adherence by individuals to the exercise program that has been so carefully designed? How can individuals be motivated to work so that their optimal level of fitness can be realized?

Goal setting is important in promoting adherence to an exercise program. According to Swain and Leutholtz, as a professional, the most important

Many adults exercise with sufficient intensity, duration, and frequency to realize health benefits.

consideration in setting goals is that you allow participants to set the goals for themselves, with appropriate guidance from you.[9] Goal-setting is discussed in Chapter 9.

Swain and Leutholtz identify social support as one of the key elements in behavior change, for example, moving from inactivity to an active lifestyle.[9] Social support from family members, friends, and professionals reinforces individuals' efforts and can be used effectively to help individuals stay active. Involving friends and family in the exercise program and working out with a partner are just two ways in which professionals can use social support to their advantage.

Physical education, exercise science, and sport professionals must plan strategies to promote adherence to an exercise program and incorporate those strategies into program design. Dishman estimates about 50% of individuals fail to adhere to their exercise programs.[10] Use of reinforcements, such as contracts and incentives, help improve adherence. Self-efficacy, an individual's confidence that he/she can perform a specific behavior (e.g., exercise) is one of the most important determinants of adherence.[11] Since high levels of self-efficacy are associated with adherence, physical education, exercise science, and sport professionals must take steps to help individuals gain confidence in their ability to exercise and successfully engage in various forms of physical activity.

Physical educators, exercise scientists, and sport leaders must be aware of physiological principles when designing an exercise program. The principles of overload and specificity must be followed. Consideration also must be given to individual differences. Behavioral strategies such as goal setting and positive reinforcement can facilitate exercise adherence. Physical educators, exercise scientists, and sport leaders should also realize the importance of being a good role model for a healthy lifestyle.

Planning a Fitness Program

To achieve and maintain fitness, individuals must exercise on a regular basis. They must exercise sufficiently to cross the threshold of training; to achieve optimal results, they must exercise within the fitness target zone. When professionals prescribe an exercise program for an individual, they must specify the frequency, intensity, time, and type of exercise. These variables are used in constructing an exercise prescription or program for an individual.

Each fitness component has a specific threshold of training that must be achieved. The *threshold of training* is the minimum level of exercise needed to achieve desired benefits. The *target zone* begins at the threshold of training and defines the upper limits of training.[12] To achieve fitness benefits, individuals must exercise with sufficient intensity, duration, and frequency to stay within the target zone. Exercise beyond the upper limit may be counterproductive. The target zone defines the optimal level of exercise.

Frequency refers to the number of exercise sessions per week—for example, 3 to 5 times per week. Achieving and maintaining health fitness requires that the individual exercise on a regular basis.

Intensity is the degree of effort or exertion put forth by the individual during exercise. It is how hard a person works. For example, the intensity of effort put forth by a runner can be described as 80% of his or her maximum effort, and the effort put forth during strength training can be described as weight lifted—for example, 80 lb. Intensity is often viewed as the most important of the exercise variables.

Time is the duration or the length of the activity. Time is how long an exercise must be performed to be effective. Time is frequently expressed in units of time, such as 40 minutes of exercise.

Type is the mode of exercise being performed. Since fitness development is specific, different types of activities build different components of fitness. Activities such as jogging, rowing, bicycling, stretching, and weight training are types of exercise that can be used to realize specific fitness gains. The selection of the type of exercise should be guided by the fitness goal to be achieved.

The acronym *FITT* can be used to help remember these prescriptive variables. These exercise variables are interrelated and can be manipulated to produce an exercise program appropriate to an individual's needs and to the outcomes wanted. For example, cardiovascular improvement can be realized by jogging (type) at 70% effort (intensity) for 40 minutes (time) 5 times a week (frequency) or at 85% intensity for 20 minutes 4 times a week. Individuals who are just starting a program to improve their fitness may be more successful if they exercise at a lower intensity for a longer session. Individuals who are obese may find it beneficial to exercise for shorter periods (duration) but more often during the week (frequency).

The interactive nature of the exercise components allows for the design of exercise programs to meet unique needs. Individualization is very important. Personal characteristics such as fitness status, medical status, and age must be considered when prescribing exercise. Individuals who have lower initial fitness levels require a lower level of intensity when beginning a program than individuals who are fit. Medical conditions such as heart disease, diabetes, and asthma must be taken into account when designing an exercise program. Appropriate modifications must be made so that the individual can participate safely. Individuals beginning an exercise program at middle age or older may need to start at a lower intensity. It is important to note that gender is not a limiting factor; men and women respond equally to training.

The participant's fitness needs and goals also must be considered when planning an exercise program. The program must be designed to provide opportunities for the development of the fitness quality the participant desires to improve. Selected activities should be specific to the goal. For example, if the participant's goal is to improve stamina or cardiorespiratory endurance, the activities selected should stimulate the circulatory and respiratory systems (e.g., running or swimming) and the exercise components manipulated to allow the participant to achieve this goal.

Enjoyment is another critical factor in the selection of the type of exercise. Adherence to the training program is enhanced when the participant enjoys the prescribed exercise. Activities should allow participants to achieve the desired fitness goals while maintaining interest and enjoyment. Individuals who find an activity enjoyable will be more likely to continue the exercise long enough to realize desired fitness improvements and to incorporate exercise into their lifestyle to maintain these improvements.

Equally important in planning an exercise program is the provision of experiences that will promote the development of the cognitive and affective outcomes essential for lifetime fitness. Achievement of a desirable level of fitness is a significant concern, but attention also must be directed to educating participants about the principles of designing a personal exercise program, assessing their own fitness, and resolving personal fitness problems. Development of a knowledgeable, independent fitness and health consumer—an individual who can achieve and maintain fitness for a lifetime—is an important priority. People need to take charge of their own lives and assume personal responsibility for their level of fitness.

HEALTH FITNESS COMPONENTS

The components of health fitness include cardiorespiratory endurance, body composition, muscular strength and endurance, and flexibility. In

Triathletes train to develop high levels of fitness and skill in several sports.

this section, each fitness component is defined, its relationship to health delineated, methods to improve the fitness component discussed, and techniques to measure the component identified.

Cardiorespiratory Endurance

Cardiorespiratory endurance is the body's ability to deliver oxygen effectively to the working muscles so that an individual can perform physical activity. Efficient functioning of the cardiovascular system (i.e., heart and blood vessels) and the respiratory system (i.e., lungs) is essential for the distribution of oxygen and nutrients and removal of wastes from the body.

The performance of sustained vigorous physical activities is influenced by the efficiency of the cardiorespiratory system. The more efficient the system, the greater the amount of physical activity an individual can perform before fatigue and exhaustion occur. Performance diminishes greatly when sufficient oxygen cannot be provided by the cardiorespiratory system to the working muscles.

Cardiorespiratory endurance is regarded as the most important component of health fitness. Because of the benefits derived from improved cardiorespiratory function—such as the potential for reducing the risk of cardiovascular disease, improving work capacity, and providing greater resistance to fatigue—this component, if properly developed, can make a major contribution to an individual's health.

Health fitness can help prevent hypokinetic disease. Hypokinetic diseases are caused by insufficient physical activity. Persons who have hypokinetic diseases frequently experience loss of flexibility, cardiovascular degeneration, bone and muscle weakness, and bladder and bowel malfunctions. One risk factor that contributes to premature susceptibility to heart disease and stroke is lack of physical activity. Moreover, it is believed that hypertension and obesity, which are also risk factors associated with heart disease, can be helped by participation in regular physical activity.

Cardiorespiratory endurance is concerned with the aerobic efficiency of the body. Aerobic efficiency is the body's ability to supply fuel and oxygen to the muscles. One of the major factors influencing aerobic efficiency is the capacity of the heart to pump blood. A well-conditioned heart is able to exert greater force with each heartbeat; consequently, a larger volume of blood is pumped through the arteries and throughout the body.

Another important factor in cardiorespiratory endurance is the efficiency of the lungs. The amount of oxygen that can be supplied to working muscles is a limiting factor in performance. Oxygen is required to produce the energy needed for activity. Food is metabolized to provide needed fuel, and oxygen is essential for this process. Air is inhaled; oxygen from the air is transported to the heart and is then carried from the heart to the organs needing oxygen. From the organs the blood carrying carbon dioxide is returned to the heart and finally to the lungs, where it is exhaled.

When demands for oxygen increase, such as during strenuous exercise, the body's ability to take in and provide oxygen to the working muscles is an important determinant of the amount of work that can be performed. The greater the body's ability to take in and deliver oxygen, the longer a person can exercise before fatigue and exhaustion occur. Thus, individuals who have well-developed circulatory and respiratory systems can deliver more oxygen and therefore can exercise for a longer period.

Many benefits have been attributed to aerobic exercise. Aerobic exercise is activity that can be sustained for an extended period without building an oxygen debt in the muscles. Bicycling, jogging, skipping rope, rowing, walking, cross-country skiing, and swimming are some examples of aerobic activities.

The benefits of aerobic exercise include the ability to use more oxygen during strenuous exercise, a lower heart rate at work, the production of less lactic acid, and greater endurance. Aerobic exercise improves the efficiency of the heart and reduces blood pressure.

Cardiorespiratory endurance is important for the performance of many sport activities. In sport activities that require an individual to perform for an extended period, such as a 500-yard swim or a soccer game, cardiorespiratory endurance can have a profound impact on performance.

Individuals who have trained and developed a high level of cardiorespiratory endurance can work at a higher level of intensity without fatigue than individuals who are unfit. Additionally, fit individuals can perform more work before reaching exhaustion. Furthermore, following exercise, fit individuals recover faster than unfit individuals.

Cardiorespiratory fitness can be improved and maintained through a well-planned program of exercise. Physical activity of an appropriate intensity, duration, frequency, and type can enhance cardiorespiratory fitness.

Intensity. For development of cardiorespiratory fitness, physical activities must be of sufficient intensity. During exercise, heart rate changes in proportion to the energy requirements of the task. As the energy requirements increase, there is a corresponding increase in heart rate. Thus, heart rate can be used to monitor the intensity of exercise. (See the Measuring Your Heart Rate box.) Because heart rate slows within 1 minute following exercise, it is often recommended that the pulse be monitored for 10 seconds and then multiplied by 6 (or monitored for 6 seconds and multiplied by 10) to determine beats per minute. For an accurate reading, the heart rate should be monitored within 15 seconds of the cessation of exercise.

Exercising at a proper intensity is essential for a safe and effective workout. Intensity can be controlled by speeding or slowing the pace of the exercise. To realize training benefits, the intensity of the exercise must be regulated so that the heart rate is elevated to a predetermined level and maintained within a certain range. This level is called the threshold of training and the range called the target heart rate zone.

The American College of Sports Medicine recommends that individuals who desire to develop and maintain cardiorespiratory fitness should exercise at an intensity of 55/65%–90% of maximum heart rate (HR_{max}) or 40%/50%–85% of Heart Rate Reserve (HRR) or maximum oxygen uptake reserve ($\dot{V}O_2R$). The lower intensities, 55–64% of HR_{max} and 40–49% of HRR, are most appropriate for individuals who have a low level of fitness.[9,13]

Maximal heart rate (HR_{max}) for both males and females is estimated to be 220 beats per minute (bpm). Maximum heart rate is related to age; as individuals age, their maximum heart rate decreases. A simple way to calculate HR_{max} is 220 – age.

Heart rate reserve (HRR) is the difference or range between resting heart rate (RHR) and maximum heart rate (HR_{max}). HRR is calculated by the following formula:

$$HRR = HR_{max} - RHR.$$

There are several formulas that can be used to calculate a target heart rate (THR) to monitor the intensity of exercise. One way is to calculate a percentage of HR_{max}. This can be done using the formula shown below:

$$THR = (\text{Target Intensity})(HR_{max})$$

The THR_{max} is quick and simple to use.

Another method to calculate target heart rate is to use a formula based on the HRR. This method takes into account the individual's resting heart rate and provides a more accurate estimation than the HR_{max} formula. This formula is commonly called the Karvonen Equation and is as follows:

$$THR = (\text{Target Intensity})(HR_{max} - RHR) + RHR.$$

Examples of these calculations are shown in the Examples for Calculations of Heart Rate box.

Target heart rates allow individuals to easily monitor their exercise intensity and to make sure

Measuring Your Heart Rate

You can determine your heart rate by counting the frequency with which your heart contracts in a period of time and converting this to the standard measure in beats per minute. Make sure you press just firmly enough to feel the pulse. If you press too hard it may interfere with the rhythm.

You can detect your pulse by placing a finger or fingers on your lower arm near the base of the thumb.

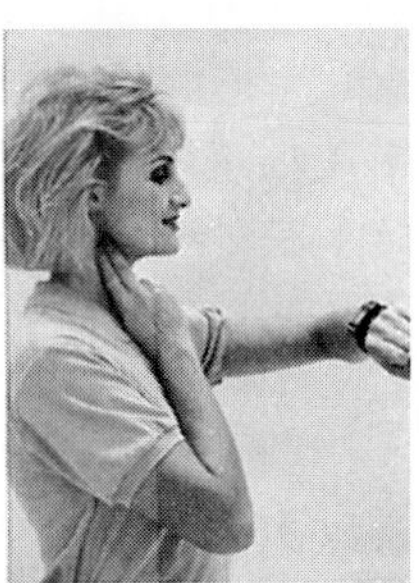

Your pulse can also be easily detected over the carotid artery in the front of the neck.

that they exercise with sufficient intensity to cross the threshold of training and that they are in the target heart rate zone.

Individuals should select an intensity that takes into account their current level of fitness and their fitness goals. Intensity can be progressively increased as conditions warrant.

The American College of Sports Medicine recommends 20 to 60 minutes of continuous aerobic activity. This amount can be accumulated during two or more sessions throughout the day but each session should be a distinct exercise period and a minimum of 10-minute bouts in duration.[9,13]

It is important to remember that the intensity and duration of the activity are critical to achieving and maintaining fitness. Generally, as the intensity of the activity increases, its duration decreases; conversely, as intensity decreases, the duration of the activity increases. Typically, for development of health-related cardiorespiratory endurance, lower intensities and longer durations are recommended. It is important to remember, however, that both the intensity and the duration of the activity must meet minimum requirements for fitness development to occur.

Frequency. Three to five exercise sessions per week are recommended by the American College of Sports Medicine to realize minimal improvement in cardiovascular fitness. Many individuals

Students at Agassiz Middle School, in Fargo, North Dakota, use heart rate monitors to measure the intensity of their efforts.

Examples for Calculations of Heart Rate using HR_{max} and HRR

Calculation of training heart rate for working at 65% intensity for a 20-year-old with a resting heart rate of 70 bpm

Heart Rate Maximum (HR_{max})

Formula	*Example*
220	220
– Age	– 20
Predicted Maximum HR	200
× % Intensity	× 65%
Training Heart Rate	130 bpm* Training Heart Rate

Heart Rate Reserve (HRR)

Formula	*Example*
220	220
– Age	– 20
Predicted Maximum HR	200
– Resting HR	– 70
	130
× % Intensity	× 65%
	84.5
+ Resting Heart Rate	+70
Training Heart Rate	154.5 → 155 bpm Training Heart Rate

*bpm = beats per minute

choose to work out more often. It is important to remember, however, that the body must have time to recover from the effects of exercise. Many persons build this recovery time into their exercise program by exercising only every other day. Although daily workouts are not required to develop health fitness, many other individuals choose to work out on a daily basis. To allow the body to recover, they often follow a strenuous workout day with a less strenuous recovery day.

Type. Aerobic activities should be used to develop cardiorespiratory endurance. Basically, aerobic activities are those in which a sufficient amount of oxygen is available to meet the body's demands. During the performance of these activities, the heart rate is maintained at an elevated level for an extended period. These activities typically involve vigorous and repetitive whole body or large muscle movements that are sustained for an extended period. Popular aerobic activities include jogging, running, walking, swimming, cycling, rowing, aerobic dance, and cross-country skiing. Because these activities are somewhat continuous in nature, the intensity of the workload can be easily regulated by controlling the pace. Intermittent activities such as racquetball, basketball, and tennis involve various intensities of effort during the course of the activity. Thus, it is more difficult to regulate the degree of effort expended during these activities. However, these activities can contribute to the improvement of cardiorespiratory endurance if they are of sufficient intensity.

In summary, to develop and maintain cardiorespiratory fitness, it is recommended that the individual exercise 3 to 5 times a week, with an intensity sufficient to elevate and sustain the heart rate in the target zone for at least 20 minutes. Exercise should involve aerobic activities that are continuous, vigorous, and, most important, enjoyable to the individual. Once a desirable level of cardiovascular fitness has been achieved, regular appropriate exercise is necessary to maintain it. Individuals who stop exercising tend to lose their fitness gains within 5 to 10 weeks. Achieving and maintaining a high level of this critical fitness component requires a long-term commitment and the incorporation of exercise into one's lifestyle.

Cardiorespiratory fitness can be measured. The best method to determine the level of cardiovascular functioning is to measure maximum oxygen consumption. The more oxygen the body is able to deliver and use, the more work the body is able to perform before becoming fatigued. Maximum oxygen consumption is the greatest rate at which the oxygen is processed and used by the body.

A bicycle ergometer can be used to determine maximum oxygen consumption.

Measurement of maximum oxygen consumption requires a sophisticated laboratory setting and well-trained personnel to monitor carefully the performance of the individual during the test. This testing is usually done on an individual basis. Following prescribed test protocols, the individual exercises on a treadmill or bicycle ergometer and breathes through a specially designed mouthpiece. Various physiological and metabolic parameters are monitored, such as heart rate, respiration rate, and rate of oxygen consumption. The exercise task is made progressively more difficult until no further increase in oxygen consumption is noted; this point is considered to be the maximum oxygen intake for the task. Although this test yields highly accurate information, it is expensive, time consuming, and requires sophisticated equipment and highly trained personnel.

There are a variety of other methods that can be used to provide a good estimate of cardiorespiratory endurance. These tests measure the maximum amount of work that can be performed over a specified period. The most commonly used tests are the 12-minute or the 9-minute run/walk, the timed 1½- or 1-mile run/walk, and the Harvard step test. These tests are most often used in school and community fitness programs. When these tests are properly conducted, results can be used to accurately estimate maximum oxygen consumption and provide an indicator of cardiorespiratory fitness.

Body Composition

Body composition is a description of the body in terms of muscle, bone, fat, and other elements. With respect to health fitness, it refers to the percentage of body weight composed of fat as compared with fat-free or lean tissue. Having a high percentage of body fat is a serious deterrent to fitness and health.

Height and weight tables traditionally have been used to determine desirable body weight. Individuals whose body weight exceeds set standards for their sex, age, and physical stature by 10% to 20% are considered overweight.[8] Persons overweight by 20% of their optimum weight are obese, and those who are overweight by more than 50% of their optimum weight are considered morbidly obese or superobese.[8]

It should be noted that being overweight can be attributed to having an excess of either fatty tissue or lean tissue. For example, certain athletes such as football players could be classified as overweight. However, when their body composition is examined, the excess weight is attributable to muscular development and their overall percentage of body fat is quite low (e.g., a professional football player can weigh 250 pounds or more, yet have only 12% body fat or less). The important consideration with respect to health fitness, therefore, is not weight but proportion of fat. The average percentage of body fat is 18% for men and 23% for women. With respect to health fitness, the desirable level of body fat for men is 12% or less and for women, 18% or less. The percentage of body fat should not be less than 3% in men and 12% in women (the higher percentage for women is necessary for protection of the reproductive organs).[8] Extremely low percentages of body fat are hazardous to one's health. It is highly important that professionals and the public realize that a certain amount of adipose tissue or fat is essential for the body to function. Body fat also serves to protect internal organs. *The goal of fitness programs is not the elimination of body fat but helping individuals attain the desirable levels of body fat.*

Body composition can also be assessed using the Body Mass Index (BMI). The National Institutes of Health (NIH) has adopted the use of the BMI to determine if an individual is at risk for poor health outcomes due to overweight or obesity.[14] BMI is calculated by dividing the weight of the individual in kilograms by the height in meters squared (for an estimate, multiply the individual's weight in pounds by 703 and then divide by the height in inches squared). For most persons, BMI more closely correlates with total body fat than the traditional height/weight tables and provides a clearer indication of disease risk.[14] However, one limitation of BMI is that it overestimates the degree of fatness of very muscular individuals. According to the NIH Clinical Guidelines, for adults, overweight is defined as a BMI between 25 kg/m^2 and 29.9 kg/m^2 and obesity is defined as a BMI of 30 kg/m^2 or greater.[14] A person who has a BMI of 30 kg/m^2 is about 30 pounds overweight; a person who weighs 221 pounds and is 6 feet tall or a person who is 5'6" tall and weighs 186 pounds has a BMI of about 30 kg/m^2.[14] For children and adolescents, overweight is defined as a BMI at or above the 95th percentile for age and sex, based on the revised Centers for Disease Control and Prevention growth charts.[15]

Poor body composition is associated with numerous health problems. In 2001, the U.S. Surgeon General issued a report—"A Call to Action to Prevent and Decrease Overweight and Obesity."[15] The epidemic of overweight and obesity assailing our nation makes the prevention and treatment of these conditions and their associated health problems an important public health goal. According to this report, in 1999, an estimated 61% of adults were overweight or obese and 13% of children and adolescents were overweight.[15]

The health consequences of overweight and obesity are enormous. Approximately 400,000 deaths per year are associated with overweight and obesity.[15] Epidemiological studies show that persons who are obese (BMI $\geq$ 30 kg/m^2) have a 50% to 100% increased risk of premature death from all causes compared to those persons with a BMI of 20 kg/m^2 to 25 kg/m^2.

Overweight and obesity are associated with increased risk for coronary heart disease, type 2 diabetes, certain types of cancer, low-back pain, respiratory problems, and musculoskeletal disorders, such as knee osteoarthritis. Both modest and large weight gains are associated with significantly increased risk of disease. For example, a weight gain of 10 to 20 pounds presents an increased risk of coronary heart disease (nonfatal myocardial infarction and death) of 1.25 times in women and 1.6 times in men.[15,16] Higher levels of weight gain of 22 pounds in men and 44 pounds in women result in an increased coronary heart disease risk of 1.75 and 2.65, respectively.[15–17] Overweight and obesity exacerbate many chronic conditions such as hypertension and high cholesterol. Additionally, overweight and obese individuals may experience social stigmatization, discrimination, and poor body image.[14] Furthermore, overweight children and adolescents are more likely to become overweight and obese adults.[15]

Determination of the cause of obesity is important. In most cases obesity can be attributed to overeating and a lack of physical activity. In a few cases, however, obesity can be the result of disease. When dealing with obesity, particularly individuals who are superobese, it is important that a physician be consulted. A physical examination and careful monitoring of eating and exercise habits are helpful in determining the cause of the problem. A qualified physician can offer guidance in designing and implementing a sound fitness program to deal with the problem of obesity.

Body composition is primarily influenced by nutrition and physical activity. Although body composition is genetically related to body type, the nature and amount of food consumed and the extent of participation in physical activity exert a profound influence on body composition. Poor nutritional practices contribute to an unfavorable body composition. Eating more calories than needed and consumption of a high-fat diet lead to high percentages of body fat. Caloric consumption should be consistent with caloric expenditure. Dietary guidelines suggest that individuals reduce their consumption of fat. The average American derives 34% of his or her calories from fat, compared with the recommended 25% to 30%, with no more than 10% from saturated fats.[19] Sedentary individuals have lower levels of caloric expenditure. Leading a physically active lifestyle can contribute to a favorable body composition.

Energy balance is important to achieving a favorable body composition. The relationship between food intake and energy expenditure is critical. This relationship is often referred to as energy or caloric balance:

Energy or caloric balance = Number of calories taken into the body as food − Number of calories expended

Energy is expended through three processes: (1) basal metabolism or maintenance of essential life functions; (2) work, which is any activity requiring more energy than sleeping and includes exercise; and (3) excretion of body wastes.

A neutral balance occurs when the caloric intake is equal to the caloric expenditure. Under these circumstances, body weight is maintained. When a positive balance exists—that is, when more calories are consumed than expended—the excess is stored as fat and body weight increases. A negative balance occurs when more calories are expended than consumed; this results in weight loss. Weight control requires maintaining the appropriate energy or caloric balance. Individuals must be careful about food intake and conscious of energy expenditures. Caloric tables are useful in monitoring the number of calories consumed. Energy expenditure tables are helpful in monitoring energy expended. These tables provide information about the calories expended both during the performance of daily living tasks such as house cleaning and during participation in physical activities such as bicycling.

Body composition can be improved. Individuals who have an unhealthy percentage of body fat can reduce it by modifying their lifestyle. Fat loss can be accomplished by several means: (1) consuming fewer calories through dieting, (2) increasing caloric expenditure by increasing the amount of exercise, and (3) combining a moderate decrease in caloric consumption with a moderate increase in exercise or caloric expenditure.

Experts recommend that fat loss be accomplished through a combination of diet and exercise. For example, if caloric intake is reduced by 200 to 300 calories per day and caloric expenditures are increased by 200 to 300 calories a day, approximately 3,500 calories—1 pound of fat—will be lost over the course of a week. Adoption of sound nutritional practices in conjunction with regular, appropriate exercise will help most individuals achieve a desirable body composition.

Exercise increasingly is being recognized as a critical component of fat loss. Often those desiring to lose fat focus on counting the number of calories consumed and neglect the exercise component. Exercise can aid in fat loss in several ways: (1) it can increase caloric expenditures (a 180-lb. person walking 4 miles in an hour will expend approximately 400 calories); (2) it can suppress appetite and thereby contribute to reduction in caloric intake; (3) it can increase the metabolic rate for some time after vigorous exercise, thereby permitting extra calories to be burned; and (4) it can contribute to health fitness. Also, because sedentary living contributes to poor body composition, incorporation of regular appropriate exercise into one's lifestyle helps to successfully manage one's body composition.

Attention to the composition of one's diet is important in attaining a healthy level of body fat. Increasingly, nutritionists are encouraging individuals to pay close attention to the fat calories they consume. Eating a low-fat diet is an effective way to manage one's percentage of body fat. A low-fat diet also reduces the risk of heart disease and cancer. Adults who are at a healthy weight and want to prevent cancer should follow a diet that provides 20% to 30% of the calories from fat. Individuals who have a high percentage of body fat and/or have heart disease should derive 10% to 20% of their calories from fat.

Individuals who try to follow a low-fat diet are typically encouraged to monitor the percentage of fat in the foods they consume and to choose foods that have 30% or less of the calories from fat. Another way to keep track of fat consumption is to count the number of grams of fat eaten each day and to keep the total number of fat grams at or below the desired level. To calculate the number of fat grams per day, use the following formula:

$$\frac{\text{Number of calories needed} \times \text{desired percentage of calories from fat}}{9 \text{ (number of calories in a fat gram)}} = \text{fat grams}$$

So, if you need 2,000 calories per day and you want to eat a diet that has 20% of the calories from fat, your calculations would reveal that you should consume 44.4 grams or less of fat per day:

$$\frac{2{,}000 \text{ calories} \times 20\%}{9} = 44.4 \text{ grams of fat per day}$$

Careful attention to dietary practices and physical activity habits is important in attaining a healthy body composition.

Note that individuals who desire to gain weight should focus on increasing lean body mass (muscle) rather than body fat. This can be accomplished by following a sound muscle training program in conjunction with an appropriate increase in caloric intake to realize a gain of 1 to 2 pounds per week. Failure to incorporate a muscle training program as part of the total program will result in excess calories being converted to fat. Thus, even though the weight gain is achieved, the percentage of body fat may be less than optimal. Therefore, a weight-gaining program should combine a reasonable increase in caloric intake and a well-planned muscle training program to achieve an optimal body composition.

Sound practices should be followed in losing fat. Experts suggest the following guidelines regarding fat loss:

1. Prolonged fasting and diets that severely restrict calories are medically dangerous. These programs result in loss of large amounts of water, electrolytes, minerals, glycogen stores, and other fat-free tissue, with a minimal amount of fat loss.
2. Moderate caloric restriction is desirable, such as consuming 500 calories less than the usual daily intake. It is important that the minimum caloric intake not go below 1,200 calories per day for a woman and 1,400 calories per day for a man, and that sound nutritional practices are followed.

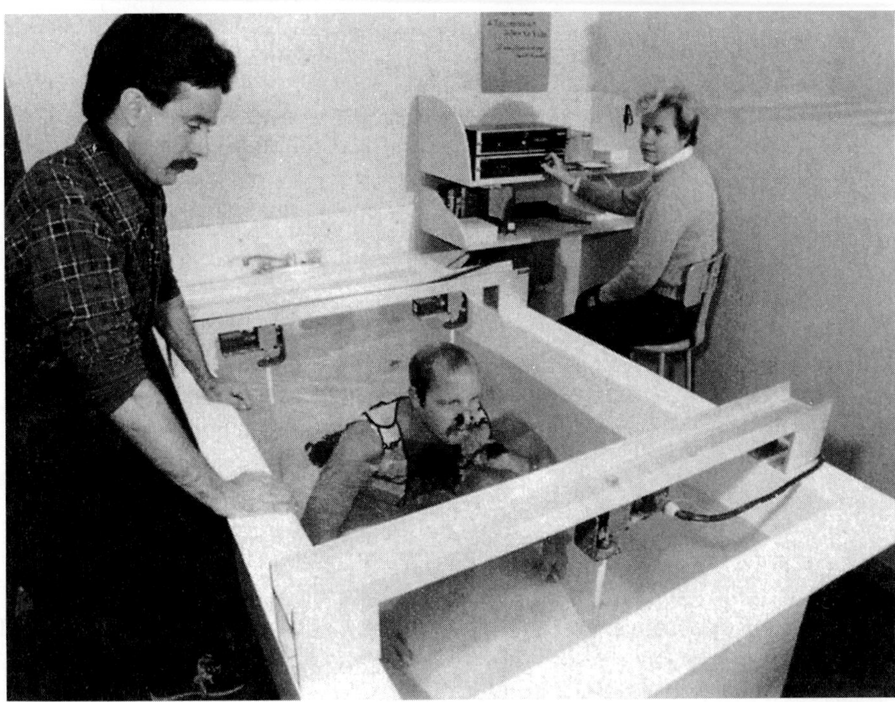

Underwater weighing is a sophisticated, accurate technique used to determine body composition.

3. Appropriate regular exercise of the large muscles assists in the maintenance of fat-free tissue, including muscle mass and bone density, and results in the loss of weight, primarily in the form of fat.
4. A sound program should be comprehensive in nature. It should include a nutritionally sound, low-fat diet with mild caloric restriction, regular and appropriate exercise to increase caloric expenditure, and behavior modification. Weight loss should not exceed 2 pounds per week.
5. Maintenance of proper weight and desirable body composition requires a lifetime commitment to proper eating habits and regular physical activity.

A word of caution: Some individuals become obsessed with weight loss, dieting, and exercise. This obsession can, in conjunction with a host of other factors, contribute to the development of an eating disorder. Two common eating disorders are anorexia nervosa and bulimia.

Anorexia nervosa is a disease in which a person develops a psychological aversion to food, resulting in a pathologic weight loss. Bulimia involves recurrent episodes of binge eating and subsequent purging by self-induced vomiting, use of laxatives, and/or excessive exercising. Both disorders have a higher prevalence among young women, although men do suffer from these conditions as well. These disorders pose a severe threat to health and require professional treatment.

Body composition can be measured. Several methods can be used to determine the percentage of body fat. One of the most accurate methods is hydrostatic weighing. This involves weighing an individual on land and then in an underwater tank. Body density is then determined, and this information is used to calculate the percentage of lean body

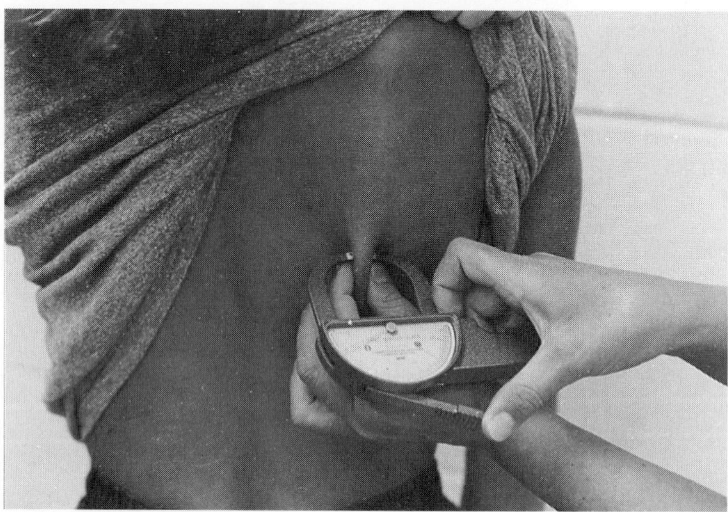

Skinfold measurements can be used to calculate a person's percentage of body fat.

weight and body fat. This technique is used most often in exercise physiology laboratories and hospitals. It requires expensive equipment and is time consuming, and thus is not practical for use with large groups of people.

Air displacement plethysmography, also known as the "Bod Pod," offers another means of assessment of body composition. Similar to hydrostatic weighing, the Bod Pod uses air instead of water. A person sits in the enclosed chamber (pod) and computerized sensors measure the amount of air displaced by the person's body. This approach offers similar accuracy as underwater weighing without requiring a person be submerged in water. It is easy to use, but its cost limits its availability. This technique is used most often in exercise physiology laboratories or clinical settings.

Of the alternative approaches to measurement, the most common is the use of skinfold measurements. Skinfold measurements are taken from several selected sites, such as the triceps, subscapular, or thigh, with skinfold calipers. Formulas are then used to calculate the percentage of body fat. This method is relatively inexpensive, can be used with large groups of people, and produces accurate information when performed by well-trained individuals.

Another approach is the use of the body mass index. *Body mass index* (BMI), a height-to-weight ratio, is calculated by dividing an individual's weight, in kilograms, by the height in meters, squared (BMI = weight/height^2). To calculate the BMI for a person who is 5'8" tall and weighs 170 lb., you would perform the following steps:

- Convert weight to kilograms by dividing pounds by 2.2 (170/2.2 = 77.3 kg).
- Convert height in inches to meters by multiplying by 0.0254 (68" × 0.0254 = 1.73 m).
- Square the height in meters (1.73 × 1.73 = 2.99 m^2).
- Divide the weight by the height squared (77.3 kg/2.99 m^2).

The BMI is 25.8. The National Institutes of Health Clinical Guidelines Classifications for BMI is shown in the Classifications for BMI box. An excessively low BMI is not desirable and can be associated with health problems such as eating disorders or chronic fatigue.

The BMI allows large populations to be quickly screened for potential health risks to body composition. However, sometimes the results can be misleading when the excess weight is lean as

Classifications for BMI

Classification	BMI
Underweight	< 18.5 kg/m^2
Normal weight	18.5–24.9 kg/m^2
Overweight	25–29.9 kg/m^2
Obesity (Class 1)	30–34.9 kg/m^2
Obesity (Class 2)	35–39.9 kg/m^2
Extreme Obesity (Class 3)	≥ 40 kg/m^2

Source: From National Institutes of Health (NIH), National Heart, Lung, and Blood Institute (NHLBI). Clinical guidelines on the identification, evaluation, and treatment of overweight and obesity in adults. HHS, Public Health Service (PHS), 1998.

opposed to fat tissue. For example, individuals who engage in a high level of strength training, such as athletes, may have a high BMI. These individuals are not at risk for obesity-related disease because their excess weight is due to lean tissue. For this reason, it is suggested that the BMI be interpreted in conjunction with other measures of body composition.

Muscular Strength and Endurance

Muscular strength is the ability of a muscle or muscle group to exert force against a resistance. Specifically, it is the maximum amount of force that a muscle or muscle group can apply against a resistance in a single effort.

The ability of a muscle or muscle group to exert force repeatedly is known as muscular endurance. Muscular endurance also refers to the capacity of a muscle or muscle group to sustain a contractive state over a period of time.

Muscular strength and endurance are specific to each muscle or muscle group. That is, different muscles in the body can have different levels of strength and endurance. Moreover, muscles used more frequently are stronger and have greater endurance than muscles used less frequently. Maintenance of strength and endurance requires that the muscles be used. When muscles are not used, strength and endurance decrease.

Many people perceive muscular strength and endurance as important only for athletes or those engaged in occupations that require heavy work, for example, construction. Although muscular strength and endurance are necessary for these people to perform their responsibilities effectively, these fitness components are also important for all people. Strength and endurance are necessary for performing everyday tasks, maintaining proper posture, and resisting fatigue. As individuals age, maintaining adequate levels of strength and endurance is particularly important, because these fitness components play a critical role in the maintenance of functional independence. Additionally, the development of adequate strength and endurance is an important objective of many rehabilitation programs.

Muscular strength and endurance are important to good health. They contribute to the maintenance of proper posture and the improvement of personal appearance. Because strong muscles provide better protection for body joints, the risk of joint injuries is decreased. Millions of Americans suffer from low-back pain. Weak abdominal muscles and poor flexibility contribute to this problem. Strengthening the appropriate muscles and developing increased flexibility can help alleviate this condition.

High levels of muscular strength and endurance are important for athletes. Many of the advances in athletic performance can be attributed to improvements in training techniques, especially the development of strength. Strength is a critical element of sport performance. Strength training for sport must be specifically related to the particular characteristics required for performance of the sport. Thus, the strength training of a sprinter will differ markedly from that of a shot putter, which will be different from that of a gymnast. For effective performance, each athlete requires the development of a high level of strength in specific muscles or muscle groups.

Strength combines with other physical elements to enhance the quality of performance. For example, power, which is strength combined with

Lifespan and Cultural Perspectives: Exercise Physiology

- What is the recommendation for physical activity needed to yield health benefits in people over the age of 65?
- How does the cardiovascular system respond to prolonged weightlessness, such as that experienced in space?
- At what age should children begin weight training? What type of weight training program is best for children?
- How do individual differences in age, sex, ethnicity, prior health status, and family background influence a person's response to physical activity?
- How does age affect aerobic capacity?
- What is the relationship between childhood physical activity levels and fitness and adult physical activity levels and fitness?

speed, is an important motor-skill fitness component. Power is the quality that permits a basketball player to jump high and to snare rebounds off the backboard, a golfer to drive a golf ball 250 yards down the fairway, or a gymnast to execute a double-back somersault. Many movements in sport require an explosive effort during execution. When force is generated quickly, the movement is known as a *power movement.* Power is critical to successful performance in many sports today, and proper strength training can enhance this component.

Isometric, isotonic, and isokinetic exercises can be used to develop muscular strength and endurance. Body movements depend on the contraction of muscles. As a muscle contracts, tension is created within the muscle and the muscle shortens, lengthens, or remains the same.

Isometric exercises. A muscle contracts isometrically when it exerts force against an immovable resistance. Although tension develops within the muscle, the length of the muscle remains relatively constant and there is little or no movement of the joint. This is also referred to as a *static contraction.*

When performing isometric exercises, the individual exerts maximum force against an immovable object and tension develops within the muscle. For example, stand in a doorway and place the palms of your hands at shoulder height against the frame. Push with all your might and feel the tension develop in your muscles. Even though you grunt and groan as you contract your muscles to their maximum, it is impossible for you to move the resistance, in this case the door frame. Another approach to performing isometric contractions is to contract one muscle against another muscle, applying an equal and opposite force; in this case, the opposing muscle serves as a resistance. For example, raise your arms to shoulder height and place your palms together. Push against your palms as you contract your muscles. There should be no movement as your muscles work against one another.

When one is performing isometric exercises, it is suggested that the muscle should generate a maximum force for 5 seconds, with the contraction repeated 5 to 10 times each day. Isometrics offer the advantage of not requiring any equipment; any immovable object or your own body serves as the resistance. One frequently cited disadvantage of isometric exercise is that strength is developed at only a specific joint angle, not through the entire range of motion. Isometric exercises were most popular in the late 1960s to early 1970s. Isometric exercises now are most often used to develop strength at a specific joint angle to enhance a particular movement or for injury rehabilitation.

Isotonic exercises. Isotonic contractions occur when force is generated while the muscle is changing in length. Movement occurs at the joint, and the muscles involved shorten and lengthen. For example, for one to lift a weight from its starting point when performing a biceps curl, the biceps muscle must contract and shorten in length. This is called

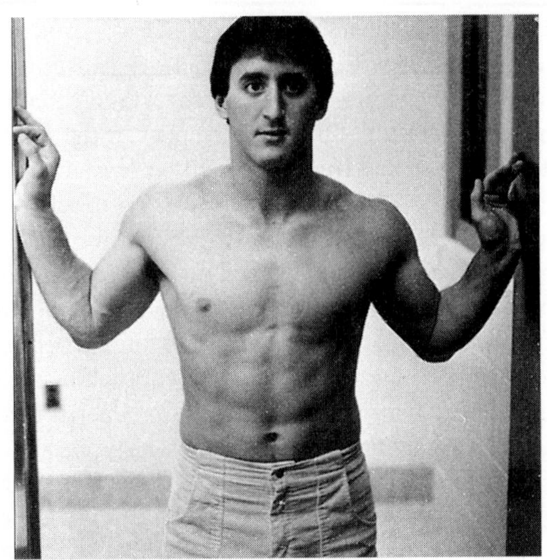

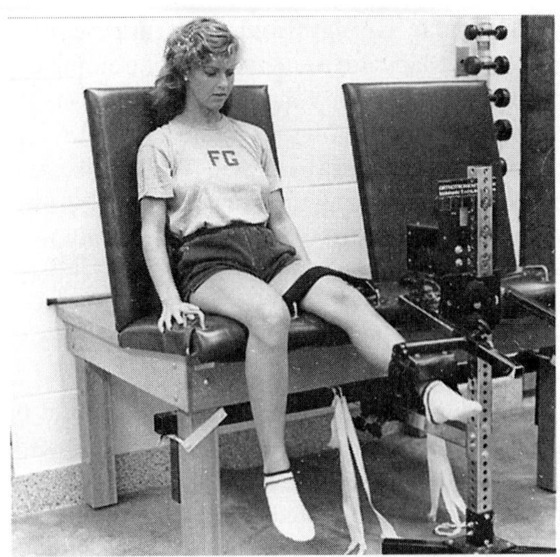

A, Isometric exercise is force exerted against an immovable resistance. **B,** An isokinetic device, such as the Orthotron, provides resistance at a constant velocity.

a *concentric contraction.* To control the weight as it is lowered back to the starting position, the biceps muscle continues to contract while gradually lengthening. This is referred to as an *eccentric contraction.* When exercising isotonically, it is essential to use both concentric and eccentric contractions for the greatest improvement to occur and also to exercise through the range of motion.

One problem associated with isotonic training is that the force applied to the weight varies throughout the range of motion. This is attributable to the effects of gravity and the system of levers within the body. Once the initial resistance is overcome, lifting the weight can be easy or difficult, depending on the position of the weight relative to the body. Thus, the muscles are not working at or near their maximum effort throughout the range of motion.

Common forms of isotonic exercise equipment are free weights, barbells, dumbbells, and various machines. Some isotonic exercise machines have been designed specifically to vary the resistance throughout the range of motion. This permits the muscles to exert their maximum effort throughout the entire range of motion.

Isotonic exercises are probably the most popular means of developing strength and endurance. Millions of people use this approach to achieve and maintain desired levels of muscular development.

Isokinetic exercises. When one is performing isokinetic exercises, the length of the muscle changes while the contraction is performed at a constant velocity. Isokinetic devices such as Cybex are designed so that the resistance can be moved only at a certain speed, regardless of the amount of force applied. The speed at which the resistance can be moved is the key to this exercise approach. Because isokinetic machines can be expensive, they are most often used in the diagnosis and treatment of various injuries.

The advantages and disadvantages of each exercise approach have been debated in the scientific literature. Many researchers have examined the various types of exercise and training approaches to determine which are safest and most effective for producing a desired gain. Understanding how to design programs using each approach and their advantages and disadvantages probably will be included in your professional preparation coursework.

Muscular strength and endurance can be improved. Many different methods of training can be effective to develop these fitness components. Although weight training is not necessary to realize gains in muscular strength and endurance, this approach is popular with many people. The term *progressive resistance exercise* is commonly used to denote weight-training programs that involve working out against a resistance that is progressively increased as the muscle adapts to the workload or resistance.

Although all principles of training should be incorporated into a weight-training program, the principle of overload is of critical importance. Improvements in strength and endurance occur only when a muscle or muscle group is worked at a higher level than that to which it is accustomed—it must be overloaded. As muscle development increases, the body adapts to the level of resistance. To further improve, the workload must be progressively increased. Once the desired level of fitness is achieved, maintenance of this level requires continued training at the current resistance.

Before a discussion of the general guidelines for training, it may be helpful to define the following terms:

- *Resistance* is the workload or weight being moved.
- *Repetition maximum (RM)* is the maximum force that can be exerted or the weight of resistance lifted. One RM is the maximum weight that can be lifted in a single effort. The intensity of the workout can be expressed as a percentage of 1 RM. For example, if a person can bench-press 200 lb, 80% of 1 RM would be 160 lb. Each repetition would be completed using this weight.
- *Repetition* is the performance of a designated movement or exercise pattern through the full range of motion.
- *Set* is the number of repetitions performed without a rest.

When planning a training program, one must consider the weight used per lift, the number of repetitions per set, the number of sets per workout, and the number of workouts per week. Because there are so many weight-training programs available, only general guidelines with respect to the intensity, duration, and frequency will be presented.

Intensity. The intensity of the workout refers to the extent to which the muscles are overloaded. Overload can be accomplished by any combination of the following: increasing the resistance or weight lifted, increasing the number of repetitions per set, increasing the number of sets per workout, increasing the speed at which the repetition is performed, and decreasing the time for rest between sets.

Programs can be designed to develop either strength or endurance or both. The differences between these programs pertain to the number of repetitions and the amount of resistance. Generally, a strength-training program emphasizes a low number of repetitions (e.g., 8 or less) with a heavy resistance (e.g., 70–80% or greater of 1 RM), whereas endurance-training programs involve performing a high number of repetitions (e.g., 12 to 20) with a low resistance (e.g., 40–70% of 1 RM). For the development of both strength and endurance, a moderate number of repetitions (e.g., 8 to 12) and a moderate resistance are used. Guidelines for strength and endurance training are shown in Figure 7-1. The weight that will create an adequate resistance varies with the individual and the goal of the program.

Time. The duration of the training program depends on the person's level of fitness, fitness goals, equipment available, and time available to work out. One to three sets are often completed of each exercise. The amount of rest between each set varies according to the individual's program.

Frequency. The training program must include time for the muscles to rest and recover from the workout while adapting to a higher physiological level. The same muscle group should not be worked on successive days. It is recommended that exercises be performed 2 or 3 days per week or every other day.

Muscular strength and endurance can be measured. Because muscular strength and en-

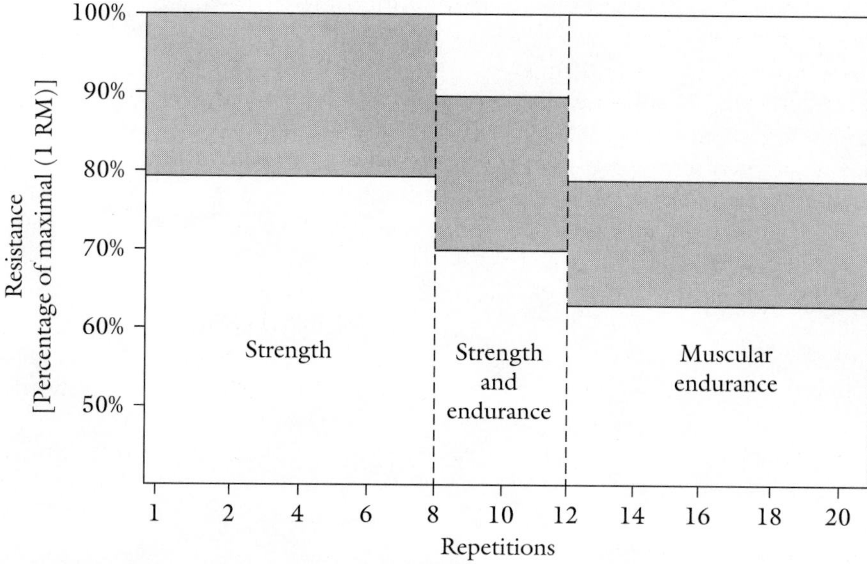

Figure 7-1 Guidelines for developing strength and muscular endurance.

durance are specific to each muscle or muscle group, the level of development can vary among the various muscles or muscle groups. Therefore, the strength and endurance of each muscle or muscle group must be measured.

Strength can be measured isometrically by using a dynamometer. As muscle contraction occurs, the force is transmitted to the instrument and can be recorded (e.g., the hand dynamometer can be used to determine grip strength). Strength can be measured isotonically by determining the maximum amount of weight that can be moved once through the designated range of motion (e.g., bench press); this is 1 repetition maximum or 1 RM.

Endurance can be measured by determining the number of repetitions of a particular movement that can be performed continuously (e.g., the number of repetitions of the bench press that can be performed with a designated resistance) or the number of repetitions performed within a specified period of time (e.g., the number of sit-ups that can be performed in 1 minute). Endurance also can be determined by measuring the time a specific contraction can be sustained (e.g., how long a static push-up can be held).

Flexibility

Flexibility can be defined as the maximum range of motion possible at a joint—that is, the extent of movement possible about a joint without undue strain. Although it is one of the most important fitness components, it is often overlooked, and consequently its development is neglected.

Flexibility is not a general quality; it is specific to a particular joint, such as the knee, or to a series of joints, such as the spinal vertebral joints. This means that an individual can have a better range of motion in some joints than in others.

The extent of movement possible at a joint is influenced by the structure of the joint. For example, the elbow and the knee are hinge joints, allowing movement in one direction only; flexion (bending) and extension (straightening) are the only movements possible. In contrast, the shoulder and hip are ball and socket joints; this joint

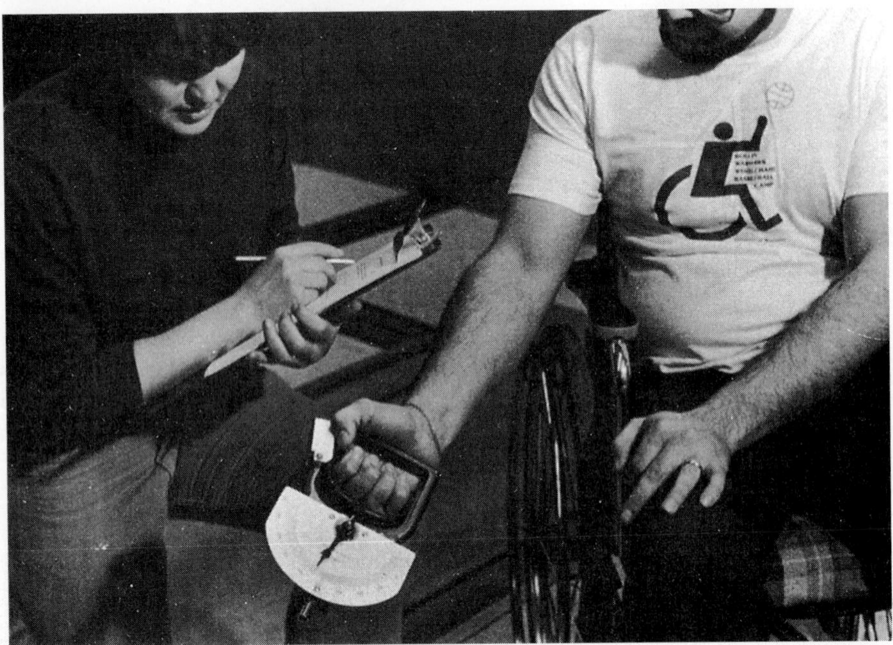

Some devices are specially designed to assess grip strength.

structure allows movement in many directions, usually with a greater range than the hinge joint. Soft tissues such as muscles, tendons, and ligaments greatly influence the range of movement possible at a joint. Flexibility is affected by the length that a muscle can stretch (i.e., its elasticity). When muscles are not used, they tend to become shorter and tighter, thus reducing the joint's range of motion.

Flexibility is essential to performing everyday tasks and is also a critical component in the performance of many sport activities. Activities such as gymnastics, yoga, swimming, karate, and dance place a premium on flexibility. Limited flexibility decreases the efficiency with which everyday and sport activities can be performed. Thus, the development of flexibility should be addressed in designing a fitness program.

Flexibility is important to good health. Flexibility is important for maintaining good posture. Poor postural alignment can cause pain and limit one's ability to move freely.

Flexibility can help prevent low-back pain. Nearly 85 million Americans suffer from episodes of low-back pain each year. This condition is caused by poor muscle development and poor flexibility. Improving muscle development and flexibility in conjunction with using proper care in sitting, standing, and lifting objects can help alleviate this condition.

Flexibility is also important for preventing muscle injuries. Poor flexibility can contribute to uncoordinated and awkward movements, thus increasing the potential for injury. Muscle soreness and body stiffness following vigorous physical activity can be alleviated by using a good stretching program to develop flexibility both before and after an activity session.

Flexibility is important for the performance of physical activities. Flexibility contributes to the efficient performance of all kinds of physical activities, including everyday tasks and sports. Flexibility helps one perform these tasks to one's fullest potential.

Flexibility is important to the performance of even the simplest everyday activities. Imagine how difficult it would be to get dressed without adequate flexibility. Developing and maintaining flexibility are critical to help elderly persons be functionally independent. Some physical conditions, such as arthritis or cerebral palsy, severely restrict flexibility. Improving flexibility to the greatest degree possible, given one's capabilities, can have a significant impact on one's quality of life—even to the extent of allowing a dependent individual to become functionally independent.

Athletes recognize the importance of flexibility in sport performance. Adequate flexibility can enhance performance capabilities by allowing the athlete to stretch and reach further, to generate more force when kicking or throwing an object, and to change positions more quickly and efficiently. Poor flexibility can adversely affect performance. For example, a sprinter may have a shorter stride length and less speed because tight hamstring muscles can adversely affect his or her ability to flex the hip joint. Because certain sports require an extremely high degree of flexibility for successful performance, stretching exercises to enhance flexibility are typically included as part of an athlete's warm-up and cool-down activities. These activities enhance the elasticity of the muscles and thus help reduce the likelihood of injury and muscle soreness.

Decreased flexibility can be caused by many factors. People who are active tend to have better flexibility than those who are sedentary. When muscles are not used, they tend to become shorter and tighter and lose elasticity. Consequently, flexibility decreases. Age is another factor that influences the extent of flexibility. It is important to encourage people to remain active as they grow older so that the effects of aging on fitness will be minimized.

Excessive amounts of body fat impede movement and flexibility. Consider the difficulty of severely obese persons when they are trying to tie their shoelaces: the fat deposits serve as a wedge between the parts of the body, thereby restricting movement.

Muscle tension can affect flexibility. Individuals who experience prolonged stress often respond by bracing or tensing the muscles in their neck, shoulders, and upper back. This tightens the muscles for long periods, thus reducing flexibility.

To be successful, athletes must develop the fitness components required by their sports.

Maintaining flexibility helps elderly people continue to function independently.

Muscle imbalance also can restrict flexibility. When weight training, for example, if an individual strengthens one group of muscles around a joint while neglecting the development of the opposing group (e.g., the quadriceps muscle group in the front of the thigh is strengthened but the hamstring muscle group in the back of the thigh is not), flexibility will be decreased. Therefore, to ensure maximal flexibility when weight training, it is important to perform each exercise correctly, through the full range of motion, and develop opposing muscle groups.

Flexibility can be improved. There are several different approaches to developing flexibility. Participating in some physical activities can promote flexibility. Swimming, for example, can improve the flexibility of several joints. Also, because the activity is non-weight-bearing, swimming in a warm pool is often recommended for people with arthritic conditions.

Flexibility also can be improved through a stretching program. Because flexibility is specific to each joint, improvement and maintenance of flexibility requires a program that incorporates specific exercises for the major joints of the body. Flexibility exercises can be performed using ballistic, static, or contract-relax stretching techniques.

Ballistic stretching. This dynamic method uses the momentum generated from repeated bouncing movements to stretch the muscle. Although it is effective, most experts do not recommend this technique because it may overstretch the muscle and cause soreness or injury.

Static stretching. An extremely popular and effective technique, static stretching involves gently and slowly moving into the stretch position and holding it for a certain period of time. Movement should take place through the full range of motion until a little tension or tightness is felt in the muscle or muscle group. As the muscle relaxes, the

The alternate toe touch is an example of a ballistic exercise, which is not recommended by experts. The sitting hamstring stretch is safer and can be performed using static stretching or the contract-relax technique.

stretch should be extended and held again. Stretching should not be painful. Care must be taken not to force the joint to move too far, which could cause an injury. Stretches should be held from 10 to 30 seconds and a minimum of five repetitions performed for each exercise. Flexibility exercises should be performed at least three to five times a week. If flexibility at a particular joint is extremely poor, a daily stretching program can be recommended. Flexibility exercises also should be performed at the start and at the end of a workout.

Contract-relax technique. When one is performing stretching exercises, it is important that the muscles involved are relaxed. The contract-relax technique facilitates the relaxation of muscles. Muscles are arranged in pairs; when one contracts, the opposing muscle in the pair relaxes (e.g., when the quadriceps muscles contract, the hamstring muscles relax). When one uses this technique to develop flexibility, the muscle opposite the one to be stretched is contracted for at least 5 seconds. This relaxes the muscle to be stretched. Then the static stretch is performed on the desired muscle. To apply this technique to the development of hamstring flexibility, an individual would contract the quadriceps muscles, thus relaxing the hamstrings. Then a static hamstring stretch is employed. This technique allows the stretch to be performed through a greater range of motion.

Because flexibility is specific, a program for improvement and maintenance of flexibility must include exercises for each movement at the joint for which flexibility is being developed.

Flexibility can be measured. Because flexibility is joint specific, there is no one test that can be used to provide an overall measure of an individual's flexibility. The goniometer, a large protractor

A goniometer can be used to measure hip flexion.

with movable arms, provides a measurement of the range of movement in terms of degrees.

There also are a number of other tests that have been developed to measure movement at certain joints and require little equipment to perform. The sit-and-reach test is used to assess the flexibility of the lower back and hamstring muscles.

CONDUCTING FITNESS PROGRAMS

Physical education, exercise science, and sport professionals must follow the principles of exercise when designing a fitness program. The principles of specificity, overload, and progression must be taken into account. Careful consideration must be given to providing for individual differences and for safety. When planning a fitness program to meet individual needs, practitioners must ensure that the participant exercises with sufficient intensity, duration, and frequency to attain desired fitness goals. Equally important to realizing long-term fitness benefits is the manner in which the program is conducted. Physical education programs in the schools, cardiac rehabilitation programs, and adult fitness programs in community, commercial, and corporate settings should be conducted in a manner that optimizes the chances for maintaining health fitness throughout life.

Guidelines for Developing Health-Related Fitness

Cardiorespiratory endurance

- Frequency: 3–5 days/week
- Intensity: 55%/65%–90% HR_{max} or 40%/50%–85% HRR*
- Time: 20–60 minutes
- Type: Aerobic activity

Muscular strength and endurance

- Frequency: 3 days/week
- Intensity: Strength requires high resistance, 6–8 repetitions
  Endurance requires low resistance, 12–20 repetitions
- Time: 1–3 sets
- Type: Isotonic or progressive resistance exercises; can also use isometric and isokinetic exercises

Flexibility

- Frequency: 2–3 days/week
- Intensity: Stretch past the normal length until resistance is felt
- Time: Hold the stretch from 5–10 seconds initially, building to 30–45 seconds
- Type: Static or contract-relax techniques

Body composition

- Maintain present level of physical activity and reduce caloric intake
- Maintain present level of caloric intake and increase level of physical activity
- Reduce caloric intake and increase level of physical activity
- Eat a diet low in fat

*ACSM Guidelines[13] state that lower intensity values—that is, 55%–64% HR_{max} or 40%–49% HRR—may be appropriate for those individuals who are unfit.

Fitness programs should include cognitive and affective educational goals as well as physical activity. For fitness to become an integral part of one's life, one must be taught fitness knowledge and an appreciation for the benefits of fitness. Participants should know (1) why fitness is important, (2) the risks associated with being unfit, (3) guidelines for designing a personal exercise program, and (4) how to evaluate and solve their own fitness problems. Program experiences should be structured to develop a positive attitude and a long-term commitment to fitness. These goals can be accomplished by fostering an understanding of the contributions of fitness to one's quality of life. Program participants should have the opportunity to develop proficiency in several physical activities that can be used throughout their lives.

Fitness should be fun. Boring and tedious exercises and calisthenics do little to develop enthusiasm for fitness. Fitness activities should meet the needs and interests of the program participants. Activities selected should be enjoyable to the individual while permitting the attainment of fitness objectives. Not everyone likes to jog; some prefer swimming, bicycling, tennis, or soccer. Practitioners should help each program participant find an activity that is enjoyable yet sufficiently strenuous to contribute to the attainment of fitness goals. When participants engage in activities that are personally satisfying, they are more likely to incorporate those activities into their lifestyle.

Fitness goals should be established and a plan of action to attain them should be developed. Specific fitness goals based on individual needs should be established for program participants. Some individuals may wish to develop an optimal level of cardiorespiratory endurance, others may hope to lose weight, and still others may strive to enhance their flexibility to perform daily living tasks more easily. Such individual objectives must be considered when conducting a program.

Goals provide a direction for participants and help to focus their energy and effort. Goals should be realistic, and a reasonable amount of time allotted to attain them. Fitness does not happen overnight—it requires effort, determination, and discipline. Once long-term goals have been established, short-term or weekly goals should be set to help move toward the desired outcome. It is important for program participants to realize that the

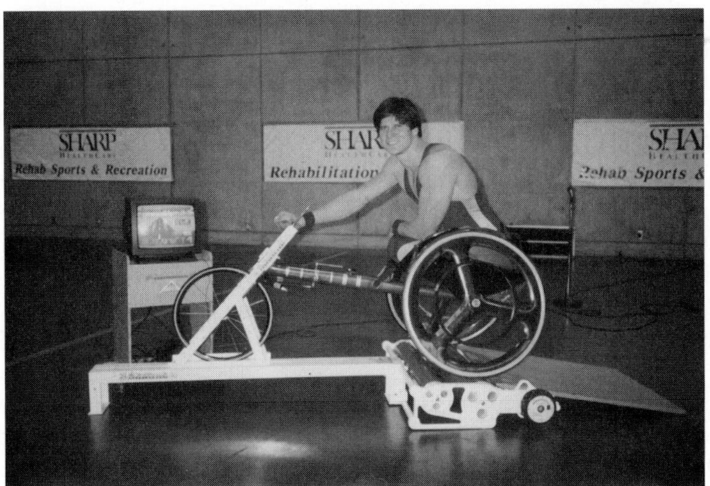

Specialized fitness equipment has been developed to meet the needs of athletes in wheelchairs. This resistance trainer, created by D & J Development, has an interactive computer that simulates road racing conditions.

development of an acceptable level of fitness requires time. It is estimated that 50% or more of the adults who start an exercise program drop out within the first month.[11] Participants should be informed that it will take time for the effects of their efforts to be noticed or felt. It may take as long as 8 weeks to experience many of the major benefits. However, by monitoring their weekly efforts, individuals will be able to see that they are making progress.

Fitness progress should be monitored. Progress should be monitored on a regular basis. This will help individuals to notice their improvement. Each participant should be encouraged to keep a personal fitness log of information, such as the number, time, and intensity of exercise sessions; calories consumed and calories expended; weight changes; and personal feelings pertaining to exercise. Monitoring progress regularly is reinforcing and provides a means of assessing one's improvement.

Fitness requires a maintenance program. Once the desired fitness goals are achieved, a maintenance program is needed. When a person stops exercising, fitness gains are lost in a short time. Just as weight lost is quickly regained if a person reverts to poor eating habits, fitness gains are quickly lost if a person reverts to poor activity habits.

Participants in a fitness program often ask, "How long do I have to keep exercising?" or "Now that I have reached my goal, what do I need to do to keep it?" or "What will happen if I stop exercising?" Fitness gains are easily lost once training stops. Cardiorespiratory gains deteriorate most quickly and can disappear within a few weeks or months of inactivity (5 to 10 weeks). Strength gains are longer lasting; some strength gains remain for 6 months to 1 year after cessation of training.[8]

Because fitness diminishes when exercising is stopped, an exercise program should be an integral part of one's life. Once the desired fitness goals are achieved, a maintenance program should be incorporated into one's lifestyle. Because it is easier to maintain fitness than to acquire it, modifications can be made in the intensity, duration, or frequency of exercise. However, minimal standards for these components should be followed and exercise must be continued on a regular basis.

Fitness improvements and maintenance are a personal responsibility. Achievement and maintenance of an optimal level of fitness require a personal commitment. Individuals must take personal responsibility for their fitness. Fitness must be valued for the important contributions it makes to one's life. Each person must realize that the benefits accrued from participation in a fitness program are indeed worthy of the effort. All persons must be encouraged to incorporate fitness activities into their lifestyle.

EFFECTS OF TRAINING

The results derived from regular periods of muscular work or exercise are many and varied. Individuals who participate regularly in exercise adapted to their needs and thereby attain a state of physical fitness may be called *trained.* Individuals who allow their muscles to get soft and flabby and are in poor physical condition can be referred to as *untrained.*

A trained individual is in a better state of physical fitness than a person whose life is sedentary and inactive. When two persons, one trained and one untrained, of approximately the same build are performing the same amount of moderate muscular work, evidence indicates that the trained individual has lower oxygen consumption, lower pulse rate, larger stroke volume per heartbeat, less rise in blood pressure, greater red and white blood cell counts, slower rate of breathing, lower rate of lactic acid formation, and a faster return to normal blood pressure and heart rate. The heart becomes more efficient and is able to circulate more blood while beating less frequently. Furthermore, in strenuous work that cannot be performed for a long period of time, the trained individual has greater endurance, a capacity for higher oxygen consumption, and a faster return to normal heart rate and blood pressure. Training results in a more efficient organism. Since improved efficiency of heart action enables a greater flow of blood to reach the muscles and thus ensure an increased supply of fuel and oxygen, more work is performed at less cost; improvements in strength, power, neuromuscular coordination, and endurance occur; coordination and timing of movements are better; and an improved state of physical fitness results.

PHYSICAL ACTIVITY RECOMMENDATIONS FOR GOOD HEALTH

As previously discussed, experts have reached a consensus that cardiovascular health benefits can be achieved by engaging in physical activity below the threshold of training necessary to produce fitness benefits. The Centers for Disease Control and Prevention, the American College of Sports Medicine, and the Surgeon General's report on *Physical Activity and Health*[2] recommend that adults should engage in 30 minutes of physical activity equal to brisk walking on most, preferably all, days of the week. Activity can be accumulated in bouts of 8–10 minutes, but 30-minute sessions are preferred. Activity of greater intensity will yield greater health benefits and is encouraged. Children over the age of 2 should accumulate at least 60 minutes a day of moderate intensity physical activity on most, preferably all, days of the week. Additional physical activity should be encouraged. The National Institutes of Health Consensus Development Conference Statement on Physical Activity and Cardiovascular Health emphasized the importance of children's and adults' accumulating a minimum of 30 minutes of physical activity on a daily basis. Active lifestyles are encouraged for people of all ages.

One way that activity for health benefits can be monitored is through the measurement of caloric expenditure. Caloric expenditure provides an indication of the energy expended. It is recommended that a minimum of 1,000–1,500 calories be expended a week in regular physical activity or no less than 1.35 calories per pound of body weight per day. For optimal health benefits, an expenditure of 2,000–3,500 calories per week is recommended. However, it should be noted that for health benefits to occur, calories must be expended by engaging in activities on most, if not all, days of the week and for long periods of time. Activity must be an integral part of one's lifestyle if these benefits are to be attained.

The important health benefits associated with engaging in resistance training to promote strength led the Centers for Disease Control and Prevention, the American College of Sports Medicine, and the Surgeon General's report on *Physical Activity and Health*[2] to recommend that adults perform strength-developing activities at least twice a week. It was recommended that at least 8–10 strength-developing activities that use the major muscle groups of the legs, trunk, arms, and shoulders be performed at each session, with one or two sets of 8–12 repetitions being performed for each exercise.

These activity recommendations offer people of all ages a multitude of options for including physical activity into their lives. It is hoped that these recommendations will encourage people who were discouraged by the difficulty of adhering to a program of vigorous exercise, such as that associated with health fitness, to include moderate amounts of physical activity into their lives.

SPECIAL CONSIDERATIONS FOR FITNESS

There are many different factors that should be considered in conducting fitness programs. Environmental conditions should be carefully weighed by program leaders. Leaders and program participants should know how to modify their exercise program based on weather conditions. They should also be familiar with the risks associated with exercising in hot and humid weather as well as extreme cold.

Program leaders and participants often want to know the answers to other areas related to fitness and performance. One area of great interest is nutrition. Proper nutrition can enhance individuals' fitness, health, and performance. Another area of interest within the realm of exercise physiology is ergogenic aids. Athletes at all levels are interested in improving their performance. Some use a variety of ergogenic aids, such as carbohydrate loading, creatine, caffeine, steroids, and sports drinks.

Environmental Conditions and Fitness

Participants' safety should always be the primary concern of professionals conducting fitness programs. Exercising in an exceptionally hot, humid environment or in extreme cold requires both short- and long-term physiological adaptations by the body. Professionals and participants should be aware of the risk these conditions impose and how fitness programs need to be modified for safe participation.

Extreme caution must be used when exercising in hot, humid weather. The body's normal temperature is 98.6°F. During exercise, as the body's temperature rises, several methods are used by the body to cool itself. The main method of cooling is evaporation. As you exercise, you perspire or sweat, and the evaporation of the sweat keeps the body temperature within normal limits. When it is hot and when the relatively humidity reaches 65%, heat loss through evaporation is less effective, and the body's ability to dissipate heat is impaired.[8] Additionally, excessive sweating and lack of fluid replacement can lead to dehydration. A person who is dehydrated stops sweating, and evaporation no longer cools the body. Heat-related problems such as heat cramps, heat exhaustion, and heat stroke can occur under hot and humid conditions.

Heat cramps are muscle cramps, typically in the muscles most used in exercise. Heat exhaustion is characterized by muscle cramps, weakness, dizziness, disorientation, nausea, elevated temperature, profuse sweating, rapid pulse, and collapse. Heat stroke is a life-threatening emergency. The symptoms include a sudden collapse, unconsciousness, rapid pulse, relatively dry skin from lack of sweating, and a core body temperature of 106°F or higher. In heat stroke, the sweating mechanism breaks down and the body is unable to dissipate heat by sweating. If heat stroke occurs, immediate action is necessary to reduce the temperature of the body and access medical care.

To prevent heat-related problems, use caution when exercising in hot, humid weather. Be sure to drink plenty of fluids before, during, and after exercise to replace fluids lost through evaporation. Water and commercial sport drinks such as Gatorade, Powerade, and Thirst Quencher are good for replenishing fluids. Exercise in the coolest part of the day, either early in the morning or in the evening. On extremely hot and humid days, participants should consider decreasing the intensity of their workout to reduce heat stress. Other considerations may involve canceling the workout or exercising indoors in a cool environment. It is also important to take time to acclimatize the body to the hot and humid weather. Acclimatization occurs usually in 5 to 7 days.[18] Exercise should be reduced from the normal level as the body adjusts to the stress of heat.

Cold weather also requires precautions be taken during exercise. Conserving heat is a major concern when exercising in cold weather. Hypothermia, the breakdown of the body's ability to produce heat, can occur when the weather is between 50°F to 60°F and it is damp and windy. Hypothermia occurs when the body temperature drops below 95°F. Shivering and loss of coordination initially occur. As the body's temperature drops further, shivering stops, muscles stiffen, and unconsciousness occurs. This is a medical emergency, and first-aid efforts should focus on raising the body's temperature and seeking immediate medical attention.

Extreme cold can also lead to frostbite. To prevent cold-related problems, participants should be aware of the conditions that contribute to hypothermia. Before exercising, individuals should check both the temperature and wind chill to determine whether it would be dangerous to exercise. Dress properly for exercise in cold weather. Hats should be worn to reduce the loss of body heat through the head. Several light layers of clothing should be worn so that the body temperature can be more easily regulated. Try to avoid getting wet in cold weather, which increases the risk for hypothermia. To prevent frostbite, wear a mask, gloves, and a hat. Be sure to take time to gradually acclimatize to exercising in the cold. In extreme conditions, consider canceling or limiting workouts or moving to an activity that can be performed indoors.

Environmental conditions pose challenges to individuals seeking to work out on a regular basis. It is important to be aware of the current weather conditions, the risks they impose, and the adaptations necessary to exercise safely. Maintaining the core body temperature, taking time to gradually acclimatize to conditions, following safety precautions, and using common sense can help reduce the health risks associated with exercising under conditions of extreme heat, humidity, and cold.

Nutrition and Fitness

Nutrition plays an important role in enhancing fitness and health. As a science, nutrition is concerned with the study of foods and their effect on the human body. The central focus of nutrition is the study of food requirements for the production of energy and the regulation of bodily processes.

"You are what you eat" is an adage that captures the critical contribution of nutrition to our health and well-being. What we eat can affect our health, growth and development, and ability to perform various activities that fill our lives. In terms of health fitness, the foods we consume directly affect our body composition and the energy we have available to engage in physical activity. The energy derived from food is measured in kilocalories, which are commonly referred to as calories. Regulating one's energy balance by carefully monitoring caloric consumption and expenditure is important in achieving a desirable level of health fitness. Individuals must also take care to consume sufficient calories so that they have the energy necessary for work and to lead a physically active lifestyle.

A nutrient is a basic substance that is used by the body to sustain vital processes such as repair and regulation of cellular functions and the production of energy. The six major categories of nutrients are carbohydrates, fats, proteins, vitamins, minerals, and water.

Carbohydrates, proteins, and fats—the three basic foodstuffs—provide the energy required for muscular work. They also have a critical role in the maintenance of body tissues and in the regulation of their functions. Carbohydrates are the major source of energy for the body, and fats are a secondary source.

Vitamins and minerals have no caloric value. Although they are required only in small amounts, they are essential to body functioning. Vitamins are needed for normal growth and development. Vitamins do not provide energy directly, but play a critical role in releasing energy from the foods that are consumed. Minerals are essential to the regulation and performance of such body functions as the maintenance of water balance and skeletal muscle contraction.

Water is the most basic of all the nutrients—it is necessary to sustain life. The most abundant of all the nutrients in the body, water accounts for approximately 60% of the body's weight. Water is necessary for all of the chemical processes performed by the body. It is essential for such functions as energy production, digestion, temperature regulation, and elimination of the by-products of metabolism.

Maintaining a proper water balance is crucial. Insufficient water causes dehydration; severe dehydration can lead to death. People who are physically active should carefully monitor their water intake to ensure that an adequate fluid balance is maintained. This is particularly critical for individuals who exercise in a hot, humid environment. Exercising under these conditions typically causes excessive sweating and subsequently large losses of water. Sufficient water should be drunk to ensure that proper fluid balance is maintained.

A well-balanced diet is necessary to obtain all the nutrients required by the body. The Food Guide Pyramid, shown in Figure 7-2, was designed by the United States Department of Agriculture (USDA) to help people eat a balanced diet that includes sufficient servings from each food group. The base of the food pyramid is the grain group, and the vegetable and fruit group occupies a position above it. Next is the dairy group and the group composed of meat, poultry, fish, dry beans,

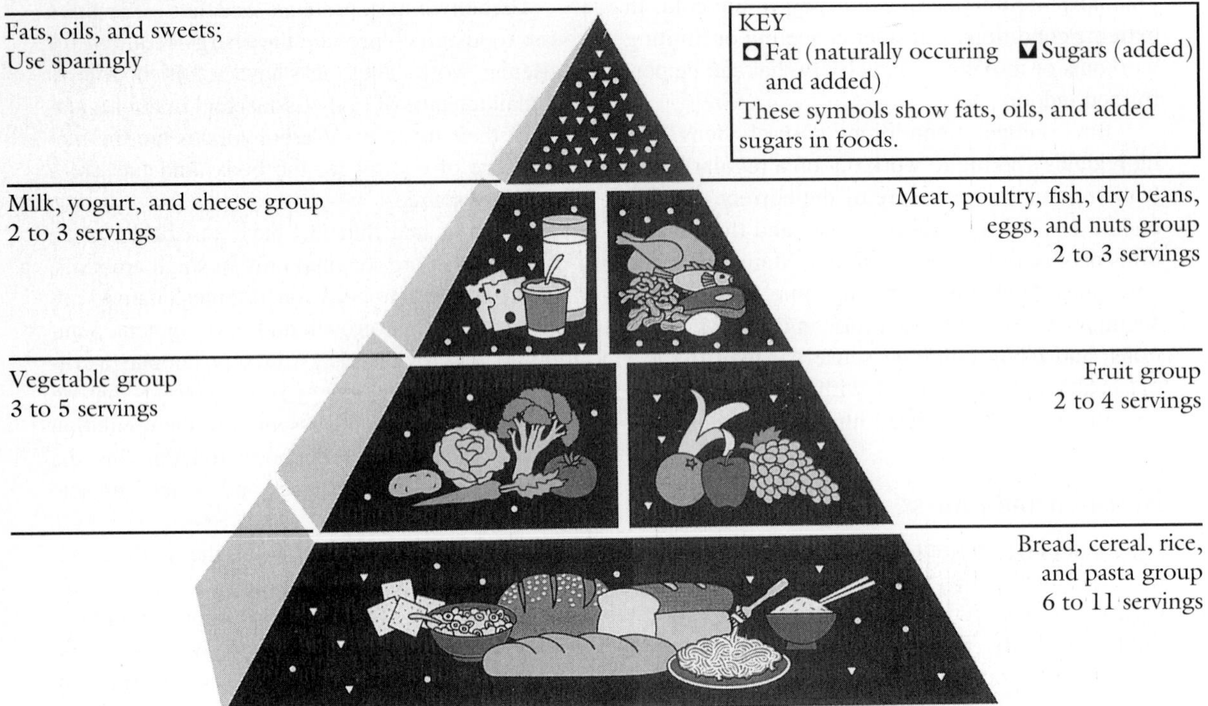

Figure 7-2 The USDA Food Guide Pyramid.

eggs, and nuts. At the top of the pyramid are fats, oils, and sweets, with an accompanying note advising that these products be used sparingly. All necessary nutrients can be obtained daily by eating a variety of foods from each of the food groups and by following recommendations for servings.

In planning a daily diet, it is also important to carefully monitor caloric intake and the amounts of carbohydrates, fat, and protein consumed. Current dietary practices and recommended dietary goals are shown in Figure 7-3. U.S. health officials have expressed a concern that the current American diet is too high in fat, cholesterol, sugar, and sodium and is lacking in carbohydrates and fiber. Although Americans lowered their percent of caloric intake from fat from 45% to 34% in 1995, the decrease was the result of increased caloric intake and not necessarily a reduction in fat consumption.[19] The total average caloric intake, as well as calories from fat, is shown in Figure 7-4.

The USDA's *Dietary Guidelines for Americans, 2000* emphasizes the **ABC**s of good health.[20] These 10 guidelines focus on building a healthy diet and lifestyle. The guidelines encourage Americans to "**A**im for Fitness" by eating healthy and being active daily. "**B**uild a Healthy Base" emphasizes using the Food Guide Pyramid to guide food choices. Lastly, Americans are encouraged to "**C**hoose Sensibly," that is, follow a diet according to the recommended percentages for fat, moderate intake of sugar and salt, and drink alcoholic beverages in moderation. This is the first time that physical activity is being included as part of the USDA's Dietary Guidelines. The *Dietary Guidelines for Americans, 2000*[20] are shown in the box on page 280.

Dietary planning requires the thoughtful application of nutritional knowledge to ensure that the diet is adequate and balanced. Individual conditions and factors such as age, sex, weight, med-

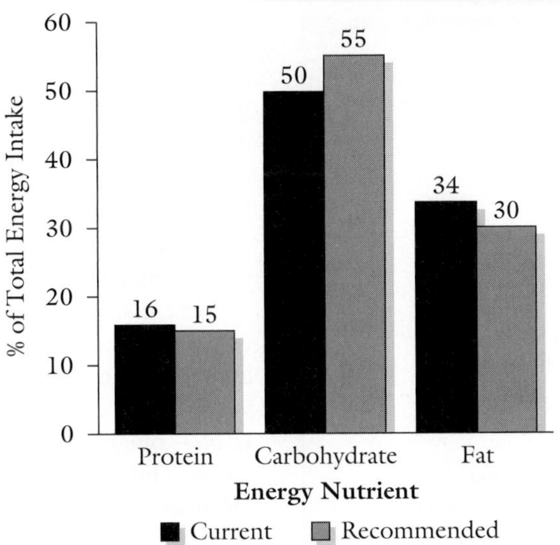

Figure 7-3 Comparison of current dietary practices and recommended dietary goals. Data from Wardlaw, GM and Insel, PM: Perspectives in nutrition, 3rd ed, St. Louis, 1996, Mosby.

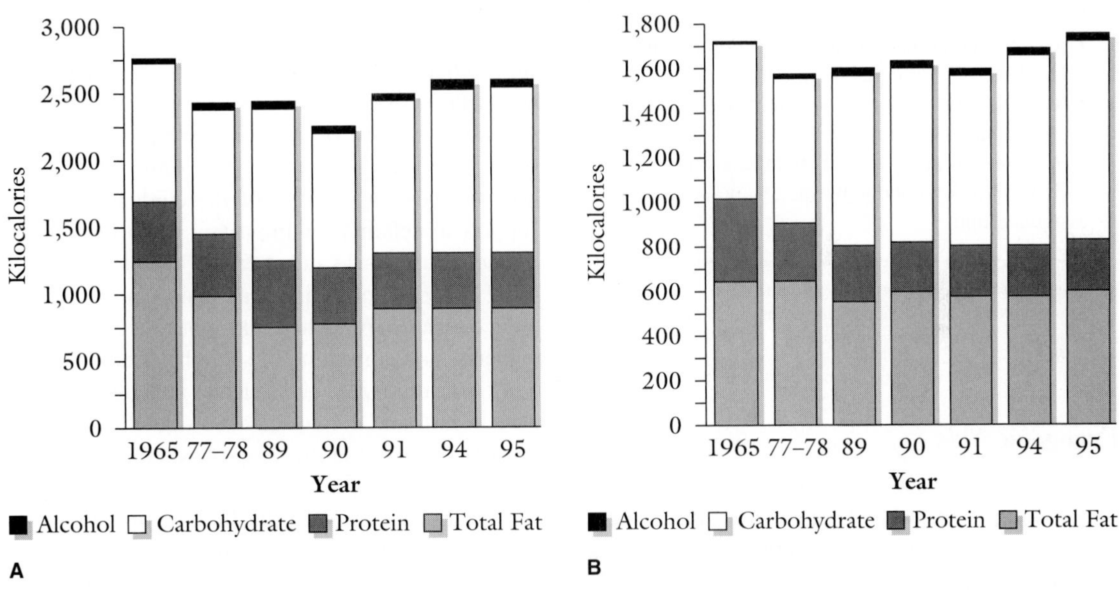

Figure 7-4 Dietary contribution to total caloric intake in American adults. **A,** Men ages 19 to 50 years of age. **B,** Women ages 19 to 50 years of age. From: U.S. Department of Agriculture, Center for Nutrition Policy and Promotion, *Nutrition Insights,* Number 5, April, 1998.

ical conditions, environment, and level of physical activity must be considered in dietary planning. Because of the significant impact of nutritional practices on health, the production of energy for physical activity, and the regulation of body composition, attaining and maintaining desirable levels of health fitness require careful attention to nutritional practices.

Dietary Guidelines for Americans, 2000

Aim, Build, Choose—for Good Health

AIM FOR FITNESS

- Aim for a healthy weight.
- Be physically active each day.

BUILD A HEALTHY BASE

- Let the pyramid guide your food choices.
- Choose a variety of grains daily, especially whole grains.
- Choose a variety of fruits and vegetables daily.
- Keep food safe to eat.

CHOOSE SENSIBLY

- Choose a diet that is low in saturated fat and cholesterol and moderate in total fat.
- Choose beverages and foods to moderate your intake of sugars.
- Choose and prepare foods with less salt.
- If you drink alcoholic beverages, do so in moderation.

Source: From US Department of Agriculture, Center for Nutrition Policy and Promotion, Dietary Guidelines for Americans, 2000. (www.usda.gov/cnpp)

Ergogenic Aids

Athletes at all levels seek different means to improve their performance. One way to improve performance is through the use of ergogenic aids. According to Powers and Howley,[21] ergogenic aids are work-producing substances or phenomena believed to increase performance. Athletes use ergogenic aids to enhance their energy use, production, and/or recovery in their quest for improved performance.

Ergogenic aids take on many different forms. There are mechanical aids, such as weight belts or breathing strips. Psychological aids, such as stress management or hypnosis, comprise another category of ergogenic aids. Pharmacological aids include drugs, some of which are legal and some that are not. Caffeine and anabolic steroids fall under this category. Physiological aids include the use of blood doping and oxygen supplementation. Lastly, nutritional aids, such as carbohydrate supplementation and creatine, are used by many athletes to enhance their performance.

Exercise physiologists study the effects of ergogenic aids on an individual's physiologic state as well as the individual's performance. They investigate the effects of ergogenic aids at multiple levels—ranging from the subcellular to systematic levels. This includes the pulmonary, cardiovascular, neuromuscular, and metabolic systems. Their investigations focus on many different aspects of ergogenic aid use. For example, they investigate the effects of different amounts or doses of the substance, the impact on both short- and long-term performance, and whether the effect is different for trained or untrained individuals.[21] They also consider whether the ergogenic aid works better for power tasks or endurance tasks and whether it has an impact on fine or gross motor tasks.[21] The researchers have found that for some of the ergogenic aids, the weight of the evidence did not support the claims for improved performance, increased muscle size and strength, or quicker recovery.[21] However, oftentimes, athletes, convinced that their chosen approach works, may use it despite evidence not supporting the sought-after benefits.

Some ergogenic aids, such as anabolic steroids, have been found to have adverse side effects. Additionally, there is the question of whether it is legal to use or on a banned substance list by various sport organizations, including the International Olympic Committee (IOC). Creatine supplements, anabolic steroids, carbohydrate loading, sports drinks, and caffeine are just a few of the many ergogenic aids used by athletes.

Caffeine

Caffeine, a stimulant, is found in a variety of foods, drinks, and over-the-counter products. The IOC classifies caffeine as a restricted drug, allowing its use up to a certain level. The standard is up to a urine level of 12 micrograms/milliliters, which is about 6 to 8 cups of coffee. Caffeine is absorbed rapidly from the gastrointestinal track, rising to a significant level in the blood about 15 minutes after consumption, with the peak concentration about 45–60 minutes after ingestion. Given this, an athlete wanting a boost in performance from caffeine needs to consume it about an hour before the event. Ingestion of the equivalent of about 2 cups of coffee has been shown to have an ergogenic effect.

Caffeine enhances the function of the skeletal muscle, increasing tension development. It stimulates the sympathetic nervous system, which typically leads to increased alertness and decreased perception of fatigue. Research suggests that caffeine can increase endurance performance. However, the ergogenic effect on performance is variable and is influenced by the dose and the amount of caffeine the athlete typically consumes. Athletes who do not regularly consume products with caffeine typically have more pronounced ergogenic effects than athletes who are regular consumers of caffeine. Additionally, athletes who abstain from caffeine for a period of days prior to its use have more pronounced effects.

Some side effects associated with the use of caffeine include very rapid heart rate, diuresis, insomnia, nervousness, diarrhea, and anxiety. Athletes who choose to use this ergogenic aid should be careful to monitor their dosage, modify the dose to take into account their pattern of caffeine consumption, and be cognizant of the side effects. Prior to using caffeine to improve performance during competition, athletes should experiment with various dosages to optimize benefits and reduce side effects.

Carbohydrate Loading

Carbohydrate loading or glycogenic supercompensation is a practice followed by athletes who compete in endurance events lasting 60 to 90 minutes or longer. Carbohydrates perform a critical role in the production of energy in the body. They are converted to glycogen and are stored in the liver and muscles. Blood glucose, a by-product of the breakdown of carbohydrates, also is important to energy production. Muscle glycogen stores are used for muscle energy metabolism, and the liver's store of glycogen is used to replace blood glucose. During prolonged exercise, such as during endurance events lasting longer than 60 to 90 minutes, the stores of glycogen decline to very low levels, contributing to muscle fatigue, performance decrement, and exhaustion.

In an effort to maximize performance, endurance athletes practice carbohydrate loading before an event. By modifying their diet to eat more complex carbohydrates than normal, athletes hope to store additional glycogen in their muscles and liver, sometimes up to four times the usual level. During competition, athletes draw on these additional stores to delay fatigue and to maintain their race pace for a longer time. In addition to modifying their diet, athletes also change their training regime to ensure that their glycogen stores are at capacity.

There are several approaches to carbohydrate loading. One approach, termed the classical approach, requires athletes to begin the process of carbohydrate loading 7 days prior to competition. Both athletes' training and diet are modified. Seven days prior to competition, athletes deplete their muscle glycogen stores by training to exhaustion. Hard training continues for the next 3 days, followed by 3 days of rest prior to competition. In addition to altering their training schedule, athletes modify their diet. Typically, on the first day when training to exhaustion occurs, athletes consume a diet consisting of about 50% carbohydrates. During the other 3 hard training days, a high fat and protein diet is eaten. The 3 days before competition, on the rest days, athletes consume a diet consisting of about 90% carbohydrates. On the day of the event, athletes eat a high carbohydrate meal, typically consuming complex carbohydrates such as grains, pasta, rice, or bagels. Not all athletes found this approach to be beneficial. Some athletes had difficulty handling the extremes in diet. Other athletes were uncomfortable stopping their training 3 days before their competition.

Researchers determined that another approach, referred to as the modified approach, could be successfully used to maximize glycogen stores.[21] This approach does not require athletes to exercise to exhaustion in order to deplete their glycogen stores, nor does it require athletes to eat extremely low or extremely high amounts of carbohydrates. Instead, athletes gradually reduce the intensity and duration of their workouts on the days preceding competition while modifying their diet to increase their carbohydrates to 70%. For example, 5 days before the event, athletes would decrease their workout time from 90 minutes to 40 minutes, while eating a 50% carbohydrate diet. After 2 days, workout time again is reduced, this time from 40 minutes to 20 minutes, while carbohydrate consumption is increased to 70%. The day prior to competition, athletes rest and continue to consume the 70% carbohydrate diet. This approach has been found to be effective in increasing glycogen stores and enhancing performance. Some athletes tolerate this approach better than the classical approach.

During the meal prior to the event, it is recommended that athletes consume between 1 and 5 grams of carbohydrate per kilogram of body weight.[21] Athletes should eat from 1 to 4 hours before exercise.[21] The meal should be easily digestible carbohydrate, but, if it is taken 1 hour before exercise, it should be in liquid form. Prior to trying carbohydrate loading before a competition, the athlete should test the procedure during practice. It should also be noted that following strenuous exercise, athletes can hasten their recovery by consuming carbohydrates.

Carbohydrates ingested during exercise delay the onset of fatigue. One way to ingest carbohydrates during exercise is through the use of sport drinks.

Hydration, Energy, and Sports Drinks

During exercise, heat is dissipated by the body to minimize the increase in body core temperature. The primary mechanism through which this occurs is the evaporation of sweat. As exercise intensity increases, so does the evaporation of sweat. Exercising in hot and humid environments increases the evaporation of sweat even more. Researchers have found that in hot weather as much as 2.8 liters per hour can be lost in sweat.[21] In events of long duration, such as a marathon, some runners can lose as much as 8% of their body weight.[21] In addition to loss of water, electrolytes that are critical to the normal function of the body are lost. Levels of electrolytes, such as sodium, calcium, chloride, and potassium, decrease. The loss of fluid and electrolytes adversely affects cellular functions. If these fluids and electrolytes are not replaced, significant health problems could arise, such as heat stroke, and performance decrements will occur.

Exercise physiologists investigate the optimal way to replace lost water and electrolytes. Fluid replacement during exercise is associated with lower heart rate, body core temperature, and levels of perceived exertion. The ease of fluid replacement depends on the activity. During intermittent activities such as soccer or football, it is easier for an athlete to replace lost fluid and electrolytes. During prolonged activities, such as marathon running, fluid replacement typically occurs on the go. Having determined that fluid replacement during exercise is beneficial, the next question is which fluid is best.

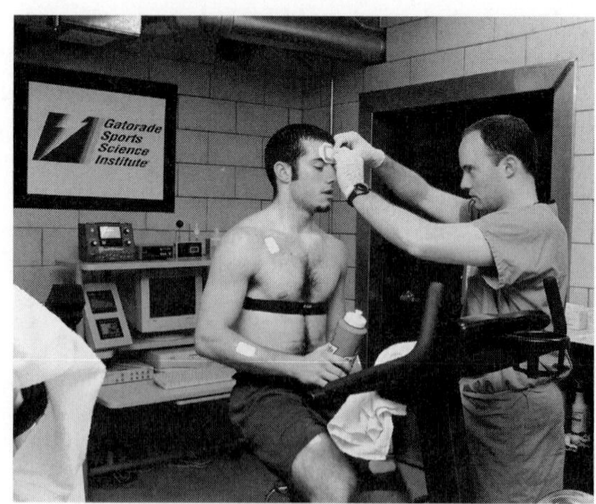

To determine the effects of a sports drink on performance, companies test athletes under various performance conditions. Here an athlete is being prepared for testing at the Gatorade Sports Science Institute.

Water is often regarded as the natural choice for fluid replacement. It is readily available and inexpensive. It is generally recommended that 4–6 ounces of water be consumed for every 15–20 minutes of exercise, especially during prolonged exercise and conditions of high heat and humidity.[21] One problem associated with using water to rehydrate is that oftentimes athletes do not drink enough water to adequately replace the fluids. To some athletes, it is not as palatable as some of the other fluid-replacement beverages so they drink an insufficient quantity. Another problem with drinking water to rehydrate is that is does not contain electrolytes nor carbohydrates.

Sports drinks are popular for maintaining hydration. They are formulated to maximize fluid absorption. Sports drinks are designed to enhance performance through replacement of lost electrolytes and supplying of additional carbohydrates to replenish glucose stores. Researchers have found that sports drinks containing 6 to 8% carbohydrates are well tolerated by athletes and provide extra energy to enhance performance.[21] Because of the variety of flavors offered, athletes find drinking sports drinks more appealing than drinking water. In events of long duration as well as under conditions of high heat and humidity, replacing fluids and electrolytes is important to alleviating dangerous conditions such as heat stroke.

Fluid replacement during exercise reduces athletes' heart rate and body temperature as well as athletes' perception of exertion. The greater the rate of fluid intake, the lower the athletes' responses.[21] Additionally, Powers and Howley report that drink temperature influences absorption rate; cold drinks are absorbed more rapidly than warm drinks.[21] For exercise lasting less than 60 minutes, replacement of fluids using water is adequate. However, when exercise lasts longer than an hour, drinks should contain sodium, chloride, and carbohydrates.

In planning for fluid replacement, the athletes' state of fitness and the intensity and duration of the event must be taken into account. Additionally, attention must be paid to environmental conditions. Environmental conditions, such as excessive heat and humidity, extreme cold, and high altitude also require increased fluid intake to avoid dehydration.

Creatine

Many individuals use nutritional supplements in hopes of enhancing their athletic performance. One popular supplement used to improve performance in events placing a premium on strength or power is creatine monohydrate.

Phosphocreatine in skeletal muscle is important to the production of ATP, a critical source of energy in high-intensity brief exercise lasting less than 5 seconds. Sprinting 50 meters in track, explosive events such as high jumping, short bursts of speed in soccer, or rapid weight-lifting movements rely on this energy source. During these intense efforts, phosphocreatine is depleted, reducing the rate of ATP production.

Phosphocreatine is a limiting factor in short-term, high-intensity events. In an effort to increase stores of muscle phosphocreatine and have more fuel available to support short, high-intensity activity, many athletes have used creatine supplementation. Additionally, many athletes use creatine supplementation in conjunction with a resistance-training program to maximize their muscular strength and increase their fat-free mass.

Compared to other supplements, there has been much research on the efficacy of creatine as an ergogenic aid.[22] Research findings have been varied, with some supporting creatine's effectiveness as an ergogenic aid in brief, high-intensity events, while other studies find less evidence to support anecdotal claims.[22] These is also less evidence that creatine supplementation can enhance performance in events lasting more than 90 seconds.[22] The American College of Sports Medicine's position is that creatine supplementation enhances exercise performance in events involving short periods of extremely powerful activity, especially during repeated efforts.[22] Additionally, research has shown individual variability in the supplement's effects, with some individuals benefiting more than others from its use.[22]

Typically, athletes go through a loading phase in which they try to maximize the amount of phosphocreatine in their muscles. They load their muscles by ingesting 5 grams of creatine 4 to 6 times a day for 5 days. This phase is sufficient to saturate the muscles and maximize the amount of phosphocreatine available for ATP production. However, in addition to using creatine supplementation prior to an event to improve performance, athletes use it to maximize the effects of their training, often in the off-season. Many athletes continue supplementation for weeks or months, ingesting several grams of creatine a day. During this phase, they engage in intense training to increase muscle strength, muscle size, and body mass.[22] Creatine supplementation allows athletes to train at higher workloads, enabling them to perform more repetitions per set of a given exercise and to recover more quickly between exercise sets.[22]

Little research has been conducted on the short- and long-term effects of oral creatine supplementation. Some athletes have experienced muscle cramping, excessive water retention, and gastrointestinal disturbances from supplementation. However, overall, it appears that creatine supplementation for up to 8 weeks does not appear to produce major health risks.[21] More research is needed on the long-term effects of supplementation.

Development of strength is one reason athletes use ergogenic aids.

Anabolic-Androgenic Steroids

Anabolic-androgenic steroids are synthetic forms of testosterone, the primary male sex steroid. Testosterone secreted by the testes is responsible for the development of masculine characteristics changes seen in adolescents and continued into adulthood. Testostereone functions both androgenically—stimulating the growth of male characteristics—and androgenically—promoting the growth of tissue, muscle mass, weight, and bone growth.[21]

Synthetic forms of testosterone were developed by scientists who sought to maximize the anabolic effects and minimize the androgenic effects.[21] Originally these synthetic forms were developed to help promote the growth of tissue in patients suffering from certain debilitating diseases. The ability of steroids to develop muscle mass and strength soon attracted the attention of athletes. Athletes began to take steroids and use heavy resistance-training programs in an effort to acquire significant strength gains.

Numerous research studies were conducted to investigate the mechanism of strength gains and various performance claims. There was considerable variation in the results of the studies. Additionally, due to ethical constraints of testing on human subjects, the dosages used in studies were the recommended therapeutic dosage. Athletes seeking to improve their performance typically self-administer 10 to 100 times the recommended dosage.[21] Many athletes did accrue significant strength gains. As the number of athletes using steroids increased, many sports governing bodies, including the International Olympic Committee, banned them.

Even though illegal, steroid use by athletes continues. Athletes and others, including adolescents, use anabolic steroids to enhance perfor-

Focus on Career: Exercise Physiology

PROFESSIONAL ORGANIZATIONS

- American College of Sports Medicine
  www.acsm.org
- American Physiological Society
  www.the-aps.org
- Exercise Physiology Academy
  www.aahperd.org → NASPE → Academies

PROFESSIONAL JOURNALS

- *American Journal of Physiology*
- *Clinical Exercise Physiology*
- *Journal of Applied Physiology*
- *Journal of Aging and Physical Activity*
- *Exercise and Sport Sciences Reviews*
- *International Journal of Sport Nutrition and Exercise Metabolism*
- *Medicine and Science in Sports and Exercise*
- *Physician and Sports Medicine*
- *Research Quarterly for Exercise and Sport*

mance and improve physical appearance. Anabolic steroids are taken orally or injected at levels many times the recommended therapeutic dosage. Typically, dosages are taken daily in cycles of weeks or months, then stopped for a period of time, and then resumed. Sometimes in an effort to obtain maximum gains while minimizing the negative effects, users combine several different types of steroids, a process referred to as stacking. Steroid abuse is most prevalent in sports where the premium is placed on strength. Power lifting, throwing events in track and field, American football, and baseball are sports in which athletes may seek to gain an advantage through the use of steroids.

Many serious side effects, some irreversible, are associated with steroid use. For both males and females, adverse side effects associated with chronic steroid use include increased risk of heart disease, liver tumors and cancer, increased cholesterol, and hypertension. Psychological effects of use include mood swings and aggressive behavior. In males, side effects include male-pattern baldness, acne, and voice deepening. Males also experience a decrease in testicular function, including a decrease in sperm production, and gynecomastia—breast development. Mood swings and aggressive behavior are also characteristic of chronic steroid abuse. Females taking steroids experience irreversible voice deepening and enlarged clitoris. Increased facial hair, decreased breast size, increased libido, increased appetite, and menstrual irregularities are also outcomes of chronic steroid use in females. Adolescent users risk a decrease in their ultimate height. Adolescents' long bones are still growing, and if they abuse steroids, the growth plates of these bones may cease growing prematurely.

The use of ergogenic aids can take many forms, be it mechanical, psychological, physiological, or pharmacological. Some ergogenic aids have been shown to be beneficial through research while others gain popularity through anecdotal evidence. Users of ergogenic aids need to be careful to understand the correct manner of usage, whether it is legal or not, and the associated health consequences.

SUMMARY

Exercise physiology is the study of the effects of exercise on the body, ranging from the level of the system (e.g., cardiovascular system) to the subcellular (e.g., production of ATP for energy) level. Exercise physiologists are interested in both the acute and chronic adaptations of the body to exercise. Professionals in physical education, exercise science, and sport build on this foundational knowledge in many different ways. Knowledge from exercise physiology is used to design effective fitness programs for people of all ages, to guide the development and implementation of cardiac rehabilitation programs, to plan programs to help children and youths to incorporate physical activity into their life, to conduct training programs for elite athletes, and to structure rehabilitation programs for injured athletes and exercise enthusiasts.

A major concern of the exercise physiologist is fitness development, maintenance, evaluation, and outcomes. Within the profession, interest has increased in health-related fitness as opposed to performance-related fitness. The components of health-related and performance-related fitness are different. And, the extent to which these components are developed depends on individuals' goals. The health-fitness components are cardiovascular function, body composition, muscular strength and endurance, and flexibility. Attainment of desirable levels of these components can enhance one's health and well-being. Individuals who are unfit are at increased risk for disease.

Many health benefits are derived from physical fitness and the incorporation of physical activity into one's lifestyle. Physical education, exercise science, and sport professionals should follow medical guidelines and sound training principles in developing and implementing physical fitness programs. Professionals should be aware of contributors to fitness, such as sound nutritional practices. Physical education, exercise science, and sport professionals must take an active role in educating the American public about proper fitness and nutritional practices.

Another area of study for exercise physiologists is ergogenic aids. Ergogenic aids, such as caffeine, creatine supplements, sports drinks, carbohydrate loading, and steroids are used to improve performance.

SELF-ASSESSMENT TESTS

These tests are designed to help you determine if you have mastered the material and competencies presented in this chapter.

1. Define exercise physiology and discuss the importance of exercise physiology to the professionals in physical education, exercise science, and sport. Investigate one of the areas of study in exercise physiology and write a short paper on a selected topic of interest to you.
2. Using the information provided in the Get Connected box, access the ACSM site and review one of the position papers. What new insights did you gain? How can you use this information as a professional? Or, access the President's Council on Physical Fitness and Sport site and read the latest research digest. What are the implications of this research for professionals?
3. In a short paper, discuss how an individual's lifestyle and habits may be a deterrent to a state of fitness and health. What rationale would you use to persuade a friend or a relative who was tired all the time, feeling overwhelmed by stress, and overweight to start a physical fitness program? What excuses may be offered for not being active? How could you counter these excuses?
4. Research information on the variety of ergogenic aids available to individuals aspiring to improve their performance. Prepare a short presentation on your selected aid, including mechanism of effect, claims for use, research on its efficacy, legality of aid, and other related areas.

REFERENCES

1. Buskirk ER: Exercise physiology, Part I: Early history in the United States. In JD Massengale and RA Swanson, editors, The history of exercise and sport science, Champaign, Ill., 1997, Human Kinetics.

2. Tipton CM: Exercise physiology, Part II: A contemporary historical perspective. In JD Massengale and RA Swanson, editors, The history of exercise and sport science, Champaign, Ill., 1997, Human Kinetics.
3. US Department of Health and Human Services: Physical activity and health: a report of the Surgeon General, Atlanta, Ga., 1996, US Department of Health and Human Services, Centers for Disease Control and Prevention, National Center for Chronic Disease Prevention and Health Promotion.
4. US Department of Health and Human Services: Healthy people 2010: understanding and improving health, ed 2, Washington, D.C., 2000, US Government Printing Office. (www.healthypeople.gov/healthypeople)
5. President's Council on Physical Fitness and Sport: Definitions: health, fitness, and physical activity, Research Digest, March 2000.
6. Kesaniemi YA, Danforth, E. Jr., Jensen MD, Kopelman PG, Lebvre P and Reeder BA: Consensus statement: dose-response issues concerning physical activity and health: an evidence-based symposium, Medicine and Science in Sports and Exercise, 33(6 June Supplement 2001), S351–S358, 2001.
7. Lee I and Skerrett PJ: Physical activity and all-cause mortality: what is the dose response relationship, Medicine and Science in Sports and Exercise, 33(6 June Supplement 2001), S459–S471, 2001.
8. Prentice W: Fitness and wellness for life, ed 6, New York, 1999, McGraw-Hill.
9. Swain DP and Leutholtz BC: Exercise prescription: a case study approach to the ACSM guidelines, Champaign, Ill., 2002, Human Kinetics.
10. Dishman RK: Determinants of participation in physical activity. In C Brochard, RJ Shepard, T Stephens, JR Sutton, and BD McPherson, editors, Exercise, fitness, and health, Champaign, Ill., 1990, Human Kinetics.
11. Marcus BH, King, TK, Bock BC, Borrelli B, and Clark MM: Adherence to physical activity recommendations and interventions. In SA Shumaker, EB Scrhon, JK Ockene, and WL McBee, editors, The handbook of health behavior change, ed 2, New York, 1998, Springer.
12. Corbin CB, Welk GJ, Corbin WR, and Welk KA: Concepts of physical fitness: Active lifestyles for wellness, ed 12, 2004, New York, McGraw-Hill.
13. Pollock ML, Gaesser GA, Butcher JD, Després J, Dishman RK, Franklin BA, and Garber CE: ACSM position stand: the recommended quantity and quality of exercise for developing and maintaining cardiorespiratory and muscular fitness, and flexibility in healthy adults, Medicine and Science in Sport and Exercise, 30:975–991, 1998. (www.acsm.org)
14. National Institutes of Health (NIH), National Heart, Lung, and Blood Institute (NHLBI): Clinical guidelines on the identification, evaluation, and treatment of overweight and obesity in adults. HHS, Public Health Service (PHS), 1998.
15. US Department of Health and Human Services: The Surgeon General's call to action to prevent and decrease overweight and obesity. Rockville, MD, US Department of Health and Human Services, Public Heatlh Service, Office of the Surgeon General, 2001. (www.surgeongeneral.gov/library)
16. Willett WC, Manson JE, Stampfer MJ, Colditz GA, Rosner D, Speizer FE, Hennekens CH: Weight, weight change, and coronary heart disease in women. Risk within the "normal" weight range, JAMA, 273(6):461–465, 1995.
17. Galanis DJ, Harris T, Sharp DS, Petrovitch H: Relative weight, weight change, and risk of coronary heart disease in the Honolulu Heart Program, American Journal of Epidemiology, 147(4):379–386, 1998.
18. Prentice WE: Fitness and wellness for life, ed 6, New York, 1999, McGraw-Hill.
19. US Department of Agriculture, Center for Nutrition Policy and Promotion, Is total fat consumption really decreasing?, Nutrition Insights (5), April 1998. (www.usda.gov/cnpp)
20. US Department of Agriculture, Center for Nutrition Policy and Promotion, Dietary Guidelines for Americans, 2000. (www.usda.gov/cnpp)
21. Powers SK and Howley ET: Exercise physiology: Theory and application to fitness and performance. St Louis, 2004, McGraw-Hill.
22. Rawson ES and Clarkson PM: Scientifically debatable: Is creatine worth its weight? Sport Science Exchange 91, 16(4), 2002. Available online at www.gssiweb.com.

SUGGESTED READINGS

Faigenbaum AD: Strength training and children's health. JOPERD 72(3):24–30, 2001.

Addresses several areas of strength training for children, including health benefits, prevention of sport-related injuries, program design, and safety guidelines.

Frontera WR: Exercise and musculoskeletal rehabilitation, The Physician and Sports Medicine, 31(12), 2003 (available online at www.physsportsmed.com).

Discusses the rehabilitation of musculoskeletal injuries, including guidelines for the acute, recovery, and function phases. Information is provided on the tailoring of exercise to fit the needs of the individual and integrating exercise with other interventions, such as mediations, physical modalities, and psychological support.

Heath GW: Epidemiologic research: a primer for the clinical exercise physiologist, Clinical Exercise Physiology, 2:60–67, 2000.

Provides an introduction to methods used in epidemiology, which gives readers some understanding and assistance in evaluating the research literature on the complex interactions between physical activity, health, and disease.

Kraemer WJ: Strength training basics. The Physician and Sports Medicine, 31(8), 2003 (available online at www.physsportsmed.com).

The basic principles of specificity, progressive overload, and variation of training are described and the development of an individualized exercise program is presented.

Knuttgen HG: What is exercise? A primer for practitioners, The Physician and Sports Medicine, 31(3), 2003 (available online at www.physsportsmed.com).

Although written for physicians, this overview of exercise provides information about exercise units, intensities of exercise, physiology of exercise, energy reservoirs, and considerations in prescribing exercise.

Medicine and Science in Sports and Exercise 2001, 33(6) June Supplement 2001.

Issue devoted to physical activity and health, focusing on the dose-response relationship or the relationship between the amount and intensity of physical activity and the health outcomes achieved. Includes papers on research methodology, whether physical activity or physical fitness is more important in accrual of health benefits, individual differences in responses, and physical activity and mortality.

Pediatric Exercise Science, 12(2), 2000.

This entire issue is devoted to reviews of research of children's and youth's engagement in physical activity. The articles include reviews of aerobic fitness, anaerobic fitness, muscular strength, and skeletal development in children.

Powers SK and Howley ET: Exercise physiology: theory and application to fitness and performance. St Louis, 2004, McGraw-Hill.

Presents a theory-into-application approach to exercise physiology, including such topics as exercise metabolism, systematic adaptations to exercise, fitness, training for performance, nutrition, and exercise for special populations.

Welk GJ and Wood K: Physical activity assessment in physical education: a practical review of instruments and their use in the curriculum, JOPERD 71(1):30–40, 2000.

Written by researchers from the Cooper Institute for Aerobic Reseach, this article presents a practical view of various means of assessing physical activity, including self-report, heart rate monitor, activity monitor, and direct observation.

Wilmore JH: Aerobic exercise and endurance. The Physician and Sports Medicine, 31(5), 2003 (available online at www.physsportsmed.com).

Describes the various responses of the body to exercise, including metabolic, neuromuscular and cardiovascular, and respiratory responses. The importance of helping individuals be active and sustain their activity as they age is discussed.

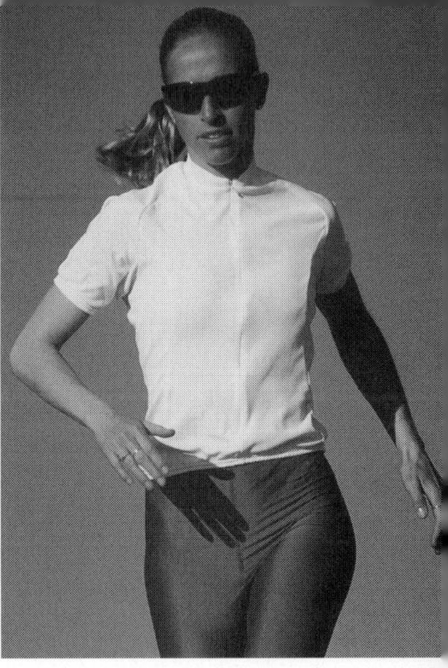

CHAPTER 8

SOCIOLOGICAL FOUNDATIONS

OBJECTIVES

After reading this chapter the student should be able to—

- Show how sport is a socializing force in the American culture.
- Discuss the nature and scope of sport.
- Trace the growth of sport in educational institutions in the United States and the attitude of educators toward this growth.
- Know the dimensions of concerns in sport today including girls and women, children, minorities in sport, violence, use of performance-enhancing substances, and sport for individuals with disabilities.

Sport is an important part of this nation's culture and other cultures throughout the world. It captures newspaper headlines, holds television viewers' attention, produces millions of dollars a year in revenue for entrepreneurs, and even impacts international affairs. The Olympic Games is one of the best-known international sports events. The Olympic Games are seen by billions of people worldwide. In 1995, NBC paid the International Olympic Committee $3.6 billion for the television rights to the Olympic Games for the years 2000 through 2008. Corporations, eager to capitalize on this large market, pay the International Olympic Committee millions of dollars to be one of many exclusive sponsors (e.g., the official credit card, film, sun glasses, etc.).

Sport exerts a strong influence on many aspects of the American lifestyle. Millions of Americans are "glued" to their chairs when featured baseball, football, basketball, and golf contests are scheduled to be televised. Advertisers target large percentages of their promotional budgets to buy airtime during sporting events to sell their wares. For example, a 1-minute advertisement aired during the 2004 football Superbowl sold for over $4 million. This rate is in sharp contrast to the $75,000 charged to advertise during the first Superbowl in 1967. Professional sports teams attract millions of spectators each year. Professional teams spend astronomical sums to obtain the best talent to sustain spectator support and interest and to ensure a profitable year for management. Newspaper coverage devoted to sports occupies more space than all

GET CONNECTED

Center for the Study of Sport in Society contains information about the center's various programs to assist athletes, articles related to the sociology of sport, and the race and gender report card, which details information about race and gender equity in sport.

www.sportinsociety.org

Disabled Sports USA Web site lets you learn about sports opportunities for persons with disabilities and volunteer opportunities and includes links to the Paralympics and disability sport and recreation links.

www.dsusa.org

National Alliance for Youth Sports gives access to information about youth sports, links, and information for kids, parents, coaches, and administrators.

www.nays.org

National Collegiate Athletic Association provides information on many different aspects of collegiate sport, including current news. Click on Education/Outreach to access information on gender equity, participation rates, drug testing, and a multitude of other topics.

www.ncaa.org

Women's Sports Foundation provides information on current issues, career opportunities, upcoming events, and links to research and topics of interest.

www.womenssportsfoundation.org/cgi-bin/iowa/index.html

the arts combined, and sports symbols and jargon infiltrate American language, art, and politics.

The big business of sport has also influenced the nature of college and secondary school sport. Schools and colleges, in an effort to field the best teams, may compromise their academic standards. It is not uncommon for academically outstanding colleges to be more widely recognized for the feats of their athletic teams.

Within the last 10 years, the number of sport participants in our society has increased dramatically. Millions of people of all ages and abilities participate in a diversity of sport activities. Because of the social, political, legal, and educational influence of sport on cultures, it is important to examine this phenomenon.

SOCIOLOGY OF SPORT

The social significance of sport in America is unparalleled.[1] As Leonard states, "Sport permeates virtually every social institution in society."[1] Sport influences and is influenced by social institutions such as economics, family, education, politics, religion, mass media, and popular culture. (See the Lifespan and Cultural Perspectives box.) "The ubiquity of sport is evidenced by news coverage, sports equipment sales, financial expenditures, the number of participants and spectators, and its penetration into popular culture (movies, books, leisure, comic strips, and everyday conversation.)"[1] Coakley notes that sports, as social phenomena, have "meanings that go far beyond score and performance statistics. Sports are related to the social and cultural contexts in which we live. . . ."[2] The prominence and pervasiveness of sport in American culture and its institutional nature led to its study from a sociological perspective. The definition, scope, historical development, and areas of study are discussed in this section.

Definition and Scope

Sociology is concerned with the study of people, groups, institutions, and human activities in terms of social behavior and social order within society.

Lifespan and Cultural Perspectives: Sociology of Sport

- Why do so few minorities and women hold coaching and administrative positions in intercollegiate and professional sports? What can be done to increase their opportunities?
- How does social class influence sport participation?
- How does disabled sport affect our perceptions of people with disabilities?
- How does sport influence our view of masculinity and femininity?
- How are children socialized into sport, and what can be done to sustain their involvement in sport?
- Do the Olympics contribute to international understanding?
- How does the use of Native American imagery in sport influence participants' and spectators' beliefs about Native Americans?
- What societal factors have contributed to parental violence in youth sports?

It is a science interested in such institutions of society as religion, family, government, education, and leisure. Sociologists are also concerned with the influence of social institutions on the individual, the social behavior and human relations that occur within a group or an institution and how they influence the behavior of the individual, and the interrelationships between the various institutions within a society, such as sport and education or religion and government.

As a medium that permeates nearly every important aspect of life, sport has led some physical educators and sociologists to believe that it should receive intensive study, particularly as it affects the behavior of human beings and institutions as they form the total social and cultural context of society. Sport sociology focuses on examining the relationship between sport and society. Coakley[3] lists the major goals of sport sociology to be an understanding of the following:

- Factors underlying the creation and the organization of sports.
- The relationship between sport and other aspects of society, such as family, education, politics, the economy, the media, and religion.
- The influence of sport and sport participation on individuals' beliefs relative to equity, gender, race, ethnicity, disability, and other societal issues.
- The social dynamics within the sport setting, such as organizational structure, group actions, and interaction patterns.
- The influence of cultural, structural, and situational factors on the nature of sport and the sport experience.
- The social processes associated with sport, including competition, socialization, conflict, and change.

Harris describes the sociology of physical activity, which includes sport, as having three main goals. These are as follows:

1. "to look at physical activity with a penetrating gaze that goes beyond our common understanding of social life.
2. to identify and analyze patterns of change and stability in physical activity.
3. to critique physical activity programs in order to identify problems and recommend changes leading to the enhancement of equality and human well-being."[4]

Sport sociologists challenge us to critically examine our common and perhaps sacrosanct assumptions about sport, to scrutinize sports from different perspectives, and to understand social problems and social issues associated with sport (e.g., relationship between wealth and opportunity in sport). Sport sociologists examine societal forces that lead to change in sport (e.g., increased

The emphasis on being number one is so strong in the United States that oftentimes other values derived from participation in sport get forgotten.

opportunities for women and changing conceptions of gender roles). Increasingly, sport sociologists seek to take a more active role in changing the status quo; they identify problems in sport and encourage changes that would transform sport and lead to equitable opportunities and promote human well-being (e.g., inequalities of opportunities experienced by racial and ethnic groups).

Historical Development

Sport sociology emerged as a distinct field of inquiry in the late 1960s. The foundation for the emergence of sport sociology, however, can be traced back to the mid- to late-1800s. During this time, social scientists studied the nature and social functions of play, games, and sport—how these activities contributed to development and the building of character and reflected the culture of the times. In 1899, Thorstein Veblen wrote *The Theory of the Leisure Class,* in which he critiqued sport practices. Veblen argued that sports represented a return to the days of barbarism.[5] Sports were a way for the upper class to show that they were rich enough to avoid work and had the time to enjoy sport in their leisure.[4] A few sociologists of this period undertook the task of writing about sport as a social phenomenon, describing the relationships between sport and social behavior. The topics of this time included an ethnographic study of Native American games, the effect of sports participation on academic performance, and the role of sport in school.[4,5] However, as Sage notes, research was sporadic and often embedded in studies of play and games.[5]

The 1950s marked a growth of interest in the sociology of sport. In 1953, physical educators Frederick Cozens and Florence Stumpf published *Sports in American Life,* which, according to noted sport sociologist George Sage, must be considered a pioneer effort to examine the social role of sport in American society.[5] Two noteworthy and often-cited studies of play also occurred during this time frame. Johan Huizinga's *Homo Ludens* in 1955 and Roger Caillois's *Man, Play, and Games* (1961)—both analyzed the role of play in culture.

In the 1960s, the growth of sport sociology was stimulated by publications and presentations that described the need for and the importance of the field. In 1965, Gerald Kenyon and John Loy authored *Toward a Sociology Sport,* which articulated the need for a discipline that focused on the social aspects of sport. In 1969, Kenyon authored *"A Sociology of Sport: On Becoming a Sub-discipline."*

The growth of interest and the desire to discuss ideas and to share research led to the development of scholarly organizations and journals. In 1964, Europeans and North Americans founded the International Committee of Sport Sociology (ICSS), which, in 1994, became the International Sociology of Sport Association (ISSA). ISSA is affiliated with UNESCO and is a subcommittee of the International Sociological Association (ISA) and the International Council of Sport Science and Physical Education (ICSSPE). In 1976, AAHPER (now AAHPERD) founded the Sociology of Sport Academy, whose mission was to promote the study of sport sociology. In 1980, the North American Society of Sport (NASSS) was established, providing another forum for discussion and dissemination of research in sport sociology.

As research grew, scholarly journals focusing on sport sociology were developed. In 1966, ICSS began publication of the *International Review of Sport Sociology,* which, in 1984, became the *International Review for the Sociology of Sport.* In 1977, the inaugural issue of the *Journal of Sport and Social Issues* appeared. The first issue of the NASSA publication, *Sociology of Sport Journal,* debuted in 1984 under the editorship of noted sport sociologist Jay Coakley. Additionally, *Quest* and the *Research Quarterly for Exercise and Sport* sometimes included articles on sport sociology.

As sport sociology emerged and evolved as a field, changes in its focus occurred. Janet Harris, in tracing the history of sociology of physical activity, which includes sport, describes the primary research emphases during various periods. The topics that have received the most attention are those related to social inequities—especially concerning gender, race, ethnicity, wealth, sexual orientation, and culture.[4] The 1970s were marked by an increased focus on socioeconomic inequalities and class relations in sport, and these topics continued to be one of the primary thrusts of research in the 1980s.[4] Also in the 1980s, more scholars began to study gender inequities in sport, and this continues to be a major focus at present.[4] Another area of study that emerged was exercise and societal conceptions of the body, topics that continue to be major research areas.[4] In the 1990s, scholars increasingly directed their attention to racial and ethnic inequities, particularly those faced by African Americans, and this research continues as one of the central topics today.[4] The globalization of sport, the impact of the media, economics, and politics on sport in different cultures, was also a focus in the 1990s, and is receiving considerable attention at present.[4]

Sport sociologists used a variety of different methods to collect quantitative and qualitative data for their research. As sport sociology emerged, expanded, and evolved, research moved from describing and analyzing sport to interpreting sport using a multitude of theoretical and methodological approaches. Today, many sport sociologists have taken a more active role—using a critical inquiry approach, they examine and interpret sport as well as make suggestions on how to solve problems in sport and seek to transform sport to be more equitable.[2,4]

Areas of Study

Sport sociologists use sociological research strategies to study the behavior of individuals and groups within the sport milieu. They are concerned with understanding the influence of social relationships, past social experiences, and the social setting of sport activities on the behavior of individuals and groups within sport. Some questions sport sociologists might address are these:

- Does participation in sport build character? Does it prepare individuals for life?
- Does sport help minorities, including women, become more fully integrated into society? How does participation in sport affect the social and economic status of minorities?

- How do the mass media affect sport?
- What are the effects of youth sport programs on the lives of participants? the participants' families?
- How are politics and sport related? religion and sport? the economic status of the community or the country and sport?
- How does interscholastic and intercollegiate sport influence the academic achievement of its participants?
- How do coaches influence the lives of their athletes?
- What will be the nature of the sport experience as we move forward in the twenty-first century?

To address these and other questions, sport sociologists may examine historical circumstances, social conditions, economic factors, political climate, and relationships among the people involved.

As a field of study, sociology of sport will likely continue to grow, expanding both in depth and breadth. However, many challenges face the field. For example, Coakley[3] points out that there is a need for further research leading to the development of theories about sport and its relationship to society and social life. Furthermore, Coakley suggests that there is a need to focus additional attention on female participants in sport and on participation in sport throughout one's lifespan (currently only childhood and early adulthood participation are highlighted).[3]

Sport can be viewed as a social institution and examined in relation to its impact on other social institutions such as the economy or the educational system. The effects of sport on participants are also a vital area of study. Before a discussion of several areas of concern to sport sociologists, it may be helpful to define sport and discuss its nature and scope.

SPORT: A DEFINITION

In order to study sport in a systematic manner, it is necessary to develop a specific definition of sport. Such a definition may, by its very nature, be limiting and restrictive. Yet it is necessary to provide a focus and a shared perspective by which to understand the relationship of sport to society.

Coakley defines sports as follows:

> Sports are institutionalized competitive activities that involve rigorous physical exertion or the use of relatively complex physical skills by participants motivated by personal enjoyment and external rewards.[2]

This definition refers to what is popularly known as organized sport activities. On the basis of this definition, three often asked questions can be addressed: (1) What kinds of activities can be classified as sport? (2) Under what circumstances can participation in activities be considered sport? and (3) What characterizes the involvement of participants in sport?

Sport Activities

What physical activities can be considered sport? Is jogging a sport? Chess? Auto racing? Weight lifting? Are participants in a pickup baseball game engaged in sport even though their activity is different in nature from the game professionals play?

Sport, as it is defined, requires that participants use relatively complex physical skills and physical prowess or vigorous physical exertion. Because these terms can be conceptualized as part of a continuum, at times it is difficult to make the distinction between physical and nonphysical skills, between complex and simple motor requirements, and between vigorous and nonvigorous activities. Because these terms are not quantified, determining what is complex physical activity and what is not can be a difficult task. Furthermore, not all physical activities involving complex physical skills or vigorous physical exertion are classified as sport. The circumstances and conditions under which these physical activities take place must be considered when classifying a physical activity as sport.

Conditions

The circumstances or context in which participation in physical activities occurs can be designated as

Sport is said to be institutionalized when there are standardization and enforcement of the rules, emphasis on organization, and a formal approach to skill development.

ranging from informal and unstructured to formal and structured. For instance, compare the nature of a playground pickup game of basketball with a scheduled game between two professional teams. The individuals involved in both situations are playing basketball, but the nature and consequences of these games are different. Thus, the question is, Are both groups of individuals engaged in sport?

When sport sociologists discuss sport, they most often are referring to physical activity that involves competition conducted under formal and organized conditions. Given this perspective, friends engaged in an informal game of basketball are not participating in sport, whereas athletes participating on the professional teams are participating in sport. From the sociological point of view, sport involves competitive physical activity that is institutionalized.

According to sociologists, institutionalization is a standardized pattern or set of behaviors sustained over a period of time and from one situation to another. Thus, competitive physical activity can be considered sport when it becomes institutionalized. Institutionalization occurs when there is standardization and enforcement of the rules governing the activity, emphasis on organization and the technical aspects of the activity (e.g., training, use of strategies, specialization and definition of the roles of players and coaches), and a formalized approach to skill development (e.g., use of experts to provide instruction). Through the process of institutionalization, unstructured and informal physical activities such as throwing a Frisbee become a sport known as *Ultimate Frisbee,* in which competition and organization are an integral part of the setting in which the activity takes place.

Participation Motives

Sport depends on maintaining a balance between intrinsic and extrinsic motivations. When the intrinsic satisfaction of being involved coexists with extrinsic concern for external rewards (e.g., money, medals, approval from parents or a coach), sport occurs. The balance does not have to be 50:50, but when one source of motivation begins to greatly outweigh the other, changes occur in the nature of the activity and the experience of the participants. When participants' intrinsic motives prevail, the organization and structure of physical activity becomes one of play. When participants' extrinsic motives such as medals or money prevail, physical activity changes from sport to what is often referred to as spectacle or work. It should be noted that during the course of a single sport event, participants may shift back and forth from intrinsic to extrinsic sources of motivation. At times participants may be absorbed in the flow of the action and revel in the satisfaction of being involved. Moments later the participants may be motivated by the desire to win a medal or receive the adulation of the crowd; the play spirit becomes replaced with the desire to reap external rewards.

In summary, according to Coakley's definition, three criteria must be met for an activity to be defined as sport. The activity must involve physical skill, prowess, or exertion; it must be institutionalized and competitive in nature; and its participants must be motivated by a combination of intrinsic and extrinsic rewards. These criteria are useful in determining whether or not a physical activity can be classified as sport. Moreover, this definition serves as a focal point for sport sociologists to scientifically examine the role of sport in people's lives and in our society.

As a field of study, sociology of sport has grown tremendously within the past three decades. Due to space limitations, an overview of only a few topics can be presented in this chapter. The topics selected were chosen to enable students to relate to them based on their past experience and the contemporary nature of the topics. Because of the number of children and youth involved in sports, this topic was chosen for inclusion. Additionally, because many students reading this textbook have participated in interscholastic and intercollegiate sports, a few of the many issues within these topics are presented. This chapter also includes a brief introduction to the topics of girls and women in sport, minorities in sport, sports for individuals with disabilities, violence in sports, and drugs in sports.

SPORT IN EDUCATIONAL INSTITUTIONS

The growth of sport in schools and colleges has been comparatively recent in the United States. The period from 1875 to 1900 saw for the first time a Harvard-Yale football game, a Big Ten Conference, and an All-American team. The advent of the radio and "lunar craters," as football coach Alonzo Stagg called the athletic arenas, resulted in an increase in "spectatoritis" and the exploitation of sport for its commercial value.

As sport programs grew, they were extended into the lower educational levels. Athletics started at the college level with a crew race between Harvard and Yale in 1852, followed by the introduction of other sports to the college campus. As higher education athletic programs gained recognition and popularity, the high schools thought that sports should also be a part of their educational offerings. Next, the junior high schools initiated interschool athletic programs, many of which were carbon copies of those in the high schools, which previously had copied the colleges. Today some elementary schools are scheduling games, as competitive sports are pushed further down the educational ladder.

From the beginning, sport was of concern to educators because of its questionable educational worth and the way it can distort a school's or a nation's sense of values. For example, as reported in *Sports Illustrated,* Yale alumni helped raise $180,000 in honor of Walter Camp for the memorial gateway to the Yale Bowl; however, Yale admirers of Josiah Willard Gibbs, one of the greatest physicists the country had produced, were unable to muster $12,000 for a more modest tribute.

Another view of sport in institutions of higher education was advanced by J. Neils Thompson, past president of the National Collegiate Athletic Association (NCAA). Thompson stated, "It seems clear that the image of the institution is clearly influenced by athletic performance. Halfbacks make

Title IX legislation stimulated the growth of girls' and women's sports at all levels.

better copy than philosophers—unfortunate perhaps, but true. Without question, the recruitment of students and the raising of financial support . . . can be favorably impacted by successful athletic programs."[6]

Despite some educators' objections, athletics and sports in the nation's schools, colleges, and universities have continued to grow. Over 6.9 million youths participate in interscholastic sports. In 2003–2004, the National Federation of State High School Associations reported that 4,038,253 boys and 2,865,299 girls participated in interscholastic athletics.[7] Thousands of young men and women participate in collegiate sports. In 2002–2003, the National Collegiate Athletic Association (NCAA), the largest governing body of college athletics, reported that 216,991 males and 160,650 females participated in intercollegiate sports.[8] Thousands of other students participate in sports in community colleges and non-NCAA member institutions. Title IX and the women's movement have become factors in the participation of an increasing number of girls and women in sports in educational institutions. It is estimated that the number of girls and women participating will gradually approach a figure equal to that of boys and men.

Today school and college athletics are experiencing difficulties beyond those provided by their educational critics. The economy, austerity budgets, student criticism, academic performance of athletes, and concerns for minority and female athletes have caused some educational institutions to curtail, abolish, or reevaluate their sport programs. Since athletics play such an important role in American culture, it is interesting to examine some of the sociological implications of sport.

Interscholastic Sports

Interscholastic sports are viewed by many, including the National Federation of State High School Associations, as an integral part of the educational experience for high school students and, increasingly, junior high/middle-school students as well.

Since the advent of Title IX in 1972, girls' and women's sports have grown in popularity. The University of Connecticut basketball players autograph photos for their fans prior to their 2004 NCAA Championship appearance.

The inclusion of interscholastic sports in the educational curriculum has typically been justified on the basis of sport contributing to educational goals.

While there is widespread support for interscholastic athletics, there has also been much criticism of these programs. Proponents of interscholastic athletics cite their valuable contributions to the educational mission of the schools. Critics take the position that sport interferes with the attainment of educational goals (see the Popular Arguments for and against Interscholastic Sport box presented by Coakley[3]).

Participation in interscholastic sports can benefit students in several ways. Participation in sport can help students develop a high level of physical fitness and attain a high degree of proficiency in selected sport skills and knowledge of various aspects of the game. Other frequently cited benefits of participation include the development of sportsmanship, cooperation, leadership, and loyalty. Sport can provide opportunities for personal growth, pave the way for the development of friendships, develop decision-making and thinking skills, teach self-discipline and commitment, enhance one's self-esteem and personal status, and promote the acceptance of others regardless of race or ethnic origins.

However, whether participation in sport enhances academic achievement is a very complex and debatable question. When viewed as a group, high school athletes generally have better grade point averages and express more interest in further education than their nonathletic peers.[3] It is important to note, however, that such differences are typically small. Moreover, academic achievement is linked to a number of factors, including academic goals, personal achievement values, and motivation. It is also difficult to isolate the influence of sport participation from other factors known to influence academic achievement such as family background, economic status, support and encouragement from significant others, and individual characteristics.

Interscholastic sport can also heighten school spirit and engender parental support. In many locales across the country, interscholastic athletics provide a focal point for the community.

It appears that interscholastic programs do not use a disproportionate share of budgetary resources when they are maintained in a proper perspective. However, it should be noted that in times of austerity they are one of the first extracurricular programs to be threatened with cutbacks.

Whether or not interscholastic sport programs help participants attain desirable educational goals, as well as provide a positive experience for those students involved, depends a great deal on the manner in which the programs are conducted. These desired outcomes do not accrue automatically as a result of participation in the program. They can, however, be realized when school administrators and coaches make a concerted and thoughtful effort to structure sport programs to provide experiences that will lead to the attainment of educational goals and fulfillment of students' needs. Lumpkin[9] offered suggestions to help promote a positive interscholastic sport experience for participants and the realization of desirable goals. (See the Interscholastic Program box.)

Interscholastic sport programs are an integral part of the educational experience for millions of

Popular Arguments for and against Interscholastic Sport

Arguments For

1. Involves students in school activities and increases interest in academic activities.
2. Builds the responsibility, achievement orientation, and physical vigor required for adult participation in society.
3. Stimulates interest in physical activities among all students in the school.
4. Generates the spirit and unity necessary to maintain the school as a viable organization.
5. Promotes parental, alumni, and community support for all school programs.

Arguments Against

1. Distracts the attention of students away from academic activities.
2. Perpetuates dependence and immaturity and focuses the attention of students on a set of values no longer appropriate in industrial society.
3. Relegates most students to the role of spectator rather than active participant.
4. Creates a superficial, transitory spirit subverting the educational goals of the school.
5. Deprives educational programs of resources, facilities, staff, and community support.

U.S. high school students and enjoy widespread support. Nevertheless, in many schools across the country, interscholastic sport programs are in serious need of reform. Some programs have little relevancy to the education process. Critics of interscholastic sport also denounce the overemphasis on winning, restriction of opportunities for students, and eligibility requirements for participation. Concern has also been voiced pertaining to drug abuse, soaring costs, pressures from parents and community supporters, and coaches' behavior.

Overemphasis on winning is one of the most frequently voiced criticisms of interscholastic sport. This disproportionate emphasis is reflected in the increased specialization in one sport by athletes, the participation of injured athletes, the subversion of the educational process, and coaches' jobs depending on their win-loss records.

Compared with just 10 years ago, more high school athletes are foregoing multisport competition and specializing in one sport.[10] Whereas in the past athletes would compete in a fall, a winter, and a spring sport, there is a trend toward competing in only one sport a year. Increasingly, athletes engage in conditioning programs and informal practices for their chosen sport in the off-season and attend specialized sport camps and play in community leagues during the summer. Proponents of sport specialization stress that such an emphasis is needed to develop proficiency in advanced skills and refine strategies, remain competitive with other teams, and increase an athlete's chances of receiving college grants-in-aid. Critics argue that specialization limits athletes' development, denying them opportunities to develop skills in other activities, participate with other athletes, and learn from other coaches. Athletes who specialize may be exploited by coaches seeking to win; they are subjected to overuse injuries, are at risk for athletic burnout (i.e., are tired and emotionally exhausted from participating), and may drop out of the sport, often near the point of reaching their fullest potential.

In an effort to win, coaches may resort to undesirable behaviors. They may pressure athletes to practice and play when injured. In an effort to maintain player eligibility, coaches may steer athletes toward easier courses, pressure teachers to pass athletes or, in some cases, alter athletes' grades.

Winning is overemphasized when teachers are hired or fired based on their coaching win-loss records rather than their abilities as teachers. Good teachers have been fired because of a poor

The Interscholastic Program

The Interscholastic Sports Program which is an outgrowth of the basic instructional program, provides additional physical education experiences in a wide range of sports. The purposes of this program should be to help participants to

Gain a better understanding of their physiological and psychological capabilities, and establish reasonable personal goals.
View winning as a means to self-improvement and not as an end in itself.
Assume leadership roles in planning and conducting intramural and interscholastic activities.
Share in the decision-making process involved in those programs.
Participate and/or compete fairly on the factors of age, ability, height, weight, physiological maturity, and strength.
Benefit from the expertise of coaches who are certified teachers possessing either a major or a minor in physical education and/or state coaching certification.
Receive appropriate medical attention before, during, and after intramural/interscholastic sports programs.

1. Medical examinations should be required for all who participate in interscholastic activities.
2. A physician's statement indicating the student's fitness for resuming participation should be required following a serious illness or injury.
3. An athletic trainer or teacher/trainer should be present at all games and practices.

From an administrative standpoint, all secondary school interscholastic contests, including postseason games, should be conducted under the jurisdiction of state high school athletic associations, and the programs should be financed by local boards of education.

From AAHPERD.

coaching record, and poor teachers have been retained because of their outstanding coaching accomplishments.

If interscholastic sports are to realize their educational potential, it is important that winning be kept in perspective. The educational goals of learning and development should be emphasized, not the win-loss record.

The restricted number of opportunities for participation is another criticism of interscholastic sports. Interscholastic sports programs usually offer limited opportunities for participation. Schools typically have both a varsity team and a junior varsity team in a variety of sports, although larger schools also may have freshman teams and reserve teams. Thus, when a given school offers both a varsity and a junior varsity basketball team for boys and for girls, perhaps as few as 48 students will have the opportunity to participate. Many students who are less highly skilled are excluded, despite their love of the game, and often no other scholastic sport opportunities are provided for them. Furthermore, in addition to consuming a great deal of the time and energy of physical education teachers, interscholastic sport teams utilize monies, facilities, equipment, and other resources that could be used for general participation. In addition, even though federal legislation has mandated that boys and girls must have equal opportunities, often the informal support and commitment so necessary to develop and maintain quality programs for females is lacking. (This is discussed elsewhere in this chapter.)

Academic requirements for eligibility are also a controversial issue. Most high schools require that students meet certain academic standards to be eligible to participate in extracurricular activities, including sports. These standards often exceed the criteria required to stay in school. Many states have adopted "no pass, no play" policies, setting forth even more stringent requirements for athletes to maintain their eligibility. These requirements vary, but typically the policy bars participation of those individuals who do not pass all of their courses or who fail to maintain a certain grade-point average during a marking period.

Advocates of this policy believe that establishing stringent standards for participation in sport programs will have a positive effect on athletes' academic performance. In order to maintain their eligibility, athletes will be motivated to pursue their studies. Critics of this policy point out that students who stay in school mainly to play sports now find themselves ineligible and may drop out of school.

The central issue of the no pass, no play controversy is, according to Siedentop,[10] the educational importance of interscholastic sport. Eligibility standards may be appropriate if sport is an extracurricular activity and participation is a privilege to be earned. If, however, sport is an integral part of the educational experience—if it has educational value—then is it appropriate to deny this experience to any student? If participation in interscholastic athletics contributes to educational goals, if the experience can promote learning and foster personal development, why should any student be denied this opportunity? Siedentop[10] also relates this argument to the exclusionary nature of interscholastic sport discussed previously. If participation in sport is an important developmental experience for adolescents, it should be more widely available so that more students, both boys and girls, can benefit.

One of the most serious problems in the schools is drug abuse. Much media attention has been focused on the use of performance-enhancing drugs, such as anabolic steroids, in professional, international, and intercollegiate sports. However, such drug use is a concern in interscholastic sports as well. It is estimated that many adolescents use anabolic steroids illegally, with girls accounting for approximately one-third of the users.[11] When taken in amounts far exceeding the recommended dosage (megadoses) and coupled with intense physical workouts, anabolic steroids can build muscle and enhance performance. The side effects associated with such large dosages are serious and lead to irreparable damage. The American Academy of Pediatrics states that the use of steroids poses a special danger to adolescents. "High school and middle school students and athletes need to be aware of the effect steroids have on growth. Anabolic steroids, even in small doses, have been shown to stop growth too soon. Adolescents also may be at risk for becoming dependent on steroids. Adolescents who use steroids are also more likely to use other addictive drugs and alcohol."[12] Coaches also must be prepared to address other serious problems, including the use of tobacco, alcohol, and illegal drugs such as marijuana, amphetamines, and cocaine. The use of supplements, such as creatine, to improve performance must also be addressed by coaches.

Soaring costs are increasingly becoming a concern in interscholastic athletics. Rising costs for injury and liability insurance as well as costs associated with providing programs for girls and for students with disabilities have caused some schools to reduce the scope of their athletic programs and/or require athletes to pay in order to participate. A "pay-to-play" policy requires students who desire to participate in sports to pay for the opportunity. Critics have decried this policy because it discriminates against students who can not afford to pay. Some schools and communities, in response, have made provisions so that economically disadvantaged students can participate in the athletic program. However, often, few of these students choose to participate.

Many pressures exert an insidious influence on interscholastic sport programs. When school administrators, community members, and parents pressure coaches to win; when the expectations of parents exert too much pressure on their children to excel; and when coaches place undue pressure on their athletes to perform, the quality of the sport experience can deteriorate rapidly. Sport becomes unrewarding and less enjoyable than it should be and harmful to the participants. The educational experience becomes subverted and educational outcomes unrealized.

The quality and nature of the leadership provided is of critical importance in determining whether educational goals will be realized. If learning is to occur and personal development is to be enhanced, then administrators and coaches must structure the program to provide experiences that will lead to the attainment of these goals.

When high school coaches exert undue pressure on athletes to perform, when they excessively control the lives of their athletes, and when they physically or verbally abuse their athletes to set an example for the rest of the team, then the educational goals of interscholastic sport will go unfulfilled. There are coaches who equate obedience with self-discipline, demand singleminded dedication to sport, and provide no opportunity for athlete involvement in decision making (such as in setting team goals or planning game strategies). These coaches may win games, but they are failing to further the aims of education. Coaches who foster personal development of their athletes by guiding them, by allowing them to make decisions and to live with the consequences of those decisions, and by enhancing the worth and dignity of each athlete will help interscholastic sport fulfill its educational mission.

Intercollegiate Sports

The nature of intercollegiate sport in the United States varies greatly. The number of sports offered by a school can range from as few as 10 teams to as many as 25 different teams for men and women.[8] In smaller institutions, the athletic program may be part of the physical education department and be funded from its budget, the coaches have faculty teaching status, and one individual may serve as the coach for two or more teams. In contrast, at larger institutions, separate athletic departments exist; athletics has its own budget and generates substantial revenue from gate receipts and contributions; coaches have no teaching status; and an individual coaches only one sport. Program philosophies vary as well; in some institutions the educational nature of intercollegiate sport is emphasized, while in other institutions sports are seen as big business. Financial assistance for athletes varies and may be directly influenced by the skill of the athlete. Some schools offer no athletic scholarships; financial assistance is based solely on financial need. Other schools offer athletes a full scholarship that covers all expenses for tuition, room, board, fees, and books. Still other schools may offer partial assistance to athletes, such as providing only a tuition waiver. Given the tremendous diversity of intercollegiate sport programs, it is reasonable to believe that the nature of the intercollegiate sport experience for participants varies widely throughout the United States.

Intercollegiate sport is regulated by three primary governing bodies: the National Collegiate Athletic Association (NCAA), the National Association of Intercollegiate Athletics (NAIA), and the National Junior College Athletic Association (NJCAA). These associations attempt to administer intercollegiate athletic programs in accordance with educational principles.

The NCAA is the largest, most powerful governing body in intercollegiate athletics. In 2003, the NCAA had over 1,000 active member institutions, divided into five divisions based on the characteristics of their athletic program.[13] Division I includes 325 schools and is divided into three divisions. Division I-A consists of 117 schools with "big money, high profile" football teams. Division I-AA is comprised of 123 schools with smaller football programs, and Division I-AAA includes 85 teams with no football programs. Division I "big-time" programs typically highlight football or men's basketball, because of their potential to generate revenue, often in the millions of dollars for successful programs. Division II and III are composed of 270 and 910 schools, respectively.

Many intercollegiate sport programs, excluding the big Division I programs, operate in a manner similar to those found in larger, big-time high school programs. These intercollegiate sport programs include some Division I programs and those generally classified as Division II and III by the NCAA, as well as those programs governed by the NAIA and the NJCAA. They offer participants similar experiences to those found in high-level interscholastic programs. However, unlike the situation with high schools, college and university coaches need to recruit athletes for these teams. Athletes who choose to attend these schools may be offered some form of financial assistance. This can range from full athletic scholarships to need-based financial assistance.

Athletes who participate in the big Division I programs generally possess a higher level of athletic talent, face a greater time commitment to their sport, receive full athletic scholarships, experience a greater amount of travel, and benefit from greater media exposure. Pressures to have a winning program are often immense, and the consequences of winning and losing are usually much greater. Economic survival for these programs frequently depends on their ability to generate revenue through gate receipts, contributions, and, increasingly, television contracts. Winning teams generate interest among fans, which increases gate receipts, which in turn provides more money to hire coaches with proven winning records to raise the athletic program to even greater heights. Commercialism and entertainment dominate; educational goals are de-emphasized and often subverted, and athletics is transformed into a business and entertainment venture.

Many of the positive educational outcomes ascribed to participation in interscholastic sport programs can be realized when intercollegiate programs emphasize the attainment of educational goals. Similarly, many of the problems associated with interscholastic programs are evident in intercollegiate programs throughout the country. The overemphasis on winning, concerns about the academic achievements of athletes and their eligibility for participation, and the use of drugs are some of the problems associated with intercollegiate sports.

As with interscholastic sport, overemphasis on winning can lead to the subordination of educational goals. Such goals as sportsmanship, character development, and social development may be abandoned when winning becomes the most important objective. Desire and pressure to win may lead to the subversion or violation of rules in an effort to recruit the best athletes and maintain their eligibility.

The academic achievement of intercollegiate athletes is a major concern. There are many student-athletes who exemplify the true meaning of the word—they have combined sports and academics successfully. A prominent example is former U.S. Senator Bill Bradley, who played basketball for Princeton University, was named a Rhodes scholar, and had an outstanding professional basketball career before entering government service. In many colleges and universities, the academic achievements of athletes are comparable to those of their nonathlete peers. Studies have shown that the academic performance of athletes on women's teams, NCAA Division III teams, and other nonrevenue-generating teams is comparable to other college students.

There are, however, many instances in which the term *student-athlete* is truly a misnomer; in these cases athletics is given a much higher priority than academics. This is particularly true of student-athletes in the big-time programs. Athletes in these programs, especially those in revenue-generating sports such as football and basketball, face considerable demands on their time and energy that can interfere with their academic work.

Some athletes in big-time programs can successfully balance the time-consuming demands of athletics with the rigorous demands of academics and excel in both areas. However, sometimes the pressures on coaches to win translate into pressure to keep athletes eligible. Focusing attention on eligibility rather than on learning can lead to many abuses. Coaches may recruit athletes who lack the academic preparation needed to succeed at the challenges of college. They counsel athletes into taking easy courses, pressure professors to give them good grades, and encourage athletes to enroll in majors that require little academic effort. Unfortunately, progress toward a degree is not monitored as closely as is the maintenance of athletic eligibility. Additionally, because many black athletes are from rural and inner-city schools, where quality education programs are often lacking, a higher proportion of black athletes are affected.

In 1990, the U.S. Congress passed a law requiring all colleges and universities to make public the graduation rates of their athletes, starting in 1991. However, even the availability of this information makes it difficult to get a true picture of the graduation rates of athletes. Studies of the graduation rates of athletes yield conflicting results because of the many different methods that can be used to compute them. Furthermore, a number of factors influence graduation rates. For example, students who transfer to another institution, leave school to play on a professional team, or are dismissed for academic deficiencies—all are considered not graduating.

The 2003 NCAA Division I Graduation Rates Study data are shown in Table 8-1. These graduation rates are based on individuals who received an athletic scholarship and who graduated within 6 years of their initial college entry. The data show the following:

- Division I athletes with athletic grants graduate at a rate similar to other students, about 62% in six years after entering college compared to 60% of the general student body.
- The graduation rate for female athletes is higher than for male athletes, 70% compared with 55%. Female athletes graduated at a rate higher than other female students and at a higher rate than the general student body.
- Athletes are graduating at rates higher than students of the same racial and gender group. For example, black male athletes graduated at a rate of 48% compared with 36% for the entire black male student body. Female athletes graduated at a rate of 70%, compared with 63% of all females graduating. Black female basketball players' graduation rate was 59% compared to 47% for the entire black female student body.
- Graduation rates are lowest in the revenue-producing sports of football and basketball. Football players graduate at a rate of 55%, male basketball players at a rate of 44%, and female basketball players at a rate of 64%.
- Black athletes graduate at a rate lower than white athletes. For example, the graduation rate for black male basketball players was 42%; that for white male basketball players was 48%. Additionally, black athletes are more likely to leave school with a GPA lower than 2.0.[14]

The graduation rates show that athletic administrators need to pay greater attention to fostering, learning, and focusing on improving the educational experiences of athletes. Even though athletes are receiving greater educational support (e.g., tutors) than ever before, much more needs to be done. Failure to address these educational needs compromises the academic integrity of the institution and imperils the educational relevance of sports.

The National Consortium of Academics and Sports (NCAS), under the auspices of Northeastern University's Center for the Study of Sport in Society, seeks to "keep the student in the student-athlete" and better balance academics and athletics.[15] NCAS is an organization of 215 colleges and universities that provide former student-athletes with opportunities to continue their higher education. As a member of the NCAS, the college or university agrees to "bring back, tuition free, their own former student-athletes who competed in revenue and nonrevenue sports and were unable to complete their degree requirements. In exchange for tuition assistance, these former student-athletes are required to participate in the school's outreach and community service programs."[16] Since the formation of this program in 1985, more than 10,000 former student-athletes and more than 6,000 professional athletes have returned to school to complete their degrees.[15] The NCAS schools have donated more than $130 million in tuition fees to this endeavor. Many athletes dropped out of college once their eligibility was completed. The NCAA has also started new degree completion grants for athletes who have completed their eligibility and are 30 or fewer credits away from graduation.

In an effort to help remediate the academic abuses associated with big-time, revenue-producing sports and to restore academic integrity, the NCAA, in 1983, adopted a rule establishing minimum standards for freshman athletes to be eligible to participate on varsity teams at Division I institutions.

TABLE 8-1 Graduation Rates for Division I Student-Athletes and General Student Body Entering College in 1997 and 1984*

Student Group	Percentage of Students Graduating Who Entered in 1997		Percentage of Students Graduating Who Entered in 1984*	
	Student-Athletes	General Student Body	Student-Athletes	General Student Body
Student-Athletes	62	60	52	53
Males	55	57	47	51
White Males	59	60	55	54
Black Males	48	36	33	28
Females	70	63	62	54
White Females	72	65	66	57
Black Females	62	47	45	34
Male Basketball Players	44	57	38	51
White Male Basketball Players	48	60	53	54
Black Male Basketball Players	42	36	29	28
Female Basketball Players	64	63	53	54
White Female Basketball Players	67	65	66	57
Black Female Basketball Players	59	47	42	34
Football Players	55	57	47	54
White Football Players	65	60	56	56
Black Football Players	48	36	35	33

* Based on 2003 NCAA Division I Graduation-Rates Summary Data reflect individuals who received an athletic scholarship and who graduated within 6 years of their initial college enrollment. The data from 1984 are before Proposition 48 took effect in 1986.

Commonly known as Proposition 48, this rule stipulates that in order to be eligible to participate in sports, a first-year athlete must enter college with a 2.0 grade point average (GPA) in 11 specified core high school courses and achieve a minimum score of 700 on the Scholastic Aptitude Test (SAT) or 15 on the American College Test (ACT). Implemented in 1986, this rule permitted students who met only one of the requirements to be accepted at a college and given athletic aid, but they were not permitted to practice with their teams during their first year and had to forfeit one year of eligibility.

The NCAA hoped that Proposition 48 would send a strong message to high schools and their athletes that academic achievement was a prerequisite for students participating in Division I athletics. It was further hoped that this rule would help colleges and universities break the habit of recruiting athletes who had neither the academic background nor the potential to graduate within a 4- or 5-year period. It also provided first-year athletes who needed it a year to strengthen their academic abilities without the added pressures and commitments associated with sports.

Since the inception of Proposition 48 in 1986, additional rulings, such as Proposition 42, by the NCAA have led to more stringent qualifying criteria. Athletes who fail to qualify no longer can receive athletic financial assistance during their first year. However, they are eligible for institutional financial aid that must come from approved nonathletic sources.

In 1993 the NCAA increased the initial eligibility requirements. Starting in 1995, under Proposition 16, to be initially eligible, freshmen had to graduate from high school and meet GPA requirements in 13 core academic courses and achieve the required score on the ACT or SAT. This is a sliding scale; the higher the high school student's GPA, the lower the required standardized test score minimums. For example, students with a GPA of 2.5 or above need an SAT score of 820 or an ACT sum score of 68 to be initially eligible. Students who had a lower GPA in the core courses, such as 2.0, are required to attain a score of 1010 on the SAT or an ACT sum score of 86.

The NCAA has implemented other efforts to improve the academic performance of athletes, such as more stringent continuing-eligibility requirements. These requirements include requiring athletes to designate a specific major leading toward a degree by the beginning of their third year of enrollment, successfully complete 24 credit hours that count toward a specific degree each year, maintain specific GPA requirements, and achieve benchmarks of 25%, 50%, and 75% of degree requirements before the start of the third, fourth, and fifth years, respectively. As stronger initial- and continuing-eligibility requirements took effect, many institutions expanded their academic support services for athletes.

In 1996, the NCAA established the NCAA Eligibility Clearinghouse. All high school students wanting to play sports at Division I or II schools must register and be certified by the clearinghouse. The clearinghouse reviews the high school courses taken by the athletes to make sure they fulfill the core course requirements. Grade point averages and ACT/SAT scores are also reviewed to determine whether the student meets the eligibility requirements.

Proposition 16 and its predecessors are controversial. Critics charge that they discriminate against economically disadvantaged students who were not fortunate enough to have received a strong high school preparation for college or those who do not have the resources to retake the standardized tests or pay for commercial test preparation courses. In 2001, the NCAA released its latest study of Division I initial eligibility. The NCAA reported that when Proposition 16 went into effect, there was an initial spike or rise in ineligibility. However, since that time, the rate of ineligibility for all ethnic and family income groups has declined.

There are disparities in ineligibility rates that provoke thoughtful questions. The overall ineligibility rate was 6.8%.[16] The ineligibility rate for black student-athletes was 20.6%, compared to 9.2% and 3.7% for Hispanic and white student-athletes, respectively.[17] Disparities were seen by income as well. The ineligibility rate for student-athletes whose family income was less than, $30,000 a year was 16.7% compared to 2.1% for student-athletes whose family income was $80,000 or more a year.[17] Further concerns are voiced about the cultural bias of the standardized tests, in particular the SAT. The requirement that a student achieve a score of 820 on the SAT or 68 on the ACT, regardless of academic credentials, is the most controversial of the rulings. According to critics, the SAT discriminates against blacks and women. The average SAT scores for most minority groups are lower than for white students.[17] Females score significantly lower than males. For both the SAT and the ACT, average scores increase as family income increases.[17] Scores are significantly lower for most minority groups and women.[18] The standardized test requirement has been challenged in the courts, and the NCAA is currently studying the requirement.

Have Proposition 48 and Proposition 16 been successful in improving the academic performance of athletes? The graduation rates for 1984, the period before the implementation of Proposition 48, are shown in Table 8-1. After Proposition 48 took effect, the graduation rates for student-athletes have risen from 52% to 62%, while the rates for the student body rose from 53% to 60%. The graduation rate for male black basketball players and black football players rose from 29% to 42% and from 35% to 48%, respectively. Since the enforcement of Proposition 48, approximately 75% of the athletes affected by this ruling have achieved good academic standing in their universities. Having a year to concentrate on academics seems to be beneficial to the athletes. Furthermore, in addition to becoming more concerned about the academic abilities of recruited athletes, some universities have established or expanded academic support services for athletes.

Supporters of this ruling suggest that it has had a favorable impact at the high school level.[18] Young athletes appear to recognize the need to take high school core courses and to regard standardized tests more seriously. Coaches appear to be more encouraging of academic efforts, and academic support services have been developed to help high school athletes strengthen their academic skills.

The long-term effectiveness of Proposition 48 remains to be seen. It is hoped that it will lead to improved educational programs, to an increased emphasis on academic achievement for athletes at both the high school and the collegiate levels, and to restoring much-needed academic integrity to intercollegiate athletic programs.

Several other problems beset big-time intercollegiate sports, including the fact that sports have become big business. This commercialism has led to financial concerns receiving a greater priority than the education and personal development of the athletes. Television contracts increase the pressure to have a winning program in order to reap greater financial benefits. Media coverage of sport continues to grow. The recent NCAA $6.2 billion, 11-year contract with CBS reflects the tremendous interest in the commercial value of intercollegiate sports. Almost 80% of the NCAA's revenue comes from television rights.

The explosive growth of gambling nationwide and the increase in sports wagering are viewed by the NCAA as a threat to collegiate athletics. The FBI projected that $2.5 billion was illegally wagered on the 1995 NCAA Division I Men's Basketball Championship, second only to money gambled on the National Football League's Superbowl. A survey by the University of Cincinnati of more than 600 Division I football and men's basketball players showed that 25% had gambled money on other college sport events, 4% had bet on a game in which they played, and 5% had received money from a gambler not to play well in a game.[20] The growth of Internet gambling provides another avenue for those wishing to bet on collegiate sports, one that is very difficult to monitor. The NCAA has taken a strong position on gambling, stating that it has "the potential to undermine the integrity of sports contests, and jeopardizes the welfare of student-athletes and the intercollegiate athletics community."[19]

There is increasing concern about the exploitation of athletes. Some intercollegiate athletes can generate millions of dollars for their institution, but the only compensation permitted under NCAA rules is tuition, room, board, books, and fees. Even at the most expensive of institutions, when the total cost of the athletic scholarship is divided by the number of hours athletes are required to devote to their sport, the pay per hour is low.[10] Although critics say it is difficult to place a value on the benefits of a college education, oftentimes athletes are strongly encouraged to focus their energies and efforts on sports instead of academics. Moreover, the educational abuses cited detract from the nature of the educational experience. All too often athletic departments are concerned with athletes' academic status only until their 3 or 4 years of eligibility are used up; after this period, their concern about the academic progress of athletes is minimal. Most adversely affected by this practice are athletes from lower socioeconomic backgrounds and those who have received poor preparation for college from their high schools. These athletes often do not have the financial resources to pay for the extra semesters needed to graduate. Furthermore, because much of their efforts had previously been devoted to sports rather than academics, they may find it difficult to cope with the academic demands without the extra assistance (e.g., tutors) previously available to them as members of sport teams.

Several other issues in intercollegiate sport must be addressed. The media have increased the public's awareness of violations of recruiting regulations. Illegal recruiting practices, such as cash payments to prospective athletes, must be stopped. Drug abuse also is a problem. Athletes, in an effort to enhance their performance, may abuse such drugs as amphetamines and anabolic steroids. Although drug testing policies and procedures have become more stringent, methods to mask the use of drugs have become more clever. The effect of win-loss records on the retention of coaches, the role of coaches within the institutions of higher education, and the role of alumni and other influential supporters in the hiring and firing of coaches must be carefully evaluated and monitored.

The 1980s and the early 1990s have been marked by calls for the reform of intercollegiate athletics. Abuses have become so serious and so widespread that the academic integrity of educational institutions sponsoring these programs is challenged. In 1990, the U.S. Congress called for monitoring athletes' graduation rates. In 1991, the Knight Foundation Commission on Intercollegiate Athletics released a report calling for the reform of intercollegiate athletics. University presidents were called upon to exercise greater control over their sports programs, both in terms of fiscal responsibility and academic integrity.[19] Greater attention must be focused on containing the spiraling costs of intercollegiate athletics. Equally important, careful attention must be given to enhancing the academic performance of student athletes. The NCAA has passed legislation that focuses on providing opportunities and conditions that foster better academic achievements by student-athletes. Among these rulings are the elimination of the athletic dormitories, reductions in the number of hours practiced per week and in the length of the season, and more stringent monitoring of the student-athlete's academic progress toward a degree.

In 2001, 10 years after it issued its landmark 1991 report, the Knight Foundation Commission on Intercollegiate Athletics released another report entitled *A Call to Action: Reconnecting College Sports and Higher Education*.[20] The 2001 report stated, "While the NCAA and individual schools have made considerable progress . . . the problems of big-time college sports have grown, rather than diminished. The most glaring problems—academic transgressions, a financial arms race, and commercialization—are all evidence of the widening chasm between higher education's ideals and big-time college sports."[20]

In examining the widening chasm between the goals of education and big-time athletics, the Knight Commission noted the following:

- Big-time athletic programs operate with little interest in scholastic matters beyond the maintenance of athlete eligibility. The graduation rates for football players and men's basketball players are dismally low.
- The ever-growing "arms race" of spending has led to rapidly rising expenditures. Only about 15% of athletic programs at all levels operate in the black. Deficits are growing each year. Some programs have sought to control expenses by dropping minor sports. Many big-time programs are refurbishing or building new stadiums and arenas; in some cases, they are naming them after corporate sponsors. Over 30 college football and men's basketball coaches are paid a million dollars or more a year—more than anyone in the college or university, including the president.
- Big-time college sports resembles the professional model of sports. Commercialization of college sports led to vastly larger television and athletic shoe contracts and to more and more space in the stadiums and arenas being sold to advertisers. Corporate trademarks and sponsors' logos appear on athletes' uniforms and equipment.

After reviewing the academic performance of student-athletes, the escalating spending on athletics, and the growing commercialization of intercollegiate sport, the Knight Commission recommended a "one-plus-three" model to reform collegiate athletics. The "one" was the establishment of a Coalition of Presidents who would work in concert with such groups as the American Council on Education to restore athletics as an integral part of the educational enterprise. The coalition would address the "three"—academic reform, de-escalation of the athletics arms race, and de-emphasis of the commercialization of intercollegiate athletics. In terms of academic reform, the key point is that "students who participate in athletics deserve the same rights and responsibilities as all other students."[20] Some of the recommendations to accomplish this goal are as follows:

- Tie championships and postseason opportunities to graduation rates. By 2007, teams that graduate less than 50% of their players would be ineligible for conference championships or postseason play.
- Hold athletes accountable, the same as other students, with respect to criteria for admission, academic support services, choice of major, and satisfactory progress toward a degree.
- Reduce the length of the season and postseason competition and lessen practice time commitments to allow athletes a reasonable chance to complete their degree.
- Encourage the NBA and the NFL to develop minor leagues to provide another route to professional careers.

The second key point is that to keep expenditures under control, the coalition should insist that "athletic department's budgets be subject to the same institutional oversight and direct control as other university departments."[20] Among the recommendations to the coalition to accomplish this goal are the following:

- Reduce expenditures associated with big-time football and basketball, including reducing the number of scholarships awarded in Division I-A football.
- Ensure that compliance with Title IX and support of women's programs does not become an excuse for soaring costs, while expenses in big-time sports continue unchecked.
- Bring coaches' compensations in line with existing compensation norms across the institution.
- Distribute television revenue from the NCAA Division I Final Four based on an institution's improving academic performance, enhancing the athletes' collegiate experience, and achieving gender equity.

Lastly, with respect to commercialization, the fundamental issue is "colleges and universities must take control of athletics programs back from television and other corporate interests."[20] With respect to this goal, the coalition should do the following:

- Insist that institutions alone be the determiner of when games will be played and how they will be broadcast, rather than allowing television to dictate terms.
- Prohibit athletes from wearing corporate trademarks or sponsors' logos on their uniforms.
- Actively work to ban legal gambling on collegiate athletics.

Additionally, the Knight Commission recommends that an independent watchdog body be formed to monitor big-time sports programs. The Knight Commission calls for a concerted effort to reaffirm the role of athletics within the educational institution and emphasizes the critical need for reform of a system that is increasingly distancing itself from the educational model of sport and embracing the professional model.

Many other suggestions have been offered by individuals concerned about the abuses associated with intercollegiate athletics. These include elimination of first-year eligibility, further limitations on practice and game schedules, stricter academic standards for eligibility, tying athletes' graduation rates to the number of athletic scholarships that can be offered, and providing coaches with some form of job security to encourage them to more strongly support athletes' academic endeavors and achievements. Other voices have been raised on behalf of athletes' rights, calling for elimination of exploitative, discriminatory, and prejudicial practices directed against minorities and the reduction of gender inequities.

Like interscholastic sports, intercollegiate sports have the potential to contribute to the educational goals of the institutions that sponsor them. Whether these educational goals are attained depends on the leadership. When winning is overemphasized, commercialism is rampant, and athletes are exploited, the educational relevance of these programs is called into question. When winning is placed in perspective, when academic achievement is strongly supported, and when athletes are encouraged and given opportunities to develop to their fullest potential, then the educational mission of intercollegiate athletics will be fulfilled.

Since Title IX, sports opportunities for girls and women have increased. Sports are no longer just for fathers and sons.

GIRLS AND WOMEN IN SPORT

Prior to the 1970s, opportunities for girls and women to compete in sports were limited. Within the past 30 years, there has been a dramatic increase in girls' and women's participation in sports. This increase is visible at all levels of competition—the Olympics, professional and amateur sports, intercollegiate and interscholastic sports, and youth sports.

The relatively recent increase in participation by girls and women in the United States can be attributed to several factors. These include federal legislation, the women's movement, the fitness movement, and an increased public awareness of female athletes.

Federal legislation, specifically Title IX of the Educational Amendment Act, was one of the most influential factors because it mandated equal treatment for women and men in programs receiving federal assistance. Passed in 1972, Title IX prohibits discrimination on the basis of sex in any educational program or activity receiving federal financial assistance. It states that "no person in the United States shall, on the basis of sex, be excluded from participation in, be denied the benefits of, or be subjected to discrimination under any educational program or activity receiving federal assistance."

Because Title IX is politically controversial and the guidelines complex, implementation and enforcement of this law are difficult. After its implementation, access to sport opportunities for women increased. However, it should be noted that in 1984, in *Grove City College v. Bell,* the U.S. Supreme Court ruled in favor of a narrow interpretation of Title IX, stating that it should be regarded as program specific. Thus, only programs directly receiving federal aid are required to comply with Title IX regulations, not the institution as a whole. Because athletic programs typically receive little if any direct federal funding, the threat of losing funding for noncompliance and nonsupport of women's athletics is not a substantial one. Subsequently, the 800 cases of alleged sex discrimination that were being investigated by the U.S. Department of Education's Office for Civil Rights were either narrowed in scope or withdrawn. Four years later, in 1988, the Civil Rights Restoration Act was passed. This law provided for a broad interpretation of Title IX by mandating equal opportunity for both sexes in all programs in any organization that received federal funds. In 1991, the Office of Civil Rights announced that investigation of Title IX athletic complaints would be one of its priorities.

In 1997, 25 years after Title IX, Donna Lopiano, Executive Director of the Women's Sports Foundation, stated that more than 90% of the schools and colleges were not in compliance with Title IX.[15] Is your high school or college in compliance? The Office of Civil Rights has a three-pronged test to determine if an institution is in compliance. A school must meet one of these three tests to be within the law:

1. *Proportionality.* Are the opportunities for males and females substantially proportionate to the school's full-time undergraduate enrollment? Recent court decisions indicate that being within 5 percentage points is acceptable and within the law. Thus, if 49% of the enrollment is female, between 44% and 54% of the athletes should be female.
2. *History and continued practice.* Even though a school has a disproportionate number of male athletes, as long as the school is adding more women's sports and has added one recently, generally within the last 3 years, the school would probably be considered in compliance.
3. *Accommodation of interests and abilities.* If the school can demonstrate that the women do not have enough ability or interest to sustain additional teams, the school would be considered in compliance. However, if there are club teams playing sports, this could indicate to the court that there is sufficient interest to support another team.

Great strides have been made toward equity. Much more needs to be done to create additional opportunities for participation in sports at all levels.

The impact of Title IX has resulted in noticeable increases in participation of girls and women at both the interscholastic and intercollegiate level. The growth of participation by girls in interscholastic sports following the passage of Title IX can be seen in Figure 8-1. At the intercollegiate level, there was an increase in the number of intercollegiate teams for women, the hiring of qualified coaches, and the offering of athletic scholarships to outstanding high school women athletes. In 1972, 32,000 women competed in intercollegiate sports; the NCAA reported that nearly 160,650 women participated in its athletic programs in 2002–2003. Spectator interest in women's sports has grown as well. This has resulted in increased attendance at games. For example, in 1999–2000, perennial national power Tennessee averaged more than 15,000 fans for its home basketball games. Television coverage of women's sports has increased; the NCAA championships in swimming and diving, basketball, gymnastics, volleyball, and track and field have been televised in recent years. Even coverage of regular season events has expanded.

The women's movement has encouraged increased participation in athletics by women. It has helped redefine societal, occupational, and family roles for women and has given women more control over their lives. The idea that women are enhanced as human beings when they are given opportunities to develop competence has encouraged women of all ages to pursue an increasingly wide array of interests, including sport. Moreover, the changing cultural image of women athletes has contributed to the growth of women's sports. Whereas women athletes were once perceived by many as unfeminine or were stigmatized for engaging in high levels of competition, athletic participation by women is now regarded as acceptable. Ideas about what is masculine and what is feminine are based on societal definitions and may be needlessly restrictive, creating barriers to participation.[3] In the future, as society's attitudes continue to change, more people may come to perceive sport not as a masculine activity but rather as a human activity.

Playing sports can be an empowering experience for girls and women by changing their

Figure 8-1 Participation in high school athletics by girls and boys, 1971–2004.
From National Federation of State High School Athletic Associations, High School Athletics Participation Survey, 2003–2004.

perceptions of themselves. Sports can engender feelings of competence, promote confidence, and help girls and women see themselves as more in control of their lives. This is important because, quite often in our society, girls and women are portrayed as weak, dependent, and powerless. The President's Council on Physical Fitness Report, *Physical Activity and Sport in the Lives of Girls,* released in 1997, used an interdisciplinary approach to examine the impact of physical activity and sport on the lives of girls. The report emphasized the contributions physical activity and sport can make to the "complete girl"—her social, physical, emotional, and cultural environment—rather than to just one aspect of the girl's life. Some conclusions follow:

- Exercise and sport participation can be used as a therapeutic and preventive intervention to enhance the physical and mental health of adolescent girls.
- Exercise and sport participation enhance mental health by offering adolescent girls opportunities to develop positive feelings about their body, improved self-esteem, tangible experiences of competency and success, and enhanced self-confidence.
- Sports contribute to educational goals. Compared to their nonathletic peers, high school female athletes have higher grades, lower dropout rates, and are more likely to go to college.
- Poverty substantially limits many girls' access to physical activity and sport. This is particularly true for minorities, who are overrepresented in lower socioeconomic groups.
- The potential for girls to derive positive experiences from physical activity and sport is limited by lack of opportunity and stereotypes.[21]

The benefits of participation are great. Physical education and sport professionals must create greater opportunities for participation and work to remove barriers that limit participation.

Since the 1970s, the fitness movement has encouraged many women to participate in physical activities, including sport. Many women started engaging in jogging, walking, aerobics, and swimming to realize the associated benefits of fitness, particularly to feel good and look better. Although there is still an emphasis on engaging in physical activities to look better and to preserve one's youthfulness, there is also a growing emphasis on the physical development of the body. Additionally, many women have moved from engaging in fitness activities to engaging in competitive athletics; joggers have gone on to participate in road races, marathons, and even triathlons. Interest in fitness has also led to an increase in the number of women participating in community sport programs in such sports as softball, volleyball, and basketball.

As participation by girls and women increases, there will be more women athlete role models. The increased coverage and publicity given to women athletes have allowed girls and women to read about the achievements and watch the performance of women athletes in a wider range of sports than ever before. The accomplishments of the Olympic gold medal American female athletes in softball, soccer, swimming, track and field, gymnastics, basketball, skiing, and other sports may encourage many girls to participate in sports and pursue their athletic ambitions.

Professional opportunities for women are also increasing. In 1996, two professional women's basketball leagues—the American Basketball League and the Women's National Basketball Association (WNBA)—were organized offering elite women athletes the opportunity to continue to participate in their sport. The American Basketball League folded after the 1998–1999 season. The WNBA has grown rapidly. Its 16 teams, organized into two conferences, attracted 2.5 million spectators during the 2000 season. Television coverage of the WNBA reached nearly 60 million viewers.[22] Women now also have the opportunity to play professional soccer in the United States. In 2001, the Women's United Soccer Association (WUSA) launched its inaugural season. The eight-team league featured players from the U.S. World Cup Championship Team and many top international players. The 87 games drew over 700,000 fans, with an average attendance of 8,295.[23] Twenty-two games were nationally televised on TNT and CNN/SI.[23] Over 5 million viewers tuned in to these broadcasts. In 2001, WUSA and PAX Television reached an agreement to televise the full schedule of WUSA matches during 2002 and 2003.[23] Unfortunately, in 2004, due to financial issues, the league ceased operation. It is hopeful that financial backing can be found and the WUSA can once again operate. Although professional opportunities for women are increasing, they are still limited.

Legislation, the women's movement, the fitness movement, and increased visibility accorded female athletes have done much to expand opportunities for women in sport. However, while opportunities for girls and women in athletics have increased tremendously over the past three decades, whether participation rates will continue to grow for women depends to a great extent on the expansion of opportunities for involvement and the support and encouragement of female athletic endeavors. Some factors that may limit participation are financial constraints, overt and subtle resistance to comply with government policies and legislation, a decline in women's coaches, and the continued trivialization of women's sports.[3]

Financial considerations may serve to limit opportunities for participation by girls and women. When school, collegiate, and community athletic programs are threatened with cutbacks, programs for girls and women are most at risk for losing financial support. Because these programs are newer and not as established as similar programs for men and boys, they have had less time to gather administrative and community backing and may not be able to elicit sufficient support to survive cutbacks. Participation opportunities for females also may be adversely affected because the establishment and development of new programs generally requires greater financial support and resources than do

TABLE 8-2 Top 10 High School Sports for Boys and Girls for 2003–2004

Boys		Girls	
Sport	**Participants**	**Sport**	**Participants**
Football (11-player)	1,032,682	Basketball	457,986
Basketball	544,811	Outdoor track and field	418,322
Outdoor track and field	504,801	Volleyball	396,322
Baseball	457,146	Fast-pitch softball	362,468
Soccer	349,785	Soccer	309,032
Wrestling	238,700	Tennis	167,758
Cross country	196,428	Cross country	166,287
Golf	163,341	Swimming and diving	144,565
Tennis	152,938	Competitive spirit squads	89,443
Swimming and diving	96,562	Golf	63,173

Data from National Federation of State High School Associations, High School Athletics Participation Survey, 2003–2004.

established programs. Because many programs for females are new or in the process of development, successful growth of these programs requires financial commitment. Yet, despite the need, programs for females tend to be funded at lower levels than programs for males. This lack of funding hampers program growth and adversely affects opportunities for participation and quality competition.

In spite of the passage of Title IX and improvements in opportunities, sex discrimination is still a feature of many athletic programs. New laws are often met with resistance and questions about how to implement them. Additionally, people tend to be reluctant to change the status quo. Individuals with a vested interest in maintaining the status quo may use their power and control of financial resources to thwart the progress of women's programs. Women across the nation at all levels of competition are still denied fair treatment. Such discrimination can be as blatant as the refusal to fund a program. But lack of equality often occurs in less noticeable forms, such as the provision of quality equipment, supplies, and uniforms; the assignment of games and practice time; the use of facilities and locker rooms; the allocation of equal funds for travel and the availability of travel opportunities; the access to quality coaches, size of coaching staff, and compensation of coaches; the opportunity to receive support services such as academic tutoring; the administration of medical and training services; and the publicity accorded to individual athletes and the team.

Despite prohibitions by Title IX against discrimination, women still do not receive equitable treatment in sport. Furthermore, violations of Title IX are often not prosecuted vigorously. Commitment, time, and effort are needed to ensure compliance with the law and ensure that the spirit of the law becomes an integral part of athletic programs at all levels. Table 8-2 shows the popularity differences in boys' and girls' sports.

Discrimination is also noticeable in sports outside the school setting. At the international level, for example, where efforts to bring about changes have not been supported by legislation, women typically have fewer events in which to participate and are less likely to be rewarded for their efforts than men. Even though changes have occurred during the past two decades, women are still underrepresented in international sport. In the Summer Olympic Games, women have fewer events than men and fewer participants. Figure 8-2 shows the number of events open to men and women in the Summer Olympics. In the 2000

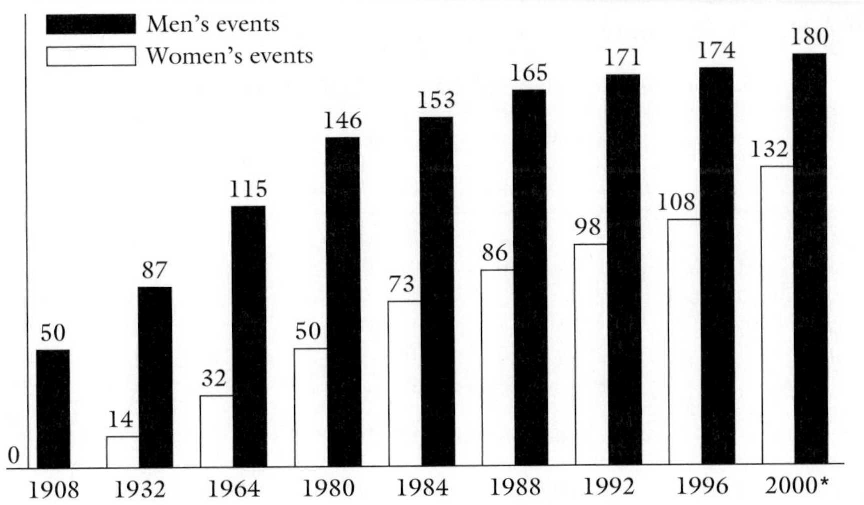

*Twelve events in 2000 were mixed, or open, to both men and women. These 12 have been added to both totals for men and women. This procedure of adding mixed events to the total events for women and men was also used for each of the other Olympics in the graph.

Figure 8-2 Number of Summer Olympic events open to women and to men.*
Courtesy of J. Coakley: Sport in society: issues and controversies (8th ed.) McGraw-Hill, 2004, N.Y.

Summer Olympic Games in Sydney, 6,582 men competed compared to 4,069 women. In the 1996 Olympic Games in Atlanta, the U.S. team had 382 men and 280 women, compared with 342 men and only 96 women in 1972. In the 1996 Games in Atlanta, women made up 36.5% of the athletes compared with only 28.5% of the participants in the 1992 Olympics in Barcelona. Moreover, the male-dominated International Olympic Committee (IOC) is slow to approve additional events for women. The IOC finally approved the 1,500 meter run (the metric mile) for the 1972 Games in Munich, the 3,000 meter run and the marathon for the 1984 Games in Los Angeles, the 10,000 meter run for the 1988 Games in Seoul, and the 5,000 meter run for the 1996 Games in Atlanta. The slowness to approve is difficult to understand because women have been competing in these events internationally for many years.

Today there are fewer female coaches for women's sports than in the years following the passage of Title IX. Despite the fact that women's sport programs have increased, the proportion of women in coaching and athletic administrative positions has declined. For example, at the intercollegiate level, Acosta and Carpenter[24] reported that the percentage of female coaches of women's sport programs decreased from 90% in 1970 to 58% in 1978 to 47.7% in 1996. In 2004, the NCAA reported that only 41.3% of women's teams were coached by women and only 2.5% of women coaches were minorities.[25] (See Table 8-3.) This is one of the lowest percentages of head coaches that has been reported to date. As you can see from tracking the percentages across the years, head coaching opportunities for women are decreasing. And, although men serve as head coaches for 58.7% of women's teams, only 3.5% of women are head coaches of men's teams.[27] In 1972, 90% of the women's intercollegiate athletic programs were headed by female athletic administrators. The NCAA report revealed that 17.4% of director of athletics positions are held by women; about one-third of the associate director and assistant director positions were held by women.[25] Current president of the National Association of Collegiate Women

TABLE 8-3 NCAA Demographic Information (%)

Selected Athletic Administrative Staff 2003–2004* (%)

	White		Black		Other Minority		Total	
	Men	Women	Men	Women	Men	Women	Men	Women
Director of Athletics	77.5	17.4	2.7	0.2	1.5	0.6	81.7	18.3
Associate Director of Athletics	58.1	33.0	5.2	1.5	1.3	1.0	64.5	35.6
Assistant Director of Athletics	60.2	30.2	4.8	2.0	1.7	1.0	66.9	33.1
Sports Information Director	84.4	12.3	0.9	0.7	1.3	0.4	86.6	13.4
Strength Coaches	77.2	11.0	8.5	0.2	2.8	0.2	88.7	11.3
Head Athletic Trainer	68.8	26.6	1.2	0.5	2.0	0.9	72.0	28.0

Head Coaches 2003–2004* (%)

	White		Black		Other Minority		Total	
Men's Teams	Men	Women	Men	Women	Men	Women	Men	Women
All Divisions Percentages (%)	88.2	3.1	4.8	0.3	3.5	0.1	96.5	3.5
Division I	87.6	1.9	7.2	0.5	2.6	0.0	97.4	2.4
Women's Teams								
All Divisions Percentages (%)	52.5	38.8	3.4	1.6	2.8	0.9	58.7	41.3
Division I	51.4	37.9	4.0	3.0	2.6	1	58.0	41.9
Basketball								
Men's All Divisions	86.0	0.0	12.3	0.0	1.7	0.0	100.0	0.0
Men's Division I	76.4	0.0	23.2	0.0	0.4	0.0	100.0	0.0
Women's All Divisions	35.9	56.0	2.9	3.9	0.6	0.7	39.4	60.6
Women's Division I	29.9	59.4	1.9	7.7	0.8	0.4	32.6	67.5
Football								
All Divisions	97.7	0.0	1.6	0.0	0.8	0.0	100.1	0.0
Division I	96.8	0.0	2.2	0.0	1.1	0.0	100.1	0.0

(continued)

Athletic Administrators, Peg Bradley-Doppes, in a speech before the Knight Commission in 2000, asked that the Knight Commission "reaffirm the policies that will reinforce principles related to gender equity, diversity, ethics, and integrity in educational sport environments."[26]

Reasons for the underrepresentation of women in these positions have been debated widely, and the results of the research are confusing. However, one reason that is frequently cited is the lack of well-qualified women coaches and administrators. Recently, several programs have been implemented in the United States in an effort to recruit and train more women coaches. It is also important to note that the lack of visibility of women coaches and administrators within the sport structure provides few

TABLE 8-3 NCAA Demographic Information (%) *(continued)*

Student-Athlete Ethnicity 2002–2003 (%)

	White		Black		Hispanic		Other Minorities and Nonresident Aliens	
	Men	Women	Men	Women	Men	Women	Men	Women
All Divisions	71.6	78.9	17.9	10.5	3.5	3.0	7.0	7.6
Division I	62.6	71.9	24.6	14.8	3.3	2.9	9.5	10.4
Basketball								
All Divisions	50.3	65.9	41.8	26.6	2.4	2.4	5.5	5.1
Division I	32.3	48.7	57.9	40.9	1.3	1.7	8.5	8.7
Football								
All Divisions	62.1		31.4		2.6		3.9	
Division I	49.3		43.8		2.2		4.7	

From National Collegiate Athletic Association 2003–2004 race demographics of NCAA member institutions' athletics personnel, NCAA, 2004, Indianapolis, IN. National Collegiate Athletic Association 2002–2003 participation statistics report, NCAA, 2003, Indianapolis, IN.

*Information for Athletic Administration Staff and Head Coaches exclude historically black institutions. Percentages are slighty higher when historically black institutions included.

role models for females who aspire to careers in these areas. Other reasons include the persistence of traditional stereotypes of women and resistance of those in power, predominately males, to provide opportunities for women.

One of the concerns raised by some opponents to the implementation of Title IX was that compliance with Title IX, specifically the expansion of sport opportunities for girls and women, would substantially reduce opportunities for boys and men. In 2001, the United States General Accounting Office (GAO) released its report on gender equity entitled *Intercollegiate Athletics: Four-Year Colleges' Experiences Adding and Discontinuing Teams.*[27] This report monitored changes in athletic programs for the two largest intercollegiate athletic associations, the NCAA and the NAIA, for a period covering 18 years, from 1981 to 1982 through 1998 to 1999. Several of the GAO findings are listed below:

- The number of women participating in intercollegiate athletics increased substantially—from 90,000 to 163,000, an 81% increase. Men's athletic participation experienced a modest 5% increase, from 220,000 to 230,000.
- Women's teams increased from 5,695 to 9,479, an increase of 3,784 teams. Men's teams increased by 36 teams, from 9,113 to 9,149 teams. Although women have more teams than men, they still have fewer participants because of the large number of men participating in team sports with large squad sizes, such as football.
- Both men's and women's sports added teams. The sport added most frequently for both men and women was soccer. Women's soccer increased from 80 teams to 926 teams in 1998 through 1999. Men's soccer increased by 135 teams, from 744 teams to 879 teams.
- Both men's and women's teams were discontinued. Among women's sports, gymnastics

was most often dropped, decreasing from 190 teams to 90 teams. Fencing teams also decreased for women from 76 teams to 45 teams. For men's sports, wrestling experienced the largest decrease from 428 teams to 257 teams. Men's gymnastics also decreased from 82 teams to 26 teams and men's tennis dropped from 952 teams to 868 teams.

- Since 1982 to 1993, 962 institutions added teams and 307 discontinued teams. Most schools, 72%, were able to add teams—usually women's teams, without discontinuing any teams. Schools added nearly three times as many women's teams as men's teams—1,919 teams for women compared to 702 teams for men. Schools discontinued more than twice as many men's teams; 386 men's teams were discontinued compared to 150 teams for women.
- Among the institutions that added teams, the two most often cited factors that influenced the decision were the need to address student interest in a particular sport and the need to meet gender equity goals and requirements. Overall, 52% of the schools cited student interest as a great factor and 47% of the schools indicated the need to meet gender equity goals and requirements as the reason for adding women's teams. Reasons for adding a women's team varied by the size of the institution. For example, at the NCAA Division I-A level, 82% of the schools cited gender equity considerations compared to 35% of the schools at the Division III level.
- Of the schools that discontinued a men's team, 33% cited a lack of student interest as a factor, 31% cited gender equity concerns, and 30% reported a need to reallocate the athletic budget to other sports as factors influencing their decision.
- Major factors associated with discontinuing men's sports varied by the size of the institution. Fifty-four percent of NCAA Division I-A schools reported that meeting gender equity goals and requirements influenced their decision, whereas 44% of Division III schools most often cited absence of sufficient student interest, as influencing a decision to discontinue a team.

Schools that expanded their athletic options for women by adding teams and not discontinuing men's teams used a variety of strategies to accomplish this task. Most often, the schools obtained additional revenue for the program expansion rather than containing costs and reallocating revenue. Division I-A schools tended to rely on generating revenue from other sports and from outside sources.[27] At smaller schools, such as Division III and NAIA schools, additional monies from the institution's general fund and reallocation of existing resources provided the funds to support the growth of athletic opportunities for women.[27]

Although some schools have been successful in increasing opportunities for women and men, there is concern that, as Bradley-Doppes states, "schools are choosing to cut programs rather than ask all teams to operate on smaller pieces of the financial pie. In fact, schools are spending more money on men's sports than ever. . . . The 1999 NCAA Revenue and Expenses of Division I and II Intercollegiate Athletics Programs study revealed that in Division I-A institutions the average total operating expenses for women's sports were $3,741,000, while average total operating expenses for men's sports were $9,544,000."[27] Almost three times as much money is being spent on men's sports compared to women's sports.

The 2001 Knight Commission Report recommended that efforts should be made to ensure that "the legitimate and long-overdue need to support women's athletic programs and comply with Title IX is not used as an excuse for soaring costs while expenses in big-time sports are unchecked."[20] More opportunities for both men and women to participate in sports can be achieved by reducing excessive funding of sports rather than denying opportunities to participate. This could be achieved in many different ways, such as holding the line on spending in men's sports, generating new revenue sources to support women's sports, and decreasing excessive spending by limiting squad sizes, decreasing the number of scholarships, or by trimming excesses from existing budgets, such as teams spending the night in hotels before a home game. Remember that Title IX prohibits discrimination on the basis of sex, and that federal regulations require that both men and women be provided with equitable opportunities, including opportunities to participate in intercollegiate athletics.

Although women's participation in sport has increased dramatically during the last 30 years, the accomplishments of female athletes are often trivialized and ridiculed by both men and women. For example, women often have to suffer with team names and mascots that belittle physical competence and minimize the achievement of female athletes. To illustrate, at one university, the men's teams are referred to as the Bears and the women's teams as the Teddy Bears; other examples are the Blue Hawks and Blue Chicks, the Rams and Rambelles, and the Tigers and the Tigerettes. Were the men's and women's teams at your high school or college referred to by different nicknames? If so, what messages do these names send to the public about the abilities of the athletes and the seriousness of their endeavors?

Other factors that have contributed to the inequities experienced by women in sport are myths about the consequences of athletic participation and the physical, social, and psychological characteristics of women. Examples of these myths include the belief that strenuous participation in sport can lead to problems in childbearing (it has been shown that athletes who are in excellent physical condition have shorter and easier deliveries and experience fewer problems such as backache after the birth of a child) and the belief that the fragile bone structure of women makes them more likely to experience injuries than men (when both men and women athletes experience similar training regimens and care and practice under the leadership of qualified coaches, injury rates are similar for both sexes in any given sport). Other myths perpetuate the belief that participating in sports can threaten one's femininity (women athletes typically do not see their involvement as a threat to their image). Although research and education have done much to dispel these myths, they still persist and serve to needlessly limit participation by women.

Events of the past 30 years have served to increase opportunities for participation by women in sport at all levels. Federal legislation, the women's movement, the fitness movement, and increased visibility and recognition of the achievements of women athletes have helped females of all ages to benefit from opportunities to participate in sports. However, while progress has been made, continued increases in participation by women will depend on eliminating barriers to involvement such as financial constraints, less than full compliance with Title IX, lack of women coaches and administrators, minimization of women's accomplishments, and unfounded beliefs or myths. Coakley[3] notes that gender equity is a complex issue and suggests that the following guideline from the 1993 NCAA Gender Equity Panel may be helpful in thinking about this issue: "An athletics program is gender equitable when either the men's or women's sports program would be pleased to accept as its own the overall program of the other gender." Qualified and committed leadership is needed to change the structure of sport programs in order to reduce inequities and to further eliminate barriers to participation so that all individuals, regardless of sex, can enjoy the benefits of sport.

MINORITIES IN SPORT

Sport is often extolled as an avenue by which to transcend differences in race and cultural backgrounds. It has been said, for example, that "sport is color blind"—that on the playing field a person is recognized for ability alone and rewards are given without regard to race and class. The widely televised performances of black and Hispanic male athletes in such sports as baseball, basketball, track and field, boxing, and football suggest to millions of viewers that sport is relatively free of the prejudice and discrimination often found in other areas of society. Despite a commonly held belief that sport allows individuals to accept one another on the basis of their physical competence, close scrutiny of the sport phenomena reveals that sport organizations are typically characterized by the same patterns of prejudice and discrimination found in the surrounding society.

Historically, sport in the United States has been characterized by racism and prejudice. While blacks and other minorities have a rich history of sport participation, prior to the 1950s, minorities were rarely given access to mainstream sport competition in the professional leagues, colleges and universities, and schools. Members of minorities organized their own leagues and competed within them; for example, blacks had their own basketball and baseball leagues. The integration of professional sport did not occur until 1946, when Jackie Robinson "broke the color barrier" by playing for the then Brooklyn Dodgers. Integration of intercollegiate sports occurred later and was particularly slow to occur in the South. The U.S. Supreme Court's decision in *Brown v. Board of Education* in 1954, as well as the civil rights movement of the 1970s, slowly led to the integration of schools and the opening of doors to sports for minorities.

Currently, the participation of black athletes remains concentrated in a few sports. Black athletes are overrepresented in certain sports such as football, basketball, and baseball. These sports typically require no expensive equipment or training, have coaches readily available through the public schools, and offer visible role models to aspiring athletes. Black athletes are underrepresented in such sports as volleyball, swimming, gymnastics, soccer, golf, and tennis. The expenses increasingly required for many of these sports, such as private lessons and elite coaching, expensive equipment, funds for travel, and club memberships, as well as the virtual lack of role models in these sports, discourage minority participation. Participation by black women has been very limited, and accomplishments of black women athletes are typically accorded little attention.

Minority men and women are significantly underrepresented in coaching and managerial positions in sports at all levels. For 14 years, Dr. Richard Lapchick has authored a racial and gender report card that provides a comprehensive analysis of opportunities for women and minorities in sports. College sports and professional sports organizations are assigned a grade based on their hiring practices. The grades range from A+ to F, with one grade given for gender, one for race, and a combined grade. Professional sports included in this study include Major League Baseball (MLB), National Basketball Association (NBA), Women's National Basketball Association (WNBA), Major League Soccer (MLS), and National Hockey League (NHL).

The 2001 Racial and Gender Report Card (RGRC), while revealing significant areas of concern, also revealed record levels of hiring within the college and professional levels for minorities and women.[15] The latest study, the 2003 Racial and Gender Report Card, revealed that since the 2001 RGRC there has been a decline in opportunities for women and, in some cases, people of color. The 2003 RGRC revealed some positive findings, indicating areas in which progress is being made. Among the 2003 areas of concerns and highlights are the following findings:

- The participation of African Americans in all sports except for professional and collegiate basketball and baseball declined from previous years.
- Compared to 2001, minorities had fewer opportunities in top-management positions in college and professional sport, including general managers, team vice presidents, and college athletic directors.
- The number of Latino players in MLB, MLS, and Division I college baseball reached all-time highs.
- Within the three biggest professional leagues, an all-time high number of 24 head coaches/managers were people of color. The NBA had 12 and the NFL three African American head coaches; MLB had six African Americans and three Latinos serving as managers.
- Even after 30 years following the advent of Title IX, women head less than 45% of head coaching positions for women's college teams.
- The WNBA was found to have the best record for diversity, which reflects the combined opportunities for gender and race. The WNBA percentages for people of color and women

As college football teams changed their offensive strategies so that quarterbacks became more like running backs, more African Americans were recruited for the position.

occupying professional positions in the league offices were 45% and 95%, respectively. The WNBA had the highest percentage for women. The WNBA earned a grade of A–, the highest combined grade of all organizations.

- The NBA's record for race was the best of all organizations. Eighty percent of its players are people of color; forty-eight percent of its head coaching positions and 33% of the assistant coaching positions are occupied by people of color. Additionally, 28% of the league office professional staff, 17% of the general managers, and 19% of the team senior administrative positions are held by people of color. Additionally, three people of color are team presidents. With respect to opportunities for women, the NBA provided the most opportunities within the men's leagues. The NBA ranked second among all organizations, earning a grade of B+.[28]

The RGRC shows where progress has been made and identifies areas in which opportunities for minorities and women must be improved. Lapchick notes with concern the efforts to weaken Title IX and affirmative action programs, action that may limit opportunities for minorities and women.

Analysis of the data from the NCAA 2003–2004 Demographic Study of Athletic Personnel[25] shows that minorities have limited opportunities in collegiate sports (see Table 8-3 for information about administrative positions, head coaching positions, and student-athlete ethnicity).[29] The data revealed that:

- For all divisions, only 5% of director of athletic positions are held by minorities and only 18.2% of these positions are held by women. Only about 9% of the associate director of athletics and assistant director of athletics positions are held by minorities, and women hold about one-third of these positions.
- For all divisions, only 8.7% of the head coaches of men's teams are minorities, although 28.4% of men student-athletes are minorities. At the Division I level, 9.8% of head coaches of men's teams are minorities, although 37.4% of Division I men student-athletes are minorities.
- For all divisions, only 8.7% of the head coaches of women's teams were minorities, although 21.1% of women student-athletes are minorities. At the Division I level, 10.8% of the head coaches of women's teams were minorities and 28.1% of women student-athletes are minorities.
- For men's basketball, for all divisions, 14.0% of head coaches are minorities, compared to 49.7% of men basketball players; at Division I 23.6% of head coaches were minorities, and 67.7% of Division I men's basketball players are minorities.
- For women's basketball, for all divisions, 8.1% of head coaches were minorities, compared to 34.1% of women basketball players; at Division I level, 10.8% of the coaches were minorities, compared to 51.3% of the women basketball players at this level.
- For men's football, for all divisions, 2.4% of head coaches were minorities and 37.9% of the athletes were minorities; at the Division I level, 3.3% of the head coaches were minorities, compared to 50.7% of the Division I football players.

In 2002, at the 117 Division I-A schools, there were even fewer black coaches. There were only five black head coaches, representing about 3% of all coaches. At this level, 50.5% of the players are black and over 57% of the players are minorities. In 2002, the University of Notre Dame hired Tyrone Willingham, who is black, as its head coach; however, since Willingham left Stanford for the position at Notre Dame, minority representation in coaching at this level did not increase. Fired by Notre Dame in 2004, Willingham signed with Washington.

Professional sports also reflect a lack of opportunities for minorities. For example, in 2001, in the NFL, there were only three black head coaches, less than 10%, in a sport where over 60% of the players are black and 70% of the players are minorities.

The lack of opportunities for minorities reflects forms of discrimination. Although, as the 2003 *Gender and Race Report Card*[28] indicates, opportunities for minorities and women in sports have increased, there are considerable inequities in opportunities for minorities and for women.

The impact of societal beliefs about different racial and ethnic groups can be seen in the pattern of positions and roles played by athletes from different racial and ethnic backgrounds. Coakley uses the terms *race logic* and *race ideology* to refer to a "complex set of beliefs shared by many people and used to describe and interpret people, behaviors, and events in racial terms."[2] In some team sports, such as baseball, football, and women's volleyball, racial and ethnic stereotypes are reflected in the positions played by the athletes. Players from certain racial or ethnic groups are disproportionately represented at certain positions in a phenomenon known as stacking. For example, in professional baseball, black players are most heavily concentrated in the outfield positions, whereas white players are concentrated at the positions of pitcher, catcher, and the infield, although less so at first base. Whites are disproportionately represented in positions requiring leadership, dependability, and decision-making skills, while black players are overrepresented in positions requiring speed, agility, and quick reactions.[2]

In women's intercollegiate volleyball, blacks are disproportionately represented at spiker, while whites are overrepresented at setter and bumper.[2] Stacking patterns are widespread and occur in other sports and in countries throughout the world (e.g., in British soccer, black West Indians and Africans are overrepresented in the wide forward position, while white players are overrepresented at the goalie and midfielder position).[2] Stacking reflects stereotypical beliefs about different racial and ethnic groups—for example, that blacks are better jumpers, while whites are better leaders. Although stacking is one of the most studied topics in sociology of sport, there are serious disagreements about why stacking patterns exist. But even though a consensus is lacking about the causes of stacking, it is important to recognize that stacking perpetuates patterns of prejudice and discrimination in sport.

Increased recognition has been given to the problems confronting black and other minority athletes in collegiate sports. Some frequently cited problems are disparity in treatment by coaches, pressures to sacrifice educational goals for athletic goals, difficulty in overcoming an educational background that ill-prepared them for college, social isolation, and prejudicial attitudes held by coaches and teammates. Although desegregation has opened doors, it has not eliminated prejudice and discrimination.

Native Americans have long participated in sports, often uniting physical activities with cultural rituals and ceremonies.[30] Although many Native Americans have achieved success in sports, little recognition has been given to their accomplishments. Public acclaim most often has focused on the few Native Americans, such as Jim Thorpe, who were outstanding athletes on segregated government-sponsored reservation school football and baseball teams. On the whole, participation by Native Americans in most sports has been and continues to be limited.

Poverty, poor health, lack of equipment, and a dearth of programs are factors that often serve to limit Native American sport participation. Concern about loss of cultural identity, prejudice, lack of understanding, and insensitivity by others toward Native Americans act in concert with the other factors previously mentioned to curb sport involvement.

One example of this lack of sensitivity is the use of school names and mascots that perpetuate the white stereotypes of Native Americans. Team names such as Indians or Redskins or a team mascot dressed up as a savage running around waving a tomahawk threatening to behead an opponent reflects distorted beliefs of Native Americans. Such inappropriate or distorted caricatures of Native Americans who, as school mascots, are painted on gymnasium walls and floors, do little to increase student and public awareness of the richness and diversity of Native American culture. It is even more ironic that this occurs in institutions that by definition exist to educate people about the different cultures within the world in which they live. These stereotypes are often accepted as valid depictions of native people and serve to demean the cultural heritage and history of Native Americans.

Concerned American Indian Parents is a group committed to the elimination of Native American stereotypes in advertising and sport. The poster shown on page 324 is one example of this group's efforts to heighten public awareness of the racism experienced by Native Americans that has become an accepted aspect of sport in the United States. As Coakley[3] writes:

> The use of the name Redskins cannot be justified under any conditions. To many Native Americans, redskin is as derogatory as "nigger" is for black Americans. It is symbolic of such racism that the capitol city of the government that once put bounties on the lives of native peoples has a football team named the Redskins. It symbolizes a continuing lack of understanding of the complex and diverse cultures and the heritage of native peoples and is offensive to anyone aware of the history of native peoples in North America.

In 2001, the United States Commission on Civil Rights issued a statement on the use of Native American images and nicknames as sports symbols. The commission called for an end of the use

A poster used by the Concerned American Indian Parents to increase the public's awareness of racism toward Native Americans.

of Native American images and team names by non-Native schools. The commission believes that:

> the use of Native American mascots and their performances, logos, images and nicknames by schools are [*sic*] both disrespectful and insensitive to American Indians and others who object to such stereotyping. The stereotyping of any racial, ethnic, religious or other groups, when promoted by our public educational institutions, teaches all students that stereotyping of minority groups is acceptable—a dangerous lesson in a diverse society. Schools have a responsibility to educate their students; they should not use their influence to perpetuate misrepresentations of any culture or people.[31]

In addressing the contentions of schools that continue to use Native American imagery under the claim that their use stimulates interest in Native American culture and is a form of honoring Native Americans, the commission points out that these schools have failed to listen to Native American groups and civil rights organizations that oppose the symbols. Furthermore,

> these false portrayals prevent non-Native Americans from understanding the true historical and cultural experiences of American Indians. Sadly, they also encourage biases and prejudices that have a negative effect on contemporary Indian people. These references may encourage interest in mythical "Indians" created by the dominant culture, but they block genuine understanding of contemporary Native people as fellow Americans.[31]

Many state education departments have issued directives urging schools to ban the use of Native American imagery for mascots, team names, and logos. The commission does not see this as a trivial matter. The use of the imagery is offensive and must stop. Finally, the commission stated,

> The Commission has a firm understanding of the problems of poverty, education, housing, and health care that face many Native Americans. The fight to eliminate Indian nicknames and images in sport is one front of the larger battle to eliminate obstacles that confront American Indians. The elimination of Native American nicknames and images as sports mascots will benefit not only Native Americans, but all Americans. The elimination of stereotypes will make room for education about real Indian people, current Native American issues, and the rich variety of American Indians in our country.[31]

Stereotypes are the foundation of prejudice and racism. Attitudes change slowly. This is particularly true concerning prejudicial beliefs about different racial and ethnic groups. As discussed in Chapter 3, cultural competency is important in the fields of physical education, exercise science, and sport. Understanding and respecting cultures' worldviews is critical in addressing issues of opportunity and equity. In an era when our society is becoming increasingly multicultural and diverse, it is important that we, as physical education, exercise science, and sport professionals, step up and take a leadership role in this issue. As Staurowsky points out, "Professionals from the allied fields of sport science and physical education are perhaps positioned better than anyone else to provide leadership on this issue, given the integral role we play in facilitating athletic opportunities for students. By calling for elimination of stereotypes in the form of American Indian images, we can contribute positively to the education of all of our children, Indian and non-Indian alike."[32]

SPORT FOR INDIVIDUALS WITH DISABILITIES

Individuals with disabilities, like girls and women, had limited opportunities for participation in athletics prior to the 1970s. Changing societal attitudes, the use of sport for rehabilitation, and federal legislation have contributed to the growth of competitive sport opportunities for the disabled. Professional organizations such as AAHPERD advocate participation in physical education and athletics for all individuals, including those with disabilities.

An estimated 28 million people 3 years of age or older have serious limitations affecting their performance of physical activities. About 3.5 million of these persons are school aged. Federal legislation has had a significant impact on the schooling of individuals with disabilities. P.L. 94-142, Education for All Handicapped Children Act, mandated a free and appropriate education in the least restrictive environment for students with disabilities. Provision for instruction in physical education was specifically mentioned in this law. The Rehabilitation Act, specifically Section 504 of P.L. 93-112, stated that students with disabilities must have equal opportunity and access to extracurricular activities including intramurals and athletics. The Amateur Sports Act of 1978, P.L. 95-606, called for the United States Olympic Committee (USOC) to assist amateur athletic programs for individuals with disabilities and, where feasible, to expand the opportunities for meaningful participation by athletes with disabilities in competitions for able-bodied athletes.

Participation also has been encouraged by changing societal attitudes. Changes toward a more humanistic educational philosophy and society's recognition of the rights of individuals with disabilities were seen. Society's acceptance of individual differences and understanding of the capabilities of individuals with disabilities grew. These factors contributed to the integration of individuals with disabilities into society.

Changes occurred slowly. Orr[33] believes that the reluctance of school personnel to provide sport opportunities for disabled persons results from myth, superstition, and sport control. In elaborating on the myth surrounding the handicapped athlete, Orr writes:

> The imposed myth is that the handicapped person participating in sports is inferior and different from the so-called "normal" athlete. The reality is that while the handicapped person usually does not have equal marks in performance of a quantitative nature, the qualitative performance may equal or surpass any other athlete. The effect of the myth has been to obstruct opportunity for the handicapped as time, energy, and funds have been funneled in other directions.

Participation on interscholastic and intercollegiate teams by individuals with disabilities has been slow to increase. However, in recent years regional, national, and international competitions for individuals with disabilities have flourished. One of the most visible competitions has been the Special Olympics. The Special Olympics are sponsored by the Joseph P. Kennedy, Jr., Foundation. This foundation has focused more attention on sport for persons with disabilities than any other single organization or legislation.

The Special Olympics were organized in 1968. They were designed to provide youths 8 years of age and over who are mentally impaired with opportunities to participate in a variety of sport and games on local, state, regional, national, and international levels. Thousands of people volunteer to coach youngsters in Special Olympic events such as track and field, swimming, gymnastics, floor hockey, and volleyball. The volunteers include professional athletes in many areas of sport.

As a consequence of the Amateur Sports Act, a Committee of Sports for the Disabled was established as part of the USOC.[34] Some of the committee's responsibilities included promoting sport for disabled individuals; conducting research and disseminating information on various aspects of competition such as sports medicine, equipment design, and performance analysis; and publicizing the accomplishments of athletes with disabilities. Seven major amateur sport organizations for individuals with disabilities were recognized. One of the criteria for recognition as a major sport organization was that the organization had to offer national competition in two or more sports that are included in the program of the Olympic or the Pan American Games. These organizations are the National Association of Sports for Cerebral Palsy, American Athletic Association for the Deaf, National Handicapped Sports and Recreation Association, the National Wheelchair Athletic Association, United States Amputee Association, United States Association for Blind Athletes, and Special Olympics.

The Paralympics are recognized by the International Olympic Committee and provide international competitions for elite athletes with disabilities. Competitors include athletes who are blind, physically disabled, and amputees and who have cerebral palsy. Competitions are held in the Olympic host country following the Olympic Games. The 2004 Paralympic Games in Athens involved more than 4,000 athletes with disabilities and 2,000 team officials from 130 countries. The athletes competed in 18 sports and contested 550 medals. Over 100,000 people filled the stadium for both the opening and the closing ceremonies. Advanced training methods and high-tech equipment contributed to many outstanding performances. The paralympics reflect the importance of focusing on the possibilities and potential of people with disabilities, rather than stigmas surrounding disabilities. Sports are an important vehicle to promote equality, inclusion, accessibility, and awareness about the potential of people with disabilities.

Although sport opportunities are being provided for many youths with disabilities, the need to establish and conduct more sport programs is urgent if the sport needs of all individuals with disabilities are to be met. It is also necessary to encourage athletes with disabilities to participate with able-bodied athletes when feasible.

SPORT FOR CHILDREN AND YOUTH

For many Americans, participation in youth sport activities is an integral part of growing up. It is estimated that over 20 million boys and girls participate each year in youth sports, that is, organized sport activities that take place outside the school setting.[35] Furthermore, it is estimated that over 3 million volunteer coaches are involved with these programs. Youth sport ventures are organized around such sports as football, baseball, softball, tennis, ice hockey, golf, gymnastics, soccer, and swimming.[36] An increasing number of opportunities for girls to participate in these programs at all levels is being offered, and it appears that many more children are beginning to compete in these programs at younger ages.

While participation in youth sports has grown tremendously over the past decade, there is widespread concern about the nature and outcomes associated with these programs. Even though these programs are extremely popular, considerable criticism is voiced about the manner in which they are conducted. As you read about the benefits, harmful effects, and criticisms of youth sport programs, it may be helpful to keep in mind your own experiences and those of your friends in youth sport. Consider the following questions:

- What did you like most and least about your experiences?
- What did you learn from participating in youth sports?
- How did your parents influence your participation and what was the extent of their involvement with the program?
- How would you characterize the nature and effectiveness of the coaching you received or observed?
- How did you, your teammates, parents, and coaches respond to your successes and failures?
- At what age did you discontinue your participation in youth sports and what were the reasons for stopping?
- What changes would you make in the organization of the program to make the experience a more positive one for all involved?

As with school sports, many benefits have been ascribed to participation in youth sport programs. Proponents of youth sports emphasize that they promote physical fitness, emotional development, social adjustment, a competitive attitude, and self-confidence. In addition, youth sport programs provide opportunities for the development of physical skills, encourage the achievement of a greater level of skill, give children additional opportunities to play, and offer a safer experience than participation in unsupervised programs.

And, as with school sports, one of the greatest criticisms of youth sports is its overemphasis on winning. Critics also voice concerns that children's bodies may be underdeveloped for such vigorous activities, that there is too great an emotional strain and pressure on the participant, and that the players are too psychologically immature to compete in such a setting. Youth sport programs are cited as being too selective and excluding too many children who would like to participate and as promoting specialization at too early an age. Additional criticisms are directed toward overenthusiastic coaches and parents who take winning too seriously, who pressure children to achieve, and who place their needs before the needs of the child.

Overemphasis on winning has led to many of the abuses found within youth sport programs. The desire to win has led coaches to employ such behaviors as conniving to get the best players in the league on their team, holding lengthy practice sessions and endless drills to perfect skills, and berating children for their mistakes. Many physical education and sport professionals decry the overemphasis on winning. They believe that youth sport programs should be developmental in nature—that is, they should be organized and conducted in such a way as to enhance the physical, cognitive, and affective development of each child and youth participant. This development is particularly critical during the child's younger years. The fun of playing (rather than the beating of an opponent) should be stressed, participation opportunities for many children of all abilities should be provided (rather than limiting participation to the gifted few), and the development of skills within the sport and in other sports should be stressed (rather than specialization).

Too often, our attention is focused on the game or winning, leading us to overlook important messages from the athlete.

Specialization is another frequently voiced concern. During their early years, children should be given an opportunity to develop proficiency in fundamental motor skills and be exposed to a variety of sports. Some children are guided at an early age into a specific sport, such as soccer, or into a specific position within a sport, such as a pitcher. This early specialization deprives children of an opportunity to develop an interest and skills in a variety of sports.

Concern about specialization has further increased within the last decade. During this time there has been a growth of private sport leagues and clubs that emphasize the development of skills in a particular sport. This often leads to beginning high-level sport instruction and competition at an early age; children may begin as early as 3 years of age in such sports as swimming, gymnastics, skating, and soccer.[10] Training is serious and often occurs on a year-round basis. Physically, children may be at risk for the development of overuse injuries because they are often involved in practicing on a daily basis for several hours at a time. Psychologically, these participants may experience burnout from doing the same thing year after year. They may drop out before reaching their optimal level of performance, even after many years of successful participation.

Some professionals in the field of physical education, exercise science, and sport take the position that competitive sport for youth is not inherently bad or good. Instead, they point out that

The quality of leadership exerts a significant influence on the outcomes experienced by youth sports participants.

sport is what one makes it. Under sound leadership, if the welfare of the child is the primary consideration, if the environment is warm and supportive, and if the sport is administered in light of the needs and characteristics of the participants, much good can be accomplished. However, if poor leadership is provided, harmful effects will accrue.

Many recommendations have been set forth by professionals to improve youth sports. Professionals suggest that programs be structured so that children can experience success and satisfaction while continuing to develop their abilities. This may mean modification of the rules, equipment, and playing area to promote success and participation rather than failure and elimination. For example, simplified and fewer rules, smaller balls, smaller fields, bigger goals, batting tees rather than pitchers, rule changes to facilitate scoring, and a requirement of equal playing time for all participants are some of the ways that youth sports programs can be changed to make the experiences more positive for all participants.

Programs should be structured to include elements that children find enjoyable within their own informal games. Plenty of action, opportunity for involvement, close scores to keep the game exciting and interesting, and friendship are important to children; these elements should be infused into youth sport programming.[6] Children also should be given opportunities to be involved in decision making, such as deciding what strategies to use or planning a practice session. They can also be given the responsibility for self-enforcement of rules during the game.

As previously mentioned, the quality of leadership can exert a significant influence on the outcomes children derive from participating in youth sports. Coaches within the youth sport programs are typically volunteers, often parents, who have received little if any training on how to coach children. Recognizing this, professionals within the field have directed increased attention toward the development of coaching education programs. These programs emphasize understanding the growth characteristics and developmental needs of children, modifying existing programs to meet these needs, incorporating proper training techniques into the design of the program, and supporting the efforts of children while providing developmentally appropriate opportunities to help them become better players. Enhancing children's self-esteem, recognizing their accomplishments, and praising their efforts are more appropriate than ridiculing, shaming, and belittling their achievements and attempts.

Under qualified leadership, many of the problems associated with youth sport programs can be rectified. Implementation of these recommendations can maximize the positive experiences and minimize the negative experiences of youth sport participants. The key to successful youth sport programs is putting the needs of the child first. Programs should be designed to meet the children's needs, not those of adults. Youth sport programs should be organized on a developmental model, not a professional model. Programs should focus on fostering children's physical, cognitive, and affective development. The whole child as a moving, thinking, feeling human being should be considered when designing and conducting youth sport programs.

VIOLENCE

Violence is one of the major problems facing sport today. It is particularly noticeable in professional contact sports such as football and hockey. Physical and psychological intimidation of one's opponent is considered an essential part of professional basketball. Yet do such forms of intimidation lead to violence? Have coaches gone too far in "psyching" up their teams to go out and "kill" their opponents? In some contact sports, such as hockey, some players are even designated as "enforcers"—charged with protecting their own players and aggressively intimidating their opponents. However, violence is not limited to contact sports; bench-clearing brawls occur with greater frequency in even noncontact sports such as baseball. Has violence gotten out of control?

The media has done much to bring incidences of sport violence to the public's attention. Newspapers and sport periodicals give readers glowing, blow-by-blow accounts. Television glamorizes such events, often replaying them in slow motion. Special videos are being produced that show incident after incident of players using violence and force in pursuit of victory.

What impact has violence at the professional level had on other levels of sport? Some experts have expressed concern that the popularity and visibility of professional athletes lead athletes at lower levels of competition to imitate their actions, including their violent behavior. Other athletes, including those at the high school and even the youth sport level, may emulate the playing style of sport professionals. Thus, violence permeates other levels of sport and its impact on the nature of the game grows.

Spectator violence is also a concern, as media coverage of violent behavior at sport events throughout the world verifies. At some events, fans have stampeded the field and, in the process, trampled other fans to death. Outbreaks of fights among fans are reported. Experts have found that spectator violence is related to the actions of the players during the contests. In essence, player violence tends to increase the likelihood of violence by fans during and following the game. The media's promotion of games for their potential for violence tends to encourage spectator violence. The potential for violence also increases when fans believe that their team was robbed of a score or a victory by incompetent or unfair officiating. Crowd dynamics also influence the occurrence of spectator violence, including the amount of alcohol consumed, the importance of the contest, the demographics of the crowd, crowd size, and seating arrangements.

Violence between players and spectators is a concern as well. One recent distressing incidence of violence between professional players and fans occurred on November 19, 2004. During a Detroit Pistons versus Indiana Pacers game at the Palace of Auburn Hills in Detroit, a brawl erupted. A hard foul to Pistons' center Ben Wallace by Pacers' forward Ron Artest led to Ben Wallace's retaliating with a hard shove to Artest's neck. Events escalated from there, with opposing players shoving each other, fans heckling the players and throwing objects onto the court. Artest, hit by a drink thrown by a fan, ran into the stands to confront the individual he believed had thrown it. More players followed into the stands, and fans spilled onto the court. Punches, shoves, and kicks were exchanged between players and fans in the ensuing violent brawl that lasted over 10 minutes. NBA Commissioner David Stern acted quickly, suspending five Pacers and four Pistons for over 140 games. Artest was suspended for the remainder of the season, one of the harshest suspensions in NBA history. By his actions, Commissioner Stern sent a strong message that such behavior was not only inappropriate, but unacceptable. According to Stern, "The line is drawn, and my guess is that it won't happen again—certainly not to anybody who wants to be associated with our league."[37] Additionally, in the days following what some have deemed the worst brawl in the history of the NBA, criminal charges were filed against players and fans involved. The charges typically were for assault and battery.

Parental violence during youth sport events appears to be occurring with distressing frequency. Increasingly the media carry stories about parents attacking the coach, beating the umpire, and/or engaging in fights with parents of the opposing team. One of the most shocking incidents occurred in 2000, when a parent, Thomas Junta, fought another parent, Michael Costin, who was supervising the youth ice hockey practice in which the sons of both men participated. The argument was over rough play on the ice. Unconscious after the beating, Costin was hospitalized and died the next day. After a jury trial, Junta was found guilty of involuntary manslaughter, and on January 25, 2002, Junta was sentenced to 6 to 10 years in state prison. What impact did this tragedy, which received national attention, have on parental violence in youth sports? Unbelievably, two days after the sentencing, a brawl broke out among 30 parents during a match at a youth hockey game in Colorado. Four parents, including an off-duty police officer, were charged with disorderly conduct. Strong leadership is needed to eliminate parental violence in youth sports, and parents need to be held accountable for their actions. Policies must be established that will serve the best interests of the youth who are participating in these programs.

It is important to note that the environment in which the contest takes place contributes to its potential for violence. As Coakley[3] points out, spectators bring the issues and ideologies that are reflective of the events within their communities to sport events. When conflict and violence are an integral part of a community, the likelihood of spectator violence at a local sporting event increases. For example, highly publicized contests between rival high schools where high levels of racial and ethnic tension exist in the communities have led to violence. In some communities, efforts to prevent violence at school sporting events have led to the banning of all spectators from the events or the playing of events at neutral sites.

The question of how to deal with the problem of violence in sport has no single, simple solution. Experts are in agreement, however, that some type of control must be instituted, and it must start with persons who love sport and want to protect it from intrusions that will lower its value. They point out that violence is to be abhorred, particularly because it interferes with proper play, detracts from excellent athlete performance, and is barbaric in nature. Most spectators, it is suggested, do not want to see players hurt or crippled. They want to see clean, hard tackles and hard body checks. This is the essence of the game and sport itself.

It has been suggested that to reduce violence stricter penalties should be imposed at all levels of sports. Indeed, athletes in some sports and at some levels of competition are being penalized more severely for violent acts. However, the real and best solution to the problem of violence is a change in attitude on the part of all persons concerned. If subscribed to by professional and amateur players, coaches, spectators, sport entrepreneurs, and the public in general, the ideals of playing within the spirit and the letter of the rules, defeating one's opponent when at one's best, and having respect for other players will reduce the violence marring the playing fields and sport arenas today.

The potential for spectator violence can be reduced when some forethought is given to the factors that contribute to violence and thoughtful planning results in steps to minimize the occurrence of these factors. Reducing violence among contestants, decreasing the media hype that portrays the contest as a confrontation among hostile opponents, using competent officials to control the flow of the game, and taking preventive crowd-control measures can decrease spectator violence. Violence can also be decreased by formulating better relations between the teams and the community and by athletes' taking steps to become actively involved in the community in which they play and live.

PERFORMANCE-ENHANCING SUBSTANCES IN SPORT

Citius, altius, fortius—the Olympic motto of "Swifter, higher, stronger"—embodies the quest for excellence for many athletes. At the elite level, where races are won by a thousandth of a second, a gold medal by a tenth of a point, and fame achieved by a fraction of a centimeter, athletes are constantly experimenting with new ways to enhance their performance. Today, being swifter, higher, and stronger than one's competitors may lead athletes to seek "better performance through chemistry" and use/abuse performance-enhancing substances. Unfortunately, the use/abuse of performance-enhancing substances is not just a problem at the elite level, but one that has filtered down to athletes at the collegiate and even high school levels.

Professional leagues, sporting bodies, the International Olympic Committee, and the NCAA are among the organizations that have antidoping policies, with accompanying long lists of banned substances. Among those substances are anabolic steroids, human growth hormone, and amphetamines, as well as their derivatives. Athletes take these and other substances, often at many times the recommended doses, in an effort to gain strength, increase power, work harder during training, and/or enhance their endurance. The ultimate goal is to improve one's performance.

Sport sociologists study the use of these performance-enhancing substances by athletes. They seek to answer such questions as "If sports build character, why do athletes cheat and use banned substances?" or "Why do some athletes seek an unfair advantage by using banned substances?" Noted sport sociologist, Jay Coakley, in a discussion of deviance in sport, invites us to look at the use performance-enhancing substances in sport as a form of deviance associated with overconformity to the high power and performance sport ethic.

Coakley defines the sport ethic as a "set of norms that many people in power and performance sports have accepted as the dominant criteria for defining what it means to be an athlete and to successfully claim an identity as an athlete."[38] The four norms associated with the sport ethic are making sacrifices, striving for distinction, taking risks and playing through the pain, and accepting no limits in pursuit of the "dream."

When athletes embrace the sport ethic, they give sport priority over all aspects of their life. They pressure themselves to live up to their own expectations as well as those of their coaches and their teammates. They make the sacrifices necessary and are willing to pay the price to play. Athletes strive to achieve distinction, constantly seeking to improve and achieve at the highest level. Athletes take risks; they do not back down from a challenge. Courage enables them to overcome fear and accept risk of failure. It is courage that enables athletes to play in pain. Lastly, athletes pursue their dream with dedication, believing success is possible for those willing to work hard to achieve it.

When athletes go to the extreme to conform to the sport ethic, this overconformity carries with it significant risks to their health and well-being. Examples of overconformity that present health risks to athletes include severely restricting food and prolonged exercising in rubber suits to make weight in wrestling, running an excessive number of miles in training for cross-country, and using huge doses of pain killers to play when injured. Why do athletes, often unquestioning, take such risks?

According to Coakley, one reason for overconformity is that athletes will do anything to stay involved in sport because the sport experience is so exhilarating.[38] Second, athletes perceive that their chances of staying involved and competing at higher and higher levels are enhanced when they overconform to the sport ethic.[38] Coaches want dedicated, committed athletes, willing to sacrifice all for the love of sport. Lastly, continued involvement where normative boundaries are exceeded infuses drama and excitement into athletes' lives.[38] This increases their commitment and investment in sport as well as bonding them to other athletes. Overconformity to the sport ethic is to many athletes not deviant behavior but an affirmation of their athletic identity.[38]

The use of banned performance-enhancing substances falls within the range of deviant overconformity to the sport ethic. It is not, as some would suggest, because athletes are not disciplined enough to achieve gains through hard work. Nor is it really a desire to cheat. Athletes view performance-enhancing substances as a means to gain an edge. Some see the use of such substances as the avenue to being able to play at the highest possible level, an opportunity to stay involved in a sport they love. Athletes who are deeply committed to their sport often will do whatever it takes to achieve distinction.

How widespread the use of banned performance-enhancing substances is among athletes is difficult to determine. One way the sports world has sought to cope with the use of illegal performance-enhancing is through drug testing. Two of the many drug testing agencies are the World Anti-Doping Agency (WADA) and the United States Anti-Doping Agency (USADA). They conduct drug testing for athletes involved in Olympic sports.

Drug testing is controversial. Critics consider drug testing a violation of privacy rights, and in some societies it violates cultural norms. Additionally, as rapidly as new tests are being developed for banned substances, athletes switch to an undetectable drug or use masking drugs to obscure test results. Drug testing is also costly, and paying for testing draws on funds that could be used to provide health programs for athletes. Proponents of drug testing see it as necessary in order to protect the health of athletes. Death and serious health problems have been associated with the use of performance-enhancing substances in sport. Testing is also necessary to guarantee a level playing field, where the winners are those who have toiled diligently to develop their skills rather than those athletes who have access to performance-enhancing substances.

Educational programs and treatment approaches have been used to try to stem the use of illegal performance-enhancing substances. Strong punishment for violators, such as a lifetime suspension or a 2-year ban from competition, stands as a strong deterrent to the use of illegal performance-enhancing substances. Despite these and other approaches, news headlines continue to report stories of track stars, football players, baseball standouts, elite cyclists, and other athletes found to be using illegal drugs to gain a performance edge.

As medical science becomes more sophisticated and as new scientific advances, such as genetic manipulation, challenge our imagination, we must critically assess the norms governing the sports experience. Coakley suggests that critical reflection on existing norms is important, and rules and limits must be set if deviant overconformity is to be controlled.[38] According to Coakley, "Controlling deviance requires a critical examination of the values and norms in sport, as well as the restructuring of the organizations controlling and sponsoring sports."[38] In order to transform sports and deal with current and future challenges, all those involved in sports should think critically about the meaning, purpose, and organization of sports and take an active role in addressing these challenges in order to maintain the integrity of sports performance.

Focus on Career: Sport Sociology

PROFESSIONAL ORGANIZATIONS

- International Sociology of Sport Association www.uq.edu.au/~asjmckay/info.htm
- North American Society for the Sociology of Sport playlab.uconn.edu/nasss.htm
- Sport Sociology Academy www.aahperd.org → NASPE → Academies

PROFESSIONAL JOURNALS

- *International Review for the Sociology of Sport*
- *Journal of Sport and Social Issues*
- *Research Quarterly for Exercise and Sport*
- *Sociology of Sport Journal*
- *Quest*

SUMMARY

Sport is an important part of American culture. As a social institution, sport influences and is influenced by other institutions in our society, such as politics, education, family, religion, and the media. Its pervasiveness has led to the study of sport from a sociological perspective.

Sport has a significant role in educational institutions. Over 6 million youths play sports at the high school level. At the collegiate level, thousands of men and women compete. Sport can have both a positive and negative influence on the lives of its participants. Among the problems associated with sport in educational institutions are an overemphasis on winning, athletic goals overshadowing academic goals, soaring expenditures, continued growth of big-time sport, and inequities in opportunities for women and minorities.

Sport sociologists are interested in transforming sport, changing the nature of sport so that it is more equitable and beneficial for those involved. Racism, including the use of Native American imagery, is one of the topics studied by sport sociologists. Among other topics studied are gender issues, opportunities for girls and women in sports, sport for persons with disabilities, violence in sport, and the use of performance-enhancing substances.

It is important for physical education, exercise science, and sport professionals to understand the significant role of sport as an institution in our society. In the future, it is hoped that physical education, exercise science, and sport professionals will take a more active role in creating greater opportunities for all people in sport.

SELF-ASSESSMENT TESTS

These tests are designed to help you determine if you have mastered the materials and competencies presented in this chapter.

1. Discuss the role of sport in American culture and its impact on various institutions in society, such as economics, education, family, and the media.
2. Discuss the sociological implications of educational sport. What are the benefits and possible disadvantages of participating in educational sport? Reflect carefully on your personal experiences in sport. How did they contribute to your personal development and educational goals?

3. Use the information provided in the Get Connected box to explore more deeply the extent of participation by girls and women in sport. What are the benefits of participation? How can participation be increased further, especially among underrepresented population groups such as minorities and girls and women from low socioeconomic backgrounds? What can be done to increase the number of women in coaching and athletic administration?
4. Use the Internet or library to search for current information about violence in sport, youth sport, or use of illegal performance-enhancing substances in sport. Share your findings with the class.

REFERENCES

1. Leonard II WM: A sociological perspective of sport, ed 5, Boston, 1998, Allyn and Bacon.
2. Coakley J: Sport in society: issues and controversies, ed 7, New York, 2001, McGraw-Hill.
3. Coakley J: Sport in society: issues and controversies, ed 6, Dubuque, Iowa, 1998, WCB/McGraw-Hill.
4. Harris JC: Sociology of physical activity. In SJ Hoffman and JC Harris, Introduction to kinesiology: studying physical activity, Champaign, Ill., 2000, Human Kinetics.
5. Sage GH: Sport sociology. In JD Massengale and RA Swanson, editors: The history of exercise and sport science, Champaign, Ill., 1997, Human Kinetics.
6. Coakley J: Sport in society: issues and controversies, ed 2, St Louis, 1982, Mosby.
7. National Federation of State High School Associations: 2003–2004 High School Participation Survey. (www.nfhs.org)
8. National Collegiate Athletic Association: 2003 NCAA Participation. (www.ncaa.org)
9. Lumpkin A: Physical education and sport: a contemporary introduction, ed 2, St. Louis, 1990, Mosby.
10. Siedentop D: Introduction to physical education, fitness, and sport, Mountain View, Calif., 1998, Mayfield.
11. Centers for Disease Control and Prevention: Prevent alcohol and drug use fact sheet 11 risk behaviors. (www.cdc.gov/nccdphp/dash/yrbs/trend.htm)
12. American Academy of Pediatrics: Steroids: play safe, play fair. 2002. (www.aap.org/family/steroids.htm)
13. National Collegiate Athletic Association: Composition of the NCAA 2001 membership. (www.ncaa.org)
14. National Collegiate Athletic Association: 2001 NCAA division I graduation rates report. (www.ncaa.org)
15. Center for Study of Sport in Society: 2001 racial and gender report card. (www.sportinsociety.org/ncas.html)
16. National Collegiate Athletic Association: Initial eligibility. (www.ncaa.org)
17. The National Center for Fair and Open Testing: What's wrong with the NCAA's test score requirements? (www.fairtest.org)
18. Knight Foundation: Report of the Knight Foundation Commission on Intercollegiate Athletics, 1991. Available from the National Collegiate Athletic Association.
19. National Collegiate Athletic Association: Sports wagering, Kansas, 1997, National Collegiate Athletic Association.
20. John S. and James L. Knight Foundation: A call to action: reconnecting college sports and higher education. Knight Commission, June 2001. (www.knightfdn.org)
21. The President's Council on Physical Fitness and Sports: Physical activity and sport in the lives of girls, Washington, D.C., 1997, President's Council on Physical Fitness and Sports.
22. Women's National Basketball Association. (wnba.com)
23. Women's United Soccer Association. (www.wusa.rog)
24. Acosta RV and Carpenter LJ: Women in intercollegiate sport: a longitudinal study—nineteen

year update, 1977–2004. Available at www.arcade.uiowa.edu/proj/ge/Acosta/womenspt.html#Overview

25. National Collegiate Athletic Association: 2003–2004 race demographics of NCAA member institutions. (www.ncaa.org)
26. National Association of Collegiate Women Athletic Administrators: A time of opportunity, challenge, change and transformation in intercollegiate athletics, 2000. (www.ncawaa.org)
27. United States General Accounting Office: Intercollegiate athletics: four-year colleges' experiences adding and discontinuing teams, Washington, D.C., March 2001, United States General Accounting Office.
28. Lapchick RE: 2003 Racial and Gender Report Card, The Institute for Diversity and Ethics in Sport, University of Central Florida, 2004.
29. National Collegiate Athletic Association: 1982–2004 participation statistics report. (www.ncaa.org)
30. Oxedine, JB: American Indian sports heritage, Champaign, IL, 1988, Human Kinetics.
31. The United States Commission on Civil Rights: Commission statement on the use of Native American images and nicknames as sports symbols, Washington, D.C., 2001, United States Commission on Civil Rights. (www.usccr.gov)
32. Staurowsky, EJ: American Indian imagery and the miseducation of America, Quest, 51, 382–392, 1999.
33. Orr RE: Sport, myth, and the handicapped athlete, JOPERD 55(2):34–46, 1979.
34. DePauw KP: Commitment and challenges: sport opportunities for athletes with disabilities, JOPERD 55(20):34–46, 1984.
35. Patel DR, Greydanus DE, and Pratt HD: Youth sports: more than just sprains and strains. Contemporary Pediatrics, March 2001.
36. Martens R: Youth sport in the USA. In M Weiss and D Gould, editors: Sport for children and youth, Champaign, Ill., 1986, Human Kinetics.
37. Lapchick, RE: Rough play is out of bounds, ESPN.Com, Page 2. November 24, 2001.
38. Coakley J: Sport in society: issues and controversies, ed. 8, New York, 2004, McGraw-Hill.

SUGGESTED READINGS

Ashe AR, Jr: A hard road to glory: a history of the African American athlete, New York, 1988, Warner Books.

The involvement of African Americans in sports from 1619 to 1988 is chronicled.

Baca LR: Native images in schools and the racially hostile environment, Journal of Sport and Social Issues, 28:71–78, 2004.

Title VI of the Civil Rights Act of 1964 prohibits discrimination on the basis of race, color, or national origin in federally funded programs, which include the public schools. Some Native American students attending schools that use stereotypical images of Indians, as well as their parents, find that the use of these images create a negative, hostile environment. The author discusses the application of legal standards pertaining to a racially hostile environment to schools.

Brittain I: Perceptions of disability and their impact upon involvement in sport for people with disabilities at all levels, Journal of Sport and Social Issues, 28:429–453, 2004.

Societal perceptions of people with disabilities and their involvement in disability sport are discussed, including how media coverage tends to portray participation in ways that reinforce the medical model of disabilities.

Coakley JJ: Sport in society: issues and controversies, ed 8, New York, 2004, WCB/McGraw-Hill.

An excellent critical analysis of the many issues within sport today, including educational sport, youth sport, racism, gender issues, politics, and the media and sport.

Coventry BT: On the sidelines: sex and racial segregation in television sports broadcasting, Sociology of Sport Journal, 21:322–342, 2004.

Examines the relationship between different job classifications in sports broadcasting, race, and gender. Women and people of color were found to be concentrated in lower positions in the field.

Donnelly P: Approaches to social inequality in the sociology of sport, Quest 48:221–242, 1996.

After a discussion of how social inequality in sport can be analyzed, ways in which sport can be used to promote social equality are presented.

Duderstadt, JJ: Intercollegiate athletes and the American university: A university president's perspective, Ann Arbor, MI, 2000, University of Michigan Press.

Critically examines the role of the university president in the management of intercollegiate athletics. The author suggests that action be taken to realign athletics with the educational mission of institutions rather than allowing its role as entertainment to continue to expand.

King CR: This is not an Indian: Situating claims about Indianness in sporting worlds, Journal of Sport and Social Issues, 28:3–10, 2004.

Reviews the history and significance of the use of Native Americans as mascots in sports, including an examination of the literature.

Landers MA and Fina GA: Learning life's lessons in tee-ball: the reinforcement of gender and status in kindergarten and sport, Sociology of Sport Journal 13:87–93, 1996.

This article describes how status and gender roles are reinforced by children's earliest sport experiences: tee-ball.

Marzano-Parisoli MM: The contemporary construction of a perfect body image: body building, exercise addiction, and eating disorders, Quest, 53:121–135, 2001.

Discusses the influence of culture on the body, in terms of ideal appearance and social norms and rules. Explores the similarities between anorexia and addictive exercise behaviors and the consequences for individuals.

Staurowsky EJ: American Indian imagery and the miseducation of America, Quest 51:382–392, 1999.

Critical examination of the use of Native American images, logos, and mascots in education from the perspective of cultural literacy.

CHAPTER 9

SPORT AND EXERCISE PSYCHOLOGY

OBJECTIVES

After reading this chapter the student should be able to—

- Describe the psychological benefits of participation in sport and physical activities.
- Understand the different theories of behavior and their potential application to exercise adherence.
- Discuss the roles of anxiety, arousal, and attention in the performance of motor skills and the application of intervention strategies to enhance performance.
- Understand goal-setting and how it can be effectively used in physical education, exercise, and sport.
- Describe self-talk and strategies to modify self-talk to enhance behavior or performance.

Sport and exercise psychology has its legacy in psychology. In the 1970s, as the academic scope of physical education grew, sport psychology emerged as a subdiscipline. Initially, sport psychologists focused on competitive sport and the elite athlete. As the subdiscipline grew, sport psychologists became interested in studying participation in exercise and other facets of physical activity. Additionally, their focus broadened from working with elite competitors to include people of all ages and abilities. The name of the subdiscipline today, sport and exercise psychology, reflects this expanded focus.

This chapter provides a short introduction to sport and exercise psychology. It includes a brief overview of the development of the subdiscipline. Selected topics within sport and exercise psychology are briefly discussed; space limitations preclude the inclusion of more topics and limit the depth of discussion. Given that caveat, this chapter presents information on the psychological benefits of physical activity, exercise adherence, personality, anxiety and arousal, attention, goal-setting, self-talk, and various intervention strategies. It is hoped that this brief glimpse will stimulate your interest in this area and encourage further study.

GET CONNECTED

Association for the Advancement of Applied Sport contains information on sport psychology, certification information, code of ethics, and information about graduate programs in sport psychology.

www.aaasponline.org/index2.html

Mind Tools provides an overview of sport psychology as well as information about goal-setting, imagery and simulation, focus and flow, and achieving excellence.

www.demon.co.uk/mindtool/page11.html

American Psychological Association Exercise and Sport Psychology site gives information about career opportunities in sport and exercise psychology and provides a list of sport and exercise psychology links and a list of conferences and meetings.

www.psyc.unt.edu/apadiv47

Athletic Insight is an online sport psychology journal, offering articles on various topics, such as mood regulation, children in sport, and professional issues, as well as links to related sites.

www.athleticinsight.com

SPORT AND EXERCISE PSYCHOLOGY

Sport and exercise psychology is a rapidly growing subdiscipline of physical education, exercise science, and sport. Initially, this subdiscipline was closely aligned with motor learning; however, during the last two decades it has evolved as a distinct field of study. The definition and scope, historical development, and areas of study within sport and exercise psychology are described briefly in this section.

Definition and Scope

Sport and exercise psychology is defined by Vealey as "the systematic scholarly study of the behavior, feelings, and thoughts of people engaged in sport, exercise, and physical activity."[1] According to the Association for the Advancement of Applied Sport Psychology (AAASP), sport and exercise psychology focuses on the psychological and mental aspects of participation in sport and exercise, seeking to understand how psychological processes influence and are influenced by participation.[2] The International Society of Sport Psychology states that "this dynamic field can enhance the experience of men, women, and children of all ages who participate in physical activity, ranking from those who do so for personal enjoyment to those who pursue a specific activity at the elite level."[3]

The scope of sport and exercise psychology is quite broad, encompassing both theoretical and applied approaches and reflecting close ties to the discipline of psychology. The initial work in the subdisicpline focused on sport and elite athletes. Today, the focus has expanded and includes the psychological dimensions of competitive sport participation and engagement in fitness, exercise, and physical activity. Sport and exercise psychology seeks to understand, influence, and improve the experiences of people of all ages and abilities, ranging from the youth sport participant to the elite Olympic performer and from the elderly individual engaging in an exercise rehabilitation program following a heart attack to the healthy adult who enjoys lifting weights on a regular basis.

Historical Development

The early history of sport and exercise psychology is closely related to motor learning. As these areas of study grew in the 1970s in the United States, they

Paralympians mentally rehearse their performances before the competition begins.

began to emerge as separate subdisciplines of the academic discipline of physical education; however, in Europe today, these areas remain closely aligned under the umbrella of sport psychology.

In the late 1890s and early 1900s, physical educators and psychologists began to write about the psychological aspects of physical education and sport. The most notable of these early researchers was Norman Triplett, who, in 1898, studied the effects of the presence of other people on the performance of motor skills.[1] The influence of the presence of other people—that is, an audience, on motor performance later developed into an area of research known as social facilitation.[1]

In 1918, Coleman Griffith, commonly recognized as the "father of sport psychology," began his groundbreaking work in sport psychology as a doctoral student at the University of Illinois.[4] Later, as Director of the Athletic Research Laboratory at Illinois, Griffith engaged in research in motor learning and on the psychological aspects of sport. Additionally, Griffith taught sport psychology classes, published numerous research articles, and authored two books considered classics in the field—*Psychology of Coaching* (1926) and *Psychology of Athletics* (1928). Like the applied sport psychologists of today, Griffith's research extended outside of the laboratory setting; he observed and interviewed outstanding athletes and coaches of the time, such as Red Grange and Knute Rockne, regarding motivation and the psychology of coaching.[4] In 1938, Griffith was hired by Philip Wrigley as the Chicago Cubs baseball team's sport psychologist. In this capacity, Griffith worked with players and researched ways to enhance motivation and develop self-confidence.

From 1940 to 1965, Gill characterizes the research in sport psychology as sporadic.[4] Following World War II, colleges and universities established motor behavior research programs. As previously mentioned in the chapter on motor learning and control, Henry, Slater-Hammel, Hubbard, and Lawther were instrumental in developing research programs focusing on motor learning and performance. These research programs included some work on topics currently within the realm of sport psychology today. Another important contribution of this time was Warren Johnson's study, in 1949, of pregame emotion in football, which served as the basis for later research on emotions associated with competition.[4] Lawther's publication, in 1951, of *The Psychology of Coaching* reflected an applied sport psychology orientation to coaching athletes.

In the 1960s, several texts were published that included information about the psychological aspects of sport and learning. These books introduced both undergraduate and graduate physical education students to both motor learning and sport psychology.[4] Bryant Cratty, who became one of the most prolific authors in the field, published *Movement Behavior and Motor Learning* in 1964 and *Psychology and Physical Activity* in 1967.[4] In

Lifespan and Cultural Perspectives: Sport and Exercise Psychology

- How do sociocultural factors influence participants' adherence to an exercise program?
- Does age influence the psychological benefits derived from participation in physical activity?
- Do personality traits and psychological dispositions of elite athletes vary by ethnicity or gender?
- How can self-efficacy be developed in children with low skill ability?
- What interventions are most effective in mediating the effects of anxiety in Senior Olympic competitors?

1968, Robert Singer's textbook, *Motor Learning and Human Performance,* was published.[4] Another book published during this era caused considerable controversy—Bruce Ogilvie and Thomas Tutko's book *Problem Athletes and How to Handle Them* (1966). Gill notes that this book was criticized by scholars intent on advancing the scientific nature of sport psychology for its clinical approach and the lack of a scientific framework.[4] However, the book was popular among coaches and helped set the stage for applied sport psychology in the 1980s.[4]

The late 1960s and the 1970s marked the emergence of sport psychology as a subdiscipline of physical education. Courses were developed for inclusion within the graduate and undergraduate physical education curriculums, graduate programs were inaugurated and research programs established, professional societies were organized, and specialized sport psychology journals were created. Scholars such as Rainer Martens, Dorothy Harris, Daniel Landers, and William Morgan helped shape the direction of the field.[1,4] As the amount of research grew and interest in sport psychology developed, outlets for dissemination of research and forums for the exchange of ideas were needed. In 1965, the International Society of Sport Psychology (ISSP) was founded. Two years later, in 1967, professionals interested in motor learning and sport psychology formed the North American Society for the Psychology of Sport and Physical Activity (NASPSPA). In 1975, the Sport Psychology Academy was organized as part of NASPE, a substructure of AAHPERD. *The Research Quarterly* and journals in the parent field of psychology served as the major outlets for publication of research until the *Journal of Sport Psychology* began publication in 1979.

However, during this time sport psychology was still aligned with motor learning and drew heavily on the parent discipline of psychology for theories. Much of the work was conducted in laboratory settings, rather than within sport, and offered little help to teachers, coaches, and participants.[4] In 1979, Martens called for a greater emphasis on applied issues within sport psychology including a focus on more relevant issues, a greater emphasis on field-based rather than laboratory-based research, and the development of sport-specific conceptual models.[4] This shift in focus was reflected in the work of sport psychologists in the 1980s.

The 1980s marked a period of tremendous expansion for sport psychology. Many scholars embraced a more applied approach to sport psychology. More field-based research with sport participants was conducted, and a greater emphasis was placed on the application of research to real-world sports events. In 1986, the Association for the Advancement of Applied Sport Psychology (AAASP) was organized; it is comprised of three interrelated focus areas: intervention/performance enhancement, health psychology, and social psychology. In 1987, the inaugural volume of *The Sport Psychologist* was published, providing another outlet for scholarly work with an applied focus.

Another factor that helped shaped the field was the growing interest of more clinically trained psychologists in sport psychology.[4] Ogilvie's applied approach to sport psychology, which was not well received when initially presented, gained greater acceptance. One noteworthy contribution during this time frame was that of Richard Suinn, a clinical psychologist whose work with the United States Olympic Ski Team did much to bring sport psychology to public attention.[4] Another significant step in the growth of sport psychology occurred in 1986, when Division 47 Exercise and Sport Psychology became a formal division within the American Psychology Association.

It was during the 1980s that exercise psychology evolved as a specialized area of study. Researchers became interested in understanding the psychological aspects of fitness, exercise, health, and wellness, including psychological factors that influence participation and the influence of participation on those involved. Attention was also directed toward enhancing the experience for those participants involved in health-related physical activity. This growth of interest occurred at a time when more and more research and public attention was being directed toward the significant contribution of physical activity to health. To reflect the expanding scope of the subdiscipline, in 1988, the *Journal of Sport Psychology* was renamed the *Journal of Sport and Exercise Psychology.*

Sport and exercise psychology during the 1990s and today reflects the rich diversity of this subdiscipline, both in research and practice. As Gill writes,

> Some researchers emphasize theory-based basic research with tight controls, and search for underlying physiological mechanisms; others shun traditional research, using interpretive approaches and searching for experiential knowledge. Some are not concerned with research at all, but seek information on strategies and techniques to educate, consult, or clinically treat sport and exercise participants.[4]

Some researchers seek to focus exclusively on sport psychology; others on exercise psychology. As sport and exercise psychology continues to grow and evolve in the twenty-first century, Gill suggests that it is likely that more sport and exercise-specific approaches will develop and that there will be a greater appreciation "of the richer understanding that can be gained through collaborative research across specializations, such as exercise physiology and motor learning."[4]

Areas of Study

Sport and exercise psychology includes many different areas of study. Sport and exercise psychologists are interested in understanding factors that influence participation in sport and exercise. For example, why do some athletes "choke" under pressure? Why do some postcardiac patients fail to complete their rehabilitation program? Sport and exercise psychology also studies the psychological outcomes derived from participation. For instance, does participation in an exercise program reduce stress and alleviate depression? Does participation in youth sport build character?

Sport and exercise psychology can also help physical educators, exercise scientists, and sport leaders make modifications to sport and exercise programs to enrich the experience for the participants involved. This could include helping athletes learn techniques to regulate their level of arousal to achieve optimal performance, teaching coaches how to promote self-confidence or to motivate their athletes, or building more social support into exercise programs to promote adherence and provide greater enjoyment for the participants.

Areas of study within sport and exercise psychology include attentional focus, personality, aggression and violence, self-confidence and self-efficacy, self-talk, arousal, social reinforcement, adherence, team building, commitment, and level of aspiration. Researchers design and assess the effectiveness of various interventions to enhance performance and participation such as cognitive restructuring, mental rehearsal, and social support. Researchers are also interested in factors that cause people to become involved in sport and exercise and those factors that lead to people's dropping out or discontinuing participation.

The amount of research produced by scholars in sport and exercise psychology has grown tremendously over the past decade. Examples of questions that may be investigated by researchers include the following:

- Is the personality profile of the outstanding or elite athlete different from that of the average athlete or nonathlete?
- How does participation in an exercise program influence one's body image? Or one's feelings of self-efficacy and control?
- What are the psychological benefits derived from participation in physical activity? What is the dose-response relationship between physical activity and psychological effects?
- Does one's personality change as a result of participation in sport or an exercise program? If so, what is the nature of the change?
- In what way does anxiety influence performance in various types of sports?
- How can an athlete deal most effectively with the stress of competition? What strategy would be most helpful for an athlete to use to deal with the pressure of competition?
- What factors influence an individual's adherence to an exercise or rehabilitation program?
- Does participation in sport empower athletes with disabilities?
- How does an individual's self-confidence affect his or her performance? How can self-confidence be developed most effectively and then used to maximize performance?
- How can self-efficacy in adolescents be increased to promote the establishment of beneficial physical activity patterns?

These are only a sample of the type of questions that may be addressed by researchers in sport and exercise psychology.

Sport psychologists today work with both male and female athletes to help them perform at their optimal level. Sport psychologists work with professional sport teams, national sports teams (U.S. Olympic Teams in various sports), and intercollegiate teams. Some professional athletes or athletes that compete at an elite level, such as in figure skating, may engage the services of a sport psychologist to help them achieve their goals.

Knowledge of sport psychology is important to coaches at all levels. It can help coaches more fully understand the psychological impact of their coaching behaviors and decisions on the athletes. Coaches can incorporate information from sport psychology into their preparation of athletes for competition and use information during competition to help their teams perform at their highest possible level. Additionally, coaches may find it beneficial to understand the factors that contribute to athletes' continuing commitment to a sport and the factors that predispose athletes to discontinue sport participation.

Specialists in exercise psychology focus their efforts on individuals participating in exercise and rehabilitation programs. Researchers have sought to identify the psychological determinants of participation in physical activity and the factors that influence the completion of rehabilitation regimens. Given the documented evidence supporting the contribution of regular physical activity to health, understanding the psychological dimensions of participation is of critical importance to physical education, exercise science, and sport professionals working in these areas. Such an understanding can help practitioners design programs and structure experiences to enhance the probability that program participants will engage in physical activity to the extent necessary to realize health benefits and incorporate physical activity into their lifestyle.

Sport and exercise psychologists can provide educational and/or clinical services, depending on their credentials. Clinical sport psychologists have extensive training in psychology and are licensed by state boards to treat people with psychopathology. Clinical sports psychologists may treat participants with personality disorders, eating disorders, or chemical dependency. They supplement their training in psychology with additional training in sport and exercise psychology.

Educational sport and exercise psychologists often have a background in physical education, exercise science, and sport, with extensive training in sport and exercise psychology. They are not licensed psychologists. The Association for the

Advancement of Applied Sport Psychology (AAASP) offers a certification program for applied sport psychology that recognizes attainment of professional knowledge in sport psychology, including health/exercise psychology, intervention/performance enhancement, and social psychology. Upon meeting the requirements for certification, an individual is conferred the title Certified Consultant, Association for the Advancement of Applied Sport Psychology. Certified consultants engage in educational activities focused on the "development and understanding of cognitive, behavioral, and affective skills in participants of all ages and at all skill levels."[2] Examples of educational activities include informing individuals and groups about the role of psychological factors in exercise, physical activity, and sport or teaching participants specific psychological skills such as imagery or coping skills that they can use to enhance their participation.[2] Another activity is the education of organizations and groups in areas such as development of team cohesion, strategies to promote exercise adherence, and the modification of youth sports programs to enhance the experience for the young athletes. As the AAASP notes, "Although some individuals may possess coaching expertise and/or knowledge of the analysis and treatment of psychopathology, these two areas are excluded from the role definition association with AAASP certification."[2]

Sport and exercise psychology encompasses many areas of study. The next section will provide a brief overview of some topics within this subdiscipline.

PSYCHOLOGICAL BENEFITS OF PHYSICAL ACTIVITY

The role of physical activity in enhancing well-being is receiving increased professional and public recognition. The physiological effects of engaging in physical activity on a regular basis are well documented. There is also a growing body of evidence supporting the psychological benefits of physical activity.[5,6] Psychological benefits have been noted for both aerobic and resistance exercise. It appears that moderate-intensity exercise has the best psychological benefits.

The psychological benefits of participating in physical activity include the following:

- Physical activity improves the health-related quality of life by enhancing both psychological and physical well-being.
- Physical activity improves one's mood. Mood states influence our outlook on life, our emotions, thought processes, and behaviors.
- Physical activity appears to alleviate symptoms associated with mild depression. Physical activity may be a valuable adjunct to therapy in cases of chronic, severe depression.
- Physical activity reduces state anxiety—that is, feelings of tension, apprehension, and fear associated with various situations.
- Physical activity can be effective in managing stress. It can serve as a buffer against stress as well as provide a healthful means of stress reduction.
- Physical activity contributes to the development of the self. It enhances self-concept and improves self-esteem or feelings of worth. Physical activity promotes greater self-efficacy and self-confidence.
- Physical activities offer a means of affiliation with other human beings, an important psychological need.
- Physical activities offer participants the opportunity to experience peak moments. Peak moments are characterized by feelings of being "lost" or absorbed in the activity and "flow" or feelings of powerfulness or being able to do no wrong. Participants have reported feelings of euphoria, such as runners' high.
- Physical activity provides recreation and a change of pace from long hours of work or study. Individuals return to their daily routine feeling refreshed, both mentally and physically.
- Physical activity experiences can present a challenge that, when successfully met, provides

a sense of achievement. Some physical activities include certain elements of risk, such as mountain climbing, that provide excitement and opportunities for mastery.

- Physical activities offer aesthetic and creative experiences. Activities such as dance allow individuals to express their emotions in a nonverbal manner and provide opportunities for individual interpretation.

The psychological benefits of physical activity are being increasingly understood and offer exciting possibilities for research.

Researchers have advanced several hypotheses to explain the effects of exercise on mental health. Hypotheses have been developed that explain the mechanism of effect from a psychological or a physiological perspective. Among the psychological hypotheses offered are the cognitive behavioral hypothesis and the distraction hypothesis. One physiological hypothesis that has received considerable attention is the endorphin hypothesis.

According to the cognitive behavior hypothesis, participation in exercise promotes positive thoughts and feelings.[7] These serve to counteract negative thoughts and feelings as well as mood states associated with depression and anxiety.[7] Nonexercisers who begin and adhere to an exercise program, a task many nonexercisers perceive as difficult, experience enhanced feelings of competence and an increase in self-efficacy.[7] Increased self-efficacy is also associated with effort and persistence, factors that will help individuals continue to participate in exercise and reap the psychological benefits.[7]

The distraction hypothesis proposes that the psychological benefits of exercise accrue because engaging in exercise distracts individuals from their cares, worries, and frustrations.[8] Exercise provides individuals with a "time out" from events and issues in their life that are associated with feelings of anxiety or depression.

The endorphin hypothesis explains that psychological benefits associated with exercise are due to the increased secretion of endorphins. Endorphins are chemicals produced in the brain in response to a stimuli, including stressors. As a stressor, exercise elicits the production of endorphins. Elevated levels of endorphins are associated with improved mood and enhanced sense of well-being. Endorphins are also associated with a reduction in pain. The general well-being produced by endorphins reduces levels of depression, anxiety, and other negative mood states.[8] The popular press often refers to the improved mood associated with prolonged exercise as "runners' high." Although there is agreement that the body does produce endorphins in response to prolonged exercise, the research on the mechanism of positive effects has been equivocal.

Although many hypotheses have been advanced, the mechanism by which exercise promotes psychological benefits is not clear at this point in time. Research investigating these and other hypotheses yields conflicting results. What is known, however, is that there is a positive relationship between exercise and various psychological states. Before starting an exercise program, individuals should consult with their physician.

The value of physical activity as a therapeutic modality is increasing, and new avenues are being explored. However, Fontaine points out that several important questions need to be addressed about the therapeutic value of physical activity (PA). These questions include:

1. How and under what circumstances should PA be incorporated into therapy for patients with mental health disorders?
2. What are the long-term effects of PA on mental health disorders?
3. Does regular PA protect against developing mental health disorders?
4. What is the optimal PA prescription for various mental health disorders?[9]

Fontaine notes that despite these questions, it appears that physical activity can play an important role in the treatment of mental health disorders.[9]

Dance therapy and recreation therapy (see Chapter 14) utilize physical activity as part of therapeutic and rehabilitation processes. The role of physical activity in improving mental health and psychological well-being offers exciting possibilities in treatment and prevention.

EXERCISE ADHERENCE

An expanding area of research is investigation of exercise adherence. Researchers have found that patients' adherence to prescribed medical regimens is a great concern. Although figures vary, authorities estimate that half of all patients fail to comply with their medical treatment.[10] The past decade has brought increased recognition of the value of exercise as a therapeutic modality. Exercise is increasingly being prescribed as part of an overall treatment approach to several diseases, including cardiovascular diseases and diabetes. Unfortunately, the compliance rates for participants in exercise programs are similar to those in other medical regimens. Adherence to supervised exercise programs ranges from about 50% to 80% in the first 6 months.[10] Other researchers report that only 30% of individuals who begin an exercise program will be exercising at the end of 3 years.[11]

Knowledge that a particular behavior has either good or harmful influences on our health does not consistently affect our behavior. Most individuals are aware of the factors that detract from wellness—smoking, high-fat diet, sedentary lifestyle, and so on—yet continue to engage in these behaviors despite the health consequences. Why aren't more people active? Despite the known benefits, why are there so few participants? And what can be done about it?

How do you get people to begin to lead a more active lifestyle? How do you promote behavior change? Many theories and models of human behavior have been used to guide interventions to promote a more physically active lifestyle and encourage health-promoting behaviors. Among the

As professionals, we must develop effective behavioral strategies to help sedentary individuals adopt a healthy, active lifestyle.

models are the classic learning theories, the health belief model, social cognitive theory, the transtheoretical model, and the ecological perspective.

The classic learning theories emphasize that learning a new complex pattern of behavior, such as moving from a sedentary to an active lifestyle, is achieved by altering many of the small behaviors that compose the overall behavior. This suggests that a targeted behavior, such as walking continuously for 30 minutes a day, is best learned by breaking down this behavior into smaller goals to be achieved, such as walking for 10 minutes daily. Incremental increases, such as adding 5 minutes to daily walking a week, are then made as the behavior is gradually shaped toward the targeted goal. Rewards and incentives, both immediate and long range, serve as reinforcement and motivation for the individual to achieve and maintain the targeted behavior. Looking better, receiving a T-shirt for participation, and experiencing a feeling of accomplishment all strengthen and sustain the behavior change.

The health belief model emphasizes that the adoption of a health behavior depends on the person's perception of four factors: the severity of the potential illness, the person's susceptibility to that illness, the benefits of taking action, and the barriers to action. Incorporation of cues to action, such as listing walking on your daily "To Do" list, is important in eliciting and sustaining the desired behavior. Self-efficacy, a person's confidence in his or her capability to perform the desired behavior, is included as an important component of this model.

Social cognitive theory states that behavior change is influenced by environmental factors, personal factors, and attributes of the behavior itself. Self-efficacy is central to this model. A person must believe in his or her ability to perform the behavior (self-efficacy) and must perceive an incentive for changing his or her behavior. The outcomes derived from the behavior must be valued by the person. These benefits can be immediate in nature, such as feelings of satisfaction or enjoyment from engaging in the behavior, or long term, such as improved health from being physically active on a regular basis.

The transtheoretical model of health behavior uses the concept of "stages of change" to integrate the processes and principles of change relating to health behavior[12] (See box, p. 348). Developed by Prochaska and his colleagues, it was described by Samuelson, in 1997, as "one of the most important theoretical health promotion developments of the decade."[13]

The transtheoretical model views behavioral change as a spiraling continuum, moving from a "firm conviction to maintain the status quo by never changing, and proceeds through the conditions of someday, soon, now, and forever."[13] Prochaska's stages of change and a brief description of each are listed below[12,13]:

- Precontemplation is the stage at which people have no intention to change behavior within the foreseeable future, usually the next 6 months. People in this stage may not be fully informed about the consequences of their behavior or, based on past failures, they may doubt their abilities to change. They may be perceived as resistant or unmotivated.
- Contemplation is the stage at which people are intending to take action sometime in the next 6 months. In this stage, they are aware of and weigh the benefits and drawbacks of changing. This may produce profound ambivalence about change, and people may remain in this stage of chronic contemplation or behavioral procrastination for some time.
- Preparation is the stage at which people take small or inconsistent steps toward change, such as developing a plan to change their diet or beginning to exercise.
- Action is the point at which individuals have made modifications in their lifestyle. They are engaging in the health-promoting behavior, such as walking briskly for 30 minutes or swimming during their lunch time 3 days a week.
- Maintenance is sustaining the change in behavior for at least 6 months. During this time, people become increasingly confident that they can maintain their changes.

Transtheoretical Model and Its Application to Promotion of Physical Activity

Stage of Change	Behaviors	Suggested Approaches by Professional
Precontemplation	No intention to change behavior in next 6 months	Educate the individual and deliver a clear message about the importance of physical activity to health
Contemplation	Awareness of the problem, the pros and cons of change; intending to take action within next 6 months	Highlight the benefits of change and try to shift the decisional balance
Preparation	Taking small steps or developing a specific plan of action to begin physical activity program (e.g., check out walking routes or join fitness club)	Help individual identify the best time to walk, a safe walking route; teach individual warm-up and cool-down stretches; assist individual to develop a progressive walking plan (20 minutes moderate pace 3 times week progressing to 30 minutes brisk walking most days of week)
Action	Make modifications in lifestyle and engage in physical activity (e.g., get up an hour earlier to fit walking into day); commitment to exercise	Encourage and support individual to become active; help individual monitor physical activity; discuss modifications in program as situation changes
Maintenance	Sustaining the change in behavior for at least 6 months; becoming increasingly confident in ability to sustain change (e.g., continues to walk on daily basis); exercise becomes routine	Support individual as person remains active; explore with individual ideas for continuing to be active even when person's schedule changes and he/she can't walk at usual time, etc.
Termination	Behavior is fully integrated into lifestyle (e.g., walking is planned for as part of the day's activities); exercise patterns are integral part of life	Individual walks as part of the daily routine; offer to be available to individual as a resource
Relapse	Move to previous stage	Remind individual that relapse gives the opportunity to rethink physical activity strategy—what worked and what should be changed; encourage individual to recommence physical activity at an appropriate level

Modified from Duffy FD and Schnirring L: How to counsel patients about exercise: an office-friendly approach, The Physician and Sportsmedicine, 28(10):53–54, 2000.

- Termination is the stage in which the behavior is fully integrated into the lifestyle. People in this stage have a high degree of self-confidence that, despite temptations to relapse, they will continue the behavior.

In this approach, a relapse or discontinuation of the behavior, such as ceasing to exercise, is seen as a return from the action or maintenance stage to an earlier stage. Though relapse occurs often in many behavior changes, only about 15% of the people move all the way back to the precontemplation stage.[12] Relapse should be dealt with in a positive way so that the person does not see it as a failure and become demoralized, but rather perceives it as part of the process of change. Relapse is part of being human and presents individuals with an opportunity to learn which behavior strategies worked and which ones did not.[14]

Decisional balance and self-efficacy are important aspects of the transtheoretical model. Decisional balance involves weighing the relative pros and cons of the behavioral change: that is, perceived benefits, drawbacks, and barriers to change. The cons outweigh the pros at the precontemplation stage, and the pros outweigh the cons at the action and maintenance stages.[15] The shift in decisional balance appears to occur at the contemplation and preparation stages.[15]

Self-efficacy is a critical feature of this model. Self-efficacy is a person's confidence about his or her competence or abilities in a specific situation. In the context of behavioral change, self-efficacy is a person's belief that he or she can maintain a healthy behavior, such as exercising, or abstain from an unhealthy behavior, such as smoking. Self-efficacy is typically low at the precontemplation stage and higher in the maintenance and termination stages.

Knowledge of the individual's current stage offers an important guide for intervention programs. The type of intervention should be targeted to the stage. At the precontemplation and contemplation stages, people are not ready for the traditional action-oriented programs, such as beginning an exercise program. Stage-matched interventions, such as education, consciousness raising, and self-reevaluation, are more effective at this point. People at the preparation stage should be recruited into action-oriented programs, such as weight loss or exercise.

The transtheoretical model has most frequently been applied to the cessation of unhealthy, addictive behaviors and more recently to the acquisition of healthy behaviors such as exercise. Acquisition of a healthy behavior can also be viewed as cessation of an unhealthy behavior; that is, adopting a healthy, active lifestyle can be viewed as ending the unhealthy habit of sedentary living.[14] This model offers physical education, exercise science, and sport professionals great insight into the process of change and guidelines for developing intervention programs. This model has been used to predict the use of sport psychology consultations by collegiate athletes.[16]

Another model that has increased in popularity in the last decade is the ecological approach. One criticism of many theories and models for changing health behavior is that they emphasize individual behavior change while paying little attention to the sociocultural and environmental influences on behavior. The ecological approach emphasizes a comprehensive approach to health, including development of individual skills and creating supportive, health-promoting environments. Creating longer-lasting changes and maintenance of health-promoting habits can be enhanced by addressing environmental and societal barriers to change, such as limitations imposed by poverty on access to services or the difficulty in jogging or walking if one lives in an unsafe neighborhood. These interventions can take place in the family, school, work sites, community, and health institutions. Societal and environmental influences on health behavior must be considered by physical education, exercise science, and sport professionals.

What are factors that promote adherence, encourage persistence, and prevent dropping out? Researchers have identified several factors that predispose individuals to drop out of exercise programs. In general, the researchers found that low self-motivation, depression, and low self-efficacy were related to decisions to quit the program, as was denial of the seriousness of one's cardiac condition.[17,18,10] Higher dropout rates were found among smokers, blue-collar workers, and individuals who are either obese, exhibit the Type A behavior pattern, perceive that exercise has few health benefits, lead physically inactive lifestyles, or work in sedentary occupations. Lack of social support from significant others, family problems, and job-related responsibilities that interfered with the exercise program were also identified as factors associated with quitting. Social support from other participants was important to individuals who continued in the program. Group exercise programs usually had lower dropout rates than individually designed programs. Programs that were inconvenient to attend and that involved high-intensity exercise were associated with higher dropout rates than programs that were conveniently located and offered exercise of a less-intense nature.

Knowing the factors associated with exercise program dropout enables practitioners to target intervention strategies to those individuals at greatest risk of discontinuing their participation. Intervention strategies to improve adherence include educational approaches and behavioral approaches. Educational approaches provide participants with information to increase their knowledge and understanding. Behavioral approaches focus on increasing individual involvement in the program and creating more healthful behavior patterns. These methods use such strategies as reinforcement, contracting, self-monitoring, goal-setting, tailoring programs to meet individuals' lifestyles, and enhancement of self-efficacy. Behavioral approaches have been found to be more effective than educational approaches in promoting adherence.

Exercise adherence also can be enhanced through careful program design. One approach is structuring the program to increase the social support available to participants. Successful strategies include forming exercise groups rather than having the individual exercise alone and involving significant others, such as family members or friends, in encouraging the participant to exercise. Offering programs at times and locations convenient to the participant is important in maintaining involvement. The use of goal-setting combined with periodic assessment of progress, use of qualified and enthusiastic leaders, establishment of ongoing leader and participant communication and rapport, and inclusion of a variety of enjoyable activities to meet individual needs are some techniques that can promote exercise adherence and reduce dropout rates.

The issue of adherence to treatment is also beginning to be addressed in the realm of sports medicine. Many of the psychosocial factors that contribute to exercise adherence are also critical to the success of rehabilitation programs. There is increased recognition that sports medicine specialists' and athletic trainers' knowledge of injury mechanisms and treatment protocols is not enough to ensure successful completion of the rehabilitation program. Researchers have found that rehabilitation adherence can be enhanced through the use of such strategies as goal-setting, establishment of effective communication, tailoring the program to individual needs, monitoring progress, and building a collaborative relationship to achieve the goals of therapy.[19] Social support has also been linked to rehabilitation adherence. Social support is a complex, multidimensional construct and has been found to be related in many ways to health outcomes. With respect to rehabilitation, social support has been found to relieve distress, enhance coping, and help an injured athlete remain motivated throughout the recovery.[20] It has also been found to strengthen relationships between the injured athlete and team members, coaches, and providers of health care.[20] Understanding the significant role social support plays in exercise and rehabilitation adherence can assist physical education, exercise science, and sport professionals to develop psychosocial rehabilitation interventions.

Young professionals aspiring to work in fitness and rehabilitation fields, such as corporate fitness, athletic training, and cardiac rehabilitation, will find knowledge from the subdiscipline of sport and exercise psychology very valuable in their work.

PERSONALITY

Researchers have long been interested in personality types in sport. Some researchers sought to address the question of whether sport influences personality; other researchers have investigated whether there were personality differences between athletes and nonathletes. Still other researchers undertook the task of identifying the psychological differences between elite athletes and their less successful counterparts. One of the questions was whether it would be possible to predict the success of an athlete based on his or her personality characteristics.

Vealey describes personality as "the unique blend of the psychological characteristics and behavioral tendencies that make individuals different from and similar to each other."[1] Anshel describes personality as traits possessed by an individual that are enduring and stable.[21] Because traits are enduring and stable, they predispose an individual to consistently act in certain ways in most, but not all, situations; thus, there is a degree of predictability to an individual's actions. Anshel suggests that psychological dispositions (i.e., broad pervasive ways of relating to people and situations) may be more helpful in studying athletes' psychological characteristics.[27] Personality traits are linked to predispositions. The personality traits of dominance, trait anxiety, and internal locus of control are linked to the Type A disposition.

The early research focused on the relationship between personality traits and sport performance. Researchers addressed questions such as "Do athletes differ from nonathletes?" "Can athletes in certain sports be distinguished from athletes in other sports on the basis of their personality?" "Do individuals participate in certain sports because of their personality characteristics?" "Do highly skilled athletes have different personality profiles than less skilled athletes in the same sport?" "Are there certain personality traits that can predict an athlete's success in a sport?"[22]

Researchers' findings have revealed contradictory answers to each of these questions. In many instances problems in research design have contributed to these contradictory results. Cox,[22] after an extensive review of the research on personality and sport, offered the following generalizations about men and women athletes relative to the questions posed above:

- Athletes and nonathletes differ with respect to personality characteristics. Various researchers have reported that athletes are more independent, objective, self-confident, competitive, outgoing or extroverted, and less anxious than nonathletes.
- Sport participation has an effect on the personality development of young athletes during their formative years. Thus, youth sport experience can positively or negatively affect the development of personality.
- Athletes in one sport can be differentiated from athletes in another sport based on their personality characteristics. Perhaps the clearest example occurs between individual sport athletes and team sport athletes. It has been shown that individual sport athletes are less extroverted, more independent, and less anxious than team sport participants.
- World-class athletes can be correctly differentiated from less-skilled athletes by their psychological profile 70% of the time. Personality profiles that include situational measures of psychological states have been shown to be the most accurate in predicting level of athletic performance.

While Cox has advanced some generalizations based on an overview of research in the area, much of the research is still inconclusive.[22]

Despite the controversies and the limitations of personality trait research, there is some agreement about the psychological characteristics of highly skilled athletes. Anshel[21] reports that:

> Highly skilled athletes score relatively low in neuroticism, tension, depression, anger, fatigue, and confusion. They tend to score very high in self-confidence, self-concept, self-esteem, vigor, need achievement, dominance, aggression, intelligence, self-sufficiency, mental toughness, independence (autonomy), sociability, creativity, stability, and extroversion. A composite of the psychological profiles of elite athletes reveals a person who is mentally healthy, physically and psychological mature, and committed to excellence.

Anshel points out that these characteristics serve as a model of the elite athlete, but the value of applying these characteristics as the basis for athletic selection, promotion, or elimination is questionable.[21]

As interest in personality in sport grew, different approaches began to be utilized to study personality and psychological characteristics of athletes. The interactionist approach views behavior as being influenced by both the traits of the individual and situational and environmental factors. The study of personality states is another approach that has been undertaken by researchers to study athletes. Unlike traits, which are relatively stable, states fluctuate and are a manifestation of the individual's behaviors and feelings at a particular moment, reflecting the interaction of traits and situational factors. For example, anxiety has both a trait dimension (how you typically respond to situations) and a state dimension (how you feel at this moment or at particular point in time, such as before the start of the competition).

The emergence of cognitive psychology offers another perspective to understand the behaviors, feelings, and thoughts of athletes. According to this theory, individuals continuously process information from the environment, interpret the information, and then behave based on their appraisal of the situation. Cognitive psychology recognizes that individuals' thoughts about themselves and the situation influence their actions. Vealey[1] reports that researchers using the cognitive approach were able to distinguish between successful and less-successful athletes. Compared to less-successful athletes, successful athletes are

- possess more self-confidence,
- employ more effective coping strategies to maintain their optimal competitive focus despite obstacles and distractions,
- more efficiently regulate their level of activation to be appropriate for the task at hand,
- tend to be more positively preoccupied with their sport, and
- have a high level of determination and commitment to excellence.[21]

Anshel discusses psychological predispositions of highly successful athletes.[21] These athletes are characterized by risk-taking. Risk-taking involves engaging in actions that can lead to bodily harm and psychological harm, such as failure. Elite athletes take greater and more frequent performance risks than their less-successful competitors and enjoy that challenge of competitive sport. Highly competitive, they strive for success and measure their success by performing at their personal best rather than by just winning alone. Elite athletes are highly self-confident and possess a high degree of self-efficacy, a conviction that they can successfully perform the skills to yield the desired outcome. High expectations for success contribute to their achievement. However, they also have the ability to cope with failure and learn from their mistakes. They are able to shift their attention to the critical cues in the environment as the situation demands. Additionally, elite athletes can effectively manage their stress through the use of appropriate coping techniques and intervention strategies (e.g., self-talk, relaxation).

The research on personality and psychological characteristics of athletes, while at times presenting conflicting results, does offer us some insights into the psychological characteristics and thoughts of athletes. Differences in traits, predispositions, and cognitions influence athletes' behaviors and experiences in sport. What can be said with some degree of assurance is that each athlete must be treated as an individual.

ANXIETY AND AROUSAL

The goal of coaches, teachers, and sport psychologists is to optimize an individual's performance. To achieve this goal they must consider the effect of anxiety and arousal on performance. Anxiety, as defined by Levitt,[23] is a subjective feeling of apprehension accompanied by a heightened level of physiological arousal. Physiological arousal is an autonomic response that results in the excitation of various organs of the body. Examples of this phenomenon seen in athletes are sweaty hands, frequent urge to urinate, increased respiration rate, increased muscle tension, and elevated heart rate.

Anxiety is commonly classified in two ways. Trait anxiety is an integral part of an individual's personality. It refers to the individual's tendency to classify environmental events as either threatening

Optimal arousal is important for superior performance. The level of optimal arousal varies according to the individual and the sport.

or nonthreatening. State anxiety is an emotional response to a specific situation that results in feelings of fear, tension, or apprehension (e.g., apprehension about an upcoming competition). The effects of both state and trait anxiety on motor performance have been studied by sport psychologists.

Coaches and teachers continually attempt to find the optimal level of arousal that allows individuals to perform their best. An arousal level that is too low or too high can have a negative impact on performance. A low level of arousal in an individual is associated with such behaviors as low motivation, inattention, and inappropriate and slow movement choices. A high level of arousal in an individual can cause deterioration in coordination, inappropriate narrowing of attention, distractibility, and a lack of flexibility in movement responses. It is important for each individual to find his or her optimal level of arousal for a given activity. However, no one knows for sure exactly how to consistently reach this ideal state. A variety of approaches have been employed by physical education, exercise science, and sport professionals in pursuit of this goal. These techniques include "pep talks," use of motivational slogans and bulletin boards, relaxation training, imagery, and in some cases the professional services of a sport psychologist.

Sport psychologists and researchers have studied the relationships among anxiety, arousal, and sport performance. Cox,[22] after a review of the research in this area, offered the following ideas:

- Athletes who feel threatened by fear of failure experience a high level of anxiety. Fear of failure can be reduced by defining success in individual terms and keeping winning in perspective.
- Athletes who possess high levels of trait anxiety tend to experience high levels of state anxiety when confronted with competition. Coaches who are aware of their athletes' levels of trait anxiety can better understand how they are likely to respond in a competitive situation. This knowledge will help coaches select appropriate strategies to adjust athletes' levels of state anxiety and arousal to an optimal level.
- Athletes' perceptions of a given situation influence their level of state anxiety. Not all athletes react to the competitive situation in the same manner. Each athlete perceives the same situation in a different way. Coaches must be aware that when placed in the same competitive situation, athletes experience different levels of anxiety. That is why "psych" talks may be an effective means of regulating the arousal level of some athletes and ineffective with other athletes. Techniques must be tailored to the individual athlete and the situation.
- An optimal level of arousal is essential for peak performance. The individual characteristics of the athlete, the nature of the skill to be performed, and the competitive situation influence the level of arousal needed.
- As the arousal level increases, athletes tend to exhibit the dominant or habitual response. Under the stress of competition, they tend to revert to skills they are most comfortable performing. Thus, if a volleyball player has been recently trained to pass the ball in a low trajectory to the setter, under the stress of competition, the player may revert to the safer, easier-to-perform, high-trajectory pass.

Research in sport psychology suggests several ways that coaches can help their athletes achieve their optimal performance, whether it is to decrease their level of arousal and anxiety or increase it. One way to determine whether an athlete is "feeling up" as opposed to "uptight" is to help athletes accurately identify their feelings, encourage them to monitor their feelings and arousal levels prior, during, and after competition and to help them learn and use appropriate strategies to enable them to reach their optimal state.

Anshel[21] identifies several different approaches that can serve to reduce anxiety and arousal. These approaches include the following:

- Use physical activity to release stress and anxiety. Warm-ups can provide an effective means to reduce stress; however, be careful that it is not too emotionally or physically intense that it leads to the depletion of the athletes' energy.
- To reduce the anxiety associated with the performance of new tasks and activities, develop, teach, and practice a precompetition routine so that it is comfortable and familiar to the athletes.
- Simulating games in practice allows athletes to rehearse skills and strategies until they are mastered.
- Tailor preparation for the competition to the individual athlete. Athletes prepare for competition in different ways. Some athletes prefer to sit quietly before the competition, relax in their own way, and reflect on what they need to do in the upcoming events. Other athletes thrive on an exciting, noisy locker-room atmosphere and a high emotional pep talk from the coach. Individualize, whenever possible, athletes' preparation.
- Focus on building self-confidence and high but realistic expectations. Personal insecurities, self-doubts, low self-esteem, and fears about the competition heighten anxiety. Highlighting the athletes' strengths, reviewing game strategies, and expressing confidence in the athletes' abilities and efforts help promote positive thoughts, alleviate doubt, and decrease negative thinking.
- Assist athletes to cope with errors by keeping errors in perspective. Help the athletes to stay focused on the present and future events when an error occurs, rather than dwelling on past events. Emphasize the opportunity to learn from mistakes, and help athletes avoid negative self-statements, which tend to exacerbate anxiety and disrupt performance.

There are a host of additional strategies that coaches can use to help athletes manage their anxiety and arousal. Once again, coaches must be prepared to work with athletes as individuals and determine which approach best suits each athlete.

What can coaches do to "psych up" a team? Increasing the team's and athletes' levels of arousal is sometimes necessary. Anshel suggests that coaches take into account each athlete's ability level, age, psychological needs, and skills to be performed.[21] Remember that athletes respond differently to various techniques and need different levels of arousal to perform different tasks.[21] Coaches can also use a multitude of different strategies to increase arousal, including increasing the intensity of their voice, using loud and fast-paced music, setting specific performance goals, and using the warm-up to help athletes adjust their level of arousal.[21] Some coaches show videotapes of the opponents, whereas other coaches may show highlights of the athletes' successful performances.[21]

Managing anxiety and arousal is a challenging task. Coaches must recognize that athletes' perceptions of a situation influence their anxiety and arousal. Individual differences in athletes' physical and psychological states require that techniques to help athletes achieve their optimal performance must be individualized. Anxiety can affect other factors that influence an athlete's performance, such as attention.

ATTENTION

An individual's performance is greatly influenced by his or her attention to the task. As previously discussed, an individual must locate, select, and focus on relevant cues to be successful in per-

Psychological skills can help athletes maximize their performance.

forming the task (skill or game). Not only must the individual discriminate between relevant and irrelevant cues, but also he or she must maintain the necessary attentional focus for the task. If an individual focuses on the irrelevant cues or fails to maintain the appropriate attentional focus, the performance will be less than optimal.

Nideffer[24] defined attention as the ability to direct senses and thought processes to particular objects, thoughts, and feelings. Attention can be described in terms of two dimensions—width and direction. (See Figure 9-1.) The width dimension varies from broad to narrow. The direction dimension may be described as external (i.e., focusing on environmental cues) or as internal (i.e., focusing on thoughts, emotions, and sensations). In any particular situation, an individual's attention may be described as broad external, broad internal, narrow external, or narrow internal. An individual who has a broad external focus is directing his or her attention to a wide range of environmental cues; an individual who has a broad internal focus is directing his or her feelings to a multitude of internal thoughts and sensations. In contrast, an individual who has a narrow external focus is concentrating on a few selected environmental cues; an individual who has a narrow internal focus is concerned with selected internal cues and thoughts.

To be successful, an individual must match his or her attentional focus to the task demands that often change as the performance progresses. Thus, to be successful, the individual must be able to switch rapidly back and forth between the various attentional styles at will. Let us use batting a pitched ball for an example. As the batter stands outside the batter's box awaiting his or her chance to hit, attention may have a broad internal focus. As the batter waits, he or she is reviewing the coach's directions and the strategies previously favored by the pitcher. The batter internally constructs the current situation, identifying the number of outs and the position of the runners on base. The batter then prepares a strategy. The focus is then narrowed to specific thoughts (narrow internal focus). As the batter stands in the box, he or she may adopt a broad external focus to predict the type of pitch by concentrating on cues from the pitcher. As the ball is released, attention shifts to a narrow external focus as the batter follows the path of the ball.

In an effort to assess individuals' attentional style, Nideffer developed the Test of Attentional

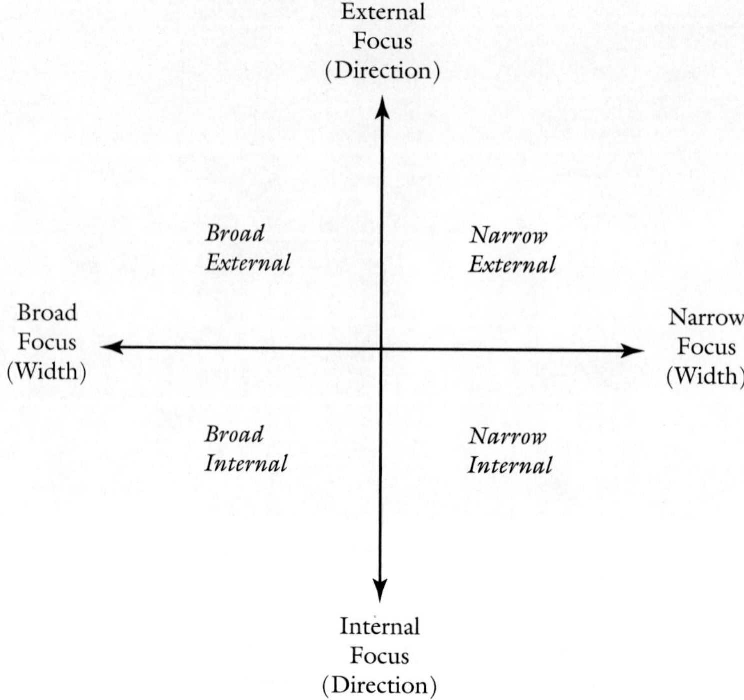

Figure 9-1 Dimensions of Attention

and Interpersonal Style (TAIS).[24] The TAIS comprises six scales designed to measure the width and direction dimensions of attention. The broad external scale, the broad internal scale, and the narrow scale (this scale includes both external and internal dimensions) represent effective attentional styles. Three scales reflect ineffective attentional styles. The overloaded external focus assesses the amount of confusion from trying to process too many environmental cues at the same time, while the overload internal focus represents the confusion from trying to think too much. Last, the underinclusive attentional focus reflects an excessive narrowing of attention, often referred to as tunnel vision.

The TAIS measures attention in general situations. Researchers measuring attention in sport situations have modified Nideffer's TAIS to reflect situations encountered in specific sport environments. Researchers have developed attention tests in the areas of tennis,[25] riflery,[26] volleyball,[27] diving,[27] soccer,[27] baseball,[27] and field hockey.[27] Physical educators need to be cognizant of the attentional requirements of various sports and sport skills, as well as the ability of each individual to attain and sustain the appropriate attentional focus.

An individual's focus of attention may be affected by a variety of factors. One factor that has a critical impact on attention is anxiety. Anxiety tends to narrow and internalize an individual's attentional focus. Sport and exercise psychologists use a variety of techniques to help athletes achieve and maintain the proper attentional style.

GOAL-SETTING

Goal-setting is important in many of the different environments in which physical education, exer-

Setting goals is the first step toward achievement. Participants in the Tenneco Health and Fitness program record their progress.

cise scientists, and sport leaders work. Goal-setting can be used to help students in school physical education, athletes on sports teams, clients rehabilitating an injury, or adults involved in fitness programs. Goal-setting is important both as a motivational strategy and as a strategy to change behavior or enhance performance. It is also used as an intervention strategy to rectify problems or to redirect efforts.

Types of Goals

According to Weinberg, a goal can be defined as "that which an individual is trying to accomplish; it is the object or aim of an action."[28] Goal-setting focuses on specifying a specific level of proficiency to be attained within a certain period of time.[28] Goals can be categorized as outcome goals, performance goals, and process goals.

Outcome goals typically focus on interpersonal comparisons and the end result of an event. An example of an outcome goal is to win first place at the senior games regional track meet at the end of the season. Whether an outcome goal is achieved or not is influenced in part by the ability and play of the opponent.

Performance goals refer to the individual's actual performance in relation to personal levels of achievement. Striving to increase ground balls won in lacrosse from 5 to 10, decreasing the time to walk a mile from 20 minutes to 15 minutes, increasing the amount of weight that can be lifted following knee reconstruction, and improving one's free-throw percentage from 35% to 50% are examples of performance goals.

Lastly, process goals focus on how a particular skill is performed. For example, increasing axial rotation in swimming the backstroke and following through on the tennis backhand are two examples of process goals that focus on the improvement of technique. As technique improves, improvements in performance are likely to follow.

How Goal-Setting Works

Goal-setting leads to improved performance. Locke, Shaw, Saari, and Latham[29] identified four distinct ways in which goal-setting influences performance.

It focuses attention, mobilizes effort, nurtures persistence, and leads to the development of new learning strategies.[29]

Goal-setting leads to the focusing of attention on the task at hand and on the achievement of the goal related to that task. When there are no specific goals, attention has a tendency to wander, drifting from one item to the next without any particular attention or intent. When specific goals are set, individuals can direct their attention to that task and its accomplishments. For example, a volleyball player who has a goal of getting 15 kills in a match can then focus his efforts on the specific elements of the skill that will help accomplish this goal.

Once a goal is determined, to achieve the goal, individuals must direct their efforts toward its attainment. This mobilization of effort, in and of itself, can lead to improved performance. Knowing what you want to accomplish and having specific strategies to achieve it influence motivation and increase effort.

Not only does goal-setting focus one's attention and mobilize one's efforts, but it encourages persistence. Persistence is critical. Often the attainment of goals involves a concentrated effort over an extended period of time. There may be periods of frustration and failure as individuals learn new strategies or challenge themselves to higher levels of achievement. Individuals need to persist in pursuit of their goals.

Development of relevant learning strategies is an essential aspect of goal-setting. Strategies can include learning new techniques or changing the manner in which a skill is practiced. Strategies can also include developing a plan by which incremental changes in performance or behavior can be attained. For example, an individual desiring to lose 30 pounds through a combination of healthy dieting and increased physical activity may need to learn strategies to select healthier foods, to develop and modify a walking program, and to learn how to continue to maintain the weight loss once it is accomplished.

Properly implemented, goal-setting can lead to improvements in performance and changes in behavior. Goals can be outcome, process, or performance oriented. Goal-setting improves performance by directing attention, mobilizing effort, encouraging persistence, and introducing new strategies. Goal-setting requires careful planning if it is to be effective as a motivational strategy or intervention strategy.

Principles of Effective Goal-Setting

Several principles provide guidance for physical educators, exercise scientists, and sport leaders involved in goal-setting. It is important that the goal-setting program be structured and implemented correctly, because a decrement in performance can actually occur from improper goal-setting. To help you get started with goal-setting, think SMART. SMART is an acronym suggested by Weinberg and Gould[30] to help professionals remember the critical characteristics of effective goals. Goals should be Specific, Measurable, Action oriented, Realistic, and Timely.

Specific goals have been linked to higher levels of performance than no goals or general do-your-best-type goals. While do-your-best goals may be motivating and encouraging, they do not have as powerful an impact on performance as having specific goals. Furthermore, general goals such as "I want to be a better swimmer" or "I want to be healthier" are not as effective as specific goals. It is hard to monitor general goals or to know what types of changes need to be made to achieve them. A specific goal, such as a swimmer stating, "I want to reduce my time in the 200 freestyle to 1 minute 56 seconds from 2 minutes 5 seconds by the championships," is more likely to result in improvements in performance.

Additionally, measurable goals allow progress to be more easily monitored. Measurable goals provide individuals with feedback, which helps motivate them and sustain involvement. An individual who sets a goal of walking 30 minutes a day for 5 days of week at a brisk pace of 12 minutes a mile or less can easily monitor whether progress is being made toward goal attainment. Action goals, also referred to as observable goals, are goals that can be assessed through observation of a person's actions. By viewing the person's actions, you can determine whether or not the individual is exhibiting the desired goal or behavior.

Identification of the time frame for achievement is a critical part of goal-setting. Will the goal be accomplished by the end of the season? Or within 1 month? The time frame should be long enough so that it gives a reasonable time to accomplish the goal. If the time frame is too short, it appears unrealistic, which may cause the individual to give up prematurely. If the time frame is too long, there is a tendency to procrastinate.

Goals that individuals establish should be moderately difficult so that the individuals feel challenged and have to extend themselves to achieve the goals. Goals must be perceived by individuals to be realistic and achievable with effort, persistence, and hard work.

Both Weinberg[29] and Cox,[7] noted sport psychologists, suggest several other principles that should be incorporated into goal-setting in addition to the SMART goal characteristics. These include writing goals down, incorporating different types of goals into the program, setting short-term and long-term goals, providing individual goals within the group context, determining goals for both practice and competition, ensuring goals are internalized by the individuals, regularly evaluating progress, and providing for individual differences.

Goals should be written down and monitored regularly to determine if progress is being made. Some swimmers religiously chart each practice, writing down times for each set of repeats in a swim diary. Other swimmers may only chart their meet performances. What's important is that the individual knows his or her goal, writes it down, and tracks its progress consistently.

A variety of goals should be integrated into the goal-setting plan. A combination of outcome, performance, and process goals is recommended. When individuals set goals based on their own performance, they feel more in control. Goals based on outcome measures, such as winning and losing, can lead to a loss of motivation and higher levels of anxiety.[7] The reason is that there are many aspects of an outcome goal that individuals can not control, such as their opponents' ability. Furthermore, using a combination of different types of goals presents individuals with additional opportunities for success. For example, a swimmer can finish third and fail to achieve an outcome goal of finishing first in the event, but feel successful by posting a personal best time for the event, a performance goal.

Setting a long-term goal provides a direction for individuals' efforts. In addition to long-term goals, short-term goals should be established. Short-term goals play an important role in goal achievement. They serve as stepping stones to the long-term goal. Short-term goals provide individuals with benchmarks by which to judge their progress. This form of feedback serves to keep motivation and performance high. It allows individuals to focus on improvement in smaller increments and helps make the long-term goal task seem less overwhelming.

Goals should be set for different circumstances. Goals are important for both practice and competition. What happens in practice is reflected during performance in competition. Daily practices are a critical component of competitive success. If a tennis player wants to improve his first serve percentage during competition, this goal should be given attention during practice. Practices also provide the opportunity to work on other goals that contribute to team success, such as working hard or communicating more with teammates.

Goals can also be set for teams. Team goals provide a focus for practice goals. For example, if the lacrosse team's goal is to be ranked number one in the conference on winning ground balls, practice time should be allocated to the achievement of that goal. Additionally, individual performance goals that contribute to the achievement of the team goal, such as working on skills to increase the percentage of ground balls won, should receive attention.

Social support is acknowledged as an important factor in goal achievement. Social support has been found to be critical in achieving rehabilitation goals as well as health goals. For example, in cardiac rehabilitation programs, where individuals set goals related to fitness and nutrition, eliciting the support of a spouse or significant other increases the likelihood that individuals will achieve their goals. Expressions of social support, such as genuine concern and encouragement, also help individuals remain motivated and committed when they are discouraged or frustrated or hit a performance plateau.

Acceptance and internalization of goals by the individual is one of the most critical aspects of goal-setting. Individuals must commit to the goals and invest themselves in their attainment. Allowing individuals to set their own goals increases their commitment to their achievement. Goals set by others, such as a personal trainer or a coach, may cause individuals not to feel ownership of the goals. Ownership can be enhanced by using a collaborative approach to goal-setting. If goals are not determined by the individual, but are assigned by others, professionals should make sure that the individual commits to the assigned goal.

Provision for frequent evaluation needs to be incorporated into the goal-setting plan. Evaluative feedback helps individuals assess the effectiveness of their goals and whether or not their goal-achievement strategies are working. Additionally, goal-setting is a dynamic process. Frequent evaluation allows both short- and long-term goals to be adjusted to reflect progress, the changing circumstances of the individuals, or the effectiveness of learning strategies.

Individual differences need to be taken into account when goal-setting. Some individuals thrive on challenges and welcome goals whose achievement, although attainable, will be difficult. Other individuals require a boost in self-confidence and may benefit from a goal-setting approach that uses many short-term goals, the achievement of which enhances their feelings of competence. Individual circumstances should be reflected in goal-setting.

Physical education, exercise science, and sport professionals may find goal-setting to be an integral part of their work. A summary of goal-setting is presented in the table Guidelines for Goal-Setting. Goal-setting can be used effectively in many different ways to help individuals improve their performance or change their behaviors relative to physical activity.

ENHANCING PERFORMANCE THROUGH SELF-TALK, A COGNITIVE STRATEGY

What thoughts run through your head before an athletic performance? As you sit and wait to give a 10-minute speech in front of a class, what are you thinking? As you set out on your daily 3-mile jog, what conversations do you have with yourself in your head? What did you say to yourself as you took a test for this course? Cognitive approaches in sport and exercise psychology focus on understanding the relationship between individuals' thoughts, feelings, and behavior or performance.

What individuals say to themselves during performance can be positive or negative. These thoughts and associated feelings can influence self-confidence, which, in turn, impacts performance. Who would you rather have take a penalty kick in soccer—a soccer player who steps up to take the shot and thinks, "I consistently make this shot in practice; I can do it" or a player who steps up to take the shot and thinks, "What if I miss?" Which player's self-talk is more conducive to successful performance? Understanding and modifying individuals' self-talk is one focus of cognitive sport and exercise psychology.

According to Williams and Leffingwell, "Self-talk occurs whenever an individual thinks, whether making statements internally or externally."[31] Self-talk is thoughts that occupy individuals' mind or spoken words, and they can be positive or negative in nature. Positive self-talk does not guarantee an outstanding performance, but it does enhance factors associated with better performance, such as self-confidence and a task-relevant focus of attention.[31] Sport and exercise psychologists use a vari-

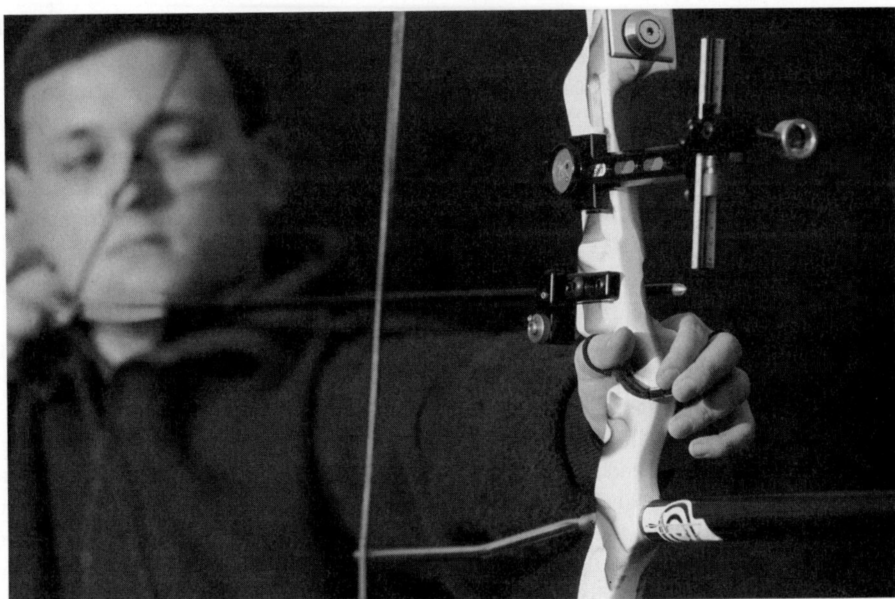

Self-talk can help individuals focus their attention and concentrate on relevant cues.

ety of strategies to promote positive self-talk and to counteract the effects of negative self-talk.

Types of Self-Talk

There are several different types of self-talk. Task-relevant statements reinforce technique. For example, a volleyball setter may use the cue "diamond" to remind himself of the correct hand position. Positive self-statements refer to talk that encourages effort or persistence or reinforces feelings of confidence. A cross-country runner, facing an uphill stretch during the last kilometer, may say to herself, "I can do it," as a way of encouraging herself to push through to the finish. A third form of self-talk is mood words—words designed to elicit an increase in intensity or arousal. "Turn it on," a swimmer says to himself as he completes the last 50-yards of a 1,500-yard freestyle race.

Application of Self-Talk

There are several uses of self-talk. Self-talk can be effective in enhancing skill acquisition, focusing attention, modifying activation, and promoting self-confidence.[31] Self-talk is not only for athletes, but is also useful for individuals engaging in a variety of physical activities.

Self-talk can be useful when learning a new skill or modifying a previously learned skill or habit. Self-talk can range from rehearsing key words of the steps involved in a skill to the use of a cue word such as "step" to serve as a reminder of what to do. It is important that the self-talk focus on the desirable movement versus what not to do. For example, if a tennis player wants to toss the ball higher in preparation for the serve, appropriate self-talk would be "High toss," not "Don't toss the ball so low."

Focusing attention is another effective use for self-talk. During practices or competition, athletes' attention may wander or be directed inappropriately. Cue words such as "focus" help athletes regain their concentration. Self-statements can also be used to help athletes focus on relevant task cues such as "mark up" or "adjust position relative to the ball."

The right intensity at the right time is critical in performance. Self-talk can be used by athletes to modify their intensity or level of arousal so that it is at an optimal level. Self-statements may be helpful in decreasing activation ("relax") or increasing it ("get psyched").

Promoting self-confidence is an effective use of self-talk. Self-confidence is influenced by a variety of factors, such as performance outcomes or skill ability. Self-confidence is also influenced by self-talk. Individuals' self-talk affects their self-confidence, either positively or negatively. Self-confidence is undermined with negative self-talk and feelings of doubt. Although self-criticism can provide an important source of feedback to improve later performances, it is important that it not be overgeneralized ("My shot went wide because of the direction of my follow-through" versus "I'm a terrible player"). Positive self-talk enhances feelings of competence. Self-statements prior to and during competition should be positive in nature and engender high levels of motivation and effort.

Modifying Self-Talk

Some individuals may not even be aware of their self-talk or its potential to impact performance. Sport and exercise psychologists work with individuals to help them use self-talk effectively. For individuals who have negative self-talk, steps can be taken to help them make changes. Williams and Leffingwell identify several approaches to modifying self-talk: thought stopping, changing negative thoughts to positive thoughts, countering, and reframing.[31]

Thought-stopping uses a trigger or cue to immediately interrupt unwanted thoughts when they occur. An athlete who hears herself begin to say "I can't . . ." can interrupt this negative thought by saying to herself or out loud the word "Stop" or by visualizing a red traffic stop sign. Interrupting the negative thought before it leads to negative feelings and adversely influences behavior can have a beneficial effect on performance. With consistent use of thought-stopping, the frequency of unwanted negative self-talk can be decreased.

Replacing negative thoughts with positive thoughts is another approach. With this approach, negative self-statements are immediately followed by positive self-statements. For example, a basketball player who misses a foul shot may make the negative statement "I never am good from the foul line." The player can replace that negative statement with "I made five of my eight shots tonight. With more practice, I can increase that percentage." Compared to thought-stopping, this approach encourages individuals to replace a negative thought with a positive one, rather than simply stopping the negative thought.

Countering focuses on challenging individuals' beliefs that lead them to accept negative statements as being the truth. Countering uses facts, reason, and rational thinking to refute negative thoughts. Once these negative thoughts are refuted, individuals are more accepting of positive self-statements. For example, an athlete may perceive herself as someone who "chokes" under pressure. This belief can be countered by examining the athlete's past performances in pressure situations. When the evidence is reviewed, it shows that the athlete actually performs well under pressure, especially in critical games. Now the athlete is helped to replace the negative thought with "I know I can come through under pressure."

The technique of reframing focuses on altering individuals' view of the world or changing their perspective. Through this approach, negative statements are changed to positive statements by interpreting the situation differently. An athlete who is nervous and perceives his pounding heart as reflecting his anxiety can reinterpret this as " I'm geared up and ready to go." Athletes fearful of competition and the associated stress of winning and losing can be helped to reinterpret competition as a challenge and the opportunity to test themselves while providing the additional benefit of identifying areas of improvement.

Changing the self-talk of individuals presents a challenge to sport and exercise psychologists. First, individuals may not be aware of their negative self-talk. Before modifying self-talk, sport and exercise psychologists need to help individuals realize that self-talk can be self-defeating and adversely influence performance. Exploring the underlying beliefs that perpetuate negative self-talk, such as low self-esteem, is also an important part of the process. In some cases, dealing with the underlying cause of the negative self-talk will require additional interventions. Another challenge is that thought patterns are deeply ingrained and changing them, just like changing any other habit, requires motivation, learning new skills, practice, and patience.

For greatest effectiveness in modifying negative self-talk, Williams and Leffingwell suggest using a combination of thought stoppage, changing negative thoughts to positive thoughts, reframing and countering.[31] Self-talk is only one cognitive approach that can be used to enhance the performance of individuals as well as their personal development.

The use of self-talk is not limited to the realm of athletics. Students in physical education classes can be taught to use cognitive strategies, such as self-talk, to enhance their feelings of competence as movers. When starting a new activity unit, some students might engage in self-talk such as "I'm no good at this." This negative statement and others like them result in loss of motivation and lack of effort. Instead, students can be helped to reframe their self-talk and to see that the new unit presents them with an opportunity to improve their skills or learn new ones.

Self-talk can play a critical role in the adoption of a physically active lifestyle. Middle-aged individuals just beginning an exercise program after 2 decades of inactivity may experience self-defeating thoughts that ultimately may lead to their discontinuing participation. "I can't do this—I was never athletic anyway" may precipitate participant dropout. Self-talk may also affect participation in rehabilitation programs. For example, a gymnast rehabilitating a shoulder after rotator cuff surgery may be beset with self-doubts about whether he will be able to return to competition. Negative self-talk such as "This is a waste of time" may lead to less than full effort being expended during the performance of the rehabilitation exercises. As a professional, you need to recognize that such negative self-talk can have an adverse impact on achievements by participants in your programs. With training, physical educators, exercise scientists, and sport professionals can learn how to effectively modify self-talk to enhance the experiences of participants in their programs.

INTERVENTION STRATEGIES

In recent years coaches, teachers, and sport psychologists have turned to a variety of intervention strategies to help athletes achieve their optimal performance. As discussed earlier, anxiety and arousal can have harmful effects on athletes' performance. Athletes' performance can also suffer due to lack of motivation, poor level of self-confidence, and, because of the intimate relationship between the mind and the body, negative thoughts and feelings about themselves and their capabilities. With the help of appropriate intervention techniques, athletes learn skills and strategies to regulate their physiological and psychological state to achieve optimum performance.

Sometimes athletes experience excessive anxiety and arousal, which causes a deterioration in their performance. Intervention strategies focusing on reducing this level would benefit these athletes. One way to deal with elevated levels of arousal is through the use of a variety of relaxation techniques. These techniques teach the individual to scan the body for tension (arousal is manifested in increased muscular tension) and, after identifying a higher-than-optimal level of tension, to reduce the tension to the appropriate level by relaxing. Once specific relaxation techniques are learned, this process should take only a few minutes. Types of relaxation training include progressive relaxation, autogenic training, transcendental meditation, and biofeedback. A note of caution is in order here, however. Athletes should be careful not to relax or reduce their level of arousal too much because this will have a harmful influence on their performance.

In recent years, the use of cognitive strategies to facilitate optimum performance has gained increased acceptance. Cognitive strategies teach

Focus on Career: Exercise and Sport Psychology

PROFESSIONAL ORGANIZATIONS	• Association for the Advancement of Applied Sport Psychology www.aaasponline.org/index2.html • American Psychological Association—Division 47 Sport and Exercise Psychology www.apa.org/about/division/div47.html • North American Society for Psychology of Sport and Physical Activity www.naspspa.org • Sport Psychology Academy www.aahperd.org → NASPE → Academies
PROFESSIONAL JOURNALS	• *Journal of Applied Sport Psychology* • *Journal of Sport and Exercise Psychology* • *Research Quarterly for Exercise and Sport* • *The Sport Psychologist*

athletes psychological skills that they can employ in their mental preparation for competition. In addition to focusing on alleviating the harmful effects of anxiety and arousal, these cognitive strategies can also be used to enhance motivation and self-confidence and to improve performance consistency. These approaches include cognitive restructuring, thought stopping, self-talk, hypnosis and self-hypnosis, goal-setting, and mental imagery.

Some cognitive intervention techniques focus on changing athletes' thoughts and perceptions. Self-talk, previously discussed, is an example of a cognitive intervention technique. Cognitive strategies can also be used to alter athletes' perceptions of events, thus reducing anxiety. Affirmation of athletes' ability to succeed in an upcoming competition is another cognitive strategy frequently used to promote optimal performance.

Imagery is the visualization of a situation. This technique has been used in a variety of ways to enhance performance. It can be used to mentally practice skills or to review outstanding previous performances. By remembering the kinesthetic sensations associated with the ideal performance, the athlete hopes to replicate or improve performance. Imagery has also been used as an anxiety-reduction technique. The athlete visualizes anxiety-producing situations and then "sees" himself or herself successfully coping with the experience, thus increasing confidence to perform successfully in similar situations.

Intervention strategies have proved useful in helping athletes maximize their performance. These strategies are not only for athletes but also have implications for all participants in physical activities and sport. For example, the beginning jogger may derive as much benefit from goal-setting as the high-level performer. The practitioner using these strategies must be cognizant of individual differences; otherwise, performance may be affected adversely.

The growth of sport and exercise psychology has provided physical education, exercise science, and sport professionals with a clearer understanding of various psychological factors that may affect an individual's performance. Sport and exercise psychologists have been able to enhance individual performance through the use of a diversity of intervention strategies. Although much of the work done in the area of sport psychology has been with athletes, many of the findings and techniques are applicable to participants in a variety of physical activity settings such as school, community, and corporate fitness programs. As the field of sport and exercise psychology continues to expand, practitioners will gain further insight into how to enhance the performance of all individuals.

SUMMARY

Sport and exercise psychology is concerned with the application of psychological theories and concepts to sport and physical activity. Although the physiological benefits of physical activity are well documented, physical education, exercise science, and sport professionals also need to be familiar with the psychological benefits of engaging in physical activity on a regular basis. Unfortunately, too many adults are inactive, and many adults who start a physical activity program drop out. Exercise adherence focuses on understanding the factors that influence initiation and continuation of physical activity programs. Several theories have been used in research on physical activity participation and health behavior change, including classic learning theories, health belief model, transtheoretical model, social cognitive theory, and ecological perspective.

Sport psychologists have studied many different areas relative to athletic performance, including personality, anxiety and arousal, and attention. Goal-setting and control of self-talk are two approaches used to help individuals improve their performance. To help athletes perform at their best, sport psychologists assist athletes to learn and use a variety of intervention strategies. Some of the findings of sport psychologists, methodology, and intervention strategies can also be used in other physical activity settings to help us better understand and enhance the experiences of participants in our physical activity programs.

SELF-ASSESSMENT TESTS

These tests are designed to help you determine if you have mastered the materials and competencies presented in this chapter.

1. Justify the claim that participation in physical activity can have positive psychological benefits.
2. Using the information provided in the Get Connected box, access the MindTools or Athletic Insight site and read about one of the topics in sport and exercise psychology. Choose a topic that interests you. Then write one to two pages summarizing what you have learned and discussing how you can apply that information in your professional career.
3. Too many people are inactive on a regular basis. Furthermore, many people who begin an exercise program drop out. Using the information on exercise adherence, create a brochure that highlights both the physiological and psychological benefits of regular physical activity. Then include in your brochure information that would encourage people to begin and stay involved in a program (e.g., small groups with individually designed exercise programs). Be sure to include images and pictures highlighting physical activity and a "catchy" title.
4. In recent years, the field of sport psychology has expanded tremendously. As a practitioner, whether a teacher, coach, adapted physical educator, athletic trainer, or exercise physiologist, you are concerned with optimizing individuals' performance. Discuss the roles of anxiety, arousal, attention, self-talk, and goal-setting in the performance of motor skills and the use of intervention strategies to enhance performance.

REFERENCES

1. Vealey RS: Psychology of sport and exercise. In SJ Hoffman and JC Harris, editors: Introduction to kinesiology: studying physical activity, Champaign, Ill., 2000, Human Kinetics.
2. Association for the Advancement of Applied Sport Psychology. (www.aaasponline.org)
3. International Society of Sport Psychology. (www.issponline.org)
4. Gill D: Sport and exercise psychology. In JD Massengale and RA Swanson, editors: The history of exercise and sport science, Champaign, Ill., 1997, Human Kinetics.
5. US Department of Health and Human Services: Physical activity and health: a report of the Surgeon General, Atlanta, Ga., 1996, US Department of Health and Human Services, Centers for Disease Control and Prevention, National Center for Chronic Disease Prevention and Health Promotion.
6. Berger BG: Psychological benefits of an active lifestyle: what we know and what we need to know, Quest 48:330–353, 1996.
7. Cox RH: Sport psychology: Concepts and applications, ed. 5, New York, 2002, McGraw-Hill.
8. Petruzzello SJ: Exercise and sports psychology. In SB Brown, Introduction to exercise science, Philadelphia, 2001, Lippincott Williams & Wilkins.
9. Fontaine, KR: Physical activity improves mental health, The Physician and Sportsmedicine 28(10):83–84, 2000.
10. Brannon L and Feist J: Health psychology: an introduction to behavior and health, ed 2, Belmont, Calif., 1992, Wadsworth.
11. Dishman RK and Sallis JF: Determinants and interventions for physical activity and exercise. In C Brochard, RJ Shephard, and T Stephens, editors, Physical activity and health, fitness, and health: international proceedings and consensus statement, 214–238, Champaign, Ill., 1994, Human Kinetics.
12. Prochaska JO and Velicer WF: The transtheoretical model of health behavior change, American Journal of Health Promotion 12:38–48, 1997.
13. Samuelson M: Commentary: changing unhealthy lifestyle: who's ready . . . who's not?: an argument in support of the stages of change component of the transtheoretical model, American Journal of Health Promotion 12:13–14, 1997.
14. Duffy FD, with Schnirring L: How to counsel patients about exercise—An office-friendly approach, The Physician and Sportsmedicine 28(10):53–54, 2000.
15. Herrick AB, Stone WJ, and Mettler MM: Stages of change, decisional balance, and self-efficacy across four health behaviors in a worksite environment, Journal of Health Promotion 12:49–56, 1997.
16. Leffingwell TR, Rider SP, and Williams JM: Application of the transtheoretical model to psychological skills training, The Sport Psychologist, 15:168–187, 2001.
17. King AC, Blair SN, Bild DE, Dishman RK, Dubbert PK, Marcus BH, Oldridge NB, Paffenbarge RS, Jr., Powell KE, and Yaeger KK: Determinants of physical activity and intervention in adults, Medicine and Science in Sports and Exercise Supplement 24(6):S221–S236, 1992.
18. Nieman, DC: Fitness and sports medicine: an introduction, Palo Alto, Calif., 1990, Bull.
19. Fisher AC, Scriber KC, Matheny ML, Alderman MH, and Bitting LA: Enhancing athletic injury rehabilitation adherence, Journal of Athletic Training 28(4):312–318, 1993.
20. Bianco T and Eklund RC: Conceptual considerations for social support research and exercise settings: the case of sport injury, Journal of Sport and Exercise Psychology, 23:85–107, 2001.
21. Anshel MH: Sport psychology from theory to practice, Scottsdale, Ariz., 1997, Gorsuch Scarisbrick.
22. Cox RH: Sport psychology concepts and applications, Dubuque, Iowa, 1994, Wm. C. Brown.
23. Levitt EE: The psychology of anxiety, Hillsdale, N.J., 1980, Earlbaum.
24. Nideffer RM: Test of attentional and interpersonal style, Journal of Personality and Social Psychology 34:394–400, 1976.
25. van Schoyck SR and Grasha AF: Attentional style variations and athletic ability: the advantage of a

sport specific test, Journal of Sport Psychology 3:149–165, 1981.

26. Etzel EF: Validation of a conceptual model characterizing attention among international rifle shooters, Journal of Sport Psychology 1:281–290, 1979.
27. Fisher AC: Tests of attentional style for volleyball, diving, soccer, baseball, and field hockey, Ithaca College, Ithaca, N.Y.
28. Weinberg RS: Goal setting in sport and exercise: research to practice. In JL Van Raalte and BW Brewer: Exploring sport and exercise psychology, ed. 2, Washington, DC, 2002, American Psychological Association.
29. Locke EA, Shaw KN, Saari LM, and Latham GP: Goal-setting and task performance, Psychological Bulletin 90:125–152, 1981.
30. Weinberg RS and Gould D: Foundations of sport and exercise psychology, Champaign, IL, 1999, Human Kinetics.
31. Williams JM and Leffingwell TR: Cognitive strategies in sport and exercise psychology. In JL Van Raalte and BW Brewer: Exploring sport and exercise psychology, ed. 2, Washington, DC, 2002, American Psychological Association.

SUGGESTED READINGS

Anshel MH: Sport psychology from theory to practice, Scottsdale, Ariz., 1997, Gorsuch Scarisbrick.

An applied approach to sport psychology, covering such topics as characteristics of successful athletes, management of anxiety and arousal, attribution, motivation, aggression, leadership, and youth sports.

Berger BG: Psychological benefits of an active lifestyle: what we know and what we need to know, Quest 48:330–353, 1996.

Discusses the four psychological benefits associated with an active lifestyle: enhanced mood, stress reduction, more positive self-concept, and higher quality of life.

Bianco T and Eklund RC: Conceptual considerations for social support research and exercise settings: the case of sport injury, Journal of Sport and Exercise Psychology, 23:85–107, 2001.

Explores the different dimensions of social support, the role of social support in rehabilitation, and questions and areas for future research.

Cardinal BJ and Kosma M: Self-efficacy and the stages and processes of change associated with adopting and maintaining muscular fitness-promoting behaviors, Research Quarterly for Exercise and Sport 75:186–197, 2004.

Constructs from the Transtheoretical Model were successfully applied to the promotion of muscle fitness. The researchers also found self-efficacy to be important in the adoption and maintenance of muscle fitness.

Cox RH: Sport psychology: concepts and applications, ed 5, New York, 2002, McGraw-Hill.

In an easy-to-understand format, Cox discusses key psychological concepts and their application to sport, including motivation, aggression, anxiety, self-confidence, and intervention strategies.

Hutchinson GE and Mercier R: Using social psychological concepts to help students, JOPERD 75(7):22–27, 2004.

Motivation theory, achievement goal theory, goal-setting, self-assessment, positive self-talk, and suggestions to integrate psychological concepts into physical education are discussed.

Iso-Ahola SE and St. Clair B: Toward a theory of exercise motivation, Quest 52:131–147, 2000.

The motivational foundations of exercise behavior are examined, and differences between routine exercises and nonroutine exercises discussed. The authors explore the concept of whether exercise could become an automatic behavior, and the important role of enduring goals, self-determination, and intrinsic motivation.

Shumaker SA, Schron EB, Ockene JK, and McBee WL: The handbook of health behavior change, ed 2, New York, 1998, Springer.

Introduces theoretical models of health behavior change, presents adherence issues within different populations, and applications of models to different health behaviors, including physical activity, eating, tobacco use, sexual practices, and stress management.

Van Raalte JL and Brewer BW: Exploring sport and exercise psychology, ed. 2, Washington, DC, 2002, American Psychological Association.

Performance enhancement, promotion of well-being, clinical issues in sport and exercise psychology, suggestions for working with specific populations, and professional issues are addressed within this text.

PART III

Careers and Professional Considerations

In Part II the historical and scientific foundations of physical education, exercise science, and sport were described. In recent years the expansion of the knowledge base has led to the development of subdisciplines in physical education, exercise science, and sport. This expansion, coupled with the tremendous growth of interest in sports and fitness in our society, has resulted in the development of many career opportunities for qualified physical education, exercise science, and sport professionals.

In Part III, diverse career opportunities within the fields of physical education, exercise science, and sport are described. This section begins with a discussion of career preparation, professional responsibilities, and leadership development in Chapter 10. Chapter 11 discusses traditional career opportunities, such as teaching and coaching in the schools. The expansion of physical education, exercise science, and sport programs to nonschool settings and to people of all ages has resulted in teaching and coaching opportunities outside of the school setting. The tremendous interest in physical fitness and health has stimulated the growth of fitness-, health-, and therapy-related careers. These careers are examined in Chapter 12. Chapter 13 describes career opportunities in media, management, performance, and other related areas. The pervasiveness of sport in our society, combined with the growth of the communications media, has encouraged careers in sport communication, while the development of sport as big business has created a need for professionals trained in sport management. Opportunities for people interested in pursuing careers as performers have also increased during the last decade.

CHAPTER 10

CAREER AND PROFESSIONAL DEVELOPMENT

OBJECTIVES

After reading this chapter the student should be able to—

- Identify career opportunities in physical education, exercise science, and sport.
- Self-assess strengths, interests, goals, and career preferences.
- Understand his or her professional preparation curriculum.
- Discuss the role of practical experience in professional preparation.
- Describe strategies to enhance his or her marketability.
- Identify leadership skills for physical education, exercise science, and sport professionals.
- List professional organizations in physical education, exercise science, and sport.

Career opportunities in physical education, exercise science, and sport have never been greater. Traditional careers of teaching and coaching have expanded from schools and colleges/universities to nonschool settings, such as community centers (e.g., YMCA) and commercial clubs (i.e., gymnastics or tennis). Many physical education, exercise science, and sport professionals are pursuing careers in the fitness field, working in health clubs or corporate fitness centers. Other professionals are employed in the areas of sport management, sports medicine, and sport media. The increased specialization within the fields of physical education, exercise science, and sport has created additional career opportunities. For example, biomechanists may work for sporting goods companies designing and testing sport equipment and apparel such as running shoes. Exercise physiologists may be employed in a corporate fitness center, hospital cardiac rehabilitation program, or a sports medicine clinic. Career opportunities for a student who has studied physical education, exercise science, and sport have never been greater. Professional preparation for a career in physical education, exercise science, and sport will be discussed in this chapter.

GET CONNECTED

Career Planning Web site offers information on careers, resume writing, job searching, graduate schools, legal issues, continuing education, minority opportunities, and a host of other topics.

http://careerplanning.about.com

Occupational Outlook Handbook, revised every two years, provides career information, including job responsibilities, working conditions, education needed, earnings, and future outlook in many occupations.

www.bls.gov/oco/

Professional Organizations—these Web sites give information about the mission of the organization, services, membership, publications, limited access to resources, and educational opportunities.

AAHPERD	**www.aahperd.org**
NATA	**www.nata.org**
ACSM	**www.acsm.org**
NASPSPA	**www.naspspa.org**
AAASP	**www.aaasponline.org**
IAPS	**www. dmu.ac.uk/ dept/ schools/ pesl/ affiliat/ iaps.htm**
NASSH	**www.nassh.org**
NASSS	**www.uwm.edu/~aycock/nasss/nasss.html**
NASSM	**www.nassm.com**

Gradschools.com lists links to graduate programs, including programs in dance, exercise sciences, kinesiology, physical education, sport psychology, and sports administration.

http://gradschools.com

CAREERS IN PHYSICAL EDUCATION, EXERCISE SCIENCE, AND SPORT

Career opportunities in physical education, exercise science, and sport have expanded tremendously during the past 30 years. The expanded career opportunities are a result of several factors. First, although many people are inactive, millions of Americans from all segments of society engage in fitness activities on a regular basis. These individuals participate in a variety of activities, including working out at health and fitness clubs and engaging in community and commercial fitness programs. This has led to a need for competent physical education, exercise science, and sport professionals to design, lead, and evaluate physical activity programs. Additionally, people seeking to use their leisure time in an enjoyable manner have sought out physical activities and sports. Qualified individuals are needed to conduct recreational programs and to teach lifetime sport skills. The increased interest in competitive sports by all segments of the population has served as the impetus for the growth of competitive sport programs, sport clubs, and leagues and the associated career opportunities in coaching, sport management, officiating, and athletic training. Finally, the increase in the depth and breadth of knowledge in physical education, exercise science, and sport has led to the further development of subdisciplines and expanded career opportunities such as biomechanists, sport psychologists, exercise physiologists, and adapted physical activity specialists.

Career opportunities in physical education, exercise science, and sport are limited only by one's imagination. Lambert[1] points out that one's definition of physical education can limit or expand one's horizons. Defining physical education only as "the teaching of sports, dance, and exercise in the public schools" can limit job opportunities to

Tenneco employees work out on their indoor track.

the traditional teaching-coaching career. However, if you define physical education as the "art and science of human movement," "sport education," "fitness education," or "preventive and rehabilitative medicine," many career possibilities become evident. Similarly, defining physical education as the "study of play," the "study of human energy," "perceptual-motor development," or as an "academic discipline that investigates the uses and meanings of physical activities to understand their effects and interrelationships with people and their culture" opens up other avenues of employment. Possible career opportunities are listed in the Physical Education, Exercise Science, and Sport Career Opportunities box. This list is by no means exhaustive but will help readers realize the number and diversity of career opportunities in physical education, exercise science, and sport. These career options will be discussed further in other chapters. Careers involving the teaching and coaching of physical activity skills in a variety of settings are discussed in Chapter 11. Health- and fitness-related careers are described in Chapter 12. Career opportunities in sport management, sport media, and other areas are addressed in Chapter 13.

You also can use your imagination to create new job opportunities suited specifically to your abilities and interests. The growth of the knowledge base combined with the expansion of our services to diverse populations has created many new and exciting career opportunities. By combining your abilities within a subdiscipline with your interest in working with a specific population and age group and within a particular setting, you can create a career opportunity uniquely suited to you. The Creating Career Opportunities in Physical Education, Exercise Science, and Sport box will assist you in exploring these various career options.

The broadening of career opportunities in physical education, exercise science, and sport is an exciting development. Selecting a career from the many available options requires careful consideration of a number of factors.

Choosing a Career

Have you already chosen a career in physical education, exercise science, and sport? Perhaps you decided years ago to pursue a career in teaching, athletic training, or sport broadcasting. On the other hand, you may be like many other students—undecided about a specific career. However, you do know that the fields of physical education, exercise science, and sport are of interest, and you have decided to explore the many options in this area. Whether you are committed or undecided about a career, college offers a wonderful opportunity to broaden your base of knowledge about careers in these dynamic fields and to explore the growing number of opportunities that are available.

How do you choose a career from the many available? First, it is recommended that you select a career pathway as opposed to a specific job. A ca-

Physical Education, Exercise Science, and Sport Career Opportunities

Teaching Opportunities

School Setting	Nonschool Setting
Elementary School	Community Recreation/ Sport Programs
Junior High School	Corporate Recreation Programs
High School	Commercial Sport Clubs
Junior/Community College	Youth-Serving Agencies
College and University Basic Instruction Programs	Preschools
Professional Preparation Programs	Health Clubs
Adapted Physical Education	Military Personnel Programs
Overseas School Programs	Resort Sport Programs
Military School Programs	Geriatric Programs
	Correctional Institution Programs

Coaching Opportunities

Interscholastic Programs	Commercial Sport Clubs
Intercollegiate Programs	Community Sport Programs
Commercial Sport Camps	Military Sport Programs

Sport Media Opportunities

Sport Journalism	Sport Broadcasting
Sport Photography	Sport Art
Sport Writing	

Fitness and Health-Related Opportunities

Cardiac Rehabilitation	Space Fitness Programs
Sports Medicine	Corporate Fitness Programs
Movement Therapy	Sports Nutrition
Health Clubs	Athletic Training
Community Fitness Programs	Weight Control Spas
Worksite Health Promotion	Military Personnel Programs
Personal Training	

Sport Management Opportunities

Athletic Administration	Sport Organization Administration
Sport Facility Management	Health Club Management
Commercial Sport Club Management	Sports Information
Community Recreation/ Sport Management	Sport Retailing
Intramurals/Campus Recreation	Corporate Recreation
	Resort Sport Management

Sport-Related Opportunities

Sport Law	Sport Officiating
Professional Athlete	Dancer
Entrepreneur	Sport Statistician
Research	Consulting
Sport Psychologist	

reer pathway allows you to pursue many different jobs within a specific area, such as sport management. Second, you can remove some of the stress and anxiety associated with choosing a career by realizing that a career decision is not irreversible. Many students change their minds about the career they desire several times during the course of their college education. Third, a career is not a lifelong commitment. Changing careers has become increasingly common. Some people deliberately plan to pursue one career for a while to provide a foundation for a second career. For example, a student may choose to pursue a career as a teacher and coach for several years before returning to school for training as a sport psychologist. The practical experience gained from coaching enhances the individual's new career as a practicing sport psychologist with a professional team. Additionally, you should periodically evaluate your satisfaction from your chosen career. If you feel little satisfaction

Creating Career Opportunities in Physical Education, Exercise Science, and Sport

Explore career options by combining an area of study with a population group, an age group, and a setting/environment that matches your individual interests. Add additional items to each column as you think of them.

Area of Study	Population	Age	Setting
Adapted physical activity	Athletes	Adolescents	Athletic contests
Biomechanics	Cardiac risks	Adults	Clinic
Exercise physiology	Disabled	Children	College/university
Motor development	Inmates	Youth	Community
Motor learning	Military	Infants	Corporation
Sport history	Obese	Elderly	Correctional institution
Sport management	Patients		Geriatric center
Sports medicine	Students		Health/fitness club
Sport nutrition	Healthy fit		Health spa/resort
Sport pedagogy	Healthy unfit		Home
Sport philosophy	Chronically diseased		Hospital
Sport and exercise psychology			Media setting
Sport sociology			Park
Measurement and evaluation			Professional/sport organization
			Research laboratory
			Retail establishment
			School
			Space
			Sport facility

Create your own job title and define your responsibilities. In the example that follows, exercise physiology is combined with an interest in working with youths with disabilities in the home setting to create a job as a personal fitness trainer to an adolescent with a disability, working in the youth's home.

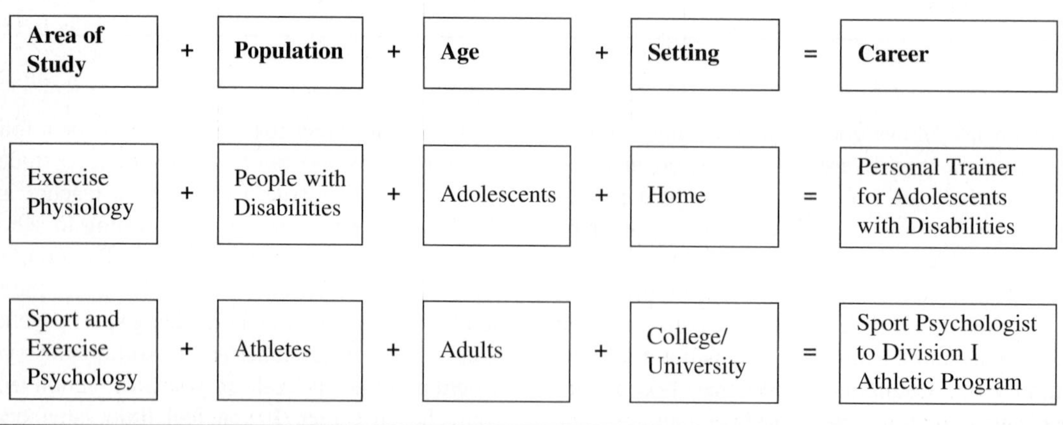

from your career, you may want to pursue opportunities in other career fields.

Choosing a career is a decision-making process. This involves gathering facts, evaluating information, and making a selection from the alternatives available to you. The most important factors influencing your choice of a career are your strengths, interests, goals, and preferences.

Having a realistic perception of your strengths and abilities is important in finding a satisfying and fulfilling career. In selecting a career, you should draw on your current strengths and abilities as well as the ones that you have the potential and desire to develop. Identifying your strengths and abilities involves the process of self-assessment. Self-assessment should be positive and ongoing.

Ask yourself the following questions about your strengths and abilities:

- What are my strengths?
- What are my best personal characteristics?
- What personal abilities are reflected in my accomplishments?
- What abilities would I like to improve?
- What do I like to do?

Reflect on the compliments you have received from your parents, teachers, and peers to gather additional information about your abilities. Have you received frequent compliments on your leadership? On your organizational ability? On your work with very young children?

You must also consider your academic abilities and interests.

- What are your academic strengths? Math? Science? Computers? History?
- What areas of study do you enjoy? Music? Language? Math? Psychology?
- What special talents or skills do you possess? Are you an accomplished photographer? Golfer? Painter? Basketball player? Web page designer?
- What talents and skills are you interested in developing?

Your decision to pursue a career in the area of physical education, exercise science, and sport reflects your interest in this area. Pursuit of a career in this area also reflects to a great extent an interest in working with people.

In weighing your career options, ask yourself what your personal and professional goals are.

- What are your goals?
- What are you striving to accomplish at this point in your life? What do you wish to accomplish in 5 years, in 10 years, or in 20 years?

Obviously your goals will have a great deal of impact on your selection of a career.

Finally, what are your preferences in terms of your lifestyle and your work?

- Do you want to work in an urban, suburban, or rural setting?
- What kind of environment do you want to live in?
- What ages of people do you prefer to work with?
- Do you prefer to work with people in groups or on an individual basis?
- What kind of facility do you want to work in? School or college gymnasium? Hospital? Health spa? Community center? Corporation?
- What are your salary expectations? Would you be comfortable with a salary based on commissions? Merit?
- Is salary the most important consideration in your selection of a career, or do you value other rewards associated with the job more? For example, is the personal satisfaction gained from helping a cardiac patient resume a normal activity level more important than your salary?
- What hours and days of the week do you prefer to work?
- How much vacation time would you like each year? Would you be satisfied having two or three weeks off a year, or does two months off appeal to you more?
- How important is job security? Career advancement? Fringe benefits?

As a result of this self-assessment process, you will become more cognizant of your strengths, interests, goals, and lifestyle and work preferences. If you had difficulty in determining your personal characteristics, you may want to take advantage of services offered by the career planning office or the counseling center at your college or university. Trained personnel can help you recognize your assets and articulate your goals. You can take a variety of paper-and-pencil or computerized inventories to help identify your abilities and preferences for different types of careers. One test commonly used is the Strong-Campbell Interest Inventory. Computerized inventories, such as Discover, are being used with increased frequency.

Talking and soliciting advice from others may also be helpful in the process. Discuss your self-assessment findings with your family, professors, and your friends. Listen to the advice they have to offer, but remember that ultimately the career decision is yours alone to make. You are the one who has to find the career satisfying and rewarding.

Information about yourself—your abilities, interests, goals, and preferences—should be matched to the characteristics of your prospective career. For example, you can combine your organizational ability with your mathematical ability to pursue a career in sport management. However, before you can accurately match your own assets with a career, you need to obtain further information about your possible vocation.

Matching assets with careers requires an understanding of the nature of the career you are considering. This information is available from a variety of sources. Career planning or counseling center personnel are excellent resources. They can provide you with information about careers and job characteristics as well as prospects for employment in your selected career. College and university libraries are also a good source of information. Ask the reference librarian for assistance if necessary.

Two publications that might be helpful are the *Occupational Outlook Handbook*[2] and the *College Placement Annual.*[3] The *Occupational Outlook Handbook* is published annually and provides information about the job market in numerous areas. It is also available on the World Wide Web. The *College Placement Annual* provides information on potential employers in your specific interest area. Another source is the *Encyclopedia of Associations*[4], this reference lists professional organizations active in your career area. For example, a search for fitness lists the American Council on Exercise and the American College of Sports Medicine, just to name a couple. If you want further information about wellness, you can write to the Wellness Council of America. Browsing through the athletic section of the encyclopedia, you will discover career opportunities that perhaps you never even realized existed. An expanded version, *Associations Unlimited,* can be accessed online.

Another excellent way to find out about potential careers is to talk to practitioners. Most people will be happy to talk with you about their career and share their perceptions. Ask practitioners the following questions:

- What is a typical workday like?
- What are the specific responsibilities of the job?
- What do you like and dislike about your work?
- What are the rewards associated with this career?
- What are the negative aspects of this line of work?
- What motivated you to seek employment in this area?
- How did you prepare yourself professionally for this position?
- What is the typical beginning salary associated with this position? What fringe benefits are available?
- What opportunities are there for advancement in this field? What are the qualifications for advancement?
- To what professional organizations do you belong? What conferences or workshops do you typically attend?
- What advice would you give someone seeking to enter this field?

Try to talk to several people in the same career area, because individuals' perceptions will vary as will their experiences.

Still another way to find information about various careers is through your own practical experience. This will be discussed later in the chapter.

Your professional preparation courses will also provide you with information about various career opportunities and their requirements. It is hoped that reading this text and participating in this class will assist you in making a career choice or in solidifying one made previously.

After gathering information about yourself and the characteristics of the career you are choosing, try to make a match between your assets and the requirements and characteristics of your potential career. Although you may already have a career in mind, as you embark on your professional preparation program, be open minded, flexible, and ready to explore other career opportunities that interest you.

Maximizing Professional Preparation

The process of preparing for a career is referred to as professional preparation. Professional preparation is the attainment of knowledge necessary to be an educated person as well as knowledge essential to understanding the field of physical education, exercise science, and sport.

Professional preparation also includes maximizing strengths and developing abilities with reference to one's chosen career. In addition to providing the knowledge and skills necessary to be a successful practitioner, professional preparation may be thought of as the process of increasing personal competence as well as your marketability. When viewed from this perspective, professional preparation includes not only your coursework and academics but related career experiences as well.

Education

Typically, professional preparation curriculums were oriented toward preparing individuals for careers in teaching and coaching. The growth of the subdisciplines and the changing job market have stimulated the development of curriculums to prepare individuals for these expanded opportunities in physical education, exercise science, and sport.

Professional curriculums have traditionally focused on preparing students for careers in teaching and coaching.

Although professional preparation curriculums at different institutions vary, these curriculums do have some commonalities.

Liberal Arts Professional preparation curriculums typically include liberal arts courses. Liberal arts courses provide the opportunity to obtain a broad base of knowledge. These courses are the sciences, math, languages, English, art, and music. Certain liberal arts courses may be required of all students; these can be referred to as the core curriculum. For example, all first-year students may be required to take a writing course and a speech course. Additional liberal arts courses are often mandated, depending on the major area of study. Some courses of study and state accreditation may mandate specific courses, whereas others may allow students to elect the liberal arts courses they wish to take; sometimes a certain number of courses may be required and a certain number deemed elective.

Professional Courses Building on this liberal arts foundation are the professional physical education, exercise science, and sport courses. Professional theory courses focus on conveying knowledge within the discipline of physical education, exercise science, and sport. Professional theory courses required for physical education, exercise science, and sport majors pursuing the same career paths may vary among institutions.

The professional theory courses provide students with knowledge relative to the discipline and are designed to prepare majors for their chosen career. Some courses outside the realm of physical education, exercise science, and sport are required as well. Usually the courses and the sequence in which they are to be taken are specified. Thus, students preparing for a career in teaching and coaching may take courses in physical education that include curriculum design, teaching methods, activity courses, performance analysis courses, and coaching courses; courses taken outside the area include education courses and psychology courses. Students preparing for a career in exercise science may take professional science courses and outside courses focusing on exercise science (e.g., chemistry and physiology), psychology, and nutrition. In addition to the required professional courses, students may take electives in this area.

Electives Most curriculums have electives, although the number of electives varies from program to program and from institution to institution. Electives may be used to pursue a special interest, to broaden your liberal arts background, and/or to enhance your marketability by complementing and strengthening your career preparation.

Electives should be chosen carefully to help you achieve your goals. If you anticipate attending graduate school, check carefully to see if you have satisfied all the prerequisites for admission. Stu-

Computer skills are a necessity for physical education and sport professionals. This student is using a computer to complete a biomechanical movement analysis.

dents who are planning on pursuing graduate study in another area to complement their degree may have to satisfy several requirements. For example, someone majoring in athletic training who wishes to obtain a master's degree in physical therapy may have to take additional courses in biology, chemistry, and physics. You can use your electives to take these courses.

Minors An increasing number of students are taking advantage of their electives to pursue minors and/or concentrations or areas of specialization. (Different institutions define these terms differently, so you should be familiar with how these terms are used at your own institution.) By doing so, they broaden their career options and increase their marketability. Some physical education, exercise science, and sport major curriculums require a minor or a concentration. Sport management majors frequently are required to have a minor in business or to take a substantial number of business, economic, accounting, and management courses. Sport communication majors may have a minor in journalism, photography, or speech. Exercise science majors may minor in science or perhaps nutrition and health.

In some states, if physical education teaching majors take enough credits in a second specific academic area, they can become certified to teach in that area as well. Often, the number of credits required for certification is only a few more than the number required to complete a minor at your institution. Thus, physical education teacher majors can become certified to teach math, science, or health. Using credits judiciously can pay big dividends for all students, regardless of their course of study.

Practicums Provision for practical experiences has become a common feature of many physical education, exercise science, and sport curriculums, regardless of the career being pursued. In teaching, this practical experience has long been a tradition and is referred to as student teaching. Student teaching typically takes place in the latter part of the student's junior year or during the senior year; this experience may last for a quarter or for a semester. In recent years a concerted effort has been made by professionals to provide their prospective teachers with practical or field-based experiences prior to their student teaching. This allows students to practice the teaching skills learned in their courses and can help them solidify their career decision.

Practical experiences associated with non-teaching physical education, exercise science, and sport programs are commonly referred to as fieldwork or internships. Fieldwork is typically shorter in duration than an internship; an internship may be similar in length to the student teaching experience. These courses focus on placing students in a practical setting on or off campus. Exercise science majors enrolled in fieldwork may work with clients in a commercial fitness center or health club. As interns, exercise science majors may work in a hospital cardiac rehabilitation program or in a corporate fitness center. Sport management majors may intern with a professional athletic team, whereas sport media majors may gain practical experience with a radio or television station. Athletic trainers usually gain practical experience on campus, putting in hundreds of hours working in the training room and serving as the trainer for various athletic teams. Many professionals view the practical experience gained through fieldwork, internships, and student teaching as vital in career preparation.

Certifications

You can also enhance your professional credentials by taking advantage of various certification programs offered through the college or university and by outside agencies. For example, many students take first aid courses offered by the American Red Cross as part of their curriculum. However, you can also become certified as an instructor in first aid by taking one additional Red Cross course. This instructor certification will allow you to teach first aid and certify your students as meeting the standards of the American Red Cross. The Red Cross offers instructor certification in cardiopulmonary resuscitation (CPR), permitting you to

Certifications, such as those offered by the American Red Cross in swimming, and practical experience can be assets in preparing for a career.

teach and certify people in this important skill. Certification in this area is also offered by the American Heart Association. If you are planning a career in exercise science, such as a corporate fitness center instructor, certification in CPR and first aid will allow you to train employees in these lifesaving areas. These certifications are also helpful if you are pursuing a teaching-coaching career. Even if your institution does not offer these courses, your local American Red Cross can provide you with the necessary training in a short period of time.

If you are interested in a career in athletic training or in exercise science, you may want to consider becoming certified as an Emergency Medical Technician (EMT). The National Athletic Trainers Association (NATA) offers certification for athletic trainers. To be certified, individuals must complete an approved course of study, accumulate a certain number of hours of practical experience, and pass the certification exam (for current requirements and more detailed information, contact NATA or www.nata.org).

The American College of Sports Medicine (ACSM) offers a certification program for individuals interested in sports medicine, fitness, or exercise science. ACSM certification is organized into two specific tracks, with each track offering different levels of certification, and each level reflecting increased competency and responsibility. The Health and Fitness Track certifications are "designed primarily for individuals who wish to work in preventive health programs, which are aimed at low- to moderate-risk individuals or individuals with controlled diseases in corporate, commercial, hospital-based and community settings."[5] The three certifications within this track include ACSM Group Exercise Leader, ACSM Health/Fitness Instructor, and ACSM Health Fitness Director. The Clinical Track certifications are "designed for those individuals who work in clinical settings where the participants are engaged in cardiac or pulmonary rehabilitation or have a chronic disease such as diabetes. Participants in these clinical settings will, in most cases, be at increased risk for exercise-related events."[5] The three certifications within this track are ACSM Exercise Specialist, ACSM Program Director, and ACSM Registered Clinical Exercise Physiologist (for current requirements and more detailed information contact ACSM or www.acsm.org).

Certifications also can be obtained in specific sport areas. For example, you can work toward becoming certified as a golf professional or a scuba instructor. Certification by the American Red Cross as a Water Safety Instructor will enable you to teach all levels of swimming. Aerobic dance certification is becoming increasingly popular. Certification and training programs are offered by many professional organizations, such as the Aerobics and Fitness Association of America (AFAA). Officiating ratings in various sport areas can also be attained from the specific sport officiating governing body.

Some of these certifications may be available through your institution. If not, you can attain these certifications on your own through appropriate agencies and professional organizations. Be sure to check, however, to ensure that the certifying agency is reputable and the certification is highly regarded by professionals in the field. It may be helpful to check with your instructors and practitioners in the field about the appropriate credentials and certifications.

Academic Performance

A major determinant of your career opportunities and professional success is your academic performance. Potential employers view academic performance as a strong reflection of a prospective employee's abilities and often as a reliable indicator of one's potential to succeed. You should make a commitment to your academic performance at the start of your college years. Additionally, your academic performance may affect your ability to enroll in graduate school.

Many students enter graduate school immediately after completing their undergraduate degree. The increased specialization within the fields has made graduate school a necessity for some students and an attractive option for those seeking to increase their knowledge in their area of interest. Attending graduate school for further work in exercise physiology, biomechanics, sport management, sport psychology, sports medicine, adapted physical education, and pedagogy is the choice of many undergraduates. However, this option may not be open to someone who has a poor academic record. Most graduate schools require a minimum grade-point average (GPA) of 3.0 on a 4.0 scale. An even higher GPA may be required for you to get into the graduate school of your choice. Your undergraduate academic average may influence whether or not you are awarded a graduate assistantship to defray the expenses of graduate study. Graduate assistantships are also highly prized because of the practical experience they afford the recipient.

Personal Development

Development of personal skills and abilities is an important part of the educational process. As part of the self-assessment process, you were able to identify areas of strength and areas needing improvement. Additionally, you should carefully consider how you can develop transferable job skills, skills that can be used in many different positions. Communication skills, leadership skills, and skills in human relations are applicable to working with people in many different settings. The Transferable Skills box identifies these transferable and highly marketable job skills.

Effective physical education, exercise science, and sport professionals can educate and motivate others to adopt a healthy, active lifestyle. Are you a role model for a healthy lifestyle? Do you incorporate physical activity into your life on a daily basis? Eat a low fat diet? Deal with stress in a healthy manner? Research conducted by Eastern Washington University showed that although an applicant's fitness level is not normally listed as an official job criterion or even discussed at a job interview, it is an important factor in hiring. In 1990, the university initiated a Fit for Hire program designed to help majors achieve a healthy lifestyle and recognize those who exemplify active living.[6] Three basic components are included in the program: fitness testing, lifestyle or wellness assessment, and individual advising.[6] Students

Transferable Skills

Transferable skills are those skills that have application to many different careers. They can be developed through course work, related experiences, and personal activities. Examples of how these skills are important to professionals in different careers in physical education, exercise science, and sport are provided.

Speaking
Develop your skills as a public speaker through classwork and leadership experiences. Learn how to prepare remarks, effectively communicate ideas, and motivate people. (Applications: Coach appearing before the school board to justify his/her budget, sports information director giving an update on the local television station.)

Writing
Write often and learn how to write for different audiences. Shape your skills by writing letters to the editors of the college newspaper and to publications that you read routinely. Write a newsletter for a club or organization to which you belong. (Applications: Writing a brochure to promote your personal training business; publishing a newsletter for participants in a corporate fitness program.)

Teaching/Instructing
Refine your ability to explain things to people of different ages. Much of our work involves educating individuals with regard to skills, fitness, and healthy lifestyle. Develop your ability to share information and instruct. (Applications: Teaching students in the school setting; instructing an athlete how to rehabilitate an injured knee.)

Interviewing
Learn how to obtain information from people through direct questioning. Learn how to put a person at ease even when talking about difficult subjects. (Applications: Intake interviews for fitness and rehabilitation programs; athletic administrator gathering information to resolve a problem.)

Public Relations
Accept roles in which you must meet or relate to the public, such as greeting people, answering the phone and dealing with complaints, fundraising, and making presentations to the public. (Applications: Staff administrator in a professional organization engaging in athletic fundraising.)

Leadership
Assume responsibility for directing an event, supervising the work of others, initiating an activity and directing it to completion. Learn how to advocate on behalf of yourself or others, promote change. (Applications: Advocating for additional community sports opportunities for people with disabilities; directing a corporate fitness program.)

Budget Management
Gain experience in working with a budget, even if it is small. Manage how the funds are dispersed, balance the "books," prepare reports. (Applications: Facility management; ticket sales.)

Negotiating
Learn how to bring opposing sides together, help people discuss their differences, and resolve difficult situations; learn how to negotiate with those in power. (Applications: Resolving conflicts among employees of a fitness club; negotiating with the publisher of the local paper for more coverage of your events.)

Organizing
Take charge of an event. Manage projects and learn how to delegate and follow through. (Applications: Organize a community health awareness fair or host conference for local teachers to share ideas and activities.)

Computer and Analytical Skills
Develop skills in word processing, spreadsheet, data base, presentation software; data analysis and presentation; Web page construction. (Applications: Construct a database to monitor the progress of your personal training clients; develop a Web page to promote your program.)

Modified from Career Planning and Placement presentation and handout, Ithaca College, Ithaca, N.Y.

who satisfy program requirements are issued a Fit for Hire certificate. The certificate lets employers know that the students are fit and are role models.

As a student, it is important that you become familiar with your curriculum so you can plan your education and strengthen your qualifications for your chosen career. Most institutions assign professors to serve as academic advisors. Work closely with your advisor in planning your program of study. Take advantage of all your education has to offer to become an educated individual and a professional. Create options along your chosen career pathway through judicious selection of courses and commitment to your academics. Your activities and related experiences also can contribute to your professional development.

Participation in athletics can later prove valuable in securing employment as a coach.

Related Experiences

Your activities and related experiences can significantly enhance your career preparation. Your extracurricular activities can help you develop skills that are relevant to your chosen career. Perhaps it would help to view your extracurricular activities as an unofficial fieldwork or internship of sorts. Certainly, participation on an intercollegiate athletic team as a player, manager, or statistician can enhance your expertise in that sport. Your experience as a sport photographer, sport writer, or editor of the campus newspaper provides you with excellent training for your career in sport media. Being active in the physical education majors club, if your institution has one, contributes to your professional growth. Serving as a member of the student government may develop leadership, planning, and organizational skills applicable to a diversity of careers.

Your work experience can contribute to your professional development as well. Work experience gained through part-time and summer employment can give you valuable on-the-job experience. Although employment opportunities may be difficult to secure, try to find work that relates to your career goals. In the summer, gain experience teaching and organizing activities for people of all ages by working in a community recreational program. Or try to get a job working in a fitness or health club, teaching clients how to use the various pieces of exercise equipment, supervising their workouts, and teaching aerobic dance. To gain practical experience, you may want to consider foregoing a higher paying job in favor of working the career-related job and getting a second job to make ends meet.

Another source of practical experience is on-campus jobs. If you have financial need, you may qualify for a work-study job. As a first-year student, you may not be able to get the job you want and have to settle for working in the cafeteria, but after your first year you will have a better chance to secure the job you desire. Work-study jobs may be available as an intramural assistant, researcher, tutor, lab assistant, or computer assistant. Of course, you must have the skills to perform the job or the willingness to learn if afforded the opportunity to do so. Another campus employment opportunity open to qualified students is being a resident assistant in the dormitories. As a resident assistant, you will learn how to work closely with people and develop counseling and programming skills.

Volunteering is another means to gain practical experience. Although volunteering does not pay you any money, try to view it as an investment in your future. Perhaps you would have liked to work for the summer at a corporate fitness center, but have found that the center is unable to hire you due to budgetary constraints. Ask if the center would be willing to accept your services as a volunteer. This means that if you need money for tuition and related costs, you may have to work nights and weekends to secure the necessary funds for school. However, volunteering may pay big dividends when it comes to your career. One word of advice: Even if you are a volunteer, devote as much time and energy to the job as if you were a paid employee. You are being viewed by the management as a potential employee. Perhaps if you do a good job this summer, you may be hired on a regular basis for the next summer. Volunteering is a good way to gain entry into your career field. Considering a career in sport broadcasting? Volunteer to be a "go-fer" at a local television station to gain exposure to life behind the scenes. Perhaps this will put you in the right place at the right time to take advantage of any opportunities that may come your way. Volunteering will also allow you to make professional contacts for the future.

As mentioned previously, fieldwork and internships are a good way to gain practical experience. If they are not mandated by your program, find out if you could do one for credit or on a volunteer basis. Many professional organizations are delighted to provide internship experiences for volunteers. AAHPERD, for example, offers internships to interested students. Contact professional organizations within your field of study to see if they would be willing to accept an intern.

Consider volunteering to work with one of your professors on a research project he or she is conducting in your area of interest. If you are attending an institution with a master's or doctorate program in physical education, exercise science, and sport, volunteer to help one of the graduate students collect data for a research project. This research experience will prove enlightening and can be helpful when you are involved in your own graduate education. Again, a reminder: Make a commitment to the research project and let the researcher know you can be counted on to fulfill your responsibilities.

Extracurricular activities, work experiences, and volunteer activities can contribute to your professional development. These practical experiences provide you with the opportunity to work in your chosen career, learn necessary skills, and develop professional contacts. Even though you are just starting your professional preparation for your career, it is not too early to start thinking about being a professional and planning for the future.

Professional Involvement

Start early to become a professional. Professional activities are a source of knowledge and growth. One way to start is by becoming active in the physical education, athletic trainers, sport management, or exercise science majors club at your institution. If there is not a professional club, try to start one with the help of fellow students and interested faculty.

Join the national association affiliated with your career choice (e.g., AAHPERD, ACSM, or NATA). Many professional organizations offer student memberships at reduced rates. Attend the national conventions where you will have the opportunity to meet professionals, make personal contacts, and attend meetings and workshops on research findings and new techniques. In addition to national meetings, many organizations have state or regional associations that hold their own conventions. These may be more convenient to attend and allow you to meet professionals within the same geographical area. Association members, as part of their membership fee, receive professional periodicals. For example, AAHPERD members can select JOPERD, the *Journal of Physical Education, Recreation, and Dance,* or *The Research Quarterly for Exercise and Sport* as one of their publications.

Start to build a professional library. In addition to the professional periodicals to which you subscribe, organize and retain your class notes, handouts, and texts. Many a student who threw out notes for a particular class or sold textbooks found it meant a lot of additional work and money later on when the materials were needed for a job. These materials serve as resources when you are starting out in your career. Undergraduate notes and materials may prove helpful in your course work in graduate school.

Attaining a Professional Position

Whether you are seeking full-time employment following graduation, part-time or summer employment, an internship, a graduate assistantship, or a position as a volunteer, obtaining the desired position requires a well-planned, concerted effort. Highly desirable positions attract numerous applicants, and competition is strong. Therefore, it is important to market yourself effectively and prepare thoroughly for this effort.

Preparing yourself to attain a professional position can be viewed as a 4-year ongoing effort. Each year can be viewed as a stepping stone toward achieving your long-term goal of employment as a professional or entry into graduate school. A 4-year timeline for achieving your goal is presented in Table 10-1. If you proceed in a systematic manner, you will maximize your professional preparation and enhance your marketability.

Resume-Building

Early in your educational career you should begin the process of developing a resume. A resume is a summary of your qualifications and experiences. To facilitate the writing of your resume, keep a record of all your activities on an ongoing basis throughout your career. People who fail to do so often inadvertently exclude important activities or honors from their resume because they have been forgotten. Some examples of activities that are important to include are honors, athletic participation, employment, professional memberships, and volunteer activities.

One way to keep track of your activities is to use an index card system. Label a file folder "Resume," and each time you participate in a professional activity, engage in an extracurricular activity, or are awarded an honor, make note of it on an index card and put it in the folder. Some students use a computer to effectively keep track of their accomplishments and activities.

Make sure the information you record, whether it is on an index card or a computer, is accurate and complete. For student teaching, internships, work, and related experiences, be sure that you have the correct title, the correct spelling of the organization, the address, and the name and the title of the person who supervised you. Carefully and accurately portray the responsibilities you performed and give the relevant dates. For example, if you just completed an internship at Xerox Corporation in its corporate fitness program, you would write in your resume file:

> Internship at Xerox Corporation. Industrial Drive, Rochester, NY, 14859. Supervisor: Dr. Richard Smith, Director of Corporate Fitness. Responsibilities: Assisted with the administration of stress tests; designed individual exercise prescriptions; supervised individual exercise programs; counseled participants in the areas of nutrition, smoking cessation, and stress management. Dates: January–May 2005.

Have you ever been awarded any honors, such as being named to the Dean's List? Make note of it: Dean's List, Fall 2004. Write down extracurricular activities on a yearly basis as well—intramurals, intercollegiate athletics, physical education majors club member, representative to student government, attendance at the state Association for Health, Physical Education, Recreation, and Dance convention, volunteer for Special Olympics, and so on. Make note of the dates that you attained certifications as well: For example, "2005: certified by the American

TABLE 10-1 Four-Year Timeline for Professional Preparation

Focus	First Year	Second Year	Third Year	Fourth Year
Academic	Learn about requirements of your major, including liberal arts and professional courses; determine how many electives you have to explore areas of interest or to use for a minor.	Begin working on requirements for a minor; carefully monitor your academic performance; remember that many graduate schools require a minimum GPA of 3.0 for admission.	Determine prerequisites for graduate school and plan how to satisfy them. Check to make sure that you are on track to graduate; take advantage of opportunities to join academic honor societies.	Review carefully your requirements for graduation to make sure you have completed them.
Career Goals	Identify short- and long-term career goals.	Identify a unique skill and formulate a plan for its development.	Work on strengthening your transferable skills; reevaluate your short- and long-term career goals.	Solidify career goals for the next 1 year and for the next 5 years.
Campus Activities	Become involved in some capacity in one sport or one fitness-related activity.	Continue involvement in sport and fitness activity; add involvement in another campus organization or other activities.	Undertake some leadership activity in a professional organization, such as chairing a committee or being an officer.	Advance in leadership responsibilities by taking on more challenging and responsible positions.
Professional Activities	Join your majors club; join a local affiliate of a professional organization (e.g., state athletic trainers organization).	Join a national professional organization; attend a professional conference and take advantage of special opportunities for students.	Attend a professional conference and become involved in the organization in a leadership capacity.	Attend a professional conference; take advantage of placement opportunities offered by professional organizations.
Volunteer Activities	Check out opportunities for volunteering in school and hometown communities.	Volunteer for a few hours a week in an organization of interest to you (e.g., Special Olympics, American Heart Association).	Increase volunteer hours or consider volunteering in a different area of interest.	Undertake some leadership responsibilities as a volunteer (e.g., volunteer recruitment).

Related Work	Seek out related work experiences during the school term or summer.	Work in related area during the summer or the school year (e.g., aerobics instructor on campus, fitness trainer in a health club).	Advance in responsibilities you undertake at work; consider a different job to broaden your expertise.	Continue to work and expand responsibilities undertaken; advance to a position of leadership or supervision.
Practicums	Explore practicum opportunities, including both short- and long-term opportunities.	Participate in a short-term practicum, such as fieldwork.	Investigate internship opportunities in your major. Continue to participate in practicum experiences.	Complete full-time internship or student teaching experience lasting at least 10 weeks.
Career Planning	Visit your career planning office. Take advantage of self-assessment and guidance programs to clarify your interests, strengths, and areas needing improvement.	Write a draft of your resume and have it reviewed by a professional or career planning counselor.	Take advantage of career planning seminars on interviewing, writing cover letters, and conducting effective job searches. Update your resume.	Update your resume. Attend on-campus job fairs. Take advantage of alumni networks. Use career planning, the Internet, and other resources to identify potential job openings.
Networking	Get to know faculty and students within your school; interview practitioners about their work.	Take advantage of local professional opportunities, such as conferences, to meet professionals in your field.	Widen your professional contacts and expand your network.	Network with faculty, professionals, friends, and family to identify employment opportunities.
Certifications	Identify certifications that will enhance your professional skills and contribute to your marketability.	Begin to acquire certifications such as CPR, first aid, or water safety.	Add additional certifications as appropriate. Find out the requirements to take major certification exams in your career field—athletic training, fitness, and teaching.	Take certification exams for athletic training, fitness, and teaching.
Application for Employment after Graduation	Become familiar with employment opportunities in the field.	Practice job search skills in securing summer employment, fieldwork, and internship experiences.	Establish a credential file. Secure letters of recommendation for your file.	Apply for jobs.
Application for Graduate School	Become familiar with areas of advanced study within the field.	Explore graduate school options and identify general program prerequisites; develop a plan to satisfy prerequisites.	Write for graduate school applications and determine entrance requirements. Take examinations for entry.	Apply for graduate school and assistantships.

Red Cross as a Community CPR Instructor." It is also helpful to make a note of your special skills, such as speaking a foreign language or a high level of competency with computers.

There are many different formats for writing a resume, depending on the purpose for which it is being used. For example, resumes can be used to obtain an interview, as a follow-up to an interview, as a means of highlighting your qualifications for the position, and as a complement to a letter of application. Career planning and counseling centers offer students guidelines for constructing resumes. A sample resume is shown in Figure 10-1. There are also computer programs available that can be used to write a resume.

Customize your resume for the particular position that you are pursuing. This may involve developing several different resumes, tailoring your background, strengths, and experience to fit the position being sought. Your index cards or computer records serve as a master list from which to select information and activities to present the best picture of you to the potential employer and enable you to include all relevant information on the resume. Preparing your resume on a computer will allow you to easily edit it and to create different versions. There are also several online sites that help you write a resume.

Resumes should be prepared meticulously and proofread several times to ensure that there are no errors. The resume serves as a writing sample and reflects how well you can communicate. It also reflects your neatness and attention to detail. Organize the resume so that the reader's attention is easily drawn to the most important information. Print your resume on high-quality, standard-size bond paper using a high-quality photocopier or laser printer.

Portfolios

Portfolios are used by some individuals to showcase their work and document their attainment of stated standards for the field. Although primarily used in teaching, other physical education, exercise science, and sport professionals, such as those entering the field of sport media, may find portfolios useful to highlight their qualifications for a job and document their professional competence and achievements.

To create a portfolio, samples of work—artifacts—are collected over the 4-year professional preparation program. Artifacts can include a wide variety of objects, such as essays (e.g., professional philosophy), samples of work (e.g., case study or unit plan), videotapes (e.g., instructional videotape of you leading an exercise class or teaching a class in a public school), photographs (e.g., programs in action or a bulletin board you designed), computer disk (e.g., Web page of an instructional unit), and published works (e.g., journal article or news article you authored). Additionally, your resume, a statement of professional philosophy, transcript, copies of relevant certifications (e.g., teaching license or ACSM certification), and letters of recommendations are included. These artifacts should represent a sample of your abilities, strengths, quality of work, and attainment of specific competencies for the field. Often, a 3-ring binder, with a clear cover insert on the front, is used for the portfolio. Artifacts are typically placed in plastic sheets before being inserted into the binder. A table of contents and section dividers separate artifacts and organize them for easy review. A brief explanation of the artifacts included in the section and their importance and significance helps the reader—the potential employer—to understand the material presented. The portfolio used for employment should be neat, free from grammatical and spelling errors, and easy for the employer to use. Not all artifacts are used in construction of a portfolio for employment, only those relevant to the specific situation. The portfolio can be sent to the potential employer either in advance of the job interview or presented during the job interview. Some individuals choose to develop electronic portfolios, making their credentials easily accessible online.

Placement File

As a senior, open up a placement file at your institution's placement office. Placement files generally

ROBYN LEE WEST

School Address	Permanent Address
221 Eastview Road, Apt. 1	312 Cherry Lane
Ithaca, NY 14856	Floral Estates, NY 11003
Phone: 607-111-5555	Phone: 516-222-5555

CAREER OBJECTIVE	To teach physical education in an elementary school, work with children with disabilities to improve their motor performance, and coach soccer and track
EDUCATION	Ithaca College, Ithaca, NY, May 2004 Bachelor of Science in Physical Education Provisional certification K–12 Minor in Health Concentration in Adapted Physical Education
PROFESSIONAL EXPERIENCE	Student teacher, Pine Elementary School (1/3–3/7 2004) Student teacher, Cayuga High School (3/10–5/14 2004) Fieldwork in adapted physical education, United Children's Center (1/4–5/2 2003) Youth Bureau volunteer soccer coach (Fall 2001, 2002) Counselor for children with special needs, Floral Estates Youth Summer Camp (Summers 2001–2003)
HONORS AND AWARDS	Dean's List (Fall 2001, 2003; Spring 2002) Who's Who in American Colleges and Universities Ithaca College HPER Professional Achievement Award
COLLEGE ACTIVITIES	Physical Education Majors' Club (2000–2004; Vice-President 2002–2004) Intercollegiate Soccer Team (2000–2003; Captain 2003) Intercollegiate Track and Field Team (2001–2002) Intramural volleyball and basketball official (2001–2003) Peer counselor, Health Center (2000–2002) President's Host Committee for Admissions (2000–2002)
CERTIFICATIONS	American Red Cross Community First Aid Instructor American Red Cross Water Safety Instructor American Red Cross Adapted Aquatics Instructor American College of Sports Medicine Health Fitness Instructor Rated official in volleyball and basketball
PROFESSIONAL AFFILIATIONS	American Alliance for Health, Physical Education, Recreation, and Dance New York State Association for Health, Physical Education, Recreation, and Dance American College of Sports Medicine Finger Lakes Board of Officials
REFERENCES	Available from the Placement Office, School of Health Sciences and Human Performance, Ithaca College

Figure 10-1 Sample resume

contain demographic information, a resume, and letters of recommendation. Letters of recommendation should be solicited from people who are well acquainted with your abilities. Professors familiar with your work, student teaching or internship supervisors, and individuals for whom you worked or volunteered may be able to accurately assess your abilities and qualifications for employment or further study.

Searching for a Job

Many sources will assist you in locating job openings. College/university placement offices maintain job listings and update these on a continuing basis. Some professional organizations offer placement services to their members and periodically disseminate information about job openings. AAHPERD, the National Athletic Trainers Association (NATA), and the American College of Sports Medicine (ACSM) offer placement services and job listings to their members. Newspapers, state employment offices, and some state education departments have lists of job openings. Job listings are also posted on the World Wide Web.

Networking is one of the most important job search strategies. Contact faculty members, friends, relatives, former employers, and practicum supervisors to see if they know of any job openings. It is through personal contacts that people learn about jobs before they are even advertised. Attending conferences or participating in professional organizations is a great way to build contacts and expand your network. Be sure to follow up on all leads in a timely manner.

Applying for a Job

Once you are aware of possible vacancies, send a copy of your resume along with a cover letter requesting an interview and/or application. The cover letter's purpose is to interest an employer in hiring you. When possible, address the letter to a specific person. It should set forth the purpose of the letter, refer the reader to the resume to note certain qualifications particularly relevant to the position, and relate why you are interested in the position, emphasizing your career goals and potential contributions to the organization. The letter should close with a request for action, either an interview or an application, and should thank the reader for his or her time.

Interviewing

If you are invited for an interview, prepare carefully—in other words, do your homework. Find out as much as possible about the organization, the job responsibilities, and other relevant information. Before the interview, take some time to formulate answers to commonly asked interview questions. The following list contains some common questions.

- What are your career plans and goals?
- When and why did you select your college major?
- How has your education prepared you for this job?
- Which of your experiences and skills are particularly relevant to this job?
- What are your greatest strengths? What are your major weaknesses?
- What is your professional philosophy? Can you give an example of how your philosophy has guided your actions?
- What jobs have you held? How did you obtain them, and why did you leave? What would your former supervisors tell us about your job performance?
- What can you tell me about yourself?
- What accomplishments have given you the greatest satisfaction?
- What have you done that shows leadership, initiative, and a willingness to work?
- What salary do you expect to receive? How many hours per week do you expect to work?
- Why should I select you above all other candidates for this position?
- What questions do you have about our organization?

As part of the preparation process, you also should prepare a list of questions to ask the interviewer. Some possible questions follow:

- What are the opportunities for personal growth?
- What are the training programs or educational opportunities offered to employees?
- What are the challenging aspects of this position?
- What are the organization's plans for the future?
- What qualities are you looking for in new employees?
- What characteristics distinguish successful personnel in your company?
- How would you describe the organization's management style?
- How would you best use my skills within the organization?

Develop additional questions appropriate to the specific job for which you are interviewing.

First impressions are critical, so create a positive one by your professional appearance, attitude, and personality. Dress appropriately for the interview. To be sure to be on time, plan on arriving ahead of the scheduled appointment time. Greet the interviewer with a firm handshake and be courteous, poised, interested, responsive, and enthusiastic. Be prepared to discuss your accomplishments, skills, interests, personal qualities, and work values in an honest, self-confident manner. Be self-assured, not arrogant or aggressive. Listen to each question carefully and take some time to formulate a thoughtful, concise answer. Remember that you are being evaluated not only on your achievements, but on your ability to think and communicate. At the close of the interview, thank the interviewer for his or her time.

Follow-Up

Follow each interview with a thank-you letter. The letter should stress your interest in the position and highlight important topics that you believe went particularly well in the interview. Be sure to thank the interviewer for his or her time and consideration. If you decide after the interview that the position is not for you, thank the interviewer for his or her time and say politely that you are not interested in the position.

Accepting a Position

When offered a position, again carefully weigh the characteristics of the job with the results of your self-assessment pertaining to your skills, interests, personal and work values, and career goals. If you accept the position, your letter should confirm previously agreed-on terms of employment and reflect your excitement at meeting the challenges of the position. If you decide to decline the offer of employment, the letter of rejection should express your regrets as well as your thanks to the employer for his or her time, effort, and consideration.

Attaining a desired position requires a commitment to marketing yourself effectively. Actively seeking information about position vacancies and diligently pursuing all leads are important for conducting a successful job search. Your resume should truthfully portray your abilities and accomplishments and be tailored to fit the position. Prepare thoroughly for each interview and present yourself as a young professional. Make your final decision thoughtfully and communicate this decision to your potential employer in a professional, timely manner.

LEADERSHIP AND PROFESSIONAL DEVELOPMENT

Developing professionals with strong leadership abilities is critical to the future of the field of physical education, exercise science, and sport. The advancement of knowledge, the growth of programs to reach people of all ages, and the significant contribution to society depend on professional leadership. It is important that professionals entering the fields of physical education, exercise science, and sport take an active leadership role in the field.

Leadership is critical to the success of physical education, exercise science, and sport programs. Willis and Campbell describe leadership as a key factor in sustaining participants' involvement in exercise.[7] "No other factor has quite the potential to elicit change in a client as a competent and enthusiastic exercise leader."[7] Mack describes leadership as the distinguishing factor among great coaches. Many coaches are equally good as tacticians with an extensive knowledge of their sports. What separates the great coaches from good coaches is their uniqueness as leaders.[8]

Although physical education, exercise science, and sport programs vary considerably, leadership is critical for achieving program success. Although some would say that leaders are born, not made, great leaders themselves would tell you that effective leadership is a skill that can be learned.[8] Smith points out that leaders are people "remarkably like the rest of us, but with a difference that they know the skills and techniques of leadership."[9]

Definition of Leadership

The term *leadership* refers to the art of influencing people to work together harmoniously to achieve set goals that they endorse. According to Smith, "Leaders have the ability to develop a vision, the skill to articulate that vision in practical terms, and the skill to direct and assist others in executing various aspects of that vision."[9] The leader of a group influences group members' feelings, beliefs, and behavior. A leader can help a group to achieve its goals with a sense of unity and provide an opportunity for members to achieve self-realization. Leadership involves motivating and vitalizing the members of a group to contribute a maximum effort. It taps vital resources and encourages higher levels of achievement. It eliminates inertia, apathy, and indifference and replaces them with inspiration, enthusiasm, and conviction. It provides for self-fulfillment and satisfying endeavor. It results in power *with* the members, not power of the leader.

The leader should be very conscious of the need for self-realization by each member of an organization or profession. Each individual needs to believe that he or she counts for something, is recognized, and has a sense of worth. At the same time, the leader needs to recognize that each individual has different interests, needs, abilities, attitudes, talents, capacities, and creative powers to contribute. The true test of leadership is the number of people's lives it enriches. It is a process of helping people to discover themselves.

Many traits, qualities, characteristics, and skills have been used to describe effective leaders. Early research on leadership focused on describing personality traits possessed by effective leaders. Current research suggests that effective leadership is highly interactive. Personal behaviors interface with situational factors to determine the leadership behaviors that will be most effective in a given situation. Thus, a physical education, exercise science, and sport professional possessing certain characteristics may be more effective as a leader in one situation but not as effective in another situation. The characteristics of the group (e.g., class, team, exercise participants) also influence the behaviors necessary for effective leadership. Among the specific characteristics of the group that are important to consider are gender, age, ability level, personality, ethnicity, and experience.[10] The challenge to professionals is to determine which leadership behaviors will be most effective in a specific situation.

Many people believe that leaders are born, not made. However, research on the qualities, traits, and skills of leaders reveals that these are evidently behaviors that can be learned and developed. Smith, in disputing the "born to lead" myth, states, "Leadership skills can be described and learned. The key to leadership lies in not having the right stuff from birth, but in getting it."[9] Thus, it is within the power of aspiring professionals in physical education, exercise science, and sport to develop and improve these essential behaviors for strong leadership.

Because of the interactional nature of leadership, not all leadership qualities and skills will be needed in every situation. They will be needed to varying degrees depending on the specific situation and the preferences and needs of the group members. However, professionals who do take the time and put forth the effort to develop these qualities, traits, and skills will be effective in a greater variety of situations.

Leadership Qualities, Traits, and Skills

Many qualities have been used to describe effective leaders. Weinberg and Gould note that there is not one distinct set of essential core qualities that assure a person will become a leader.[10] However, they note that leaders seem to have the following qualities in common: intelligence, assertion, empathy, intrinsic motivation, flexibility, ambition, self-confidence, and optimism.[10] These qualities are viewed as necessary, but not sufficient, qualities for leadership. Effective leadership stems from matching the qualities to the situations and the characteristics of the members of the group.

Many other qualities have also been associated with effective leaders. Hard work, determination, and perseverance are frequently cited characteristics. According to Anshel, respected coaches possess these leadership characteristics: genuine concern for people, respect for others, ability to teach, knowledge of the sport, and excellent communication skills.[11] Relationships are based on a long-term commitment to the program and to the attainment of team and individual goals. Fairness in decision making, social support, and positive reinforcement also are important. These characteristics can enhance the effectiveness of all physical education, exercise science, and sport professionals.

Another perspective on leadership is offered by Peterson and Bryant, in a discussion of leadership within the health/fitness environment.[12] Although Peterson and Bryant address the importance of effective leadership relative to success as a personal trainer, their ideas regarding leadership are applicable to physical education, exercise science, and sport professionals working within the realm of health, fitness, and wellness. According to Peterson and Bryant, to be successful as a personal trainer, it is imperative that a personal trainer understand and develop effective leadership.[12] To be effective as a leader, you must be able to "influence the way people influence themselves."[12]

Peterson and Bryant point out that there is no one single recipe for leadership. The traits and qualities to be a successful leader "vary from situation to situation and from individual to individual."[12] Leadership is like a mosaic comprised of different traits. As situations change, so does the mosaic of effective leadership.[12] However, Peterson and Bryant state that skillful leaders possess some, if not all of these attributes:

- Values-oriented behavior and ethically guided principles (e.g., integrity, trustworthiness).
- Adequate preparation, including well-defined goals, ability to prioritize time and resources to achieve goals, and flexibility to adopt to changing circumstances.
- Self-discipline, including a strong work ethic and commitment to doing what is necessary to get the job done and a moral ethic to guide actions. Self-control is important, and influences one's response to situations; utilization of time and resources; acceptance of responsibility for time and resources; and ability to maintain focus.
- Knowledge serves as a source of competency and credibility. Competence engenders respect and enhances one's credibility as a leader.
- Performance-oriented attitude that leads to the creation and definition of a vision, development of a plan to attain that vision, and ongoing assessment of progress. Passion and dedication

Leaders have a vision, a strong belief in the value of their endeavors, and a commitment to their profession. Head Coach, Mike Krzyzewski, Duke University, exemplifies leadership.
Photo courtesy Duke University Sports Information.

help ensure that plans are successful. Vision is the "touchstone that helps guide the behavior of the leader."

- Effective communication encompasses several essential skills, which have an impact on leadership. These include verbal communication, listening, written communication, feedback, electronic communication, and nonverbal communication.
- Motivational abilities enable leaders to help clients achieve personal goals and help organizations attain their vision. Effective leaders understand and respond appropriately to the unique needs and other factors that affect the motivation of individuals within the health/fitness environment.
- Problem-solving skills enable leaders to solve problems in a timely, systematic manner while remaining focused on what's important in each situation.
- Opportunistic outlook that enables leaders to identify and take advantage of opportunities that will have a positive impact on their professional lives, the lives of their clients, and the organization.
- Courage is "the personal strength that enables a leader to handle fear, make difficult decisions, take risks, confront change, accept responsibility, and remain self-reliant. . . . It empowers individuals to be themselves, follow their conscience (instincts), and purse their visions."[12]

Physical education, exercise science, and sport professionals must develop the qualities and attributes essential to the leadership mosaic. Leadership contributes to your effectiveness as a practitioner, and it is important to take steps to develop your leadership abilities.

McIntyre,[13] in a discussion of leadership skills for administrators in physical education, suggests that leadership skills can be taught through developmental programs. These skills are also appropriate for an individual seeking to become a leader in the profession. Among these skills are peer skills, leadership skills, conflict resolution skills, information-processing skills, decision-making skills, and introspective skills.[13]

Peer skills relate to establishing and fostering effective group and individual peer relationships. *Leadership skills* include developing a variety of leadership styles, performance evaluation skills, planning skills, and skills to foster positive morale. *Conflict resolution skills* are needed to deal with group conflict in a positive manner. *Information-processing skills* involve the gathering of information, evaluation of information, formulation of action plans based on the information, and dissemination of information to others. *Decision-making skills* typically follow the model of problem identification, generation of alternative solutions, evaluation of the outcomes of possible solutions, and selecting a solution from among the alternatives. Finally, *introspection skills* include sensitivity to one's own behavior and its effects on others. Development of these skills will enhance one's ability to be a leader in the profession.

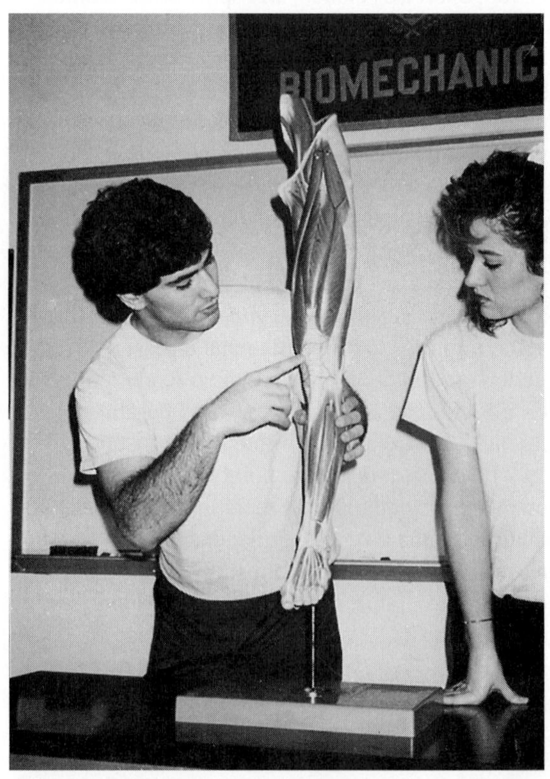

A leader must understand the scientific foundations of his or her field.

Mack describes leadership skills as a coach's greatest asset.[8] In a coaching situation, leadership may be the critical factor in determining success. Coaches need to utilize their leadership skills not only in competition but every day in practice. Mack's principles of effective leadership have great relevancy for professionals in physical education, exercise science, and sport. These principles include the following:

- *Create a vision and commitment.* Creating a vision is the most critical of all leadership skills. Effective leaders create a shared vision and foster a sense of commitment. They align and motivate the group toward the attainment of the vision.
- *Maintain integrity.* Effective leaders have a strong sense of ethics and moral values. They remain firmly committed to their beliefs and never compromise their values.
- *Lead by example.* Effective leaders model the behaviors they seek to develop in their group members. They "practice what they preach"; they "walk the talk." They understand the powerful effects of their actions. They serve as an energizing force.
- *Give credit for success and accept responsibility for failure.* Effective leaders recognize the contributions of others to their successes. They acknowledge their failures and learn from their mistakes.
- *Praise the contributions of the group.* Effective leaders try to catch group members doing something right. The use of positive reinforcement engenders enthusiasm, builds self-confidence, and fosters commitment.
- *Communicate effectively.* Effective leaders display skillful use of a wide array of communication techniques, including listening.
- *Delegate.* Effective leaders delegate wisely, giving group members tasks to complete and responsibilities to fulfill. They facilitate the completion of the tasks by giving members the necessary resources, encouraging their efforts, and supporting their actions.
- *Practice the Golden Rule.* Treat others as you wish to be treated. Be respectful, considerate, and kind. The age-old Golden Rule "Do unto others as you would have them do unto you" offers leaders a good standard to follow in their endeavors.
- *Create an environment for self-motivation.* Although leaders are often given credit for motivating others, most motivation comes from within the individual. Effective leaders nurture the strengths of the group members, provide meaningful yet challenging opportunities to achieve success, and promote the development of self-confidence and independence.

Many qualities, characteristics, traits, principles, and skills of effective leadership have been discussed.

Smith suggests that while effective leaders have a variety of behaviors and techniques in their repertoire, it may be easier to understand leadership by focusing on the core roles a leader must fulfill at all levels of leadership responsibility, whether in a group or within the profession. These roles include the vision role, the relationship role, the control role, the encouragement role, and the information role.[9]

The *vision role* requires that the leader clearly communicate his or her vision to the group. Activities associated with this role are creating a vision statement, setting specific goals contributing to the attainment of the vision, and motivation. In the *relationship role,* the leader fosters relationships that help move toward achievement of the goal. Fulfilling this role involves nurturing relationships within the group, team building, and networking to gain support.

In the *control role,* the leader prioritizes activities to be undertaken and problems to be resolved, as well as determines the resources that will be committed to their solution. This role also encompasses decision making, delegation, and conflict management. In the *encouragement role,* the leader recognizes the contributions of members to the group, reinforces efforts through giving incentives and rewards, and supports actions that move the group forward toward its goal. In fulfilling the *information role,* the leader maintains the channels of communication within the group and the organization and makes sure that the members of the group have the necessary information to fulfill their responsibilities.

Physical education, exercise science, and sport professionals can use Smith's leadership approach to help them work effectively with people under their direction. These roles may be useful to a teacher in helping children to improve their skills, an exercise leader working with program participants, or an administrator seeking to work effectively within a sport organization.

Professionals in physical education, exercise science, and sport should carefully assess their leadership behaviors and develop a plan to strengthen them further as they continue their career. Mack writes, "Failure to hone leadership skills is an opportunity lost."[8] Physical education, exercise science, and sport professionals should actively seek out experiences and opportunities that allow them to further develop as leaders.

Opportunities for leadership development are plentiful. Smith advises that individuals take the opportunity to practice leadership skills at all levels of responsibility, from working with one person to working at the highest level of an organization.[9] For example, an aspiring professional can learn leadership skills by helping a roommate begin and continue an exercise program, by assisting a friend to learn a new sport, by volunteering to serve as a coach of a youth sport team, or by officiating at intramurals. Taking on progressively more challenging leadership roles in various campus, community, and professional organizations allows a professional to develop further and refine his or her leadership abilities. It is also important to seek to develop leadership skills that are missing from your leadership repertoire.

Professionalism

Professionalism is a deep commitment to all aspects of the fields of physical education, exercise science, and sport. Professionalism means many different things to people and includes several dimensions. Professionalism means exhibiting high levels of professional competence and conduct, possessing required credentials, presenting accurate and truthful information about the programs and services provided, and exemplifying a commitment to a healthy, active lifestyle. Professionals

Conventions offer professionals opportunities for communication and fellowship.

demonstrate an enthusiasm for their work, an interest in new developments, leadership skills, and involvement in the further advancement of the field.

Accountability

Professionals exhibit accountability. They fulfill their many professional obligations in an exemplary fashion. Programs are planned, have established goals, are implemented according to current standards of professional practice, are conducted in the best interests of the participants, are monitored for quality on a continuous basis, and are evaluated periodically using accepted assessment techniques. Equally important, the public statements and claims that professionals make about their credentials, programs, and outcomes are accurate and truthful.

Cultural Competency

Cultural competency is important for professionals. As described in Chapter 3, our society is becoming increasingly diverse. Physical education, exercise science, and sport professionals need to be able to effectively provide services in multicultural environments. Professionals need to become attuned to issues of language, culture, and ethnicity and sensitive to cultural beliefs regarding the cause, prevention, and treatment of illness and maintenance of good health. Physical education, exercise science, and sport professionals must develop cultural competency so that they can help address health disparities in our population. Culturally competent health care has been shown to have a positive impact on the health of minority populations. Sensitivity, respect for culture, and integration of cultural beliefs into preventive (e.g., worksite health promotion programs) and rehabilitative (e.g., cardiac rehabilitation) programs can help physical education, exercise science, and sport professionals meet the needs of all people.

Ethics

Professionals adhere to ethical standards of conduct in their dealings with participants in their programs. These ethical standards serve as guidelines for actions and aid in decision making. Interactions with participants in programs should be appropriate. For example, many codes of conduct and common professional consensus prohibit inappropriate personal relationships between coaches and their athletes, disclosure of confidential information about an employee by a worksite health professional, or discrimination by athletic trainers in their treatment of starting and nonstarting athletes (see Table 10-2). Actions toward program participants and other professionals in the field reflect honesty, respect, and fairness.[14]

Role Modeling

Professionals remember that they are in a position of influence and serve as role models for participants in their programs. Initially, young professionals may want to discount the idea that appearance is important and believe that competence is what matters the most. Yet first impressions and appearances do influence people's perceptions and beliefs. What impression does a sloppily dressed, overweight, out-of-shape, smoking, inarticulate physical education, exercise science, and sport professional make on participants in their program? Compare that impression to the one made by a professional who is nicely groomed, well-spoken, fit, dynamic and enthusiastic and possesses good health habits. Which professional has more credibility? Effective professionals are exemplary role models; they "practice what they preach."

It is important for physical activity professionals to model an active lifestyle and physical fitness. NASPE, in a position paper entitled *Physical Activity and Fitness Recommendations for Physical Activity Professionals* states:

> Participation in regular physical activity at a level sufficient to promote health-related physical fitness is an essential behavior for all professionals in all fields of physical activity at all levels (this includes coaches, K–12 teachers, physical education and kinesiology faculty in higher education, fitness professionals, athletes, all advocates of a physically active lifestyle).[22]

TABLE 10-2 Examples of Codes of Ethics and Conduct for Physical Education, Exercise Science, and Sport Professionals

Organization	Examples
National Association for Sport and Physical Education (NASPE) Code of Conduct for Sport and Physical Educators	• "Sport and Physical Education practitioners . . . maintain their professional and personal standing through the highest standards of ethical behavior." • "Sport and Physical Education practitioners . . . seek out and implement, appropriate instructional methods that reflect best practice in teaching physical education and coaching sport."
National Association for Sport and Physical Education (NASPE) Coaches Code of Conduct	• "Coaches have the knowledge and preparation to lead their teams" as outlined in the National Standards for Athletic Coaches. • "Coaches are responsible to ensure that the health, well-being, and development of athletes take precedence over the win/loss record."
Association for the Advancement of Applied Sport Psychology (AAASP) Code of Ethics	• "AAASP members recognize that differences of age, gender, race, ethnicity, national origin, religion, sexual orientation, disability, language, or socioeconomic status can significantly affect their work. AAASP members working with specific populations have the responsibility to develop the necessary skills to be competent with these populations, or they make the appropriate referrals."
North American Society for Sport Management (NASSM) Canons or Principles	• "That professionals shall (a) hold as primary their obligations and responsibilities to students/clients; be a faithful agent or trustee when acting in a professional matter; (b) make every effort to foster maximum self-determination on the part of students/clients; (c) respect the privacy of students/clients and hold in confidence all information obtained in the course of professional service; and, (d) ensure that private or commercial service fees are fair, reasonable, considerate, and commensurate with the service performed and with due respect to the students/clients to pay."
National Athletic Trainers' Association (NATA) Code of Ethics	• "Members shall accept responsibility for the exercise of sound judgment. Members shall not misrepresent in any manner, either directly or indirectly, their skills, training, professional credentials, identify or services." • "Members shall maintain and promote high standards in the provision of services."
American College of Sports Medicine (ACSM) Code of Ethics	• "Members should continuously strive to improve knowledge and skill and make available to their colleagues and the public the benefits of their professional attainment."
IDEA Health and Fitness Professionals Code of Ethics for Group Exercise Leaders	• Group Fitness Instructors should "uphold a professional image through conduct and appearance. (a) Model behavior that values physical ability, function, and health over appearance. (b) Demonstrate healthy behaviors and attitudes about bodies (including your own). Smoking, substance abuse and unhealthy exercise and eating habits should be avoided. (c) Encourage healthful eating for yourself and for others. (d) Dress in a manner that allows you to perform your job, while increasing the comfort level of class participants. Be more conservative in dress, decorum and speech when the class standard is unclear. (e) Establish a mood in class that encourages and supports individual effort and all levels of expertise."

Data from references 15 through 21.

Personal trainers and other physical activity professionals should engage in regular physical activity at a sufficient level to promote health fitness. Modeling what we preach enhances our credibility as professionals.

In support of this position, NASPE notes that modeling is an important factor in changing the behaviors and attitudes of others. Modeling influences health practice, motor skill acquisition, and adoption of a physically active lifestyle. Physical activity professionals are important models for the individuals with whom they work. They should model the most current recommendations for improving health and fitness. This includes accumulation of at least 30 minutes a day of moderate physical activities on most days of the week and vigorous aerobic activities 3 to 6 times a week. Additionally, professionals should engage activities to improve muscle fitness 2 to 3 times a week and flexibility exercises 3 to 7 times a week. Besides modeling appropriate behavior and commitment to what they preach, professionals will realize the associated health benefits. Additionally, they will enjoy greater credibility and exemplify the value of a physically activity lifestyle.

Involvement

The fields of physical education, exercise science, and sport are growing rapidly. Professionals are committed to staying up to date with new research findings and changing techniques. They are interested in learning and take advantage of continuing education courses, workshops, conferences, and professional journals to stay abreast of the latest changes. Professionals take an active role in advancing the field through conducting and sharing research, exploring new ideas, and undertaking leadership responsibilities at various levels (e.g., local to regional to national levels). Through networking, professionals exchange ideas and support each other's efforts.

Service

Professionalism includes service not only to the profession but to society. Professionals recognize their responsibility to be involved in community service, not only to offer leadership in their area of expertise, but to participate in activities that enrich the community as a whole. Professionals advocate for increased opportunities in physical activity and sport for those who have been denied or have limited access to services.

Professionalism is a concept with many different meanings. Professionalism reflects commitment to the field and people whom they serve, respect and consideration for others, and responsibility to oneself, others, and society.

PROFESSIONAL ORGANIZATIONS IN PHYSICAL EDUCATION, EXERCISE SCIENCE, AND SPORT

Professional organizations play an important role in the growth and development of the fields of physical education, exercise science, and sport. Many of the greatest changes in the field have their beginnings in organizational meetings and conferences. Scholarly research, curriculum development, certification requirements, and hundreds of other topics are discussed in detail at conferences and other activities associated with professional organizations. The physical education, exercise science, and sport fields, both in the United States and in other countries of the world, have an imposing list of associations concerned with every aspect of the field.

All physical education, exercise science, and sport professionals should belong to the national and state associations in their areas of interest. If all professionals belonged to and worked for their professional organizations, the concerted effort of such a large professional group would result in greater benefits and more prestige for the field.

Why Belong to a Professional Association?

Belonging to a professional organization has many advantages.

1. *It provides opportunity for service.* With the many offices, committee responsibilities, and program functions that professional associations provide, the individual has an opportunity to serve to better this field of work.
2. *It provides an opportunity to shape the future of the profession.* Members can work actively to influence the direction of the field in the future. This can be accomplished through involvement in committees, task forces, and governance. Members can also be active in influencing legislation that will benefit the profession. For example, NASPE, an association of AAHPERD, is actively crusading for daily physical education for all schoolchildren and is using its congressional lobby as one means to achieve this objective.
3. *It provides a channel of communication.* Communication in a field is essential so that members may keep abreast of the latest developments in techniques, of new emphases in program content, and of the many other trends that emerge continually in a growing field. Organizations provide effective channels of communication by way of publications, meetings, and announcements. The World Wide Web is a growing channel of communication. Many organizations have Web sites and post information for professionals on these sites.
4. *It provides a means for interpreting the field.* Physical education, exercise science, and sport must be interpreted to the public on national, state, and local levels. This interpretation is essential to achieve public support for the services rendered by the professional practitioner. The professional association provides an opportunity for the best thinking and ideas to be articulately interpreted far and wide. As a result of such endeavors, the profession can achieve recognition, respect, prestige, and cooperation with other areas of education, professions, and the public in general.
5. *It provides a source of help in solving professional problems.* Often, physical education, exercise science, and sport professionals encounter professional problems. Through their officers, members, conferences, and other

Professional organizations publish periodicals that help disseminate information to members and foster communication among professionals.

activities, professional associations can play an important role in solving these problems. The associations can be of assistance, for example, in solving a professional problem involving the administration of an adapted physical activity program or even a personal problem with liability insurance.

6. *It provides an opportunity for fellowship.* Through association conferences and meetings, physical education, exercise science, and sport professionals get to know others doing similar work; and this common denominator results in friendships and many enjoyable professional and social occasions. The opportunity to build and sustain networks is an important benefit of belonging to a professional organization.
7. *It provides a forum for research.* Professions must continually conduct research to determine the effectiveness of their programs, the validity of their techniques, and the quality of their contributions to society. Professional associations aid in the dissemination of research findings through conferences, workshops, newsletters, and publications. They also support research efforts by promoting collaborative projects and/or by offering grants to help defray costs. Through research, associations also must seek knowledge that will enable the profession to move ahead and expand its services.
8. *It provides a means for distributing costs.* The work undertaken by a professional association is intended to benefit the members. This work requires money. By joining a professional association, professionals rightfully assume their responsibility to share in these costs. If one participates in the benefits, one should also share in the costs of achieving these benefits.
9. *It is valuable in gaining employment.* Through organizations, physical education, exercise science, and sport professionals can develop professional contacts that may prove useful in gaining employment. Through such contacts, professionals can learn of prospective employment opportunities or obtain a letter of recommendation for a desired position. Many professional organizations offer placement services for their members. They send their members updates of job openings, have job openings posted on their Web sites, and have placement services at their national conventions. These services help a person in gaining his or her first job, as well as in changing jobs.

Numerous professional organizations exist within the realm of physical education, exercise science, and sport to meet the diverse interests and needs of professionals in the field. From the many organizations available, you should select carefully those that best meet your needs and interests. Become involved. Be a committed, active professional willing to work hard to shape the direction and future of these dynamic fields.

Professional Organizations

It would be difficult to discuss all the organizations that pertain to the physical education, exercise science, and sport fields. The growth of these fields has led to the formation of numerous organizations; it seems that for every specialized area of study, as well as for each sport, there are organizations for interested professionals.

You can find out about organizations in your areas of interest in several ways. First, talk to other professionals, such as faculty at your undergraduate institution, that may share the same interests. Talk to practitioners in your prospective field of employment and find out the organizations in which they hold membership. Second, you can search the World Wide Web for organizations in your area of interest. Third, a comprehensive listing of all organizations in the United States is given in the *Encyclopedia of Associations.* The listing for each organization includes the purpose of the organization; name, address, and phone number of the person to contact for further information; size of the membership and the association staff; and publications of the association. The *Encyclopedia* is probably available at the reference desk or in the reference section of most college and university libraries.

The American Alliance for Health, Physical Education, Recreation and Dance (AAHPERD), the American College of Sports Medicine (ACSM), and the National Athletic Training Association (NATA) will be described here. Examples of associations for individuals interested in sport and exercise psychology, sport sociology, sport philosophy, and sport history are mentioned. Finally, examples for professionals interested in specific sport areas are provided. Since many professional organizations now have Web sites, it is easy to obtain information about professional organizations and even to visit online.

American Alliance for Health, Physical Education, Recreation and Dance (AAHPERD)

AAHPERD was established in 1885, under the title of American Association for Advancement of Physical Education. AAHPERD is committed to developing and maintaining healthy, active lifestyles for all Americans and to enhancing skilled and aesthetic performance. AAHPERD's mission is to "promote and support creative and healthy lifestyles through high-quality programs in health, physical education, recreation, dance, and sport and to provide members with professional development opportunities that increase knowledge, improve skills, and encourage sound professional practices."[23] AAHPERD has over 30,000 members representing many different areas of interest within health, physical education, recreation, and dance. These include administrators, teachers and coaches at all levels, sports medicine professionals, athletic trainers, dancers, fitness professionals, recreators, and physical activity specialists.

AAHPERD comprises six national organizations.

- The American Association for Leisure and Recreation (AALR) is concerned with the promotion of leisure services at the community and national levels and recreation education within schools.
- The Association for the Advancement of Health Education (AAHE) is involved with the conduct of health education programs in schools, colleges, and communities as well as being concerned with addressing societal health issues, such as drinking and driving, and promotion of health-oriented legislation.
- The American Association for Active Lifestyles and Fitness (AAALF) consists of various special interest groups, such as the Council on Outdoor Education and the Council of Aging and Adult Development, and administrative groups such as the College and University Administrators Council.
- The National Association for Girls and Women in Sport (NAGWS) focuses on improvement of leadership sport opportunities for girls and women at all levels of competition.
- The National Association for Sport and Physical Education (NASPE) is concerned with the promotion of physical education and sport at all levels. NASPE's special interest groups include the Academies (e.g., Curriculum and Instruction,

Sport Philosophy), Physical Education Councils (e.g., Council on Physical Education for Children), and Sport Councils (e.g., National Council of Secondary School Athletic Directors).
- The National Dance Association (NDA) seeks to promote dance both within the educational setting and on the community and national levels.

The Research Consortium is also an important part of the Alliance. The Research Consortium provides services and publications that assist professionals to become aware of new research in the fields. The Consortium promotes the exchange of ideas and the dissemination of scientific knowledge.

Nationally, AAHPERD is divided into six district or regional organizations. The Eastern, Southern, Central, Midwestern, Southwestern, and Northwestern districts have a similar purpose to that of AAHPERD and elect officers and hold district conventions. These district organizations provide leadership opportunities for professionals and allow AAHPERD to present programs specific to regional needs.

State associations provide services to professionals in each state. Membership in the state organization requires a fee; membership in the national organization is optional. State associations provide wonderful opportunities for young practitioners to become involved in their profession.

The publications of the Alliance serve to disseminate knowledge about the field to its many members. Among its many publications are *JOPERD (Journal of Physical Education, Recreation, and Dance), the Research Quarterly for Exercise and Sport, Strategies, Update, and Health Education.* In addition, AAHPERD publishes many other materials pertinent to the work of the Alliance, such as the National Content Standards for Physical Education.

The services performed by the Alliance include the following:

- Research on a variety of topics and the dissemination of research through conferences, workshops, and published materials.
- Professional development through numerous conferences, workshops, and training sessions.
- Advocacy at all levels of government and with other national agencies on behalf of members for such issues as gender equity, coaching certification, and maintenance of educational programs.
- Job placement services and professional development services offered to members.
- Recognition of excellence through presentation of numerous awards.

The AAHPERD Student Action Council (SAC) is an organization of students that works for the benefit of its members through student involvement. The group's objectives include (1) greater student involvement in AAHPERD, (2) promotion of professionalism among majors, and (3) promotion of professional interest groups. The Alliance in cooperation with SAC has made available special membership plans for students.

The national office of AAHPERD is located at 1900 Association Drive, Reston, VA 20192–1598 (Phone 800-213-7193). (www.aahperd.org)

American College of Sports Medicine (ACSM)

ACSM, founded in 1954, is the largest sports medicine and exercise science organization in the world. The purpose of ACSM is to promote and integrate "scientific research, education, and practical applications of sports medicine and exercise science to maintain and enhance physical performance, fitness, health, and quality of life."[24] From astronauts to athletes to those people chronically diseased or physically challenged, ACSM seeks to find methods that enable people to live longer, work more productively, and enjoy a better quality of life.

Nationally, ACSM is divided into several regional chapters, such as the Mid-Atlantic Chapter of ACSM. Many states have their own chapters as well. The 18,000 members of ACSM include physicians, fitness professionals, cardiac rehabilitation specialists, sports medicine practitioners and athletic trainers, physical education teachers, and coaches. The Association for Worksite Health Promotion became part of ACSM in 2002. ACSM is affiliated with the International Federation of Sports Medicine (IFSM), an organization that has played an important role for many years in Europe and South America.

ACSM supports many different activities related to health, fitness, exercise, and sports medicine. These activities include the following:

- Promoting public awareness and educating about the benefits of physical activity and exercise for people of all ages and abilities.
- Sponsoring certification programs for professionals interested in preventive and rehabilitative exercise.
- Holding conferences and workshops throughout the year for professionals in the field.
- Publishing journals, including *Medicine and Science in Sports and Exercise, Sports Medicine Bulletin,* and the *Encyclopedia of Sport Sciences and Medicine.*
- Supporting scientific studies and encouraging research efforts to advance the field.
- Cooperating with other organizations concerning sports medicine and related areas.

The mailing address of ACSM is 401 W. Michigan Street, Indianapolis, IN 46206–3233 (Phone: 317-637-9200). (www.nata.org)

National Athletic Trainers Association (NATA)

The mission of NATA, founded in 1950, is to "enhance the quality of health care for athletes and those engaged in physical activity and to advance the profession of athletic training through education and research in the prevention, evaluation, management, and rehabilitation of injuries."[25] There are more than 28,000 members nationwide and 22,000 of the membership are certified by the NATA Board of Certification, earning the title *certified athletic trainer* (ATC). In 1990, athletic training was recognized as an allied health profession by the American Medical Association.

NATA establishes the standards for athletic trainers through its education programs. Nationwide, over 100 colleges and universities offer NATA-approved curricula. Each year, 1,200 to 1,500 athletic trainers earn certification through its program.

NATA provides a variety of services to their members, including the following:

- Establishment of professional standards and a code of ethics for athletic trainers.
- Administration of the certification program.
- Continuing education opportunities through conventions and workshops.
- Annual conventions for the benefit of its members.
- Advocacy efforts to influence legislation beneficial to the field.
- Promotion of athletic training through public relations efforts.
- Job placement services for its membership.
- Publication of journals and newsletters, including the *Journal of Athletic Training,* a quarterly scientific journal, and *NATA News,* a monthly membership magazine.

For further information, contact NATA at 2952 Stemmons Freeway, Dallas, TX 75247–6916 (Phone: 800-TRY-NATA) (www.nata.org)

Organizations for the Subdisciplines of Physical Education, Exercise Science, and Sport

Many of the subdisciplines of physical education, exercise science, and sport also have professional organizations or associations. The number of these specialized organizations continues to grow each year as professionals with specific areas of interest start new organizations in their areas of expertise. Examples of five of these specialized organizations are provided in this section.

North American Society for the Psychology of Sport and Physical Activity (NASPSPA) was founded in 1965. NASPSPA is a "multidisciplinary association of scholars from the behavioral sciences and related professions. The society functions to:

- Develop and advance the scientific study of human behavior when individuals are engaged in sport and physical activity.
- Facilitate the dissemination of information.

- Improve the quality of research and teaching in the psychology of sport, motor development, and motor learning and control."[26]

NASPSPA provides opportunities for physical education, exercise science, and sport professionals interested in motor behavior and the psychology of sport and exercise to exchange ideas, present research, and stay abreast of the latest developments in the field. It also offers members access to employment services.

NASPSPA journals reflect the two major interest areas of its membership. NASPSPA's journals include *Motor Control* and the *Journal of Sport and Exercise Psychology.* The society publishes a newsletter to keep its members informed about news in the areas of interest. NASPSPA holds an annual convention, usually in the early summer. For more information about NASPSPA, access their Web site (www.naspspa.org).

The **International Association for the Philosophy of Sport** (IAPS) has as its primary purpose to "foster philosophic interchange among scholars interested in better understanding sport."[27] The forerunner of this organization was the Philosophic Society for the Study of Sport, which was founded in 1972. The central focus of the organization is the scholarly investigation of sport at all levels, including practical implications. IAPS publishes the *Journal of the Philosophy of Sport,* and a newsletter for its membership. IAPS's conferences provide members with an opportunity to share their research and exchange ideas. More information about IAPS can be obtained from its Web site (www.dmu.ac.uk/dept/schools/pesl/affiliat/iaps. htm).

The **North American Society for Sport History** (NASSH) was founded in 1972. According to its mission statement,

> "the purpose of the North American Society for Sport History is to promote, stimulate, and encourage study and research and writing of the history of sport; to support and cooperate with local, national, and international organizations having the same purposes. The Society conducts its activities solely for scholarly and literary purposes and not for pecuniary profit."[28]

NASSH seeks to encourage the study of sport, exercise, and physical activity within different time spans and diverse historical contexts. NASSH promotes research and the teaching of the history of sport, exercise, and physical activity through its annual conferences and *Journal of Sport History.*[28] Its newsletter and annual proceedings keep members informed about the society's activities and new research in sport history. For more information, visit the Web site (www.nassh.org).

The **North American Society for the Sociology of Sport** (NASSS), founded in 1980, is concerned with promoting study of the sociology of sport. According to its mission statement, NASSS

> "is organized exclusively for educational purposes to promote, stimulate, and encourage the sociological study of play, games, and sport, to support and cooperate with local, national, and organizations having the same purposes, and to organize and arrange meetings and issue publications concerning the purpose of the Society. The Society shall recognize and represent all sociological paradigms for the study of play, games, and sport and will promote scholarly activity and exchange among these alternative paradigms and perspectives."[29]

NASSS promotes scholarly endeavors and interchange through its annual conferences, *Sociology of Sport Journal,* newsletters, maintenance of a directory of experts, and Sociology of Sport listserv. More information about NASSS can be found on the NASSS Web site (www.uwm.edu/~aycock/nasss/nasss.html).

The **North American Society for Sport Management** (NASSM) was founded in 1985. NASSM's purpose is to

> "promote, stimulate, and encourage study, research, scholarly writing, and professional development in the area of sport management (broadly interpreted). Members of the Society are concerned about the theoretical and applied aspects of management theory and practice specifically related to sport, exercise, dance, and play as these enterprises are pursued by

> all sectors of the population. The Society endeavors to support and cooperate with local, regional, national, and international organizations having similar purposes and organizes and administers meetings to promote its purposes."[30]

The majority of NASSM's members are sport management educators who teach and conduct research at colleges and universities. Its official scholarly journal, *Journal of Sport Management,* supports both quantitative and qualitative research from a variety of perspectives focusing on topics within the broad realm of sport management. Some areas of study include sport and the law, sport marketing, leadership, and management. Membership is open to students enrolled in sport management programs of study. Its annual conference, as well as its sport management electronic forum, provides members with opportunities to discuss their research, exchange ideas, and collaborate on projects of mutual interest. For more information, visit the Web site (www.nassm.com).

Sport Organizations for Coaches and Interested Professionals

Numerous organizations are affiliated with specific sport areas. Many of these organizations sponsor annual conferences and clinics for interested professionals, conduct certification programs, and publish newsletters and journals related to the sport. Professionals who are coaching or teaching in the specific sport are good sources of information about these sport associations. Another source is the *Encyclopedia of Associations* or *Associations Unlimited* online. For example, a professional interested in the sport of swimming would find the following professional organizations listed in the *Encyclopedia:*

- American Swimming Coaches Association
- Aquatics Exercise Association
- College Swimming Coaches Association of America
- National Interscholastic Swimming Coaches Association of America
- United States Masters Swimming
- United States Swimming, Inc.
- United States Diving, Inc.
- United States Synchronized Swimming, Inc.

A professional interested in the sport of tennis may find membership in one or more of these organizations helpful:

- Intercollegiate Tennis Coaches Association
- Sports on Wheels
- United States Professional Tennis Registry
- United States Professional Tennis Association
- United States Tennis Association
- United States Tennis Writers Association
- Women's Tennis Association

Some professional organizations may have certain requirements for membership, whereas others may be open to any interested individuals. They provide a wonderful means to network with other professionals, learn new skills and techniques, and stay up to date with new advances in the sport.

SUMMARY

Many exciting career opportunities are available today for persons interested in pursuing a career in physical education, exercise science, and sport. Teaching and coaching in schools at all levels remains a popular career choice. Teaching and coaching opportunities have also expanded to nonschool settings. With the growth of the fields of physical education, exercise science, and sport, additional career opportunities are available for qualified individuals in fitness, health promotion, cardiac rehabilitation, athletic training, sport management, and sport media, to name a few of the many career choices available.

Selecting a career pathway from the many available options requires careful consideration of many factors. To make an informed decision, you must gather information from the appropriate sources and evaluate it. Your personal strengths, interests, goals, and preferences are the most important considerations in choosing a career. In selecting a career, you must also consider information about the career itself. This information may be gathered through research and by talking to practitioners in your prospective career.

Professional preparation for a career involves academic studies, related experiences, and professional activities. Planning for a career demands understanding the nature of the work to be performed and the requirements of the job. As you read about different career opportunities in physical education, exercise science, and sport, be flexible and open minded and explore career opportunities that interest you.

Professional leadership is needed to ensure the continued growth and vitality of the field of physical education, exercise science, and sport. Leadership is also critical in helping participants in our programs achieve desired goals. Leaders are not born, but made. Leadership qualities and skills can be developed and improved by professionals who desire to enhance their effectiveness.

There are many advantages to belonging to a professional organization. Professional organizations provide opportunities for service, facilitate communication, and provide a means to disseminate research findings and other information to professionals. Membership in a professional organization provides opportunities for networking and a resource for resolution of problems and may enhance one's employment opportunities.

Numerous professional organizations exist. To find out about a professional organization in one's specific area of interest, one can consult a professional or practitioner in the field, the *Encyclopedia of Associations,* or the World Wide Web.

Self-Assessment Tests

These tests are designed to help you determine if you have mastered the materials and competencies presented in this chapter.

1. Identify five career opportunities in physical education, exercise science, and sport. Using the information provided in the Get Connected box, access the *Occupational Handbook* site and search for information about physical activity careers. Find out the skills required, potential employers, future outlook, and salary associated with each career.
2. Using the questions provided in the text as guidelines, assess your strengths, interests, goals, and preferences. Based on this information, what careers might you choose? If you choose, share this information with a fellow student and solicit each other's input regarding possible careers.
3. Develop a multi-year plan to enhance your credentials. Specifically, in addition to the requirements of your professional preparation program, what other opportunities will you pursue (e.g., certifications, extracurricular activities, employment) to enhance your professional qualifications?
4. Through self-reflection, determine what leadership qualities and skills you possess. What qualities do you need to develop?
5. Carefully read the statements in Table 10-2 regarding codes of ethics and conduct for professionals. Working as a group, select one career area and develop a five-point code of conduct for that career.
6. Using the information provided in the Get Connected box, access the list of associations. Locate information about two associations in your areas of interest. Find out the fees for membership, membership benefits, and publications.

References

1. Lambert CL: What is physical education? JOPERD 51(5):26–27, 1980.
2. US Department of Labor: Occupational outlook handbook, current edition, Washington, D.C., Department of Labor.
3. College Placement Council: CPC annual, current edition, Bethlehem, Pa., College Placement Council.
4. Akey DS, editor: Encyclopedia of associations, Detroit, Gale Research Co., current edition.

5. American College of Sports Medicine Certifications. (www.acsm.org)
6. Krause JV and Melville DS:Fit for hire—a model for promoting the health and fitness of physical education students. JOPERD 64(4):61–65, 1993.
7. Willis JD and Campbell LF: Exercise psychology, Champaign, Ill., 1992, Human Kinetics.
8. Mack R: Leadership skills: a coach's greatest asset, Coach 16(4):3–4, 1996.
9. Smith DM: The practical executive and leadership, Lincolnwood, Ill., 1997, NTC Business Books.
10. Weinberg RS and Gould D: Psychology of exercise and sport, Champaign, Ill., 1995, Human Kinetics.
11. Anshel MH: Sport psychology: From theory to practice, ed 3, Scottsdale, Ariz., 1997, Gorsuch Scarisbrick.
12. Peterson JA and Bryant CX: A personal trainer's guide to effective leadership, Fitness Management, October 2001.
13. McIntrye M: Leadership development, Quest 33(1):33–41, 1981.
14. Stoll SK and Beller JM: Professional responsibility—a lost art, Strategies 9(2):17–19, 1995.
15. American Alliance for Health, Physical Education, Recreation and Dance, National Association for Sport and Physical Education: Code of conduct for sport and physical educators, Reston, Va., 1999, AAHPERD. (www.aahperd.org)
16. American Alliance for Health, Physical Education, Recreation and Dance, National Association for Sport and Physical Education: The coaches code of conduct, Reston, Va., 2001, AAHPERD. (www.aahperd.org)
17. Association for the Advancement of Applied Sport Psychology: ethical principles and standards of the association for the advancement of applied sport psychology. (www.aaasponline.org)
18. North American Society for Sport Management: Position statement. (www.nassm.com)
19. National Athletic Trainers' Association: Code of ethics. (www.nata.org)
20. American College of Sports Medicine: Code of ethics. (www.acsm.org)
21. IDEA Health and Fitness Professionals: Code of ethics for group exercise leaders (www.ideafit.org)
22. NASPE. Physical activity and fitness recommendations for physical activity professionals, College and University Physical Education Council, NASPE, 2002.
23. American Alliance for Health, Physical Education, Recreation, and Dance. (www.aahperd.org)
24. American College of Sports Medicine. (www.acsm.org)
25. National Athletic Trainers' Association. (www.nata.org)
26. North American Society for the Psychology of Sport and Physical Activity. (www.naspspa.org)
27. International Association for the Philosophy of Sport. (www.dmu.ac.uk/dept/schools/pesl/affiliat/iaps.htm)
28. North American Society for Sport History. (www.nassh.org)
29. North American Society for the Sociology of Sport. (www.uwm.edu/~aycock/nasss/nasss.html)
30. North American Society for Sport Management. (www.nassm.com)

SUGGESTED READINGS

Bolles RN: What color is your parachute? a practical manual for job-hunters and career changers, Berkeley, Calif., current edition, Ten Speed Press.

This book provides practical guidelines for obtaining a job and/or changing careers. The resource section of the book is comprehensive and a valuable guide for obtaining career information.

Cardinal BJ: Role modeling attitudes and physical activity and fitness promoting behaviors of HPERD professionals and preprofessionals, Research Quarterly for Exercise and Sport, 72:84–90, 2001.

To determine whether HPERD professionals and preprofessionals "practice what they preach," Cardinal examined the relationship between role modeling attitudes, regular physical activity, and body mass index. He found that the study's participants engaged in regular physical activity and had acceptable BMIs.

Cardinal BJ and Cardinal MK: Role modeling in HPERD: do attitudes match behavior, JOPERD, 72(4):34–39, 2001.

Modeling behaviors that promote physical activity and fitness is often cited as an important responsibility of HPERD professionals. This article explores attitudes of HPERD professionals toward role modeling, including whether role modeling is valued, which forms of physical activity HPERD professionals should engage in, and whether professionals should be expected to uphold a fitness standard.

College Placement Council: CPC annual, current edition, Bethlehem, Pa., College Placement Council.

Available through the career planning office, this annual periodical offers advice on career planning, the job search, and graduate school.

Horton ML: Digital portfolios in physical education teacher preparation, JOPERD 75(9):35–39, 2004.

Electronic or digital portfolios provide an excellent way for preservice teachers as well as professionals in other fields to provide evidence of their competencies and showcase their accomplishments.

Melograno VJ: Preservice professional portfolio system, Reston, VA: 1999, National Association for Sport and Physical Education.

This helpful handbook guides the preservice teacher step-by-step through the development of a portfolio system—multiple portfolios to serve specific needs. It includes information on planning, selection of artifacts, and organization.

Stoll SK and Beller JM: Professional responsibility—a lost art, Strategies 9(2):17–19, 1995.

Professional responsibility is discussed with reference to personal morality, professional ethics, and social responsibility.

CHAPTER 11

TEACHING AND COACHING CAREERS

OBJECTIVES

After reading this chapter the student should be able to—

- Describe the advantages and disadvantages of pursuing a teaching career in a school or nonschool setting.
- Describe the similarities and differences between teaching and coaching.
- Discuss the problem of burnout and its effects on teachers and coaches.
- Discuss strategies to maximize opportunities for employment in a teaching or coaching position.

Teaching and coaching opportunities for physical education, exercise science, and sport professionals have expanded from the school to the nonschool setting and from school-aged populations (i.e., 5 to 18 years) to people of all ages, ranging from preschoolers to senior citizens. Although traditional opportunities in the public school are available, professionals are seeking other avenues for teaching and coaching careers. The national interest in fitness and sport has contributed to the opening of these alternative areas of employment. Moreover, the continued emphasis on fitness, physical activities, and sport opportunities for all age groups presents an encouraging employment picture to potential physical education teachers and coaches.

The challenge to those who wish to enter the teaching or coaching professions is reflected in the words of Aristotle. He said that those who educate children well are to be honored more than those who produce them, for those who produce children give them only life, but those who educate them give them the art of living well.[1] A physical education teacher or coach has the responsibility to inspire students or athletes with the desire to learn, to have them recognize the need to develop physical skills and be physically active, and to see that each one develops to his or her capacity.

Cultural competency is important for both teachers and coaches (see Chapter 3). In our increasingly multicultural society, both teachers and coaches must be committed to conducting culturally responsive programs

GET CONNECTED

National Association for Sports and Physical Education (NASPE), an association of AAHPERD, presents information about its Academies, Physical Education Councils, and Sports Councils, as well as access to position papers, standards for teachers and coaches, and publications.

www.aahperd.org → NASPE

PE Central site serves as a major resource for physical educators of all levels, offering access to lesson plans for all levels of physical education and adapted physical education, information on assessment, positive learning environment, professional links, jobs, and resources.

www.pecentral.org

PE Links4U offers information, lesson ideas, and tips for teachers and coaches of all levels as well as current news in the field of physical education and sport. Areas include technology, interdisciplinary learning, coaching, teaching, and current events.

www.pelinks4u.org

National Consortium for Physical Education and Recreation for Individuals with Disabilities site presents information about the Adapted Physical Education Standards Project, fact sheets, monographs, and links to resources.

http://ncperid.usf.edu

that are sensitive to the needs of students and athletes from diverse cultural backgrounds. This includes being committed to the equitable treatment of all persons, regardless of race, gender, socioeconomic background, abilities, sexual orientation, and religion.

THE TEACHING PROFESSION

Teaching has been the traditional focus of the field of physical education and sport. Even though many types of jobs are now available in the field, many young people still choose to teach and to coach. The school setting remains the most popular setting for teaching, and job opportunities look promising. It is estimated that during the next decade, 2 million new teachers (all subjects) will need to be hired to replace the generation of teachers about to retire and to respond to a growing need. The 1990s saw a surge of interest in teaching.

Teaching in the school and nonschool setting has many benefits as well as some drawbacks. Regardless of the setting, effective teachers hold high expectations for their students, keep them involved in relevant learning activities, and create an atmosphere that promotes learning. Beginning teachers possess competencies in many different areas that enable them to enhance student learning. The use of developmentally appropriate teaching practices helps teachers more effectively address the needs of their learners.

Choosing a Teaching Career

Teaching offers many rewards, regardless of whether it takes place in the traditional school or an alternative nonschool setting. Probably most important is that it offers an opportunity to help shape people's lives and promote a healthy lifestyle. Students select teaching as a career for many reasons.

Many physical educators want to teach because of their love of children and their desire to help others. The conviction that involvement in a sound physical education program can have a significant impact on the quality of life of its participants motivates some individuals to enter the teaching profession. Prospective teachers who have been fortunate to reap the benefits of participation in a quality physical education program often express the desire to share with others the same benefits that they themselves have realized. Other individuals, who had poor experiences while students in physical education, enter the teaching profession because they want to improve physical education programs so that the benefits of quality programs can be attained.

Certainly personal interests, likes, and dislikes influence one's decision to enter the teaching profession. Many choose to teach physical education because of their love for sport and perhaps the desire to transmit this love to others. The opportunity to be outdoors, to work out and stay physically fit, and to have fun are often given as reasons for entering the teaching profession.

The nature of the job attracts many individuals. In the school setting, the long vacations, the informality of teaching in the gymnasium as compared with the classroom, and the security offered by tenure are some of the benefits that prompt some people to seek a teaching career. Others may enter teaching because they desire to coach, and in many schools teaching is a requirement for coaching. Teaching may also be used as a stepping stone to other careers, such as athletic administration.

Many of these reasons for entering the teaching profession are valid for those seeking to work in nonschool settings. The opportunity to capitalize on one's proficiency in a sport, the desire to share the benefits of participation with others, and the love of working with people may motivate physical educators to prepare for a teaching career in a nonschool setting.

The rewards that accrue from teaching depend to a large degree on the individual and what each person makes of his or her opportunities. The inner rewards, plus the financial and other benefits, can be great for the person who applies himself or herself diligently and sincerely to teaching.

What Are the Benefits and Drawbacks Associated with Teaching?

The teaching profession is considered a service-oriented profession. As with other service-oriented professions, those who enter teaching must often be satisfied with intrinsic rather than extrinsic rewards. Several benefits are associated with teaching physical education in the school setting.

Salaries associated with teaching vary widely. According to the American Federation of Teachers (AFT), in 2002–2003 the average teacher salary was $45,771.[2] The highest average salaries were found in California ($55,693), Michigan ($54,020), and Connecticut ($53,962).[2] The lowest average teacher salaries were found in South Dakota ($32,414), Oklahoma ($33,277), and North Dakota ($33,869).[2] The AFT estimates that the average beginning salary for 2003–2004 was $30,496.[2] In 2002–2003 the highest average beginning teacher salaries were found in Alaska ($37,401), New Jersey ($35,673), and the District of Columbia ($35,260).[2] The lowest average beginning teacher salaries were found in Montana ($23,052), Arizona ($23,548) and North Dakota ($23,591).[2]

At first glance, teachers' salaries appear to be low compared to those offered in other professional careers. However, remember that teachers typically work 9 months or about 180 days a year. Additionally, many teachers receive additional compensation for coaching or for directing/supervising extracurricular activities, such as intramurals and fitness clubs or even advising the student yearbook staff. When looking at teacher salaries, remember that cost of living varies considerably from place to place. The long vacation periods provide the opportunity to earn additional money, to travel, or to continue one's education. Although teaching is not a lucrative career, the financial picture in many cases is not bleak as is sometimes thought.

Second, teaching in an educational setting offers job tenure. The primary objective of tenure is to enhance the academic freedom of teachers. However, it can also be perceived as providing teachers with job security. Tenure is typically granted in the public schools after 3 years of satisfactory service to the school district. At the college and university level, tenure is typically granted after 6 years.

Many other benefits associated with teaching attract young people to the field. The intrinsic rewards are great. These include the opportunity to serve as a role model to young people. As many of you know from your own experiences, teachers can exert a great influence on the lives of young students, contributing greatly to their development. Others are attracted to the field because of the chance to teach a diversity of activities. For many young people, one great benefit to teaching physical education is that it offers them the opportunity to coach.

On the other hand, one should be aware that there are several disadvantages to pursuing a teaching career in a school setting. Although the public's confidence in teachers appears to be improving, the lack of wholehearted commitment has resulted in problems of morale, lack of financial support, and pressure to do more with less money and to get by with often inadequate facilities. The teacher is often beset with discipline problems, confronted with overpopulated classes that contain unmotivated students, and required to absorb teaching loads that are too heavy. Teachers often do numerous tasks not related to teaching, such as lunchroom and study hall supervision, hall duty, and playground or bus patrol.

Several benefits are associated with teaching in the nonschool setting. Examples of teaching opportunities in the nonschool setting include working as a tennis or golf professional and teaching in a community recreation program, YMCA/YWCA, or commercial sport club such as a gymnastics club, swim club, or racquetball club. First, since participation in these programs is voluntary, the teacher generally works with individuals and students who are highly motivated and eager to be involved in the activity. Second, many physical educators elect to teach in the nonschool setting because of the opportunity to specialize; many physical educators like the idea of teaching just one activity, such as golf, tennis, or swimming. However, many nonschool settings such as YMCA/YWCA and community recreation programs require the ability to teach a diversity of activities.

There are some drawbacks to teaching in the nonschool setting. Unlike teaching in the schools, there is a lack of job security. The number of participants enrolled in a program may determine whether it continues to be offered and may also determine the teacher's salary. Salaries vary widely as well. In contrast to school, where the working hours are confined to weekdays (unless one is coaching), working hours at a nonschool setting may be late afternoons and evenings and often weekends. Working hours need to be responsive to the hours the clients have available for leisure time pursuits. Work may also be seasonal, but this depends on the nature of the activity and the location. For example, golf professionals in the Northeast may find work only from May to September, but those pursuing this profession in the South may be able to work year round.

Prospective teachers should identify their reasons for entering the teaching profession as well as evaluate the benefits associated with this career in terms of their personal priorities and goals. Advantages and disadvantages are associated with teaching in both the school and nonschool settings. These must be considered in making a career choice.

What Is Effective Teaching?

Teaching can be defined as those interactions of the teacher and the learner that make learning more successful.[3] Although it is possible for learning to occur without a teacher's involvement, it is generally accepted that teachers facilitate the acquisition of knowledge, skills, and attitudes. Teachers who are effective use a variety of pedagogical skills and strategies to ensure that their students are appropriately engaged in relevant activities a high percentage of the time, hold positive expectations for their students, and create and maintain a classroom climate that is warm and nurturing.[4]

Salient teacher behaviors can be divided into several broad areas: organization, communication, instruction, motivation, and human relations. These characteristics are common to effective teachers, regardless of the skill to be learned, the age of the students, or the setting in which the teaching occurs.

Organizational skills are very important in establishing the learning environment and facilitating

Physical education teachers and coaches must be well prepared for working in their field. This prospective teacher is receiving feedback from her instructor about her practice teaching.

student involvement in activities. The manner in which the teacher structures instruction is of major importance. To be effective the teacher must ensure that the lesson to be presented relates to the stated objectives, meets the needs of the individual learners, and is presented in a logical, systematic manner. Through efficient and thorough planning, effective teachers minimize transition time (i.e., the time to move students from place to place) and management time (i.e., time used for tasks such as taking attendance). Lessons are planned to ensure that students receive maximum opportunities to practice relevant skills and experience success. Actively supervising and monitoring student performance and providing students with appropriate feedback are characteristics of successful teachers. Skilled teachers bring each lesson to an end by summarizing what has been accomplished and by providing students with an assessment of their progress toward the stated objectives.

Communication skills needed by the teacher include verbal and nonverbal expressive skills, written competencies, and the ability to use the various media. Effective verbal communication skills are essential in the teaching process. The ability to speak clearly and project one's voice in a pleasing manner is essential. Other attributes of a successful teacher are the abilities to give clear, precise directions and explanations and to use terminology and vocabulary that are appropriate to the activity and the level of the learners. The teacher's ability to use questions to elicit student input, to promote student involvement, and to clarify student understanding of the material being presented enhances the effectiveness of the learning process. Effective teachers are also aware of the influence of their nonverbal behavior on the students and learning process. Use of eye contact, smiles, and pats on the back are some of the methods of communicating with students in a nonverbal manner. Through their verbal and nonverbal behaviors, effective teachers model the kinds of behaviors they wish their students to exhibit, such as interest in and enjoyment of the activity and respect for other persons' opinions and needs. Effective teachers communicate enthusiasm through both their verbal and nonverbal behavior.

Written communication skills are essential, especially in the planning and evaluation phase of teaching. Those teachers who possess effective written communication skills are able to express themselves clearly. The ability to communicate with supervisors, participants, and interested others will help to establish a more successful program.

Expertise in the use of various instructional media techniques is a quality of effective teachers. Use of transparencies, slides, movie projectors, and videotape equipment requires skills that should be mastered early in one's career. Appropriate use of media can enhance and accelerate student learning.

Competency in a variety of instructional skills is essential for effective teaching. When planning experiences for students, effective teachers use their knowledge of the content to be taught, in conjunction with instructional objectives and students' needs, to provide appropriate experiences leading to the attainment of stated goals. Effective teaching requires the ability to sequence movement tasks by increasing difficulty and complexity as students progress, and by providing opportunities for students not only to develop skills but to apply them. Good teachers not only must be able to implement planned experiences effectively but also must be flexible so that they can appropriately modify planned experiences to suit the needs of the students and the situations that arise within the learning environment.

Effective teachers are able to maintain an orderly, productive learning environment, handling discipline problems appropriately while encouraging and providing opportunities for students to learn responsibility and to be accountable for their actions. A wide variety of teaching methods and instructional strategies are judiciously employed to maximize students' active and successful engagement in relevant tasks. The ability to present clear explanations and offer accurate demonstrations contributes to learning. Effective teachers actively monitor their students' performance and are concerned about the quality of their efforts. Teachers are aware of, and capably respond to, the myriad events that occur within the instructional environment; this quality, "with-it-ness," is often described as "having eyes in the back of one's head." Evaluation skills are also important. Teachers must be able to observe and analyze student performance, focusing on the critical elements in relationship to the goal, with feedback reinforcing or modifying responses as necessary.

The communication of high expectations for each student is also important. Teachers should hold high expectations for both student learning and behavior. Positive expectations, including the belief that all students are capable of learning, are important in establishing a warm, nurturing classroom climate and a productive learning environment.[4]

The ability to motivate students to perform to their potential is the goal of every teacher. Skillful teachers use a variety of teaching techniques to stimulate interest in participation and seek creative techniques to involve students in the learning process. They also use appropriate reinforcement techniques to maintain student involvement and promote a high level of student effort. These may include checklists, contracts, award systems, and verbal and nonverbal feedback. Praise is used thoughtfully; it is contingent on the correct performance, specific in its nature and intent, and sincere. Successful teachers continually update their lessons in an effort to meet students' needs and to make the material presented relevant and challenging to the students.

Effective teachers possess superior human relations skills. They listen to students and accept students as individuals, treating them as such. They strive to instill in each student a sense of self-worth. Effective teachers show concern for the well-being of each student in their classes and endeavor to provide students with opportunities that will enhance their self-confidence. The ability to establish and maintain rapport with students and staff and readiness to acknowledge one's own mistakes are also characteristics that many successful teachers possess. A sense of humor is a welcome attribute as well.

In summary, effective teachers are able to successfully utilize a variety of skills pertaining to organization, communication, instruction, motivation, and human relations. However, effective teaching requires more than these skills; it requires the ability to assess accurately the needs of the moment and to tailor these skills to the specific context and situation. Although many of these skills appear to be innate to certain individuals, all of them can be developed or improved by individuals who desire to become effective teachers.

Competencies for Beginning Teachers

What should beginning teachers know? What should they be able to do? How well should they be able to perform these tasks? What is competent beginning teaching? In an effort to address these questions, a committee of teachers, teacher educators, and state agency officials met to determine what constitutes competent beginning teaching. As a result of these shared efforts, in 1992, the Interstate New Teacher Assessment and Support Consortium (INTASC) identified the knowledge, dispositions, and performances that beginning teachers at all levels and across all subject areas should demonstrate.

In 1995, the National Association of Sport and Physical Education (NASPE) developed standards for beginning physical education teachers. These standards identified what competencies should be possessed by beginning physical education teachers.

INTASC

INTASC's performance-based standards represent a common core of teacher knowledge that transcends different disciplines, grade levels, and states. Guiding the development of these standards was one key premise: "An effective teacher must be able to integrate content knowledge with the specific strengths and needs of students to assure that all students learn and perform at high levels."[5]

INTASC's standards provide information for beginning teachers about behaviors and expectations for performance. According to INTASC standards, beginning teachers should have an understanding of the content they are teaching, the ability to work with diverse learners, and competency in a variety of instructional strategies.[5] Beginning teachers also need to be able to motivate students, actively engage students in learning, and create a positive learning environment.[5] Beginning teachers use a multitude of communication strategies to foster inquiry, active engagement, and self-motivation.[5]

As beginning teachers plan for instruction, they take into account the subject matter, the needs of the students, the curriculum goals, and the community in which students live.[5] Formal and informal assessment strategies are used to ensure the intellectual, social, and physical development of students.[5]

Beginning teachers strive to learn from their experiences, engaging in systematic reflection of their teaching, considering the effects of their choices and actions on their students, parents, and other professionals in the school.[5] Beginning teachers seek opportunities to grow professionally, further developing their skills and acquiring new competencies.[5] Recognizing that teachers are part of a learning community, beginning teachers foster relationships with school colleagues, parents, and agencies within the community, seeking to expend students' learning opportunities and support their well-being.[5]

These standards identified what beginning teachers should know, the skills they should possess, and expectations for performance. INTASC standards have helped shape teacher preparation programs as well as teacher licensing.

Competencies for Beginning Physical Education Teachers

What competencies should beginning teachers possess? In 1995, the National Association for Sport and Physical Education (NASPE)[6] developed standards for beginning physical education teachers. The NASPE Content Standards (see Chapter 2) were closely considered in developing these standards. Nine standards were identified. The standards relate to competencies in the following areas:

- Content knowledge.
- Growth and development.

Beginning Physical Education Teacher Standards: National Association for Sport and Physical Education (NASPE) Selected Standards

Standard 1. Content Knowledge. The teacher understands physical education content, disciplinary concepts, and tools of inquiry related to the development of a physically educated person.

Disposition 2. The teacher has enthusiasm for the importance of physical education as a means of developing a physically educated person.

Standard 2. Growth and Development. The teacher understands how individuals learn and develop, and can provide opportunities that support their physical, cognitive, social, and emotional development.

Knowledge 3. The teacher has knowledge of expected developmental progressions and ranges of individual variation and can identify levels of readiness.

Standard 6. Planning and Instruction. The teacher plans and implements a variety of developmentally appropriate instructional strategies to develop physically educated individuals.

Performance 10. The teacher creates short- and long-term plans that are linked to learner needs and performance and adapts plans to ensure learner progress, motivation, and safety.

Standard 8. Reflection. The teacher is a reflective practitioner who evaluates the effects of his/her actions on others and seeks opportunities to grow professionally.

Disposition 1. The teacher is committed to ongoing self-reflection, assessment, and learning.

Standard 9. Collaboration. The teacher fosters relationships between colleagues, parents/guardians, and community agencies to support learner's growth and well-being.

Performance 3. The teacher identifies and uses community resources to enhance physical activity opportunities.

NASPE: National standards for beginning physical education teachers, Reston, Va., 1995, AAHPERD.

- Diverse learners.
- Management and motivation.
- Communication.
- Planning and instruction.
- Learner assessment.
- Reflection.
- Collaboration.

Associated with each standard are dispositions, knowledge, and performance competencies. Dispositions are fundamental attitudes and beliefs about teaching that underlie the professional and ethical basis for practice. Knowledge is the subject matter that a beginning teacher needs to know and understand. Performance refers to the demonstrated outcomes or teaching skills that the teacher should exhibit or possess. Examples of the standards and sample dispositions, knowledge, and performance competencies are shown in the Beginning Physical Education Teacher Standards box.

Developmentally Appropriate Physical Activity Experiences

Traditionally, the teaching of motor and sport skills has taken place in physical education programs and in athletic programs associated with the schools. However, in the past decade there has been a proliferation of programs to teach movement and sport skills outside of the school setting. Some examples are preschool and day-care motor-development programs, community youth sport programs, exercise programs in senior citizen centers, recreational programs in community settings, private sport clubs, and corporate fitness programs. These programs encompass people of all ages and abilities.

Strong leadership and appropriate program design are important if these physical activity programs are to provide a positive experience for the participants and achieve desired outcomes. How then should these programs be structured to enable the maximum amount of learning to occur and to provide an enjoyable experience for the participants? Perhaps some guidance can be gained from a document entitled "Developmentally Appropriate Physical Education Practices for Children," written by the Council on Physical Education for Children (COPEC), a unit of the National Association of Sport and Physical Education (NASPE), an association of AAHPERD.[7] This document outlines appropriate and inappropriate practices in teaching physical education to young children. Although it was designed for school physical education, many of the guidelines presented are appropriate for physical education programs for all school levels and physical activity programs for people of all ages in community and commercial settings.

Selected guidelines, modified to include all people and settings, are presented in Table 11-1. As you read each guideline, first reflect on your own experiences in physical education classes and determine whether the practices you experienced were appropriate or inappropriate. Next, reread the guidelines and expand your thinking to conceptualize how these guidelines would apply to leaders (teachers) and participants in a variety of different physical activity programs. For example, what are the implications of these guidelines for the conduct of interscholastic sports, youth sport programs, programs for the elderly, corporate fitness programs, cardiac rehabilitation programs, and preschool motor development programs?

As professionals, we can play a significant role in the nation's health by conducting programs to help participants acquire the skills, knowledge, and attitudes to incorporate physical activity into their lives. For us to contribute in a meaningful way, however, we must make sure our programs are of high quality and appropriate to the needs of the participants.

Noted fitness leader and author Charles Corbin offers sage advice for teachers regarding the conduct of physical education programs.[8] The assumption that promoting lifelong physical activity is the primary goal of physical education programs is a premise that should underlie our programs at all levels.[8] As Corbin notes, this primary goal is consistent with the NASPE guidelines.[8] The focus on promoting lifelong physical activity supports the public health role of physical education and is congruent with the emphasis on using physical activity to promote better health for youth as advocated by the Centers for Disease Control and Prevention.[8] Quality programs should progressively build toward this goal, with physical education at each level of instruction helping students acquire the skills, knowledge, and attitudes to be physically active for a lifetime.

TEACHING RESPONSIBILITIES

Teachers in both school and nonschool settings perform a myriad of tasks every day. Prospective teachers need to be cognizant of their responsibilities. In addition to actually teaching, teachers perform many administrative and professionally related tasks. Gensemer[9] groups the activities of teachers into three areas: instructional tasks, managerial tasks, and institutional tasks. Instructional tasks are responsibilities and activities that relate directly to teaching. These tasks include explaining and/or demonstrating how to perform a skill, describing how to execute a particular strategy in a game, evaluating students' performance, motivating students through the use of various techniques, and using questions to check students' comprehension of the material being presented to determine the clarity of the presentation and to elicit student input.

Managerial tasks are activities related to the administration of the class. In the school setting, these activities may include taking attendance, dealing with discipline problems, and patrolling the locker room. In a nonschool setting such as a commercial health club or sports center, managerial responsibilities may include setting up and dismantling equipment, equipment repair, handing out towels, distributing workout record sheets, and recording individuals' progress.

Table 11-1	**Developmentally Appropriate Physical Activity Program Practices**	
Program Component	**Appropriate Practice**	**Inappropriate Practice**
Curriculum	The physical activity curriculum has a scope and sequence that is based on goals and objectives that are appropriate for the participants. It includes a balance of activities designed to enhance the cognitive, motor, affective, and physical fitness development of each participant.	The physical activity curriculum lacks developed goals and objectives and is based primarily on the leader's interests, preferences, and background rather than those of the participants.
Development of movement concepts and basic skills	Participants are provided with frequent and meaningful age-appropriate practice opportunities that enable individuals to develop a functional understanding of movement concepts (body awareness, space awareness, effort, and relationships), and build competence and confidence in their ability to perform a variety of motor skills (locomotor, nonlocomotor, and manipulative).	Individuals participate in a limited number of activities in which the opportunity for them to develop basic concepts and motor skills is restricted.
Cognitive development	Physical activities are designed with both the physical and the cognitive development of participants in mind; leaders provide experiences that encourage individuals to question, integrate, analyze, communicate, apply cognitive concepts, gain a multicultural view of the world, and integrate physical activity experiences with their other life experiences.	Leaders fail to recognize and explore the unique roles of physical activities that allow individuals to learn to move while also moving to learn. Individuals do not receive opportunities to integrate their physical activity experiences with other experiences.
Affective development	Leaders intentionally design and teach activities that allow participants the opportunity to work together to improve their social and cooperation skills. These activities also contribute to the development of a positive self-concept. Leaders help all individuals experience and feel the satisfaction and joy that results from regular participation in physical activity.	Leaders fail to intentionally enhance the affective development of individuals when activities are excluded that foster the development of cooperation and social skills. Leaders ignore opportunities to help individuals understand the emotions they feel as a result of participation in physical activity.
Concepts of fitness	Individuals participate in activities that are designed to help them understand and value the important concepts of physical fitness and the contribution they make to a healthy lifestyle.	Individuals are required to participate in physical fitness activities, but are not helped to understand the reasons why.

Adapted from: *Developmentally Appropriate Physical Education Practices for Children,* Council on Physical Education for Children, National Association for Sport and Physical Education, American Alliance for Health, Physical Education, Recreation, and Dance. Modified to reflect developmentally appropriate physical activity programs for people of all ages in a diversity of settings.

Continued

TABLE 11-1 —cont'd

Program Component	Appropriate Practice	Inappropriate Practice
Physical fitness tests	Ongoing fitness assessment is used as a part of the ongoing process of helping individuals understand, enjoy, improve, and/or maintain their physical health and well-being. Test results are shared privately with individuals as a tool for developing their physical fitness knowledge, understanding, and competence. Individuals are physically prepared for the fitness assessment tests.	Physical fitness tests are given infrequently, solely for the purpose that they are required. Individuals are required to complete a physical fitness test battery without understanding why they are performing the tests or the implications of their individual results as they apply to their future health and well-being. Individuals are required to take physical fitness tests without adequate conditioning.
Calisthenics	Appropriate exercises are taught for the specific purpose of improving the skill, coordination, and/or fitness levels of individuals. Individuals are taught exercises that keep the body in proper alignment, thereby allowing the muscles to lengthen without placing stress and strain on the surrounding joints, ligaments, and tendons (e.g., sitting toe touch).	Individuals perform standardized calisthenics with no specific purpose in mind (e.g., jumping jacks, windmills). Exercises are taught that compromise body alignment and place unnecessary stress on the joints and muscles (e.g., deep knee bends, ballistic or bouncing stretches).
Fitness	Fitness activities are used to help individuals increase personal physical fitness levels in a supportive, motivating, and progressive manner, thereby promoting positive lifetime fitness attitudes.	Physical fitness activities are used by leaders as punishment for individuals' misbehavior (e.g., individuals running laps or doing push-ups, because they are off-task or slow to respond to instruction or the leader wants to teach them a lesson).
Assessment	Leaders' decisions are based primarily on ongoing individual assessments of persons as they participate in physical activities (formative evaluation), and not on the basis of a single test score (summative evaluation). Assessment of individuals' physical progress and achievement is used to personalize instruction, plan the program, identify individuals with special needs, and evaluate program effectiveness.	Individuals are evaluated on the basis of fitness test scores or on a single physical skill test.
Regular involvement	Individuals participate on a regularly scheduled basis because they recognize that it is an important part of their life and essential to their health.	Individuals participate infrequently or fail to recognize the value and contribution of regular participation to their life and health.

Continued

TABLE 11-1—cont'd

Program Component	Appropriate Practice	Inappropriate Practice
Active participation	All individuals are involved in activities that allow them to remain continuously active. Classes are designed to meet an individual's need for active participation in all learning experiences.	Activity time is decreased because of waiting for a turn, insufficient equipment, or organization into large groups. Individuals are eliminated from activities with no chance to reenter the activity.
Activities	Activities are selected, designed, sequenced, and modified by teachers and/or individuals to maximize learning and enjoyment.	Activities are taught with no obvious purpose or goals, other than to keep individuals "busy, happy, and good."
Equity	All individuals have equal access to activities. All individuals are equally encouraged, supported, and socialized toward successful achievement in all realms of physical activities, regardless of race or sex. Statements by leaders support leadership opportunities and provide positive reinforcement in a variety of activities that may be considered equitable.	Individuals' opportunities are limited because of traditional roles (feminine or masculine) and stereotypes. Prejudice and discrimination reduce opportunities for equitable participation.
Success rate	Individuals are given the opportunity to practice their skills at high rates of success adjusted for their individual skill levels.	Individuals are asked to perform activities that are too easy or too hard, causing frustration, boredom, and/or misbehavior. All individuals are expected to perform to the same standard with no allowance for individual abilities and interests.
Time	Individuals are given the opportunity to participate daily at a scheduled time; the length of time is appropriate for the developmental level of the individual.	There is no provision for regular physical activity. Individuals' age and maturational levels are not taken into account when the physical activity program is developed.
Facilities	Individuals are provided an environment in which they have adequate space to move freely and safely.	Classes are held in spaces not free from obstructions where opportunities to move are restricted.
Equipment	Enough equipment is available so that each individual benefits from maximum participation. Equipment is appropriate to each individual's size, skill, and confidence level so that they are motivated to participate.	An insufficient amount of equipment is available for the number of individuals present. Equipment used is inappropriate and may hamper skill development or injure or intimidate individuals.

Institutional tasks are activities related to the institution in which teaching occurs: that is, the school or organization for which the teacher works. In the school setting, teachers may be expected to assume hall duty or lunchroom supervision, attend curriculum or departmental meetings, and conduct parent-teacher conferences. Many physical educators note that counseling students about matters that affect the development of their physical selves and advising students on personal problems occupy a

Locker room supervision is one of a teacher's managerial responsibilities.

great amount of their time, but the opportunity to be of service to students in this manner is rewarding. In the nonschool setting, teachers may also perform institutional duties such as checking membership cards at the front desk, mailing promotional brochures to attract new members, and filling out a variety of reports. In some situations, managerial and institutional responsibilities occupy more of a teacher's time than actual teaching.

Teachers have numerous professional responsibilities in addition to the responsibilities previously described. Teachers may conduct research in an effort to push back the frontiers of knowledge. Another professional responsibility is to interpret the worth of physical education and sport to the public. This requires that physical educators be well versed in the scientific foundations of the discipline so that they may accurately interpret the worth of physical education and sport to others. Physical educators need to be cognizant that the programs they conduct reflect the aims and the worth of the field. Physical educators symbolize their commitment to the profession by being role models for what they preach; they should exemplify a healthy, active lifestyle. Professionals need to take advantage of opportunities to speak to educators, the community, and civic and other groups about their field of endeavor.

Many physical educators may also have community responsibilities. These are usually engaged in voluntarily. However, the special qualifications and skills of physical educators make them a likely target for requests from community groups to assist with youth and other sport programs such as Little League or adult recreational programs. Physical educators should be interested in providing leadership for such community programs. By exercising a leadership role, they can help ensure that such programs are organized and administered in the best interests of youths and adults. By their participation, physical educators are afforded an opportunity to interpret physical education and sport to the public in general. In doing so, physical educators become respected and important leaders in the community and gain greater support for their program.

Lifespan and Cultural Perspectives: Pedagogy

- How do the genders, race, or ethnicity of teachers and students affect their interactions?
- What are the consequences of burnout on teachers' and coaches' behaviors and their students'/athletes' learning?
- How do expert and novice teachers differ in their design and implementation of lessons?
- How does a student's ability influence a teacher's interaction?
- What challenges do beginning teachers face? How can we, as physical education teacher educators, prepare them for these challenges?
- Does grouping by skill ability enhance skill learning?
- How can more minorities be encouraged to enter physical education and coaching?
- How do students spend their time during instruction, and how can learning opportunities be increased?
- How does cultural competency influence adherence to physical activity programs for adults?
- How do teachers' personal preferences for sports affect their curriculum decisions?
- How can physical education be used to promote student responsibility?
- What is the most effective way to design instruction to meet the needs of students with specific disabilities?
- How can physical educators more effectively promote lifelong physical activity?

Teachers' responsibilities are not limited to teaching. They perform a wide variety of activities during the course of their workday. Managerial, administrative, institutional, and professional responsibilities are associated with teaching. The exact nature of these tasks may vary from setting to setting. Teaching opportunities in school and nonschool settings and with people of all ages will be discussed in the following section.

TEACHING CAREERS

If teaching is your career goal, there are many different opportunities for work. Traditionally, physical education teachers have worked in the school setting with children and youths. Today, however, there are teaching opportunities available in many settings outside of school, giving teachers the wonderful opportunity to work with people of all ages. (See Lifespan and Cultural Perspectives box.)

Teaching in the School Setting

Teaching positions in the school setting are available in public and private school systems, higher education, and specialized schools. Public and private schools are organized according to various administrative patterns. The traditional grade configuration is elementary school, which is composed of kindergarten and first through eighth grade, and high school, which is composed of grades 9 through 12. Another pattern that is used is the elementary, junior high, and high school configuration (i.e., grades K to 6, 7 to 9, and 10 to 12). An increasingly common pattern incorporates the middle school; here the grade configuration becomes K to 5, 6 to 8, and 9 to 12.

The number of preschool programs in the United States is growing rapidly. Currently 4-year-olds are enrolled in public school programs in more than 30 states. Some schools even enroll 3-year-olds. The National Education Association (NEA) recommends that a greater emphasis be placed on early childhood education for all children.[10] The growth of preschool programs has created additional opportunities for physical educators to work with young children to develop motor skills and promote the development of a healthy lifestyle.

In higher education, professional opportunities include teaching in 2-year junior colleges or community colleges and 4-year colleges or universities. There are also teaching positions for those professionals who want to work with persons with disabilities and for those who aspire to instruct in a professional preparation program. Teaching opportunities also exist in specialized schools, such as vocational and technical schools, as well as in developmental centers.

Teaching in an Elementary School

Physical education in an elementary school is emerging as the art and science of human movement. Quality elementary school programs and teachers seek to instill in children the why of movement, the how of movement, and the outcomes or physiological, psychological, and sociological results of movement. A primary objective of these programs is the sound development of movement skills and motor patterns that make up the movement repertoire of human beings.

Providing a quality physical education program for young children is critical. Participation in a quality program during these formative years will likely instill in the child a love for physical activity that may last a lifetime and a favorable attitude toward physical education. If the experience is negative, the youngster may come to hate physical education as well as physical activity, a feeling that could remain with him or her for life. Because of the close relationship between physical activity and health, this could have a significant impact on the quality of the child's life.

Movement experiences are recognized as educationally desirable in the early life of the child. This is the time when a solid movement foundation can be developed, providing children with a base for future physical development and achievement in various forms of physical activity. Furthermore, it is through movement that children express themselves, are creative, develop self-image, and gain a better understanding of their physical selves. It is through such movement experiences that young children explore, develop, and grow in a meaningful manner.

In the primary grades K to 3, great emphasis is placed on learning fundamental motor skills such as running, jumping, climbing, throwing, catching, kicking, and striking. Children participate in guided discovery and problem-solving activities focused on movement concepts, including body awareness, spatial awareness, qualities of movement, and relationships. Conceptually based programs further enhance the child's understanding of movement. Perceptual-motor activities help children to develop such necessary skills as eye-hand and eye-foot coordination, laterality and directionality, and tracking of an object.

The primary grade curriculum is concerned with developing within each child a positive self-image as a mover. Attention also should be given to developing desirable social skills, such as working with others. Individualized learning, in which students learn at their own pace, is compatible with problem solving, guided discovery, and a creative approach to learning for primary school children.

In the upper elementary school grades, the physical education curriculum focuses on refining fundamental motor skills and applying these skills to the development of sport-related skills. During this time, all children should be given the opportunity to participate in a wide range of sport and physical activities rather than be encouraged to specialize in a few selected sports. A school curriculum that offers soccer and football in the fall, basketball and volleyball in the winter, and softball and track in the spring is not providing the diversity of activities necessary to ensure optimum skill acquisition at these grade levels. In addition to being exposed to traditional team sports, students at this level should receive instruction in dance, gymnastics, and individual activities (e.g., track and, whenever possible, aquatics). Acquisition of knowledge relative to physical education and the development of qualities of good sportsmanship, leadership, and fellowship should be encouraged.

Specific state requirements should be considered in structuring the elementary school physical education program. Although there is no national curriculum, elementary school physical educators may find the guidelines developed by the Council on Physical Education for Children (COPEC), a substructure of NASPE of AAHPERD, helpful in designing and implementing their programs. COPEC recommends that a quality instructional program provide opportunities for each child to develop motor skills and efficient movement patterns,

Young children like to test their abilities, such as balance, in a variety of environments.

attain a high level of fitness, learn to communicate through movement, acquire self-understanding, interact socially, and achieve desired psychomotor, cognitive, and affective outcomes. COPEC guidelines also suggest that elementary school children participate in a quality physical education program for a minimum of 150 minutes per week.

Many reasons are given by physical educators for preferring teaching in the elementary schools. At this level, students typically are motivated, eager, and enthusiastic and take pride in their progress. Children at this age enjoy being active and have boundless energy. Many physical educators enjoy the challenge of working with children during their most impressionable and formative years. The rapid, visible skill improvement typical of elementary school students is rewarding and motivating to the teacher.

Teaching in a Middle School or Junior High School

Teaching students enrolled in a middle school or junior high school presents a unique series of challenges to physical educators. Students are in a period of their development that is fraught with physical, social, and emotional changes. Because of the anatomical and physiological characteristics of this age group, activities must be selected with care. Students at this level are in a period of rapid growth that causes them difficulty in coordinating their actions and often results in awkwardness and excessive fatigue. Students are faced with the task of coping with the myriad changes associated with puberty, including the development of secondary sex characteristics. Social and emotional changes are also experienced. The desire to be independent and the influence of peers are particularly strong. Physical educators need to be aware of and sensitive to the many changes students are experiencing. Students may often seek out the physical education teacher for guidance and support during this time of transition.

At this level, physical education programs should include a balance between individual and dual sport activities such as aquatics and tennis and team sport activities such as soccer and basketball. Dance, gymnastics, and fitness activities also should be an integral part of the curriculum. It is important to build on the skills and positive experiences of the elementary school level. Those students who have not progressed as rapidly as their peers in motor development should receive special attention to help them improve their skills. Students' knowledge of physical education should be further expanded and opportunities to apply this knowledge be provided. During these school years, students begin to specialize in certain physical activities and actively pursue those interests.

NASPE's Committee on Middle School Physical Education recommends that middle-school physical education programs provide opportunities for each student to engage in activities that promote motor skill and fitness development throughout life. Programs at this level should advance knowledge of physical education while enhancing social and emotional development through increased self-responsibility and self-direction. Within the physical education program, students should be grouped by interest and ability, and careful attention should be given to avoiding sex-role discrimination and stereotyping. A minimum of 250 minutes of physical education per week, distributed over at least 3 days, is recommended. Additional opportunities for students to participate in physical activity experiences should be provided through intramural programs, club activities, and, when appropriate, interscholastic sports.

Teaching in a High School

At the high school level, students exhibit increased physical, mental, social, and emotional maturity. This is the time of transition from adolescence to adulthood.

One of the primary goals for physical educators teaching at the secondary school level is to socialize students into the role of participants in physical activities suited to their needs and interests. Pangrazi and Darst[11] state that "the most important goal of a secondary physical education program should be to help youngsters incorporate some form of physical activity into their lifestyle." This means that teachers must design and implement physical education programs in such a manner that the students' attitudes, knowledge, and skills are developed with a view to realizing this objective. Pangrazi and Darst[11] contend that the ultimate measure of a successful high school physical education program is the "number of students who incorporate physical activities such as exercise, sport, dance, and outdoor adventure activities into their lifestyles."

The curriculum is generally oriented toward lifetime sports, although team sports also may be popular. It is critical that the physical educator take into consideration the interests and needs of the students in planning the curriculum. During this time, students should have the opportunity to develop sufficient skills so that when they leave school they will have the desire and the knowledge to participate in physical activities and sport successfully and enjoyably. Because many students do not continue on to college, it is essential that they acquire the competencies and interest before they leave high school.

NASPE's Secondary School Physical Education Council recommends that programs at the high school level focus on refining skills in a wide range of activities and on developing advanced skills in lifetime activities personally selected by the student. Students should learn how to develop personal programs to gain and maintain optimal levels of fitness throughout their lifetime. Knowledge of the scientific principles related to physical education, self-direction in the conduct of individual physical activity programs, and an appreciation of the role of physical activity and sport in society are also outcomes of a quality secondary school physical education program. It is recommended that daily physical education be provided for all students. The length of the class period, the size of the class, and the quality standards used for credit should be comparable with those used for other subject areas within the curriculum.

Many high school physical education programs, while required of the students, offer students the opportunity to select units in which they want to participate. An increasing number of schools have expanded their course offerings by using off-campus community facilities such as a golf course, an ice rink, an aquatics center, or a ski

A physical education instructor directs students in an exercise class at Ithaca College.

slope. The trend is toward providing students with increased knowledge and understanding of physical education concepts. This is often accomplished by offering minicourses on topics of interest, such as fitness or weight management, or by the integration of concepts, such as those pertaining to force production, into regular activity classes. Intramurals, interscholastic sports, and sport clubs offer students additional opportunities to participate in sport, develop expertise, and realize other desirable outcomes.

Teaching Physical Education in Higher Education

Prospective physical education teachers may also take advantage of opportunities to teach in higher education. Opportunities may be found to teach at 2-year community colleges or at 4-year colleges or universities. Often a master's degree in an area of physical education is a prerequisite to obtaining a job at this level. In some institutions, coaching responsibilities may be associated with teaching positions, whereas in other institutions, coaches carry no teaching responsibilities.

The status of general or basic instruction physical education programs* in colleges and universities in the United States has changed in recent years. At one time, many colleges and universities required all students to take a physical education course each semester—for example, one course a semester for two years. Today physical education at this level is usually voluntary, thus placing responsibility on the physical education department to offer courses that are appealing to students. Because of this need, curriculums at this level tend to be more flexible and to change more often in response to students' interests and needs.

Lifetime sports and recreational activities are emphasized at this level, including such activities as tennis, golf, self-defense, aerobic dance, and

*These programs are designed to serve all students on campus and are not to be confused with programs designed to educate prospective physical education and sport majors; those programs are referred to as professional preparation programs.

personal fitness; outdoor pursuits such as canoeing, camping, and rock climbing; and aquatic activities. Students may have the opportunity to enroll in theory courses. Class topics may include health concepts, cardiovascular fitness, principles of exercise, biomechanical principles, and development of personalized fitness programs. Some colleges offer courses called Wellness for Life or Fitness for Life. These courses combine theoretical information with laboratory experiences designed to help students acquire the knowledge and skills necessary to lead a healthy lifestyle.

Sport clubs provide interested participants an opportunity for social group experiences and enjoyment of a particular sport activity. Intramurals and intercollegiate sports play an important part in college and university physical education programs. They offer students additional opportunities for participation according to their abilities, needs, and interests.

Teaching Physical Education and Sport in Professional Preparation Programs

Professional preparation programs are designed to prepare students for careers in physical education, exercise science, and sport. Professionals who aspire to teach at the college and university level and are interested in shaping the direction of their field by preparing future leaders have many opportunities to render this valuable service in the more than 700 institutions that offer such programs.

The qualifications for teaching in professional preparation programs include advanced degrees, a strong academic record, an interest in and understanding of college students, a broad view of educational problems, and, many times, previous experience at elementary or secondary school levels. The college teacher must be particularly well versed and highly competent in the field.

A professor in a professional preparation program may teach theory courses in the subdisciplines and related areas such as history and philosophy of physical education, assessment, motor control, motor learning, motor development, biomechanics, exercise physiology, curriculum and methods, organization and administration, sociology of sport, sport psychology, and adapted physical education. These individuals typically possess doctorate degrees in their areas of expertise. Individuals who aspire to teach in professional preparation programs may also teach professional activity and skills courses, as well as courses in coaching methods. These individuals usually possess a high degree of skill in their areas of expertise. Professionals teaching activity and skills courses possess master's degrees, and some individuals may have earned doctorate degrees.

In addition to their teaching responsibilities, teachers are expected to conduct research, participate on department and college or university committees, and advise and counsel students. These teachers are expected to write for professional publications, perform community service, consult, and participate in the work of professional organizations.

The services rendered by physical educators in professional preparation programs can be rewarding. By a teacher's providing experiences that will help develop desirable qualities, competencies, and attributes in students preparing to become leaders in the field, and by doing an outstanding job in this training experience, a teacher's work will live on forever in the lives of students and other leaders of future generations.

Teaching Adapted Physical Activity

Teaching physical education to students with disabilities is another career opportunity. Students with disabilities include those with mental and emotional impairments, physical challenges such as cerebral palsy or amputation, vision and hearing problems, speech disorders, learning disabilities, and other health impairments such as asthma, heart problems, and cancer. Adapted physical activity focuses on adapting or modifying physical activity to meet the needs of students. "Good" physical education is adapted physical education, for the heart of quality physical education and adapted physical activity is education that is developmentally appropriate for the needs of the individual student. With the advent of P.L. 94-142 and other legislation, students with disabilities have the opportunity to participate in physical education.

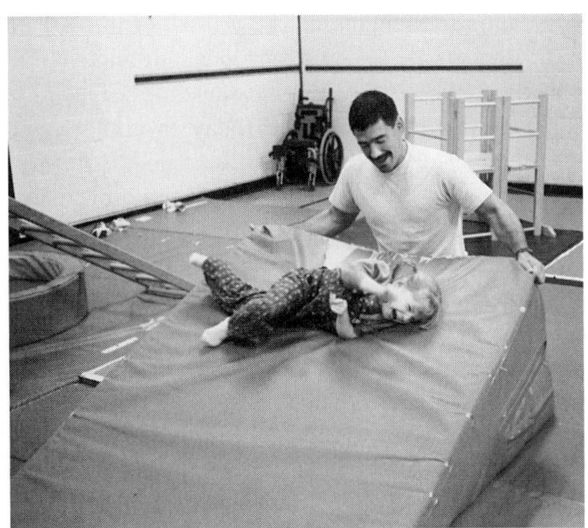

Adapted physical education focuses on modifying activities to meet students' needs.

By law, each identified student with a disability must have an individualized education plan, or IEP. Physical education is mandated by law to be included in each student's educational program. Physical education teachers have the opportunity to participate in the design of the individual plan.

There are several approaches to the inclusion of children with disabilities into the educational setting, including physical education. The least restrictive environment approach places students with disabilities in an educational setting that matches the students' abilities and provides as much freedom as possible. For some students, this may be a placement, with or without an aide, in a "regular" physical education class with peers who are not disabled, or it may be placement into a special class or adapted physical education. These classes are generally smaller and contain only children with special needs. The placement of students with disabilities into the regular class is referred to as "mainstreaming."

In the 1990s, some educators have advocated that students with disabilities be placed in the regular class setting, including physical education. This inclusive approach insists that all students, regardless of their disability and its severity, be placed in the regular classroom in the neighborhood school. Supplemental aids and services are used to help students with disabilities achieve success in the regular class setting. There is considerable debate within many communities about the use of inclusion. Many regular teachers do not feel qualified to include children with special needs in their classes. They feel they lack the specialized training to provide them with a quality educational experience.

Physical education teachers may render many different services to individuals with disabilities. Some schools or school districts have an adapted physical education specialist who provides direct services to individuals with disabilities. In other settings, the adapted physical educator serves as a consultant to help other teachers provide needed services.

All physical education teachers should be prepared to work with students with disabilities. Physical educators will be involved in the writing of IEPs. These plans may focus on helping students to correct physical conditions that can be improved with exercise, assisting each student to achieve the highest level of physical fitness within his or her capabilities, aiding the student to identify physical activities and sports suited to his or her abilities and interests, and providing each student with positive experiences conducive to the development of a healthy self-concept.

Prospective physical education teachers interested in working with individuals with disabilities should prepare for this opportunity by taking additional course work in the area of adapted physical activity and special education. Try to obtain practical experience working with individuals with disabilities as part of your preparation for a physical education career.

Physical education teachers can also become certified as adapted physical educators. The Adapted Physical Education National Standards Project was designed to ensure that physical education for students with disabilities is provided by qualified physical educators. As part of this project, national standards were developed and a certification examination was designed to measure knowledge of these standards. The first exam was given in May 1997.

Physical educators interested in taking the certification examination must demonstrate that they have a bachelor's degree in physical education, 200 hours of documented practicum experience in adapted physical education, and have successfully completed at least one 3-credit-hour survey course in adapted physical education. They should also study the Adapted Physical Education National Standards to make sure that they have the broad-based knowledge of physical education required of adapted physical education specialists. Teachers who pass the exam are certified for 7 years and can use the acronym CAPE (Certified Adapted Physical Educator) after their name. They are listed in the National Registry of Certified Adapted Physical Educators that is distributed to each state education department. They also receive 1-year free membership in the National Consortium for Physical Education and Recreation for Individuals with Disabilities (NCPERID).

Currently there are almost 50 million persons in the United States with disabilities. A majority of those who are school aged are receiving their education in regular educational settings. It is important that all people preparing to teach physical education be able to teach individuals with special needs.

A diversity of opportunities exists for individuals interested in teaching in the school setting. These opportunities involve teaching people of all ages. Many opportunities also can be found for the physical educator who is interested in working overseas. Teacher exchange programs and the Peace Corps offer the opportunity to teach in elementary and secondary schools, as well as colleges and universities, in other countries. The United States Armed Forces also operates elementary and secondary schools on overseas bases for students of personnel; it is not necessary to be a member of the military to teach in these schools. Job possibilities are numerous for the prospective physical education teacher who actively seeks a position teaching in the schools.

Teaching in Nonschool Settings

Obtaining teacher certification in physical education opens up many doors for you. Opportunities to teach physical education outside of the school setting continue to increase. The growth of interest in sport by people of all ages has stimulated the growth of these other teaching avenues. Teaching opportunities may be found today in commercial sport clubs, community recreational and sport programs, resorts, the Armed Forces, senior citizen and retirement centers, and correctional institutions.

The requirements for employment in these positions, working conditions, salaries, and other benefits vary widely. Some of these teaching positions require a high level of expertise in a particular sport, whereas others require individuals able to teach a diversity of activities. Working hours vary a great deal as well. For some positions, hours are often dictated by the times clients or students are available. If one is working with youths, hours are likely to be after school and on the weekends. If one is working with adults, hours tend to be on the weekends and in the evenings. Daytime work is also available, however. These positions may pay on an hourly basis, have a set salary (which can vary from $15,000 to $25,000 a year or more), or may pay based on the number of students taught. Benefits may vary from none to complete medical, dental, and life insurance plans.

Some teaching positions in nonschool settings require that individuals assume other responsibilities as well. These may include public relations work, soliciting memberships, record keeping, and equipment and facility maintenance.

Some work may be seasonal in nature, depending on the climate and/or type of facility. For example, if you were a teacher and/or director of aquatics at an outdoor facility in the northeastern United States, your employment would probably last from June to September; working at an indoor facility in the Northeast would likely result in a year-round position. In the Southwest, the same job might be year round, regardless of the type of facility.

Because these jobs, in essence, require teaching skills, many physical educators who desire to teach in the nonschool setting also complete the requirements for teaching certification. By doing so, they increase their range of job opportunities. Other physical educators, having prepared for teaching in the schools, look to these other avenues

Physical educators may find teaching and coaching opportunities outside the school setting. This instructor, for example, teaches in a preschool gymnastics program.

of employment when they are unable to find a teaching position suited to their needs and interests or as a means of part-time and summer employment. Many employers hiring physical educators to fill these positions also view favorably the credentials of those applicants able to list a teaching certificate on their resume. For some positions special certificates may be required, such as certification by the Professional Golfers' Association (PGA) or Ladies Professional Golfers' Association (LPGA) as a golf professional.

The physical educator should also understand why adults and youths seek instruction. Adults seek instruction at these organizations for many reasons. First, they may not have had instruction in the activity or activities during their youth in their physical education classes. Second, they may seek instruction for their own personal growth and pleasure. Instruction may be sought for social reasons, such as the desire to be able to participate in specific activities with friends and family. For example, some adults may seek instruction in golf to be able to successfully participate with business associates in this accepted social activity. The desire to improve and refine one's performance by seeking instruction from a professional is often cited as the reason for enrolling in instructional classes.

Youths enroll in these organizational programs and classes for many of the same reasons as adults. Additionally, youths may enroll in certain activity classes because instruction or interscholastic competition in that activity is not offered in their school. Youths desiring to develop more advanced skills such as in gymnastics or to compete in certain sport activities such as swimming may find that these organizations offer experiences that meet their needs. Youths and their parents may seek expert instruction because of aspirations to be a professional player such as in golf and tennis or because of the desire to successfully compete for a college scholarship in certain sport areas; they may find nonschool instructional opportunities essential to the realization of these goals.

Teaching in Commercial Sport Clubs

In recent years the number of commercial sport clubs and facilities has grown tremendously. Tennis and racquetball clubs, gymnastics clubs, swimming clubs, country clubs offering golf and tennis, karate and judo schools, and bowling establishments are examples of commercial sport enterprises.

Since commercial sport clubs usually focus on a particular sport, physical educators who desire to teach in such an organization should possess a high level of expertise in a particular sport. In many instances this expertise can be gained through participation in intercollegiate athletics. Many physical educators also have gained expertise by participating in private clubs such as gymnastic clubs during their youth and continuing their participation throughout their college years. Teaching responsibilities may include private lessons as well as group lessons. There may be the opportunity to coach high-level performers as well. Additional responsibilities may include setting up tournaments such as in a tennis and racquetball club, selling sport equipment and apparel such as in a golf pro shop at a country club, or transporting individuals to competitions such as in a swimming club or a gymnastics club. Many commercial clubs also expect the teachers to assume managerial responsibilities at times.

Employers, in addition to requiring a high level of expertise as a condition of employment, may also require certification. In the aquatics area, certification as a water safety instructor, lifeguard instructor, and in pool management may be required. Certification as a golf professional such as through the PGA and LPGA may be necessary. Where not required, certificates may enhance one's employment opportunities.

Teaching in Youth and Community Organizations

The Young Men's Hebrew Association (YMHA), the Young Women's Hebrew Association (YWHA), the YMCA, and the YWCA and similar organizations such as Boys' Clubs, Girls' Clubs, and the 4-H Clubs serve both the youth and adult populations in the community. Religious training was originally the main purpose of many of these organizations. However, sport and fitness are now an important part of their programs. Included in the programs are classes in various physical activities; athletic leagues for industry employees, youth, and adults; and young people's groups. The cost of financing such organizations is usually met through membership dues, community and business contributions, and private contributions.

These organizations are designed to improve participants socially, physically, morally, mentally, and spiritually through their programs of physical activity. Usually these organizations employ physical educators and recreation specialists to teach a wide diversity of activities. In many communities, events are scheduled from early morning to late at night—early-bird swim at 6 A.M. for business and professional people before work and late-hour racquetball games. Besides instructing clients in sport activities, the physical educator may have the opportunity to serve as a coach of a team. Many youth clubs offer young people and adults the opportunity to compete on athletic teams at the local, state, regional, and national levels. Additional responsibilities include developing health and fitness programs, managing facility and budget, and supervising personnel. Many centers, in addition to physical activities, offer programs in exercise and fitness evaluation, cardiac rehabilitation, and health counseling. A background in these areas as well as in teaching would be helpful in seeking employment. Although salaries vary, they are comparable to public school teaching positions.

Although the YMCA, YWCA, YMHA, and YWHA certainly constitute widespread organizations, they are not the only community organizations offering employment opportunities to the physical educator. Other opportunities include working for town and city recreation departments, community centers, youth centers similar in nature to the YMCA/YWCA, and playgrounds. Some of these opportunities may be seasonal, generally available in the summer, but the trend is for more and more programs to operate year round. These programs provide instruction in physical activities for people of all ages, recreational sport leagues, and recreational activities. In addition to jobs teaching and coaching for these organizations, other job possibilities include the supervision of personnel and program development.

Teaching opportunities outside of the school setting include working with adults providing specialized instruction in many different activities. This yoga instructor assists a student in attaining the correct posture.

Teaching in Centers for the Elderly

In recent years, elderly persons have received considerable attention from the U.S. government and other agencies. The elderly comprise over 11% of the population, and this percentage is increasing yearly. There is also concern for the physical fitness of elderly persons and their need to be physically active to maintain a state of optimum health. In recent years programs for elderly persons offered by recreational agencies, retirement centers, and health-care facilities have expanded in the number and types of offerings.

Many of these programs offer instruction in physical activities suited to the abilities and interests of the participants. Exercise is frequently included in these programs. In addition to the physical benefits, physical education programs provide the opportunity for socialization. Physical educators interested in working in such programs may benefit from classes in adapted physical education, sociology, psychology, and gerontology.

Teaching in Resorts

The increase in leisure time has stimulated an increase in the travel and tourism industry. The number of resorts has grown, and many resorts offer instruction in various physical activities as part of their programs. Activities offered may include sailing, scuba, tennis, golf, swimming, water skiing, and snow skiing. Expertise in specific sport areas is required for employment in these resorts. Instruction is usually done in small groups or in private lessons. Additionally, responsibilities may include managerial activities and directing social activities. Pay varies, and depending on the location of the resort, work may be seasonal, although many resorts operate year round. Working in a resort offers many desirable side benefits, such as working in an attractive location and usually lush surroundings, and the opportunity to work with changing clientele.

Teaching in the Military

The Army, Navy, Marines, Air Force, Coast Guard, and National Guard have extensive physical activity programs that aid in keeping service personnel in good physical and mental condition. In addition to the personnel used to direct the fitness and physical training programs of these organizations, physical educators are needed to instruct service personnel in physical activities and sport for use in their leisure time. The military sponsors extensive recreational programs on its bases, and qualified personnel are needed to direct these programs. Coaches are also needed to assist military athletes in their training for competitions throughout the world. The military also sponsors schools for children of military personnel. Physical educators who desire to teach overseas may wish to consider employment in these schools. For many of these positions, physical educators do not have to belong to the military.

Physical educators interested in further information about these opportunities should talk to their local military recruiter.

TEACHING CERTIFICATION

Each state has established minimum requirements that must be met by prospective teachers before they become legally certified to teach. The certification of teachers protects schoolchildren by ensuring a high level of teaching competency and the employment of qualified personnel. Many states require that candidates for teaching positions take a standardized test, such as PRAXIS. These standardized tests usually consist of a core battery that tests general knowledge (e.g., knowledge pertaining to art, literature, history, science), communication skills, and professional knowledge. Some states require that students take an additional test in their speciality area, such as physical education. Different states have different passing score requirements for the standardized tests. Some states have their own certification examinations. For example, New York requires that teachers take the New York Teacher Certification Examinations.

Because certification procedures and requirements vary from state to state, prospective teachers should obtain the exact requirements from their college or university or by directly contacting the state education department. Because of variations in state requirements, a certificate to teach in one state is not necessarily valid in another state. However, reciprocity among states in a region is increasingly common. Sometimes, where there is not reciprocity, prospective teachers can become certified in another state by merely taking a few additional required courses.

Teaching certificates are required to teach in the public schools. Some private schools may not require their teachers to possess a certificate. Teaching certificates are also an asset to individuals desiring to teach in nonschool settings. Prospective employers may be impressed by candidates who have fulfilled the necessary requirements for certification.

COACHING CAREERS

Many prospective physical educators aspire to a career as a coach. Because a teaching certificate is required by many states to coach, many aspiring coaches enroll in a program of study leading to a teaching certificate in physical education. Some of these prospective coaches seek a dual career as a teacher and a coach, whereas others desire solely to coach and view a teaching career as a means to attain their ultimate ambition.

Within the last three decades, coaching opportunities have increased tremendously. The passage of Title IX legislation promoted the growth of interscholastic and intercollegiate competition for girls and women. The increased interest in sport by people of all ages also served as a stimulus to increase opportunities in competitive athletics.

As with teaching, coaching opportunities today exist in both the school and nonschool setting. In the school setting at the interscholastic level, coaches work with middle-school, junior high school, and high school athletes. Intercollegiate coaching opportunities are found in 2-year

More and more people with disabilities are participating in sports and taking an active role in coaching. Helping to lead the way is Brad Parks, founder of the National Foundation for Wheelchair Tennis.

community colleges as well as 4-year colleges and universities.

Outside of the school settings are many different coaching opportunities. Some young people aspire to coach at the professional level. An increasing number of coaching opportunities are available in commercial or private clubs, such as coaching elite gymnasts or young tennis professionals. Community-based programs offer a multitude of coaching opportunities.

In the past two decades, participation in sport by older adults and people with disabilities has increased. For example, in 1999, more than 12,000 world-class senior athletes participated in the U.S. Summer National Senior Games—the Senior Olympics. This is one of the premier competitions for athletes age 50 and over. The Special Olympics for individuals with mental retardation, the Paralympics, and the Games for the Deaf are attracting record numbers of participants. Coaching opportunities within these populations are increasing as these athletes strive to be their best.

Teaching responsibilities may be associated with coaching. At the interscholastic level, it is expected that coaches will teach classes in the school; often coaches teach physical education. At the collegiate level, some coaches are hired solely to coach and have no teaching responsibilities. At other higher education institutions, coaches may have teaching responsibilities in the general physical education program or in the professional preparation program. Administrative responsibilities also may be associated with coaching.

Choosing a Coaching Career

Individuals aspire to a coaching career for many reasons: their love for the sport, their own previous involvement on athletic teams, and the enjoyment they derived from participation. The desire to continue this involvement and association with athletics, perhaps to share some of what one has learned through athletics, is a strong motivating factor in selecting a coaching career. Individuals may choose to coach because of the profound influence one of their coaches had on their lives. Having a coach who was a positive role model and a desire to emulate this individual can influence one's decision to pursue a coaching career.

Many choose to coach because of their love of children. The opportunity to work with highly skilled and motivated individuals is often cited as a reason for coaching. Many coaches enter the profession because of their belief that participation in athletics can be a positive experience; they are committed to providing opportunities by which young people can develop to their fullest potential, both as athletes and as individuals.

Coaching is a highly visible occupation. Coaches may have a great deal of influence and power within both the institution and the community. The excitement, attention, influence, and recognition associated with coaching make it an attractive career choice.

What Are the Benefits and Drawbacks of Coaching?

Like teaching, a coaching career has both advantages and disadvantages. Many intrinsic rewards are associated with coaching. The opportunity to work with athletes and strive side by side with them to achieve their fullest potential, the excitement of winning and the satisfaction associated with giving the best of oneself, and the respect accorded to a coach are some of the intrinsic benefits of coaching.

Several drawbacks are associated with coaching. The hours are often long and arduous. The practice hours and the hours spent coaching during a competition are the most visible indications of the amount of time involved in coaching. Untold hours may be spent in preparing practices, reviewing the results of games and planning for the next encounter, counseling athletes, performing public relations work, and, at the collegiate level, recruiting.

Salaries vary greatly depending on the level coached, the sport coached, and the coach's position as head or assistant coach. Salaries at the high school level can range from a small stipend to a

Coaches fulfill many different responsibilities, including helping athletes put winning and losing in perspective.

few thousand dollars, whereas coaches at the collegiate and professional levels may have contracts worth hundreds of thousands of dollars.

A high turnover rate is associated with coaching. Unlike teachers, coaches are often placed under tremendous pressure to achieve—to have a winning season. Many coaches are fired because of a lackluster win/loss record or for having a poor working relationship with the administration or alumni. Other coaches choose to leave the profession voluntarily, overwhelmed by the pressures and exhausted by the demands, suffering from burnout, disenchanted with the profession, or desirous of a career change.

Role conflict is one problem some teachers and coaches struggle with in an effort to balance their jobs as teacher and coach. Individuals occupy many different roles in our society, both personally and professionally. Both positions or roles—teaching and coaching—carry with them responsibilities and associated expectations for performance. Both roles carry a multitude of responsibilities that often consume many hours—preparing lessons, formalizing practice plans, teaching classes, conducting practices, and a myriad host of other demands. Additionally, personal and external expectations relative to performance induce pressure. Teachers are expected to teach challenging lessons to all students, maintain discipline, participate on school committees, and fulfill many other functions. Coaches are expected to conduct practices in preparation for games, motivate athletes to achieve, interact with the public and press, and many times go on the road to scout the opponent. These and many more demands are coupled with the pressure to win.

Sometimes the pressure to do it all and do it well can be overwhelming. Role conflict occurs when teachers/coaches, in an effort to fulfill the demands associated with these two roles, have to make choices about how to apportion their time and effort in order to juggle the demands of these multiple roles. The perceived value of each of the roles affects how teachers-coaches choose to balance their demands. Teachers hired to instruct physical education and committed to delivering a quality physical education try to maintain that goal in the face of pressures to produce a winning team as a coach. To resolve this conflict, some teachers choose to spend less time on their teaching, perhaps to the extent that they offer a "roll out the ball" physical education program. This compromise in use of time and values allows teachers to spend more time on their coaching, a role for which there is often more public recognition and reward. However, achieving success in coaching, one role, may be the result of reducing effort directed toward the other role, teaching. Trying to resolve this conflict between multiple roles can be stressful and can result in a decrease in the quality of performance. Yet many teachers and coaches successfully balance the demands and conduct high-quality physical education programs while helping students to achieve in the athletic arena.

Teaching and Coaching

Because coaching is in essence teaching, the qualities that exemplify good teachers—organizational, communication, human relations, instructional, and motivational skills—may also be characteristics of effective coaches. Coaches must be able to organize their practices to provide maximum opportunities for all players to learn the skills and strategies essential for play. They must be actively engaged in monitoring the efforts of their athletes. They must be able to communicate what is to be learned in a clear manner and provide athletes with appropriate feedback to improve their performances. Coaches must instill in each athlete a feeling of self-worth and self-confidence, and be able to motivate all players to put forth their utmost effort to achieve their goals.

Many qualities characterize the outstanding coach. First, this person has the ability to teach the fundamentals and strategies of the sport: he or she must be a good teacher. Second, the coach understands the player: how a person functions at a particular level of development, with a full appreciation for skeletal growth, muscular development, and physical and emotional limitations. Third, he or she understands the game coached. Thorough knowledge of techniques, rules, and so on is basic. Fourth, the coach is a model for the players, a person of strong character. Patience, understanding, kindness, honesty, sportsmanship, sense of right and wrong, courage, cheerfulness, affection, humor, energy, and enthusiasm are imperative.

Although coaching is similar in nature to teaching, there are some dissimilarities. Both teachers and coaches are engaged in instructional activities and both must provide opportunities for the learners—students and athletes—to attain the skills and knowledge presented. However, coaches must have the expertise to teach their athletes more advanced skills and are held much more accountable for their athletes' learning than teachers are for their students. The caliber of a coach's instruction is scrutinized by both the administration and the public. If a coach has failed to prepare the athletes for competition or their learning appears inadequate (by the often used standard of the win/loss record), the coach may be dismissed. Teachers, on the other hand, have less pressure and less accountability for their students' learning, and even if their success rate is not high, they will most likely be allowed to retain their position. The coach must work in a pressure-filled arena, whereas the teacher works in a less-stressful environment.

Teachers must work with a diversity of skill levels and interests within their classes. Students may be mandated to take gym class and may be difficult to motivate. In contrast, coaches work with highly skilled athletes who often possess a high level of commitment to their sport. Their decision to participate is voluntary, and they may be united in their effort toward a common goal. Thus, although there are some similarities between teaching and coaching, there are some striking differences.

Coaching Responsibilities

Many responsibilities are associated with coaching. As in teaching, these responsibilities may be classified as instructional, managerial, and institutional in nature.

The coach's instructional responsibilities include conducting practice and coaching during the game. Although the coach is working with highly skilled athletes, the coach must be a good teacher to instruct the athletes in the more advanced skills and strategies necessary to perform at this level. During practices and games, the coach must motivate the athletes to put forth their best effort so that their optimal level of performance can be achieved. In many cases, these instructional responsibilities may be the least time consuming of all the coach's responsibilities.

Many coaches spend untold hours evaluating practices and the results of competitions and then using this information to plan for forthcoming practices and competitions. For those coaches fortunate enough to have assistant coaches, time must be spent with them reviewing this information and delegating responsibilities for future practices and games. Team managers may relieve the coach of many of the necessary but time-consuming managerial tasks such as dealing with equipment or recording statistics. Additionally, the coach must take care of the necessary public relations functions such as calling in contest results, giving interviews, and speaking in front of groups. Where allowed, recruiting occupies a tremendous amount of time. Phoning prospective athletes, arranging for campus meetings, talking with parents, and scouting contests for potential athletes adds many hours to the day.

The institutional responsibilities are many as well. Interscholastic coaches are expected to take part in many school activities in addition to their teaching responsibilities. Intercollegiate coaches may be expected to attend athletic department meetings or represent the institution on a community committee.

Many other responsibilities and expectations are associated with coaching. Coaches occupy highly visible positions in their institution. In institutions of higher education, it is not uncommon for more students to recognize the face of the football or basketball coach than the face of the college president. The coach is expected to reflect a positive image and reflect the values associated

Coaches spend countless hours preparing for games and practices.

with sport. The actions of the coach as the team wins or loses will influence the public's opinion of the sport program. Establishing and maintaining positive relationships with the community, alumni, and parents is often seen as vital to a coach's success in generating support for the athletic program. Because of their influence and visibility, coaches may be sought after to take an active part in community and civic affairs. They may be called on to train volunteer coaches for community recreational and sport programs or to spearhead a fund-raising drive for United Way.

Many other duties are incumbent on the coach by virtue of his or her position. The coach, because of the close relationship that develops from the many hours of working with his or her athletes toward a common goal, often undertakes the role of counselor with athletes or assumes the role of a surrogate parent. Athletes turn to their coach for advice about myriad problems. Athletes may have problems associated with their athletic performance or financial, academic, and/or personal concerns. Because of their positions as leaders, coaches are viewed as role models. They are expected to exemplify the highest standards of conduct and are under pressure to live up to these expectations.

Coaches must fulfill many professional responsibilities. Coaches must attend sport and rules clinics so that they are aware of the current trends and latest rule changes in the sport. They are often active in professional organizations related to the sport they coach as well as professional organizations such as AAHPERD. They may be called on to serve as clinicians at some of these groups' meetings or asked to write an article for a professional journal.

The responsibilities and expectations associated with coaching are many. Instructional, managerial, institutional, community, and professional responsibilities compose the work of the coach.

University of Tennessee Head Women's Basketball Coach Pat Head Summitt demonstrates leadership and commitment to her sport and her athletes.

Securing a Coaching Position

Depending on the level you wish to coach, you can take several steps to enhance your chances of securing the coaching position you desire. First, coaching requires a great deal of expertise. Playing experience in the sport you wish to coach may be helpful in this respect. Attending clinics and workshops on advanced techniques and rules may add to your knowledge. Consider becoming a rated official in your sport. Take advantage of coaching certification and licensing programs, such as the one offered for soccer by the United States Soccer Federation. Second, particularly for coaching at the interscholastic level, a teaching certificate may be required. However, this depends on the state in which you wish to coach. Coaching at the intercollegiate level often requires a master's degree.

Prospective coaches should consider developing expertise in a second sport, preferably one that is not in season at the same time as your major sport. For example, if one aspires to coach soccer, a fall sport, one should develop expertise in a spring sport such as lacrosse, baseball, or softball.

In many institutions, at both the interscholastic and intercollegiate levels, coaches may be required to coach two sport activities or sometimes be the head coach in one sport and serve as an assistant coach in a second sport. At other institutions, a coach may be involved in one sport throughout the year because of the length of the season.

Practical experience is helpful as well. Volunteering to serve as an assistant coach or working with a youth sport program as a coach during your undergraduate preparation is a step in the right direction and is an invaluable experience. It is important that prospective coaches realize that oftentimes one must be willing to work in other positions in the coaching organization before achieving the head coaching position desired. Serving as a junior varsity coach, working as a graduate assistant coach, or accepting a position as an assistant coach can be helpful in attaining a head coaching position at the desired level.

Certification of Coaches

Criteria for certification of coaches at the interscholastic level vary from state to state. In 1987, only 21 states mandated that interscholastic coaches possess a teaching certificate, although not necessarily in physical education.[10] Furthermore, the increased need for coaches and the lack of teachers available to fulfill these needs has led to the hiring of many nonteacher coaches. In 1997, the number of states allowing nonteacher coaches was 49.[12] As a result, many individuals who hold coaching positions lack the professional preparation and competencies so necessary to conduct educationally sound and safe programs. To address the lack of preparation, 28 states require coach education.[12]

Additionally, concern has been expressed by professionals regarding the qualifications and preparation of youth sport coaches. Millions of children participate in youth sport; millions of adults serve as volunteer coaches. Some of these coaches have excellent credentials and do an outstanding job in keeping winning in perspective and enhancing the development of the young athletes entrusted to their care. Other coaches lack preparation in safety, skill development, organization, training and conditioning, and the needs of young athletes. To address these concerns, coaching standards and numerous coaching education programs have been established.

The National Association for Sport and Physical Education (NASPE) developed National Standards for Athletic Coaches to provide a national framework for organizations and agencies that provide coaching education and training (see the National Standards box). Knowledge, skills, and values associated with effective and appropriate coaching of athletes were organized into 37 standards, grouped into eight domains. The eight domains are as follows:

- Injuries: Prevention, Care, and Management.
- Risk Management.
- Growth, Development, and Learning.
- Training, Conditioning, and Nutrition.
- Social/Psychological Aspects of Coaching.
- Skills, Tactics, and Strategies.
- Teaching and Administration.
- Professional Preparation and Development.

These standards are not a coaching certification program but a framework for the education of coaches.[13]

In 2001, the Coaches Council of NASPE published The Coaches Code of Conduct, to which coaches at all levels should be held accountable.[14] The Coaches Code of Conduct is designed to maximize the mental, physical, and social development of athletes. In addition to possessing the competencies outlined in the National Standards for Athletic Coaches, coaches should adhere to the 18 standards of conduct. Examples of the standards are listed below:

- "Coaches are responsible to ensure that the health, well-being and development of athletes take precedence over the win/loss record.
- Coaches accept that they do serve as role models and there must be congruency between their actions and their words.

National Standards for Athletic Coaches Domain and Sample Standards

Domain: Injuries: Prevention, Care and Management

Standard 5 Be able to plan, coordinate and implement procedures for appropriate emergency care.

Domain: Risk Management

Standard 9 Understand the scope of legal responsibilities that comes with assuming a coaching position, i.e., proper supervision, planning and instruction, matching participants, safety, first aid and risk management.

Domain: Growth, Development and Learning

Standard 14 Understand the social and emotional development of the athletes being coached, know how to recognize problems related to this development, and know where to refer them for appropriate assistance when necessary.

Domain: Training, Conditioning and Nutrition

Standard 25 Demonstrate effective motivational skills and provide positive, appropriate feedback.

Domain: Skills, Tactics and Strategies

Standard 33 Organize, conduct and evaluate less practice sessions with regard to established program goals that are less appropriate for different stages of the season.

Domain: Teaching and Administration

Standard 34 Know the key elements of sport less principles and technical skills as well as the various teaching methods less that can be used to introduce and refine them.

Domain: Professional Preparation and Development

Standard 36 Demonstrate organizational and less administrative efficiency in implementing sports programs, e.g., less event management, budgetary procedures, facility maintenance, participation in public relations activities.

NASPE: National Standards for Athletic Coaches, Reston, Va., 1994, AAHPERD.

- Coaches exemplify honesty, integrity, fair play, and sportsmanship regardless of the impact that might have on the outcome of the competition.
- Coaches maintain a professional demeanor in their relationships with their athletes, officials, colleagues, administrators and the public, and treat them with respect and dignity.
- Coaches are committed to the education of their athletes and should encourage academic achievement."[14]

The Coaches Code of Conduct, in conjunction with the National Standards for Athletic Coaches, provides coaches with guidelines for their behavior and for enhancing the experience of athletes in their programs.

There are several coaching certification programs sponsored by private and professional organizations. The American Sport Education Program (ASEP) is the most widely used coaching education program in the United States. Rainer Martens, founder of ASEP, states: "ASEP is committed to improving amateur sport by encouraging coaches, officials, administrators, parents, and athletes to embrace the 'athletes first, winning second' philosophy, and by providing the education to put the philosophy to work."[15] ASEP provides education at three levels: volunteer level primarily for youth sport coaches, leader level for leaders of scholastic and club sports, and master level for those who aspire to higher levels of competency. Educational programs are designed for sport parents, sport coaches, and sport directors. ASEP provides training in coaching the young athlete, coaching principles, sports first aid, drugs and sport, teaching sports skills, and a variety of sport sciences. Some ASEP courses can be completed online. ASEP has been selected by the National Federation of State High School Associations, the YMCA, and thousands of high schools for their coaching education programs.

The National Youth Sports Coaches Association (NYSCA) has been active in the training, support, and continuing education of coaches of youth sports teams. NYSCA reports that 1.3 million individuals have become NYSCA certified coaches since the inception of the program in 1981.[16] Volunteer coaches attend training clinics, pass an exam, and sign a pledge committing them to uphold the standards set forth in the NYSCA Code of Ethics. As a continuing member, coaches receive the quarterly *Youth Sports Journal,* excess liability insurance, and accident/medical insurance.

Other coaching certification programs are available, such as PACE (Program for Athletic Coaches Education), a branch of the Institute for the Study of Youth Sports. PACE seeks to provide "interscholastic coaches with the latest information pertaining to their day-to-day responsibilities.[17] Specific sports also may have certification programs for their coaches. Coaching certification programs may also be offered at the local level—for example, by the recreation department in charge of youth sports in a community.

Young professionals aspiring to coach should prepare carefully for assumption of this important responsibility. They may accomplish this through an undergraduate professional preparation program or by enrolling in a coaching certification program. Athletic participation and the practical experience of working as an assistant coach or a volunteer youth sport coach in a community program can enhance the professional qualifications of prospective coaches.

BURNOUT

Burnout is a problem among teachers and coaches. Noted researcher Christina Maslach defines job burnout as "a psychological syndrome in response to chronic interpersonal stressors on the job. The three key dimensions of this response are an overwhelming exhaustion, feelings of cynicism and detachment from the job, and a sense of ineffectiveness and lack of accomplishment."[16] Exhaustion refers to "feelings of being overextended and depleted of one's emotional and physical resources."[18] Cynicism is reflected in "a negative, callous, or excessively detached response to various aspects of the job."[18] Reduced efficacy or accomplishment refers to "feelings of incompetence and lack of achievement and productivity at work."[18] Because burnout can have a devastating effect on dedicated individuals, young professionals need to be aware of the causes and consequences of burnout and strategies they can use to prevent its occurrence.

There are many causes of teacher burnout: lack of administrative support, lack of input into the curriculum process, and public criticism and the accompanying lack of community support. Inadequate salaries, discipline problems, too little time to do the ever-growing amount of work, large classes, and heavier teaching loads may also contribute to this problem. The lack of challenge, inadequate supervisory feedback, and the absence of opportunities for personal and professional growth also may lead to burnout.

In the coaching realm, burnout may be caused by seasons that seem to go on without end, administrative and community pressures, and time pressures. Teacher-coach role conflict may also lead to burnout. This role conflict occurs when a disparity exists between the expectations associated with being a teacher and a coach; this results in a multitude of simultaneous, somewhat diverse demands. The teacher-coach, unable to satisfy these demands, experiences role conflict.

In both the teaching and coaching realms, personal problems may interact with professional problems to exacerbate burnout. Personal problems such as family conflicts, money difficulties, or perhaps even divorce or problems with relationships may cause additional stress for the individual. These stresses coupled with professional problems may hasten the onset of burnout.

Excessive demands can lead to burnout among teacher-coaches.

The consequences of burnout are many and are often quite severe, affecting teachers as well as their students. Burnout is associated with absenteeism, intent to leave the job, and actual job turnover.[18] For people who continue to work, burnout leads to lower productivity and effectiveness.[16] Burnout can adversely affect instruction. Burned-out teachers may cope with the demands of teaching by sitting on the sidelines, going through the motions of teaching by "throwing out the ball." Infrequent and careless planning of classes, complacency, and behavioral inflexibility may occur as well. Teachers' interactions with their students may also suffer. Burned-out teachers may treat their students in a depersonalized manner, providing them with little encouragement, feedback, and reinforcement of their efforts, and many have lower expectations for student performance. Teachers who are burned out may feel dissatisfied with their accomplishments and believe they are wasting the best years of their lives. Burnout can result in deterioration of health. Insomnia, hypertension, ulcers, and other stress-related symptoms may manifest themselves in burned-out teachers.

What can be done to cope with burnout? The varied causes and consequences of burnout require a diversity of solutions. Supervisors such as principals and athletic directors can play a crucial role in the prevention and remediation of burnout. Supervisors can provide teachers and coaches with meaningful in-service programs, focusing on developing a variety of teaching and coaching techniques, learning efficient time management, and acquiring effective communication skills. They can also provide teachers and coaches with more feedback about their performance, which can serve as a stimulus for growth. Teachers and coaches can seek out new ideas, professional contacts, and opportunities through participation in professional organizations and conferences. Taking some time off to revitalize oneself during the summer is also a successful strategy. Developing and participating in hobbies or nonwork-related activities are helpful ways to deal with burnout. Establishing and maintaining an appropriate level of fitness, practicing proper nutrition, and getting enough sleep are also positive approaches to dealing with burnout.

Some teachers and coaches seek to cope with the consequences of burnout by adopting inappropriate solutions such as alcohol or drugs. The pervasiveness of burnout and the serious consequences for the teachers, coaches, students, and athletes should make dealing with burnout an important professional priority.

INCREASING YOUR PROFESSIONAL MARKETABILITY

If you are interested in a teaching career in the public schools or in nonschool settings, you can often enhance both your marketability and your ability to teach by building on your assets and interests. Through careful planning of your study program and wise use of your electives and practicum experiences, you can easily improve your chances of gaining the professional position you desire. Many of the same strategies are applicable to coaching as well.

You should enhance your opportunities to teach in the public schools in several ways. One way is to build on talents or skills you already possess. For example, the need is great for bilingual educators. Perhaps you have gained proficiency in a second language because of your family background, the location in which you grew up, or foreign language courses you studied in secondary school. These language skills can be built on with further course work at the college or university level.

Second, additional course work can be beneficial in broadening the abilities of the prospective teacher. Courses in the area of adapted physical education are an asset whether or not one is interested in working only with special needs children. Since adapted physical education emphasizes individualized instruction, the knowledge gained from its study can be applied to all children, including those with special needs mainstreamed into or included in regular physical education classes. Additional courses in health may be helpful because physical educators are often expected to teach one or two health classes. The close relationship between wellness and fitness makes knowledge of health important to the practitioner.

Another possibility, depending on the state in which you plan to teach, is to gain certification to teach in a second academic area. If you enjoy other areas such as math, science, or health, dual certification would enable you to qualify for additional jobs such as a teaching position that has a teaching load of one-third math and two-thirds physical education or one-third health and two-thirds physical education. Certification in driver education is also a popular choice that enhances one's credentials. To gain dual certification, you are required to take several courses in your alternate area of study. Often the number of courses required for certification may not be many more than are required by your college or university for a minor. The education department in the state in which you plan to teach can provide you with additional information about the requirements for certification.

Individuals interested in teaching in a nonschool setting can enhance their marketability in just the same way as individuals preparing for a teaching position in the public schools. Depending on where one seeks employment, having a bilingual background might be an asset. Experience in adapted physical education will be useful in working with individuals of different abilities and ages. Courses in math and business may be helpful if one is employed by a commercial sport club or fitness center or community sport program, where the position often involves managerial duties. Because many of these organizations offer some type of health counseling and because of the interest of many of the clientele in health, courses in health will be an asset as well. Many employers may view possession of a teaching certificate by someone seeking to teach in these nonschool settings as an asset. Expertise in one or several sport areas

Focus on Career: Teaching and Coaching

PROFESSIONAL ORGANIZATIONS

- American Alliance for Health, Physical Education, Recreation and Dance
  www.aahperd.org
- National Association for Sport and Physical Education
  www.aahperd.org → NASPE
  - Curriculum and Instruction Academy
  - Physical Education Councils
  - Sport Councils
- American Association for Active Lifestyles and Fitness
  www.aahperd.org → AAALF
  - Adapted Physical Activity Council
  - Aquatic Council
- National Education Association
  www.nea.org
- American Federation of Teachers
  www.aft.org

PROFESSIONAL JOURNALS

- *Adapted Physical Activity Quarterly*
- *JOPERD*
- *Journal of Teaching in Physical Education*
- *Palestra*
- *Research Quarterly for Exercise and Sport*
- *Sports and Spokes*
- *Strategies*
- *Teaching Elementary Physical Education*

may also be a plus, as is possession of specialized certifications.

In the coaching realm, one's previous experience as an athlete in the sport is an asset. Many former athletes have capitalized on their experience to secure coaching positions. Previous work as an assistant or head coach certainly is in one's favor. Professional contacts, official ratings in a sport, and membership in a professional organization are helpful in getting hired or advancing. Many states require that coaches hold teaching certification; holding such certification gives one more flexibility in selecting from job opportunities.

Finally, one can enhance one's credentials by gaining as much practical experience as possible, working with people of all ages and abilities. This holds true whether you are seeking work in a school or nonschool setting or in coaching. This experience can be gained through volunteer work, part-time employment, summer employment, or through supervised field experiences sponsored by your college or university. Being able to cite such practical experiences on your resume may prove invaluable when you are seeking to gain employment. Membership in professional organizations and professional contacts may also be helpful in your securing employment.

Teachers and coaches can improve their marketability by acquiring skills in the use of technology. Technology can help teachers and coaches enhance their instructional effectiveness and manage their time more efficiently. Many teachers are

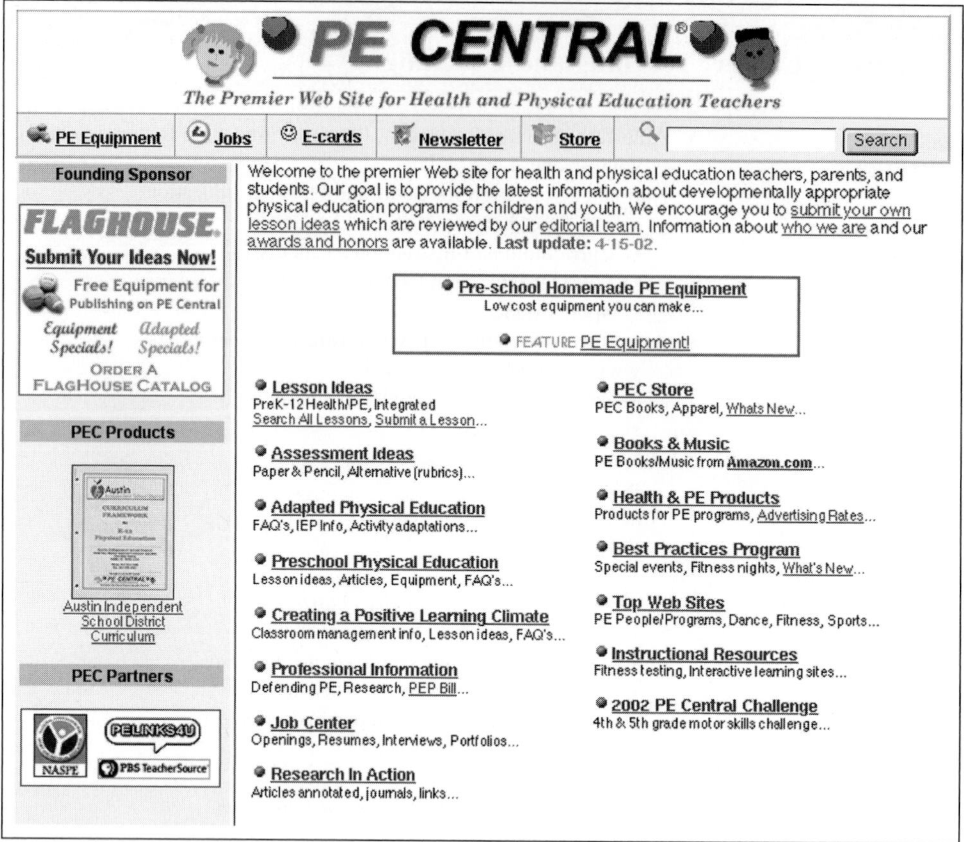

Figure 11-1 PE Central is a popular Web site for physical educators. Used by permission of PE Central (www.pecentral.org), the premier Web site for health and physical education teachers.

now using heart-rate monitors in their classes. These monitors, which attach to the student's wrist, provide immediate and ongoing feedback to students about their heart rate. Some heart-rate monitors store the information so that it can be downloaded to a computer and later analyzed by the teacher. Some teachers use hand-held computers to gather information about a student's performance of different skills during class. Other teachers use computers for a myriad of tasks, such as record keeping, grading, and creating newsletters to promote their programs.

Coaches can use laptop computers and video-editing technology to prepare scouting reports on their opponents. Spreadsheets help coaches quickly calculate statistics and keep track of their budgets. College coaches especially benefit from the use of databases to manage their recruiting activities.

The use of the World Wide Web as a resource for teachers and coaches is growing. There are many Web sites for physical education teachers to use as resources and a means to communicate with other teachers throughout the country. *PE CENTRAL* (Figure 11-1), established by Dr. George

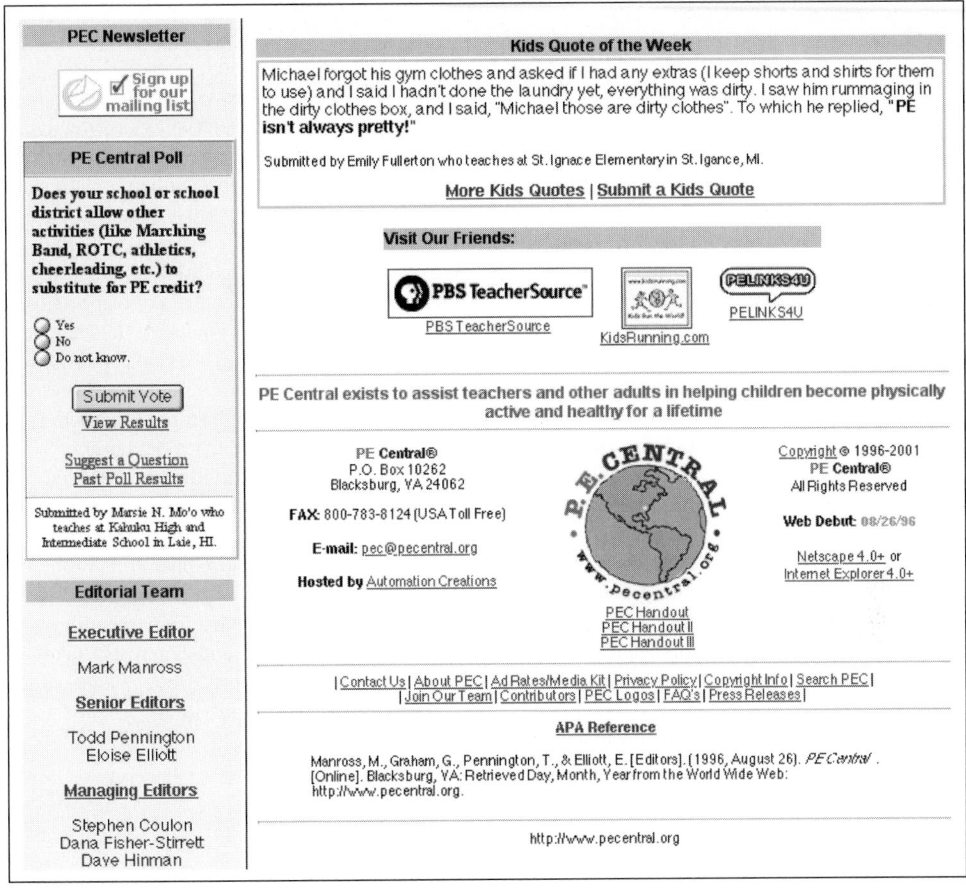

Graham and the doctoral students in the health and physical education program at Virginia Tech, is one of the premier Web sites for physical educators. It offers teachers access to lesson plans, instructional resources, assessment ideas, professional information on conferences and workshops, job openings, equipment purchasing, and related Web sites. Through its listserv, physical education teachers can share information and engage in problem solving with other teachers throughout the nation.

Coaches find that the Web offers them the opportunity to share information with coaches throughout the world. A coach may find posted on the Web information about drills, training techniques, and upcoming conferences and clinics. Through several different sites on the Web, college coaches can contact and recruit prospective athletes. Through various sport-specific listservs, coaches can communicate with colleagues worldwide.

Prospective teachers and coaches can enhance their marketability. Building on your skills, taking additional courses, and gaining as much practical experience as possible will increase your options and enhance your opportunities for employment.

SUMMARY

Teaching and coaching opportunities have broadened from the traditional school setting to the nonschool setting and from school-aged populations to people of all ages, ranging from preschoolers to senior citizens. Teaching opportunities in the school setting are available at the elementary level, secondary level, and in higher education. Prospective teachers may also teach physical education in adapted physical education programs and in professional preparation programs. In the nonschool setting, opportunities exist in commercial sport clubs, community and youth agencies, resorts, corporate fitness programs, the Armed Forces, and preschool and day-care motor development programs. Many individuals choose a teaching career because of their strong desire to work with people, because of personal interests, and because of the nature of the job. Individuals desiring to pursue a teaching career, regardless of setting, should be cognizant of the numerous advantages and disadvantages of such a career.

Many prospective physical educators aspire to a career as a coach. Some seek a dual career as a teacher and a coach, whereas others desire solely to coach and view a teaching career as a means to attain their ultimate ambition. The prospective coach should be knowledgeable of the benefits and drawbacks of this career.

In an effort to improve teaching, researchers have sought to identify characteristics of effective teachers. They determined that effective teachers possess organizational, communication, human relations, instructional, and motivational skills. Teachers have a myriad of responsibilities; their responsibilities may be classified as instructional, managerial, and institutional in nature. Coaching is similar in many respects to teaching. Effective coaches possess many of the characteristics of effective teachers and must assume many of the same responsibilities as well.

One problem that has become increasingly prevalent among teachers and coaches is burnout. Burnout is physical, mental, and attitudinal exhaustion. The causes of burnout are many, and personal problems may interact with professional problems to exacerbate burnout. There are a variety of solutions to this problem.

Many strategies can be used by prospective teachers and coaches to enhance their marketability. They can build on their talents and interests, take additional course work in a supporting area, and gain as much practical experience as possible.

SELF-ASSESSMENT TESTS

These tests are designed to help you determine if you have mastered the materials and the competencies presented in this chapter.

1. In light of the qualities of effective teachers and their responsibilities, assess your own qualifications for this field of endeavor.
2. Discuss the advantages and disadvantages of pursuing a teaching or coaching career in a school and a nonschool setting. If possible, try to interview a physical educator or coach presently working in each setting.
3. Using the information provided in the Get Connected box, access the *PE CENTRAL* or *PE Links 4U* sites on the World Wide Web. Explore the information contained within each site. Write a 1- to 2-page paper on the usefulness of the World Wide Web to teachers and coaches.
4. Using the information provided in the Get Connected box, access the AAHPERD Web site and read the National Standards for Athletic Coaches and the Coaches Code of Conduct. Carefully review your own athletic experiences and compare the actions and behaviors of your coaches to the standards. Did your coaches meet these standards? Where did they fall short? Discuss the importance of standards for coaches, especially at the youth sport level.

REFERENCES

1. Bucher CA and Koenig CR: Methods and materials for secondary physical education, St. Louis, 1983, Mosby.
2. American Federation of Teachers, Teacher salaries report 2000. (www.aft.org)
3. Wuest DA and Lombardo BJ: Curriculum and instruction: the secondary school physical education experience, St. Louis, 1994, Mosby.
4. Siedentop D: Developing teaching skills in physical education, ed 3, Palo Alto, Calif., 1991, Mayfield.
5. Interstate New Teacher Assessment and Support Consortium Standards. Retrieved 12/10/04. (http://www.ccsso.org/content/pdfs/corestrd.pdf)
6. National Association for Sport and Physical Education: National standards for beginning physical education teachers, 1995, American Alliance for Health, Physical Education, Recreation and Dance.
7. American Alliance for Health, Physical Education, Recreation and Dance: Developmentally appropriate physical education practices for children, Reston, Va., 1992, AAHPERD.
8. Corbin CB: Physical activity for everyone: what every physical educator should know about promoting lifelong physical activity, Journal of Teaching in Physical Education 21:128–144, 2002.
9. Gensemer RE: Physical education: perspectives, inquiry, and applications, Philadelphia, 1985, W. B. Saunders.
10. National Education Association: Building blocks for success, 2002. (www.nea.org)
11. Pangrazi RP and Darst PW: Dynamic physical education curriculum and instruction for secondary school students, Minneapolis, 1985, Burgess.
12. American Sport Education Program: 1997 national interscholastic coaching requirements report: a shared mission, Champaign, Ill., 1997, Human Kinetics. (www.asep.com/)
13. National Association for Sport and Physical Education: National standards for athletic coaches, 1994, American Alliance for Health, Physical Education, Recreation and Dance.
14. National Association for Sport and Physical Education, Coaches Council: The coaches code of conduct, 2001, American Alliance for Health, Physical Education, Recreation and Dance. (www.aahperd.org)
15. American Sport Education Program: About ASEP and human kinetics, 2001, Human Kinetics. (www.asep.com)
16. National Youth Sport Coaches Association. (www.nays.org/coaches/index.cfm)
17. Institute for Youth Sport: PACE. (http://ed-web3.educ.msu.edu/ysi)
18. Maslach C: Job burnout. Annual Review of Psychology, Annual 2001.

SUGGESTED READINGS

Corbin CB: Physical activity for everyone: what every physical educator should know about promoting lifelong physical activity, Journal of Teaching in Physical Education 21:128–144, 2002.

Provides ideas for change to support the primary role of physical education—the promotion of lifelong physical activity. Ideas include narrowing our focus to a few objectives, shifting the emphasis from the promotion of fitness to encouraging physical activity, and emphasizing the development of skills that will enable youth to be physically active throughout their lifespan.

Drewe, SB: An examination of the relationship between coaching and teaching, Quest 52:79–88, 2001.

Explores the relationship between teaching and coaching, including the commonalities and contrasts, as well as the differences between the concepts of education and training and the importance of the educational role of coaches.

Jones RL, Armour KM, and Potrac P: Understanding the coaching process: a framework for social analysis, Quest 54:34–48, 2002.

Suggests that coaching can be analyzed using three interrelated concepts—role, interaction, and power and that these concepts reflect the social and cultural contexts, personal experiences, professional philosophy and practice, and their interaction.

Kozub FM and Poretta D: Including athletes with disabilities: interscholastic athletic benefits for all, JOPERD 67(3):19–24, 1996.

This article discusses the continuum of opportunities for participation by students with disabilities, benefits for participants, and suggestions for coaches.

Mavi HF and Sharpe T: Reviewing the literature on teacher and coach expectations with implications for future research and practice, Physical Educator, 57:161–168, 2001.

Reviews expectancy literature, discusses the dangers of the self-fulfilling prophecy, and offers professionals a list of strategies to ensure positive interactions with all students/athletes.

Potrac P, Brewer C, Jones R, Armour K, and Hoff, J: Toward a holistic understanding of the coaching process, Quest 52:186–199, 2001.

Addresses the humanistic nature of the coaching process, specifically identifying the coach's instructional behaviors during practice, striving to understand why coaches behave the way they do, and describing the impact of their instructional strategies on athletes.

Rink J: Teaching physical education for learning, ed 5, McGraw-Hill, 2005, New York.

Designed for teachers of physical education K–12, this text presents theories and teaching strategies for the design of effective instruction.

Rink JE: Investigating the assumptions of pedagogy, Journal of Teaching in Physical Education 20: 112–128, 2001.

Explores the relationship between learning theories and teaching methodology in physical education.

Senne TA: On your mark . . . get set . . . go!: a guide for beginning physical education teachers, NASPE, 2004, Reston, Va.

Offers ideas to help physical education majors transition to the world of teaching, information on how to develop a classroom management plan, socialization and its role in teaching, professional development, and ideas for getting off to a good start during the first days of school.

Sherrill, C: Adapted physical activity, recreation, and sport: Cross-disciplinary and lifespan, ed 5, McGraw-Hill, 2001, New York.

Comprehensive approach to the broad area of adapted physical activity, including development, descriptions of specific disabilities with implications for instruction, and assessment.

Stoot SA, editor: Preparing for a professional career in physical education, Journal of Teaching in Physical Education 12(2): Theme Issue, 2001.

This volume is devoted to the challenges of the beginning teacher, including professional isolation and philosophical conflicts. Teachers strive to incorporate managerial and pedagogical skills to teach effectively and meet the challenges of working with diverse learners. It is important to continue to take responsibility for continued professional growth throughout one's career.

CHAPTER 12

FITNESS- AND HEALTH-RELATED CAREERS

OBJECTIVES

After reading this chapter the student should be able to—

- Discuss the responsibilities of a fitness or an exercise specialist.
- Describe the various employment opportunities for a fitness or an exercise specialist.
- Discuss the responsibilities of physical education, exercise science, and sport professionals working in a health-related career.
- Describe the opportunities available to an individual desiring to pursue a therapy-related career.
- Discuss the various strategies that can be used to enhance one's professional marketability in fitness-, health-, and therapy-related careers.

Within the past decade, there has been a dramatic increase in interest in preventive medicine and a greater public awareness of the values of physical activity. Research has substantiated the benefits of exercise and appropriate physical activity in reducing the incidence of cardiovascular disease and in enhancing the rehabilitation of those experiencing this common malady. The increased public awareness of the role of physical activity in health promotion and disease prevention, coupled with the interest in fitness by many segments of society, has stimulated the growth of community, commercial, and worksite health promotion and fitness programs. As a result, employment opportunities for professionals with preparation as exercise and fitness specialists have grown tremendously. The number of physical education, exercise science, and sport professionals who have found employment opportunities working in preventive and rehabilitative physical activity programs has risen sharply, and it appears that this trend will continue in the years ahead.

Another field that has experienced growth is athletic training. Although professional and college athletic teams have typically employed athletic trainers, their employment at the secondary school level is rising. Furthermore, the public's increased participation in a variety of sport activities and the medical

GET CONNECTED

American College of Sports Medicine gives information about the organization, membership, certification, research reports, publication, and official position papers on a variety of topics.

www.acsm.org

American Council on Exercise contains information on certification, fitness news and facts, and trends. Access the press releases to read information about research projects, such as the most effective exercises or tests of claims made for different fitness products.

www.acefitness.org

FitnessManagement.com offers access to fitness statistics, current news, and a library with articles on many topics including aerobics, cardiac rehabilitation, club management, certification, and resistance training. You can also subscribe to a bi-weekly newsletter.

www.fitnessworld.com

National Athletic Trainers' Association provides information on the NATA, membership, certification, position papers, and listing of undergraduate and graduate schools offering an approved NATA curriculum.

www.nata.org

National Strength and Conditioning Association site presents information on membership, certification, and research abstracts.

www.nsca-lift.org

profession's interest in sport have led to increased employment opportunities for qualified athletic trainers in commercial sports medicine clinics, physical therapy clinics, hospitals, and even in corporate worksite programs.

Employment opportunities also have become more available for qualified individuals in weight-control health spas, resorts, and health clubs. Qualified individuals may be employed as dance exercise specialists, exercise leaders, exercise test technologists, and weight management counselors.

An increasing number of medical and health care professionals, as well as members of the general public, realize the significant physical and psychological benefits gained by individuals who participate in regular, appropriate physical activity. There is greater recognition of the therapeutic values of movement in helping individuals attain an optimal state of well-being, as well as recover from an illness. Careers in movement therapy, recreation therapy, and dance therapy are available to physical education, exercise science, and sport professionals who desire to work in a therapeutic setting. Aquatic therapy is also a growing area of interest.

FITNESS- AND EXERCISE-RELATED CAREERS

The awareness of the benefits of physical activity by the public, corporate sector, and medical profession has stimulated the growth of preventive and rehabilitative physical activity programs. Students aspiring to pursue careers in this growing area should familiarize themselves with the types of programs typically offered and the nature of responsibilities associated with them, the many career opportunities available, and strategies to prepare themselves for a fitness- and exercise-related career.

Preventive and rehabilitative exercise programs differ in their focus and in the nature of the participants; the setting in which these programs are conducted often is different as well. Preventive exercise program specialists work with healthy

Members work out at the state-of-the-art Taking Care Center, in Hartford, Connecticut. In addition to the exercise equipment and indoor track, it has a pool and an aerobics studio.

adults to increase their level of fitness and realize concomitant gains in health. Rehabilitative exercise program specialists work primarily with individuals who exhibit the effects of coronary heart disease; they focus on helping these individuals attain a functional state of living and an enhanced quality of life. Preventive exercise programs are commonly found in corporate fitness centers, commercial fitness centers, and community agencies such as the YMCA/YWCA. An increasing number of hospitals are now offering wellness programs. Rehabilitative exercise programs are most often found in hospitals, although some may be found in medical clinics or community agencies or are affiliated with corporate fitness centers.

Preventive and rehabilitative programs often vary in their scope and comprehensiveness. However, some commonalities may be discerned. Although these programs typically focus on improvement of fitness, they may include other components such as educational programs, health promotion programs, and lifestyle modification.

Comprehensive wellness programs are growing in popularity. The fitness component of these programs most likely includes some assessment of the individual's current level of fitness, prescription of a program of exercise and activity, opportunities to engage in exercise and activities, and periodic reevaluation of the individual's level of fitness. Educational efforts may focus on instructing individuals on the principles underlying the performance of exercises and physical activity so that they may learn to properly plan their own exercise and activity programs. Health promotion efforts may include health education, such as providing participants with nutritional information, as well as measures focusing on the early detection of disease, such as hypertension screening and cancer detection. Lifestyle modification may include counseling individuals regarding stress management, weight control, smoking cessation, and alcohol and drug abuse. In addition to these program components, recreational sport opportunities may be offered.

The trained exercise professional must be able to evaluate each participant's fitness level. This PepsiCo staff member is administering the sit-and-reach test to a program participant.

Cooper and Collingwood[1] noted that fitness and wellness programs vary in their structure and offerings. In an effort to maximize the benefits to be realized from participation and to promote adherence to these programs, the Institute for Aerobics Research identified several elements as "generic" services for such programs. Programs should make provisions for medical screening of their participants to ensure that they are safe exercise risks. Program personnel should also evaluate participants' levels of fitness and their lifestyles. Exercise programs should focus on individual goal setting; thus, exercise and nutritional prescriptions should be developed for each individual. To motivate participants to get started on their programs, supervised group exercise and activity programs should be offered. To sustain changes in fitness and lifestyle, educational classes should be held and provisions should be made for motivation and reinforcement of participants' efforts. Feedback should be ongoing in nature. These generic elements are critical to the success of preventive exercise programs and seem appropriate for rehabilitative programs as well.

The trained fitness professional working in preventive and rehabilitative exercise programs must be able to perform a wide variety of tasks and be capable of assuming responsibility for numerous aspects of the exercise program. Sol[2] identified the responsibilities of an exercise program specialist as follows:

- Direct the exercise program, which may be oriented to prevention and/or rehabilitation.
- Train and supervise staff.
- Develop and manage the program budget.
- Design and manage the exercise facility and laboratories.

- Market the exercise program.
- Evaluate—in conjunction with a physician—each participant's medical and activity history, a graded exercise test, the pulmonary function tests, and assorted fitness tests.
- Develop individual exercise prescriptions for participants.
- Evaluate and/or counsel participants, on request, about nutrition, smoking, weight control, and stress.
- Accumulate program data for statistical analysis and research.
- Maintain professional affiliations.
- Perform other program-specific duties.

The responsibilities that each professional in the program will be asked to assume depend on several factors. These factors include the scope and comprehensiveness of the program, the number of participants, the size of the staff, and qualifications of other staff members. In programs that have a broad range of services, a large number of participants, and several staff members, responsibilities tend to be more specialized. One staff member may direct the program, administer the budget, market the program, and conduct in-service training for other program staff. Some staff members may have as their sole responsibility the conducting of graded exercise tests and the writing of exercise prescriptions. Still other staff members lead the fitness classes and may provide instruction in activities. Providing participants with counseling for lifestyle modification or educating participants about exercise may be the responsibility of other staff members. Finally, another professional may be assigned to accumulate data and conduct statistical analyses. In programs that are narrower in scope or are conducted for fewer participants, the staff tends to be smaller and one professional will perform many more functions.

Opportunities for qualified individuals may be found in a diversity of preventive and rehabilitative exercise programs offered in a variety of settings. These include worksite health promotion and fitness programs, commercial and community programs, and rehabilitation programs. Some individuals are finding employment as personal fitness trainers. Salaries range from \$20,000 to over \$40,000 a year, depending on the qualifications of the individual, responsibilities assigned, and nature of the job.

Worksite Health Programs

Worksite health promotion programs have grown dramatically over the past decade. Physical activity and fitness programs are typically an integral part of health promotion efforts at the work site. Worksite health promotion programs vary greatly in their scope and the type of health promotion activities offered.

The proportion of work sites offering physical activity and fitness programs has grown from 22% in 1985 to 46% in 1998 and 1999. The larger the employer's workforce, the more likely it is the employer has a physical activity and fitness program. Thirty-eight percent of small corporations (50–99 employees) have worksite programs compared with 68% of large corporations (more than 750 employees).[3]

Worksite physical activity programs are a critical component of the national health promotion and disease prevention program because they have the potential to reach a large percentage of the population. Today's workforce comprises 142 million men and women, the majority of whom spend most of the day at the work site. The work site offers an effective way to reach these adults and to provide them with education and access to the means to adopt and maintain a healthy lifestyle. Onsite programs are convenient for employees and offer the peer social support so important for continued participation.

Corporations invest in worksite health promotion programs because it makes economic sense. Quality worksite health promotion programs contribute to high productivity and help contain costs. Improvements in job performance, increases in productivity, and reduced absenteeism are some of the benefits for companies that choose to invest in health promotion programs.[4,5] Corporations also sponsor health promotion programs as a cost

Aerobic dance is a popular offering at health spas, fitness clubs, and corporate fitness centers.

containment measure. Health-care costs are spiraling, and health insurance premiums continue to rise astronomically. Workplace programs have been associated with reduced injury rates, lower workman's compensation costs, and reduced health care costs.[4,5,6]

Reports show that the benefits realized from worksite programs vary widely. Benefit/cost ratios are most widely used to determine the economic benefits. A benefit/cost ratio divides the money saved by the money spent; a ratio of $3.43 means that for every $1 spent, $3.43 was saved. Benefit/cost ratios for physical activity programs range from 0.76 to 3.43.[7] When physical activity programs were included as part of a comprehensive health promotion program, benefit/cost ratios ranged from 1.15 to 5.52.[8] Recent studies have reported benefit/cost ratios averaged savings ranging from $3.93 to $5.07 for every dollar invested in health promotion.[9] Shepard reported that the "cumulative benefit was estimated to be $500 to $700 per worker per year, enough to cover the cost of a modest wellness program."[5] However, researchers suggest that increasing productivity as little as one-third of 1% could pay for the health promotion program.[10] Furthermore, the benefits that can be achieved from increasing productivity are 10 times greater than the savings realized by reducing medical costs.[11]

Corporations may also invest in worksite health promotion programs because of the benefits in terms of human relations and enhancement of morale. Worksite health promotion programs are also important in recruiting and retaining employees. In 1995, the International Society of Certified Employee Benefit Specialists found that wellness and health promotion ranked 10th among 30 top employee benefit health priorities.[12]

Worksite health promotion programs vary widely in comprehensiveness—that is, the number and nature of activities offered. In 1997, the Association for Worksite Health Promotion estimated the percentage of work sites offering different types of health promotion activities.[12] The top 10 activities and the percentage of work sites offering them are listed below:

- Job hazard/injury prevention (66%).
- Exercise/physical fitness (43%).
- Smoking control (42%).

- Stress management (39%).
- Alcohol/other drugs (38%).
- Back care (34%).
- Nutrition (32%).
- High blood pressure (31%).
- AIDS education (30%).
- Cholesterol screening (29%).

A 1999 survey of over 1,500 businesses revealed additional information about the types of wellness programs offered by employers. Over 50% of employers offered programs related to back care. Exercise/physical fitness, smoking control, and stress management were offered by about 35% of employers.[13] Programs about nutrition and substance abuse, AIDS education, information about sexually transmitted diseases, and education and screening about cholesterol were offered by about 25% of employers.[13] As you can see from the offerings, many health promotion programs focus on other health-related areas in addition to fitness.

Physical education, exercise science, and sport professionals aspiring to work in worksite health promotion programs may find themselves working as part of a comprehensive health promotion team. As a member of a health promotion team, professionals may benefit from additional training in wellness areas such as health, nutrition, and stress management.

The Wellness Council of America (WELCOA)[14] offers several suggestions to enhance the success of wellness and health promotion programs. These include the following:

- Make the program voluntary.
- Continually market the program.
- Be sensitive to individual differences with respect to age, culture, and health status.
- Evaluate the program often.
- Make sure that the program staff model healthy behavior.
- Recognize and reward people who develop the programs.
- Maintain good records in order to properly evaluate the program.
- Offer a balance between programs that are fun and those that are clinically significant.
- Personalize the programs to the employee's needs.

Worksite health promotion programs offer a great opportunity to improve the health of the nation. However, the effectiveness of this effort must be measured not only in the number of worksite programs but the degree of involvement of employees.

Worksite health promotion programs, especially for physical fitness and activity, are most effective when they can attract at-risk employees, that is, those employees who will benefit the most from the program.[5] At-risk employees are those members of the workforce who are sedentary and/or obese, possess high cholesterol levels, are hypertensive, experience high levels of stress, and smoke.[15] It has been found, however, that participants in the fitness program tend to already be healthier than nonparticipants.[5,15] Efforts should be directed at attracting at-risk individuals into the fitness program. Physical education, exercise science, and sport professionals must realize that part of their job responsibilities will be the active and ongoing recruitment of employees to participate in the program. Once employees have begun a program, efforts need to be directed at maintaining involvement so that desirable health benefits can be achieved.

Worksite facilities vary greatly. Some corporations have invested in multimillion dollar facilities—gymnasium, pool, indoor track, aerobics studio, racquetball courts, weight rooms, and playing fields for sport activities. Facilities at other corporations are more modest, perhaps only a weight room and a multipurpose gymnasium.

Within the last decade, there has been an increase in worksite health promotion and fitness programs for school faculty and staff. These programs vary in nature and scope. Like those found in corporate settings, school programs focus on protecting and improving employees' health status. These worksite programs are seen by professionals in the health field as an integral part of a comprehensive school health program.[16]

Colleges and universities also are offering programs for their employees. These programs typically emphasize prevention and improvement of health through appropriate lifestyle management. Some institutions offer wellness and fitness programs to their students, on either a credit or noncredit basis. The emphasis is on learning skills and acquiring knowledge to lead a healthy, active life.

Many work sites offer recreational sport programs as well. These recreational programs may include softball and bowling leagues, as well as competitive teams. Instruction in physical activities may be offered to employees.

Opportunities for employment in worksite programs are increasing for qualified professionals. A physical education, exercise science, and sport professional may work as a group aerobics or group exercise instructor. As a professional, you may work with people of all fitness levels and all ages, or you may offer specialized classes for women who are pregnant or for persons with lower back pain. Class offerings vary widely, ranging from low-impact aerobics to high-intensity cardiovascular workouts and from water-based resistance programs to cycling.

Another opportunity is to work as the director of the employee fitness or wellness program. In this capacity, you may lead a variety of wellness and fitness classes, train and supervise other instructors in the program, and educate employees on a variety of topics, such as worker safety or stress management.

Worksite health promotion programs also employ exercise physiologists. Exercise physiologists administer and evaluate exercise tests and supervise exercise sessions. Exercise physiologists work with both healthy individuals and those with special medical concerns. Depending on the scope of the worksite health promotion program, exercise physiologists may direct a cardiac rehabilitation program.

Commercial and Community Fitness Programs

The number of fitness programs has grown dramatically within the past decade. Both commercial and community programs have increased, involving people of all ages. In 2003, the International Health, Racquet, and Sportsclub Association (IHRSA) reported that there were a record number of clubs and fitness centers—23,500 (including YMCAs and community centers). There were nearly 39.4 million members, with individuals aged 35 to 54 comprising 37% of the members and individuals aged 18 to 34, 34% of the members.[17] The largest surge in membership has been in the over 55 years of age group. In 1987, adults aged 55 and older accounted for 9% of the membership; in 2000, this group represented 17% of all members.[17] Membership by children under 18 is increasing and is currently 12% of the membership.[17]

In 2003, the U.S. health club industry had total revenues of $14.1 billion, and a payroll of about $5 billion.[17] There were nearly 200,000 full-time employees and over 740,000 part-time employees.[17] Since 1987, the number of members who use the health club more than 100 days a year has soared by 175% to 14.6 million in 2003.[16] The average attendance per member climbed from 72 to 92 days per year.[17] The average retention rate of the members is 63%.[17]

The types of programs offered at clubs and fitness centers are extremely diverse. Graded exercise tests, individualized fitness evaluation and prescription, educational programs, and lifestyle modification are some services offered by more comprehensive programs. Group exercise programs of all sorts, ranging from aerobic dance class to yoga instruction to cardiac rehabilitation to sport specific training, are offered to members. Resistance training has increased in popularity. Programs that are less comprehensive may offer fewer choices for their members. As with the employee fitness programs, there is a trend toward offering wellness programming. More clubs are offering personal training services and over 50% of the clubs surveyed reported that personal training is one of their most profitable services.[17]

Fitness programs tailored to meet the needs of different age groups are becoming more common. Toddler and preschool programs, as well as programs for the aged, are being offered by both community and commercial agencies and, increasingly, by schools. Professionals working within these programs must be particularly attuned to the developmental characteristics of the age group and adapt programs accordingly.

An increased number of fitness programs are available to address the fitness needs of individuals with disabilities. For example, the Fitness Clinic for Physically Disabled at San Diego State University (SDSU), established in 1983, provides fitness programming to individuals with a wide range of physical disabilities.[18] Fitness programming at the clinic focuses on both improvement of fitness and functional independence. Improvement of functional independence allows participants in the program to assume a greater responsibility for their personal care and other activities of daily living. For individuals with severe limiting conditions, such as quadriplegia and multiple sclerosis, increasing their basic muscular strength, endurance, and balance allows them more independence and greatly enhances the overall quality of their lives. The Fitness Clinic also provides a wonderful practicum experience for SDSU students enrolled in adapted physical education, athletic training, and prephysical therapy programs to apply their fitness and therapeutic skills.

A growing site for community wellness and fitness programs is the hospital setting. These wellness centers integrate recreational and clinical services, incorporating features normally found in health clubs and community centers. These centers are big, multipurpose, with gyms, jogging tracks, state-of-the art exercise equipment, aerobic studios, and sometimes a pool.[18] This growth was stimulated in part by health-care reform and the emergence of managed care. This gave hospitals the incentive to focus on prevention to keep people from coming to the hospital in the first place. Through creation of wellness centers, hospitals could capitalize on changes in health care. These centers offer an array of services, from prevention programs to rehabilitation services, and require professionals that can competently fulfill many different responsibilities.[19]

Professional responsibilities within commercial enterprises and community programs are similar to those associated with worksite programs. Employment opportunities within these areas have grown dramatically within the past few years.

One factor that may counter the growth of employment opportunities is the tremendous increase in the sales of home exercise equipment. Many

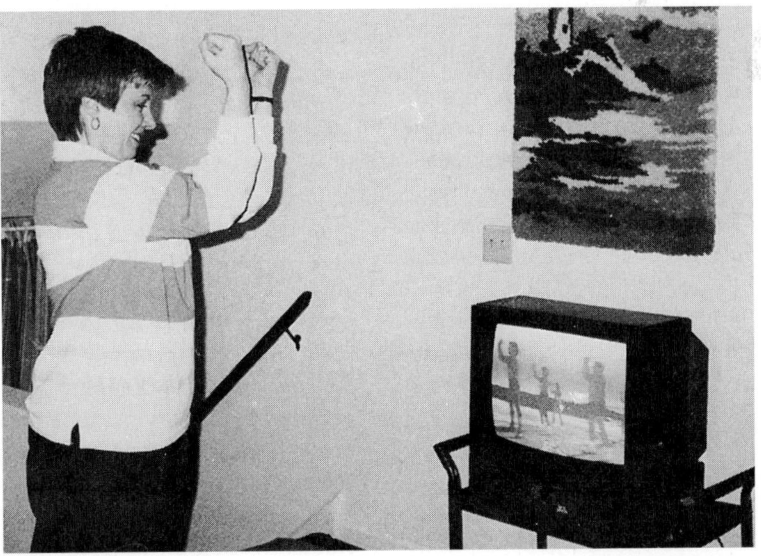

Many people prefer to exercise at home rather than at a club or other facility.

adults who in the past would have paid a membership fee to participate in these programs have chosen to invest the money in home exercise equipment, such as home gyms, bicycle ergometers, treadmills, and rowing machines. These individuals prefer the convenience of being able to exercise at home. Some professionals have capitalized on this trend by working as personal trainers, offering one-on-one fitness instruction in the home.

Personal trainers work with individuals typically in the home or club setting. Personal trainers tailor the fitness program to meet the client's needs.

Personal Trainers

A number of physical education, exercise science, and sport professionals have pursued careers as personal fitness trainers. They meet with clients individually in their homes on a regular basis, sometimes as often as 5 or 6 days per week. For each client, the personal trainer conducts a fitness assessment, develops specific goals and designs a program leading to their attainment, coaches the individual through the workout, and monitors progress. Additional services often include nutritional counseling. Personal trainers can earn from $25 to over $100 an hour.

Some fitness programs and health clubs are also offering members the services of a personal trainer at an additional cost. Members like the one-on-one attention offered by a personal trainer, believing it enhances their motivation and their effort in performing their program.

Some personal trainers work for a health club or fitness center. Members have the option of paying an additional fee to utilize the services of the personal trainer. Other physical education, exercise science, and sport professionals run their own personal training business; they may be the sole provider of care or have other professionals who work for them.

One new trend is the use of the Web for personal training. Clients who live too far away from a club, prefer to work out at home, or are too busy to visit a fitness center sign up with a personal trainer online. Via e-mail or phone, the personal trainer and the client establish fitness goals, and then the trainer prescribes a fitness regimen tailored for the needs of the client. Clients typically e-mail their personal trainer the results of each workout, and the personal trainer monitors the clients' progress—e-mailing workout modifications and encouragement. Hiring a virtual personal trainer saves money—the cost is about $30 to $40 a month compared to $25 or more per hour at the club or home.

Strength and Conditioning Professionals

According to the National Strength and Conditioning Association, strength and conditioning professionals "assess, motivate, educate, and train athletes for the primary goal of improving sport performance."[20] Strength and conditioning professionals work with interscholastic, intercollegiate, amateur, and professional athletes. They are employed in colleges and universities, high schools, sports medicine and physical therapy clinics, and health and fitness clubs.

Strength and conditioning professionals have a rather varied job description. They assess athletes' health status and fitness levels by conducting a multitude of tests, including evaluation of sport-specific abilities. Based on the results of the assessment, they design and implement safe and effective training programs to maximize performance and help athletes achieve their goals. Additionally, they provide guidance to athletes, as well as their coaches, in areas such as injury prevention and nutrition.[20] They work closely with coaches, athletic trainers, medical staff, and nutrition specialists to ensure the health and well-being of athletes. Record keeping, management of the fitness facility, and administration of the program often are part of the strength and conditioning professionals' responsibilities.

Many strength and conditioning professionals work with collegiate athletes, although an increasing number of professionals work in scholastic settings. Recognizing the critical role that fitness and sport-specific conditioning can play in enhancing performance and helping athletes remain healthy and injury-free, many colleges and university athletic departments hire strength and conditioning specialists.

The National Strength and Conditioning Association identifies several competencies needed by strength and conditioning coaches. Strength and conditioning professionals need competency in the scientific foundations of sport/exercise science and nutrition. Competency is also needed in the practical/applied areas of the field, such as exercise leadership and program design. Sport/exercise science competencies include an understanding of human physiology, exercise physiology, motor learning, sport pedagogy, and biomechanics, and the ability to utilize these understandings in the design and implementation of muscular strength and endurance training programs, as well as aerobic and anaerobic fitness programs.[19] Sport and conditioning professionals must be able to utilize techniques from sport psychology to maximize the training and performance of athletes.[19] Professionals must also be cognizant of risks and the effects of performance-enhancing substances.[19] In terms of nutrition, strength and conditioning professionals should be knowledgeable of how nutrition affects health and performance.[20]

Within the applied realm, strength and conditioning coaches need to be able to design training programs that take into account an athlete's health status, current fitness level, and training and performance goals. They need to be knowledgeable about many different forms of exercise including flexibility, plyometrics, strength training, and conditioning, and be able to instruct athletes in these exercise techniques including spotting when appropriate.[20] Competencies also include assessment and evaluation, as well as administration and record keeping.[19]

Physical education teachers, coaches, exercise and fitness specialists, physical therapists, and athletic trainers pursue opportunities as strength and conditioning professionals. Certification as a strength and conditioning specialist is often required for many of these job opportunities.

Rehabilitation Programs

As the role of exercise in the rehabilitation of individuals with illness, particularly cardiovascular diseases, has become increasingly well documented, the number of rehabilitation programs has grown. Typically, rehabilitation programs are offered at hospitals and clinics, although some programs may be offered through community agencies such as the YMCA/YWCA. Besides the development of fitness, health promotion and lifestyle modification are integral parts of these programs.

Clinical exercise physiologists work in rehabilitation settings. In 1996, the American College of Sports Medicine formally approved a statement of the scope of practice of clinical exercise physiologists. According to ACSM,

> [t]he Clinical Exercise Physiologist works in the application of exercise and physical activity for those clinical and pathological situations where it has been shown to provide therapeutic

> or functional benefit. Patients for whom services are appropriate may include, but not be limited to those with cardiovascular, pulmonary, metabolic, immunological, inflammatory, orthopedic, and neuromuscular diseases and conditions. This list will be modified as indications and procedures of application are further developed and mature. Furthermore, the Clinical Exercise Physiologist applies exercise principles to groups such as geriatric, pediatric, or obstetric populations, and to society as a whole in preventive activities. The Clinical Exercise Physiologist performs exercise evaluation, exercise prescription, exercise supervision, exercise education, and exercise outcome evaluation. The practice of Clinical Exercise Physiologist should be restricted to clients who are referred by and are under the continued care of a licensed physician.[21]

The scope and responsibilities of clinical exercise physiologists are quite broad. Clinical exercise physiologists work closely with physicians and medical personnel to meet the needs of their diverse clientele. To plan rehabilitation programs, clinical exercise physiologists must be familiar with the medical aspects of their clients' disease or condition, cognizant of the limitations faced by clients, and aware of drugs commonly used to treat the disease or condition and their effects. Clinical exercise physiologists must be prepared to help their clients deal with some of the psychological aspects associated with participation in an exercise program, such as the often-expressed fear that exercise will lead to another heart attack.

Career Preparation

Preparation for a career in this area requires a strong background in the exercise sciences and fitness and practical experience. Students will also benefit from obtaining certification from a recognized organization and becoming involved in professional organizations.

Preparation

Today many colleges and universities offer undergraduate and graduate degrees in health promotion-, fitness-, or exercise-related areas. Undergraduate degree programs are available in exercise science, fitness and cardiac rehabilitation, clinical exercise science, adult fitness, corporate fitness, and fitness programming. Although the requirements for the degree vary by institution, in the typical program the student takes core courses such as foundations of exercise science, anatomy and physiology, kinesiology, biomechanics, exercise physiology, injury prevention and care, sport and exercise psychology, sport sociology, and assessment.

In addition to these core courses, more in-depth instruction is provided in exercise science, focusing on assessment of cardiopulmonary function and health status, exercise prescription, exercise leadership, and fitness programming. Certification in cardiopulmonary resuscitation (CPR) is commonly required. Because of the strong relationship of this field to health promotion, students may take courses in nutrition, drug education, pharmacology, and stress management. In completing their preparation, students may find it helpful to take several psychology courses, such as motivation, behavior modification, and individual and group counseling. Computer science courses, statistics, and research methodology are helpful to students in preparing for the administrative and evaluative responsibilities associated with a position in this field. Finally, business courses assist students in dealing with the myriad responsibilities associated with exercise programs, such as budgeting, marketing, and personnel supervision.

To provide students a supervised practical experience in which they have the opportunity to apply and further develop their competencies, most programs require an internship. This internship can take place in a diversity of settings, such as a hospital, corporate fitness center, campus fitness program, or commercial enterprise. The internship typically occurs near the end of the program and serves as a capstone experience.

Also, many programs across the country offer a graduate degree in this area. These programs provide advanced training and an opportunity to specialize. Programs are offered in exercise physiology, fitness programming, cardiac rehabilitation,

Weight training for children is becoming popular. Professionals working with young children and adolescents must be aware of their special needs.

strength development and conditioning, fitness management, corporate fitness, health fitness, and health promotion. These programs may require that students complete an internship, research project, and/or thesis to graduate.

Certification

Certification programs offered by professional organizations have grown within the last 10 years. These programs try to ensure that individuals who receive certification have the necessary skills and knowledge to competently plan and administer programs (see Table 12-1).

The American College of Sports Medicine (ACSM) offers one of the most widely recognized certification programs for professionals in this field. Established in 1972, the ACSM certification program encompasses both preventive and rehabilitative exercise programs, offering three levels of certification within each program track. The Health and Fitness Track certifications are designed for individuals working in fitness programs in which the exercise participants are apparently healthy, have a controlled medical condition for which exercise is not prohibited, and engage in exercise for the maintenance of health.[22] The three certifications included within this track are ACSM Group Exercise Leader, ACSM Health/Fitness Instructor, and ACSM Health/Fitness Director. The Clinical Track certifications are for "individuals who work in clinical settings to provide cardiac or pulmonary rehabilitation or exercise programs for persons who have a chronic disease, such as diabetes."[22] The three certifications associated with the Clinical Track are ACSM Exercise Specialist, ACSM Program Director, and ACSM Registered Clinical Exercise Physiologist. Certifications within both program tracks reflect a progressive level of skills, competency, knowledge, and experience. Additionally, the ACSM offers a Registry for Clinical Exercise Physiologists that promotes ethical standards and competent health and medical services and requires that professionals provide services to patients in a compassionate and respectful manner.[20]

TABLE 12–1 Health and Fitness Certifications

Organization	Selected Certifications

American College of Sports Medicine	• Health and Fitness Track
	  • ACSM Group Exercise Leader
	  • ACSM Health/Fitness Instructor
	  • ACSM Health/Fitness Director
	• Clinical Track
	  • ACSM Exercise Specialist
	  • ACSM Program Director
	  • ACSM Registered Clinical Exercise Physiologist

National Strength and Conditioning Association	• Certified Strength and Conditioning Specialist • Certified Personal Trainer
The Cooper Institute for Aerobics Research	• Physical Fitness Specialist • Master Fitness Specialist • Master Fitness Specialist—Law Enforcement • Health Promotion Director
YMCA	• YMCA Group Exercise Instructor* • YMCA Personal Training Instructor* • Fitness Specialist* • YMCA Martial Arts Exercise Instructor* • Youth Fitness Instructor* • Active Older Adults Exercise Instructor (Land)* • Active Older Adults Water Fitness Instructor* • Healthy Back Instructor* • Prenatal Exercise Instructor* • YMCA Water Fitness Instructor* * Instructor Trainer Courses also offered
Aerobics and Fitness Association of America	• Primary Aerobic Instructor • Personal Trainer/Fitness Counselor • Weight Training • Emergency Response Certification
American Council on Exercise	• Personal Trainer • Group Fitness Instructor • Lifestyle and Weight Management Consultant • Clinical Exercise Specialist

*Many organizations offered other certifications as well as specialty certifications and leadership certifications.

ACSM certification requires satisfactory performance on both a written and a practical examination. Prior to the examination, optional workshops and seminars are usually offered that cover the competencies for each level of certification. Information about certification can be obtained from ACSM's Web site (www.acsm.org).

Other organizations have also developed certification programs, including the YMCA, the American Council on Exercise (ACE), the Aerobics and Fitness Association of America (AFAA), and the National Strength and Conditioning Association (NSCA).

The YMCA offers certifications for individuals who work in the many types of health and fitness programs offered by the organization. Among the certifications offered are those for Personal Training, Fitness Specialist, Group Exercise Instructor, and Water Fitness Instructor. The YMCA also offers fitness certifications designed for professionals working with different population groups; these include the Youth Fitness Instructor, the Active Older Adults Exercise Instructor (Land), the Active Older Adults Water Fitness Instructor, and the Prenatal Exercise Instructor. Additionally, the YMCA provides leadership training in specific fitness areas; for example, you can become certified as a Youth Fitness Instructor Trainer, enabling you to direct a workshop designed to certify individuals as Youth Fitness Instructors. To help instructors stay up-to-date and learn new techniques, the YMCA offers continuing education workshops. Information on certifications can be obtained from the YMCA (www.ymca.net).

ACE offers four types of certifications for fitness professionals. The Personal Trainer certification is for individuals who provide one-on-one fitness training. The Group Fitness Instructor is for fitness instructors who lead group exercise programs. The Lifestyle and Weight Management Consultant Certification is for those individuals who want to offer comprehensive weight management consulting that addresses nutrition, behavior modification, and fitness. The ACE Clinical Exercise Specialist certification is designed for personal trainers who have the experience, skills, and knowledge to work with special populations, including individuals who suffer from chronic disease or who have an injury. It is an advanced personal trainer certification that reflects the individual's ability to screen, assess, design, implement, and evaluate exercise programs to meet the needs and match the abilities of special population groups. ACE offers a variety of training workshops and opportunities to gain expertise in speciality fitness areas. ACE can be found on the Web at www.acefitness.org.

AFAA conducts a certification program, training workshops, and continuing education workshops for fitness professionals. Certification programs include Primary Aerobic Instructor Certification, Personal Trainer/Fitness Counselor Certification, Weight Training Certification, and Emergency Response Certification. Speciality workshops in prenatal fitness, aqua fitness, senior fitness, mat science, and resistance training are offered. Certification requires a written and a practical exam. AFAA workshops and home study programs may also be applied toward American College of Sports Medicine continuing certification. AFAA also offers continuing education via the Web. AFAA can be contacted via the Web at www.afaa.com.

NSCA's focus is on strength development to improve athletic performance and physical fitness. Membership in the NSCA brings together professionals in the areas of sport science, athletic training, and fitness industries. Two certifications are offered: Certified Strength and Conditioning Specialists (CSCS) and Certified Personal Trainer (NSCA-CPT). Candidates for CSCS certification must hold a bachelor of arts or science degree or be enrolled as a senior at an accredited college or university, be CPR-certified, and pass the exam. The NSCA-CPT is designed for professionals who train clients in a one-on-one situation, such as in a client's home, in a fitness or health club, and in organizations such as the YMCA. These professionals often have areas of expertise to accommodate the diverse needs of their clients. They may work with clients who have orthopedic, cardiovascular, and weight problems or who are elderly or have physical disabilities. Both certification programs require practical and written exams. NSCA also sponsors conferences and offers continuing education. NSCA can be contacted via the Web at www.nsca-lift.org.

The Cooper Institute for Aerobics Research offers certification in many different health and fitness areas. The Cooper Institute's foundation certifications include Physical Fitness Specialist and Master Fitness Specialist, with the Master certification representing increased levels of knowledge and competency. The two other foundation certifications are Health Promotion Director and Physical Fitness Specialist—Law Enforcement. The Cooper Institute also offers specialty certification courses, providing additional opportunities for professionals to gain knowledge and receive certification in areas of expertise. These include Counseling Healthy Behaviors, Team Building, Biomechanics of Resistance Training, and Fitness Specialist for Older Adults. The Cooper Institute also sponsors workshops enabling health and fitness professionals to keep abreast of the latest developments in the field. For more information, visit the Cooper Institute's Web site (www.cooperinst.org).

As the number of certification programs continues to grow, students are cautioned to check the quality of the program with professors and professionals in the field before pursuing certification. And, as Siedentop points out, "Remember that a 1-week 'intensive' workshop does not provide the level of preparation that a physical education major receives during a 4-year college program."[23]

Professional Organizations

Membership in professional organizations and establishment of professional affiliations are important for young professionals. Membership will facilitate the development of professional contacts. It provides the opportunity to update one's skills and knowledge through continuing education programs, workshops, and conventions. Students preparing for a career in this area may find membership in AAHPERD, ACSM, and NSCA, to be a valuable professional experience.

Many employment opportunities are available to men and women at the college and university level.

HEALTH-RELATED CAREERS

Health-related career opportunities in the realm of physical education, exercise science, and sport have expanded. Careers in athletic training have become increasingly available. Career opportunities also exist for physical educators, exercise scientists, and sport leaders in health and weight-control clubs and spas.

Athletic Training

In recent years, employment opportunities have increased for professionals with expertise in athletic training. Traditional employment opportunities can be found at the college and professional levels. Employment opportunities at the secondary school level also exist and are growing, although there are still many high schools that do not employ athletic trainers. It is likely that employment opportunities at this level will increase in the near future as states and school systems, concerned about the safety of their athletes and their legal liability, mandate the hiring of certified athletic trainers for interscholastic sports.

Another avenue of employment that is available to athletic trainers is in sports medicine clinics. These clinics can be commercial enterprises, affiliated with hospitals or associated with physical therapy practices. The increase in sport participation by all segments of society has resulted in the need for qualified individuals to evaluate, treat, and rehabilitate injuries.

A new avenue of employment for athletic trainers is in the corporate setting. Companies are realizing that in-house rehabilitation programs, like fitness programs, are cost-effective. Some companies are hiring athletic trainers to work in onsite fitness/rehabilitation centers.[24] It is anticipated that employment opportunities within this setting will expand within the next 10 years.

An athletic trainer's responsibilities are numerous and varied in nature, focusing primarily on the prevention of injury and the rehabilitation of

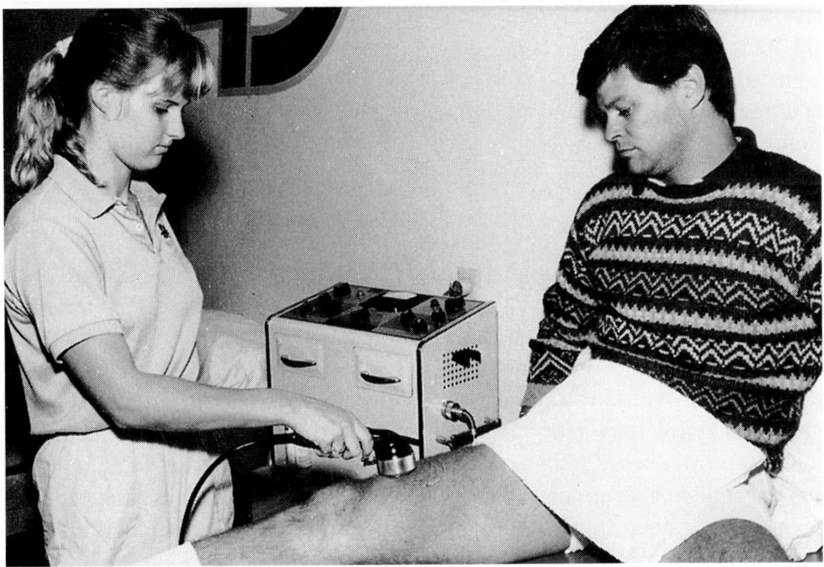

A primary responsibility of athletic trainers is to administer prescribed treatments.

injured athletes. In terms of injury prevention and safety, the athletic trainer performs such preventive measures as taping the ankles and knees of athletes prior to practices and competitions. The athletic trainer works closely with coaches in designing and supervising conditioning programs. Advising coaches and athletes regarding the prevention of injuries is an important responsibility of the athletic trainer. Athletic trainers may also assist in preseason physicals. Checking equipment and checking facilities for safety are tasks often performed by the athletic trainer.

The athletic trainer is often the first person to reach an injured athlete. Thus, the athletic trainer must be prepared to deal with a variety of emergencies. The athletic trainer diagnoses injuries and refers athletes to the appropriate medical personnel for treatment. Working closely with the physician, the athletic trainer implements the prescribed rehabilitation program and administers the appropriate therapeutic treatments. The athletic trainer closely monitors the athlete's efforts and progress during the rehabilitation program. Rehabilitation may be a long and arduous process, and the athletic trainer may need to motivate and encourage the athlete during this trying period to put forth the necessary effort to attain complete recovery. Keeping accurate records of athletes' injuries, the treatment program prescribed, and each athlete's progress during the rehabilitation program is part of the athletic trainer's job.

In addition to competencies pertaining to training, an athletic trainer must possess excellent interpersonal skills. The athletic trainer must work closely with the coaches and the team physician. Establishing and maintaining good rapport with these individuals contributes to a harmonious working relationship. Often the athletic trainer is placed in a position of telling a coach that an athlete cannot practice, play in an upcoming game, or return to the competition after an injury. Professional competency and a good rapport help make these difficult tasks a bit easier. The athletic trainer often finds himself or herself serving as a counselor to the athletes. Athletes may talk to the athletic trainer about problems relating to their own performance or that of their teammates or about problems on the team. The athletic trainer must be able to deal with the concerns of injured athletes; injured athletes may be fearful that they may not be able to return to 100% of their ability, that the injury will limit their performance in some way. The athletic trainer may also be sought out by athletes for advice about their personal and academic problems. The athletic trainer must be able to deal with these numerous problems and concerns in an appropriate and professional manner.

The hours worked by trainers are long. In addition to being in the training room before practice and on the sidelines during practice and competition, the trainer must often spend several hours in the training room at the conclusion of practices and competitions, dealing with any injuries that may have occurred and giving treatments. Trainers may have to come in on weekends for practice or contests and to give athletes treatments. During the season the athletic trainer travels with the team, and this travel can be quite extensive. Because athletic trainers frequently work several sport activities during the year, the season can go on without end. Less visible responsibilities also consume quite a bit of the athletic trainer's time. Cleaning up the training room, rerolling bandages, sterilizing the whirlpool, and ordering supplies are some of the other responsibilities of the athletic trainer. The long and demanding hours and lack of days off have resulted in some athletic trainers experiencing burnout, just as teachers and coaches do. (See Chapter 11 for a further discussion of burnout and its solutions.) Despite the long hours and other demands, many individuals pursue careers in athletic training because of the opportunity to help athletes attain their fullest potential and their desire to be closely associated with athletics. The intrinsic rewards, such as the satisfaction in helping an injured athlete return to competition quickly and at full potential, are many.

At the professional level, the athletic trainer's responsibilities include injury prevention and the care and rehabilitation of injured athletes. At the collegiate level, the athletic trainer's responsibilities may be expanded to include teaching courses in the physical education or health program. In an institution that offers an approved athletic training curriculum, athletic trainers can teach courses within the curriculum as well as supervise student athletic trainers.

At the secondary level, an athletic trainer may be employed in several different capacities. A school may employ a full-time athletic trainer, or the district may employ a full-time athletic trainer to serve all of the schools within the district. An individual may also be hired as a teacher/athletic trainer. Therefore athletic trainers may find it advantageous to possess a teaching certificate in physical education or another academic area. Some schools may contract with a sports medicine center for an athletic trainer and for related services.

Athletic trainers affiliated with clinics generally work fewer hours than individuals in a school or professional setting, and their work schedule is often more regular. Trainers who work in these settings typically work on a one-on-one basis with the athlete. However, an increasing number of schools and community sports programs are contracting with these clinics for services. Therefore, hours worked and working schedules may be similar to those of trainers employed in a school setting.

Salaries for athletic trainers vary widely. The work setting, responsibilities, and amount of experience possessed by the individual influence the salary. The National Athletic Trainers' Association 2000 Salary Survey revealed that athletic trainers with 5 or fewer years of experience averaged $27,623 a year. Athletic trainers with 20 or more years of experience averaged $62,975 (these figures include salary and benefits).[25]

The National Athletic Trainers Association (NATA) offers a certification program in athletic training; increasingly this certification is becoming required to obtain a position. Effective in 2004, in order to obtain certification, an individual must be a graduate of an approved athletic training curriculum. An approved athletic training curriculum includes courses in biological and physical sciences, psychology, first aid, and specific courses relative to training. Certification requires membership in NATA and passing a written and a practical exam. Information regarding certification procedures can be obtained from the NATA (www.nata.org).

Some athletic trainers choose to continue their education and attain a master's degree in physical therapy to add to their skills. Prospective athletic trainers interested in pursuing work in physical therapy should check early in their undergraduate career with institutions offering master's degrees in physical therapy as to requirements for admission, including course prerequisites. Often, courses in physics, chemistry, and math are required for admission to these schools. By knowing the prerequisites early, students may be able to use these courses as electives in their undergraduate professional preparation program. Other athletic trainers choose to continue their education by enrolling in a program leading to a master's degree in athletic training. Being active in professional organizations provides the opportunity to continue one's education through attendance at professional meetings and workshops.

Health and Weight-Control Clubs and Spas

The number of health and weight control clubs and spas has increased greatly during the last decade. Many commercial enterprises have been established to capitalize on people's desire to be physically fit, healthy, and to look their best. Spas can be found at resorts, hotels, mineral springs, and aboard cruise ships. Some spas are residential and others are club and day spas. Some of these businesses are independently owned, whereas others are franchises. It is a multibillion dollar industry. As a result, some health and weight-control clubs and spas are only seeking the public's dollar rather than trying to be of service. However, many spas are reputable, are hiring trained personnel, and have excellent programs. Physical education, exercise science, and sport professionals not only will find an opportunity for employment in health and weight-control clubs and spas, but they also can contribute by upgrading the standards of these businesses.

The activities and services offered by health clubs and spas vary widely. Fitness activities are an integral part of many spas. Some spas may even offer graded exercise tests as part of their program. Many spas provide their clients with instruction and the opportunities to practice a variety of sport activities such as tennis, racquetball, volleyball, and swimming. Aerobic dance, swimnastics, weight training, and a diversity of exercise classes are common. Facilities may include pools; racquetball, handball, squash, and tennis courts; and such amenities as whirlpools, saunas, steam rooms, tanning booths, and massages. Health-promotion activities such as diet and nutritional counseling, stress management, and massage are often offered to the clients.

In recent years, the number of resort-type spas has grown; individuals desiring to shape up and lose weight check into the spa and stay from one

Lifespan and Cultural Perspectives: Fitness, Exercise, and Health

- How can access to health and fitness facilities be improved for underserved populations?
- What modifications to adult exercise tests (e.g., treadmill tests) need to be made to safely and accurately assess fitness in children and adolescents?
- What factors influence employees' use of corporate wellness programs?
- How does one's body image influence enrollment and continued participation in a health club?
- What are the effects of long-term resistance training on fitness levels, body image, and self-concepts of adolescents? Adults over 55?

These women are participating in a fitness program at a spa.

to several weeks. Another pronounced trend is the growth of commercial diet centers and weight-control spas and clubs. Like health clubs and spas, these may be independently owned or franchises. The focus of these businesses is on weight reduction. Exercise classes and fitness activities, similar to those offered in health clubs and spas, may be part of the weight reduction programs at these commercial enterprises.

The growth of these health and weight-control clubs and spas has led to a diversity of employment opportunities for physical education, exercise science, and sport professionals interested in working in these health-related careers. Responsibilities associated with these positions vary widely. Professionals may gain employment in these commercial enterprises as activity instructors or as exercise leaders. They may be responsible for leading an aerobic dance class or for setting up a weight-training program for clients and monitoring their performance. In large clubs, professionals may be responsible for training the club's instructors in various exercise techniques and supervising their work with the club's clients. Where weight control and nutritional counseling are primary concerns, professionals may evaluate the clients' dietary habits, design a diet to help them reach their goal, plan individual exercise programs to be followed in conjunction with the diet, and offer nutritional counseling. In many cases, the professional will be required to attend in-service workshops on the specific diet approach espoused by the business and will also receive training in nutritional counseling and psychological techniques such as behavior modification.

Physical education, exercise science, and sport professionals may also be employed to manage these facilities. Even if professionals are employed as fitness instructors, they have many other responsibilities that are managerial in nature. These responsibilities may include record keeping, training and supervising employees, developing and implementing social programs, and membership solicitation. The varied responsibilities associated with these jobs suggest that in addition to courses in fitness, students should take courses in health, business, psychology, and recreation. Salaries can range from $25,000 to $45,000. Hours and days worked vary. As the interest in being fit and healthy in our society grows, opportunities for employment in these settings appear to be excellent.

Indoor rowing machines are popular among fitness enthusiasts. Competitions allow participants to test their ability.

THERAPY-RELATED CAREERS

Increasingly, movement in its many forms is being used as a means of therapy. Dance therapy, recreational therapy, and movement therapy are recognized as means of improving the physical, mental, emotional, and social well-being of individuals of all ages.

Dance Therapy

The use of dance has proved very helpful in alleviating physical, emotional, and social problems. It has received wide acceptance as a psychotherapeutic means of physical and emotional expression. Through dance, the patient or client has freedom of movement and gains a sense of identity. Dance encourages individuals to recognize their emotions and express them. Through dance, by varying movement qualities, individuals can convey their feelings and ideas to others and perhaps portray emotions that they cannot verbally express. Dance provides a means not only to express one's feelings and emotions to others but also a means of gaining insight into oneself. Dance, by its very nature, can promote sensitivity and awareness.

Dance therapy is one of the fastest-growing professions. It is used in rehabilitation centers, psychiatric centers, geriatric programs, hospitals, and in programs for persons with disabilities. Dance therapy is used with all segments of the population from very young to very old persons. Certification standards for dance therapists have been established by the American Dance Therapy Association (ADTA) (www.adta.org).

Recreational Therapy

Therapeutic recreation is concerned with problems of individuals with physical, mental, and social disabilities and with elderly persons. Recreation therapists work in community and institutional settings where these individuals are located. Therapists use techniques of play and other recreational activities to help individuals achieve appropriate goals in physical, emotional, mental, and social development. Games, sports, arts and crafts, and social activities are modified to meet the needs of the patients or clients so that the goals of the program can be realized. Job opportunities for recreation therapists exist in nursing homes, senior citizen centers, child- and day-care centers, recreational programs, YMCAs/YWCAs, hospitals, clinics, and private agencies.

Degree programs in therapeutic recreation are available. However, there are employment opportunities for physical education, exercise science, and sport professionals who have the background and desire to work in this area. Physical educators and sport leaders working in a community recreation agency may direct therapeutic recreation

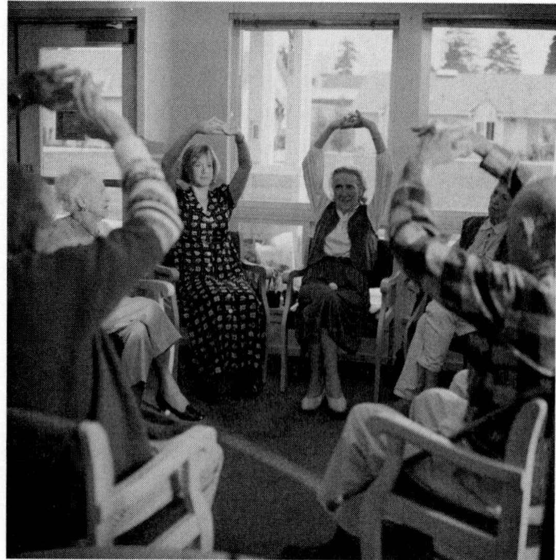

Exercise is important for people of all ages. Flexibility exercises help the elderly retain their range of motion, allowing them to be more independent.

programs in addition to teaching physical skills and leading activities. More information about therapeutic recreation is available from the American Therapeutic Recreation Association (www.atra-tr.org) and the National Therapeutic Recreation Society (www.nrpa.org).

Kinesiotherapy

According to the American Kinesiotherapy Association, a "kinesiotherapist is a health care professional who, under the direction of a physician, treats the effects of disease, injury, and congenital disorders, through the use of therapeutic exercise and education."[26] According to the Commission on Accreditation of Allied Health Education Programs, kinesiotherapists "emphasize (a) prevention of deconditioning and debilitation and (b) development and maintenance of functional fitness in persons with chronic disease or disability."[27] The American Medical Association reports that the types of treatments used by kinesiotherapists focus on "therapeutic exercise, ambulation training, geriatric rehabilitation, aquatic therapy, prosthetic/orthotic rehabilitation, psychiatric rehabilitation, and driver training."[28]

Kinesiotherapists are employed in many different settings, including medical centers, hospitals, sports medicine facilities, rehabilitation facilities, schools, private practice, and as exercise consultants.[27] The average starting salary for kinesiologists is about $28,000 a year, but varies according to the job setting and associated responsibilities.[28]

The American Kinesiotherapy Association offers certification for qualified individuals. Kinesiotherapists may have a degree in physical education or exercise science and must meet specific coursework requirements. Additionally, to qualify for certification, an individual must successfully complete a 1,000-hour clinical internship at an approved site and pass a national certification exam. To maintain their certification, kinesiotherapists must participate in continuing education every year. For more information, contact the American Kinesiotherapy Association (www.akta.org).

Physical Therapy

Physical therapists provide services directed at the restoration, maintenance, and promotion of overall health. Physical therapists work with individuals of all ages to prevent or limit physical disabilities of patients who are injured or who are suffering from disease.[29] Physical therapists work with their patients to restore function, improve mobility, and limit pain.[29]

After reviewing patients' medical histories, physical therapists assess the patients' abilities, including strength, range of motion, balance, coordination, posture, and motor function. A treatment plan is developed and implemented. Treatments might include exercises to help patients who have been immobilized regain their strength, flexibility, and endurance. To help patients improve their ability to function, physical therapists use many techniques, such as electrical stimulation, hot packs, cold compresses, ultrasound, traction, and massage.[29] Physical therapists teach patients how to effectively and efficiently use adaptive and as-

Some physical education, exercise science, and sport professionals build on their undergraduate preparation and obtain a degree in physical therapy.

sistive devices, such as crutches and prostheses.[29] Physical therapists also teach patients exercises to do at home.

Physical therapists often practice as part of a health-care team that includes physicians, therapists, educators, occupational therapists, and speech-language pathologists. Some physical therapists are generalists who treat a wide range of patients and needs. Others are specialists, focusing on pediatrics, geriatrics, orthopedics, sports medicine, and cardiopulmonary physical therapy. Physical therapists are employed in many different settings, most often in hospitals, clinics, and private offices. Some physical therapists work in homes. Salaries vary widely, ranging from mid-$30,000 to over $85,000 annually.[29]

Some physical education, exercise science, and sport professionals decide to build upon their education and attain a master's degree in physical therapy. For those who aspire to continue their education in this area, it is important to note that physical therapy programs have strict admission requirements. Biology, chemistry, and physics are just some of the many requirements that must be satisfied. Additionally, most programs require prospective students to work as volunteers in a physical therapy setting for a specified number of hours. For more information about physical therapy, contact the American Physical Therapy Association (www.apta.org).

• • •

Individuals interested in pursuing careers in dance therapy, recreation therapy, and kinesiotherapy may benefit from courses in adapted physical education, psychology, health, recreation, and counseling. Some physical education, exercise science, and sport professionals build on their background in physical education, athletic training, or exercise science at the undergraduate level to pursue master's degrees in physical or occupational therapy. Physical education, exercise science, and sport professionals aspiring to continue their studies and pursue careers in these areas should, early in their professional preparation, identify courses that are needed as prerequisites for entry into master's degree programs in these areas. Students may then use these prerequisite courses as electives in their undergraduate curriculum.

As recognition of the therapeutic, recreational, and social benefits of movement increases, employment opportunities for physical education, exercise science, and sport professionals in these areas will expand.

INCREASING YOUR PROFESSIONAL MARKETABILITY

Students who are interested in fitness-, health-, or therapy-related careers can do much to increase their professional marketability. Taking additional course work, pursuing certification, building on their talents and interests, and gaining practical experience will enhance the credentials of individuals seeking a position in these areas.

Additional courses in health will increase one's marketability. Conducting health-promotion programs—nutritional counseling, weight management, substance abuse, smoking cessation, and stress management—is often a responsibility associated with positions in this career area. Thus, courses in nutrition, stress management, pharmacology, and drug education are helpful to students preparing for careers in these areas. Courses in counseling, psychology, and sociology will be helpful as well. Prospective professionals need to develop the skills necessary to help individuals change their fitness and health habits. By understanding various decision-making approaches, motivational techniques, and behavior-modification strategies, physical education, exercise science, and sport professionals can help their clients achieve their goals, whether these goals are increased fitness, weight loss, or learning to manage stress. Because many fitness- and health-related careers include responsibilities such as budgeting, program promotion, membership solicitation, and bookkeeping, courses in business and computer science help professionals perform these aspects of the job.

Attaining certification may also increase one's marketability. In many exercise specialist and fitness-related jobs, ACSM certification is becoming an increasingly common requirement. Even if such certification is not required for employment, certification as a Health/Fitness Instructor, for example, may be viewed positively by a prospective employer. Although certification in CPR and first aid may be required, it may be helpful to pursue additional certification as a CPR or First Aid Instructor. These certifications enable one to teach CPR or first aid in a corporate fitness center. Professionals interested in working as exercise specialists or athletic trainers may wish to become certified as EMTs. This will provide additional expertise in the area of emergency care. Belonging to professional organizations such as AAHPERD, ACSM, NSCA, or NATA will also allow one to take advantage of workshops and clinics in one's area of interest.

Building on one's interests and strengths through extracurricular and outside experiences can contribute to one's professional expertise. If you are interested in weight training, for example, and work out frequently, take the time to learn about the different approaches to weight training. Expertise in dance is necessary for those seeking a career in dance therapy and can also enhance the skills of individuals seeking to work in corporate and community fitness centers and preschool programs. Aerobic dance has become a very popular approach to fitness and is often used in fitness centers.

Gaining practical experience through internships, fieldwork, volunteering, or part-time and/ or summer employment can enhance one's marketability. There is no substitute for experience. Take advantage of the opportunities to work in potential places of employment to gain insight into the day-to-day work. Working as an assistant to a recreational therapist or physical therapist in a hospital, assisting in a sports medicine clinic, supervising clients working out in a health spa, and interning in a corporate fitness center provide practical experience and the opportunity to put theoretical knowledge gained in your undergraduate preparation into practice, as well as teach you the skills necessary for employment in these positions. Through various practical experiences, professional contacts can be developed as well.

Focus on Career: Health, Fitness, Sports Medicine

PROFESSIONAL ORGANIZATIONS	• American College of Sports Medicine www.acsm.org • National Athletic Trainers' Association www.nata.org • National Strength and Conditioning Association www.nsca-lift.org • American Association for Active Lifestyles and Fitness www.aahperd.org → AAALF
PROFESSIONAL JOURNALS	• *Clinical Exercise Physiology* • *Journal of Athletic Training* • *Journal of Sport Rehabilitation* • *Journal of Strength and Conditioning Research* • *Medicine and Science in Sports and Exercise* • *The Physician and Sports Medicine* • *Strength and Conditioning Journal*

Physical education, exercise science, and sport professionals can increase their opportunities for employment in fitness-, health- and therapy-related careers by several means. Taking additional course work, building on one's interests and strengths, attaining relevant certifications, and gaining practical experience are strategies that will enhance your marketability.

SUMMARY

Within the past decade, opportunities for physical education, exercise science, and sport professionals desiring to pursue a career as a fitness or exercise specialist have increased tremendously. Career opportunities exist in preventive and rehabilitative exercise programs. Preventive exercise programs are conducted by corporations, community agencies, and commercial fitness clubs. Rehabilitative exercise programs are typically conducted in a hospital setting, but may be affiliated with corporate fitness programs and community agency programs.

Opportunities for physical education, exercise science, and sport professionals to pursue health-related careers have also grown rapidly. Professionals possessing qualifications in athletic training may find employment working with athletic programs at the professional, collegiate, and, increasingly, the secondary level. Employment opportunities also are available in sports medicine clinics, physical therapy clinics, and hospitals. Physical educators, exercise science, and sport leaders have also been successful in securing employment in health and weight-control spas and clubs.

The recognition that participation in movement and physical activities has therapeutic and psychological benefits as well as physical benefits has stimulated the growth of therapy-related careers. These include careers as dance therapists, recreational therapists, and physical therapists. Kinesiotherapy is also a potential career for physical education, exercise science, and sport professionals.

If you are seeking employment in fitness- and health-related careers, you can increase your marketability by taking additional course work in health, business, and psychology. Gaining as much practical experience as possible will also be an asset in securing employment.

It appears that opportunities for qualified individuals in fitness- and health-related careers will continue to increase in the future.

SELF-ASSESSMENT TESTS

These tests are designed to help you determine if you have mastered materials and competencies presented in this chapter.

1. Describe the responsibilities of a fitness or an exercise specialist. If possible, interview a professional in this career regarding his or her responsibilities and qualifications.
2. Describe the various employment opportunities for a fitness or exercise professional. Review the want ads in several large city papers for two weeks for employment opportunities in this area or search for jobs online; describe the positions that you found available and qualifications required for employment.
3. Using the information provided in the Get Connected box, read about one of the certification programs available through the American College of Sports Medicine, American Council on Exercise, National Athletic Training Association, the Cooper Institute for Aerobics Research, and the National Strength and Conditioning Association. For the association you have selected, investigate the certification programs, benefits offered to members, and opportunities for continuing education. How could this certification be beneficial to you in your chosen career?
4. Using the information provided in the Get Connected box, locate new research, industry news, and position papers pertaining to health and fitness. Summarize your findings in a brief report.

REFERENCES

1. Cooper KH and Collingwood TR: Physical fitness: programming issues for total well-being, JOPERD 55(3):35–36, 44, 1984.
2. Sol N: Graduation preparation for exercise program professionals, JOPERD 52(7):76–77, 1981.
3. US Department of Health and Human Services: Healthy people 2010, ed 2, Washington D.C., 2000, US Government Printing Office.
4. DiNubile NA and Sherman C: Exercise and the bottom line: promoting physical and fiscal fitness in the workplace: a commentary, The Physician and Sportsmedicine 27(2), 1999.
5. Shepard RJ: Do work-site exercise and health programs work? The Physician and Sportsmedicine Online, February 1999.
6. Riedel JE, Lynch W, Baase C, Hymel P, and Peterson KW: The effect of disease prevention and health promotion on workplace productivity: a literature review, American Journal of Health Promotion 15(3): 167–191, 2001.
7. President's Council on Physical Fitness and Sports: Economic benefits of physical activity, Washington, D.C., 1996, The President's Council on Physical Fitness and Sports Physical Activity Research Digest.
8. US Department of Health and Human Services: Physical activity and health: a report of the Surgeon General, Atlanta, Ga., 1996, US Department of Health and Human Services, Centers for Disease Control and Prevention, National Center for Chronic Disease Prevention and Health Promotion.
9. Aldana, SG: Financial impact of health promotion programs: a comprehensive review of the literature, American Journal of Health Promotion 15:4, 2001.
10. Learning about health and productivity: The Health Enhancement Research Advocate 3(1), 2000.
11. Editor's notes: American Journal of Health Promotion, Jan/Feb, 2001.
12. Association for Worksite Health Promotion: The benefits of worksite health promotion, 1997, Association for Worksite Health Promotion.
13. Chapman LS: Guidelines for health promotion in worksite settings, The Art of Health Promotion 6(6):6–9, 2003.

14. Wellness Councils of America: Health, wealthy and wise—fundamentals of workplace health promotion, Omaha, Nebr. 1993, Wellness Councils of America.
15. Lewis RJ, Huebner WW, and Yarborough CM, III: Characteristics of participants and nonparticipants in worksite health promotion, American Journal of Health Promotion 11:99–106, 1996.
16. Drolet JC and Fetro JV: State conferences for school worksite wellness: personal health practices of conference participants, Journal of Health Promotion 24(3):174–178, 1993.
17. International Health, Racquet, and Sport Club Association: Industry statistics. 2002. (www.ihrsa.org)
18. Aufsesser PM and Burke JP: The fitness clinic for physically disabled, Palestra 13:18–20, 1997.
19. Cohon A: Special treatment: hospital wellness centers, Athletic Business 21(7):31–34, 1997.
20. National Strength and Conditioning Association. (www.nsca-lift.org)
21. American College of Sports Medicine endorses clinical exercise physiologist profession. (www.acsm.org)
22. ACSM Certifications. (www.acsm.org)
23. Siedentop D: Introduction of physical education, fitness, and sport, Mountain View, Calif. 1990, Mayfield.
24. Zimmerman GR: Industrial medicine and athletic training: cost effectiveness in the nontraditional setting, Journal of Athletic Training 28(2):131–136, 1993.
25. NATA 2000 Salary Data Survey Results: National Athletic Trainers' Association. (www.nata.org)
26. American Kinesiotherapy Association. (www.akta.org)
27. Commission on Accreditation of Allied Health Education Programs: Kinesiotherapist, 2002. (www.caahep.org)
28. American Medical Association: Kinesiotherapist. (www.ama-assn.org)
29. Bureau of Labor Statistics, US Department of Labor, Occupational Outlook Handbook, 2004–2005 ed., Physical Therapists. Retrieved on December 21, 2004. (www.bls.gov/ovo)

SUGGESTED READINGS

Aldana SG, Merrill RM, Price K, Hardy A, and Hager R: Financial impact of a comprehensive multisite workplace health promotion program, Preventive Medicine 40:131–138, 2005.

This study provides information about the effectiveness of a school district wellness program. The researchers found no significant differences in health-care costs for participants, but did find that program participants missed three fewer workdays than nonparticipants, a savings of $15.60 for every dollar invested.

Aufsesser PM and Burke JP: The fitness clinic for physically disabled, Palestra 13:18–20, 1997.

Information about the fitness clinic for the physically disabled is presented, including program goals and the value of the program for young professionals.

Cohon A: Special treatment: hospital wellness centers, Athletic Business 21(7):31–34, 1997.

Hospital wellness centers are growing and offer additional opportunities for professionals in physical education and sport.

Durrett A: Starting a worksite wellness business. IDEA Health and Fitness Source, June 1999.

This article is for fitness professionals who want to enter or expand their services into worksite health promotion. To enter this field, professionals need to become knowledgeable about cost-saving benefits of worksite programs and types of programming that work best in this setting and develop a business plan to market their services.

Huddleston E: Fitness at work, Athletic Business, 2001. (Online at www.athleticbusiness.com)

Articulates the benefits of worksite programs and includes examples to illustrate different programs in action.

McDermott L: A qualitative assessment of the significance of body perception to women's physical activity experiences: revisiting discussions of physicalities, Sociology of Sport Journal 17:331–363, 2000.

Explores how women's perceptions of their bodies influence their initiation of physical activity and how physical activity affects their perceptions of their bodies. Included is a discussion of the significance of participation to women involved in aerobics and wilderness canoe-tripping.

Pelletier KR: A review and analysis of the clinical- and cost-effectiveness studies of comprehensive health promotion and disease management programs at the worksite: 1998–2000 Update, American Journal of Health Promotion 16:107–116, 2001.

This review of 15 studies of worksite health promotion programs highlights methodological issues, identifies outcomes, and, as Pelletier reports, offers moderate to strong evidence that these comprehensive programs are both clinically effective and cost-effective.

Pierce P and Herman S: Obtaining, maintaining, and advancing your fitness certification, JOPERD 75(7):50–55, 2004.

Certification is defined, the certification process explained, and several certifying organizations described. The authors emphasize the importance of professional development once certification is attained.

Rupp JC, Campbell K, Thompson WR, and Terbizan D: Professional preparation of personal trainers, JOPERD, January 1999, 54–57.

Some physical education, exercise science, and sport professionals have embarked on a career as a personal trainer. This article discusses need qualifications, legal liability, and future directions.

Walk SR: Peers in pain: the experiences of student athletic trainers, Sociology of Sport Journal 14: 22–56, 1997.

This article provides insights about the experiences of student athletic trainers who work with their athlete-peers, including information about their expectations, management of injuries, and risks involved in sport.

CHAPTER 13

SPORT CAREERS

OBJECTIVES

After reading this chapter the student should be able to—

- Identify opportunities for professionals in sport management and entry-level positions in these careers.
- Describe career opportunities in sports media and explain how preparation in physical education, exercise science, and sport can assist individuals in these careers.
- Describe career opportunities in performance and other sport-related careers.
- Discuss how professionals can increase their professional marketability.

Participation in fitness activities and sport at all levels is at an all-time high, and it appears that participation will continue to increase in the future. One indication of this growth is the sale of fitness and sports products. According to the Sporting Goods Manufacturers Association (SGMA), in 2003 the sporting goods industry enjoyed nearly $50 billion in wholesale business.[1] Some highlights that reflect the state of the industry in 2003 include:

- Sales of sport apparel totaled $22.8 billion. Sales of active sportswear—that is, sportswear likely to be used to participate in fitness and sports activities—exceeded $12.7 billion.
- Sales of athletic footwear rose to $9.73 billion, up from $9.34 billion in 2002. Running/jogging shoes ($2.77 billion), basketball shoes ($2.07 billion), and cross-training/fitness shoes ($1.06 billion) topped the market. SGMA notes that athletic footwear is a fashion product and estimates that less than 30% of athletic footwear is actually used for sport and fitness activities.
- Retail sales of sport licensed products in the United States and Canada reached $12.1 billion. Products with team logos and/or stars' names on them from the National Basketball Association, National Hockey League, NASCAR, and college and universities are popular and sales continue to rise.
- Sport equipment sales reached $17.5 billion. Sales of exercise equipment machines led this category, topping $3.8 billion; golf equipment sales ranked second at $2.42 billion dollars.

GET CONNECTED

Athletic Business site allows free registration and access to the archives of articles on a variety of sports issues pertaining to equity, management, coaching, fitness, and professionalism.

www.athleticbusiness.com

North American Society for Sport Management contains information about the organization, membership, publications, and conferences.

www.nassm.com

ESPN and CNN—Sports Illustrated sites provide up-to-date information about sports and sports issues.

http://msn.espn.go.com/main.html

http://sportsillustrated.cnn.com

Women's Sports Foundation site gives access to research, information about career opportunities in sports, articles on a variety of topics, and internships.

www.womenssportsfoundation.org

- In the exercise equipment category, consumer spending accounted for 81.3% of the total expenditures. Treadmill sales led this category, accounting for 26.4% of exercise equipment sold. The next two largest categories were home gyms, reaching sales of $305 million, and exercise cycles, $200 million.

As can be seen from these figures, interest in sports and fitness is tremendous, and the industry has become a big business. As participation and the sporting industry continue to grow, career opportunities in the various areas of sport management will expand.

Spectator interest in all sports at all levels is rising. Many sports recorded record-high attendance at contests. The NCAA's women's basketball Final Four championships continue to sell out, as do the men's Final Four championships. The Women's Basketball League (WNBA) draws nearly 2 million fans a season. Nearly 20 million fans attended regular season NBA games. Almost 15 million attended regular season NFL games. The growth of spectator interest in sport at all levels widens the career opportunities for physical education, exercise science, and sport professionals.

The media—television, newspapers, magazines, books, and movies—have come to play an increasingly important role in the realm of sports. Sports coverage by the various media continues to grow and has become big business. Two of the greatest areas of growth are cable television and the Internet. Monies paid by television for broadcasting rights to certain sports provide a good example of the magnitude of media involvement in sports. For example, the National Football League will get at least $17.6 billion from four television networks for the rights to broadcast games through 2005. Contrast that to 1960 and 1961 when the NFL received $600,000 for the television rights. NBC spent $2.6 billion dollars to secure the broadcast rights for the Olympic Games through the year 2008. CBS paid $6 billion dollars to telecast the NCAA men's basketball tournament for 11 years. ESPN paid $200 million for the right to cover the NCAA Division I Basketball Championships.

Premier sporting events, such as the Olympics, Super Bowl, NCAA Basketball, National Basketball League Playoffs, Major League Baseball's World Series, and soccer's World Cup are watched by millions, even billions of people worldwide. For example, the National Basketball Association

(NBA) playoffs on NBC were watched by nearly 600 million viewers; NBA programming is seen in nearly 200 countries in 41 languages. Media coverage of women's events is also increasing and is gaining in popularity. For example, broadcasts of the WNBA are seen in over 125 countries. As media coverage continues to grow, so will opportunities for qualified professionals seeking a career in this area.

Sport at many levels is big business. In 2001, it was estimated that amateur, college, and professional sports generated $48 billion in sales.[2] The NFL takes in the most revenue, estimated to be about $5 billion in 2004.[3] Today, professional athletes are paid astronomical sums of money. For example, from 2003 to 2004, the median salary for the National Hockey League New York Rangers was $2.8 million.[4] In 2004, the total payroll for Major League Baseball's New York Yankees was estimated at $1.84 million, and the median salary was reported to be $3.1 million.[4] In 2001, it was reported that the average salary for the Women's National Basketball Association was $55,000. Successful professional tennis players and golfers, both men and women, earn millions each year.

Product endorsements provide additional monies for athletes, while increasing the companies' bottom line. In 2004, it was reported that Nike has earmarked $1.6 billion for long-term endorsements for this year, an increase of $192 million from the past year.[5] Tiger Woods has a 5-year $100 million contract with Nike, among other sponsors, and was estimated to have earned over $55 million in endorsements in 2001, more than he earned on tour. Other high-profile athletes with lucrative endorsement deals include LeBron James, Derek Jeter, Michael Vick, and Michael Jordan. Additionally, many companies are expanding into the international market to promote their products. Reebok signed Yao-Ming for an estimated $100 million.[5] The NBA continues to strive to increase its $2.4 billion in international licensing.[5] Nike and Adidas compete to increase their share of the international soccer market. In 2003, Nike's share of the European soccer market was estimated to be 34% compared to 30.2% for Adidas.[5] Since the 2002 World Cup, Nike has increased its share of the soccer business by 100%, accruing an estimated $100 billion in annual sales.[5]

As you can see from the statistics, the sport is a mega-business, one that is constantly expanding. The magnitude of the industry as well as its diverse nature offers students with an interest in sport a multitude of career opportunities. Before describing some of the many opportunities available, a short overview of sport management, an ever-expanding area of study is presented. Examples of careers associated with sport management, including sport media, are next highlighted. In addition to careers in these areas, some individuals aspire to careers as performers. Others pursue careers in officiating and sports law. Entrepreneurship captures the interest of other individuals, who develop their own business or services.

SPORT MANAGEMENT

Sport management is a rapidly growing area of knowledge. Professional opportunities for individuals trained in this area are diverse and challenging. Sport management can be defined in many different ways. According to DeSensi, Kelley, Blanton, and Beitel, sport management is "any combination of skills related to planning, organizing, directing, controlling, budgeting, leading and evaluating within the context of an organization or department whose primary product or service is related to sport."[6] Opportunities within this broad field include but are not limited to the management of facilities, hotels, resorts, fitness facilities, clubs, merchandising, and sports at all levels and within the public as well as the private sectors.

The growth of the sport business industry, a multibillion-dollar-a-year industry, has created additional opportunities within the field. Given the expanding dimensions of sport, Parkhouse and Pitts suggest that a more contemporary definition of sport management may be needed. They define sport management as the following:

> Sport management is the study and practice involved in relation to all people, activities, organizations, and businesses involved in

> producing, facilitating, promoting, or organizing any product that is sport, fitness, and recreation-related; and, sport products can be goods, services, people, places, or ideas.[7]

Sport can include a wide range of activities, ranging from the spectator sport industry and its focus on consumer entertainment to the fitness and sport industry and its focus on consumer participation.

A conceptual analysis of the dimensions of sport management developed by Blann is shown in Figure 13-1.[8] Sport management is conceptualized as encompassing the sport work, organized sport, management of sport experiences, and the sport enterprise.

During the past three decades, the academic study of sport management has grown tremendously. Historically the study of sport management, like that of the other subdisciplines, was based in physical education. Today, sport management continues to grow and develop its own specialized programs of study.

There are several major professional organizations for sport management professionals. The North American Society for Sport Management (NASSM) was established in 1985 to promote sport management and to encourage the growth of research, scholarly writing, and professional development in the field. NASSM sponsors an annual conference and publishes the *Journal of Sport Management.* The National Association for Sport and Physical Education (NASPE), one of the associations of the American Alliance for Health, Physical Education, Recreation and Dance, established a Sport Management Council (SMC). The SMC strives to provide the development of quality programs in sport management, to work to develop research and projects of benefit to professionals, and

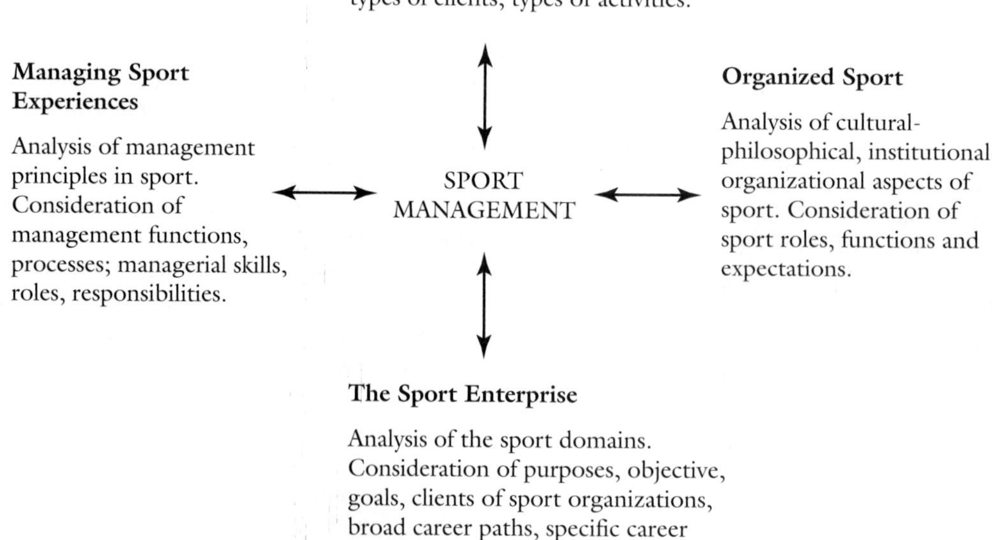

Figure 13-1 Four-factor analysis of sport management.

to establish mutually beneficial relationships with professionals in sport industry. Two other associations deal with specific aspects of the sport management field. The Sport and Recreation Law Association (SRLA) focuses on the legal aspects of sport. In addition to their annual conference, SRLA publishes the *Journal of Legal Aspects of Sport.* The Sport Marketing Association provides professionals an opportunity to interact with others who share a similar interest in sport marketing.

As the area of sport management evolved from physical education, new programs were developed to prepare professionals in this specialized area. Today there are over 200 programs offering degrees in sport management at the undergraduate and graduate levels. In an effort to ensure that students entering the field were prepared with the appropriate knowledge and skills, a joint task force was established by NASPE and NASSM to develop standards for sport management professional preparation programs.

NASPE-NASSM defines sport management as "the field of study offering specialized training and education necessary for individuals seeking careers in any of the many segments of the industry."[9] The NASPE-NASSM Task Force developed a comprehensive set of competencies to be included in a sport management professional preparation curriculum. The undergraduate content areas include:

- Sociocultural dimensions.
- Management and leadership in sport.
- Ethics in sport management.
- Marketing in sport.
- Communication in sport.
- Budget and finance in sport.
- Legal aspects of sport.
- Economics in sport.
- Governance in sport.
- Field experience in sport management.[9]

The field experience is considered a critical aspect of preparation for a career in the sport management. An internship is commonly required. Students usually work in a sport management setting for a semester or summer, working at least 40 hours a week and accumulating at least 400 hours. This experience is supervised by a faculty member from the undergraduate institution, as well as by a professional at the internship site. Additional practical experiences can be gained by students through fieldwork (short periods of supervised work in a professional setting), by volunteering, or by working in a sport management position during the summer or on a part-time basis during the school year. Practical experiences are also a good way to investigate the growing number of career opportunities in this rapidly expanding field.

The increased growth of athletics, sport participation by all segments of our society, and sport-related businesses has created a need for individuals trained in sport management. There are many different career paths that students with an interest in sport management can pursue. The dynamic nature of the field and the growth of the field lead to new career and plentiful career opportunities for students well prepared in this area. Figure 13-2, developed by Blann, shows some of the sport management career paths.[10] Employment opportunities include sport administration, management of sport clubs and facilities, sport and leisure social services, sport marketing, and sport communication.

Individuals interested in pursuing a career in sport management need to realize that they will likely begin their career working in an entry-level position, often with limited responsibilities. From this position, competent individuals can work their way up the career ladder to middle- and top-management positions. Each step up the ladder typically requires assuming increased and more broad-ranging responsibilities. Salaries in this field vary widely, ranging from $24,000 to $40,000 per year, although some salaries may be greater than $100,000 a year.

CAREERS IN SPORT MANAGEMENT

Athletic administration, campus and corporate recreation management, sport facilities management, sport retailing, and sport tourism opportunities are described in the next section. Additionally,

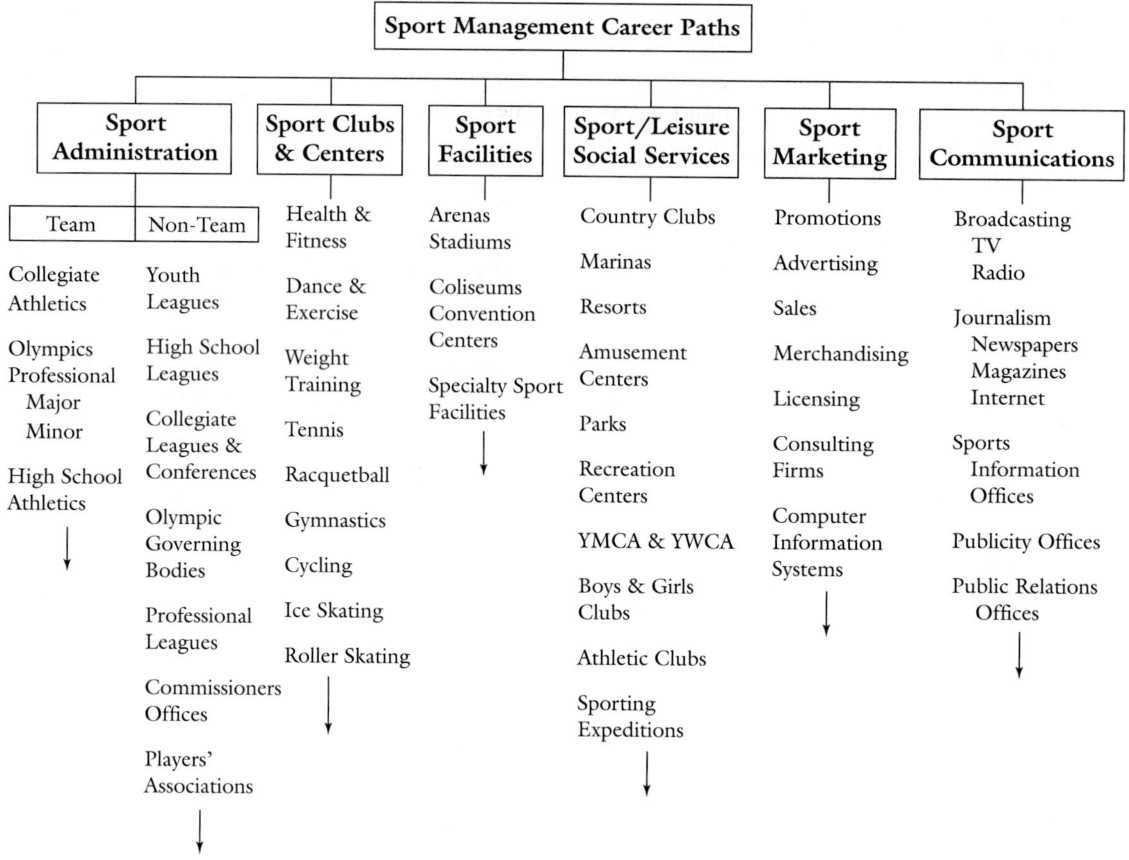

Figure 13-2 Sport management career paths.

a myriad of opportunities exist for qualified individuals in professional organizations, conferences, and leagues.

Athletic Administration

There are many job opportunities in the field of athletic administration. At the high school level, administrative positions are available as an athletic director and, depending on the size of the school, as an assistant athletic director. At the collegiate level, many administrative opportunities exist, with the number of administrative positions and associated responsibilities depending on the nature and size of the athletic program. Among the administrative positions are athletic director, associate athletic director, and assistant athletic director. Other administrative positions that might be found in collegiate athletic programs include program fund-raising director, marketing director, recruiting coordinator, compliance coordinator, and academic counseling coordinator. Not all colleges and universities have these positions; oftentimes, the athletic director and his or her associate/assistant director may fulfill the responsibilities associated with these positions.

The director of athletics is responsible for the administration of the athletic programs. This position may be found at high schools as well as at colleges and universities. Typically, at the high school level, the athletic director may be employed as a teacher and, in smaller schools, also as a coach. At the collegiate level as well, athletic directors also may have teaching and coaching responsibilities. In many schools, however, particularly those with large competitive programs, the athletic director may have as his or her sole responsibility the conduct of the competitive program. In many instances, athletic directors have associate and assistant athletic directors to help them in the performance of their work.

The athletic director is responsible for performing a myriad of tasks. The athletic director may delegate these tasks to assistants or perform them himself or herself. The athletic director is responsible for the administration of men's and women's athletics. This includes both the hiring and ongoing supervision of coaches and assistant coaches. The athletic director must be knowledgeable regarding the rules and regulations governing athletic competition, including rules pertaining to the recruitment and eligibility of athletes. Other tasks are scheduling of athletic contests; arranging for officials; and, for competitions involving travel, planning for transportation, lodging, and meals.

The athletic director is also responsible for the safety of the coaches, athletes, and spectators at home contests. This involves working closely with security personnel and making careful provisions for crowd control. At home contests, the athletic director supervises the ticket office and concessions. The athletic director must work closely with other personnel involved in athletics such as the athletic trainers and sport information directors. Establishing a good working relationship with the facilities manager and maintenance staff is important as well.

Development and management of the athletic budget is an important function of the athletic director, who is often expected to work as a fund raiser. Establishing and maintaining good relationships with the community, local support groups such as Booster Clubs, and alumni are seen as vital to the success of the athletic program. The athletic director must also attend professional meetings to keep abreast of changes in rules and governance.

In large athletic programs, such as those at major colleges and universities, there may be a fairly large administrative staff with specific job responsibilities assigned to each person. Many large institutions employ associate and/or assistant athletic directors. A few institutions employ directors of fund-raising who are charged with obtaining money to supplement the athletic budget. Some institutions have employees who monitor the institution's compliance with the growing number of rules and regulations of the athletic governing bodies, most notably the National Collegiate Athletic Association (NCAA).

More and more institutions have academic support programs for their student-athletes. Through these programs, student-athletes have access to tutoring, supervised study tables, and courses in life skills. The academic coordinator also works with faculty and other academic resources across campus to help student-athletes fulfill their academic obligations. Some tutors travel with the team, providing student-athletes with academic support when they are on the road for an extended period of time. Some institutions have an administrator who coordinates the academic support program; in other institutions, this responsibility is undertaken by the athletic director or one of his or her assistants. Opportunities exist within these programs for program coordinators, tutors, and instructors of life skills courses.

Salaries associated with the various jobs in athletic administration vary widely, depending on the extent of the responsibilities and the size of the program. Salaries can range from $25,000 to over $100,000. For individuals who enjoy working with athletics, jobs in athletic administration can be very rewarding.

Students interested in pursuing a career in athletic administration may find it helpful to know that at the high school level, directors of athletics typically have a degree in physical education and coaching experience. At the collegiate level, athletic directors may have a physical education degree, a sport management degree, or a business degree. Additionally, oftentimes an advanced degree, either a master's or doctoral degree, is required. Students aspiring to a career in athletic administration may want to take advantage of opportunities to intern or volunteer at their college or a high school athletic department. Additionally, the NCAA offers scholarships for post-graduate internships in athletic administration.

Director of Intramurals and/or Campus Recreation

College and university intramural programs and campus recreation programs have expanded in recent years. Traditional intramural programs have grown to include a variety of recreational opportunities. Wellness and fitness offerings, such as step aerobics, are also becoming popular. These programs have also expanded to include not only students but faculty, staff, and other campus personnel.

Many titles have been used to describe the individual charged with the administration of these programs. These titles include Director of Intramurals, Director of Recreational Sports, and Director of Campus Recreation. Depending on the institution, the intramural and campus recreation programs may be administered through student services, the physical education department, or the athletic department. In schools with large programs, the director may have an assistant or several staff members to help conduct the program.

Responsibilities associated with this position are wide ranging. One of the primary responsibilities is to promote participation. This requires scheduling activities and tournaments that are of interest to students, publicizing programs, and working closely with campus groups such as residential life and student government to promote these programs. Training and supervision of officials are essential if programs are to run smoothly and safely. The director may also be responsible for instructional programs and the supervision of sport and recreation clubs. Often the director is assigned to supervise physical education and athletic facilities and open recreation programs such as recreational swimming. This may entail the training and supervision of numerous students to serve as lifeguards, gymnasium supervisors, or building security guards.

The intramural director may or may not have teaching responsibilities, depending on the size of the program. Programs are usually offered from late afternoon to late at night; frequently in schools with limited facilities, intramurals cannot start until the athletic teams have finished their practices. Programs also may be offered on weekends. Professionals who are interested in promoting educational values through activities and in providing opportunities for others to experience the satisfaction derived from participation will find working in intramural and campus recreation programs an enjoyable career. The National Intramural-Recreational Sports Association provides additional information on career opportunities and programming (www.nirsa.org).

Director of Corporate Recreation

More and more companies are providing recreational and sport opportunities for their employees. As the number of programs has increased, so has the need for qualified professionals to direct these activities. The responsibilities associated with this position are similar to those associated with the director of intramurals and/or campus recreation. These responsibilities include establishing a program of activities, setting up athletic teams, scheduling contests, providing for instruction, and supervising personnel. As corporate recreation programs continue to grow, so will opportunities for qualified professionals.

Sport Facilities Management

Facilities manager positions can be found in a diversity of settings. Facilities managers are traditionally employed by colleges and universities. Facilities managers are needed to direct community, municipal, and commercial facilities such as aquatic centers, ice arenas, domed stadiums, sports complexes, and golf courses. The growing number of fitness centers and health clubs has also increased opportunities for individuals interested in facilities management.

The 70,000-seat Edward Jones Dome is home to the NFL's St. Louis Rams. Job opportunities in professional sports have increased in the last decade.

Depending on the size of the sport facility, nature of programs, and number of individuals using the facility, the sport facilities manager may perform all the responsibilities by himself or herself or may have an assistant or several staff persons under his or her direction. In some situations, the facilities manager may have additional responsibilities; for instance, in a fitness club the facilities manager may also teach exercise classes or monitor individuals' workouts.

One of the primary concerns of the sport facilities manager is the safety of individuals using the facility. This involves making sure that the facility and equipment are maintained according to accepted standards. Knowledge of building codes, health and sanitation requirements, and certain laws is necessary in this position. In facilities that are used for competitions, such as stadiums, the facilities manager must make provisions to ensure the safety and well-being of spectators as well as participants. The manager must be concerned with crowd control and is responsible for security personnel. The facilities manager also is concerned about the business aspects of managing the facility, and he or she can have an impact on the financial success of the facility. The facility must be scheduled for maximum use to ensure a profitable financial status. The manager may also supervise other financial aspects of the facility such as ticket sales, concessions, and parking. As the number of facilities continues to grow, opportunities in this area for qualified personnel will expand.

Sport Retailing

Sales of sporting goods—equipment, apparel, and shoes—are at an all-time high. Exercise equipment and golf equipment top sporting goods sales. Sales of sports apparel, sports active wear, athletic footwear, and licensed sports products sales are in the billions. Sport retailing is a booming business. Additionally, the enormous growth of women's sports since the enactment of Title IX has created new markets for sporting goods. Manufacturers are now designing equipment and apparel specifically for girls and women, rather than downsizing boys' and men's products. The public's growing interest in sport, fitness, and physical activities has stimulated sales, and the traditional markets such as schools, colleges, and universities, and professional teams have remained strong. Consequently, job opportunities in sport retailing, in both management and sales, have increased and will continue to grow.

The area of sport retailing has several opportunities. Jobs are available as salespersons selling directly to the consumer in sporting goods stores. Job opportunities also are available as manufacturers' representatives. An individual employed in this capacity, perhaps as a representative for Nike, may sell to buyers for sporting goods stores and to athletic teams in a certain region. Manufacturers' representatives are committed to increasing their company's share of the market. This position entails a great deal of travel. Hours may be spent on the phone setting up appointments with potential buyers and following up on sales calls. Whether a manufacturer's representative is successful depends to a great extent on the quality and reputation of the product he or she is selling and the establishment of personal contacts with buyers for these stores and institutions. Manufacturers' representatives may often submit bids for equipment and goods wanted by stores and institutions. Successful bidding requires that the salesperson be able to meet the buyer's specifications for the equipment and goods at the lowest cost. Manufacturers' representatives may also set up sales booths for their companies at conventions such as the AAHPERD National Convention. Other opportunities in sport sales include positions as a manager or owner of a company.

Job opportunities in sport retailing may involve direct sales, retail management, and serving as a manufacturer's representative.

Salaries for sales positions vary widely. Salespersons may receive a set salary. More often, however, their income is based on commissions and bonuses for the sales they have completed; thus, their income may vary widely from month to month. Salespersons who travel may receive a company car or an allowance for the use of their personal car, as well as an expense account. Salespersons may receive free equipment and goods or be able to purchase them at substantial discounts.

Being a salesperson requires that an individual be extremely knowledgeable about the products that he or she is selling. The consumer in a sporting goods store often expects the salesperson to be an expert on all types of equipment. Buyers for institutions and stores expect manufacturers' representatives to know all the specifications for the equipment and goods they are selling. A background in physical education and sport is helpful in understanding the demands and nature of various sport areas and the requirements for equipment and goods for these kinds of sports. Courses in business management and accounting are helpful for salespersons. Being a salesperson requires strong interpersonal skills and the ability to identify individuals' needs and to sell them a product that meets their needs. As the interest in sport, physical activities, and fitness continues to grow, opportunities for salespersons will expand as well. For more information about the state of the sporting goods industry, contact the Sporting Goods Manufacturers Association (www.sgma.com).

Career Opportunities in Professional Organizations

Qualified physical education, exercise science, and sport professionals may find employment in one of the many professional or specific sport organizations such as AAHPERD, NCAA, National Federation of State High School Associations (NFSHSA), Ladies Professional Golf Association (LPGA), National Hockey League (NHL), or United States Tennis Association (USTA). Other jobs are available in athletic conferences, such as in the offices of the Big Ten or the Big East. Foundations, such as the Women's Sports Foundation, are yet another place for employment.

The jobs available in professional organizations vary, depending on the nature of the organization and its size. Entry-level managerial positions may be available dealing with the day-to-day operations of the organization. Other positions may entail fund-raising, handling public relations, conducting membership drives, and directing special projects. If the organization sponsors a national convention, professionals are needed to assist in this endeavor; providing support and guidance to members preparing for local and regional conventions and coordinating meetings of the organization may also be part of one's responsibilities. Writing for the organization's newsletter and editing its periodicals are also jobs performed by individuals working for professional organizations. Professionals are also needed to serve as liaisons with the various committees of the organization. Still other positions in the organization may involve conducting special research projects, gathering data, and performing statistical analyses.

Individuals interested in this kind of career can obtain further information by contacting professional organizations in their area of interest or speaking to knowledgeable faculty. Some organizations, such as AAHPERD, the NCAA, the Women's Sports Foundation, and the United States Olympic Committee, for example, may offer internships to students. Students interested in internships should write to the organization requesting information on these opportunities.

Sport Tourism

A growing area of specialization is sport tourism. Gibson defines sport tourism as "leisure-based travel that takes individuals temporarily outside of their home communities to participate in physical activities, to watch physical activities, or to venerate attractions associated with physical activities."[11] Gibson identifies three types of sport tourism—active sport tourism, such as when participants travel to take part in a sport event (e.g., Boston Marathon); event sport tourism, such as participants' traveling to watch an event (e.g., NCAA Final Four Basketball Tournament); and nostalgia sport tourism, such as participants' traveling to visit sport attractions (e.g., Baseball Hall of Fame).[11]

Globally, sport tourism is a multibillion-dollar business. Sport tourism is one of the most rapidly growing segments of the $4.5 trillion global travel and tourism industry.[12] For some countries, sport tourism is a major product, accounting for 25% of all tourism receipts.[12] Sport tourism is popular in

Lifespan and Cultural Perspectives: Sport Management, Media, and Performance

- What are the societal, personal, and situation factors that lead individuals to pursue a career as a professional athlete?
- How do the media influence gender, race, and cultural stereotypes of participants in sport?
- What are societal factors that contribute to the low numbers of women and people of color in athletic administration?
- Does the media's coverage of disabled sports reinforce or change society's perceptions of individuals with disabilities?

the United States. In 1999, the Travel Industry of America reported that in a 5-year period, between 1994 to 1999, 75.3 million American adults traveled in order to watch an organized sport event or to take part in a sport event.[11]

The growth of sport tourism has created a multitude of job opportunities for qualified individuals. Event and travel coordination, marketing, and promotion are just a few of the many aspects of the sport tourism industry that provide exciting and challenging careers. Salaries and hours worked vary widely, based on the magnitude of the event, its popularity, and its location.

CAREERS IN SPORT MEDIA

The pervasiveness of interest in sport in our society coupled with the growth of the communication media—television, radio, newspapers, and magazines—has contributed to the growth of career opportunities in sport communication. The last decade has also seen an increase in sport coverage by the media. The growth of media specifically dealing with sport has been phenomenal. For example, the number of sport periodicals has grown, including the number of periodicals dealing with specific sport areas such as running, body building, skiing, swimming, and bowling. Cable television channels such as ESPN provide round-the-clock coverage of sport. The growth of the Internet and the increasing sophistication of the World Wide Web created a whole new host of media opportunities and related occupations. The ability of the World Wide Web to serve as a site for information containing text, graphics, sound, and video makes it an exciting medium for sport. This growth has led to a number of career opportunities in sports media.

An individual interested in sports media can pursue many careers. These careers include sport broadcasting, sportswriting, sports journalism, sport photography, and sports information.[13] A job as Web developer is another career option.

Sport Broadcasting

Sport broadcasting is one career opportunity that has become increasingly popular. Sport broadcasting opportunities may be found with radio and television stations, including cable television, at local, regional, and national levels. Sport broadcasting requires not only knowledge of the game but also the ability to communicate in a clear, articulate fashion.

Preparation in physical education, exercise science, and sport will be helpful to the sportscaster. Sportscasters need to be knowledgeable about the skills, strategies, tactics, and rules used in sport, including the techniques of officiating. A background in physical education, exercise science, and sport enables the sportscaster to be cognizant of the sport skills used in the competition

Sportscasters must give the audience play-by-play information, as well as insight into the game and the athletes' efforts.

and be readily able to detect errors in the athletes' performances. Studying physical education, exercise science, and sport provides the sportscaster with an understanding of the manner in which athletes train for competition, the physiological effects of performance, and psychological insight into the athlete's actions. Sportscasters must be able to relate this information to the public in easily understood terms, providing the public with insight into the nature of the competition and the essence of the athletes' efforts. Familiarity with the sport enables the sportscaster to fluidly and accurately describe the play-by-play or moment-to-moment action and to present to the listening and watching public a vibrant portrayal of the athletes' actions.

Sportscasters need to have an in-depth knowledge of sport; in the eyes of the public the sportscaster is regarded as an expert on the sport he or she is covering. Therefore, it is important that the sportscaster have an extensive preparation in sport. In a physical education, exercise science, and sport preparation program, the potential broadcaster may be exposed to the more common sports areas such as football, basketball, baseball and softball, aquatics, golf, track and field, tennis, and gymnastics. The sportscaster also needs to be familiar with other sports such as auto racing, horse racing, skiing, surfing, boxing, ice hockey, and figure skating.[13] Because instruction in many of these sports areas is typically not provided in professional preparation programs, the sportscaster must seek out experts in these sport areas for instruction, learn through on-the-job experience, or acquire knowledge by research.

Sportscasters' days are often long. Hours spent in front of the camera or the microphone are most visible. In preparing for a broadcast, the sportscaster may put in numerous hours researching the upcoming competition, compiling statistics on athletes' performances, writing scripts, rehearsing certain aspects of his or her performance, arranging and preparing for on-the-air interviews, gathering background information on the athletes, and preparing in numerous other ways. Although many top broadcasters have help with these aspects of the job, individuals just starting their career may have to do all this preparation on their

Media coverage of girls' and women's sports is increasing.

own. In fact, many individuals begin their broadcasting careers by performing just such tasks for the established broadcasters.

Individuals desiring to pursue a career in broadcasting must be able to speak well and not be inhibited by speaking into the microphone or in front of the camera. The ability to think on one's feet is important because the action must be described as it unfolds. Courses or a minor in communication, particularly courses in speaking and interviewing, is critical. Courses or a minor in radio and television is valuable as well.

Practical experience can greatly contribute to one's success in attaining an entry-level position in this career field. If your college or university has its own television or radio station, become involved in some aspect of its work. Understand that in many situations, to gain a foothold, you may find it necessary to work on behind-the-scenes chores, such as researching material for the upcoming competition, before being afforded the opportunity to work in front of the microphone. If your college or university does not have a station or you are unable to attain a position at the station, perhaps you can gain experience by volunteering to announce and provide live commentary at college or university sporting events or events at the local high school. Try to gain employment or even serve as a volunteer at a local television or radio station for the summer or on a part-time basis throughout the year. Take advantage of opportunities provided by your college or university for fieldwork or internship at radio and television stations. The prospective sportscaster should also collect samples of his or her work to share with future employers. Audiotapes and videotapes of one's performance as a broadcaster and copies of any reviews received can be an asset in gaining employment in this field.

The hours worked by a sport broadcaster may be varied; they are usually at night and on the weekends. Depending on the position, a lot of travel may be associated with the job. Rewards are great; there are opportunities to meet athletes, watch numerous contests, share one's love of sport with the listening or viewing public, and become intimately involved with the sport. Salaries vary according to one's location (i.e., working for a local station as compared to a national network); one's reputation as a broadcaster (well known or just beginning and without a reputation); and the sport covered.

Sportswriting and Journalism

Individuals with a talent for writing may decide to pursue a career as a sport journalist or a sportswriter. The sport journalist may find opportunities for work with newspapers and in sport magazines, the number of which are increasing all the time. Sport magazines such as *Sports Illustrated* may provide coverage of several areas or, like *Runner's World,* provide coverage of one specific sport.

Sportswriters and journalists may cover events live or write in-depth or feature articles about athletes or various topics in the sport world. As in sport broadcasting, covering the athletic event and reporting it is the most visible part of this occupation. Researching stories, compiling statistics, and interviewing athletes and coaches are all functions of the sportswriter and journalist. The ability to meet deadlines and to write stories under time pressures is required. The work hours, opportunities to travel, and the rewards associated with this profession are similar to those associated with sport broadcasting.

A background in physical education, exercise science, and sport is helpful to the sportswriter and journalist. It provides the writer and journalist with a broader understanding of the demands and nature of sport. For example, a sport journalist with course work in sport psychology may be better able to explain to the public why some athletes fail to perform under pressure or "choke," whereas other athletes appear to rise to the occasion. A sportswriter with an understanding of exercise physiology may be better able to explain what happens physiologically to athletes as they endeavor to complete the rigorous marathon. Sportswriters can call on their background in sport philosophy to describe the transcendental experience of an athlete winning an Olympic gold medal.

Prospective sportswriters and journalists can benefit from course work or a minor in writing and journalism. Practical experience, as in all careers, is an asset in gaining employment. Many sportswriters and journalists have gotten their start covering sports for their high school papers and have continued this work for their collegiate newspaper. Experience working as an editor of the high school or college paper is an asset as well. These experiences can help prospective sportswriters and journalists gain internships or employment with local newspapers and sport publications. To assist in gaining employment in this field, individuals should keep a well-organized scrapbook of their work.

Some physical education, exercise science, and sport professionals engage in sportswriting as a full- or a part-time career. For example, professionals may use their expertise to write textbooks and sport skills books. Another career opportunity in this area is working for a publishing company, editing physical education, exercise science, and sport texts.

Sport Photography

A career as a sport photographer may be attractive to physical education, exercise science, and sport professionals who have a strong interest in photography and the desire to communicate to others the essence and meaning of sport through photographs. Talent as a photographer is a prerequisite to such a career. Opportunities for sport photographers exist with newspapers and sport publications; many sport photographers pursue their careers independently as freelance photographers.

One's background and preparation in physical education, exercise science, and sport can enhance one's career as a sport photographer.[6] Knowing the essentials of sports skills from work completed in biomechanics can help the photographer understand the critical aspects of the skill performance and where to position himself or herself to get the best angle for the photograph. Knowledge gained from exercise physiology of the stress endured by athletes working at their utmost level of effort, understanding gained from the sociology of sport of the significance of sport in our society, and appreciation gained from sport philosophy of the personal meaning that sport holds for its participants can help the sport photographer better capture the true nature and meaning of sport in pictures.

Courses in photography, graphics, and art will be of assistance to the potential sport photographer. Take advantage of opportunities to gain practical experience. Covering sporting events for the campus or local newspapers, taking sport photographs for the yearbook, and contributing photographs to the sports information office to be used in promotional brochures are several ways to gain practical experience and exposure. Sport photographers should maintain a portfolio of their work so that potential employers may readily discern their talent.

Sports Information Director

The sports information director's primary function is to promote athletic events through the various media. Opportunities for employment as a sports information director are found mainly at colleges and universities. At the professional level, many of the same responsibilities performed by the sports information director are handled by the director of public relations.

Among many responsibilities, the sports information director must maintain records and compile statistical information on all teams. He or she must design and prepare promotional brochures; this involves writing the copy for the text, obtaining photographs of the athletes, preparing the layout, and making arrangements for printing. Preparation of programs for various contests, including obtaining advertisements for the programs, is another responsibility of the sports information director. Another responsibility is to prepare material and even design the institution's Web pages for athletics. The sports information director provides assistance to the media covering home contests, phones in contest results to various media, writes press and television releases, writes commercials, and arranges press conferences and interviews for the media with coaches and athletes. Organization of special promotional events is also the responsibility of the sports information director. In a small school, the sports information director may handle all these responsibilities personally, whereas in a larger school the sports information director may have several assistants. The hours are long, because the sports information director may be expected to personally cover many of the athletic events, and quite a bit of travel may be required.

Marketing of events, such as basketball games, is one career option in sport management.

Being a sports information director requires the ability to work closely with the members of the college and university administration, as well as the athletic administration, coaches and athletes, and members of the various media. Excellent communication skills—writing, speaking, and interpersonal skills—are essential to this profession. In addition to a background in sport, courses in public relations, advertising, writing, speech, and Web page development are helpful. Experience gained in covering high school or college sport as a sportswriter or journalist and/or as a sport broadcaster is valuable. Faced with numerous responsibilities and demands, many college sports information directors would welcome volunteers interested in working in this career field. Volunteers may be assigned to work on promotional brochures, travel with teams to cover the competition, or work with the media covering home events. Volunteers should keep a file of their work. Prospective sports information directors may wish to obtain additional information from the College Sports Information Directors of America (COSIDA) (cosida.fansonly.com).

Web Developer

The growth of the Internet and World Wide Web has created new opportunities for individuals interested in sport communication. The online sport industry is rapidly expanding, and there is a need for individuals who have the technological qualifications and sports expertise to work in this area. Web developers design, create, and update sports sites for college athletic departments, professional teams, sports organizations, newspapers, and tele-

Professional dance requires a great deal of preparation and a high level of skill.

vision networks. The Web developer writes the material, creates the layout, attractively incorporates graphics and other electronic media into the site, and uploads the site to the organization's server. The Web developer updates the site and constantly seeks to improve the site's presence on the Web.

PERFORMANCE AND OTHER SPORT CAREERS

Dance Careers

Individuals talented in the various forms of dance may aspire to careers as professional dancers. Although college and university programs offer a major or a minor in dance performance, most college-age dancers have developed their talents through many years of private lessons, often commencing at an early age. Opportunities for professional dancers may be found with dance companies, theater companies, and television shows. Resorts and clubs where nightly entertainment is offered to guests are other settings for employment.

Individuals who enjoy dance but do not aspire to careers as professional dancers may decide to transmit their love for dance to others through teaching. Opportunities for dance teachers may be found at schools, colleges, and universities. Many individuals choose to teach dance at private studios; some start their own studios as well. A career as a dance therapist (Chapter 12) is also a viable career choice.

Expanding opportunities for individuals interested in a dance-related career can be found in dance administration. Dance administration may be an attractive choice for young dancers as well as dancers who are ready to retire from their performing careers. Lee[14] states that "dancers should capitalize on their professional strengths of fund raising, promotion, management, and administrative skills while integrating their knowledge of dance in such careers in dance company management as artistic director, managing director, development officer, public relations officer, and booking agent." Further information on dance careers may be obtained from the National Dance Association (NDA) (www.aahperd.org→NDA).

Professional Athletics

Highly skilled athletes may desire to pursue a career in professional athletics. Although many aspire to a career as a professional athlete, few individuals actually attain this goal. The expansion of men's teams and greater opportunities for women desiring to compete at this level have contributed to increased opportunities for skilled athletes of both sexes to pursue a professional career. Even though the opportunities are greater than in the past, the number of positions for individuals in professional sports is very limited. The NCAA estimates that only 1.3% of NCAA men's basketball players enter the professional ranks, compared to 1% of women basketball players.[15] The NCAA estimates that the percent of NCAA football players that enter the professional ranks is 2%; baseball players have the greatest percentage entering the professional league—10.5%.[15]

The salaries paid to top professional athletes are astronomical and range from hundreds of thousands to millions of dollars. Well-known athletes earn even millions of dollars more in commercial endorsements. Other professionals may not fare as well. Baseball players may spend years in the minor leagues before being sent to the majors, and golfers may spend years on the professional tour, struggling to make ends meet, before attracting a sponsor or winning enough money to break even.[8]

Because of the limited opportunities in professional sports, and because many professional careers can be short lived, individuals who desire to pursue this career should make every effort to complete their college degree. All aspiring professional athletes should take it upon themselves to ensure that they have the skills to earn a living should they fail to attain the professional ranks or have to leave the professional arena after a few years. One effort to help former professional and collegiate athletes complete their college degree is the National Consortium for Academics and Sports (NCAS) program, which was founded by the Northeastern University Center for Sport in Society. NCAS colleges and universities bring back, tuition free, their former athletes, and help them to continue their pursuit of a college degree while working in the community addressing social issues.

Officiating Careers

Sports officiating usually starts out as a part-time job, but some individuals elect to pursue it on a full-time basis. The growth of competitive athletics at the high school and collegiate levels has created a need for qualified officials for all sports. Opportunities are also available at the professional level.

Part-time officials can increase their chances for year-round work by becoming certified or rated in two or more sports, each with a different season. Attaining a rating typically requires passing a written exam as well as a practical exam. In some sports, beginning officials must spend a certain period of time working with experienced officials before being able to officiate alone. Individuals interested in information about becoming a rated official should ask an official in the sport, a coach, faculty member, or director of recreational sports. You can also contact the local officials association or board of officials.

Individuals interested in officiating should take advantage of opportunities to practice. Officials are needed for high school and college intramurals, summer adult recreational leagues, and youth sport leagues. Volunteering to work at home contests at your college or university as a scorekeeper or in some other capacity is another way to gain experience in this area. In officiating, one must not only know the rules but possess good officiating mechanics. For example, being able to place oneself in the right position at the right time requires an understanding of the flow of the game. Practice will enhance one's officiating skills.

In addition to being knowledgeable about the rules of the sport and skilled at the mechanics of officiating, officials must be able to work under pressure. Officiating also requires good interpersonal skills and communication skills to work with coaches and athletes in highly competitive and stressful situations.

Officiating is a challenging career option that can be pursued on a full- or part-time basis.

Officials usually work on afternoons, nights, and weekends because this is when most athletic contests are conducted. Some travel is involved. Salaries have improved considerably during the last few years, and officials are often reimbursed for their travel costs. Officiating can be a challenging career on a part-time or full-time basis.

Sport Law

One career opportunity that has attracted the interest of some physical education and sport professionals is sport law. In litigation involving sport, a physical educator's background and practical experience as a teacher and a coach can be an asset.

A career in sport law is not a career that can be prepared for directly through one's undergraduate academic experiences. The practice of sport law requires the completion of law school, which typically involves a 3-year program of study. Admission to law school is very competitive. Admission requires an excellent academic average, and many law schools also have prerequisites or prefer the candidate to have certain areas of undergraduate study. For practitioners with experience seeking to change their career focus, however, sport law may be an attractive area of study. The growth of sport management curriculums has also created a need for individuals with preparation in sport law to teach courses in sport law and liability.

Another career opportunity for individuals with expertise in sport law is working with professional athletes, serving as their agents in contract negotiations.

Contract negotiation is only one of the services performed by sport agents. Sport agents may also serve as financial consultants—managing athletes' finances, investing their income, and structuring their financial portfolio for retirement. Some sport agents manage athletes' endorsements; they negotiate the endorsement contract and arrange promotional opportunities. Some sport agents perform a myriad of services, while others prefer to specialize in one area, such as contract negotiations. While you do not have to have a law degree to be a sport agent, knowledge of the law, as well as a background in business, is helpful.

A career in sport law presents an array of options for qualified individuals. Some opportunities include working as an agent, involvement in contract negotiations, litigation, and teaching.

Entrepreneur

An increasing number of professionals are using their skills and competencies to become entrepreneurs. These individuals develop services and products to meet the public's needs and interests. The broad area of physical education, exercise science, and sport offers many entrepreneurial opportunities to motivated professionals. You may choose to pursue these opportunities on a full- or part-time basis.

Perhaps the most visible of all entrepreneurs in the profession are personal trainers. As discussed in Chapter 12, these professionals work one-on-one with the client, designing and implementing fitness programs tailored specifically to the client's needs. Personal trainers typically visit the client's home to monitor the workout.

Programming in the area of fitness and health promotion offers many entrepreneurial opportunities.[16] Many individuals who are interested in improving their fitness and health are willing to pay professionals for the opportunity to learn the skills necessary to achieve a high level of wellness. Entrepreneurs can design and offer health enhancement programs to meet these needs. Programs can focus on fitness assessment and improvement, nutrition, stress management, or weight reduction. These programs can be presented to interested individuals during the afternoon or evening. These programs also can be marketed to corporations that wish to offer these services to their employees but do not have the expertise to conduct such programs. Creative individuals also can produce and market instructional books, videos, and Web sites focusing on fitness and health.

Some professionals with a strong background in exercise science and administration use their skills to serve as consultants. They visit various fitness sites, such as a health club, assess the current program, make recommendations for improvement, train employees, and organize a system for ongoing program and employee evaluation.

Another opportunity for enterprising individuals with competency in exercise science is the establishment of a mobile fitness and health appraisal business.[17] Using a van filled with appropriate equipment, the professional can travel to different work sites to offer fitness appraisal and health enhancement programs to employees.

Personal coaching is a viable opportunity for individuals with expertise in a specific sport and the ability to coach individuals to achieve a high level of performance.[17] Parents may be interested in obtaining private coaching to help their children further develop sport skills. Many amateur and professional athletes use the services of a personal coach on a regular basis. Opportunities for personal coaching are most commonly found in individual sports such as swimming, diving, golf, tennis, track and field, and ice skating, although participants in team sports (e.g., basketball) may use a personal coach on an intermittent basis to refine selected aspects of their performance.

Professionals with expertise in biomechanics can offer computerized skill analysis services to athletes, as well as to coaches interested in furthering their team's performance.[17] The athlete is videotaped and the performance is computer analyzed. The analysis is reviewed with the athlete

Summer sports camps give children and young adults an opportunity to learn new skills and develop their athleticism. University of Tennessee coach Pat Summitt lectures at a basketball camp with the assistance of her staff and players.

and suggestions for improvement are given. Instructional videotapes can be offered to complement this service. Sites for this service typically include golf courses, tennis clubs, sporting goods stores, and various other sport facilities. The professional can also contract for this service with interested individuals, such as a coach desiring an analysis of individual team members' skills or a parent wishing a more detailed assessment of his or her child's skill performance.

Throughout the United States, sport and fitness camps for individuals of all ages are proliferating. Instructional camps are available for virtually every sport, although the most popular sports tend to be soccer, baseball, softball, tennis, golf, and volleyball. The number of instructional sports camps for youths with disabilities also is growing. There are also camp programs that focus on increasing fitness and reducing weight. Although camp programs traditionally have focused on children and youth, a growing number of programs target the adult population in the areas of both sports and fitness. Directing sports and fitness camps offers many fine entrepreneurial opportunities. Because many of these programs are offered during the summer months or school vacations, teaching and coaching professionals often find employment in such programs and welcome the opportunity to supplement their salary.

There are numerous entrepreneurial opportunities for motivated physical education, exercise science, and sport professionals. Individuals aspiring to such a career must ask themselves two critical questions: (1) Do I have a viable, marketable service or product? and (2) Is there a consumer desire for the service or product? Furthermore, professionals must make sure they have the dedication, enthusiasm, initiative, and self-confidence to pursue this career successfully. The amount of financial resources necessary varies; some services, such as personal fitness instructor, require very little financial investment, whereas other services, such as a mobilized health and fitness business, require considerable capital to purchase the necessary equipment. Young professionals who are innovative and aspire to be their own bosses will find a host of entrepreneurial opportunities available to them in the twenty-first century.

INCREASING YOUR PROFESSIONAL MARKETABILITY

Individuals interested in pursuing sport communication and sport management careers can increase their professional marketability in several ways. Taking course work and minors in appropriate areas can enhance one's marketability. For individuals interested in sport media careers, courses or a minor in speech, photography, journalism, and broadcasting is an asset. Those who are interested in sport management careers can benefit from courses in business, management, law, and communication. Students also need to take courses specifically applying knowledge from other disciplines to sport communication and sport management—for example, courses in sport journalism or sport law.

Individuals interested in pursuing sport media, sport management, performance, and other sport-related careers need to be cognizant that the positions described in this section are often top-level positions. Attaining them requires a willingness to work one's way "up the ladder." Professionals typically gain access to these positions through entry-level positions. For example, if you aspire to a career as an athletic director, you may first have to work as an assistant athletic director to gain the necessary experience and skills.

Focus on Career: Sport Management, Media, and Performance

PROFESSIONAL ORGANIZATIONS

- North American Society for Sport Management
  www.nassm.org
- Sport Management Council
  www.aahperd.org → NASPE → Councils
- National Council of Secondary School Athletic Directors
  www.aahperd.org → NASPE → Councils
- National Intramural Sports Council
  www.aahperd.org → NASPE → Councils
- National Intramural and Recreational Sports Association
  www.nirsa.org
- National Interscholastic Athletic Administrators Association
  www.nfhs.org/niaaa/niaaa_about.htm
- CoSIDA—College Sports Information Directors of America
  http://cosida.fansonly.com/
- National Association of Collegiate Directors of Athletics
  http://nacda.fansonly.com/
- National Association of Collegiate Women Athletic Administrators
  www.nacwaa.org/
- Society for the Study of Legal Aspects of Sport and Physical Activity
  www.ithaca.edu/sslaspa/

PROFESSIONAL JOURNALS

- *Journal of Sport Management*
- *Journal of Legal Aspects of Sport*
- *Recreational Sports and Fitness Magazine*
- *NIRSA Journal*

Practical experience is necessary to move up the career ladder. It can be gained from volunteering one's services, summer employment, and collegiate fieldwork and internship opportunities. Practical experience not only allows one to gain and refine the necessary skills but also allows one to develop professional contacts and exposure. These skills and professional contacts contribute to one's gaining employment and advancing up the career ladder.

SUMMARY

Sport has developed into a big business. Consequently, individuals trained in sport management are needed. Qualified professionals interested in sport management may pursue careers as athletic directors, directors of intramurals and campus recreation, directors of industrial recreation, and sport facilities managers. Individuals interested in retailing may choose a career in sport business management and sport sales. Managerial opportunities are also available in professional organizations or working in sport tourism.

The intensity of interest in sport in our society coupled with the growth of the communication media has resulted in the expansion of career opportunities in the field of sport media. Individuals interested in this area can pursue careers in sport broadcasting, sportswriting, sports journalism, sport photography, sports information, and Web development.

Talented individuals may elect to pursue careers as performers. Other sport-related careers that may be attractive to qualified individuals are sport officiating and sport law.

Physical education, exercise science, and sport professionals can use many strategies to enhance their professional marketability. Taking course work in supporting areas and gaining practical experience help individuals attain the position that they desire after graduation.

SELF-ASSESSMENT TESTS

These tests are designed to help you determine if you have mastered the materials and competencies presented in this chapter.

1. Discuss how a background in physical education, exercise science, and sport can be an asset to individuals pursuing a diversity of sport media careers.
2. If possible, interview individuals working in sport management positions. Ask each person to define his or her responsibilities and the skills that are the most helpful in the performance of the job. Determine the entry-level positions in this area. Ask each individual for suggestions about advancing to top-level managerial positions in the field.
3. Discuss the positive and negative aspects of pursuing a performance career. Since performance careers may be of short duration, how can individuals prepare for another career after the culmination of their performance career? Access Northeastern University's Center for the Study of Sport in Society Web site at www.sportinsociety.org and read about the National Consortium for Academics and Sports program to help athletes continue their higher education and complete their degree. What are some strategies that can be used to help current and former student-athletes attain their educational goals? You may find it interesting to read about the other programs under the auspices of the Center for Sport in Society, and you can also access late-breaking sports news as well as highlights from the Racial and Gender Report Card.
4. Using the information provided in the Get Connected box, locate an article on a topic of interest related to sport management, sport media, dance, officiating, or athletics. Write a brief summary of the article, identifying five key points and what you have learned.
5. Search the World Wide Web to identify different job opportunities in sports. Note the requirements for each position, as well as responsibilities associated with each job. Share your information with the class.

REFERENCES

1. Sporting Goods Manufacturers Association, 2002. (www.sgma.com)
2. Hoover's Online: Professional sports. (hoover-sports-ind.htm)
3. Saporito B: The American money machine. November 29, 2004. (www.time.com/time/insidebiz)
4. Sport Statistics Online. USAToday. Retrieved December 20, 2004. (www.usatoday.com)
5. Harrow R: Retail wars and sports: competition for expanding revenue. November 12, 2004. (cbs.sportsline.com).
6. DeSensi J, Kelley D, Blanton M, and Beitel P: Sport management curricular evaluation and needs assessment: a multifaceted approach, Journal of Sport Management 4(1):31–58, 1990.
7. Parkhouse BL and Pitts BG: History of sport management. In BL Parkhouse, The Management of Sport: its Foundation and Application, ed 4, New York, 2005, McGraw-Hill.
8. Blann, W. Four factor analysis of sport management, Personal communication, December 20, 2004.
9. NASPE-NASSM. NASPE-NASSM Sport management curriculum standards and program review. Reston, VA, 2000, AAHPERD.
10. Blann, W. Sport management career paths, Personal communication, December 20, 2004.
11. Gibson HJ: Sport tourism: an introduction to the special issue, Journal of Sport Management 17:205–213, 2003.
12. The business of sport tourism, October 2004. (www.sportbusiness.com)
13. Lambert C: Sports communications. In WJ Considine, editor: Alternative professional preparation in physical education, Washington, D.C., 1979, National Association of Sport and Physical Education.
14. Lee S: Dance administrative opportunities, JOPERD 55(5):74–75, 81, 1984.
15. Estimated probability of competing in athletics beyond high school interscholastic level, NCAA. (www.ncaa.org)
16. Westerfield RC: Entrepreneurial opportunities in health education, JOPERD 58(2):67–70, 1987.
17. Pestolesi RA: Opportunities in physical education: what the entrepreneur can do, JOPERD 58(2):68–70, 1987.

SUGGESTED READINGS

Cuneen J.: Adding rigor to the sport management internship: introduction. JOPERD 75(1), 2004.

Introduces a series of articles in this issue of JOPERD focusing on various aspects of the sport management internship, including the issue on academic credit, securing an internship, and quality control in the administration of internship.

Fischer D: The 50 coolest jobs in sports, New York, 1997, Arco.

Advice on how to get your dream job in sports, responsibilities associated with each position, and quotes from people working in the field give readers insight on the many opportunities available today in the sport industry.

Gladden JM, Irwin RL, and Sutton WA: Managing North American major professional sport teams in the new millennium: a focus on building brand equity. Journal of Sport Management 15:297–317, 2001.

The growth of major league professional sports in the 1990s was phenomenal. However, the twenty-first century brings new challenges to the marketing and maintenance of the success of professional franchises.

Klenosky DB, Templin TJ, and Troutman JA: Recruiting student athletes: a means-end investigation of school-choice, Journal of Sport Management 15:95–106, 2001.

The study investigates the factors that affected the school choice decisions of Division I football players.

BL Parkhouse, The management of sport: its foundation and application, ed 4, New York, 2005, McGraw-Hill.

Provides information about the foundations of sport management, including historical development, structure and policy, economics and finance, marketing, professional relations, field experiences, and career opportunities.

Popke M: Setting their sites, Athletic Business, November 2001.

Facility operators are using the Internet to market their facilities and programs, finding that maintaining a high-profile Internet presence can yield big dividends.

Smith DR, Ciacciarelli A, Serzan J, and Lambert D: Travel and the home advantage in professional sports, Sociology of Sport Journal 17:364–385, 2000.

Is there a home advantage in professional sports? A discussion of factors that contribute to the home team advantage, including travel and social factors.

Stratta TMP: The needs and concerns of students during the sport management internship, JOPERD 75(20):25–32.

Highlights concerns raised by students and describes how students' needs can be more successfully met during the internship experience.

Walton T: The Sprewell/Carlesimo Episode: unacceptable violence or unacceptable victim? Sociology of Sport Journal 18:345–357, 2001.

Discusses the media's coverage and attitude toward violence in sport and how media representations continue to support race, gender, and class ideologies.

Williams J: Sport management internships: agency perspectives, expectations, and concerns, JOPERD 75(2):30–34, 2004.

Offers the agency's perspective on expectations, issues, and responsibilities associated with mentoring a sport management intern.

PART IV

Issues, Challenges, and the Future

Physical educators, exercise scientists, and sport leaders need to be aware of the issues and challenges facing the field today. If professionals hope to influence the future direction of physical education, exercise science, and sport in our society, they must lead the way.

Following an overview of issues in physical education, exercise science, and sport today, Chapter 14 examines five of the issues confronting professionals. Four of the challenges to physical education, exercise science, and sport professionals are addressed as well. Chapter 15 discusses trends and the future of physical education, exercise science, and sport.

CHAPTER 14

ISSUES AND CHALLENGES

OBJECTIVES

After reading this chapter the student should be able to—

- Discuss the role of physical education, exercise science, and sport professionals in the consumer education movement relative to physical activity and fitness.
- Discuss how professionals can promote the development of values in physical education, exercise science, and sport.
- Interpret the role and contribution of physical education, exercise science, and sport professionals in the conduct of youth sport programs.
- Identify suggested names for the field currently entitled physical education, exercise science, and sport and discuss the implications of the growth of the fields.
- Discuss the gap that exists between research and practice, and describe how this gap can be lessened.
- Identify and describe strategies that professionals could use to promote quality daily physical education throughout the country.
- Explain the importance of advocacy in a variety of physical activity settings.
- Define the role of physical education, exercise science, and sport professionals in attaining the specific fitness and exercise goals delineated in the report *Healthy People 2010.*
- Describe specific strategies that could be used to help promote lifespan involvement in physical activity and sport.

Many issues and challenges confront physical education, exercise science, and sport today. As professionals, we need to be cognizant of the issues concerning the profession at all levels. As a professional, you will likely be perceived by the public as an expert in matters involving physical education, fitness, and sport. As such, you need up-to-date information on current issues so that you may give accurate, knowledgeable, and easily understood answers to the public's queries. This requires that you keep abreast

GET CONNECTED

Character Counts Web site includes essays on character, sport in American life, and Pursuing Victory with Honor coaching program—Arizona Accord—and character education based on the six pillars of character—trustworthiness, respect, responsibility, fairness, caring, and citizenship.

www.charactercounts.org

National Collegiate Athletic Association posts information on many different aspects of intercollegiate athletics, including current news, education and outreach topics, and contemporary issues.

www.ncaa.org

Unlock Research brings to physical educators information pertaining to research reports, texts, and journals in an accessible, easy-to-use format. It is designed to support the endeavors of physical educators who want to review and think about research and how it can contribute to effective instruction.

www.unlockresearch.com

American Heart Association site highlights information about many different aspects of coronary heart disease, including statistics, diseases, advocacy, publications and resources.

www.americanheart.org

PELinks4U offers information on a variety of topics related to physical education, coaching, adapted physical education, interdisciplinary efforts, and technology in physical education.

www.pelinks4u.org

of events and developments through newspapers, television, the World Wide Web, professional journals, and professional meetings and conferences.

Physical education, exercise science, and sport professionals are facing a great number of challenges. As professionals, we must take an active role in meeting these challenges. This requires commitment and professional leadership at all levels. The continued growth of the field, its vitality and its future, depends on professionals' commitment and leadership.

This chapter focuses on some issues and challenges confronting physical education, exercise science, and sport. To address all of these issues and challenges would require a separate text. The purpose of this chapter is to introduce some of the issues facing the field today and to discuss five of the issues at greater length. This chapter concludes with a discussion of four of the challenges to the fields of physical education, exercise science, and sport and its members.

ISSUES IN PHYSICAL EDUCATION, EXERCISE SCIENCE, AND SPORT TODAY

Numerous issues confront professionals in physical education, exercise science, and sport today. Some of these issues are presented here, with the goal of creating an awareness of the problems and stimulating further efforts to address them.

Problems within sport exist at all levels, from professional athletics to youth sports. At the professional level, gambling and drug abuse have commanded a great deal of attention, as have astronomical player salaries and striking players and game officials. Increased player violence has raised concern, and growing fan violence has led some teams to curb the sale of alcohol at events. In professional tennis, concern about competitors burning out at an early age has led to attempts to curtail the playing schedules of young athletes and to establish minimum age requirements for players to join the tour. Questions also have been

Violence is a problem in sports today.

raised about the responsibility incumbent on professional athletes to serve as role models to the nation's youth.

Collegiate athletics have attracted attention as well. The increasing professionalization of collegiate athletics has been decried by many. In many institutions, collegiate athletics have become big business, raising the concern that athletics is overemphasized at the expense of academics. Scandals involving the recruitment of athletes, tampering of grades on transcripts to ensure the admission of athletes to schools or their continued eligibility, questions about the academic progress of athletes, and illegal drug use to enhance performance have drawn national attention. Sport governing bodies have sought to rectify these problems by imposing stricter regulations and establishing more stringent academic requirements for student-athletes. However, questions about the place of athletics in educational institutions continue to be raised.

At the high school level, questions have been raised about the academic qualifications of athletes as well. The practice of extending favorable treatment to athletes, such as issuing them passing grades when it is not warranted, has resulted in some cases of graduating athletes who are illiterate. Efforts to address this problem have included the adoption of "no-pass, no-play" rules whereby students must maintain a certain academic average to participate in extracurricular activities. In some school districts, budgetary constraints have led to "pay-to-play" rules requiring that students must pay a fee to participate in extracurricular activities, including athletics. Many believe that overinvolvement of parents and community members in conjunction with an overemphasis on winning has detracted from the educational value of sport. In recent years, concerns have also been expressed about the increase in specialization: Athletes are focusing on one sport throughout the entire year instead of participating in two or three sports per year.

Serious concerns have also been raised regarding the conduct of youth sports. One major problem is the overemphasis on winning, especially at the younger levels. This emphasis has led to the abandonment of the developmental approach to sport, which stresses age-appropriate activities and coaching, in favor of the professional approach, which focuses on winning. Youth sport programs could not exist without the thousands of adult volunteers who serve as coaches. Although many of these coaches do an outstanding job, some youth coaches lack the necessary preparation to teach skills, treat injuries, and meet the important developmental needs of children. Communities are offering educational programs for youth sport coaches to help them acquire the necessary skills and understandings to foster a positive sport experience for the young athletes involved. Well-intentioned, but overly involved parents also contribute to problems in this area when they impose pressure on their children to win or use their children to live out their own unfulfilled athletic dreams.

Current issues are by no means limited to sport. The status and nature of school physical education programs at both the elementary and secondary levels are being challenged. Physical education programs and teachers face problems similar to those experienced in other academic areas—increased calls for accountability, dwindling economic resources, the need to deal daily with student violence and drug abuse, insufficient parental support, increasingly difficult student discipline, and career burnout. Additionally, physical education faces some unique problems. Class sizes are often larger and more heterogenous than classes in other subject areas. Administrative and teacher support for physical education is often lacking. The many and diverse expectations associated with the multiple roles of teacher and coach may lead to difficulty in meeting these competing demands. There is an ongoing debate among professionals in our field regarding the goals of physical education, desired outcomes and their priority, and the content of the curriculum. Last, physical education is typically undervalued as a school subject, often being perceived as a frill and of little educational value.

Physical education faces tremendous challenges to its integrity as a school subject and increased pressure to fight for its place in the school curriculum. It is ironic that, at a time when the American public's interest in fitness is at an all-time high, support for physical education in the schools is eroding. The public has an increased awareness of the concomitant health benefits to be gained from participation in fitness and physical activities and public health reports, such as *Healthy People 2010,* call for increasing daily physical education. Yet support is often lacking for physical education, which can provide students with the skills, knowledge, and understanding essential to leading a physically active lifestyle throughout their lifespan.

The growing educational reform movement and its increased emphasis on academics threaten school physical education programs. Time allocated for physical education in the curriculum, which is often less than for other subject areas, may be further reduced as the reform movement takes hold. Only 1 in 4 high school students have physical education daily. Participation in daily physical education declined from over 40% in 1991 to less than 30% in 2003. As we begin the twenty-first century and increasingly embrace technological approaches to education, children may attend school only 3 days a week and work the remainder of time at home using interactive computers, cable television, and distance learning. Physical education, exercise science, and sport professionals will need to find different settings and use new approaches to reach these students.

The growth of nonschool physical education and sport opportunities is of concern as well. Many of these nonschool programs are conducted by individuals without training in physical education, exercise science, and sport. The growth of commercial sport clubs, fitness centers, and health clubs in response to the public's demand for instruction in sports and fitness development has led to the employment of some individuals without adequate professional preparation in the field. Physical education, exercise science, and sport professionals need to establish leadership in this area.

The growth of interest in competitive sport and fitness has led to the expansion of opportunities available for people of all ages and abilities. Yet we must give greater attention to meeting the needs of special population groups—the elderly and people of all ages with disabilities. As the growth of commercial programs continues, we must make sure that community programs remain strong so that opportunities are available for those who do not have the ability to pay. The evidence supporting the value of regular physical activity and the contribution of physical activity to health is overwhelming. Although the research shows that the fitness movement involves participants from every population group, individuals who are young, male, white, upper-middle class, suburban, and highly educated are more likely to be involved. Greater efforts must be made to reach all segments of the population—the poor, the elderly, members of minority groups, and individuals with disabilities.

As the emphasis on health promotion and disease prevention continues to increase and the role of physical activity becomes more clearly defined, the schools have the ability to play a more significant role in attaining the nation's public health goals. The schools provide a means to reach millions of children and youth and teach them the skills, knowledge, and positive attitudes necessary for a lifetime of physical activity. Additionally, although the role of personal responsibility is emphasized in health promotion endeavors, it is important not to become insensitive to the impact of social conditions, especially poverty and discrimination, on health status. Providing access to services for all Americans is a pressing need.

Equity is another issue that must be addressed by our field. Although it has been over 30 years since the enactment of Title IX, unequal opportunities for males and females in sports still exist. Although sport participation among females increased dramatically during the three preceding decades, inequalities still exist in participation opportunities, budget, facilities, and administrative and coaching positions, as well as in other areas of the sporting enterprise.

Racism is another issue that must be confronted. Desegregation of sports has opened doors for participation of minorities in sports. However, participation has not led to the elimination of prejudice, stereotyping, and exploitative practices. Discrimination and exclusionary practices have limited opportunities for minorities in administrative and coaching positions in sports. Professionals in physical education, exercise science, and sport have spoken strongly about the need to recruit minorities into higher education and prepare them for a multitude of careers in this field.

This section has provided an overview of some of the problems and issues confronting the fields of physical education, exercise science, and sport today. Many solutions have been offered for these situations. However, the success of any solution requires the commitment of professionals who are dedicated to the improvement of the fields. This past section gave a brief overview of some of the problems and issues facing physical education, exercise science, and sport professionals today. The remainder of the chapter will examine in some detail four of the issues confronting physical education, exercise science, and sport and four of the challenges that need to be met by professionals in the fields.

Many issues confront physical education, exercise science, and sport professionals. About 20 years ago, the American Academy of Kinesiology and Physical Education, which is comprised of individuals who have made significant contributions to the profession, identified several urgent issues that should be addressed by our field. These included the need for physical educators to become more active in educating consumers about physical activities, the need for increased emphasis on affective behavior in physical education, and the need for physical educators to assume a more active role in conducting youth sports programs.[1] Our field has grown tremendously during the past 20 years, but these issues, somewhat redefined, are still important today. They remain important because of the wide impact addressing these issues will have on participants in our programs and our expanding field. The five issues that will be discussed in the next section are leadership in the physical activity movement, promotion of values and ethical behavior, leadership in youth sports, the growing discipline of physical education, exercise science, and sport, and closing the gap between research and practice.

Many challenges also confront physical education, exercise science, and sport professionals today. Four of these challenges will be addressed in the last section of the chapter. Professionals must become more active in making daily quality physical education programs in the nation's schools become a reality. They also must become more active in advocacy efforts to promote physical education programs. Professionals are challenged to attain the national health objectives and to promote lifelong involvement in physical activity and sport for all people.

Leadership in Physical Activity

Physical education, exercise science, and sport professionals must step forward and assume a greater leadership role in promotion of physical activity. Substantial evidence supports the positive contribution of physical activity to health and quality of life. Physical inactivity has been related to premature mortality and morbidity, which exert a tremendous toll on society, both in human terms and monetary costs. Individuals who engage in physical activity on a regular basis reduce their risk for many chronic diseases and increase their chances for living a long, healthy life.

As physical education, exercise science, and sport professionals, we are in a unique position to take a more central, active role in responding to society's needs and engaging its members in physical activity so that they can realize the powerful, concomitant health benefits. We have a responsibility to educate the public about the benefits of physical activity and fitness, and we must make a greater effort to disseminate a national message about the relationship between physical activity and health. One way we can do this is to take part in the activities of the National Coalition for Promoting Physical Activity (NCPPA).

NCPPA was founded by the American College of Sports Medicine, the American Heart Association, and the American Alliance for Health, Physical Education, Recreation, and Dance in 1998. Its mission is "to unite the strengths of public, private, and industry efforts into a collaborative partnership to inspire and empower all Americans to lead physically active lifestyles to enhance their health and quality of life."[2] Over 150 organizations are now members of NCPPA, working "to improve the nation's health by increasing physical activity at the national, state, and local levels."[2] Physical education, exercise science, and sport professionals and others interested in healthy lifestyles engage in a variety of activities, such as event planning and advocacy, to promote physical activities.

During the past two decades, we have witnessed dramatic increases in participation in fitness and physical activities by people of all ages. An unprecedented proliferation of programs and products designed to capitalize on these interests has occurred. Although many programs are sound in nature and products are safe and live up to their claims, there are some programs that are not reputable and the validity of claims for some products is highly questionable.

Commercial sports clubs, community fitness centers, health and fitness clubs, and health spas all offer opportunities for people to engage in physical activities. Some of the programs offered are highly reputable, meet the health and fitness industry standards, and are staffed by qualified personnel. On the other hand, there are programs that advertise their services as leading to quick and dramatic results, fail to meet industry standards, and are staffed by personnel hired more for their appearance than their credentials.

Programs that fail to comply with health and fitness standards present a risk to exercise participants. For example, a 2002 study by Costanzo, Rustico and Pescatello[3] evaluated 14 community facilities offering exercise programs to older adults, 66% of whom were over 75 years of age. The researchers found that only five of the 14 facilities required participants to fill out preactivity health questionnaires, only three administered informed consents, and not one of the facilities followed a medical clearance policy.[3] "Only two facilities had defined emergency policies, and none conducted emergency drills. One site conducted exercise programs with instructors trained in cardiopulmonary resuscitation. Professional certified exercise instructors leading all exercise programs were observed in one facility."[3] The researchers noted that most of the facilities failed to comply with existing professional health and fitness standards.

Although some organizations, such as the International Health, Racquet and Sportsclub Association (IHRSA), establish standards for clubs and others offer guidelines for exercise leaders and participants' safety, such as the American College of Sports Medicine, there is no way to determine the number of programs that comply with accepted standards. For persons who want to begin a physical activity program, where can they turn to find out whether the program meets industry standards or if the staff is certified? What type of certification should the staff have? Is the program safe? Will the program enable them to accomplish their goals?

Along with the proliferation of physical activity programs came the growth of fitness and health products, now a multibillion-dollar-a-year industry. The marketplace offers the consumer a wide choice of exercise equipment, Web sites sell diet products and fitness services, infomercials extol the merits of various types of ab machines, and magazine ads exhort readers to try products that guarantee weight loss. Books, magazines, and periodicals concerned with health, fitness, self-improvement, and sport are bestsellers. Videotapes of celebrity experts leading specially designed workout programs are popular purchases for those people who like to work out at home. How are consumers to know what works and what doesn't?

Given the wide range of programs and products relating to physical activities and fitness, it is important that the members of the public make an educated choice from among the services and goods available; participation in programs that fail to meet recognized standards of care or the use of products that are of questionable value can have harmful results. Physical education, exercise science, and sport professionals can play a critical role in educating consumers about physical activities and fitness.

Physical education, exercise science, and sport professionals must be more active in making the public aware of their expertise in physical activity. Now is the time for us to step to the forefront and take a more significant role in promoting physical activity, leading the fitness movement, and exerting a significant influence on its direction.

Corbin,[4] in a *Journal of Physical Education, Recreation, and Dance* editorial, asks, "Is the fitness bandwagon passing us by?" Corbin points out that physicians, self-appointed experts, and movie stars are at the vanguard of the fitness movement. Many of these people lack the qualifications, training, and expertise to be directing this movement. Corbin asks, "What is the problem?" He states:

> While many physical educators are experts, many are not. Some have no desire to be! I *am not* arguing that we should devote all our efforts to physical fitness or exclude other important educational objectives. I *am* arguing that one of the most important social services we can provide is to teach about fitness and exercise. Like no other profession, we should be knowledgeable in this area.

Corbin suggests that professionals can do several things to "lead the parade." Physical education, exercise science, and sport professionals should actively seek leadership roles in the fitness movement. First, as experts, professionals should be cognizant of current findings in the field. Second, the public needs to be made aware that physical education, exercise science, and sport professionals are experts in this field and are a resource for answers as well as advice. Professionals should educate their students and the public to be wise consumers of exercise programs and products. Additionally, professionals should provide their clientele with the knowledge and the skills to solve their own exercise and physical activity problems and to evaluate their own fitness needs.

Ewers[5] echos Corbin's call for physical education, exercise science, and sport professionals to lead the "exercise parade." He encourages physical education and sport professionals to be "pace setters" by "practicing what you know and believe about the benefits of movement." Physical education, exercise science, and sport professionals must take a more active role in the physical activity movement. As professionals we must provide leadership for this movement because it falls within our domain. We must take advantage of this interest in fitness and physical activity to educate people of all ages about fitness and physical activities and to teach them skills necessary for lifetime participation and healthy lifestyles.

Teaching Values in Physical Education and Sport

The development of values, character, and ethical decision-making skills has long been touted as one of the primary purposes of school physical education programs and one of the lasting outcomes of athletic participation. Professionals have promoted our programs as the means to develop such commendable values as cooperation, self-discipline, hard work, fair play, emotional control, and teamwork. The enhancement of self-esteem and self-confidence has also been cited as an outcome of participation in physical education and sport. How-

An overemphasis on winning can detract from the nature of the sport experience.

ever, there appears to be a gap between rhetoric and the reality of practice, a discrepancy between the outcomes claimed for physical education and sport and the behaviors practitioners and participants exhibit. While many practitioners believe that ethical and moral development are important, oftentimes they fail to structure their programs to achieve these outcomes or their actions belie their words.

The effects of physical education class on the affective development of students at all levels must be carefully considered by teachers. If we are committed to the enhancement of self-esteem and the promotion of respect for self and others, why are practices that humiliate, embarrass, or belittle students used or tolerated? Many adults have vivid childhood memories of standing alone in the midst of the gym and being the last chosen for the team, completing a relay race long after all the other students had finished, or predictably being the first student eliminated in a game. Do these practices, and others like them, enhance individual development? How do these practices contribute to the promotion of lifespan involvement in physical activity for all people?

In recent years, ethical and moral abuses associated with sport at all levels have gained increased notoriety. Sport has long been extolled as a vehicle for building character and teaching such values as sportsmanship, fair play, honesty, and integrity. Athletes are often placed on a pedestal and viewed as role models for traditional American values. Yet there is a disparity between the educational values claimed and the behaviors exhibited by athletes and coaches.

The academy, concerned about the moral and ethical abuses in physical education and sport, encourages professionals to take action to remedy these abuses. First, although physical education and sport programs offer the opportunity to teach values, these outcomes must be actively sought and planned to fulfill the potential of our field to contribute to affective development. The greatest gains in this area will be realized when physical education and sport professionals structure their experiences to promote the development of values and ethical judgments. We can not assume that these outcomes will occur automatically as a result of involvement in physical education and sport. Situations that promote the development of the desired values must be carefully planned for, and professionals should take advantage of teachable moments to promote desired behavior. Appropriate behavior should be acknowledged and reinforced.

Professionals can also use a curriculum that focuses on development in the affective domain. One example is the Teaching Personal and Social Responsibility Model developed by Don Hellison. Hellison's model helps students learn responsibility by progressively giving them greater amounts of responsibility and carefully shifting a significant portion of decision making to them.[6] Students move through different levels of responsibility—from irresponsibility to responsibility.[6] Students also move from gaining respect for themselves to extending that respect to others.[6] Hellison successfully incorporated this model and other approaches into his work with underserved youth in a diversity of settings and programs ranging from adventure experiences to coaching clubs.

By choosing to use models that emphasize affective development through physical activity, we can play a greater role in helping underserved youth in our society. Thomas Martinek and Hellison point out that millions of children and youth in our country live in poverty.[7] Despite the risks associated with being poor, many of these youngsters are resilient and are able to overcome their adverse circumstances and "bounce back."[7] Martinek and Hellison suggest that the development of social and psychological factors associated with resiliency can be fostered through carefully designed school and community physical activity programs.

Sports has tremendous potential to build character, foster moral development, promote responsibility, and teach positive life skills to its participants. Attainment of these outcomes can be enhanced when winning is placed in perspective. In 1999, the Citizenship Through Sports Alliance noted the troubling "decline of sportsmanship and ethical conduct in sports, a deterioration that permeates sports competition from the youth leagues to the professional leagues. The breakdown in sportsmanship extends beyond the courts and fields [and] involves athletes, their families, coaches, officials, fans, institutional administrators, corporate sponsors, the media and the public at large."[8] To address these concerns and to refocus sports organizations on the ethical and character-building potential of sport, the United States Olympic Committee (USOC) coaching division and Character Counts! Sports, a project of the Josephson Institute of Ethics, held a meeting of sports leaders in May 1999 in Arizona. At this meeting, leaders of Olympic, professional, intercollegiate, interscholastic, and youth sports organizations drafted and issued a statement of 16 principles that clearly define what it means to pursue victory with honor (see the Arizona Sports Summit Accord box). The Arizona Sports Summit Accord has been adopted by an increasing number of sports organizations, including the NCAA Division I-A Athletic Directors Association, the NAIA, many state high school athletic associations, and youth sport organizations.

"Pursuing Victory with Honor," an initiative of the USOC and Character Counts! Sports, emphasizes that the character-building aspects of sport can be achieved by focusing on ethical standards and sportsmanship. Winning is important, and the passionate pursuit of victory by coaches and athletes contributes to the enjoyment and value of sports. Pursuing Victory with Honor views ethics as essential to true winning. According to this initiative, "the best strategy to improve sports is not to de-emphasize winning but to more vigorously emphasize that adherence to ethical standards and sportsmanship in the honorable pursuit of victory is essential to winning in the true sense. It is one thing to be declared the winner; it is another to really win. Victories attained in dishonorable ways are hollow and degrade the concept of sport."[9] When winning is conceptualized in this manner, sports' contribution to affective development is enhanced.

Professional preparation programs should help their graduates acquire the competencies necessary not only to teach skills and knowledge but also to promote the development of values and ethical judgments. If we profess to contribute to the development of the whole person, then professionals must be prepared to do so. Just as it is important to plan for the development of values in our programs and not leave development to chance, it is equally important to prepare professionals to undertake this task and not to assume that they know how to do so.

The academy also urges that the profession establish criteria by which to select appropriate moral and ethical values to be developed. Formal plans for instruction to promote the development of these values should be designed. Additionally, it is recommended that the field develop additional means and methods to assess efforts to promote development in these areas.

Although the academy directs its comments to school physical education programs and athletics, its collective wisdom holds an important message for professionals in both school- and non-school-based programs for people of all ages. We must pay close attention to the affective dimension of behavior. If our goal is to promote a physically active lifestyle, we must engender the following affective goals in program participants: (1) confidence in their abilities as movers, (2) a sense of self-worth, and (3) an appreciation of the value of health and the contribution of physical activity to personal well-being. We must empower participants to take responsibility for their lives. Perhaps we must redirect some of our programming efforts to provide more individualized learning that focuses on abilities of people and provides increased opportunities to develop competence in activities that are personally meaningful and satisfying.

Leadership in Youth Sport

Participation in youth sport programs has grown dramatically in the past decade. Most communities now offer youth sport programs, often in several sports and with varying levels of competition. It is estimated that close to 25 million boys and girls participate in these programs. Adult volunteers, without which these programs could not function, number approximately 3 million.

The generally stated purpose of youth sport programs is to promote the healthy physical, psychological, and social development of participants. Additionally, a positive experience in youth sport can lay the foundation for a lifetime of participation in physical activity. Although this goal is worthy, youth sport programs have been severely criticized by educators, physical educators, physicians, parents, and the media for the manner in which this goal has been approached and for the failure in many cases to achieve it. The criticism has been directed at the overemphasis on winning and competition, which makes it difficult to attain many of the stated developmental objectives. "Untrained adult volunteers are often the focus of this criticism. The lack of volunteers' knowledge about growth and development factors, psychological processes, training principles, nutrition, equipment use, safety, and injury prevention and treatment has precipitated the criticism."[10]

Because of the controversy surrounding youth sport programs and criticism directed at their endeavors, the American Academy of Kinesiology and Physical Education recommended that professional preparation programs provide prospective teachers and coaches with more information about teaching the young child. The developmental approach to skill acquisition, practical opportunities for students to work with young learners of all skill levels, and remediation techniques for gross motor skills should receive more emphasis in undergraduate professional preparation. The academy also urged that professionals assume a greater role in the conduct of these programs.[1,11] Physical education, exercise science, and sport professionals have the knowledge and expertise to ensure that all participants have a satisfying and beneficial experience in youth sport. There are several ways that professionals can help make the sport experience a more positive one for children and youths. Professionals can work collaboratively with youth sport program administrators and volunteers to develop sound program guidelines. The Bill of Rights for Young Athletes, developed by AAHPERD, offers coaches and parents guidance in structuring the sport experience to achieve more positive outcomes (see the Young Athletes' Bill of Rights box).

Professionals can serve as a resource for program personnel. Through leading in-service workshops, professionals can share with the adult volunteers information about skill development, psychological development, officiating, and safety and first aid that is essential to the conduct of sound programs. Professionals can also assist in developing minimal competencies in skill and knowledge and possibly establishing certification programs for volunteers. Training volunteers to attain these standards is another way that professionals can contribute to the development of sound programs. The American Sport Education Program,[12] one of the most widely used programs, can

CHARACTER COUNTS!

The Arizona Sports Summit Accord

PREAMBLE

At its best, athletic competition can hold intrinsic value for our society. It is a symbol of a great ideal: pursuing victory with honor.

The love of sports is deeply embedded in our national consciousness. The values of millions of participants and spectators are directly and dramatically influenced by the values conveyed by organized sports. Thus, sports are a major social force that shapes the quality and character of the American culture.

In the belief that the impact of sports can and should enhance the character and uplift the ethics of the nation, we seek to establish a framework of principles and a common language of values that can be adopted and practiced widely.

IT IS THEREFORE AGREED:

1. The essential elements of character-building and ethics in sports are embodied in the concept of sportsmanship and six core principles: trustworthiness, respect, responsibility, fairness, caring, and good citizenship. The highest potential of sports is achieved when competition reflects these "six pillars of character."
2. It is the duty of sports leadership—including coaches, athletic administrators, program directors and game officials—to promote sportsmanship and foster good character by teaching, enforcing, advocating and modeling these ethical principles.
3. To promote sportsmanship and foster the development of good character, sports programs must be conducted in a manner that enhances the mental, social and moral development of athletes and teaches them positive life skills that will help them become personally successful and socially responsible.
4. Participation in athletic programs is a privilege, not a right. To earn that privilege, athletes must conduct themselves, on and off the field, as positive role models who exemplify good character.
5. Sports programs should establish standards for participation by adopting codes of conduct for coaches, athletes, parents, spectators and other groups that impact the quality of athletic programs.
6. All sports participants must consistently demonstrate and demand scrupulous integrity and observe and enforce the spirit as well as the letter of the rules.
7. The importance of character, ethics and sportsmanship should be emphasized in all communications relating to the recruitment of athletes, including promotional and descriptive materials.
8. In recruiting, educational institutions must specifically determine that the athlete is seriously committed to getting an education and has or will develop the academic skills and character to succeed.

assist professionals in this endeavor. This program provides a comprehensive, progressive sequence of objectives and knowledge to be used by program directors and professionals in the training of youth sport volunteers.

Vern Seefeldt, former director of the Institute for the Study of Youth Sports, addressed the controversial nature of youth sport. While many adults applaud the benefits of participation in youth sport programs, opponents of youth sport allege that the detrimental effects far outweigh the benefits. Seefeldt suggests that youth sport programs are "neither inherently good nor bad. Like other educational endeavors, their value depends on the quality of adult leadership and the supporting environment."[10]

The Arizona Sports Summit Accord (continued)

9. The highest administrative officer of organizations that offer sports programs must maintain ultimate responsibility for the quality and integrity of those programs. Such officers must assure that education and character development responsibilities are not compromised to achieve sports performance goals and that the academic, emotional, physical and moral well-being of athletes is always placed above desires and pressures to win.
10. The faculties of educational institutions must be directly involved in and committed to the academic success of student-athletes and the character-building goals of the institution.
11. Everyone involved in athletic competition has a duty to treat the traditions of the sport and other participants with respect. Coaches have a special responsibility to model respectful behavior and the duty to demand that their athletes refrain from disrespectful conduct including verbal abuse of opponents and officials, profane or belligerent trash-talking, taunting and unseemly celebrations.
12. The leadership of sports programs at all levels must ensure that coaches, whether paid or voluntary, are competent to coach. Minimal competence may be attained by training or experience. It includes basic knowledge of: 1) the character-building aspects of sports, including techniques and methods of teaching and reinforcing the core values comprising sportsmanship and good character; 2) first-aid principles and the physical capacities and limitations of the age group coached; and 3) coaching principles and the rules and strategies of the sport.
13. Because of the powerful potential of sports as a vehicle for positive personal growth, a broad spectrum of sports experiences should be made available to all of our diverse communities.
14. To safeguard the health of athletes and the integrity of the sport, athletic programs must discourage the use of alcohol and tobacco and demand compliance with all laws and regulations, including those relating to gambling and the use of drugs.
15. Though economic relationships between sports programs and corporate entities are often mutually beneficial, institutions and organizations that offer athletic programs must safeguard the integrity of their programs. Commercial relationships should be continually monitored to ensure against inappropriate exploitation of the organization's name or reputation and undue interference or influence of commercial interests. In addition, sports programs must be prudent, avoiding undue financial dependency on particular companies or sponsors.
16. The profession of coaching is a profession of teaching. In addition to teaching the mental and physical dimensions of their sport, coaches, through words and example, must also strive to build the character of their athletes by teaching them to be trustworthy, respectful, responsible, fair, caring and good citizens.

Courtesy of the Josephson Institute of Ethics, Marina Del Ray, Calif. For more information visit Character Counts ! Sports at www.charactercounts.org

Seefeldt encourages program volunteers to focus on promoting the continued sport involvement of children rather than emphasizing winning. Coaches must be aware of the reasons children participate in these activities. "Children become involved in sports to have fun, learn specific motor skills, socialize with their friends, and experience the excitement of competition on their own terms. These objectives are so wholesome and compelling that coaches should strive to incorporate them into every practice and contest."[10]

If youth sport is to achieve the desired outcomes, three interdependent changes are necessary according to Seefeldt. First, youth sport program directors must "resist the temptation to maintain the status quo."[10] Changes must be made in youth sport programs to accommodate children of all abilities and interests, not just those children

Young Athletes' Bill of Rights

1. Right to the opportunity to participate in sports regardless of ability level.
2. Right to participate at a level that is commensurate with each child's developmental level.
3. Right to have qualified adult leadership.
4. Right to participate in safe and healthy environments.
5. Right of each child to share in the leadership and decision-making of their sport participation.
6. Right to play as a child and not as an adult.
7. Right to proper preparation.
8. Right to have an equal opportunity to strive for success.
9. Right to be treated with dignity by all involved.
10. Right to have fun through sport.

From *Youth Sports Guide for Coaches and Parents,* AAHPERD.

who are highly skilled and competitive. Second, more research must be undertaken. Research is essential if programs are to be based on sound principles. Numerous questions require answers. Areas that need to be addressed include the nature and extent of injuries, optimal ages for learning specific skills, length of practices and duration of playing season, influence of different coaching methods on children's behavior and psychological development, and team selection for greatest equality. Third, sound training programs for youth sport coaches and personnel need to be developed and implemented. These programs should focus on the acquisition of basic competencies in skills, teaching, knowledge, first aid, and psychology that are prerequisites for coaching. In-service workshops are needed to help the millions of adult volunteers acquire these competencies.

Rainer Martens, founder of the American Sport Education Program, also endorses the importance of providing physical activity experiences for children and youth that will "turn kids on to physical activity for a lifetime."[13] According to Martens, to accomplish this objective, physical education and sport professionals must take into account several behavioral principles: (1) the Modeling Principle, which states that children model the behavior of significant others in their lives, (2) the Reinforcement Principle, which emphasizes that children are more likely to repeat behaviors for which they are positively rewarded and to avoid behaviors for which they are punished, and (3) the Self-Determination Principle, which recognizes that children typically prefer activities that they select themselves rather than those activities imposed upon them.[13] However, Martens states that the two most fundamental principles influencing participation in physical activity are the Self-Worth Principle and the Fun Principle.

The Self-Worth Principle recognizes that we all need to feel we are competent, have the opportunity to experience success, and believe that we are worthy individuals. Martens explains, "If children initially have positive experiences when being physically active, whether it be in sports or other forms of physical activity, the internal feedback of accomplishment and the external recognition of success deliver a powerful message of achievement and thus greater worthiness."[13] This promotes future participation in physical activity. On the other hand, when children's experiences in physical activity are negative, their feelings of competency are diminished and they become less likely to seek out physical activities. They turn to other activities to engender their feelings of self-worth.

Martens views the Self-Worth Principle as the most important principle to increase the participation of children in physical activity, not only in their childhood but throughout the lifespan.[13] Children experience diminished self-worth when participating in physical activities that are too developmentally advanced for them. Additionally, children often are placed in competitive sports programs before they have developed the necessary skills or are psychologically ready to compete with others. Openly criticizing children's performance and belittling their accomplishments rather than applauding their progress contribute to diminished self-worth.

The Fun Principle is integral to promoting involvement in physical activity. Though we know this, we often fail to apply this principle in designing and conducting physical activities for children. Martens asserts, "As we take the fun out of physical activities, we take the kids out of them. They turn their interests elsewhere."[13] How do we take the fun out of physical activity? Martens believes that professionals and adults take the fun out of physical activities and sports by overorganizing the activities, by constantly instructing and evaluating rather than allowing children to play and to apply what they have learned without fearing the consequences of failing or performing poorly. Often there is a discrepancy between the goals of the adults involved in running the activity and the children participating; adults focus on performance while the children focus primarily on having fun. Teaching skills by using boring drills, developing fitness by using calisthenics, using physical activity as a punishment, and placing children in a position of being publicly embarrassed by their performance are some ways in which fun is taken out of physical activity.[13]

How can we promote children's participation in physical activity and improve the quality of their experience? Martens suggests that adults need to keep their long-term objective of encouraging children to be active for a lifetime foremost in their minds. He writes:

> When this objective is foremost in the minds of adult leaders, then the emphasis shifts from the outcome of participation to the quality of the experience during participation. If that experience is positive, if that experience enhances children's perceptions of self-worth, or if that experience is fun, then children are far more likely to continue that activity, and to do so for a lifetime.[13]

As professionals, we can take an active role in promoting physical activity programs for children that incorporate these principles and have the vision of lifetime physical activity as the primary objective. This active role extends to making a commitment to provide training for adult volunteers in youth sports so that they understand the importance of these principles and how to apply them to their situation. Furthermore, it is important as professionals to allow children to have some say about the activities in which they participate and to give children the opportunity to experience a wide range of activities so that they can find activities that are enjoyable and satisfying to them.

It is important as professionals in the field to understand how children perceive the actions of adults involved in youth sports. To find out what problems children perceive in youth sports, Stuart interviewed 15 children, ranging from 10 to 12 years of age, who had youth sport experience.[14] The children were asked to describe things in their team sport experiences that they perceived to be a problem. The issues identified by the children revolved around three primary themes: fairness of adult actions, negative game behaviors, and negative team behaviors.

With respect to the issue of fairness of adult actions, actions by referees, coaches, and parents were mentioned. Referees were perceived as unfair when they made errors and failed to correct them or when they appeared to favor the other team by not calling certain fouls. Coaches' actions were also perceived as unfair. According to the players, coaches showed favoritism in selecting individuals for the team and in the amount of playing time given to team members. Parent pressure to play a certain sport was seen as unfair because it did not consider the child's preferences.

Negative game behaviors were also cited as a concern. These behaviors included the use of trash talk to intimidate and opponents trying to hurt each other, such as purposely tripping another person to prevent that person from getting the ball. Spitting into one's hands before shaking hands following the conclusion of an event was seen as a violation of sportsmanship.

Negative team behavior encompassed many different behaviors, including teammate misbehavior, selfishness, ridiculing teammates, losing self-control, and dishonesty. These behaviors were reflected in such actions as fighting in practice, which led to the team's not playing well. Another example is not involving everyone in practice or the game; this was perceived as having a negative effect on the entire team. Being jealous of a teammate led one child to lie about the time of the game so that her teammate would not be there on time.

It is important that professionals understand how children perceive their youth sports experiences if we are to address issues within this arena. Children's perceptions offer us valuable insight about how the nature of the youth sport experience can be changed to create more positive experiences for all those involved.

Youth sport programs have grown dramatically, and this growth will likely continue. If children are to benefit from participation in these programs, professionals need to take a more active role in their direction. Sound training programs for the millions of volunteers need to be developed and implemented so that the sought-after physical, psychological, and social benefits are realized, and, most importantly, so that millions of children become lifetime participants in physical activity and sports.

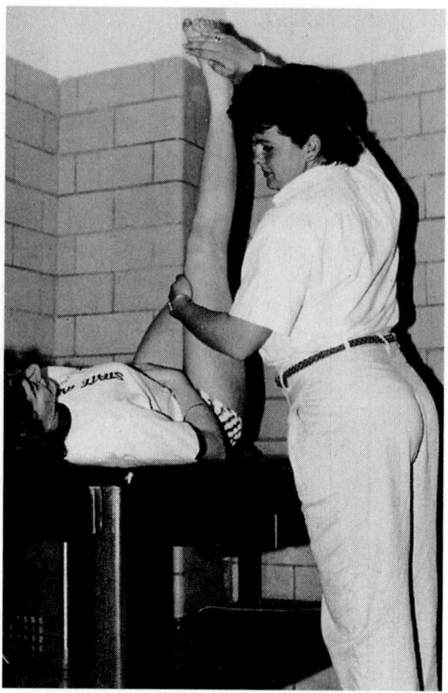

Professionals have adopted titles that more accurately reflect what they do. Athletic trainers, for example, help athletes prevent and manage injuries.

The Growing Fields

Since the early 1960s, the body of knowledge about physical education, exercise science, and sport has expanded tremendously. Because of the proliferation of research and scholarship, the theoretical base of physical education, exercise science, and sport is becoming increasingly sophisticated and complex.

The expansion of the depth and breadth of knowledge has led to the development of subdisciplines within the fields of physical education, exercise science, and sport that have emerged as areas of study in their own right. These distinct subdisciplines, which once were joined under the umbrella of physical education, have become separate, specialized areas with their own research traditions, professional organizations and publications, and specialized occupations. This specialization is currently increasing. Specialized areas of study are now emerging within the subdisciplines; for example, cardiac rehabilitation is becoming a specialized area within the subdiscipline of exercise physiology.

Many professionals have voiced concern about the increasing fragmentation and specialization of the discipline.[15,16] Lack of communication and cooperation among the increasingly specialized areas is a major concern. Moreover, the increased splintering of physical education, exercise science, and sport into narrow specialties may be harmful to our central mission of helping individuals learn the skills, knowledge, and understandings necessary to move effectively, to enhance health and well-being, and to be physically active throughout their lifespan.

It must be remembered that we as professionals are concerned with the development of the whole person through the medium of human movement, not just with the development of children's motor skills, physical fitness in adults, or psychological skills enabling elite athletes to perform at an optimum level. It is important not to forget that these specialized areas are actually parts of the greater whole. It is equally important that we not lose sight of our purpose.

Despite the calls for integration by many professionals, it is likely that the specialized areas of study will continue to further develop and become increasingly separate. However, there is a positive trend toward inter- and cross-disciplinary research. There is a growing realization of the need to help professionals integrate the growing knowledge base to respond better to the needs of the individuals with whom they work.[16] This integration of knowledge would take into account the population being served, the population's needs, and the setting in which the services are provided. Calls also abound for closing the gap between research and practice, with a greater effort being made to link theory and practice.

Many professionals are becoming dissatisfied with the traditional term used to represent the field: *physical education.* Within the past 30 years, our professional emphasis on teacher preparation has changed. Whereas teacher preparation was once the primary focus, it is now only one of many professional programs. Professional preparation programs have become increasingly diversified. The emergence of the exercise and sport sciences has led to many new professional programs, such as cardiac rehabilitation, adult fitness, sport management, sports medicine, and sport communication. Many professionals feel that the term *physical education* does not accurately describe the current nature of the field. They believe a new term is needed to represent this field more accurately and to describe what professionals in the field do.

Today, practitioners in the schools continue to refer to themselves as physical educators. However, professionals working with other populations and in other settings have adopted different terms to represent the specialized nature of their work. These professionals may refer to themselves as athletic trainers, sports medicine specialists, adapted physical educators, exercise physiologists, sport psychologists, sport sociologists, fitness instructors, sport specialists, recreation leaders, and so on.

Many terms have been suggested to describe the academic discipline of what has been traditionally called "physical education." In 1989, the American Academy of Kinesiology and Physical Education endorsed *kinesiology* as the new umbrella term for the field. Kinesiology, defined as the art and science of human movement, was believed to reflect the true focus of our efforts. Other terms frequently used are *physical education and sport, sport sciences, exercise science, human movement sciences, and exercise and sports sciences.* Massengale points out that the "lack of a common conceptual label to represent the evolving discipline" has allowed literally hundreds of descriptors to be used, much to our disadvantage.[16] This situation has led to "a confused identity that lacks an accurate concept of who we are, what we do, and where we are going."[17] It is important that we agree on a common conceptual label that reflects our mission and our identity. Corbin suggests that the term *physical activity* be used as a conceptual focus for our endeavors.[18] As a conceptual label, physical activity could provide a means to draw together all of our subdisciplines, allowing us to deliver specialized services to different populations through the medium of physical activity.[17]

The Gap between Research and Practice

One of the major problems facing the profession is the need to close the gap between research and practice.[19] A significant time lag is often seen between the publication and presentation of research and the utilization of relevant findings. If our programs, regardless of their setting, are to be based on sound principles, then this gap must be narrowed.

Factors responsible for the gap between research and practice are many. Some of these factors may be attributed to the practitioner, while others are associated with the researcher. One factor contributing to this gap is inadequate knowledge of research by the practitioner.[20] Practitioners, in both their undergraduate and graduate preparation, may not have been adequately instructed in research methods and the technical and conceptual skills necessary to conduct and interpret research. Locke writes, "The ordinary teacher, unfamiliar with basic terms and subtle distinctions in the vocabulary of research, is likely to find the usual research report nearly incomprehensible."[20] The lack of preparation hinders communication between researchers and practitioners and the consumption of research reports by practitioners. Practitioners who receive a sound background in research and statistics will be better equipped to communicate with the researcher who conducted the study and to interpret the findings.

Another factor that contributes to the gap is a negative attitude toward research held by practitioners. This attitude may deter them from using information revealed through research. Several reasons have been suggested to account for this negative attitude, including the view that research is irrelevant and impractical to the concerns of practitioners,[20,22] an inadequate understanding of research,[21] and failure to answer specific questions practitioners want answered[23] such as those about the teaching-learning process. Whatever the reason for this negative attitude, it militates against the effective use of research findings that may optimize learning.

The lack of time and resources to apply research findings to practical situations also contributes to the gap between research and practice.[23] For example, it is often heard that teachers are too busy to deal with theoretical matters; they must concentrate on daily tasks. In addition to teaching, teachers often are assigned homeroom duty, bus duty, locker room duty, hall duty, or study hall supervision, and may have coaching responsibilities as well. These extra, but required, responsibilities fill up the teacher's day and inhibit the implementation and utilization of research by the teacher. The lack of facilities and equipment with which to implement many of the research findings exacerbates the problem. Other physical education, exercise science, and sport professionals face similar constraints.

Application of research findings to practical settings is also hindered by the limited availability of the research findings. Many researchers publish their results in prestigious professional journals, many of which are not readily available to practitioners. Another source of research is theses and dissertations. Although theses and dissertations are available at college and university libraries, these unpublished sources of research are not readily available to practitioners at a distance from these sites. One promising development is the growth of the Internet as a medium for the dissemination of research findings. Online access to research and significant documents, such as *Physical Activity and Health: The Surgeon General's Report,* will make it easier for practitioners to keep abreast of current developments.

The relatively poor quality of some research and relatively few conclusive research findings contribute to the gap between research and practice. Many research studies suffer from inadequacies, especially with regard to methodological concerns. Locke notes: "Research that is poorly designed, inadequately reported, and seriously misleading constitutes a major impediment to the intelligent guidance of physical education."[20] The fact that different researchers reach disparate conclusions regarding the same research topic makes it difficult for practitioners to apply these findings in a practical setting. The conflicting results of studies present problems for practitioners who wish to use the findings to guide and support their endeavors.

Finally, the unwillingness of researchers to be concerned with the application of their findings contributes to the gap between research and practice. The failure of investigators engaged in basic research to be concerned with the application of their findings might be a cause of a lag in some cases. Complicated theoretical propositions that are sometimes advanced by researchers engaged in pure or basic research without some explanation of their practical uses are of little value to practitioners. If significant information provided by basic researchers is to be useful, investigators engaged in basic research should devote a portion of their time to development and dissemination.

How can we close the gap between research and practice? We have taken the initial steps by recognizing that the gap does exist. There are several means by which this gap can be reduced. Professional preparation programs can do a better job in preparing professionals to read and interpret research. A thorough background in research and statistics will enable physical education, exercise science, and sport professionals to develop a knowledge of research theory and statistics, locate research reports, and evaluate research studies and interpret their findings. Another approach is for practitioners and researchers to work cooperatively on joint research projects. Researchers also must make a concerted effort to bridge this gap. Researchers should endeavor to address the practical implications of their work when reporting their investigations in journals.

Although it is difficult to delineate the size of the chasm between research and practice, it is important that both researchers and practitioners work to bridge it. Over the last 10 years, we have experienced a tremendous growth in knowledge. If this knowledge is to influence the manner in which professionals conduct their programs, a concerted effort must be undertaken to narrow the gap between research and practice.

Finally, individuals are needed to serve as translators of research findings. These translators consolidate research findings, identify practical applications, and disseminate this information to practitioners in an easy-to-understand format. This job needs to be done on a large scale if research findings are to be put to use without the normal research lag. One step in this direction is the effort by the editorial board of JOPERD. In 1985, the editors instituted a new feature, "Research Works." This feature is designed to present research findings in an applied format, specifically discussing the importance of these findings to the practitioner.

In the mid-1990s, the Research Consortium of AAHPERD began publication of *Physical Activity Today,* a research-to-practice newsletter that is distributed to AAHPERD members. The easy-to-read newsletter provides a wonderful way to disseminate research findings to practitioners.

Larry Locke and his colleagues Dolly Lambdin, Stephen Silverman, and Waneen Wyrick Spirduso sought to address both the problems of research translation and accessibility by developing a Web site to bring research to practitioners in a user-friendly fashion. Debuting in 2003, the site *Unlock Research: Research for Physical Educators* (www.unlockresearch.com) was designed "to provide encouragement and support to physical educators who wish to retrieve, review, and think about research reports that might be helpful in the conduct of their professional work."[25] The site offers findings from research studies that may provide ideas and inspiration to physical educators seeking ways to enhance their professional practice.[25] Additionally, the site offers nontechnical skills to assist physical educators to interpret research and find practical value from the findings.[25]

CHALLENGES

The challenges facing physical education, exercise science, and sport professionals will increase as we move into the future. Only four of the many challenges will be discussed in this section: providing high-quality, daily physical education; promoting our programs; working to achieve the nation's health objectives; and encouraging lifespan involvement for all people.

High-Quality, Daily Physical Education

The provision of high-quality, daily physical education programs in the nation's schools is a challenge to all physical educators. There is evidence that many of the nation's children and youth are inactive and unfit.[26] Inactive lifestyles, sedentary leisure pursuits, and the lack of quality and regular physical education programs in the schools contribute to the poor fitness level of American children and youth.

There is increasingly strong support that regular and appropriate physical activity can contribute

A. Community members exercising at the Northwest Community HealthCare Wellness Center, Arlington Heights, Illinois, have over 70 pieces of cardiovascular equipment available for their use. **B.** The strength training equipment, including variable resistance and free weights, reside on the fitness floor below an elevated 1/12-mile cushioned indoor track.
Photos courtesy of Northwest Community HealthCare Wellness Center, Arlington Heights, Illinois.

to good health and enhance the quality of life for individuals of all ages.[24] There is also increased recognition that to achieve the maximum benefits of exercise an individual must begin to exercise early in life and continue to exercise throughout the lifespan. Daily physical education in school is one of the best means to help individuals learn the skills, knowledge, and values necessary to incorporate physical activity into their lifestyle.

Inadequate time for physical education in the schools is a serious problem. In an effort to address this problem, the United States Congress, in 1987, passed the National Physical Education Resolution or House Concurrent Resolution 97. This resolution encourages state governments and local educational agencies to provide high-quality daily physical education programs for all children in grades K through 12. Because the federal government usually recommends educational actions rather than mandating them, this resolution has no force of law. However, it is being used nationally by concerned teachers and parents as a lobbying tool to convince state and local educational policymakers to require daily physical education in all schools.

There is also concern about the quality of the programs offered in schools. Although there are many exemplary programs throughout the United States, many programs are of low quality. The adverse effects of low-quality programs are not limited just to the children and youth in these programs. Poor-quality programs contribute to the administrators', teachers', and parents' perceptions that physical education programs have little to offer students in our schools. Furthermore, the effects are long-lasting. Children and youth who have low-quality physical education experiences may get "turned off" to physical activity for a lifetime. Moreover, as adults, they may see little need to support physical education programs in the schools, even though the programs may have changed since they were students.

The National Association for Sport and Physical Education (NASPE) established content standards for physical education programs that clearly identified "what students should know and be able to do" as a result of participation in a high-quality physical education program.[27] These standards identified what students should learn with adequate support and sustained effort. According to NASPE, a physically educated person:

- "Demonstrates competency in many movement forms and proficiency in a few movement forms.
- Applies movement concepts and principles to the learning and development of motor skills.
- Exhibits a physically active lifestyle.
- Achieves and maintains a health-enhancing level of physical fitness.
- Demonstrates responsible personal and social behavior in physical activity settings.
- Demonstrates understanding and respect for differences among people in physical activity settings.
- Understands that physical activity provides opportunities for enjoyment, challenge, self-expression, and social interaction."[27]

A variety of activities should be included within the physical education curriculum, carefully selected for their contribution to the attainment of the NASPE standards and to learning in the cognitive, affective, and psychomotor domains. Periodic assessment of achievement allows teachers to monitor students' progress toward attainment of the standards.

NASPE has also identified additional aspects of a quality physical education program. According to NASPE, a quality physical education program does the following:

- Provides evidence of its effectiveness through the assessment of outcomes that have been achieved.
- Provides daily opportunities for the development of movement skills and physical fitness.
- Fosters an understanding of why, when, and how physical activity can be incorporated into a lifestyle.
- Focuses on the health-related benefits of physical activity and how these benefits can be acquired and maintained.
- Promotes the development of movement skills for participation beyond grades K through 12.
- Accommodates the needs and developmental levels of all students regardless of physical and mental ability levels.
- Teaches students how to apply the concepts of proper exercise in their daily lives.[28]

The incorporation of all these activities, the inclusion of these program components, and the realization of the maximum benefits from participation in a high-quality physical education program depend on the program being offered on a daily basis for a sufficient amount of time throughout all the school years. Equally important, physical education should be taught by certified physical education instructors. Just as noncertified and unqualified teachers are not tolerated in other academic areas, they should not be tolerated in physical education. Qualified and dedicated leadership is needed if the benefits associated with daily high-quality physical education programs are to be achieved. The characteristics of a quality program are summarized in the box on p. 526.

Each physical education teacher must be willing to take part in the crusade for daily high-quality physical education. Evidence supporting the value of regular and appropriate physical activity continues to mount. Furthermore, there is recognition that health behaviors are formed at an early age and that it is easier to shape positive health behaviors in children than to change unhealthy ones in adults. Moreover, while the current societal interest in wellness and fitness remains strong, now is the time to engender support for daily high-quality physical education programs. Improving the status of physical education in the schools and helping make the dream of daily, high-quality physical education a reality for all children and youth are important priorities for all physical education, exercise science, and sport professionals.

Advocacy

Advocacy is an important responsibility of physical education, exercise science, and sport professionals. The decline of physical education programs in the schools, the increased privatization of sports resulting in decreasing opportunities for

What Constitutes a Quality Physical Education Program?

According to NASPE guidelines, a high-quality physical education program includes the following components:

OPPORTUNITY TO LEARN:
- Instructional periods totaling 150 minutes per week (elementary) and 225 minutes per week (middle and secondary school).
- Qualified physical education specialist providing a developmentally appropriate program.
- Adequate equipment and facilities.

MEANINGFUL CONTENT:
- Instruction in a variety of motor skills that are designed to enhance the physical, mental, and social/emotional development of every child.
- Fitness education and assessment to help children understand, improve, and/or maintain their physical well-being.
- Development of cognitive concepts about motor skill and fitness.
- Opportunities to improve their emerging social and cooperative skills and gain a multicultural perspective.
- Promotion of regular amounts of appropriate physical activity now and throughout life.

APPROPRIATE INSTRUCTION:
- Full inclusion of all children.
- Maximum practice opportunities for class activities.
- Well-designed lessons that facilitate student learning.
- Out-of-school assignments that support learning and practice.
- No physical activity for punishment.
- Uses regular assessment to monitor and reinforce student learning.

From National Association for Sport and Physical Education, *What Constitutes a Quality Physical Education Program?* 2002, Reston, VA, American Alliance for Health, Physical Education, Recreation, and Dance.

individuals with limited economic resources, and the growing need for health promotion and physical activity programs in the worksite, community, and medical settings make it important that each professional take a role in promoting the value of our programs. Advocates need a strong voice to clearly articulate the benefits of participation in quality physical education, exercise science, and sport programs. Additionally, addressing the health disparities among population groups and inequities of opportunities for women, minorities, and people with disabilities in sport requires that we be willing to work as agents for social change and for social justice. We must assume more social responsibility and take a more active leadership role if we are to accomplish our mission of lifespan physical activity for all people.

The Advocacy Institute defines advocacy as the "pursuit of influencing outcomes—including public policy and resource allocation decisions within political, economic, and social systems and institutions—that directly affect people's lives."[27] Advocacy consists of organized efforts to change "what is"—to "highlight critical issues that have been ignored and submerged, to influence public attitudes, and to enact and implement law and public policies so that the vision of 'what should be' in a just, decent society becomes a reality."[29] The overarching framework for advocacy is human rights. Advocates seek to influence and play a role

Physical education and sport professionals should also be community leaders. These volunteers are helping children warm up before the community's Special Olympics Race for the Gold.

in the decision making of relevant institutions; they challenge the dominance of those with political, economic, and/or cultural power and through their efforts bring an improvement in people's lives.[27,30]

Advocacy is the use of communication to influence others and "to make your views or the views of those you represent count in the decision-making process."[31] The National Dance Association believes there is a role for everyone in advocacy, and activities can range from researching an issue, writing press releases, presenting your case to a group, talking to a legislator, planning special events, securing a grant, maintaining a Web site, networking with individuals, forging new partnerships with organizations, or working to stay abreast of current issues.[31] It is important that we communicate our message effectively via various formats and media to the public and decision makers if we are to bring about change.

Physical education, exercise science, and sport professionals must undertake a greater role as advocates for social justice. As Dr. Martin Luther King, Jr. said, "Injustice anywhere is a threat to justice everywhere."[32] Inequities persist despite our professed societal value of equality and the passage of legislation, such as the Civil Rights Act, Title IX, and the Americans with Disabilities Act. Much more needs to be done. We promote lifespan involvement in physical activity for all people as important to their health and well-being, yet there are tremendous disparities in physical activity and disease conditions according to race, ethnicity, sex, age, education, sexual orientation, ability/disability, and income. Sports participation for males and females of all ages has increased dramatically, yet opportunities at all levels of sport and within sport administration and the sport industry remain inequitable.

We view school physical education as the means to provide all children with the skills, knowledge, and attitudes to participate in lifelong physical activity. As Larry Locke points out, the public schools provide us with a means to reach across barriers of race, ethnicity, gender, social class, and economic conditions to reach millions of children and youth.[33] In theory, the schools afford us the opportunity to ensure that all children learn what they need to know to be physically active for a lifetime. Yet, in reality, the physical education experience of children and youth in inner-city schools in Los Angeles is likely to be quite different from that of students in an upper-class suburb of Chicago or those of students in a rural area of Maine.

As physical education, exercise science, and sport professionals, it is our professional responsibility to address these inequities. Are you ready to make a commitment to social justice and diversity? Are you ready to work in some way to close the gap between the "haves" and the "have-nots?" What will you do to promote daily, high-quality physical education K–12 for all children and youth? What will you do to ensure greater opportunities in sport for girls and women, for people with disabilities, and for minorities? What steps will you take to ensure that all high schools have certified athletic trainers on their staff? Are you ready to take an active role in working to ensure that medical insurance will cover preventive physical activity programs or that worksite health promotion programs will be open to all employees, not just the upper management?

As physical education, exercise science, and sport professionals, we must be ready and willing to work as agents of social change—as advocates to change public policies, to increase access for underserved populations, to provide services to those in need, and to empower people to make a difference in their own lives. We must not only be concerned with strengthening our programs, but with increasing access for all segments of our population to our services.

Public relations is an important component of program promotion and advocacy efforts. Now is the time to capitalize on the widespread public interest in sport, physical fitness, and health. Professionals teaching in the school setting; instructing in community and recreational sport programs; working in commercial sport clubs, fitness centers, and health spas; and directing corporate and community fitness programs must use public relations techniques to market their programs. Professionals must inform the public and prospective clientele of the values that accrue from participation in a sound physical activity and exercise program.

In the school setting, where physical education is often regarded as an extra or is cut to make more time for academic subjects, where budgetary cutbacks are becoming increasingly common, and where class sizes are expanding, teachers must be willing to advocate on behalf of their programs to gain the personal and budgetary support of school administrators, politicians, and parents. Dunn states that "the school board is recognized as one of the most influential organizations for developing and shaping policy at the local level. Without the support and advocacy of the local board, efforts to promote physical education and healthful activity will not be achieved."[34] Other legislative bodies and state education commissions must also be addressed because of the power they wield as decision-making bodies.[34]

Advocacy involves more than just promoting your program; advocacy requires a commitment to conducting a high-quality program so that it might stand as visible testimony to community leaders and decision makers of the benefits of physical education. Physical education has changed considerably in the 30 years or so since the adult public participated in these programs during their school years. Physical educators must be willing to demonstrate how physical education programs have changed by allowing the adults to observe their programs, by conducting demonstrations and other promotional activities, and by talking to parents and community groups.

Professionals can take advantage of special events and activities to increase visibility, generate excitement, promote physical education and sport, and increase awareness of the contribution of regular physical activity to health. In May, NASPE/AAHPERD sponsors National Physical Fitness and Sports Month and May 1 through May 7 is designated National Physical Education and Sport Week. Professionals are urged to use these events to showcase their programs and to educate the public about the contribution physical education makes to children's and youth's lives. Two other activities that physical educators can use to promote physical education and highlight the contribution of physical activity to the prevention of cardiovascular disease are Jump Rope for Heart and Hoops for Heart, joint projects of AAHPERD and the American Heart Association. Both programs are educational/fund-raising events, held each year in thousands of schools across the nation. Students learn about health and the importance of regular physical activity, participate in rope-jumping and basketball activities, and raise funds through pledges. Since 1978, over $325 million has been raised for cardiovascular research and prevention efforts.

The National Girls and Women in Sports Coalition sponsors its annual National Girls and Women in Sports Day to celebrate female athletic achievements, to highlight the importance of sports and fitness participation of all girls and women, and to raise awareness of the continuing struggle for equality and access for females in sport even now, 30 years after the passage of Title IX. Advocacy and awareness are critical in achieving equality for females in sports. The coalition urges all women's sports advocates to make every day Girls and Women in Sports Day by continuing to work to increase opportunities for girls and women in sports.[35]

Advocacy can result in the passage of federal and state legislation that has a favorable impact on physical education programs. One example of this effort is the passage by the U.S. Congress of the Physical Education for Progress Act, now known as the Carol M. White Physical Education Program. This bill provides millions of dollars a year in grants (PEP Grants) for schools to revitalize their physical education programs. This act underscores the importance of physical education and its contribution to our nation's well-being.

Advocacy is just as important in physical activity programs that are conducted outside of the school setting. Advocacy in these settings can take many different forms. Professionals may work to initiate programs, to expand services offered within programs, and to increase access to programs by underserved populations. Additionally, professionals must work to promote and market their programs.

As you view this father and his daughter finishing this "fun" mile, remember that it is important to encourage parents to be active role models for their children. Children whose parents are active are more likely to be active than are children of sedentary parents.

Prospective clientele for community and commercial programs must be aware of the nature of the programs offered and the benefits to be derived from participation in such programs. In the corporate fitness setting, professionals must promote the values and benefits to be derived from participation to management as well as to employees. Corporate management personnel will be reluctant to invest corporate resources, particularly money, to support these programs if they are not aware of their value and/or if the stated benefits are not achieved.

Physical education, exercise science, and sport professionals must become more powerful

David Fischer, author of *The 50 Coolest Jobs in Sport, Do Curve Balls Really Curve?,* and *365 Amazing Days in Sports,* at work. David combined his undergraduate degree in physical education with his strong interest in journalism to pursue a writing career. Many exciting careers await qualified professionals.

advocates on behalf of their programs and take a greater role in promoting the incorporation of physical activity as part of daily living.[36] Booth and Chakravarthy urge professionals to take a greater part in the war against Sedentary Death Syndrome (SeDS), a phrase they coined to describe "sedentary lifestyle-mediated disorders that ultimately result in increased mortality."[34] SeDS disorders include cardiovascular disease, certain types of cancer, Type 2 diabetes, and lower quality of life. Advocates for health promotion should use strategies that emphasize the cost-benefits of moderate physical activity—the substantial benefits that will accrue from reduction in health care costs and indirect costs associated with poor health as well as gains in quality of life. Activism and advocacy efforts should be directed at incorporation of physical activity into one's lifestyle.

Professionals should utilize specific strategies for different age groups in advocating physical activity for health. For example, Booth and Chakravarthy suggest that for children and adolescents we should promote lifetime physical activity in physical education classes; for older adults, they recommend free access to strength training equipment and recreational facilities.[36] Additionally, professionals must make efforts to lobby decision-makers—legislators, corporate heads, and community leaders—to support a physically active America.[36] Professionals should not overlook the use of the various media to educate the public about the large body of scientific evidence supporting the significant contribution of a physically active lifestyle to good health.[34]

Active involvement by physical education, exercise science, and sport professionals is critical to attaining our goal of lifespan involvement in physical activity for all people. Every physical education, exercise science, and sport professional is urged to be an active member in his or her own community, "advocating for the inclusion of appropriate physical activity for health."[34] Contact organizations that promote physical activity and health and "advocate that these organizations become more proactive in presenting the facts . . . to those decision makers who in turn can make policies to facilitate a more physically active lifestyle, and thereby play a direct part in facilitating a healthier and more prosperous America."[36] Active professional involvement will help us reduce the morbidity and mortality associated with chronic disease and help people of all ages live healthier lives.

Many professional organizations have developed advocacy kits and materials to help professionals clearly present their case, whether it be for daily, high-quality physical education; fitness instruction; or athletic training in the high schools. These kits are either free or low cost, and vary in content, but may include videos, CD-ROMs, PowerPoint presentations, position papers, suggested activities, press releases, and public service announcements. Professionals can also find information to support their advocacy efforts from government sources and publications, such as the Centers for Disease Control and Prevention or *Healthy People 2010* and the Surgeon General's report on *Physical Activity and Health.* Physical education, exercise science, and sport professionals need to become directly involved in advocacy efforts—advocacy is an important professional responsibility.

Achievement of National Health Goals

Another challenge facing physical education, exercise science, and sport professionals is working collaboratively with other health professionals toward the achievement of the national health goals set forth in the Surgeon General's report *Healthy People 2010*.[37] The *Healthy People 2010* goals reflect a commitment to improve the nation's health through a comprehensive health promotion and disease prevention effort. *Healthy People 2010* identified two overarching goals to be achieved by 2010. The goals are "to help individuals of all ages increase life expectancy *and* improve their quality of life" and "to eliminate health disparities among segments of the population, including differences that occur by gender, race or ethnicity, education or income, disability, geographic location, or sexual orientation."[37]

Increasing the amount of time physical educators spend teaching lifetime sports is important to lifespan involvement.

Healthy People 2010 identified 28 focus areas, one of which was physical activity. For each focus area, specific objectives were identified, the attainment of which would lead to an improvement in the health of the nation's people.

The current fitness status of the American people, the trends set forth by these reports, and the specific objectives are described in Chapter 3. The objectives for the year 2010 were based on the assumption that increases in appropriate physical activity by people of all ages will result in concomitant health gains. The reports also assumed that the primary motive for participation in physical activity will be a personal commitment to improve one's health and enhance the quality of one's life. The objectives for the year 2010 focus on improvement of the health status of all Americans, regardless of age; reduction of risk factors through increased participation in appropriate physical activity; increased knowledge of the public and professionals about the role of exercise in the promotion of health; and improvement of access and expansion of services.

The *Healthy People 2010* specific objectives for physical activity were described in Chapter 3.

Briefly, in terms of risk reduction, the objectives call for reducing the proportion of adults who engage in no leisure-time physical activity and increasing the proportion of adults who engage in moderate physical activity for at least 30 minutes a day and vigorous physical activity on a regular basis. Other objectives for adults emphasize increasing the proportion of adults who engage in activities to promote flexibility and muscular strength/endurance.

Healthy People 2010 recognizes that the adolescent years are critical years for the promotion of lifelong physical activity. Physical activity generally decreases during this time, so *Healthy People 2010* seeks to reverse this trend by targeting specific objectives to adolescents. Physical activity objectives for adolescents call for increasing the proportion of adolescents who engage in 30 or more minutes of moderate physical activity at least 5 days per week and encouraging more adolescents to engage in vigorous physical activity to promote cardiorespiratory fitness. In order to promote more active behavior during leisure time, *Healthy People 2010* calls for a reduction in the amount of time adolescents spend watching television and limiting time spent on other sedentary activities.

Healthy People 2010 objectives also focus on physical education. Increasing the number of the nation's schools that require daily physical education for all students is one objective for 2010. Additional objectives related to the physical education call for increasing the proportion of adolescents who participate in daily physical education as well as increasing the amount of time during physical education class when these students are active.

Providing access to physical activity facilities is critical to promoting physical activity and reducing disparities among different segments of the population. To address these issues, *Healthy People 2010* called for improving the public's access to school facilities outside of the regular school day—before and after school, on weekends, during vacations, and throughout the summer. Increasing the number of worksites that offer physical activity and fitness programs offers additional opportunities for individuals to be active during the day. Promoting physical activity within the community is encouraged by seeking to have more people of all ages walk and bike to their destinations, rather than going by car or bus.

Other *Healthy People 2010* focus areas include objectives related to promoting physical activity. Of particular relevance are those objectives associated with educational and community-based programs. These include increasing the number of school health programs that educate students about problems associated with physical inactivity and providing more information to college students about health risks, including problems associated with inadequate physical activity. Other objectives call for more work sites to offer comprehensive health promotion programs and increasing the number of employees who participate in these programs. Another community-based effort is increasing the number of hospitals that provide health promotion programs for staff and community members.

Addressing the needs of community members, especially underserved populations, is called for in the *Healthy People 2010* objectives. The development of comprehensive and multifaceted health promotion programs in local communities is emphasized. One objective calls for increasing the number of community health promotion and disease prevention programs, which could include physical activity, that provide culturally appropriate and linguistically competent care.

As you can see, physical education, exercise science, and sport can make important contributions to the improvement of the health status of the American public. Professionals should take an active role in working with other health professionals to attain these objectives. Moreover, our involvement in attaining these objectives will contribute to increased public recognition of the worth and value of our fields. Additionally, one benefit that will accrue from our participation in this endeavor is increased employment opportunities.

Employment opportunities for qualified professionals will increase, and new career opportunities will develop. The objective of promoting daily physical education will result in a demand for more teachers. Instructors also will be needed to teach physical activities to adults and the elderly and educate them about the benefits of such activities. The growth of corporate health promotion and fitness programs will create a need for more professionals qualified in this area. More hospitals are adding health promotion and fitness programs for their employees, patients, and community members.

Can we attain the objectives for 2010? There has been some progress toward attaining the specific physical activity objectives (see Chapter 3). For example, deaths from coronary heart disease have declined, worksite health promotion programs have increased, and some progress has been made in promoting involvement in moderate and vigorous physical activity. However, the decline in daily physical education is disturbing. Obesity has increased for both children and adults, and much more improvement needs to be made in the physical activity patterns of children and adults. Inequities in health and physical activity still persist. There is much more to be done to achieve our health goals. Professional organizations such as AAHPERD and ACSM provide us with strong leadership. However, whether or not we can achieve the stated objectives for physical activity depends on each professional's commitment to attaining these objectives and to advocacy to increase programs and opportunities for all people.

Physical education, exercise science, and sport professionals must make a commitment to serve as role models for healthy, active lifestyles. In a position statement on Physical Activity and Fitness Recommendations for Physical Activity Professionals, NASPE states,

> Participation in regular physical activity at least at a level sufficient to promote health-related physical fitness is an essential behavior for professionals in all fields of physical activity at all levels (this includes coaches, K–12 teachers, physical education and kinesiology faculty in higher education, fitness professionals, athletes, all advocates of physically active lifestyles).[38]

As physical education, exercise science, and sport professionals, we must take the mantle of leadership and undertake the responsibility of being role models. Research shows that role modeling is an important factor in changing human behaviors. Role models can influence attitudes and behaviors related to health practices, acquisition of motor skills, and adoption of physical activity patterns.[38] Physical education, exercise science, and sport professionals should teach and model currently recommended physical activity behaviors for improving health and fitness (e.g., participation in moderate physical activities for at least 30 minutes a day on all of most days of the week).[38] This will have a "positive influence on those who expect fitness and exercise leaders to be leaders in their profession and to set a positive example for young people and the community."[38] When we, as professionals, lead an active lifestyle it enhances our credibility among the public and vividly demonstrates the value of being physically active.[36]

Being a role model requires that we make a commitment. Wilmore[39] states:

The growth of community and commercial sport programs has enabled more children to receive instruction and develop a lifelong interest in sport and fitness activities.

> Each of us in the profession must make a personal commitment to achieve or maintain a good level of physical fitness. How can we be effective in promoting health and fitness if our bodies are not living testimonies of our commitment? What we are communicates so much more than what we say!

As professionals, we must practice what we preach.

Although modeling is only one factor that contributes to learning and behavior change, NASPE notes that "modeling an appropriate fitness level and an active lifestyle needs to be considered a significant factor in encouraging young people, colleagues, and communities to do the same."[38] Modeling can have a "powerful influence on youth and our success in advocacy for our profession to the public."[39] Actions speak louder than words. What is your commitment to serving as a model of a healthy, physically active lifestyle?

Winners belong to every age group.

Lifespan Involvement for All People

One of the most heartening changes in our fields within the last 20 years has been the expansion of physical education, exercise science, and sport programs to people of all ages and to a diversity of settings. Traditionally, our programs have focused on children and youth and have been conducted in the school and community-recreation settings. However, within the last two decades, the scope of our programs has expanded tremendously.

The expanded focus has led to providing services to new populations. Services have expanded to encompass individuals of all ages. Programs have been developed for infants and toddlers as well as for adults and senior citizens. There has been a greater effort to meet the needs of all people, regardless of their skill level, fitness status, and abilities.

There is an increased recognition that regular and appropriate physical activity can make a vital contribution to the health and lives of all people. It can enhance the quality of one's life as well as its longevity. Additionally, it has become increasingly apparent that our efforts should focus on early childhood education and intervention. Individuals gain the maximum benefits from exercise and physical activity when they begin at an early age and continue their participation throughout the lifespan.

During childhood, fitness and leisure habits are developed; once developed, they become difficult to change. Moreover, it has been shown that such insidious diseases as obesity and coronary heart disease can begin in childhood. Therefore, it is important that efforts be made to assist children in acquiring the skills, knowledge, and positive attitudes conducive to good health. Children must be educated to form good health and physical activity habits early in life. Physical educators, parents, and other health professionals should focus their efforts on helping children adopt an active rather than a sedentary lifestyle and on providing them with the skills and knowledge to effectively manage their lifestyles as adults.

It is important to note that the number of programs being provided for preschoolers is growing; it is likely that the number of these programs will increase in the next decade. Motor development programs are being offered to infants and toddlers in hospital and clinical settings. Preschools and day-care centers are incorporating physical education programs into their curricula. NASPE recently released physical activity guidelines for infants, toddlers, and preschoolers. The guidelines stress the importance of being physically active from the beginning of life and offer recommendations regarding the amount and type of physical activity for each age group.[40]

In the past decade, the fitness and wellness movements have encouraged an increasing number of adults to incorporate regular physical activity into their lifestyles. Many adults are now engaging in physical activities and exercise of sufficient intensity, duration, and frequency to realize health benefits. Unfortunately, many more adults are not. The majority of adults lead sedentary lives or exercise only moderately. The incidence of physical inactivity increases with age and is influenced by such factors as gender, race, ethnicity, socioeconomic status, educational level, occupation, and geographic location. (See Chapter 3 for further information.) As professionals, we need to help these people change their physical activity and health habits and adopt health-enhancing lifestyles. Creative educational and individualized physical activity and health promotion programs are needed to accomplish this objective.

As we begin the twenty-first century, the proportion of elderly in the population continues to increase. By the year 2025, it is estimated the elderly will compose 18.5% of the population. Furthermore, the elderly will be increasingly healthy and vigorous. Physical education, exercise science, and sport professionals must be prepared to meet the physical activity and leisure needs of this population group. Research shows that people with healthy habits live longer, are functionally independent for a greater period of time, and experience a higher quality of life. Never has our potential to improve the health and well-being of this population group been greater. We must reach out and involve members of this age group in our programs.

The last decade has also seen an increase in physical education, exercise, and sport opportunities available to individuals with disabilities. Participation in physical activity and sport makes a significant contribution to the health and fitness of individuals with disabilities. However, the benefits extend further. Dunn and Sherrill[41] state that, for some individuals with disabilities, engaging in physical activities contributes to their ability to perform the tasks of daily living, such as dressing, bathing, and preparing for work. Fun, enjoyment, and satisfaction from meeting challenges are other meaningful outcomes of participation. Participation in sport, an important institution of our society, enables individuals with disabilities to become more involved in family and community activities and thus become normalized. For example, children who have a visual impairment can use their proficiency in swimming both to compete and take part in water activities enjoyed by their families. For some individuals with disabilities, participation in sport contributes to self-actualization and feelings of empowerment.

Sport involvement among people of all ages continues to increase. Millions of children throughout the country participate in youth and interscholastic sports. Intercollegiate athletic participation continues to rise. Communities are developing more sport opportunities for adults of all ages. Competitive and recreational leagues offer adults the opportunity to continue their participation in organized sports at a desirable level of intensity. Masters' competitions and competitions for seniors in a variety of sports and at a number of levels—local, state, national, and international—allow many adults and senior citizens across the country to continue their sport involvement. Sport organizations for individuals with disabilities also provide opportunities for competition in a wide range of individual and team sports.

As we continue to expand our focus to meet the needs of new populations, we must also continue to broaden our programs. Because the populations that are served are increasingly heterogeneous, a greater diversity of programs is needed to meet their needs. The minority population is increasing and their needs must not be overlooked. Changes in program content and the manner in which programs are conducted will be necessary to meet a wide range of individual differences. Culturally competent physical education, exercise science, and sport professionals are critical to promoting the involvement of minorities and underserved populations in our programs. This is essential if we are to eliminate health disparities and increase involvement in physical activity. Additionally, we must increase our efforts to recruit minorities into careers in our field; they are presently underrepresented.

Ensuring access to our programs is critical as they continue to expand from the school setting to the community, from the public sector to the private sector. The school setting will be used increasingly as a site for community programs for individuals of all ages. Programs in day-care centers, preschools, hospitals, developmental centers, senior centers, nursing homes, community settings, and corporations will continue to expand. Commercial programs in the private sector will continue to increase. Health clubs, fitness centers, private clubs offering sport instruction, and private sport leagues will develop more programs to meet the needs of paying clients. As programs expand to meet the needs of various populations, it is important to ensure that all individuals have access to these programs. Fitness and health opportunities should also be available to those who do not have the means to pay. Fitness and health opportunities should be available to all individuals regardless of socioeconomic background.

As the scope of physical education, exercise science, and sport increases and as the focus of the programs offered expands, it is important that professional programs prepare students to capably assume responsibilities within these growing areas. Professional preparation programs have traditionally focused on preparing students to work with children and youth within the school setting. Today, professional preparation programs must provide students with the skills and knowledge necessary to conduct effective programs with different population groups and across the lifespan.

Promoting lifespan involvement in physical activity is a challenge to all physical education, exercise science, and sport professionals. Lifespan involvement can enrich the life and enhance the health of every person—regardless of age, gender, race or ethnicity, income, education, sexual orientation, religion, geographic location, or disability. As *Healthy People 2010* states, the diversity of our nation's population is one of its greatest assets, but it also represents one of the biggest challenges we

Focus on Career: Health Promotion and Leisure

PROFESSIONAL ORGANIZATIONS

- American Public Health Association
  www.apha.org
- American Association for Leisure and Recreation
  www.aahperd → AALR
- American Association for Health Education
  www.aahperd → AAHE
- National Recreation and Parks Association
  www.nrpa.org/

PROFESSIONAL JOURNALS

- *Parks and Recreation Magazine*
- *American Journal of Public Health*
- *American Journal of Health Education*

must face in improving the nation's health.[35] Every person in every community in the United States deserves the right to equal access to comprehensive, culturally competent, community-based health care.[37] Physical activity programs are an important part of health promotion and disease prevention efforts. Making lifespan involvement a reality for all people requires qualified and dedicated physical education, exercise science, and sport professionals willing to work toward attaining this goal.

SUMMARY

Following an overview of selected issues in physical education, exercise science, and sport today, five issues were examined in more detail. First, physical education, exercise science, and sport professionals must assume a greater leadership role in the physical activity movement. Second, more emphasis should be placed on promoting morals and ethical values in our programs. Third, we need to assume a greater role in the conduct of youth sports programs. Fourth, as our fields continue to grow in scope and expand their focus, we need to more clearly define who we are, what it is that we do, and how we can work together better. Lastly, as research continues at an unprecedented rate, we must take additional steps to close the gap between research and practice.

Many challenges face physical education, exercise science, and sport professionals. Four particularly important challenges were discussed. First, professionals are faced with the challenge of promoting daily, high-quality physical education in the schools. The second challenge is to become more actively involved as advocates for our programs. Professionals in all settings must actively promote their programs. The third challenge is to attain the goals set forth in the report *Healthy People 2010.* These specific physical activity objectives focus on improving the health status of all Americans by increasing the span of healthy life. If these objectives are to be achieved, each professional must make a personal commitment to work with professional organizations to accomplish this task and to be a role model exemplifying a healthy, active lifestyle. Last, promoting lifespan involvement in physical activity requires professionals to provide a diversity of services to individuals of all ages. Physical education, exercise science, and sport has the potential to enhance the health and quality of life of people of all ages. Helping individuals to realize this potential is one of our biggest challenges.

The issues and challenges confronting professionals are many. If we are to deal with them, physical education, exercise science, and sport professionals must be knowledgeable about their fields and be willing to assume leadership positions. The manner in which professionals deal with these issues and meet the challenges confronting them will influence the future of physical education, exercise science, and sport.

SELF-ASSESSMENT TESTS

These tests are designed to help you determine if you have mastered the materials and competencies presented in this chapter.

1. Discuss the role of the physical educator, exercise scientist, and sport leader in the physical activity movement. What can we do to "lead the parade"?
2. Explain how professionals can promote the development of values in their programs, regardless of the setting.
3. Discuss how professionals can help adult volunteers conduct sound youth sport programs. Discuss the need for professionals to help in the conduct of youth sport programs in light of your own youth sport experiences.
4. How can the growing disciplinary knowledge be integrated to help practitioners effectively accomplish their responsibilities?
5. Identify strategies to reduce the gap between research and practice.

6. What specific strategies could be employed to encourage the state legislature and the local school boards to mandate daily physical education?
7. Discuss the importance of advocacy programs in the physical education, exercise science, and sport setting of your choice. What local organizations exist in your current community that offer health promotion programs? How would you work to organize these groups into a coalition to promote physical activity?
8. Describe how physical educators, exercise scientists, and sport leaders, through various programming efforts, can help individuals attain the fitness and physical goals set forth in *Healthy People 2010.* What strategies could be used to promote greater access to these programs for underserved populations?
9. Describe various strategies that can be utilized to promote lifespan involvement for people of all ages, abilities, races and ethnicities, genders, and socioeconomic backgrounds.

REFERENCES

1. Park RJ: Three major issues: the Academy takes a stand, JOPERD 54(1):52–53, 1983.
2. National Coalition for Promoting Physical Activity, 2002. (www.ncppa.org)
3. Costanzo DG, Rustico DM, and Pescatello LS: Community older adult exercise programs: an evaluation of compliance to professional standards, Journal of Aging and Physical Activity 10:76–92.
4. Corbin CB: Is the fitness bandwagon passing us by? JOPERD 55(9):17, 1984.
5. Ewers JR: You must be present to win, Quest 49:238–250, 1997.
6. Hellison D: Teaching responsibility through physical activity, Champaign, Ill., 1995, Human Kinetics.
7. Martinek TJ and Hellison DR: Fostering resiliency in underserved youth through physical activity, Quest 49:34–49, 1997.
8. Character Counts. (www.charactercounts.org)
9. Josephson M: Pursuing victory with honor: a training program for coaches on ethics, sportsmanship, and character-building in sport, 2002. (www.charactercounts.org)
10. Seefeldt V: Why are children's sports programs controversial? JOPERD 56(3):16, 1985.
11. The American Academy of Physical Education: The Academy papers: reunification, no. 15, Reston, Va., 1981, AAHPERD.
12. American Sport Education Program, Champaign, Ill., current edition, Human Kinetics.
13. Martens R: Turning kids on to physical activity for a lifetime, Quest 46:303–310, 1996.
14. Stuart ME: Moral issues in sport: The child's perspective, Research Quarterly for Exercise and Sport 74:445–455, 2003.
15. Sage GH: The future and the profession. In JD Massengale, editor: Trends toward the future in physical education, Champaign, Ill., 1987, Human Kinetics.
16. Siedentop D: Introduction to physical education, fitness, and sport, Mountain View, Calif., 1990, Mayfield.
17. Massengale JD: Doing PE at the new university, Quest 52:102–109, 2002.
18. Corbin CB: Promoting lifelong physical activity: education's challenge for the new millennium, Paper presented at the National Conference for Promoting Lifelong Physical Activity, Salt Lake City, Utah, October, 1998. (Cited in Massengale JD: Doing PE at the new university, Quest 52:102–109, 2002).
19. Bucher CA and Thaxton NA: Physical education and sport: change and challenge, St. Louis, 1981, Mosby.
20. Rothstein AL: Practitioners and the scholarly enterprise, Quest 20:59–60, 1973.
21. Locke LF: Research in physical education, New York, 1969, Teachers College Press.
22. Stadulis RE: Bridging the gap: a lifetime of waiting and doing, Quest 20:48–52, 1973.

23. Barnes FP: Research for the practitioner in education, Washington, D.C., 1963, Department of Elementary School Principles, National Education Association.

24. Broderick FP: Research as viewed by the teacher, Paper presented at the AAHPER National Convention, Detroit, 1971.

25. Locke, L. Unlock research: research for physical educators. Unlock Research. (www.unlockresearch.com)

26. US Department of Health and Human Services, Physical activity and health: a report of the Surgeon General, Atlanta, Ga., 1996, US Department of Health and Human Services, Centers for Disease Control and Prevention, National Center for Chronic Disease Prevention and Health Promotion.

27. National Association for Sport and Physical Education: Moving into the future: national content standards for physical education, St. Louis, 1995, Mosby Year Books.

28. The National Association for Sport and Physical Education: Fit to achieve educational information, Reston, Va., 1989, AAHPERD.

29. Advocacy Institute: What is advocacy? From Cohen D: Part I: Reflections on advocacy, Bloomfield Press, Conn., 2001, Kumarin Press. (www.advocacy.org)

30. DePauw KP: Futuristic perspectives for kinesiology and physical education, Quest 50:1–8, 1998.

31. National Dance Association: Advocacy kit: you can make a difference, National Dance Association. (www.aahperd.org→NDA)

32. Advocacy Institute: Become a leader for social justice: fight for what you believe in, Washington, D.C., 2001, Advocacy Institute.

33. Locke LF: Advice, stories, and myths: the reactions of a cliff jumper, Quest 50:238–248, 1998.

34. Dunn JM: Communicating with school boards: position, power, perseverance, Quest 51:157–163, 1999.

35. National Girls and Women in Sports Day Central—Celebrating 30 Years of Title IX. (www.aahperd.org/ngwsdcentral)

36. Booth FW and Chakravarthy MV: President's Council on Physical Fitness and Sport: Research Digest: Cost and consequences of sedentary living: new battleground for an old enemy, 3(16), March 2002.

37. US Department of Health and Human Services: Healthy People 2010, ed 2, With understanding and improving health and objectives for improving health, 2 vols, Washington, D.C., 2000, US Government Printing Office.

38. National Association for Sport and Physical Education: Physical activity and fitness recommendations for physical activity professionals, NASPE, 2002. (www.aahperd.org)

39. Wilmore JH: Objectives for the nation: physical fitness and exercise, JOPERD 53(3):41–43.

40. National Association for Sport and Physical Education: Active start: physical activity guidelines for children birth to age five. Reston, Va., 2002, AAHPERD. (www.aahperd.org→ naspe)

41. Dunn JM and Sherrill C: Movement and its implication for individuals with disabilities, Quest 48:378–391, 1996.

SUGGESTED READINGS

American Sport Education Program, Champaign, Ill., Human Kinetics Publishers.

This multilevel program is designed to help coaches gain a basic understanding of the knowledge necessary to coach athletes at various levels and in a diversity of sports. Further information about this extensive coaching program can be obtained from Human Kinetics (www.asep.com).

Bennett RS and Wughalter EH (Co-editors): Social justice and diversity, Quest 51(4), 1999.

This entire issue is devoted to social justice and diversity. Among the topics covered are inclusion paradigms in physical education, physical activity and women with disabilities, American Indian imagery, homophobic discourse surrounding the female athlete, and media portrayals of Tiger Woods.

Costanzo DG, Rustico DM, and Pescatello LS: Community older adult exercise programs: an evaluation of compliance to professional standards, Journal of Aging and Physical Activity, 10:76–92, 2002.

This research study found that community facilities housing exercise programs for older adults were not in compliance with health and fitness industry standards. Areas of noncompliance included failure to adhere to a medical clearance policy and the use of noncertified instructors to teach exercise classes.

Daley AJ: School-based physical activity in the United Kingdom: can it create physically active adults? Quest 54:21–33, 2002.

From the standpoint of public health, school-based physical activities can contribute to lifetime participation. However, schools need to establish policies and procedures to ensure that extracurricular activities happen on a regular basis and that programs are rebalanced to ensure more opportunities that meet the needs and interests of a greater proportion of the student body. Schools also need to work with other agencies to promote a more active lifestyle.

Dunn JM and Sherrill C: Movement and its implication for individuals with disabilities, Quest 48:378–391, 1996.

The authors discuss the important contributions physical activity and sport make to the lives of individuals with disabilities. The benefits of participation for individuals with disabilities include health and fitness, ability to perform tasks of daily living, fun and enjoyment, normalization, empowerment, and opportunity to participate with friends and families in sport.

Ewers JR: You must be present to win, Quest 49: 238–250, 1997.

Ewers discusses the importance of our profession directing its energies and resources to meeting the physical activity needs of the growing healthy elderly population.

Irwin CC, Symons CW, and Kerr DL: The dilemmas of obesity: how can physical educators help? JOPERD 74(6):33, 2003.

Stresses that rising levels of obesity provide an important opportunity for physical educators to be involved in reducing obesity incidence. As part of the comprehensive school help program, we can contribute to promoting a healthy, productive lifestyle. To create a more positive physical education environment for children who are obese, physical educators need to be more compassionate and understanding, individualize the curriculum, and model appropriate and healthy behaviors.

Locke LF and Lambdin D: Putting research to work in elementary physical education: conversations in the gym. Champaign, IL, 2003, Human Kinetics.

This book brings to the reader 30 studies focusing on elementary physical education, with comments from the perspective of a researcher and an elementary teacher. Topics include instruction, class management, program design, workplace conditions, student behaviors, and teacher development. It is written to help translate research findings into practice in a way that makes sense for the practitioner.

Martens R: Turning kids on to physical activity for a lifetime, Quest 46:303–310, 1996.

Martens emphasizes the importance of self-worth and fun in youth sports and as guiding principles for promoting lifelong physical activity.

McBride RE and Xiang P: Thoughtful decision making in physical education: a modest proposal, Quest 56:337–354, 2004.

Proposes that thoughtful decision making may be an appropriate framework to serve as a theoretical model for physical education. The promotion of critical thinking and decision making is a common feature of many approaches to physical education, including games for understanding and cooperative games.

Stuart ME: Moral issues in sport: the child's perspective, Research Quarterly for Exercise and Sport 74:445–455, 2003.

This study examines children's perspectives on moral issues in sport by interviewing 15 children, ranging in age from 10 to 12 years, who had competitive youth sport experience. Three overall dimensions emerged—fairness of adults' actions, negative game behaviors, and negative team behaviors. Children expressed concern about acts of intimidation, retaliation, dishonesty, poor sportsmanship, and the opportunity to make choices.

Watson DL and Hildebrand K: Advocacy: changing our professional behaviors, JOPERD 71(1), 2000.

Applies the transtheoretical model of change to the development of advocacy behaviors in HPERD professionals. Emphasizes advocacy is the responsibility of every AAHPERD professional.

CHAPTER 15

FUTURE TRENDS

OBJECTIVES

After reading this chapter the student should be able to—

- Indicate how physical education, exercise science, and sport professionals can capitalize on the increased public interest in health and physical activity.
- Discuss how the changing nature of education and technological advances will influence physical education, exercise science, and sport in the future.
- Show how physical education, exercise science, and sport professionals can establish jurisdiction over their own domain.
- Describe how physical education, exercise science, and sport can improve its delivery system.

What will our world be like in the future? And what will physical education, exercise science, and sport be like in the future? More importantly, what is our vision for physical education, exercise science, and sport in the future? To make the most of the future requires a plan for predicting what the future may be like by generating some scenarios, selecting a preferred future, and then prescribing a course of action that will lead to its attainment. Achieving the future of our choice requires strong leadership, a charted course, marshaled efforts and resources to achieve our goals, and the active involvement of professionals at all levels in pursuit of this vision.

Today our world is experiencing greater cultural diversity, tremendous demographic shifts, growing political unrest and turmoil, increasing global interdependence, dramatic advances in science and medicine with tremendous implications for health and longevity, rapid growth of technology and information science, paradigm shifts in health and health care, alterations in the nature of education at all levels reflecting new ways to access knowledge and different roles for teachers, and widening gaps between the "haves" and the "have-nots" in our society. It is hard to say what tomorrow's world will be—yet, we must be courageous and imaginative in directing and shaping that future to meet the needs of humanity. Futurists Marvin Cetron and Owen Davies state, "Our future will be constrained by demographic, economic, and political forces that should be under our control yet seldom are—but it will be driven by our expanding knowledge of science and mastery of technology."[1]

GET CONNECTED

CDC National Center for Chronic Disease Prevention and Health Promotion Adolescent and School Health is where you can find more information about the Coordinated School Health Program as well as links to research and other initiatives.

www.cdc.gov/nccdphp/dash/cshpdef.htm

National Academy Press provides free on-line access to a wide range of health publications, including health promotion.

www.nap.edu

National Association of Physical Education in Higher Education provides a forum for exchange of ideas about issues in higher education and job openings.

www.napehe.org

Scholarly Sports Sites is a comprehensive source for physical educators, exercise scientists, and sport. It provides links to related associations, archives, resources, databases and directors, Halls of Fame and more.

www.ucalgary.ca/library/ssportsite

World Health Organization site gives access to reports on the health of the world, including health disparities, current issues, and health initiatives. WHO offers a global perspective on health issues, such as aging and poverty.

www.who.org

Preparing for the future means preparing to live and work in an increasingly complex, dynamic society. Today, we must prepare for the challenges of tomorrow—although we are not quite sure what tomorrow will bring. As physical education, exercise science, and sport professionals, meeting the challenges of the future requires that we be prepared to effectively deal with change—and that we are able to successfully direct this change to accomplish our mission and achieve our goals. We must be aware of new opportunities, evaluate them, and pursue them if they would help us meet the physical activity needs of society and people of all ages.

Human beings have always been interested in the future. Today, numerous think tanks such as the Rand Corporation, the Hudson Institute, and The World Future Society focus on studying the future. Futurists, individuals who study the future, endeavor to unravel the mysteries of the years ahead.

Futurists use a variety of techniques to describe potential futures. They try to predict the course of past and current trends and identify the consequences of selected courses of action. Futurists attempt to define priorities that will lead to a future of our choice. Future studies imply the identification of both desirable and undesirable outcomes. Futurists must assume the responsibility for seeking the alternative that creates a future as close as possible to the desired outcomes.

Some individuals using methods such as expert advice, trend extrapolation, technological forecasting, and scenarios have been very accurate in forecasting the future.

Dateline 1932: Aldous Huxley[2] wrote in his book *Brave New World,* "The Director [of the school] described the technique for preserving the excised ovary alive . . . showed them how the eggs were inspected . . . immersed in a warm bouillon containing free-swimming spermatozoa. . . ."

Dateline July 25, 1978: Forty-six years later Louise Brown, the first test-tube baby (the first child in history to be conceived outside of the womb), was born in England.

Of course, all prognosticators have not been as accurate in their predictions:

Dateline 1943: Thomas Watson, chairman of IBM, states, "I think there is a world market for maybe five computers."[3]

Although errors are made in forecasting, it is still imperative to try to predict what will happen in the years ahead. Why? Because all of us are going to spend our lives in the future. Why? Because the future to some extent is known and to some extent can be controlled. Why? Because it affects our beliefs and assumptions. We can anticipate problems. We can plan. Why? Because people shape the future. The space program of the 1960s resulted in a man's walking on the surface of the moon; now NASA is in the process of completing a permanent space station in space. One scientist has stated that "an important reason for studying the future is not so we can learn what may happen, but rather to help us decide about what kind of future we want and develop ways to achieve it."

Although forecasting the future of physical education, exercise science, and sport is difficult, it is important that it be undertaken before we are overtaken by future events. One means to plan for the future is to accept the premise of futurist Daniel Bell. Bell indicates that time is not an "overarching leap" from the present to the future. Instead, it has its origins in the past, incorporates the present, and extends into the future. Physical education, exercise science, and sport professionals seeking to forecast the future of their fields need knowledge of the past and the present as well as an understanding of what futurists, scientists, and experts are predicting about the future. Insight, imagination, creativity, and vision help forecasters predict and describe scenarios for the future.

Planning for the future recognizes that rapid change is a characteristic of our way of life. With each day that passes, we live in a different world. Human beings who are age 50 or older have witnessed in their lifetime the start of the atomic age, the space age, and the computer age. They have seen more than 80 new nations appear, the world population double, and the gross world product double and then redouble. As C. P. Snow, the noted British scientist, said, "The rate of change has increased so much that our imagination can't keep up."

Recognizing that change is ever present, certain societal trends and developments can be identified that lend themselves to a better understanding of our future and that of physical education, exercise science, and sport. Examination of trends is one of the simplest forms of studying the future. It is based on the assumption that factors that have shaped the past will continue and be instrumental in forming the future. This approach has serious limitations, such as mistaking fads for real trends or allowing personal biases to cloud professional judgment.[4] However, careful examination of trends can provide us with a starting point for thinking about the future. Some selected trends and developments that are likely to have an impact on physical education, exercise science, and sport in the future include the health promotion and disease prevention movement, the educational reform movement and the changing nature of education, the growth of technology, changing demographics, and the expanding frontiers of the habitable universe.

SOCIETAL TRENDS AND CURRENT DEVELOPMENTS

As you read about trends and developments and explore the potential implications for the future of physical education, exercise science, and sport, you may find it helpful to contemplate the following questions suggested by Massengale[4]:

- If the direction of the trend continues, what will be some positive and/or negative consequences?
- If the rate or speed of the trend continues, what will be some positive and/or negative results?
- What will occur if the trend levels off or reverses itself?
- Which forces are acting to perpetuate this trend? Will these forces continue into the future?

- How much is this trend "shapable" by human action?
- What type of action would it take to modify the trend?

As you read about each trend and consider each question, try to carefully imagine the implications for professional practice and the influence it may exert on your day-to-day responsibilities as a professional within physical education, exercise science, and sport.

Health Promotion and Disease Prevention Movement

The emphasis on the enhancement of health and the prevention of disease is a significant trend in our society. Three related factors in this movement will be discussed: the wellness movement, the physical activity and fitness movement, and the health-care reform movement.

Wellness Movement

The wellness movement represents one of the most opportune moments in our history. The wellness movement stresses self-help and emphasizes that one's lifestyle—the way in which one lives—influences greatly the attainment and maintenance of personal health. This movement supports efforts directed toward health promotion and disease prevention rather than focusing on the treatment of illness. The wellness doctrine is based on the premise that it is the responsibility of the individual to work toward achieving a healthy lifestyle and an optimal sense of well-being. A healthy lifestyle should reflect the integration of several components, including proper nutrition, regular and appropriate physical activity and exercise, stress management, and the elimination of controllable risk factors (e.g., smoking, excessive alcohol consumption).

Strong support for health promotion and disease prevention efforts was given by three national health reports: *Healthy People,*[5] *Objectives for the Nation,*[6] *Healthy People 2000,*[7] and *Healthy People 2010.*[8] *Healthy People 2010* identified two overarching goals to direct our efforts—first, to help people of all ages increase life expectancy and improve their quality of life, and second, to eliminate health disparities among different population groups, including differences that occur because of gender, race or ethnicity, educational attainment, income, disability, geographic location, or sexual orientation.[8] Physical activity was listed as one of the 10 leading health indicators, and specific objectives were established focusing on improving the involvement in physical activity of people of all ages. Whether or not these specifics are achieved depends to a great extent on physical education, exercise science, and sport professionals' willingness to commit to meeting these objectives and to work cooperatively with various other professionals and professional organizations to attain them.

The corporate sector has also become interested in the wellness movement. This has led to the development of comprehensive worksite health promotion and programs for the employees. Corporations are willing to invest in these programs because they have found that they result in increased employee productivity, decreased absenteeism, better employee health, and lower insurance costs.

As more corporations institute worksite health promotion programs, physical education, exercise science, and sport professionals need to become more cognizant of the issues associated with their conduct. Roy Shepard raises some important ethical and professional issues about the "attempts to change the personal behavior of employees in the interests of a 'healthy' workplace. . . . Needs for successful wellness programs must be balanced against individual rights to remain unhealthy."[9] One concern is the tendency to attribute the development of a preventable disease to the individuals, assuming they have failed to take adequate care of their health and the illness is their own fault. But Shepard states, before adopting a "judgmental attitude," it is necessary to consider the impact of other factors on individuals' health, including their genetic profile, overall socioeconomic conditions, and adverse environmental conditions encountered in the workplace and the home.[9] Other issues raised include bias in assessment of the effectiveness of the program, directing wellness resources to those employees with the highest salaries, initial medical clearance of participants, prescribing exercise at a lower level than would yield health benefits, advocacy of the purchase of special clothing prior to the start of the program, and failure to develop an overall plan for active living.[9]

One trend is the growth of hospital fitness centers. Hospitals and managed care practices are establishing health promotion programs, including fitness. These medical fitness programs vary, but offer a vast array of services, sometimes in partnership with fitness clubs or organizations such as the YMCA. Typically, these programs take place onsite. Facilities vary but may include an indoor track, 25-meter swimming pool, cardiovascular area, aerobic dance studio, and weight-training complex. Some of the programs offer exercise stress testing, cardiac rehabilitation, sports medicine, and aquatic therapy. Exercise programs range from aerobics to one-on-one personal training. Health promotion classes, such as nutrition, diabetes management, and smoking cession may also be conducted. These programs may be open to patients, community members, or hospital staff. They are predicted to expand as hospitals increase their emphasis on health promotion and disease prevention; and this will create additional employment opportunities for physical education, exercise science, and sport professionals.

Physical education, exercise science, and sport professionals can make a significant contribution to the wellness movement. Substantial evidence supports the positive effects of regular physical activity on health and well-being. As physical education, exercise science, and sport professionals, we can help people of all ages learn the skills, knowledge, and attitudes necessary to include physical activity into their lifestyle. Most importantly, we need to help people learn how to live actively throughout their lives. During the past decade, our responsibilities have widened in scope, expanding from the development of fitness to being an integral part of health promotion and disease prevention efforts in a variety of settings.

Physical Activity and Fitness Movement

Enthusiasm for physical activity and fitness is at an all-time high in the United States today and likely will continue to increase in the future. Sales of sport equipment, apparel, and home exercise equipment have reached astronomical levels. The number of individuals participating in exercise and sport activities continues to rise, and it appears that physical activity and fitness have become an ingrained way of American life. In 1996, the landmark report *Physical Activity and Health: The Surgeon General's Report* convincingly set forth the contribution of physical activity to health. The positive effects of remaining physically active throughout one's life have motivated many adults to embark on a fitness program and millions of others to continue their participation past the typical stopping point, the end of the school years.

However, when the information about adult participation in physical activity is examined more closely, participation is not as widespread as it seems. *Physical Activity and Health* reports that more than 60% of adults are not regularly active, and 25% report participating in no physical activity during their leisure time.[10] *Healthy People 2010* reported that 40% of adults engaged in no leisure-time physical activity. Physical activity was more prevalent among men than women, among Caucasians than minorities, among younger than older adults, and among the more affluent than the less affluent.[10] As we move into the future, a greater effort must be directed at involving all segments of the population in regular physical activity.

There is concern among medical, health, and physical education, exercise science, and sport professionals that the fitness movement is not reaching many of the children and youth of our country. Given that many chronic diseases have their beginnings in childhood, it is important that children learn that good lifestyle habits, including being physically active on a daily basis, should begin

The EVA (Extra Vehicular Activity) Exercise Device is designed to study the effects of weightlessness on astronauts during long duration space flights. Researchers may study how muscle mass changes and design exercise programs to help astronauts retain their strength. Photo courtesy NASA Ames Research Center, Mountain View, California.

early in life and continue throughout their lifetime. *Healthy People 2010* revealed that 65% of students in grades 9 through 12 participated in vigorous physical activity 3 or more days per week for 20 or more minutes per occasion, and 27% of students engaged in moderate physical activity for at least 30 minutes a day on 5 or more days of the previous 7 days.[8] Only 29% of 9th- through 12th-grade students participated in daily physical education, a decrease from 41.6% in 1991. Participation in physical education decreased as grade in school increased. Another concern is the growing incidence of overweight in children and youth. About 15% of children (ages 6 to 11 years) and 15% of adolescents (ages 12 to 19 years) are overweight; the incidence of overweight has nearly doubled during the past two decades.[11]

Physical education, exercise science, and sport professionals must direct more of their efforts at preventing the decrease in physical activity as children age. Teaching students physical skills, promoting physical fitness, and helping them acquire knowledge about sports and physical activity is not enough. More attention must be directed to the affective domain—for example, enhancing students' self-efficacy, promoting self-esteem, and engendering feelings of competence. We need to restructure our traditional physical education programs to make them more responsive to the needs of children and adolescents—new activities, new approaches, greater sensitivity to individual differences, and increased emphasis on encouraging physical activity outside of the school setting. Additionally, we must make a greater effort to help adolescents make a transition from school-based physical education programs to involvement in community-based physical activity programs that would meet their needs as adults.

To promote lifespan physical activity and physical fitness, we need to take a more active leadership role in this effort. We need to more closely identify personal and societal barriers to participation in physical activity and seek to alleviate them. As advocates for lifespan activity, we need to work more closely with health-promoting organizations within the community to develop programs to address the physical activity and fitness needs of persons from infancy to old age. Additionally, we need to collaborate with community organizers and designers to help build physical activity friendly communities—safe places to walk, accessible bicycle paths, and fitness trails. More of our efforts also need to be directed toward increasing the use of the school as a site for community-based physical activity programs and developing and sustaining community recreation programs that are available to people at low or no cost.

Finally, physical education, exercise science, and sport professionals must become more involved in physical activity programs in nonschool settings that are designed to meet the needs of all persons. More physical education, exercise science, and sport programs must be established to meet the needs of the elderly, the very young, and individuals who have disabilities. These populations will continue to grow in the future, and we must do more than we are currently doing. Also, programs need to be developed to reach individuals who are economically disadvantaged; they lack the financial resources to join health clubs or pay for private sport instruction. Equity in physical activity and fitness is an important professional concern.

Health Care Reform

The 1990s was marked by calls for health-care reform. Rising health-care costs and the growing number of people who are uninsured were two of the primary factors underlying this reform movement. In 2002, health-care costs were almost $1.6 trillion dollars.[12] Health-care costs accounted for nearly 15% of the gross domestic product (GDP), up from 7% in 1970. Health-care costs continue to escalate at an astronomical rate. It is projected that health-care expenditures will reach $3.4 trillion or 18.4% of GDP by 2013. Despite the fact that the United States spends over a trillion dollars a year on health care, over 45 million Americans are uninsured.

During the last few years, numerous health-care reform bills have been introduced by Congress. The proposals vary greatly, ranging from coverage for only catastrophic illnesses to comprehensive coverage for nearly all medical services. Other differences include the degree of emphasis placed on health promotion and disease prevention services and activities.

National public health reports, such as *Healthy People 2010,* have emphasized efforts to reduce disease, disability, and death through early intervention and prevention programs. These efforts can lead to improved health status for people of all ages and reduction in health-care costs.

Health promotion and disease prevention are less costly than treatment of disease. Chronic and preventable diseases and injuries account for nearly half of all causes of mortality in the United States and almost 70% of all medical care expenditures.[13] Lifestyle behaviors (e.g., smoking, diet, and inactivity) and social conditions (e.g., poverty) play a significant role in these disease and health disparities. Yet only about 5% of the massive expenditure on health care is devoted to reducing the risks associated with these conditions.[13]

As we move toward the future, more attention, research, and resources must be directed toward understanding the behavioral and social influences on health and identifying broader public health interventions that will lead to greater improvements in health for all population groups. After an extensive review of the research, an Institute of Medicine committee charged with the identification of effective social and behavioral health interventions put forth 21 recommendations relative to the application of behavioral and social science research to improve health. According to the committee, interventions need to:

1. "focus on generic social and behavioral determinants of disease, injury, and disability;
2. use multiple approaches (e.g., education, social support, laws, incentives, behavior change programs) and address multiple levels of influence simultaneously (i.e., individuals, families, communities, nations);
3. take account of the special needs of target groups (i.e., based on age, gender, race, ethnicity, social class);
4. take the "long view" of health outcomes, as changes often take many years to become established; and
5. involve a variety of sectors in our society that have not traditionally been associated with health promotion efforts, including law, business, education, social services, and the media."[13]

The committee notes that capitalizing on the promise of social and behavioral research to improve the public's health requires innovative, collaborative approaches. Such approaches will not only improve the nation's health but lead to reductions in our spiraling health-care costs.[13]

Healthy People 2010 identified important ways that physical education professionals can contribute to our national health goals. Conducting quality school physical education programs, promoting community-based physical activity programs, and managing worksite fitness programs are just a few of the many ways that professionals can help provide individuals with the skills, understanding, and encouragement to improve their health by leading a physically active lifestyle. Implementation of the Institute of Medicine committee's social and behavioral intervention recommendations requires that physical education, exercise science, and sport professionals work collaboratively with community groups and health agencies to deliver services—to incorporate their physical activity programs within a comprehensive community health promotion program. These professionals will also need to design and implement physical activity programs targeted to meet the needs of specific populations. To be able to do this effectively, we, as professionals, must become more emphatic and understanding of the impact of societal forces on the lives and health of people.

Education

The last three decades in the United States have been marked by calls for reform of the educational establishment. Advocates for educational reform proclaimed a need to place a greater emphasis on the basic subjects such as English, mathematics, science, social studies, and computer science. Criticism was also directed at teacher competency, school leadership, and professional preparation institutions.

In the 1990s and early 2000s, national school-reform programs, such as *Year 2000 Goals* and *No Child Left Behind,*[14] focused on providing students with the skills and knowledge to be productive members of the workforce in our growing global economy. All children, regardless of race, ethnicity, gender, or socioeconomic background, are entitled to a quality education. To ensure that children were making educational progress, standards were established and periodic assessments were incorporated into educational curriculums. Schools were required to demonstrate student learning, and greater accountability measures were instituted. Emphasis was on teacher development and school-parent-community partnerships to improve learning.

According to Lewis, the rapid acceleration and growth of technology and the information era will have a tremendous impact on the nature of education and our society.[15] He writes that it is of paramount importance that all students acquire the basic skills of reading, writing, and computing. Students must be able to access information, analyze and synthesize it, and apply information in a meaningful way. As technology becomes increasingly sophisticated and our information base grows exponentially, students must have the necessary foundational skills and the opportunities

Physical education programs should help students learn the benefits of physical activity and develop skills and habits for lifelong participation in physical activity.

to improve those skills if they are to keep abreast of developments and remain productive in our workforce.

President of Forecasting International, Inc., futurist Marvin Cetron, and educator Kimberly Cetron cite four societal and economic trends that will have an enormous impact on our nation's schools. First, it is anticipated that funding for schools will become more limited.[16] Schools will be challenged to accomplish more with less. Schools can respond to this challenge by making more creative use of financial resources and maximizing the use of new technologies.[16] Schools can use the Internet to tap into information any place in the world and shift some instruction online. Teachers will increasingly serve as catalysts and mentors. In these roles, teachers will help students learn how to "collect, evaluate, analyze, and synthesize information."[16]

The second trend is that the student population will be significantly higher than anticipated during the next two decades.[16] Furthermore, the diversity of the population will increase, and minority groups will comprise a larger percentage of the population.[16] The greatest change will be in the number of Hispanic school children. It is anticipated that the percentage of non-Hispanic white school children will decrease from about 65% today to 56% by 2020 and to less than 50% by 2040.[16] Schools will be challenged to work with a more diverse student body and meet the learning needs of all their students. Individualized and student-centered instruction and a full range of educational resources are essential to educating all students.

A third trend is the impact of technology on the workplace. Technology will transform the workplace of today's students.[16] Computer competency will be mandatory for most fields.[16] This necessitates the growth of computer and technology training at the middle- and high school levels. Teachers will need to have the necessary skills to provide this training. For the majority of high school students who do not go on to attend college, establishment of high-tech vocational training will be important.[16]

Lastly, engagement in lifelong learning will become increasingly necessary.[16] Unlike generations of the past when persons remained in one career for their working lives, today's and tomorrow's generation of workers will pursue an average of five different occupations.[16] Workers will require continual retraining. This learning will take place in the schools after the normal school day as well as through industry and community partnership.[16] Learning how to learn will be a common thread weaved throughout the school curriculum in all content areas and grade levels.[16]

School structure is changing as we enter the twenty-first century. More and more states are adding public school pre-kindergarten programs for children ages 3 to 5. Calls for a longer school day and extending the school year to provide increased opportunities for learning are occurring with more frequency. Futurist Marvin Cetron[17] stated that students may spend only three days a week in school. They would spend the rest of the time at home, learning through the use of computer-facilitated instruction and distance-learning approaches. Textbooks will be supplanted by computers and multimedia learning packages. Distance learning will allow students at several schools within the district or even throughout the nation to receive instruction from a central source. This will help equalize the quality of education provided to all students. Children and youths will not be the only learners; adults will regularly return to school to keep abreast of rapidly growing advances in technology and knowledge in their field. Today, several colleges and universities offer online degrees at the bachelor's, master's, and doctoral levels.

The school's use as a community learning center and a service provider will continue to grow. The 21st Century Community Learning Centers program of the Department of Education will lead to the establishment and expansion of the school as a site for community learning. There will be an expansion of before- and after-school, weekend, and summer programs for children and youths. These programs include academic enrichment as well as recreational programs. Greater ties and increased collaboration among public and private agencies, business, institutions of higher education, and cultural and scientific organizations will expand the learning opportunities and services provided not only to children and youth but to adults.

What are the implications of these trends and the changing structure of the school for physical education? First, to retain physical education as an integral part of the educational curriculum in the future, physical educators must clearly set forth the contribution of physical education to the educational process. To solidify the place of physical education in the educational curriculum in the next decade, physical educators must educate the public and decision makers about the values to be derived from participation in physical education, both in terms of the education and the health of the individual. Physical educators can generate support for physical education in the schools by conducting sound, exemplary programs.

Second, as more adults return to school to update their skills, physical educators need to be ready to conduct instructional programs to meet adult needs. Third, just as education must teach students to be lifelong learners, so must physical education. Students in physical education class need to have knowledge as well as skills so that they may be self-educative.

Fourth, as more and more education takes place outside of the school setting in the home, physical education, exercise science, and sport professionals need to develop new programs to meet the needs of these learners. Finally, as the school continues to grow as a community center for learning for people of all ages, physical education, exercise science, and sport professionals must be prepared to conduct physical activity programs in these settings and to work collaboratively with other professionals in the community to develop comprehensive programs to meet a multitude of needs.

Technology

Technological advances will transform our lives in the twenty-first century. Cetron and Davies state, "Technology is not the only power that will shape our future for good or ill. Yet it is the critical force that more than any other single factor, although not uninfluenced by the rest, will determine what is possible for us."[1] Technology is the "one discipline whose entire purpose is to make the future different from the present."[1] The past decade has been one of rapid technological advances, many of which have had implications for the future of physical education, exercise science, and sport. Developments in computer technology combined with increasingly sophisticated research techniques have enabled us to widen our knowledge base and will contribute to further growth in the future. The Internet has and will continue to revolutionize education, communication, and many other areas of our professional endeavors in the twenty-first century.

Technology has enabled researchers and practitioners to more clearly understand the impact of physical activity on the body as well as more clearly delineate the relationship among physical activity, exercise, fitness, and health. According to Powers, Ward, and Shanely, the development of more powerful microcomputers has had an "unprecedented effect on research in the field."[18] Other technological advances in the last 30 years that have had a significant impact on the field include the "development of electronic gas analyzers and metabolic measurement carts, blood gas analyzers, computerized muscle ergometers, and the commercially available instruments of molecular biology."[18] These advances have enabled us to explore questions not previously possible, obtain more sophisticated data and perform more complex analyses, and/or reduce the amount of time needed to complete the research process.

Physical education, exercise science, and sport professionals are using computers to perform many essential tasks, such as record keeping, fitness profiling, and database management. Professionals use hand-held computers to gather information during various assessment procedures, later uploading the information to their desktop computer, and then using statistical programs to analyze their results. Software programs allow professionals to rapidly construct fitness profiles that are used to provide program participants with feedback about their fitness status. Coaches use laptop computers to input data as they scout their opponents and to quickly access game statistics during the course of the competition.

Advances in technology enable physical education, exercise science, and sport professionals to electronically monitor physical activity in real-time situations in new, easier ways. According to Healey,

> [W]earable computers and tiny programmable microprocessors are allowing mobile monitoring and real-time in situation processing of digital signals from physiological sensors and cameras. These tiny sensored-oriented computers can be sewn into clothing and embedded into accessories such as shoes or jewelry. Mobile signal processing offers an unprecedented opportunity to collect a vast amount of digital data about a person's physical activity.[19]

As individuals engage in various tasks, a record of their physical activity, including heart rate, muscle activity, and respiration is easily and noninvasively recorded. This information is "correlated with a digital photo diary composed of images from a computer controlled camera." Integrating the visual information with the physiological information, we can see how engaging in certain activities affects individuals' physiological parameters. As technology becomes more advanced, much cheaper, and more readily available, professionals can use this technology to gather physiological information on cardiac rehabilitation participants as they engage in activities during the day, monitor athletes more closely during training and performance, and accurately track the amount and intensity of physical activity accumulated by students in physical education classes.

Computer technology has facilitated improvements in performance. In biomechanics, computer-generated graphical representations of an athlete's performance are compared with a prototypical sport performance, facilitating skill analysis and enhancing corrections. Skiers practice in wind tunnels while coaches and sport scientists study their body position and technique to find ways to reduce resistance from drag and increase speed. Equipment has been designed or reengineered using computer-assisted programs, which has led to improvements in performance. For example, redesigned handlebars for cyclists create a more aerodynamically shaped body position for the racers and lead to decreased time to complete the course. Sport participants at all levels can benefit from many of these improvements.

Changes have been made in both the design of equipment and the materials used to construct the equipment. Titanium golf clubs with enlarged heads, such as Big Bertha, have displaced the steel shafts of the old-fashioned woods. Graphite-composite tennis rackets with large racket faces have replaced metal and metal-composite tennis rackets, which replaced wooden rackets years ago. Technology applied to the manufacturing of running shoes has led to increased comfort, while producing fewer injuries for runners of all abilities. Grass fields have been replaced by artificial surfaces, cinder tracks by all-weather tracks, and open stadiums by domed arenas.

Developments in biotechnology hold implications for the future of physical education and sport. Experts in tissue engineering estimate that within the next 5 to 10 years, people will routinely have tendons, cartilage, and bones grown, a breakthrough that will benefit injured athletes as well as other individuals whose injuries limit their opportunity to lead a physically active lifestyle. Today, muscle fiber typing allows researchers to identify whether an individual has a greater potential to succeed in athletic events requiring strength or endurance. Perhaps in the near future, genetic engineering will be used to program an individual's genes for success in certain sport activities. The first cloning of an adult mammal, Dolly the sheep, was heralded as the greatest scientific breakthrough of 1997. Ethicists and scientists are now engaged in sweeping debates about cloning humans. Genetic engineering can lead to the development of humans with specific traits. Hoberman states that "it is likely that this technology will be used to develop athletes before it is applied to the creation of other kinds of human performers."[20] How will we deal with these complex issues?

Developments in the field of telecommunication have and will continue to improve our ability to communicate and our delivery systems. The Internet, a web of thousands of computer networks, has dramatically changed how we interact and manage information. E-mail allows rapid, inexpensive communication with colleagues throughout the world. E-mail listservs allow individuals with common interests, such as fitness, to engage in discussions, pose questions, and share ideas.

The World Wide Web (WWW), the multimedia channel of the Internet, is used for many different purposes. Electronic professional journals and documents are posted on the Web, enhancing the dissemination of information. Personalized information services seek out specific information, update it automatically, and send it to the PC user's desktop.[3] For example, personal trainers can receive daily updates on training techniques, nutrition, and cardiovascular research. Professionals have easier access to current research and are able to retrieve needed information from virtually anywhere in the world where they have computer access. Research data can be easily shared via the Web or through file transfers.

Internet telephones and videoconferencing enhance communications with professionals throughout the world. The Web and desktop videoconferencing are increasingly being used for distance learning. Courses and even entire degree programs can be completed via the Internet. Continuing education programs offered through distance learning will increase in popularity. For example, a professional in Alaska can "attend" a workshop on fitness hosted by an organization in New York.

Multimedia instruction and interactive tutorials using CD-ROM and/or the Web will allow physical education, exercise science, and sport professionals to tailor learning to the needs of each program participant. Users benefit from enhanced presentations of information. Haggerty writes: "Is it 'better' to read a paper or dissertation about an area, say biomechanics, on a multimedia version with sound, video, graphics, and hypertext rather than on a two-dimensional printed page? What about sport history? Can video clips, sound files, and the actual works be more valuable than a textual description of them?"[3] Participants in a fitness program or schoolchildren accessing various sites on the Web or using a CD-ROM can see a heart pulsating as it beats, follow the course of circulation, and become familiar with the short- and long-term effects of exercise on this vital organ. Multimedia presentations let content be experienced in new ways.

Virtual reality is the use of computers and sensory mechanisms to create simulated, interactive 3-dimensional environments and experiences. Virtual reality can vary in its nature and its sophistication. Head-mounted displays and sensor gloves may be a part of virtual reality. Virtual reality can also be a game or a simulation. It places the body of the user directly inside of the 3-D environment. Virtual reality offers some of the most exciting possibilities for our field and is expected to grow tremendously.

Through virtual reality, real-life situations can be recreated, altered, or simulated, allowing the user to react and to rehearse constant or changing scenarios. It provides invaluable training to users and allows them to gain a vast amount of knowledge through their experiences. Bobsledders used virtual reality to train prior to the Albertville Winter Olympics. The athletes were able to rehearse their runs and experience the course in a realistic setting. Haggerty suggests that virtual reality can be used to provide athletes in many sports (e.g., batters, goalies, football players) with a variety of simulated situations to improve their performance.[3] Virtual golf simulators give golfers the opportunity to play many of the great courses while receiving feedback on their shot, distance, and errors. Simulators are being developed for other sports such as baseball and snowboarding. Other possible uses are in the training of physical education, exercise science, and sport professionals. Preservice teachers could gain experience in organizing a class and managing behavior; cardiac rehabilitation specialists could gain practice in administering various stress test protocols to patients with varying disease conditions.

Virtual reality is being developed for medical education and training, rehabilitation, and for use by individuals with disabilities. Uses include teaching palpitation, rehabilitation of a hand, and emergency medical training. These virtual reality simulations would be helpful in training athletic trainers and specialists in cardiac rehabilitation. Virtual reality is also being used to help children in wheelchairs learn how to navigate their chair with a joystick and potentially can be used to help people with disabilities participate in "virtual" sports that they can not perform in the "real" world. Although virtual reality is expensive and accessibility is limited, it is expected that virtual reality simulators will become cheaper and more readily available.

Technology offers exciting new possibilities for the field of physical education, exercise science, and sport. Computers help professionals complete their responsibilities more efficiently. Application of technology has led to improvements in sport equipment and performance, benefiting sport participants of all abilities. Biotechnology offers exciting possibilities, as well as confronting us with a host of ethical issues that must be addressed. Multimedia technology enhances learning, and distance learning increases access to learning. Telecommunications facilitate interactions with colleagues throughout the world. And virtual reality offers tremendous possibilities for training, education, and sport participation in the twenty-first century.

Changing Demographics

Demographic trends exert a tremendous influence on the structure of societal institutions and the services they provide to different populations. The age distribution of the population is shifting quite markedly. Longer life expectancies and a declining birthrate have increased the average age of the population. Today, there are more Americans over the age of 65 than under the age of 25 and this aging trend is expected to continue.[21]

American society is aging. The change is quite dramatic when viewed over the course of the century. In 1900, approximately 4% of the population were 65 or older.[21] In 1997, 12.7% of the population fell within this age group, and this is estimated to increase to 18.5% in 2025.[22] Furthermore, there will be an increasing number of very old people, many of whom will be healthy. The number of people 85 years and older is expected to increase from 3.8 million in 1996, to more than 7 million in 2025.[22] Minorities are projected to comprise 25% of the population 65 and older in 2030; this is nearly double the 13% recorded in 1996.[22]

America's population is also becoming more culturally diverse as the number of Asians, Hispanics, African Americans, and Native Americans increase. Minorities are estimated to comprise more than 40% of the U.S. population by 2035.[23] We must not continue to overlook the needs of

New technologies can help teachers give students individualized instruction.

minorities if the health of our nation is to improve and if we are, indeed, to achieve our goal of lifespan involvement in physical activity for all people. Significant racial and ethnic disparities exist in health and health care. Many minorities, especially those with limited English proficiency, face a multitude of barriers to accessing health care and receiving appropriate treatment; consequently they generally suffer worse health.[23] Addressing the needs of increasingly diverse and underserved populations is one of our greatest challenges as we move forward in the twenty-first century.

These forthcoming years will see continued changes in the structure of the family and growing societal problems that must be addressed. The number of single-parent families is rising, including the number of teenage mothers. Single-parent families and dual-career families have led to an increase in "latch-key" children—children who come home at the end of the school day to an empty house. Preschool and day-care programs are increasing dramatically. Amidst the changing nature of the family is the problem of a growing array of threats to the health and well-being of our children and youth. Drug and alcohol abuse, violence, child abuse, suicide, and risky sexual behaviors adversely impact the lives of many young people. Persons and families living in poverty face many hardships and are at increased risk for poor health.

What are the implications of these changes for the conduct of physical education, exercise science, and sport programs? We must be prepared to effectively work with the changing population groups. Quality physical activity programs are needed for the growing elderly population to enhance their health and their quality of life and to provide enjoyable recreational pursuits. Professionals in both school and nonschool settings must be prepared to conduct programs that are sensitive to the needs of an increasingly culturally diverse population. Culturally competent techniques have the potential to improve access to health care and the delivery of services to minority populations, thus contributing to the reduction of racial and ethnic disparities in health. It is important that we, as professionals, work toward attainment of cultural competency if we are committed to promoting lifespan involvement for all people.

As physical education, exercise science, and sport shifts to an industry in which people pay for desired sport services (e.g., commercial fitness clubs), we must not lose sight of the needs of the economically disadvantaged who cannot afford to pay. Providing access to physical activity programs for children and youth through school physical education programs is only one part of the answer. Professionally, we must explore innovative approaches that will help make physical activity programs available to underserved populations. We must do more to overcome community, organizational, and personal barriers to physical activity.

Lawson discusses the interdependence of schools, families, and health and calls for the planning, implementation, and assessment of new intervention strategies for children, youth, and their families that reflect this interrelationship.[24] These strategies would expand the responsibilities assigned to the schools. Preventive and educational health programs for families and children would

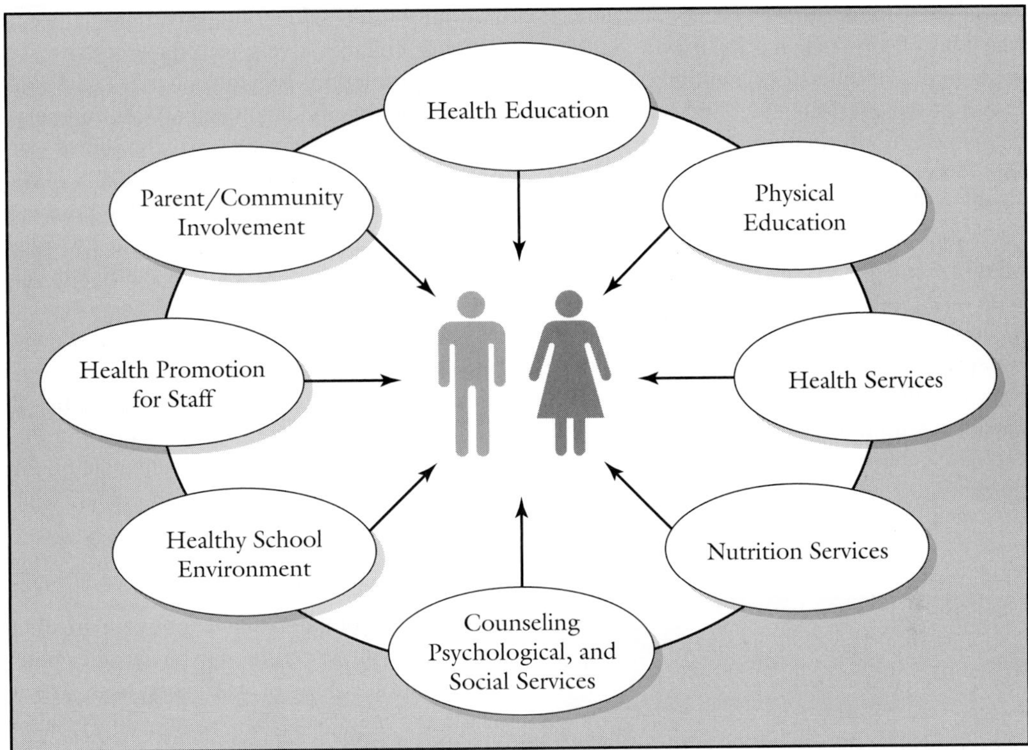

Figure 15-1 Coordinated School Health Model.
From: Centers for Disease Control and Prevention National Center for Chronic Disease Prevention and Health Promotion, Adolescent and School Health.

be established in the schools. These programs would be linked to health and social services within the community. School personnel, health care professionals, and human services providers then would work collaboratively to address the needs of the whole family within the community.

The Centers for Disease Control and Prevention Coordinated School Health Program includes physical education as one of eight components of an integrated approach to improve and maintain the well-being of children and youth (see Figure 15-1). The eight components are as follows:

- Health education.
- Physical education.
- Health services.
- Nutrition services.
- Health promotion for staff.
- Counseling and psychological services.
- Healthy school environment.
- Parent/community involvement.[25]

As you can see, physical education, exercise science, and sport professionals can contribute in many different ways to this coordinated school approach to child and adolescent health. Most directly, our primary responsibility is to teach a physical education program—a planned, sequential K–12 curriculum that promotes the optimal development of each student and provides students with the skills, knowledge, and attitudes necessary to participate in physical activity throughout their lives.

Our contributions to the coordinated school health program are not limited to physical education, however. We can make significant contributions in several other areas. In terms of health education, we can educate students about the health benefits of physical activity, how to participate in physical activity safely, and the risks associated with an inactive lifestyle. We can also incorporate nutrition information into our programs, reinforcing the importance of a healthy diet to good health and active living. The health services component focuses on appraising, protecting, and promoting student health, as well as family and community health. Fitness assessment, physical activity counseling, education, and creating linkages between school and community physical activity services and programs are several ways we can contribute within this component.

Another component is promoting the health of the staff; this provides physical education, exercise science, and sport professionals with the opportunity to conduct fitness programs for staff or work collaboratively to offer a comprehensive health promotion program. Lastly, in terms of parent/community involvement, we can serve as members of a health advisory council or participate, in our capacity as a professional working in the physical activity programs in the community, as part of a community coalition to provide services and resources to address the health-related needs of students.[25]

As we begin the twenty-first century and look beyond, we must be prepared to explore innovative approaches to providing services to people of all ages if the potential of physical education, exercise science, and sport to enhance the quality of life of all people is to be fulfilled.

Recreational activities, such as skate boarding, frequently capture youths' interest and keep them active for hours.

Expanding Frontiers

The frontiers of the habitable universe are expanding. People in the future may be living as part of a space station colony or on a moon base. The work of the astronauts and NASA has laid the basis for the future in respect to space travel. Space travel may become commonplace in the future. Citizens will be able to purchase a ticket for space travel in the space shuttle much in the same way they purchase a ticket for airline travel. In 2001, the first tourist paid $20 million dollars for a 10-day stay on the Mir space station.

The July 1976 issue of *National Geographic*[26] visualizes the outcome of a serious proposal that was developed by a group of 30 engineers and social and physical scientists. They describe what a typical colony in space will be like. Ten thousand people, their mission to build more colonies, will live under artificial gravity in an encircling tube called a *torus.* The torus is divided into six separate sections, each of which has supermarket, farming, and residential areas and such facilities as theaters, sport arenas, schools, and libraries. Sunlight is filtered and dispersed by means of mirrors that can be tilted to produce an 8-hour night every 24 hours. Farming is very productive as a result of controlled sunlight, an unfailing water supply, ample fertilizer, equable temperature, and a somewhat higher carbon dioxide content in the air than on Earth. The crop yields are many times greater than those on Earth.

A second area of the habitable universe that will be an especially exciting place to live in the future is under water. Because more than two-thirds of the planet is covered with ocean, there will be sufficient room to construct many underwater communities. Futurist Rosen reports on the work of scientist William Backley who has developed a submerged capsule equipped with observation ports that is a model for future underwater communities. A superstructure to the capsule has a helicopter landing pad and docking facilities for surface craft. The capsule is held in place by anchors and is made stable by a concrete mat suspended beneath the unit. An airlock and elevator offer easy access either to the ocean floor or to the surface. Backley's work represents a model for the construction of a future underwater colony that will have residential areas, farming, and other facilities comparable to those that will exist in space.

Physical education, exercise science, and sport professionals need to prepare themselves to help individuals attain their optimal level of fitness while living in these space and underwater environments. Space travelers to distant planets need help in keeping fit while living for long periods of time under conditions of zero gravity. Professionals must conduct research concerning the effects of weightlessness on the body and artificial gravity. Designing exercise programs to deal with differences in the environment falls within the realm of physical education, exercise science, and sport.

PREPARING FOR THE FUTURE

It is tempting to look back on these past three decades, which have been a time of tremendous growth for physical education, exercise science, and sport, and bask in the glow of such accomplishments as the celebration of the one hundredth anniversary of AAHPERD, the growth in professional stature achieved by the various subdisciplines, the tremendous expansion of our knowledge base both in depth and breadth, our efforts to develop programs to meet the needs of people of all ages in a diversity of settings, and the increase in job opportunities within the field. However, if physical education, exercise science, and sport professionals are interested in being involved in the future of their profession, they must also look at areas in which they can improve.

If the potential of our field to enhance the life of people of all ages is to be realized, we must take a more active role in creating our future and shaping our destiny. We must take a proactive, rather than reactive, stance in dealing with the issues and challenges that confront us. (See Chapter 14.) Furthermore, both individually and collectively, we must reflect more critically upon social issues related to physical education, exercise science, and sport and question long-held assumptions, sacrosanct beliefs, and traditional practices.[27] We must be introspective, engaging ourselves in a thoughtful examination of our actions and values. We also must look outwardly, beyond ourselves, and examine the broader societal issues and their impact on our lives, institutions, programs, and the people with whom we work. But we must move beyond reflection to consider alternatives to the problems that confront us. Personally and professionally, both individually and collectively, we must move toward solutions if the potential of our field is to be fulfilled.

Oberle,[28] in a discussion about the future directions for health, physical education, recreation and leisure, and dance, stressed the importance of exerting quality control within these professions. He suggested that each of the disciplines consider the following actions to enhance their effectiveness:

- Establish minimum standards of competency.
- Develop programs and services that are flexible to meet changing needs while accomplishing avowed disciplinary objectives.
- Provide meaningful programs that will meet needs today as well as tomorrow.
- Reduce ineffective programs.
- Establish minimum standards for entry into professional preparation programs.

- Provide high-quality experiences for professionals within the discipline, such as in-service education and graduate education.
- Develop a system for relicensure for all professionals, not just public school personnel.
- Establish professional accreditating agencies, as the American Medical Association has done, to ensure quality control.
- Develop high-quality model programs and build facilities that can serve as the standard for the profession.

As we move into the future, we must establish our professional stature.

A review of the past decade shows two areas—jurisdiction over the physical education, exercise science, and sport domain and the delivery system of physical education, exercise science, and sport—that need the attention of professionals. First, some of the shortcomings of each of the two areas will be described, and then a scenario will be painted for each area in the early twenty-first century.

ESTABLISHMENT OF JURISDICTION OVER OUR DOMAIN

The future of physical education, exercise science, and sport could lie in physical education, exercise science, and sport professionals' becoming the publicly recognized leaders in their field of physical activity. Many of the services with which physical education, exercise science, and sport professionals are presently associated lie within the public domain. Unfortunately, physical education, exercise science, and sport professionals are not directing these services. Muscle builders, entrepreneurs, and movie stars associated with health spas, exercise salons, and weight-reducing clinics have invaded our domain, often without proper credentials.[29] Additionally, the public is often not aware of the nature of physical education, exercise science, and sport and the tremendous worth and substance of our fields of endeavor.

If physical education, exercise science, and sport professionals are to become the publicly recognized leaders in their field, it will be because they have provided themselves with the proper credentials. The credentials necessary to achieve this leadership position are described below:

- *Credential 1.* A systematic knowledge base will exist that describes the unique social service rendered by our professionals. This knowledge base will (1) support the art and science of human movement as it relates to sport, dance, play, and exercise; (2) document the fact that physical education, exercise science, and sport foster human growth and development; and (3) convincingly show that individuals' lives can be enhanced, as well as their health, by developing the proper relationship of body, mind, and spirit.
- *Credential 2.* Physical education, exercise science, and sport will have two program priorities (although there are others) that provide consumers with self-direction in light of the emphasis on self-help medicine and the rising cost of health care. The first priority will be *knowledge*—knowledge that is (1) concerned with the science of movement and the healthful impact that proper physical activity has on the functioning of the human organism and (2) based on scientific findings that are constantly updated and provided to practitioners via retrieval systems in language that can be understood and used.

  The second priority will be *skills*—skills taught scientifically, utilizing not only the basic concepts of motor learning, but also advanced technology enabling persons to be taught more effectively and to progress more rapidly.
- *Credential 3.* Physical education teaching will become a science as well as an art. Evidenced-based effective practices will enhance learning outcomes.

As professionals, we must assume the challenge of leadership for the domain of physical education, exercise science, and sport. We must be accountable for our programs. High-quality programs are essential. We must promote our programs and take steps to ensure that the people who participate in them accrue the stated and personally desired benefits. Physical education, exercise science, and sport programs in the future will become more diverse as we expand our focus to include more populations. Professionals must be sensitive to individual needs when designing programs. Additionally, we must improve our delivery systems to more effectively serve individuals of all ages.

ENHANCEMENT OF OUR DELIVERY SYSTEMS

In the future, physical education, exercise science, and sport will need to change the manner in which it provides services, as well as the populations it serves. In other words, we need to change our delivery system.

Some remarks heard from various groups during the past few years suggest that our delivery systems need attention. Here are a few of the comments:

1. Junior high school students at a science fair where models depicting space and underwater living were on display: "How do we get our physical bodies in shape for this existence that we are very likely to experience in the years ahead?"
2. Group of physicians: "You physical and sport educators do a good job making healthy people healthier and skilled people better skilled but a terrible job making unhealthy people healthy and poorly skilled people skilled."
3. Rotary Club: "I look at school physical education and community recreation programs and can't tell the difference between the two. They overlap in the activities they offer and the people they serve. There's also a duplication of facilities and personnel. Why all this waste?"
4. Senior citizen club: "The elderly represent 11% of the population in this country. Is your profession devoting 11% of its total effort to this group?"
5. Student group: "Why don't we have a record system listing information about each person's personal physical education and sport history? We have records pertaining to people's health history. Why not a physical education and sport history record?"

The physical education, exercise science, and sport delivery system requires an overhaul; and new developments in the field of technology and communication, as well as the changing nature of education, will help us change to be more effective.

The following examples illustrate how trends and developments may shape the future of our fields.

1. The delivery system will be more responsive to individual needs. Use of technology, more personalized instructional approaches, and innovative programming will enable us to better meet the diverse needs of our increasingly heterogenous population. No longer can we rely on one program to meet all needs or, as Lawson[24] states, the "one size fits all" approach. Our delivery system will enable us to better meet the needs of various population groups, including the elderly, the very young, the growing number of ethnic minorities, and those populations historically underserved, such as the economically disadvantaged.
2. The delivery system will render services to the new frontiers of space colonies and underwater communities. Meetings will be held with futurists and scientists. Conditions that simulate space and underwater living will be established in college and university laboratories. Physical education, exercise science, and sport professionals and their students will pursue studies in these areas.
3. The delivery system will provide closer articulation between school physical education and sport programs and community programs. These programs will be combined and centrally administered. This program structure will (1) ensure efficient use of facilities, equipment, and personnel; (2) eliminate overlapping; and (3) provide for progression throughout life in the program of activities.

It will meet the needs of all individuals in the community, including those in their later years who want to become involved in physical activity, sport, and recreational activities.

Also, a computerized record system will exist for each person throughout life wherever he or she goes or lives.

4. The delivery system will make extensive use of distance learning and cable television. Programs will be packaged and syndicated. There will be such features as demonstrations of the step-by-step approach to developing skill in dance, sport, and other activities; lectures relating to such areas as exercise physiology; and demonstrations of methods by which one's physical fitness can be assessed and maintained.

   Videotape feedback of one's performance will become increasingly common, and generation of computerized models of ideal performances and actual performances will help individuals learn and improve their motor skills more easily.
5. Computers will play an increasingly important role in our delivery system. Computer information databases and services will be used to disseminate research findings, allowing professionals to more easily keep abreast of current research developments within the fields. Collaborative research endeavors with colleagues at other institutions and with practitioners at various sites throughout the world will be facilitated through telecommunication networking. Additionally, professionals can network with one another to share ideas and programs and to jointly resolve problems confronting them. Computerized resource databases will allow practitioners to more easily individualize programs to meet participants' needs. Computer recordkeeping will make it easier for practitioners to identify individuals' needs and to monitor progress toward the attainment of their goals.

As we move forward in the twenty-first century, we must change our delivery systems to use new technologies to more effectively provide services to an ever-increasing number of clientele. Our delivery systems should encourage participation and maintain involvement in our programs.

THE FUTURE

As they prepare for the future, physical education, exercise science, and sport professionals must do the following:

1. Provide themselves with the proper credentials to establish jurisdiction over their domain.
2. Utilize technological advances to improve the delivery system.
3. Prepare for space and underwater living and for changes in our society.
4. Become a positive role model for a fit and healthy lifestyle so that others will be favorably influenced to emulate this lifestyle.
5. Help persons to become increasingly responsible for their own health and fitness.
6. Recognize that individuals will live longer and become more fit and active in the years to come.
7. Provide for all persons, regardless of age, skill, disabling condition, and socioeconomic background, throughout their lifespan.
8. Remember that we are involved with the development of the whole person as a thinking, feeling, moving human being.
9. Make a commitment to conduct high-quality programs that are sensitive to individual needs so that physical education and sport's potential to enhance the health and quality of life for all people can be achieved.

Whether or not physical education, exercise science, and sport professionals meet these challenges will affect the future of our field.

Scenario planning is one approach that would allow us to see some alternative futures for physical education, exercise science, and sport. Scenario planning invites stakeholders to envision different futures based on assumptions and driving forces, such as public policy or funding. Neiner,

Howze, and Greaney[31] use scenario planning to identify ways in which a public health department could address chronic disease prevention and management with unhealthy diet and physical inactivity used as key risk factors. Neiner, Howze, and Greaney describe two potential futures: a future where there was support for physical activity and good nutrition via public policy and funding and one in which support was lacking and funding was difficult to obtain.

Some of the outcomes Neiner, Howze, and Greaney associated with strong support for nutrition and physical activity include the following:

- Increase in number of health promotion programs to promote good nutrition and physical activity.
- Increase in number of adults who exercise and eat healthily as means to prevent and control chronic disease.
- Increased support from the medical community as well as Medicare and Medicaid coverage of gym membership costs, nutrition classes, and weight-loss programs.
- Decrease in health disparities among racial/ethnic, socioeconomic, and age groups.
- Passage of a junk-food tax, from which the revenues are used to support physical activity and good nutrition initiatives.
- Offering of healthy food alternatives at all fast-food restaurants, with supersizing and the use of cartoon characters to entice children a thing of the past.
- Partnerships that involve schools, workplaces, and community agencies that lead to comprehensive approaches to addressing inactivity and poor nutrition risk factors.
- Media campaigns that use a variety of vehicles to expose the public to consistent messages that reinforce the value of an active lifestyle and good nutrition.
- Tax breaks given to owners of fitness centers and builders of recreational structures who are willing to build them in poor communities.
- Fitness staff and nutrition counselors certified in areas of expertise.
- Primary care physicians trained to counsel patients on physical activity and nutrition.
- Insurance companies required to cover the cost of physicians' referrals to registered dieticians and certified physical activity providers.[31]

The scenario recognizes that disease prevention and health promotion make economic sense and that such efforts will lead to positive gains in the health of the entire population. This approach offers a very promising future for physical education, exercise science, and sport professionals.

On the other hand, a bleaker future emerges when there is a lack of public support and funding. Some of the outcomes Neiner, Howze, and Greaney suggested that could emerge in the future include:

- Decreased funding for health promotion programs to promote good nutrition and physical activity, with the available limited funds directed toward care of those with chronic diseases.
- Growing health disparities among population groups, with the poor most affected.
- Increase in the prevalence of chronic disease factors, including sedentary behavior and poor diet.
- Lack of partnerships to promote physical activity and nutrition as agencies compete with each other for limited funding.
- Competing priorities, such as poverty, reducing political support for health programs, including those related to health promotion.
- Media campaigns to promote the value of healthy eating and physical activity not being funded.
- Consumption of fast food continuing to rise because of convenience and affordability.
- Access to physical activity venues becoming more expensive with fewer options available for those in low-income communities. Physical activity professionals not certified.
- Access to health care decreasing as the number of uninsured or underinsured individuals increase. Primary care physicians provide little counsel on physical activity and nutrition. Referrals to professionals to help patients manage their weight are not covered by insurance.[31]

This scenario reflects an orientation that will lead to higher levels of chronic diseases and increase in health disparities. This alternative future does not bode well for physical education, exercise science, and sport professionals.

Think carefully about some of the outcomes associated with each of these alternative futures. To create the future that is most beneficial to the people we seek to serve as well as to the field of physical education, exercise science, and sport, we must take an active role in its creation. We must take charge of our professional destiny and create a future that allows the full potential of physical education, exercise science, and sport to be fulfilled.

Let's remember to promote fun when we promote lifespan involvement in physical activity.

It is likely that all of us, at some time in our lives, will have a significant experience that, as years pass, will come to embody the personal meaning of physical education and sport. Noted physical education leader and author of previous editions of this text, Charles Bucher, related an experience that helped him personally and perhaps will help you to realize anew the tremendous potential of physical education, exercise science, and sport in our society. Bucher wrote the following passage about the New York City marathon, one of the largest marathons in the world:

> I was particularly enthralled as I watched the runners, some of whom took as many as five, six, and seven hours to cross the finish lines. Most runners gritted their teeth, gasped for breath, and put on an extra burst of speed as they pounded across. Some runners had given so much of themselves that they were helped onto a stretcher or were carried across.
>
> A runner from Italy, in fourth place, whipped off his sweatband and waved it to the crowd. A runner from California, in second place among the women, clenched her teeth and went the last few strides on sheer will before collapsing across the line. When a long-haired Polish woman, sweat streaming down her face, stumbled slowly toward the line, the crowd cheered and chanted, "Finish it! Finish it!" And *she did.*
>
> A few runners completed the race hand-in-hand. Some went barefoot and some carried their shoes. Each person got a tremendous cheer, but perhaps the loudest cheers of all were for two men who crossed the finish line in wheelchairs.
>
> The runners had done their best—not for acclaim, for a loving cup symbolic of supremacy, or to be a champion—but to prove to themselves that they could do it.
>
> No one could watch the sight without realizing that he or she was witnessing a great moment in America and the world.
>
> No one in physical education and sport could be a part of that experience without feeling the power and potential for our field of endeavor—the power and potential for improving the quality of life for all our citizens.

The marathon perhaps in many ways is symbolic of our society, of America, and of the qualities that we in our field try to develop. It recognizes that the training of the physical is im-

Focus on Career: Higher Education

PROFESSIONAL ORGANIZATIONS	• AAHPERD Research Consortium www.aahperd→Research Consortium • National Association for Physical Education in Higher Education www.napehe.org • American Association for Higher Education www.aahe.org • American Educational Research Association www.aera.org
PROFESSIONAL JOURNALS	• *Research Quarterly for Exercise and Sport* • *Chronicle of Physical Education in Higher Education* • *Educational Researcher* • *Quest* • *Change*

portant; but perhaps more important, it shows how the physical *can* and *should* be used as a vehicle that brings into play such desirable qualities as courage, a belief in oneself, a feeling of accomplishment, and, most important, a blending of the mind, body, and spirit in the accomplishment of worthy goals.

Physical education, exercise science, and sport are dynamic, growing fields of endeavor. Its future is very promising. An editorial by the executive directors of AAHPERD published in the *Journal of Physical Education, Recreation, and Dance* expressed a sense of optimism for the 1990s that is applicable today. It stated:[30]

> At no time in the history of American Alliance for Health, Physical Education, Recreation, and Dance have we, as executive directors of the national associations, seen more opportunities for professional growth and service within the entire profession. We are highly encouraged by the signs we see for new impact on society, stimulation of teaching and leadership personnel, development of significant projects, and potential for growth in membership. . . . Society wants and needs us. Now is the opportune time!

The vision of lifespan involvement in physical activity for all people is a powertul one, but its achievement requires dedicated and committed professionals. Excellence must be present in all our professional endeavors. After you have read this text, I hope that you, as the reader, have an appreciation for the tremendous substance and worth of the field that you have chosen to study. Physical education, exercise science, and sport has a tremendous potential to enrich and enhance the health and quality of life of all people. Whether this potential is realized depends on each professional's willingness to make a personal commitment to achieving this goal.

SUMMARY

Physical education, exercise science, and sport professionals must start planning for the future now. Such planning requires that professionals recognize that rapid change is characteristic of our way of life.

Several societal trends will influence the future of physical education, exercise science, and sport. The wellness movement and the fitness movement present excellent opportunities for professionals to involve individuals of all ages in appropriate physical activity. The educational reform movement and the changing nature of education indicate that we, more than ever before, need to inform the public and decision makers about the contribution of physical education to the educational process. The expanding frontiers of the habitable universe, developments in communications, and other technological developments will influence the future of physical education, exercise science, and sport as well.

Physical education, exercise science, and sport professionals can prepare for the future in several ways. First, professionals need to establish jurisdiction over their domain by obtaining the proper credentials and actively seeking leadership positions. Second, professionals need to improve the delivery systems. We must provide for people of all ages and utilize technological advances to facilitate learning. We must take an active role in helping individuals prepare for space and underwater living. The future of physical education, exercise science, and sport is promising, but we must take an active leadership role in shaping its direction.

Self-Assessment Tests

These tests are designed to help you determine if you have mastered the materials and competencies presented in this chapter.

1. Discuss the implications of the changing nature of education and the impact of technological developments on physical education and interscholastic sports in the future.
2. Your professor has requested that you supply information to show how physical education, exercise science, and sport can establish jurisdiction over its own domain. Prepare a report on this topic and present it to the class.
3. Develop a plan for the early 2000s that provides specific suggestions for improving physical education, exercise science, and sport's delivery system.
4. Using the information provided in the Get Connected box, access the *World Health Organization* site. Read the latest report on world health or browse through the press releases to find information on health throughout the world and the United States. Make comparisons on a specific health topic between developing countries and developed countries. Identify trends in disease treatment and prevention and discuss the implications of these trends for the people affected.
5. Using the information in the Get Connected Box, access the CDC site and read about the Coordinated School Health Program. Describe specific contributions physical education, exercise science, and sport could make to each of the eight components.

References

1. Cetron M and Davies O: Probable tomorrows: how science and technology will transform our lives in the next twenty years, New York, 1997, St. Martin's Press.
2. Huxley A: Brave new world, New York, 1932, Modern Library.
3. Haggerty TR: Influence of information technologies on kinesiology and physical education, Quest 49:254–269, 1997.
4. Massengale JD: The unprepared discipline: selection of alternative futures, Quest 40:107–114, 1988.
5. US Department of Health, Education, and Welfare: Healthy people: the Surgeon General's report on health promotion and disease prevention, Washington, D.C., 1979, US Government Printing Office.
6. US Department of Health and Human Services: Promoting health/preventing disease: objectives for the nation, Washington, D.C., 1980, US Government Printing Office.
7. Public Health Service, US Department of Health and Human Services: Healthy people 2000: national health promotion and disease prevention

objectives, Washington, D.C., 1991, US Government Printing Office.

8. US Department of Health and Human Services: Healthy people 2010, ed 2. With understanding and improving health and objectives for improving health, 2 vols, Washington, D.C., 2000, US Government Printing Office.
9. Shepard RJ: Issues in worksite health promotion: a personal viewpoint, Quest 54:67–82, 2002.
10. US Department of Health and Human Services. Physical activity and health: a report of the Surgeon General, Atlanta, Ga., 1996, US Department of Health and Human Services, Centers for Disease Control and Prevention, National Center for Chronic Disease Prevention and Health Promotion.
11. Hedley AA, Ogden CL, Johnson CL, Carroll MD, Curtin LR, and Flegal KM: Prevalence of overweight and obesity among US children, adolescents, and adults, 1999–2000, JAMA, 291, 2847–2850, 2004.
12. Centers for Medicare and Medicaid Services: Highlights—National Health Expenditures, 2002. (www.cms.gov)
13. Smedley BD and Syme SL: Promoting health: intervention strategies from social and behavioral research, American Journal of Health Promotion 15:149–166.
14. United States Department of Education. (www.ed.gov)
15. Lewis AJ: Education for the 21st century, Educational Leadership 41(1):9–10, 1983.
16. Cetron M and Cetron K: A Forecast for Schools, Educational Leadership 61(4):22–30, 2003.
17. Cetron M: Schools of the future. Presented at the Convention of the American Association of School Administrators, Dallas, August 1985.
18. Powers S, Ward K, and Shanely RA: Contemporary exercise physiology research in United States: Influence of technology, Quest 49:296–299, 1997.
19. Healey J: Future possibilities in electronic monitoring of physical activity, Research Quarterly for Exercise and Sport 71:137–145, 2000.
20. Hoberman J: Mortal engines: The science of performance and the dehumanization of sport, New York, 1992, Free Press.
21. Jones CJ and Rikli RE: The gerontology movement—is it passing us by? JOPERD 64(1):17–26, 1993.
22. US Administration on Aging and American Association of Retired Persons: A profile of older Americans, 1997, Washington D.C., 1997, US Government Printing Office.
23. Agency for Healthcare Research and Quality: Minority health: cultural competency for health care providers could reduce disparities in care related to race and ethnicity, November 2000. (www.ahcpr.gov).
24. Lawson HA: School reform, families, and health in the emergent national agenda for economic and social improvement: implications, Quest 45:289–307, 1993.
25. Centers for Disease Control and Prevention, Adolescent and School Health: Coordinated School Health Program. (www.cdc.gov/nccdphp/dash/cshpdef.htm)
26. First colony in space, National Geographic 150(1):76–89, 1976.
27. Bain LL: Beginning the journey: agenda for 2001, Quest 40:96–106, 1988.
28. Oberle GH: A future direction plan for our profession, JOPERD 59(1):76–77, 1988.
29. Corbin CB: Is the fitness bandwagon passing us by?, JOPERD 55(9):17, 1984.
30. AAHPERD Executive Directors: In our view, JOPERD 59(8):14, 1988.
31. Neiner JA, Howze EH, and Greaney ML: Using scenario planning in public health: anticipating alternative futures, Health Promotion Practice 5:69–79, 2004.

SUGGESTED READINGS

Blair SN, Franklin BA, Jakicic, JM, and Kibler B: New vision for health promotion within sports medicine, American Journal of Health Promotion 18:182–185, 2003.

Sports medicine as a broad field of endeavor can serve a large public health role and play a significant part in chronic disease management. The expanded role for sports medicine is discussed as well as barriers that prevent the inclusion of sports medicine within public health initiatives.

Corbin CB: Physical activity for everyone: what every physical educator should know about promoting lifelong physical activity, Journal of Teaching in Physical Education 21:128–144, 2002.

Offers suggestions about how we can change physical education to help youth to live actively as adults. Suggestions include recognizing unique needs, shifting our focus from fitness to physical activity, promoting self-esteem and competence, providing opportunities for girls, and helping youth make the transition from high school to community physical activity programs.

Corbin CB: The "untracking" of sedentary living: a call for action, Pediatric Exercise Science 13:347–356, 2001.

Urges that professionals seek to get adolescents back on the active track, before they become sedentary adults. Some suggestions include focusing on physical activity rather than physical fitness and helping adolescents shift from school to community physical activity programs.

Haskell WL: Physical activity, sport, and health: toward the next century, Research Quarterly for Exercise and Sport 67(Supplement):37–47, 1996.

Haskell discusses how changes in technology have contributed to sloth, lack of leisure time, physical activity in an aging society, and recommendations for enhancing health and physical performance.

Lawson HA: Looking back from the year 2082, JOPERD 53(1):15–17, 1982.

Three catalysts to change in the nature of physical education as practiced in 2082 are discussed. These are the growth of sport instruction and participation in the community, the self-help movement, and the development of the disciplinary foundation that helped stimulate the growth of alternative careers.

Mahoney DF and Howard DR: Sport business in the next decade: a general overview of expected trends, Journal of Sport Management 15:275–296, 2001.

Creative strategies are needed to thrive in the 2000s. These include using new technology, tapping new markets, capitalizing on big events, and doing a better job at targeting promotions to audiences.

Martens, R, editor: Technology in kinesiology and physical education, Quest 49, 1997 (entire issue).

This entire issue is devoted to technology and the field of physical education and sport, including articles on sport pedagogy, motor behavior, exercise physiology, and instructional technology.

Martinek V, Fu FH and Huard J: Gene therapy and tissue engineering in sports medicine, The Physician and Sports Medicine 28(2), February 2000. (online).

The potential for gene therapy in the treatment of musculoskeletal injuries in the future is presented as well as its use in combination with tissue engineering as therapy for injuries that are slow healing.

Naisbitt J and Aburdene P: Megatrends 2000: ten new directions for the 1990s, New York, 1990, William Morrow and Company.

Ten trends that will shape the future, including the global economy, the rise of women in leadership, the increased privatization of the welfare state, the increased emphasis on religion, and the growth of the individual, are presented, as well as implications for the future.

Neiner JA, Howze EH, and Greaney ML: Using scenario planning in public health: anticipating alternative futures, Health Promotion Practice 5:69–79, 2004.

Uses scenario planning to help identify two different alternatives for nutrition and physical activity based on their role in public health. One alternative assumes positive driving forces, with policy and funding support for physical activity and nutrition. The second alternative paints a different picture, revealing the consequences when fighting for funding and support is necessary.

Shepard RJ: Issues in worksite health promotion: a personal viewpoint, Quest 54:67–82, 2002.

Shepard raises ethical and professional issues, including the methods by which the benefits are calculated, the right of unhealthy employees to remain unhealthy, the importance of considering the circumstances of employees' lives before blaming them for becoming ill, barriers to physical activity, and the importance of creating innovative approaches.

Siedentop D: Lessons learned, Journal of Teaching in Physical Education 21:454–465, 2002.

Noted scholar Daryl Siedentop identifies key influences that have shaped his scholarship in physical education pedagogy over the last 25 years. Among the lessons are the importance of valuing inquiry and seeking commonalities. Effective instruction is de-

fined by sustained and deliberate practice. It is important to collaborate with the professionals you serve, and seek to be part of solutions to problems we are facing as a profession.

Smedley BD and Syme SL, editors: Promoting health: intervention strategies from social and behavioral research, American Journal of Health Promotion 15:149–166, 2001.

Presents 21 recommendations from social and behavioral research to promote health; emphasizes the importance of focusing on both individuals and the communities in which they live if improvements in health are to occur.

Teeter CR, Derrick B, and Tagtow A: A new vision for health promotion and nutrition education, American Journal of Health Promotion 18:186–192, 2003.

Further collaboration between health promotion professionals is important if they are to be effective in helping consumers accurately assess and utilize information pertaining to health and nutrition. Stresses the importance of professionals having strong academic preparation, field-based training, and continued professional development.

Welk GJ: The youth physical activity promotion model: a conceptual bridge between theory and practice, Quest 51:5–23, 1999.

Uses a social-ecological framework to present a physical activity model for children based on their unique developmental needs. The model emphasizes the importance of shifting from theory to the practice of physical activity.

CREDITS

CHAPTER 1

P. 4 © Royalty-Free/CORBIS; P. 4 © Ryan McVay/Getty Images; P. 5 Senior Citizens Center, Ithaca, NY; P. 9 © Royalty-Free/CORBIS; P. 10 From Auxter D, Pfyer J: Principles and methods of adapted physical education and recreation, ed. 6, St. Louis, 1989, Mosby; P.12 © John A. Rizzo/Getty Images; P. 13 Laura Bitting, Ithaca College; P. 14 © PhotoLink/Getty Images; P.16 © Karl Weatherly/ Getty Images; P.17 © PhotoLink/Getty Images; P.18 Duke University Sports Information; P.21 Courtesy Bill Baun Tenneco Health and Fitness Program; P.22 © Royalty-Free/ CORBIS; P 28 Fred Smith, Empire State Games, Albany, NY; P.30 © PhotoLink/Getty Images; Figure 1-1 Modified from Anderson DF, Broome EF, Pooly JC, Schrody D and Brown E: Foundations of Canadian Physical Education, Recreation and Sport Studies, Dubuque IA, 1995, WCB Brown & Benchmark.

CHAPTER 2

P.41. Deborah Wuest, P.45 © Royalty-Free/CORBIS; P.47 Joan Smith, US Master's Swimming; P. 54 Sarah Rich; P. 58 © Duncan Smith/Getty Images; P. 58 Rick Heinz, Courtesy Lois Mauch, Agassiz Middle School, Fargo, ND; P. 59 © Royalty-Free/CORBIS; P. 62 © PhotoLink/Getty Images; P. 65 Peter Mainelli, Taking Care, Hartford, CT; P. 68 © Jeff Maloney/Getty Images; Figure 2-1 Dolly Lambdin, Blanton Elementary School, Austin, Texas and the University of Texas at Austin; Figure 2-2 and 2-3 Courtesy of Cooper Institute for Aerobic Research, Dallas, TX.

CHAPTER 3

P. 80 Sarah Rich; P. 84 © Keith Brofsky/Getty Images; P. 89 Deborah Wuest; P. 97 © Ryan McVay/Getty Images; P. 101 © Royalty-Free/CORBIS; P. 102 © Photodisc; P. 105 Photodisc; P. 107 Deborah Wuest; P. 108 Suzi D'Annalfo; P. 111 Sarah Rich; P. 116 © Royalty-Free/CORBIS; P. 117 Photodisc; P. 121 © Don Tremain/Getty Images; P. 123 Photodisc; P. 128 From Auxter D, Pfyer J: Principles and methods of adapted physical education and recreation, ed. 6, St. Louis, 1989, Mosby,

CHAPTER 4

P. 140 Smith College Archives, Northampton, MA; P. 142 University of Nevada, Las Vegas; P. 143, Deborah Wuest; P. 147, Harold L. Ray, Western Michigan University, Kalamazoo, MI; P. 148 Harold L. Ray, Western Michigan University, Kalamazoo, MI; P. 149 - J. Clarence Davies Collection, Museum of the City of New York; P. American Alliance for Health, Physical Education, Recreation, and Dance; P. 153 American Alliance for Health, Physical Education, Recreation, and Dance; P. 154 Smith College Archives, Northampton, MA; P. 155 Aldrich and Aldrich; P. 157 Smith College Archives; P. 158 American Alliance for Health, Physical Education, Recreation and Dance; P. 162 Laurie Bitting; P. 166 Deborah Wuest; P. 170 Sarah Rich; P. 171 Sarah Rich.

CHAPTER 5

P. 180 © PhotoLink/Getty Images; P. 183 © Lawrence M. Sawyer/Getty Images; P. 186 © Lawrence M. Sawyer/Getty Images; P. 187 © PhotoLink/Getty Images; P. 189 Cathy Haight; P. 192 © Karl Weatherly/Getty Images; P. 202 © Jack Star/PhotoLink/Getty Images

CHAPTER 6

P. 213 William F. Staub; P. 214 © Royalty-Free/CORBIS; P. 216 © Lawrence M. Sawyer/Getty Images; P. 218 © Royalty-Free/CORBIS; P. 220 William F. Straub; P. 222 © PhotoLink/Getty Images; P. 223 Sarah Rich; P. 227 (left) William F. Straub; P. 227 (right) © Rim Light/PhotoLink/Getty Images; P. 228 © Andersen Ross/Getty Images; P. 230 William

F. Straub; P. 231 William F. Straub; P. 232 Courtesy Lee Johnson, Innovative Sports Training; P. 235 US Olympic Training Center, Colorado Springs, CO; Figure 6-1 Donald O'Connor, From Hall, S: Basic Biomechanics (2nd ed.) St. Louis 1995, Mosby; Figure 6-2 Lee Johnson, Innovative Sports Training.

CHAPTER 7

P. 248 © Jeff Maloney/Getty Images; P. 253 Deborah Wuest; P. 255 © Royalty-Free/CORBIS; P. 257 (top) From Hockey, R: The Pathway to Healthful Living, ed 7, St. Louis, 1993, Mosby; P. 257 (bottom) Jack Discher, physical education teacher, Agassiz Middle School, Fargo, ND; P. 259 From Prentice W: Fitness for College and Life, ed 4, St. Louis, 1994, Mosby; P. 270 From Safrit, M. and Wood, T.: Introduction to Measurement in Sport and Exercise Science, ed 3, St. Louis 1995, Mosby; P. 271(top) © PhotoLink/Getty Images, (middle) © Lawrence M. Sawyer/Getty Images, (bottom) © Royalty-Free/CORBIS; P. 272 National Institute on Aging; P. 273 (right, left, and bottom) From Hockey, R: The Pathway to Healthful Living, ed 7, St. Louis, 1993, Mosby; P. 275 Courtesy D and J Development, Van Nuys, CA; P. 284 Quaker Oats, Gatorade Sports Science Institute; P. 286 © Ryan McVay/Getty Images; Figure 7-1 Prentice W, Fitness for College and Life, ed 5, St. Louis, 1987, Mosby.

CHAPTER 8

P. 292 © Rim Light/PhotoLink/Getty Images; P. 295 © Lawrence M. Sawyer/Getty Images; p. 297 Bob Jackson/ Colorado Springs Gazette Telegraph, From Coakley, J: Sport in Society: Issues and Controversies, ed 5, St. Louis, 1994, Mosby; P. 298 Sarah Rich; P. 310 Joann Ward; P. 321 From Coakley, J: Sport in Society: Issues and Controversies, ed 5, St. Louis, 1994, Mosby; P. 324 Martin Williams Advertising From Coakley, J: Sport in Society: Issues and Controversies, ed 5, St. Louis, 1994, Mosby; P. 328 Photodisc; P. 329 © Ryan McVay/Getty Images; Figure 8-2. Coakley, J: Sport in society: issues and controversies, ed 7, McGraw-Hill, 2001, Dubuque, IA.

CHAPTER 9

P. 340 Sarah Rich; P. 346 © Ryan McVay/Getty Images; P. 353 © Jeff Maloney/Getty Images; P. 355 Fred Smith, Empire State Games, Albany, NY; P. 357 Courtesy Bill Baun, Tenneco Health and Fitness Program; P. 361 © PhotoLink/Getty Images.

CHAPTER 10

P. 372 Courtesy Bill Baun, Tenneco Health and Fitness Program; P. 377 University of Nevada, Las Vegas, NV; P.378. William F. Straub; P. 380 Sarah Rich; P. 383 © Photodisc; P. 394 William F. Straub; P. 396 Deborah Wuest; P. 399 © PhotoLink/Getty Images; 401 Deborah Wuest.

CHAPTER 11

P. 414 Deborah Wuest; P. 422 Mary Beth Steffan; P. 425 Deborah Wuest; P. 427 Deborah Wuest; P. 429 Sarah Rich; P. 431 Linda Castiglione; P. 433 © Ryan McVay/Getty Images; P. 434 United States Tennis Association, Cynthia Lum; P. 436 © Royalty-Free/CORBIS; P. 438 Suzi D'Annalfo; P. University of Tennessee Sports Information; P. 443 Mary Beth Steffan; Figure 11-1 Courtesy of PE Central.

CHAPTER 12

P. 453 Peter Mainelli, Taking Care Center, Hartford, CT; P. 454 Courtesy Bill Baun, Tenneco Health and Fitness Program; P. 456 Deborah Wuest; P. 459 Deborah Wuest; P. 460 © Photodisc; P. 463 Deborah Wuest; P. 466 From Arnheim D: Modern principles of athletic training, ed 6, St. Louis, 1995, Mosby; P, 467 Modern principles of athletic training, ed 6, St. Louis, 1995, Mosby; P 470 From Bucher CA: Administration of physical education and athletic programs, ed 8, St. Louis, 1983; P. 471 Concept II Rowing; P. 472 © Keith Brofsky/Getty Images, P. 473 © Royalty-Free/ CORBIS.

CHAPTER 13

P. 487 St. Louis Rams and St. Louis Visitors Bureau; P. 488 Deborah Wuest; P. 491 Christine Pritchard; P. 492 Tom Ward; P. 494 © PhotoLink/Getty Images; P. 495 © Royalty-Free/ CORBIS; P. 497 © Rim Light/PhotoLink/Getty Images; P. 498 © Keith Brofsky/Getty Images; P. 499 University of Tennessee Sports Information.

CHAPTER 14

P. 508 University of Nevada, Las Vegas; P. 513 © D. Berry/PhotoLink/Getty Images; P. 520 From Arnheim D: Modern principles of athletic training, ed 7, St. Louis,1997, Mosby; P. 524 Northwest Community HealthCare Wellness Center, Arlington Heights, Illinois; P. 527 Sarah Rich; P. 529 Phil Borgese; P. 530 David Fisher; P. 531 Suzi D'"Annalfo; P. 533 Sarah Rich; P. 534 Brad Hohenstreet.

CHAPTER 15

P. 546 NASA Ames Research Lab; P. 554 William Straub; P. 556 MHHE Images; P. 562 Deborah Wuest

INDEX

Index note: Page references with an *f* or a *t* indicate a figure or table on the designated page.

A

B

C

D

E

F

G

H

I

O

P

Q

R

S

T

U

V

W